Mac OS X Lion

ALL-IN-ONE

FOR DUMMIES®

Mac
OS X Lion
ALL-IN-ONE
FOR
DUMMIES®

by Mark L. Chambers

WILEY

John Wiley & Sons, Inc.

OS X Lion All-in-One For Dummies®

Published by
John Wiley & Sons, Inc.
111 River Street
Hoboken, NJ 07030-5774

www.wiley.com

Copyright © 2011 by John Wiley & Sons, Inc.

Published by John Wiley & Sons, Inc., Hoboken, NJ

Published simultaneously in Canada

For general information on our other products and services, please contact our Customer Care Department within the U.S. at 877-762-2974, outside the U.S. at 317-572-3993, or fax 317-572-4002.

For technical support, please visit www.wiley.com/techsupport.

Wiley also publishes its books in a variety of electronic formats and by print-on-demand. Not all content that is available in standard print versions of this book may appear or be packaged in all book formats. If you have purchased a version of this book that did not include media that is referenced by or accompanies a standard print version, you may request this media by visiting http://booksupport.wiley.com. For more information about Wiley products, visit us at www.wiley.com.

Library of Congress Control Number: 2011935816

ISBN 978-1-118-02206-1 (pbk); ISBN 978-1-118-16473-0 (ebk);
ISBN 978-1-118-16474-7 (ebk); ISBN 978-1-118-16475-4 (ebk)

Manufactured in the United States of America

10 9 8 7 6 5 4 3 2

WILEY

About the Author

Mark L. Chambers has been an author, computer consultant, BBS sysop, programmer, and hardware technician for almost 30 years — pushing computers and their uses far beyond "normal" performance limits for decades now. His first love affair with a computer peripheral blossomed in 1984 when he bought his lightning-fast 300 BPS modem for his Atari 400. Now he spends entirely too much time on the Internet and drinks far too much caffeine-laden soda.

With a degree in journalism and creative writing from Louisiana State University, Mark took the logical career choice: programming computers. (Go figure.) However, after five years as a COBOL programmer for a hospital system, he decided there must be a better way to earn a living, and he became the Documentation Manager for Datastorm Technologies, a well-known communications software developer. Somewhere in between writing software manuals, Mark began writing computer how-to books. His first book, *Running a Perfect BBS*, was published in 1994 — and after a short fifteen years or so of fun (disguised as hard work), Mark is one of the most productive and best-selling technology authors on the planet.

Along with writing several books a year and editing whatever his publishers throw at him, Mark has also branched out into Web-based education, designing and teaching a number of online classes — called *WebClinics* — for Hewlett-Packard.

His favorite pastimes include collecting gargoyles, watching St. Louis Cardinals baseball, playing his three pinball machines and the latest computer games, supercharging computers, and rendering 3D flights of fancy with *TrueSpace* — and during all that, he listens to just about every type of music imaginable. Mark's worldwide Internet radio station, *MLC Radio* (at www.mlcbooks.com), plays only CD-quality classics from 1970 to 1979, including everything from Rush to Billy Joel to the *Rocky Horror Picture Show* soundtrack.

Mark's rapidly expanding list of books includes *MacBook For Dummies*, 3rd Edition; *Macs for Seniors For Dummies; iMac For Dummies,* 6th Edition; *Build Your Own PC Do-It-Yourself For Dummies; Building a PC For Dummies,* 5th Edition; *Scanners For Dummies,* 2nd Edition; *CD & DVD Recording For Dummies,* 2nd Edition; *PCs All-in-One For Dummies,* 5th Edition; *Mac OS X Tiger: Top 100 Simplified Tips & Tricks; Microsoft Office v. X Power User's Guide; BURN IT! Creating Your Own Great DVDs and CDs; The Hewlett-Packard Official Printer Handbook; The Hewlett-Packard Official Recordable CD Handbook; The Hewlett-Packard Official Digital Photography Handbook; Computer Gamer's Bible; Recordable CD Bible; Teach Yourself the iMac Visually; Running a Perfect BBS; Official Netscape Guide to Web Animation;* and *Windows 98 Troubleshooting and Optimizing Little Black Book.*

His books have been translated into 15 different languages so far — his favorites are German, Polish, Dutch, and French. Although he can't read them, he enjoys the pictures a great deal.

Mark welcomes all comments about his books. You can reach him at mark@mlcbooks.com, or visit MLC Books Online, his Web site, at www.mlcbooks.com.

Dedication

This book is dedicated with love to Frank and Vera Judycki. They might have started out as my in-laws, but now they're MawMaw and PawPaw.

Author's Acknowledgments

Once again, the good folks at John Wiley & Sons, Inc. have made things easy on a demanding technology author! It's time to send my appreciation to those who helped make this book a reality.

As with all my books, I'd like to first thank my wife, Anne; and my children, Erin, Chelsea, and Rose; for their support and love — and for letting me follow my dream!

No project gets underway without the Composition Services team. Starting with my words and adding a tremendous amount of work, Composition Services has once again taken care of art, layout, and countless other steps that I can't fathom. Thanks to each of the team members for a beautiful book.

Next, my appreciation goes to my superb technical editor Dennis Cohen, who checked the technical accuracy of every word — including that baker's dozen of absurd acronyms that crops up in every technology book I've ever written. His eagle eye for detail and encyclopedic knowledge of everything Mac ensures that this finished book is the best it can be!

Finally, I come to Linda Morris, my hardworking and incredibly patient project editor, and my top-of-the-line acquisitions editor Bob Woerner (both of whom are also long-time friends)! My heartfelt thanks to both of them, for without their support at every step, this book wouldn't have been possible. With their help, yet another *For Dummies* title was guided safely into port!

Publisher's Acknowledgments

We're proud of this book; please send us your comments at http://dummies.custhelp.com. For other comments, please contact our Customer Care Department within the U.S. at 877-762-2974, outside the U.S. at 317-572-3993, or fax 317-572-4002.

Some of the people who helped bring this book to market include the following:

Acquisitions and Editorial

Project Editor: Linda Morris

Executive Editor: Bob Woerner

Copy Editor: Linda Morris

Technical Editor: Dennis Cohen

Editorial Manager: Jodi Jensen

Editorial Assistant: Amanda Graham

Sr. Editorial Assistant: Cherie Case

Cartoons: Rich Tennant
(www.the5thwave.com)

Composition Services

Project Coordinator: Katie Crocker

Layout and Graphics: Carl Byers,
Joyce Haughey

Proofreaders: Rebecca Denoncour,
Evelyn C. Wellborn

Indexer: BIM Indexing & Proofreading Services

Publishing and Editorial for Technology Dummies

    Richard Swadley, Vice President and Executive Group Publisher

    Andy Cummings, Vice President and Publisher

    Mary Bednarek, Executive Acquisitions Director

    Mary C. Corder, Editorial Director

Publishing for Consumer Dummies

    Kathy Nebenhaus, Vice President and Executive Publisher

Composition Services

    Debbie Stailey, Director of Composition Services

Contents at a Glance

Table of Contents

Book II: Customizing and Sharing 157

Introduction

legant.

I remember the first moment I moved a mouse across a Mac OS X Desktop. At that time, it was the beta of version 10.0 — and I very well remember the word *elegant* as my first impression. (My second impression was *UNIX done better.*)

That's really saying something because I'm an old operating system curmudgeon: I cut my computing teeth on Atari, Commodore 64, and TRS-80 Model III machines, and I still feel much at home in the character-based environment of DOS and UNIX. Of course, I've also used every version of Windows that His Gatesness has produced, including the much-improved Windows 7. And yes, I've used Mac OS since before the days of System 7, using a Macintosh SE with a 9-inch monitor (and a built-in handle).

But out of this host of operating systems, could you really call one *elegant* before now? (Even Mac OS 9 didn't deserve such a description, although it did provide the foundation of convenience and simplicity.) Mac OS X — now at version 10.7, affectionately called *Lion* — is something different: It's a fine-cut diamond amongst a handful of semi-precious stones. It's the result of an unnatural marriage, I'll admit . . . the intuitive, graphical world of Mac paired with the character-based stability and efficient multitasking of UNIX. Who would have thought that they would work together so well? Mac OS X performs like a Ferrari, and (unbelievably) it looks as good, too.

Therefore, you can imagine just how I immediately jumped at the chance to write a comprehensive guide to Apple's masterpiece. The book that you hold in your hands uses the classic *For Dummies* design; it provides you with the step-by-step instruction (plenty of which my editors grudgingly agree is somewhat humorous) on every major feature of Mac OS X. It also goes a step further from time to time, delving into why something works the way that it does or what's going on behind the scenes. You can chalk that up to my sincere admiration for everyone in Cupertino and what they've perfected.

What you *won't* find in this *All-in-One* is wasted space. All the new features of version 10.7 are here, including improvements to Apple Mail, Mission Control, and Launchpad, the awesome FaceTime application, and the latest versions of all the iLife '11 applications. Everything's explained from the ground up, just in case you've never touched an Apple computer before. By the time you reach the final pages, you'll have covered advanced topics, such as networking, AppleScript, Internet security . . . and yes, even an introduction to the powerful world of UNIX that exists underneath.

I sincerely hope that you'll enjoy this book and that it will act as your guide while you discover all the wonderful features of Mac OS X Lion that I use every day. Remember, if a Windows-minded acquaintance still titters about your iMac, I'll understand if you're tempted to drop this weighty tome on his foot. (Of course, you can also boot into Windows and watch him turn purple — truth is, he can't boot into Mac OS X on his PC.)

 The official name of the latest version is (portentous pause here, please) Mac OS X version 10.7 Lion. But who wants to spit out that mouthful every time? Throughout this book, I refer to the operating system as *Mac OS X,* or simply *Lion.*

What's Really Required

If you have a Mac that's either running Mac OS X version 10.7 (Lion) or is ready to be upgraded to it, you're set to go. Despite what you might have heard, you *won't* require any of the following:

✦ **A degree in computer science:** Apple designed Mac OS X for regular people, and I designed this book for people of every experience level. Even if you've never used a Mac before, you'll find no hostile waters here.

✦ **A fortune in software:** I do describe additional software that you can buy to expand the functionality of your Mac; however, that section is only a few pages long. *Everything else* covered in this book is included with Mac OS X Lion — and by the size of this volume, you get a rough idea of just how complete Mac OS X is! Heck, many folks buy Macs just because of the free software you get, such as iMovie and iPhoto. (Tough cookies to the vast Unwashed Windows Horde.)

✦ **An Internet connection:** Granted, you're not going to do much with Apple Mail without an Internet connection, but computers *did* exist before the Internet. You can still be productive with Mac OS X without receiving buckets of spam.

Oh, and you need to buy and download Lion from the Apple App Store, unless Lion came pre-installed on your Mac. Go figure.

About This Book

Although this book is an *All-in-One,* you can also read it in a linear fashion (straight through) — probably not in one session, mind you. (Then again, Diet Coke is cheap, so it *is* possible.) The material is divided into eight minibooks, each of which covers an entire area of Mac OS X knowledge. For example, you'll find minibooks on networking, the Apple Digital Hub suite of applications known as iLife, Apple's iWork office productivity suite, customizing your Desktop, and Internet-related applications.

Each self-contained chapter discusses a specific feature, application, connection, or cool thing about Mac OS X. Feel free to begin reading anywhere or skip chapters at will. For example, if you're already using an Internet connection, you won't need the chapter on adding an Internet connection. However, I recommend that you read this book from the front to the back, as you do any good mystery novel. (Watch out; oncoming spoiler: For those who want to know right now, Bill Gates did it.)

Conventions Used in This Book

Even *For Dummies* books have to get technical from time to time, usually involving commands that you have to type and menu items that you have to click. If you've read any of my other *For Dummies* books, you'll know that a helpful set of conventions is used to indicate what needs to be done or what you see on-screen.

Stuff you type

When I ask you to type a command or enter something in a text field (such as your name or phone number), the text appears like this: **Type me.**

Press the Return key to process the command or enter the text.

Menu commands

When I give you a specific set of menu commands to use, they appear in the following format: Edit➪Copy.

In this example, you should click the Edit menu and then choose the Copy menu item.

Display messages

If I mention a specific message that you see on your screen, it looks like this on the page: `This is a message displayed by an application`.

In case you're curious about computers

No one expects a book in the *For Dummies* series to contain techno-jargon or ridiculous computer science semantics — especially a book about the Macintosh! Apple has always strived for simplicity and user friendliness. I hereby promise that I've done my absolute best to avoid unnecessary techno-talk. For those who are interested in what's happening under the hood, I provide sidebars that explain a little more about what's doing what to whom. If you'd rather just have fun and ignore the digital dirty work, please feel free to disregard these additions (but don't tear sidebars out of the book, because there's likely to be important stuff on the opposite side of the page).

How This Book Is Organized

I've done my best to emulate the elegant design of Mac OS X by organizing this book into eight minibooks, with cross-references where appropriate.

Book 1: Introducing Mac OS X

This minibook begins with an invigorating chapter explaining exactly why you should be so happy to be a Mac OS X owner. Then I provide an introduction to the basic tasks that you'll perform — copying files, running programs, and the like. You'll also find coverage of Lion's Spotlight search engine, a guide to normal Mac OS X maintenance and troubleshooting, instructions on using the Mac OS X Help system and a chapter devoted to installing (and enjoying) Windows on your Mac.

Book II: Customizing and Sharing

Who wants to stick with the defaults? The material in this minibook leads you through the steps that you need to customize Mac OS X to your specific needs and desires . . . everything from a tweak to your background or screen saver to a description of how to set up and administer multiple accounts on a single Macintosh. You'll also find coverage of the different settings you can change in System Preferences, which is an important place in Mac OS X.

Book III: The Digital Hub

Sweet! This minibook jumps right in among the crown jewels of the Digital Hub: iTunes, iPhoto, iDVD, iMovie, iWeb, GarageBand, QuickTime Player, and the DVD Player. Taken as a suite, those first six applications make up iLife '11, and they allow you to plug in and use all sorts of electronic gadgets, including digital cameras, digital video (DV) camcorders, and MP3 players. Plus, you can edit or create your own DVDs, audio CDs, and movies.

Book IV: Using iWork

iWork '09 is rapidly becoming the favorite office productivity suite among the Apple Faithful. You'll find a chapter devoted to each application: Pages for desktop publishing, Numbers for spreadsheets, and Keynote for presentation projects. Who needs that other productivity suite? (I forget the name.)

Book V: The Typical Internet Stuff

This minibook contains just what it says. But then again, it's easy to get enthusiastic about Apple Mail, iChat (Apple's instant messaging application), and the one-on-one video conversations possible with FaceTime. I also cover Safari, Apple's hot-rod web browser. Finally, you discover more about the built-in Internet firewall and how you can use it to safeguard your Mac from Internet undesirables.

Book VI: Networking in Mac OS X

Ethernet, Bluetooth, and Bonjour are lurking in this minibook. I explain them step-by-step, in language that a normal human being can understand. Find out how to use wireless networks such as AirPort Extreme from Apple as well as how to share an Internet connection with other computers in a local network.

Book VII: Expanding Your System

Time to take things up a notch. In this minibook, I discuss the hardware and software that everyone's adding to Mac OS X and why you might (or might not) need such toys. Memory (RAM), hard drives, printers, USB, Thunderbolt, and FireWire 800 . . . they're all discussed here in detail. Consider this a banquet of expansion information.

Book VIII: Advanced Mac OS X

I know that I told you earlier that I was going to avoid techno-talk whenever possible, yet I also mentioned the advanced things that you find in this minibook, such as using UNIX within Mac OS X and using Automator to build your own custom script applications that handle repetitious tasks. If you don't mind immersing yourself in all that's technical, read here for the skinny on hosting a web site and communicating with Mac OS X by using your voice and your handwriting.

Icons Used in This Book

The icons in this book are more than just attractive — they're also important visual cues for stuff that you don't want to miss.

Mark's Maxims represent big-time-important stuff, so I call your attention to these nuggets in bold, like this:

Something *Really* Important Is Being Said that will likely affect your person in the near future. Pay attention, commit those Maxims to memory, and you'll avoid the pitfalls that the rest of us have hit on the way.

The Tip icons flag short snippets of information that will save you time or trouble (and, in some cases, even cash).

These icons highlight optional technical information for folks like me. If you also used to disassemble alarm clocks for fun when you were six years old, you'll love this stuff.

Always read this information next to this icon first! Something looms ahead that could put your hardware or software at risk.

Look to the Remember icons for those tidbits that you need to file away in your mind. Just remember to remember.

This icon denotes stuff that's, well, new in Lion. (Ahem. Paging Dr. Obvious!)

Book I

Introducing Mac OS X

The 5th Wave · By Rich Tennant

"Wow, I didn't know OS X could redirect an e-mail message like that."

Contents at a Glance

Chapter 1: Shaking Hands with Mac OS X

In This Chapter

✔ Understanding the advantages of Mac OS X

✔ Checking your system requirements

✔ Upgrading from earlier versions of Mac OS

✔ Installing Mac OS X

✔ Running Mac OS X for the first time

*I*t's human nature to require instant gratification from your software. I've seen it countless times: Someone runs a program, immediately feels comfortable with it, and then spends the rest of his days using that program religiously. Or another person plays with the same program for 120 seconds and dismisses it as too difficult or too confusing. It's rather like watching a fashion show runway in Rome or Paris: There had better be eye appeal pretty quickly or the bucks won't flow.

Ditto for modern computer operating systems. An *operating system* is the basic software that determines the look and feel of your entire computer and usually extends to the programs that you run as well. Microsoft felt the pinch of an old-fashioned operating system when Windows 98 and Windows Me were starting to appear rather plain. Then came Windows XP, where menus fade in and out like fireflies on a summer night, little puppies help you find files, and other animation abounds. With the arrival of Windows Vista (and now Windows 7), Microsoft has attempted to match some of the elegance and power of Mac OS X in the PC world . . . but to be honest, updating a PC by upgrading to Windows 7 is a little like putting on a polyester sports coat over the same tired old leisure suit — most of what changes is on the *outside*.

Apple doesn't work that way. Sure, Mac OS X looks doggone good. Forget the minimum requirement of shirt and shoes because this operating system is wearing an Armani suit. What's really exciting for Macintosh owners around the world, however, is the heart that beats *beneath* the pretty form. At its introduction, Mac OS X was quite literally an operating system revolution, and it still delivers some of the most advanced features available on any personal computer in use today while remaining as easy to use as the first Macintosh. (And yes, I do own, use, and enjoy both PCs and Macs — in the end, what's important to me is which computer docs the best job the fastest in the easiest manner.)

Now, I'm not going to just haul off and proclaim that Mac OS X can run rings around — well . . . you know, the *W* word — without solid proof. In this chapter, I introduce you to the advantages of Mac OS X and why it's such a step ahead for those running Windows. I also cover the hardware requirements for running Mac OS X version 10.7 (Lion) as well as guidelines on switching from Windows. Finally, I familiarize you with the steps that you'll encounter the first time you fire up the Big X.

Convince Me: Why Mac OS X?

Apple was one of the first to pioneer the graphical approach to computing with the appearance of the first Macintosh, so you'd expect Mac OS X to be simple to use — and indeed it is. For many folks, that's Job One. If you're one of those people, you can happily skip this section without need of further evidence because Mac OS X is undoubtedly the easiest operating system on the planet to use. (And believe me, I'm not knocking simplicity. Computers are supposed to be getting easier to use, and techno-nerds like me are supposed to be rendered unnecessary as computers advance.) Here is the mantra of the Mac — and the first of Mark's Maxims for this volume:

Make it *easy*.

Still with me? Need more testimony? Or perhaps you're just curious about the engine under the hood. Then read on — and if you're a Macintosh owner, feel free to gloat! (If you're a PC owner, there's always eBay.)

Pretty to behold

Let me illustrate with a screenshot or two. Figure 1-1 illustrates a typical screen from a day spent in Mac OS v. 9.2, the capable — albeit rather old-fashioned — version of the Mac OS operating system that shipped in the days before Mac OS X.

Compare that screen with a similar screen from the latest version of the Big X, as shown in Figure 1-2. As you can see, everything's streamlined in appearance, with maximum efficiency in mind. Tasteful 3-D abounds, from the drop-shadowed windows to the liquid-look scroll bars. Icons look like miniature works of art. Macintosh owners appreciate outstanding design — and can recognize the value of a great computer, even if it's lime green (or looks like a silver picture frame). After all, many Mac owners are professionals in the graphic arts, and Apple provides the hardware that they need — like the top-of-the-line display used with the 27-inch flat-panel Intel iMac or the killer performance of the latest Mac Pro with *twelve-core* processors.

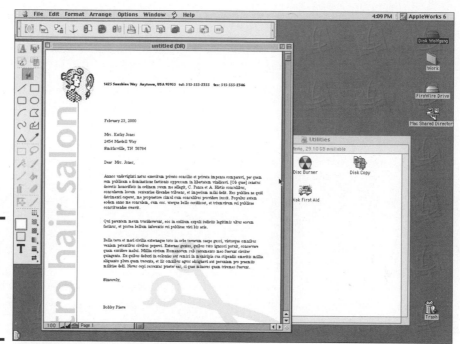

Figure 1-1:
Mac OS 9.2 was a workhorse, true, but it wasn't a work of art.

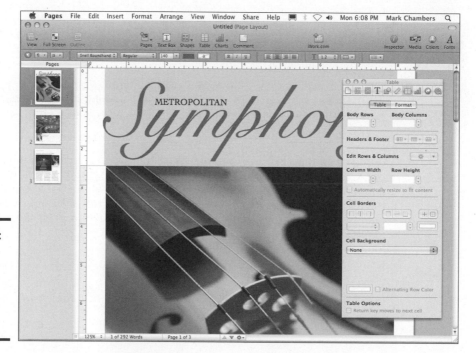

Figure 1-2:
Eye-catching? You bet! Mac OS X Lion is a knockout.

Take a look at what's going on behind the curtain — the Great Oz is actually pretty busy back there.

The allure of Aqua

The Apple software developers who introduced us to Mac OS X designed this "liquid" look from the ground up. They call it *Aqua,* and it's Lion's standard user interface.

Whoops, I just realized that I slipped a ten-cent example of techno-babble into that previous paragraph. Let me explain: A *user interface* design determines how things look throughout both the operating system itself and all applications that are written to run under an operating system (OS). This includes the buttons that you push, the controls that you click or move, and even the appearance of the windows and menus themselves. For example, if you've already begun to use Mac OS X, you've probably stopped right in the middle of a task and exclaimed to yourself, "Why, Self, look at that cool 3-D contour effect on that menu bar!" That shapely contour is a tiny part of the Aqua user interface design.

Aqua also extends to the placement of controls and how they're shown to you. For example:

✦ Mac OS X uses Aqua *sheets* (which are attached to their parent windows) to prompt you for input, such as confirming when you're about to close a document without saving it. In contrast to Windows, multiple programs can have multiple sheets open, so you can continue to work in other applications without being rudely forced to answer the query immediately.

✦ Aqua's file selection controls, such as the one in Figure 1-3, make it much easier to navigate quickly to a specific file or folder from within an application.

✦ The *Dock* is another Aqua favorite. The Dock launches your favorite applications, indicates what's running on your Mac, and allows you to switch between those programs — and all in a strip that you can relocate and customize at will. I talk about the Dock in greater detail in Book II, Chapter 2.

Consider Aqua as the *look-and-feel* of Mac OS X and virtually all applications that it runs; you can discover how to use these Aqua controls in the pages to come. Of course, Mac owners really don't have to worry about Aqua itself; the Aqua guidelines are a road map for those software developers writing applications for Mac OS X. Programs written to the common Aqua interface standard will be easier for you to use, and you'll become a proficient power user of that program much faster.

Figure 1-3:
A typical file selection dialog (done right in Aqua).

The quality of Quartz

The second ingredient in the visual feast that is Mac OS X is *Quartz Extreme* — again, I must ask your forgiveness, good reader, because I have to get a tad technical again. Quartz Extreme is a *graphics engine:* It's the portion of Mac OS X that draws what you see on the screen (in the Aqua interface, natch). Think of the engine in your car, which is responsible for making your car move. Whether your Mac is running Microsoft Word or simply idling at the Desktop waiting for you to finish your soda, Quartz Extreme is at work displaying icons, drawing shapes, exhibiting the Finder, and animating things in the Dock.

What sets Quartz Extreme apart from the ho-hum graphics engine that Windows uses? It's all about international programming standards . . . you know, those things that Microsoft would much rather you forget. To wit:

✦ **PDF:** The Quartz Extreme engine is built around the Acrobat Portable Document Format (*PDF* for short) developed by Adobe. If you've been spending any time at all on the Internet in the last ten or so years, you know that PDF files have emerged as the standard for displaying and print-ing the highest-quality electronic documents. Plus, Adobe has released a version of the free Acrobat Reader (www.adobe.com) for just about every computer on this green Earth. This means that text and graphics displayed in Quartz Extreme are razor sharp, resizable, and easily portable from one computer to another. In fact, Mac OS X displays PDF files without even requiring Acrobat, using the built-in Preview application. Figure 1-4 shows a complex PDF document that I opened in Mac OS X.

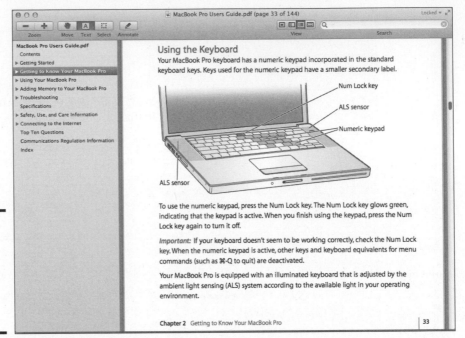

Figure 1-4:
Yep, that's a PDF document, not a scanned image!

✦ **OpenGL:** Gamers will get really excited about this one: Quartz Extreme also uses the OpenGL graphics acceleration standard, which delivers the fastest 3-D graphics on the planet. (Think photo-realistic, high-resolution graphics drawn in the blink of an eye.) In fact — and this is a really cool trick — OpenGL is even used to produce the Desktop in Mac OS X Lion.

In English, that means that today's top-of-the-line, 3-D gaming and 3-D graphics acceleration can take care of drawing *everything;* forget about waiting for windows to close or menus to appear, even when you're creating the world's biggest honking spreadsheet or building a presentation the size of Baltimore. As the Chairman of the Board would say, "We're talkin' fast, baby, like a rocket ship to the moon!"

✦ **Core Animation:** Lion includes functionality that Apple calls Core Animation, which makes it much easier for programmers to animate backgrounds and objects within their programs. Text, 3-D animation, and video now work seamlessly side-by-side, and eye-catching animations within applications, such as Time Machine, are the norm for Mac owners.

Stable, stable, stable

"So it's elegant in design. That's great, Mark, but what if Mac OS X crashes? Aqua and Quartz Extreme aren't worth a plug nickel if my mouse doesn't move and I lose my document!" Believe me, I couldn't agree more; I make my living from computers, and every time that a misbehaving program locks up one of my machines, I throw a tantrum that would make Godzilla back off. Lockups shouldn't be tolerated in this day and age.

Luckily, the folks who designed Mac OS X were just as interested in producing a rock-solid operating system as they were in designing an attractive look. (Think of Tom Cruise's face on The Rock's body.)

Mac OS X is as hard to crash as the legendary UNIX operating system — that's right, the same reliable workhorse that techno-wizards around the world use to power the Internet, where stability is all-important. In fact, Mac OS X is actually built on top of a UNIX base. It's just well hidden underneath, allowing you and me to focus on our programs and click with a mouse without knowing any of those obscure, arcane keyboard commands. You get the benefits of UNIX without a pair of suspenders, a pocket protector, or the hassle of growing a beard. (Not to mention years of computer programming experience.)

In fact, Apple has gone yet another step further in safeguarding your data in case of a power failure or misbehaving program: the *Auto Save* feature, which is new in Mac OS X Lion, automatically saves all the changes you make to your document in the background, while you work! Whenever you need to, it's a snap to revert to the document as it was when you opened it last. (I know one technology author who is downright thankful for Auto Save.)

Apple calls the UNIX foundation at the heart of Mac OS X by another nifty title: *Darwin*. I could tell you that Darwin provides the latest in 64-bit memory support and CPU management, but if you're a normal human being, your eyes will glaze over. Suffice it to say that Darwin makes the best use of your computer's memory (RAM) and your computer's brain (CPU) — Lion has been fine-tuned for processors with multiple cores, such as the Core i5 CPU from Intel. Rest assured that your web server will stay up even if your misbehaving Virtual Birdcalling simulation decides to run amok. (Emus running amok . . . how dreadful.)

Yes, yet another standard is at work here — uh-oh, Overlord Gates is truly angry now! For those who *do* have a beard and are curious about such things, Darwin uses a FreeBSD kernel, so it also inherits all the protocol standards that have made UNIX the foundation of today's Internet. You can find more about FreeBSD at `www.freebsd.org`. Because Mac OS X is developed as an open source project, software engineers outside Apple can actually contribute ideas and code, just as UNIX continues to evolve over time. (And yes, you'll even discover how to access the powerful UNIX command prompt from Mac OS X in Book VIII, Chapter 1!)

Don't forget QuickTime X!

If you've recorded or edited digital video (DV), you're probably already familiar with Apple's QuickTime MOV format. QuickTime movies are typically high resolution, relatively small, and easily created with iMovie, which I discuss in Book III, Chapter 4. Although QuickTime X isn't "on stage" all the time, as is Aqua or Quartz Extreme, it's still an important part of Mac OS X: Every time you display a video clip that you've recorded or watch a streaming TV broadcast from a web site, you use QuickTime X. (Note, however, that you don't use QuickTime X to watch DVD movies — that job is reserved for the Apple DVD Player.) QuickTime X includes support for AVC (Advanced Video Coding) for the best possible display of the latest HD (High Definition) video signals from the expensive hardware that's now appearing at your local electronics Maze o' Wires chain store.

QuickTime is actually not a new Mac OS X feature — it's been around since the early 1990s — but the latest versions of Mac OS X include the free QuickTime Player, which provides support for the latest broadcast and web video. In fact, you can set up your own TV station on the web with the tools included in the Professional QuickTime package.

To get an idea of just how well armored Mac OS X is, consider Figure 1-5. See how one program, which I call Titanic 1.0, has locked up like San Quentin. Under Mac OS 9 and older versions of Windows, your only chance at recovering anything would involve divine intervention. However, in Mac OS X, my Pages application is unaffected because it has a completely protected area of system memory to play in. (I show you how to force a misbehaving application to go away in Book I, Chapter 3.)

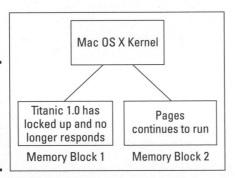

Figure 1-5: Mac OS X keeps applications separate for a reason.

By the way, Darwin makes it easy for UNIX software developers to quickly and easily *port* (or modify) all sorts of UNIX applications to work under Mac OS X. I think you'll agree that a wider selection of applications is a good thing.

Multitasking and multithreading for normal human beings

And now, for your entertainment, a short one-act play. (Yes, really. You'd be amazed at how popular this stage production has become among my readers.)

A Shakespearean Moment of Multitasking and Multithreading

Our play opens with Julius Caesar shaking his head in disgust at his Mac OS 9 Desktop.

> **Caesar:** Anon, I am only one mortal, yet my Desktop doth abound with portals to applications of all different mien. Tell me, foul beast, why thy spirit seems slow and sluggish, and my Excel spreadsheet doth crawl on its belly!

[Enter Romeo, a cocky and rather brash young Apple software developer.]

> **Romeo:** Dude, the problem is, like, your operating system. Y'see, older versions of both Mac OS and Windows ended up constantly, like, shifting your computer's attention from one app to another — Excel has to cooperate with everything else that's running in the background, like a good little corporate boy. It's less efficient and very, very '90s. Upgrade to Mac OS X, and you get *preemptive multitasking* — the app you're actually using, like, gets the lion's share of the processing time, and everything runs smoother when you need it. That's the way UNIX works.

> **Caesar:** Verily, your strange tongue doth annoy me. Guards, behead him — then obtain for me this Mac OS X.

> **Romeo:** I'm outta here — I've got a hot date — but don't forget, like, Mac OS X also uses *multithreaded processing,* so your Mac can handle different operating system tasks at the same time. It's kind of like your computer can both walk and chew gum at the same time: fast, fast, fast!

[Exit Romeo — rather swiftly — stage right.]

> **Fin**

When the play closes, we can only hope that Romeo is fast as well. (I told you it was a short play.)

The definition of Internet savvy

Remember the classic iMac advertisements that touted the one-plug approach to the Internet? That entire campaign was centered on one idea: that the Internet was *supposed* to be easy to use. The folks at Microsoft sat up and took notice when the iMac proved so incredibly successful, and Windows Vista actually reduced some of the overwhelming folderol that you had to encounter just to connect to the Internet — but Mac OS X still wipes the floor with Windows 7 when it comes to easy and complete Internet connectivity. For example:

✦ **Easy configuration:** Mac OS X sets up your entire Internet connection with a simple wizard. As long as you've got the right information handy (which your Internet service provider [ISP] should supply), it's a snap to set up.

✦ **iDisk:** What if I told you that for a reasonable yearly subscription fee, Apple can provide you with a chunk of Internet-accessible, private hard drive space — and that you can access this hard drive space from anywhere on Earth with an Internet connection? Absolutely, unbelievably, massively cool. This neat trick is called *iDisk,* and I cover it in detail in Book V, Chapter 4.

✦ **All the Internet behind-the-scenes stuff:** The Internet is basically built on a number of *protocols* (read that as *rules for exchanging all sorts of data*) — and, as I mention earlier, UNIX machines dominate the Internet. Ergo, Mac OS X on your Macintosh also provides you with support for just about every Internet protocol on the planet. Even if you don't know them by name or write your own software, the applications that you buy can use them.

✦ **A gaggle of great Internet applications:** Mac OS X ships with all sorts of Internet magic built in. For example, you'll get instant Internet and local network communication with iChat and the new FaceTime video chat application (both of which I cover in Book V, Chapter 3), Safari (covered in Book V, Chapter 5), and Apple Mail, a standard-issue, battle-ready e-mail program (which I discuss in Book V, Chapter 2). Yup, it's all free.

✦ **And Apache, sweet Apache:** Friends, as a webmaster myself, I can tell you that I was visibly moved — well, at least *exceptionally* excited — when I discovered that Mac OS X included the industry-standard Apache web server, which runs more than half of the sites on the web! (Yep, that includes `www.apple.com`.) Get all the details in Book VIII, Chapter 4.

Lots of free goodies

You don't just get Internet applications when you latch your fingers onto a box o' Mac OS X — you can start doing all sorts of neat stuff without investing one extra dollar in more software!

Remember, what you receive along with Mac OS X depends on whether you're upgrading from Snow Leopard or receiving the Big X already installed on a new Macintosh. With that in mind, check out the possibilities.

✦ **This is the iLife:** This suite of easy-to-use integrated programs is included with a new Mac, and it's practically as well known as the computer itself these days: iDVD, iPhoto, iTunes, GarageBand, iMovie, and iWeb. Each of these stellar programs is covered in full in Book III. If you've got a digital camera, an MP3 player, a USB musical keyboard, or a DV camcorder, you'll be a very happy individual. I promise.

✦ **iWork to the rescue:** If you've bought a new Macintosh with Mac OS X pre-installed, you've also received a test drive version of *iWork* (Apple's answer to Microsoft Office). Good stuff, indeed. If you don't want to spend the bucks on Office 2011, and you don't need the complex gewgaws and baroque architecture of Word, Excel, and PowerPoint, I can guarantee you that Pages, Numbers, and Keynote are powerful enough to satisfy your office document and presentation yearnings.

✦ **The obligatory games:** Apple typically chooses new games to bundle with Macs every three or four months — typically, games are selected that show off your Mac's 3-D power, as well as finger-exercising arcade challenges. Because this book isn't a game guide, I leave you to explore these games at your leisure.

What Do I Really Need to Run the Big X?

I've written a dozen other *For Dummies* books — I know, it's getting to be a habit (and a career) — and I always find the "Hardware Requirements" section a hard one to write. Why? Well, I know what Apple claims as the minimum hardware requirements necessary to run Mac OS X. But, on the other hand, I know what *I* would consider the minimum hardware requirements, and they're substantially different. Oh, well, let me list the bare bones and then I'll give you my take on what you really need. (Naturally, if Mac OS X Lion is pre-installed on your computer, feel free to tear out this page and create a handful of celebratory confetti.)

From *The World According to Jobs,* the minimum requirements are as follows:

✦ **Hardware:** You'll need any Mac with an Intel Core 2 Duo, i3, i5, i7, or Xeon processor. This means that just about any recent desktop or laptop Mac is *technically* eligible to play (although you might find the performance of a Core 2 Duo Mac mini running Lion to be unacceptable).

✦ **RAM:** You'll need at least 2GB of memory (RAM). At today's low prices, that's like buying a pizza.

✦ **Hard drive territory:** Although svelte by Windows standards, Mac OS X still needs about 8GB of free space on your hard drive.

From *The World According to Chambers,* the minimum requirements are

+ **Hardware:** I recommend a Mac with at least an Intel i3 processor. Remember, this is *my* take on what you'll need to really take advantage of Mac OS X Lion, and again, I have to say that I don't think it performs well enough on Intel Core 2 Duo computers.

+ **RAM:** Don't settle for anything less than 4GB. Again, with memory as cheap as it is these days, this is like adding extra cheese to that pizza.

Time for a Mark's Maxim:

Any techno-nerd worth the title will tell you that the *single most important key* to performance in today's operating systems is RAM — yep, it's actually more effective than a faster processor!

If you've got any extra spending cash in between your sofa cushions, spend it on RAM. (Up to an Earth-shaking 64GB of RAM on the latest Mac Pro racehorses!)

+ **Hard drive territory:** I'd recommend having

  • 15GB free for just the operating system

  • A minimum of an additional 60 to 100GB for any digital video clips, photographs, and songs you'll be collecting

Upgrading from Earlier Versions of Mac OS

Because the installation of Mac OS X Lion is handled through the Apple App Store, there's not much to tell. What's important are the steps that you should take care of *before* you start the installation. I cover those in the next section. Pay heed, or pay later. I won't go into detail about the actual installation because there really aren't any details to speak of — you'll answer a question or two and then hop up to get another cup of coffee or another caffeine-laden soda while the installer does the rest. Would anyone expect any different from Apple?

Back up — PLEASE back up

I know you're anxious to join the In crowd, and Apple makes the upgrade process as noninvasive and as safe as possible, but snafus such as power loss and hard drive failures do happen. With a full backup of your system on CD or DVD (or to an external hard drive using Time Machine), you can rest assured that you'll get your precious files and folders back in pristine shape if tragedy strikes. To be honest, you need to back up your system on a regular basis anyway. Promise me *now* that you'll back up your system, won't you?

Pet peeve number 1 . . .

The round object that you load into your CD-ROM or DVD-ROM drive is a *disc,* not a *disk,* like your hard drive or that flimsy floppy that some of the Windows horde still use.

Anyone who pretends to talk oh-so-knowingly about a *CD-ROM disk* or *DVD disk* is likely a dweeb, and in the future, you should steer as far away from that dweeb as possible.

Snuff out disk errors

Before you upgrade, I recommend that you check that hard drive for errors one last time — upgrading a disk with directory errors takes longer. If you're upgrading from an older version of Mac OS X, use *Disk Utility,* which I cover in Book I, Chapter 7. Ain't technology grand?

Plug it, road warrior

You're on the road with your MacBook Pro, and you've just bought your copy of Mac OS X Lion. You're thinking of installing your brand-spanking-new operating system . . . . Stop! NOW.

Before you decide to upgrade your Mac notebook, consider what will happen if that magical vessel containing all your files should flicker and . . . . No, on second thought, don't even *visualize* it. (Even if the battery is fully charged.) If you're installing a Mac OS X upgrade on a MacBook, MacBook Air, or MacBook Pro, make sure that it's plugged in and receiving its share of good, clean AC power from a handy, nearby wall socket. The installation process could take an hour, and there'll be constant hard drive and DVD drive activity — think "Attack of the Energy-Draining Installation from Planet Lithium." You *don't* want to try this while your notebook is operating on battery power.

What's that, you say? You'd like a comprehensive guide to your classy new Apple MacBook, MacBook Air, or MacBook Pro laptop? Look no farther than the third edition of my bestselling *MacBook For Dummies,* published in both print and electronic book format by the good folks at Wiley . . . . With a copy in hand, any road warrior will find the answers to those Persistent Laptop Questions!

Heck, a techno-purist would probably recommend that you attach your Macintosh to an uninterruptible power supply (UPS) for the installation process, but I'm not quite *that* paranoid about power outages.

Keep one thing in mind while installing Mac OS X: If you format the *destination drive* (the drive where you'll install Mac OS X), you'll lose everything that it stored. No big surprise there, and the installation program will warn you profusely about this beforehand. There's really no reason to do so unless you just crave a *clean* installation (an installation of a new operating system on a newly formatted drive, compared with an upgrade of your existing Mac OS System files). Oh, and don't forget to use Mac OS Extended (Journaled) format.

Personalizing the Big X

After the installation is complete and you have rebooted the beast, stand back and watch those beautiful rounded edges, brushed stainless-steel surfaces, and liquid colors appear. But wait — you're not quite done yet! Mac OS X needs to be personalized for you, just like your toothbrush or your SUV's six-way power seat; therefore, use the Setup Wizard that automatically appears the first time you boot Mac OS X Lion.

These wizard screens change periodically — and they're completely self-explanatory — so I won't march you through each one step by step. However, here are a few tips that provide a bit of additional over-the-shoulder help while you're setting things up.

✦ **How rude!** If you're outside the United States or other English-speaking countries, you should know that Mac OS X defaults to U.S. formats and keyboard layouts. Rest assured, though, because Mac OS X does indeed provide full support for other languages and keyboard configurations. To display these options in the list boxes, click the Show All button at the bottom of the wizard screen.

✦ **Accounts are important.** When Mac OS X asks you to create your account, don't forget your password — oh, and they're case sensitive, too, so *THIS* is different from *this* or *ThiS.* It's a good idea to enter a password hint, but don't make that hint too easy to guess. For example, *My first dog's name* is probably preferable to *Plays Seinfeld on TV.* Mac OS X uses the name and password that you enter to create your account, which you use to log in if you set up a multiuser system for several people. (More on this in Book II, Chapter 4.) *Never* write down your passwords, either; such crib sheets work just as well for others as for you.

✦ **I need to fix that.** You can click the Back button any time to return to previous wizard screens. Mac OS X, being the bright child that it is, automatically saves your choices for you, so when you click Continue to return, everything is as you left it.

✦ **Extra stuff.** Whether you decide to accept the news, offers, and related-product information from Apple is your decision. However, it's only right that I point out that you can find this same information on the Apple web site, so there's no need to engorge your e-mail Inbox unless you so desire. (In other words, I turned this off.)

✦ **Local area network (LAN) connections.** If you're connecting your Mac to a Transmission Control Protocol/Internet Protocol (TCP/IP) network (or you're using an Internet router that uses Dynamic Host Configuration Protocol [DHCP]), it's a good idea to click Yes when you're asked whether you should use the configuration supplied by the existing server.

DHCP automatically provides the computers on the network with all the settings that they need to connect. If that sounds like ancient Sumerian, find out more in Book VI, Chapter 1.

✦ **Do create your MobileMe account!** Apple's MobileMe service just plain rocks — especially the iDisk storage that you receive. Again, more on this in Book V, Chapter 4, but take my word for it. Join up, trooper. (The trial subscription is free, and it's easy to upgrade to a full membership if you decide that you like the MobileMe benefits.)

✦ **Have your Mail settings handy.** If you set up your trial MobileMe account, you can set up your @me.com address without any bother — again, this is A Good Thing. Lion will also try to configure your existing accounts automatically. However, if you're setting up an existing account, it's a good idea to make sure you have all those silly settings and numbers and names that your ISP supplied you with when you signed up. (Just in case.) This stuff includes your e-mail address, mail server variety, user account ID, password, and outgoing mail server.

Chapter 2: Navigating and Running Programs

In This Chapter

✓ **Restarting, sleeping, and shutting down Mac OS X**

✓ **Using windows**

✓ **Using menus**

✓ **Recognizing and selecting icons**

✓ **Using the keyboard**

✓ **Running applications**

✓ **Switching between programs**

✓ **Opening, saving, and quitting within an application**

As the folks in Cupertino will tell you, "It's all about the graphics." They're right, of course — Mac OS X is a highly visual operating system, and using it without a mouse or trackpad is like building Hoover Dam with a pocketknife. (And not a particularly sharp pocketknife, either.) Therefore, most of this chapter requires you to firmly grasp the little rodent — I introduce you to little graphical bits such as icons and menus, and you discover how to open windows that can display anything from the contents of a document to the contents of your hard drive.

On the other hand, any true Macintosh power user will tell you that the keyboard is still a useful piece of hardware. Because I want you to be a bona fide, well-rounded Mac OS X power user, I also demonstrate those key combinations that can save you time, effort, and possible tennis elbow from all that mouse-wrangling.

Finally, I lead you through the basic training that you need to run your programs: how to start them, how to open and save documents, and how to quit an application as gracefully as Fred Astaire on his best day.

Restarting, Sleeping, and Shutting Down

First things first. As the guy on the rocket sled probably yelled, "This is neat, but how do you stop it?" Call 'em The Big Three — Sleep, Restart, and Shut Down are the Mac OS X commands that you use when you need to take care of business away from your computer. All three appear on the friendly Apple menu (🍎) at the top-left corner of your Desktop (as shown in friendly Figure 2-1).

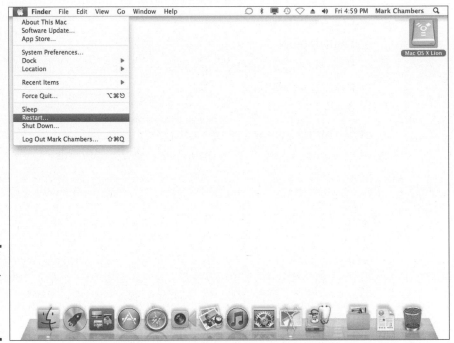

Figure 2-1: Choose your path from the Apple menu.

Each of these options produces a different reaction from your Mac:

✦ **Sleep:** You don't need a glass of water or a bedtime story when you put Mac OS X to *Sleep,* which is a power-saving mode that allows you to quickly return to your work later. (Waking your computer up from Sleep mode is much faster than booting or restarting it, and Sleep mode can conserve battery power on laptops.) Depending on the settings that you choose in System Preferences — which I discuss in Book II, Chapter 3 — your Mac can power-down the monitor and spin-down the hard drives to save wear and tear on your hardware. You can set Mac OS X to automatically enter Sleep mode after a certain amount of mouse and keyboard inactivity. To awaken your slumbering supercomputer, just click the mouse or press any key on the keyboard. MacBook owners can put their laptops to sleep by simply closing the computer; they can wake the beast by opening it back up again.

✦ **Restart:** Use Restart if your Mac has suddenly decided to work "outside the box" and begins acting strangely — for instance, if your Universal Serial Bus (USB) ports suddenly lock up or your FireWire drive no longer responds. Naturally, you first need to save any work that's open (unless your computer has locked up altogether). You also elect to restart Mac OS X when you switch startup volumes, or switch an Intel-based Mac to a Windows partition using Boot Camp. (Many applications and Apple software updates require a restart after you install them.)

✦ **Shut Down:** When you're ready to return to the humdrum, real world and you're done with your Mac for the time being, use the Shut Down option. Well-behaved Mac applications automatically prompt you to save any changes that you've made to open documents before the computer actually turns itself off. If you've configured your Mac to disable automatic login, you can shut down Mac OS X from the login screen as well.

Besides the Apple menu command, MacBook laptops have a Power key on the keyboard that you can press to display a dialog with Sleep, Restart, and Shut Down buttons. If you change your mind and decide to tie up loose ends before you leave, click the Cancel button to return to Mac OS X.

Lion's new *Resume* feature comes into play when you log out, restart, or shut down your Mac. Click the Reopen Windows When Logging Back In check box to enable it (as shown in Figure 2-2), and Lion automatically restores the state of your desktop the next time you turn on your Mac, including all your open windows and selections! Resume also works with individual applications — for example, when you quit Preview, Lion saves the current state of that application's workspace. When you launch Preview again, it displays the windows you were viewing, documents and all. (Note that an application has to be written specifically for Lion to support Resume.)

Figure 2-2:
Lion can reopen your windows after you restart or shut down.

Are you sure you want to quit all applications and log out now?

If you do nothing, you will be logged out automatically in 51 seconds.

☑ Reopen windows when logging back in

Cancel   Log Out

You can also hold down the Control key and press the Drive Eject key (which you use to load and eject discs) to display the same options.

Actually, we're not finished just yet . . .

I should probably also mention the other guys: the Log Out command (which you can find under the Apple menu) and the User Switch menu (at the right side of the Finder menu).

✔ Choose Log Out when you're running your Mac with multiple users and you want to completely pass control over to another person. All your programs will quit, and the other person can take over by logging in with his/her account. Mac OS X then reconfigures with the other user's preferences.

✔ If you've enabled Fast User Switching, another user can log in from the User Switch menu. However, your applications don't quit, you don't have to formally log out, and you can take control back when the other user is finished. (Hence the words *Fast* and *Switching* in the name.) To turn on this feature, log in with an administrator account, display the Users & Groups pane in System Preferences, click Login Options, and then select the Show Fast User Switching Menu As check box. (More on Fast User Switching appears in Book II, Chapter 4.)

A Window Is Much More Than a Frame: Navigating Windows

"And in the beginning, there was the window." As with older Mac operating systems, most of what you'll do in Mac OS X occurs within these fancy frames. And, as you might imagine, a number of controls are at your disposal, which you can use to control the size, shape, and appearance of these potent portals. In this section, I — well, to be blunt, I do windows. (No squeegee jokes, if you please.)

Opening and closing windows

Windows are generally opened automatically. Usually, a window gets opened by an application (when you first run it or it needs to display a document) or by Mac OS X itself (when the Finder opens a window to display the contents of your hard drive). The *Finder,* by the way, is the application that Mac OS X runs to display the operating system's menus and windows.

Some programs even let you open new windows on the fly; for example, Figure 2-3 illustrates a window in its purest form: a new Finder window. To display this window on your own Mac, choose File⇨New Finder Window or press ⌘+N. From here, you can reach any file on your Mac or even venture to the Internet.

Close button

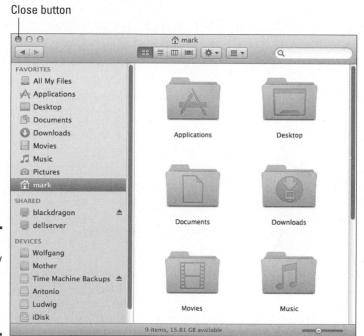

Figure 2-3:
You're ready
to navigate
with this
Finder
window.

The Command key usually has both an Apple (🍎) and a rather strange-looking symbol (⌘) on it that I often call the Spirograph.

When you're finished with a document or you no longer need a window open, you can close it to free that space on your Desktop. To close a window in Mac OS X, move your mouse pointer over the Close button; it's the red circular button at the top-left corner of the window (see Figure 2-3). An X appears on the button when you're in the zone. When the X appears, just click the mouse.

If you've been living the life of a hermit in a cave for the last two decades or so, pressing the left mouse button is called *clicking the mouse.* In the Apple universe, a standard mouse usually has at least two buttons; heck, current MacBooks don't have any buttons at all! (You tap the trackpad with one finger to click.) If you're using a pointing device with a right mouse button, a right-click usually acts the same as holding down the Control key while you click with an older one-button Apple mouse or trackpad.

Most Mac applications don't want you closing a window willy-nilly if you've changed the contents without saving them. For example, try to close a document window in Word or Pages without saving the file first. The program asks you for confirmation before it closes the window containing your Great American Novel. Most programs also have a Close command on their File menu. (Here's another indicator: Most programs display a black dot in the center of the program's Close button to indicate that there are unsaved changes.)

To close all windows that are displayed by a particular program, hold down the Option key while you click the Close button on one of the windows. Whoosh! They're all gone.

Scrolling windows

Often, more stuff is in a document or more files are on your hard drive than you can see in the space available for a window. Guess that means it's time to delete stuff. No, no, *just joking*! You don't have to take such drastic measures to see more in a window.

Just use the scroll bars that you see in Figure 2-4 to move through the contents of the window — by default, scroll bars don't appear until you move your pointer close to them. You click the *scroll box* and drag it — for the uninitiated, that means clicking the darker portion of the bar and holding down the mouse button while you move the mouse in the desired direction. Alternatively, you can click in the empty area above or below the scroll box to scroll pages one at a time.

Depending on the type of application that you're using, you might be able to scroll a window with your arrow keys as well — or perhaps use the Page Up and Page Down keys to move through a window.

Minimizing and restoring windows

The multitalented Figure 2-4 also displays another control that you can use with a window: the Minimize button. When you *minimize* a window, you eliminate it from your Desktop and store it safely in the *Dock* — that strip of icons that appears along the bottom (or the side) of your Mac OS X Desktop. In fact, a minimized window appears as a miniature icon in the Dock, so you can actually keep an eye on it (so to speak). Figure 2-5 illustrates a minimized window from Safari, which is actually displaying my web site at `www.mlcbooks.com`. To minimize a window, move your mouse pointer over the yellow Minimize button at the top-left corner of the window — a minus sign appears on the button — and then click.

Resize button

Zoom button

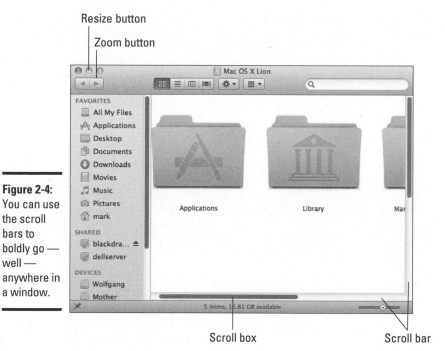

Figure 2-4:
You can use
the scroll
bars to
boldly go —
well —
anywhere in
a window.

Scroll box   Scroll bar

Figure 2-5:
Note the
miniature
web page in
the Dock —
minimizing
at work.

You're gonna love this "Easter egg" hidden in Mac OS X — if you hold down the Shift key whilst you minimize, the window shrinks in *cool* slow motion. (Who says operating systems have to be totally serious, anyway?)

When you're ready to display the window again on your Desktop — a process called *restoring* the window — simply click the thumbnail icon representing the window in the Dock, and Mac OS X automagically returns it to its former size and location.

By the way, some — note that I said *some* — applications continue to run when minimized, whereas others simply stop or pause until you return them to the Desktop. Such is the crazy world we live in.

Zooming windows

Zooming windows has a kind of Flash Gordon sound to it, don't you think? It's nothing quite that exciting — no red tights or laser guns — still, when you're trying to view a larger portion of a document, *zooming* is a good thing because it expands the window to the maximum practical size for the application that you're using (and the content being displayed). In some cases, zooming a window fills almost the entire screen; in others, the extra space would be wasted, so the application zooms the window to the maximum size that shows as much content as possible (without any unnecessary white space). In fact, the Zoom button can even be disabled by an application that doesn't want you to muck about with the window; for example, I own some games that don't allow zooming.

To zoom a window, move your mouse pointer over the green Zoom button at the top-left corner of the window. Again, Figure 2-4 (a couple of sections back) struts its stuff and illustrates the position. (Man, that is one versatile figure.) A plus sign appears on the Zoom button. Click to expand your horizons.

After you've finished with a zoomed window, you can return it to its previous dimensions by clicking the Zoom button again.

Doing the full-screen dance

Lion is the first version of Mac OS X to provide system-wide support for *full-screen* operation — that's where a single application fills the entire screen, without displaying a window frame or traditional Finder menu bar.

The method you use to switch to full-screen mode varies within applications, so there's no One Menu Command or One Keyboard Shortcut that will always do the deed. Most of the applications that are included with Mac OS X Lion use View➪Enter Full Screen, and many applications have a button you can click in the window to switch back and forth. (iPhoto is a good example.) You may also see a button with a double-diagonal arrowhead icon in the upper right corner of the window.

So how do you switch between applications if they're all in full-screen mode?

- Mouse users can move their pointers to the bottom of the screen to display the Dock, where you can click on another application to switch to it.

- You can invoke Mission Control and choose another application from there.

- If you're working with a Mac that has a trackpad (or a Multi-Touch Magic Mouse), swipe three fingers to the left or right across the surface.

- From the keyboard, use the ⌘+Tab shortcut to cycle through the applications you have running.

Those hard-working toolbars

If you're wondering what those tiny icons are at the top of many Mac OS X application windows, I won't leave you in suspense: they're called *toolbar buttons*. A *toolbar* is a strip of icons that appears in a window (usually across the top) that you can click to perform common commands, such as changing the display format or printing the current document. (The toolbar in Figure 2-4, for example, features icons to move Back and Forward, among others.) You'll encounter more toolbar technology throughout the book.

Most windows that include a toolbar also include some method of hiding the toolbar (in order to save screen real estate for your document). For example, you can toggle the display of the toolbar on and off in a Finder window from the View menu, or you can use the convenient ⌘+Option+T key shortcut to toggle the toolbar display on and off.

Moving windows

In contrast to the rather permanent windows in your home, you can pick a window and cart it to another portion of the Desktop. Typically, you do this when you're using more than one application at a time and you need to see the contents of multiple windows. To grab a window and make off with it, click the window's *title bar* — the strip at the top of the window that usually bears a document or application name — and drag the window to the new location. Then release the mouse button to plant the window firmly in the new location.

By the way, some applications allow you to arrange multiple windows in a graceful swoop with a single click of a menu. Click the Window menu and choose Arrange All to perform this magic.

I talk about Mission Control, in the section "Switching 'Twixt Programs with Aplomb." Mission Control helps you organize a large number of open windows on your Desktop. You can use it to display all open application windows so that you can pick the one you want . . . or even display all the windows opened by a specific application. Spaces allow you to create entire custom virtual desktops. (Truly cool.) Each of your Spaces desktops can contain a different set of application windows that you use for different tasks!

Resizing windows

Next, consider how to change the width or height of your window. To change the dimensions of a window to your exact specifications, move your mouse pointer over the lower-right corner of the window (which is usually marked with a number of slashed lines to indicate its status as a control), click, and drag until the window is the size that you prefer.

Switching windows

Before I move on to other graphical wonders of Mac OS X, it's important that you master how to switch between windows on your Desktop. First, remember this old Norwegian saying (or is it one of Mark's Maxims?):

Only *one* can be active at one time.™

What our Oslo friends are communicating is that only one window can be active at any time. The active window appears on top of other windows, and it's the one that you can edit by typing or by moving your mouse. (It also sports Close, Minimize, and Zoom buttons in color, or it fills the entire screen if you're working in full-screen mode.) Other windows that you have opened might be minimized, as I describe earlier, in the section "Minimizing and restoring windows," or they can be inactive (mere ghosts of themselves) and remain on your Desktop. Mac OS X dims the controls for inactive windows so that you can tell they're hanging around . . . but you can't use them at the moment. Figure 2-6 illustrates a number of open windows, with the iTunes window active.

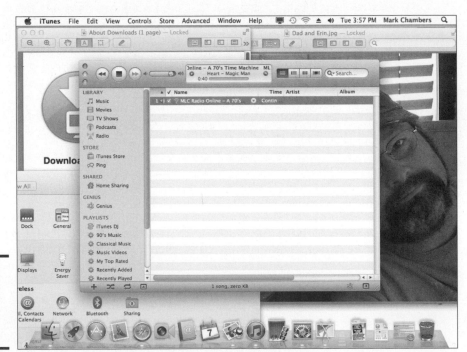

Figure 2-6: Many are open, but only one is active.

I know you're going to get tired of hearing me say this, but here I go again: Certain applications continue to run while their windows are inactive, such as iTunes, File Transfer Protocol (FTP) clients, and others. Most programs, however, stop or pause until you make their window active.

And how do you switch to — *activate* — a different window in Mac OS X? Again, Mission Control allows you to activate another window, but if the window is currently visible, you can simply click any part of that window. I generally click the window's title bar if it's visible, but any part of the inactive window will do. (You can also right-click the application's icon in the Dock and choose the desired window from the menu.) The window that you click leaps like a proud stallion to the fore, and the previously active window now skulks in the background.

You can still use a window's Close, Minimize, and Zoom buttons even when the window is inactive.

Menu Mysteries Explained

Next, I move on to menu control in Mac OS X. *Menus* are handy drop-down controls that allow you to select commands that are grouped together logically. For example, an application's File menu usually allows you to create or open a document, save a document to disk, or print the document. To pull down a menu, click the desired menu group name on the bar at the top of the screen and then click the desired menu option from the extended menu.

Figure 2-7 illustrates the Safari menu: Note the submenus designated by right-arrow icons. When you move your mouse pointer over a submenu command, you get another set of even more specific menu commands — in this case, the Services submenu command displays commands, such as Mail and Grab.

Some applications allow you to create your own custom menus; naturally, configuring a new menu system takes some time to figure out, but imagine the productivity gains that you'll enjoy! Custom menus are sleeker and easier to navigate. (However, you have to stop short of claiming that you wrote the application. Software developers get downright snippy about it.)

Mac OS X also provides another type of menu: contextual. A *contextual* menu appears when you right-click certain items on the screen, revealing commands that relate specifically to that item. (Unfortunately, the items that sport contextual menus vary from application to application, so it's best to check the documentation for a program before you spend countless hours right-clicking everything on-screen.) The same items in the right-click menu appear when you select an item and then click the Action pop-up menu, which looks like a mechanical gear. You can also hold down the Control key while clicking an item to display the contextual menu (or tap with two fingers, if you're using a trackpad).

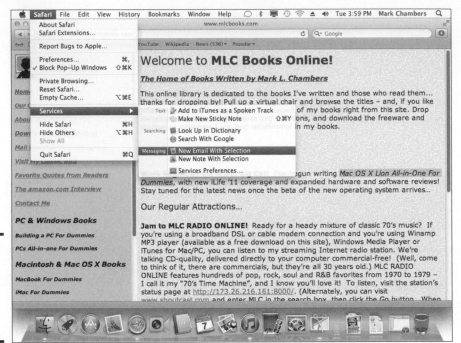

Figure 2-7:
Drilling
deeper into
Safari's
Services
menu.

Most manufacturers sell mice, trackballs, and other pointing things that include a secondary mouse button. Generally, if you have a pointing device with multiple buttons, the device displays contextual menus when you click the secondary button. Then again, you might launch Aunt Harriet into a geo-synchronous orbit, so double-check the manual for your pointing thing on the default button assignment (and how to change it, if necessary).

You'll note that many commands in menus have keyboard shortcuts. Because I hold forth on this subject in the upcoming section, "Keyboard Shortcuts for the True Power User," I hold off describing those shortcuts here.

Icons 'R Us

Icons are more than little pictures. They're . . . well . . . actually, I guess they're little pictures. However, these graphical WUDs (that's short for *Wonderful User Devices*) are really representations of the components of your Mac OS X system, and therefore they deserve a section of their own.

For complete details on what any icon is, what it represents, and what it does, click the icon once to highlight it and then press ⌘+I. This displays the Info dialog that you see in Figure 2-8, which tells you what kind of icon it is, where the item it represents is actually located, and how big it is. You also see a version number for applications — a handy way of quickly checking the version of a program you're running — and when the file was created and last modified. The Info dialog also offers other settings and options that you can display by clicking in the General section, and I cover them in other parts of the book.

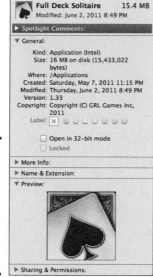

Figure 2-8:
The Info
dialog
provides the
complete
lowdown
on a Mac
application.

Hardware

Mac OS X uses icons to represent the various hardware devices of your computer, including your

+ Hard drive

+ DVD drive (if a disc is loaded)

+ iPod

You get the idea. Just double-click a hardware icon to display the folders and files that it contains, as you do with your hard drive and a disc loaded in your DVD drive.

Generally, you'll encounter hardware icons only on your Desktop or in Finder windows, or within a device or source list in applications such as iTunes and iPhoto. Figure 2-9 illustrates some of the hardware icons that live in my system.

Programs and applications

These are the fancy icons, folks. Most applications have their own custom icons, and double-clicking one will typically whisk you on your way. Mac OS X also includes a generic icon or two for applications that don't include their own custom icon. Figure 2-10 illustrates a number of my favorite program icons from all sorts of Mac OS X applications.

Running a program in Mac OS X can be as simple as double-clicking the application icon — more on this later, in the section "Houston, We're Go to Launch Programs."

Figure 2-10:
Most Lion
applications
are
represented
by custom
icons.

Files

Your hard drive will contain many thousands of individual files, and the Big X tries to make it as easy as possible to visually identify which application owns which file. Therefore, most applications use a special icon to indicate their data files. For example, Figure 2-11 illustrates several documents and data files created by a range of applications. Some cheeky applications even use more than one icon to differentiate among different file types, such as documents and templates in Microsoft Word.

Figure 2-11:
File icons generally give you a visual clue about their origin.

A number of generic file icons indicate text files, including RTF (short for rich text format) documents and PDF (Portable Document Format) documents, which use the Adobe Acrobat format.

You can open most documents and data files by double-clicking them, which automatically launches the proper application and loads the document.

Folders

Folders have a 3-D look in Mac OS X — and, as you can see in Figure 2-12, some applications even customize their folder icon!

Figure 2-12:
A selection of different generic and custom folder icons.

Major system folders — including Applications, Library, System, Users, Downloads, and Utilities — sport distinctive folder icons in Lion that help identify their contents.

To open a folder within Mac OS X, just double-click it. (Alternatively, you can click it once to select it and then press ⌘+O.) Discover more about how to control the look of folder icons in Book II, Chapter 1.

Aliases

An *alias* is a strange beast. Although it might look like a standard icon, upon closer examination, you'll notice that an alias icon sports a tiny curved arrow at the base, and the tag often appears at the end of the icon name. Figure 2-13 has roped in a variety of aliases for your enjoyment.

Figure 2-13: An alias is a pointer to another application, file, or folder.

Essentially, an alias is a link to something else on your system. For example, an Adobe Photoshop alias can run Photoshop just as the actual program icon can, but it takes up only a scant few bytes on your hard drive. (If you're a Switcher who's just crossed over from the Windows Wilderness, think *shortcut* — Windows shortcuts work in a similar manner.) The alias file is just big enough to hold the location of the actual file or folder, allowing it to yell at Mac OS X: "Hey, the Human actually wants you to run *this* or open *that thing* over there!"

Aliases come in handy for a number of reasons:

✦ **They allow you to launch applications and open files and folders from anywhere in your system.** For example, you might want an alias icon in your MP3 folder that runs the DVD-burning application Toast. With an alias icon, you can launch Toast and burn a data DVD without using Launchpad.

✦ **They can be easily deleted when no longer needed without wreaking havoc on the original application, file, or folder.** If you decide that you'd rather use iTunes to burn audio CDs, you can simply delete the Toast alias without trashing Toast itself.

✦ **Their tiny size allows you to add multiple aliases (and mucho convenience) for a single application without gulping down hard drive space.**

You might be wondering, "Why use aliases when I can just copy the actual application, file, or folder to the desired spot?" Well, indeed you can do that. However, the application might not work in its new location because you didn't copy any of the supporting files that most applications need to run. (An alias actually runs the original application or opens the original file or folder, so things should work just as if you'd double-clicked the original icon.) Additionally, remember that copying applications willy-nilly throughout your hard drive will eat up territory like a horde of angry Vikings.

If you dislike the `alias` hanging off the end of the icon name, feel free to rename it (as I show you in Chapter 3 of this minibook). The alias will continue to function nicely no matter what moniker you give it. (If you create an alias by holding down ⌘+Option whilst dragging the original icon to a new location, the alias name won't include the alias appendage.)

If the original file no longer exists, an alias naturally no longer works, either. However, Mac OS X is sharp enough to automatically "fix" an alias if you rename or move the original file, pointing it to the new location (as long as it remains on the same volume). *Slick!*

Selecting Icons for Fun and Profit

You'll often find yourself performing different actions on one icon — or a number of icons at one time. For example, you can copy or move files from one location on your hard drive to another, or delete a group of files that you no longer need. (The idea of drag-and-drop file management using icons originated on the Macintosh, but I wait until Chapter 3 of this minibook to describe these operations in detail.) In this section, I focus on the basics of selecting one or more icons to specify the files and folders you want to use for whatever you're going to do next.

Selecting a single icon

First, here are the various ways that you can select a single icon for an impending action:

✦ **Place your mouse pointer over the file and click once.** Mac OS X darkens the icon to indicate that it's selected — a mysterious process called *highlighting*.

✦ **Type the first few letters of the icon's name.** After you type a letter, Mac OS X highlights the first icon that matches that character.

✦ **If an icon in a window is already highlighted, you can move the highlight to the next icon across by pressing the right-arrow key.** Likewise, the other three directional arrow keys move the highlight in the other directions. To move through the icons alphabetically, press Tab to go forward and Shift+Tab to go backward.

Selecting multiple icons

To select a gaggle of icons for an action, use one of these methods:

✦ If the icons are next to each other, click and drag within the window (and not directly on a specific item) to highlight them all. As you drag, Mac OS X displays a selection box, and any icons you touch with that box are highlighted when you release the mouse button (as shown in Figure 2-14). Think "lasso" and you'll get the picture.

Figure 2-14: Dragging a selection box in Mac OS X.

✦ You can also select multiple adjacent icons by clicking the first item to highlight it and then holding down the Shift key while clicking the last icon in the series that you want to select.

If the icons are *not* next to each other, you can hold down the ⌘ key while you click each item that you want to select.

Just selecting an icon doesn't launch or do anything . . . you're just marking your territory.

Keyboard Shortcuts for the True Power User

Virtually all Mac OS X applications have their own *keyboard shortcuts* — a ten-cent term for a key combination that performs the same operation as a menu command or a toolbar button. Although the mouse or trackpad might seem the easier path when controlling your Mac, it's not always the fastest. Those hardy souls who venture to learn common keyboard shortcuts can zip through a spreadsheet or warp through a complex outline at speeds that no mere rodent-wrangler could ever hope to attain.

With that in mind — and with the goal of "pumping you up" into a power user — I hereby present the most common keyboard shortcuts for the Big X in Table 2-1. I've also sprinkled other keyboard shortcuts liberally through the book when I discuss other applications, but these combinations are the classics that appear virtually everywhere.

Table 2-1	Common Mac OS X Keyboard Shortcuts	
Combination Key	*Location*	*Action*
⌘+A	Edit menu	Selects all (works in the Finder, too)
⌘+C	Edit menu	Copies the highlighted item to the Clipboard
⌘+H	Application menu	Hides the application
⌘+M	Window menu	Minimizes the active window to the Dock (works in the Finder, too)
⌘+O	File menu	Opens an existing document, file, or folder (works in the Finder, too)
⌘+P	File menu	Prints the current document
⌘+Q	Application menu	Exits the application
⌘+V	Edit menu	Pastes the contents of the Clipboard at the current cursor position
⌘+X	Edit menu	Cuts the highlighted item to the Clipboard
⌘+Z	Edit menu	Reverses the effect of the last action you took
⌘+?	Help menu	Displays the Help system (works in the Finder, too)
⌘+Tab	Finder	Switches between open applications
⌘+Option+M	Finder	Minimizes all Finder windows to the Dock
⌘+Option+W	Finder	Closes all Finder windows

By the way, I should mention that many keyboard combinations use three different keys instead of just two (and a few even use four). When these shortcuts appear in a menu, they look something akin to Egyptian hieroglyphics, but you need only hold down the first two keys simultaneously and press the third key. Common "strange" key symbols that you'll see in both the Finder and most applications are shown in Table 2-2.

Dig that crazy Launchpad!

You can customize your Launchpad display by dragging icons into the order you prefer (for example, I have all the applications I use the most on the first Launchpad page). Drag an application icon to the right or left side of the screen to move it to another page.

Just like a Finder window, Launchpad also allows you to create folders to help you organize your applications. To create a folder within Launchpad, drag one application icon on top of another, and then add other icons by dragging them to the folder (or remove them by dragging them out of the folder). To run an application within a folder, click the folder icon to display the icons within it, and then click on the desired application.

Oh, and there's no need to stick with the boring folder names assigned by Launchpad! To change a folder name, click on the folder to open it, and then click the folder name to display a text editing box. Type the new moniker for the folder and press Return.

If you want to remove an application from Launchpad, click the icon and hold down the button (or continue pressing on the trackpad) until the icons start to wiggle. (Yes, you read that correctly, I said wiggle. iPhone and iPad owners know what I mean.) Click the tiny delete button that appears next to the icon — the one with the x — and the icon disappears. Press Esc to stop all that wiggling. (Note that the applications supplied with Lion can't be deleted this way.)

Table 2-2	Arcane Key Symbols
Action	*Symbol*
Control	⌃
Command	⌘
Del	⌦
Option	⌥
Shift	⇧

Houston, We're Go to Launch Programs

The next stop on your introductory tour of Mac OS X is the starting point for your applications. Although the Finder is useful, you'll likely want to actually do something with your Mac as well.

Running applications from your hard drive

You can launch an application from your hard drive by

✦ Clicking the Launchpad icon in the Dock (it's the second one along, to the right of the Finder icon) to display all of your application icons in a full-screen display. If you have more than one screen (or *page*) worth of applications, press the arrow keys to move between Launchpad pages — with a trackpad or Multi-Touch Magic Mouse, swipe two fingers to the left or right. To launch an application, just click the icon. Figure 2-15 illustrates Launchpad in action. (If you're a proud owner of an iPhone, iPad, or iPod touch, you'll be very familiar with Launchpad from the start, as it corresponds directly to the *Home screen* on those devices.)

Figure 2-15:
Launchpad is my favorite method of launching applications within Lion.

✦ Navigating to the corresponding application folder — by either clicking or double-clicking drive and folder icons — and double-clicking the application icon.

✦ Double-clicking a document or data file that's owned by the application. For example, double-clicking an MP3 audio file runs iTunes.

✦ Double-clicking an alias that you've created for the application. (Get the skinny on aliases in the earlier section, "Aliases." I'll wait.)

✦ Clicking the application's icon in the Dock (more on adding items to the Dock in Book II, Chapter 2).

✦ Selecting the application icon and pressing the ⌘+O keyboard shortcut.

✦ Adding the application to your Login Items list. (I cover the Login Items list in more detail in Book II, Chapter 3.)

Running applications from a CD-ROM or DVD-ROM

After you load a CD-ROM or DVD-ROM, you can display its contents by double-clicking the disc icon that appears on your Desktop. A Finder window opens and shows the files that reside on the disc. (See Figure 2-16.)

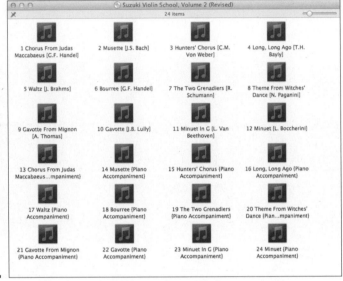

Figure 2-16:
The Finder window shows the contents of a disc when you double-click the icon.

After you locate the application you want to run on the disc, you can launch it by double-clicking it or selecting it and pressing ⌘+O.

Switching 'Twixt Programs with Aplomb

You might think that juggling multiple applications will lead to confusion, fatigue, and dry mouth, but luckily Mac OS X includes a number of features that make it easy to jump between programs that are running on your Mac. Use any of these methods to jump from open application to application:

✦ **Click anywhere in the desired window to make it the active window.**

✦ **Click the application icon in the Dock**. All applications that are running have an icon in the Dock. Depending on the Dock settings in System Preferences, the icon may also have a shiny dot beneath it to indicate that the application is open.

✦ **Press ⌘+Tab.** If you have a dozen windows open, this can get a bit tedious, which leads us to one of Lion's sassiest features, Mission Control. Figure 2-17 shows off Lion's Mission Control screen.

Figure 2-17:
Mission
Control is
Lion's new
desktop
manager.

✦ **Press F9 (or F3, depending on your keyboard) to show *all* open windows using Mission Control, grouped by application; then click the one you want.** Figure 2-16 illustrates the tiled All Window display on my Mac after I press F9. Move the cursor on top of the window you want to activate — the window turns blue when it's selected — and click once to switch to that window. You can specify which keys you want to use within the Mission Control pane in System Preferences.

✦ **Press F10 (or Control+F3, depending on your keyboard) to show all open windows from the application that you're currently using; click the one that you want to activate.** This Mission Control function is great for choosing from all the images that you've opened in Photoshop or all the Safari web pages littering your Desktop!

Along with the window switch, an astute observer will notice that the application menu bar also changes to match the now-active application.

Besides the F9/F3 and F10/Control+F3 hot keys that I just discussed, Mission Control provides one more nifty function: Press F11 (or ⌘+F3), and all your open windows scurry to the side of the screen. (Much like a herd of zebras if you dropped a lioness in the middle.) Now you can work with drives, files, and aliases on your Desktop — and when you're ready to confront those dozen application windows again, just press the keyboard shortcut a second time.

Although the Mission Control screen appears automatically when necessary, you can also launch it at any time from your Mac's Launchpad display, or by pressing the Mission Control/F9 key on your keyboard. If you're using a trackpad, display the Mission Control screen by swiping up with three fingers.

Ah, but what if you want to switch to an entirely different set of applications? For example, suppose that you're slaving away at your pixel-pushing job — designing a magazine cover with Pages. Your page design desktop also includes Photoshop and Aperture, which you switch between often using one of the techniques I just described. Suddenly, however, you realize you need to schedule a meeting with others in your office using iCal, and you want to check your e-mail in Apple Mail. What to do?

Well, you could certainly open Launchpad and launch those two applications on top of your graphics applications, and then minimize or close them . . . but with Mission Control's *Spaces* feature, you can press the Control+Left Arrow or Control+Right Arrow sequences to switch to a completely different "communications" desktop, with iCal and Apple Mail windows already open and in your favorite positions! (Figure 2-17 illustrates multiple Spaces desktops at the top of the Mission Control screen.)

After you're done setting up your meeting and answering any important e-mail, simply press Control+Left Arrow or Control+Right Arrow again to switch back to your "graphics" desktop, where all your work is exactly as you left it! (And yes, Virginia, Spaces does indeed work with full-screen applications.)

Now imagine that you've also created a custom "music" desktop for GarageBand and iTunes . . . or perhaps you paired iWeb, MobileMe, and iPhoto together as a "Webmaster" desktop. See why everyone's so excited? (Let's see Windows 7 do *that* out of the box.)

To create a new desktop for use within Spaces, click the Launchpad icon in the Dock, and then click the Mission Control icon. Now you can set up new Spaces desktops — move your pointer to the top right corner of the Mission Control screen, and click on the Add button (with the plus sign) that appears. Spaces creates a new empty desktop thumbnail. Switch to the new desktop by clicking on the thumbnail at the top of the Mission Control screen, and open those applications you want to include. (Alternately, you can drag the applications from Mission Control onto the desired desktop thumbnail.) That's all there is to it!

To switch an application window between Spaces desktops, drag the window to the edge of the desktop and hold it there. Spaces will automatically move the window to the next desktop. (Applications can also be dragged between desktops within the Mission Control screen.) You can also delete a desktop from the Mission Control screen — just hover your mouse pointer over the offending Spaces thumbnail, and then click the Delete button (with the X) that appears.

You can jump directly to a specific Spaces desktop by clicking on its thumbnail within your Mission Control screen — or you can also hold down the Control key and press the number corresponding to that desktop. Finally, you can always use the Control+Left Arrow or Control+Right Arrow shortcuts to move between desktops and full-screen applications.

Opening and Saving Your Stuff in an Application

Almost all Mac OS X applications open and save documents in the same way, whether you're creating a presentation with Keynote or expressing your cinematic side with iMovie. Therefore, I take a moment to outline the common procedures for opening and saving documents. Believe me, you'll perform these two rituals dozens of times a week, so no nodding off.

Opening a document

First, the simple way to load a document: Double-click that document in a Finder window, and . . . well, that's it. (This is my preferred method because I'm an ALT — short for *Admitted Lazy Techno-wizard* — who would rather use complex hand movements to pour myself another Diet Coke.)

To open a document the hard way — from inside an application — here's the plan:

1. **Choose File➪Open or press that handy ⌘+O key combination.**

Your Mac OS X program is likely to display the attractive Open dialog that you see in Figure 2-18.

2. **Navigate to the location of the document that you want to open.**

The pop-up menu allows you to jump directly to common locations — such as the Desktop, your Home folder, and your Documents folder — as well as places that you've recently accessed (Recent Places).

If the target folder isn't in your pop-up menu, it's time to use the Open dialog sidebar, where your hard drives, DVD drives, and network locations hang out.

3. **Click the habitat where the file will be found.**

If you're using Column view, you'll note that the right column(s) will change to show you the contents of the item that you just clicked. In this way, you can cruise through successive folders to find that elusive document. (This somewhat time-consuming process is somewhat derisively called *drilling* — hence, the importance of using Recent Items, or dragging files, locations, and applications into the sidebar at the left of the Finder.)

4. When you sight the document that you want to load, either double-click it or click once to highlight the filename and then click Open.

"Hey, the Open dialog can be resized!" That's right, good buddy — you can expand the Open dialog to show more columns and find things more easily. Click and drag the bottom-right corner of the Open dialog to resize it. (You can also switch from column view to list view or icon view or flow view, just as you can in a Finder window, using the buttons to the left of the pop-up location menu.)

Saving a document

To save a document, follow these steps:

1. Choose File⇨Save.

If you've previously saved this document, your application should immediately overwrite the existing document with the new copy, and you get to return to work . . . end of story. If you *haven't* previously saved this document, the program will display a Save dialog that's usually very similar to the Open dialog; it generally has a few more options, however, so stay frosty.

2. **Navigate to the location where you'd like to save the document and then type a filename.**

   Often, you can use a default name that's already provided by the thoughtful folks who developed the software. Note that you might be given the chance to save the document in several different formats. For example, a word processing application might allow you to save a document in RTF, HyperText Markup Language (HTML), and even bargain-basement text format.

3. **Click Save (or OK, depending on the application).**

If an application offers a Save As menu option in the File menu, you can in effect copy the document by saving a new version of the document under another name. Save As comes in particularly handy when you want to retain the original version of a document.

Quitting Applications

If I had a twisted and warped sense of humor, I'd simply tell you to quit applications by pulling your Mac's power cord from the wall socket. (Luckily, I don't.) There are, however, safer and more sane ways to exit a program — use one of these methods instead:

✦ Press the ⌘+Q keyboard shortcut.

✦ Choose the Application's named menu and then click Quit.

✦ Control-click (or right-click) the application icon in the Dock and click Quit on the pop-up menu that appears.

You can also click the Close button on the application window. Note, however, that this doesn't always completely close down the application. For example, Safari stays running even if you close the browser window. In general, if the application works within a single window (such as System Preferences), closing the window also quits the application.

As I mentioned earlier in the chapter, if the application supports Lion's Resume feature, the document you were working on will automatically be displayed when you launch the application again.

Chapter 3: Basic OS X Housekeeping

In This Chapter

- Copying, moving, and duplicating files
- Deleting and recovering files
- Renaming files
- Finding specific files
- Locking files
- Using Apple menu commands
- Using Services, the Go menu, and menu icons
- Listening to audio discs and recording data discs
- Printing within Mac OS X applications

After you master basic Mac spell-casting — things like selecting items, using menus, opening and saving documents, working with windows, and launching an application or two — it's time to delve deeper into Mac OS X. (Can you tell I'm a Dungeons & Dragons old-timer?)

In this chapter, I discuss file management, showing you the hidden power behind the friendly Apple menu. I also discuss some of the more advanced menu commands, how to print within most applications, and how to listen to an audio CD on your Mac. (It makes a doggone good stereo, especially with a good set of external speakers.) Finally, I introduce you to the built-in CD/DVD recording features within the Big X and how to add a standard USB printer to your system.

The Finder: It's the Wind beneath Your Wings

So what exactly is the Finder anyway? It's a rather nebulous term, but in essence, the Finder gives Mac OS X the basic functions that you'll use for the procedures I outline in this chapter. This über-OS has been around in one guise or another since the days of System 6 — the creaking old days when a Mac was an all-in-one computer with a built-in screen. Come to think of it, some things never change (as I glance at my iMac).

The Finder is always running, so it's always available — and you can always switch to it, even when several other applications are open and chugging away. Figure 3-1 illustrates the Dock with the rather perspective-crazy Finder icon at the far left side.

Action button

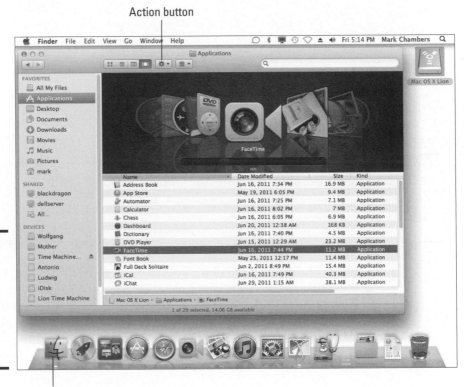

Figure 3-1: The Finder is always there, supporting you with a unique smile.

Finder icon

Is that icon supposed to be one face or two faces? I'm still confused, and I've been using the Mac now since 1989.

Don't forget that Mac OS X gives you a second method of doing everything I cover in this chapter: You can use Terminal to uncover the text-based UNIX core of Mac OS X, employing your blazing typing speed to take care of things from the command line. Of course, that's not the focus of this book, but for those who want to boldly go where no Mac operating system has gone before, you'll find more in Book VIII, Chapter 1. Despite what you might have been led to believe, power and amazing speed are to be found in character-based computing.

Copying and Moving Files and Folders

Here's where drag-and-drop makes things about as easy as computing can get:

✦ **To copy a file or folder from one window to another location on the same drive:** Hold down the Option key and click and drag the icon from its current home to the new location. (*Note:* You can drop files and folders on top of other folders, which puts the copy inside that folder.) If you're copying multiple items, select them first (read how in Book I, Chapter 2) and then drag and drop the entire crew.

"Is the Desktop a valid target location for a file or folder?" You're darn tootin'! I recommend, though, that you avoid cluttering up your Desktop with more than a handful of files. Instead, create a folder or two on your Desktop and then store those items within those folders. If you work with the contents of a specific folder often, drag it into the Favorites heading in the Sidebar (the column at the left side of any Finder window), and you can open that folder from the Finder with a single click — no matter where you are! (Alternatively, drag the folder to the right side of the Dock and drop it there, and you can open it with a single click from anywhere.)

✦ **To copy items from one window to a location on another drive:** Click and drag the icon from the window to a window displaying the contents of the target drive. Or, in the spirit of drag-and-drop, you can simply drag the items to the drive icon, which places them in the root folder of that drive.

✦ **To move items from one window to another location on the same drive:** Simply drag the icon to the new location, whether it be a window or a folder. (To move items to a different drive, hold down the ⌘ key while dragging.)

Mac OS X provides you with a number of visual cues to let you know what's being copied or moved. For example, dragging one or more items displays a ghost image of the items, and when you've positioned the mouse pointer over the target, Mac OS X highlights that location to let you know that you're in the zone. If you're moving or copying items into another Finder window, the window border is highlighted to let you know that Mac OS X understands the game plan.

In case you move the wrong thing or you port it to the wrong location, press ⌘+Z to undo the previous action.

If the item that you're dragging already exists in the target location, you get a confirmation dialog like the one you see in Figure 3-2. You can choose to replace the file, leave the existing file alone, or stop the entire shooting match.

Figure 3-2:
To replace
or not to
replace —
the choice
is yours.

Cloning Your Items — It's Happening Now!

No need for sci-fi equipment or billions in cash — you can create an exact duplicate of any item within the same folder. (This is often handy when you need a simple backup of the same file in the same folder or when you're going to edit a document but you want to keep the original intact.)

Click the item to select it and then choose File⇨Duplicate (or use the keyboard shortcut and press ⌘+D). To distinguish the duplicate from the original, Mac OS X adds the word *copy* to the end of the duplicate's icon name; additional copies have a number added to the name as well.

Alternatively, drag-and-drop aficionados can hold down the Option key and drag the original item to another spot in the same window. When you release the button, the duplicate appears.

Heck, if you prefer the mouse, you can right-click the item and then choose Duplicate from the contextual menu that appears. Decisions, decisions . . . .

Oh, and don't forget that Action button (it looks like a little gear with a downward-pointing arrow) on the Finder toolbar (refer to Figure 3-1). You can also click the Action button and choose Duplicate from the pop-up menu.

When you duplicate a folder, Mac OS X automatically duplicates all the contents of the folder as well. Remember that this could take some time if the folder contains a large number of small files (or a small number of large files). Groucho would've loved computers!

Deleting That Which Should Not Be

Even Leonardo da Vinci made the occasional design mistake — his trash can was likely full of bunched-up pieces of parchment. Luckily, no trees will be wasted when you decide to toss your unneeded files and folders; this section shows you how to delete items from your system.

By the way, as you'll soon witness for yourself, moving items to the Trash doesn't necessarily mean that they're immediately history.

Dragging unruly files against their will

In Mac OS X, the familiar Trash can appears on the right edge of the Dock — in fact, it's a spiffy-looking wire can. You can click and drag the items that you've selected to the Trash and drop them on top of the wire can icon to delete them. When the Trash contains at least one item, the wire can icon changes to appear as if it were full of trash.

You can also add a Delete icon to your Finder toolbar. For all the details, see Book II, Chapter 1.

Deleting with the menus and the keyboard

The mouse isn't absolutely necessary when deleting items. Your other options for scrapping selected files include

✦ Choosing File from the Finder menu and choosing the Move to Trash menu item

✦ Pressing the ⌘+Delete keyboard shortcut

✦ Clicking the Action button on the Finder toolbar and selecting Move to Trash from the pop-up menu

✦ Right-clicking the item to display the contextual menu and then choosing Move to Trash from that menu

Emptying That Wastepaper Basket

As I mention earlier, moving items to the Trash doesn't actually delete them immediately from your system. Believe me, this fail-safe measure comes in handy when you've been banging away at the keyboard for several hours and you stop paying close attention to what you're doing. (I usually also blame lack of Diet Coke.) More on how to rescue files from the Trash in the next section.

As you can with any folder, you can check the contents of the Trash by clicking its icon in the Dock.

After you double-check the Trash contents and you're indeed absolutely sure that you want to delete its contents, use one of the following methods to nuke the digital Bit Bucket:

✦ If the contents of the Trash are still displayed in a Finder window, click the Empty button at the upper right corner of the window.

✦ Choose the Empty Trash menu item from the Finder menu.

✦ Choose Secure Empty Trash from the Finder menu.

Believe it or not, if you use the standard Empty Trash command, you *still* haven't completely zapped that refuse! Some third-party hard drive repair and recovery programs will allow an uncool person to restore items from the Trash. Use the Secure Empty Trash method for those sensitive files and folders that you want to immediately and irrevocably delete — the data is overwritten with random characters, making it impossible to recover. (A great idea for that Mac you want to sell on eBay, no? In fact, if you like, you can reinstall Mac OS X before you ship the Mac, leaving the Setup Assistant ready-to-run for the new owner.)

✦ Press the ⌘+Shift+Delete keyboard shortcut.

✦ Click the Trash icon in the Dock, hold down the mouse button, and choose Empty Trash from the menu that appears.

✦ Right-click the Trash icon in the Dock and then choose Empty Trash from the contextual menu that appears.

Depending on the method you select and the settings you choose in System Preferences (which I cover in Book II, Chapter 3), Mac OS X might present you with a confirmation dialog to make sure that you actually want the Trash emptied.

WAIT! 1 Need That After All!

In the adrenaline-inducing event that you need to rescue something that shouldn't have ended up in the scrap pile, first click the Trash icon in the Dock to display the contents of the Trash. Then rescue the items that you want to save by dragging them to the Desktop or a folder on your hard drive. (This is roughly analogous to rescuing your old baseball glove from the family garage sale.)

Feel free to gloat. If someone else is nearby, ask her to pat you on the back and call you a lifesaver.

Renaming Your Items

You wouldn't get far in today's spacious virtual world without being able to change a moniker for a file or folder. To rename an item in Mac OS X, use one of these two methods:

✦ **With the mouse:** Click once on an icon's name (or just press Return). Mac OS X highlights the text in an edit box — type the new name and then press Return when you're done.

You want to wait a few seconds between clicks, as opposed to doing a rapid-fire double-click.

✦ **From the Info dialog:** Select the item and press ⌘+I to display the Info dialog; then click the triangle next to Name & Extension. Click in the name field, drag the mouse to highlight the text that you want to change, and type the replacement text.

Naturally, the first method is the easiest, and it's the one that I use most often.

Adding a Dash of Color

Lion also provides the ability to *color-code* files and folders to help you organize and recognize your data in a hurry. For example, why not assign the green label color to the files and folders that make up your current project? Or, if you need to mark a file for immediate attention, assign it the red label color.

To assign a label color to selected files and folders, you have three options:

✦ Click the Action button on the Finder toolbar and then click the desired color.

✦ Right-click the selection and then choose the color from the pop-up menu.

✦ Click File and choose that perfect shade from the menu.

Displaying the Facts on Files and Folders

The Finder's Info dialog is the place to view the specifics on any highlighted item (including drives and aliases). Select an item and press ⌘+I, click the Action toolbar button and then select Get Info from the menu, right-click on the item and select Get Info, or choose the Finder's File menu and then choose Get Info (see the results in Figure 3-3). If you select more than one item (up to ten items), Lion opens a separate Info dialog for each item.

You can also show an Info dialog that summarizes multiple items — this is A Good Thing if you need to see the total size for several files or folders. To display the Summary Info dialog, select the desired items, hold down the Control key and click File⇨Get Summary Info. (Yep, in case you were wondering, some of the items on the File menu do change when you hold down Control. Display the File menu and try it yourself!)

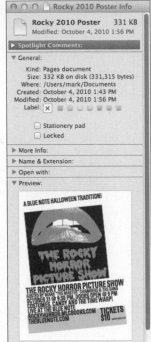

Figure 3-3:
The General
information
panel
appears first
when you
display the
Info dialog.

Mac OS X displays the General information panel when you first open the Info dialog, but other panels are usually available (depending on the type of selected items).

For most types of files and folders, the Info dialog can tell you

✦ **Kind:** What type of item it is — for example, whether it's a file, folder, drive, or alias

✦ **Open with:** What program launches automatically when you open the selected item

✦ **Size:** The total size of the item (or items, if there are more than ten) that you select

✦ **Where:** The actual path on your hard drive where the item is located

✦ **Dates:** The date when the item was created and was last modified

✦ **Version:** The application version number

✦ **Name & Extension:** The file's name and extension

✦ **Sharing & Permissions:** The privileges that control who can do what to the file (more on this later, in Book II, Chapter 6) and whether a file is locked in read-only mode

Some of this information you can change, and some can only be displayed. To banish the Info dialog from your Desktop, click the dialog's Close button.

You can hide or display various parts of the Info dialog by clicking the triangles next to each section heading.

For the rest of this section, I describe a number of tasks that you can accomplish from the Info dialog.

If you use a specific document over and over as a basis for different revisions, you can enable the Stationery Pad check box on the General information panel to use the file as stationery. Opening a stationery file automatically creates a new, untitled version of the file in the linked application; this can save you steps compared with duplicating the file or using the Save As procedure that I show you in Book I, Chapter 2.

Adding Spotlight comments

Mac OS X provides you with a Spotlight Comments field in the Info dialog, where you can add additional text that's stored along with the file (and can be matched with Spotlight). I use this feature to record the version number of manuscript chapters and programs that I create during the course of writing books.

To add a comment, follow these steps:

1. **Display the Info dialog for the item by pressing ⌘+I or choosing File⇨Get Info.**

2. **Click in the Spotlight Comments box and type the comment text.**

   If you need to expand the Spotlight Comments section of the Info dialog, click the triangle next to the Spotlight Comments heading. The arrow rotates and the Spotlight Comments box appears.

3. **Close the Info dialog to save the comment.**

Displaying extensions

Extensions are alien creatures to most Mac owners. However, these (usually) three- or four-character add-ons that follow a period at the end of a filename have been a mainstay in the Windows and UNIX environments for years. An *extension* identifies what program owns a specific file, and therefore which application launches automatically when you double-click that file's icon. Examples of common extensions (and the applications that own them) include

✦ **.pdf:** Preview, or Adobe Acrobat

✦ **.doc or .docx:** Microsoft Word

✦ **.pages:** Apple Pages

✦ **.key:** Apple Keynote

✦ **.psd:** Adobe Photoshop

✦ **.jpeg or .jpg:** Preview, or your image editor

✦ **.tiff or .tif:** Preview, or your image editor

✦ **.htm or .html:** Safari, or your web browser of choice

Why would someone want to see a file's extension? It comes in handy when a number of different types of files are linked to the same application. For example, both JPEG and TIFF images are displayed as thumbnails in a Finder window, so it's sometimes very hard to tell one from the other. With extensions displayed, it's easy to tell what type of file you're looking at.

Follow this procedure to hide or display extensions with your filenames:

1. **Display the Info dialog for the item by pressing ⌘+I or choosing File➪Get Info.**

2. **If you need to expand the Name & Extension section of the Info dialog, click the triangle next to the Name & Extension heading.**

3. **To display the extension for the selected file, clear the Hide Extension check box to disable it.**

4. **Close the Info dialog to save your changes.**

Choosing the application with which to launch a file

So what's the plan if the wrong application launches when you double-click a file? Not a problem: You can also change the linked application from the Info dialog as well. (I told you this was a handy toybox, didn't I?) Follow these steps to choose another application to pair with a selected file:

1. **Click the Action button on the Finder toolbar and click Get Info to display the Info dialog for the item.**

2. **Click the triangle next to the Open With heading to expand it.**

3. **Click the pop-up menu button.**

   Mac OS X displays the applications that it feels are best suited to open this type of document.

4. **Select the application that should open the file.**

To go completely hog-wild and choose a different application, select Other from the Open With pop-up menu. Mac OS X displays a Choose Other Application dialog, where you can navigate to and select the application you want. (If the application isn't recognized as *recommended,* click the Enable pop-up menu and choose All Applications.) After you highlight the application, click the Always Open With check box to enable it and click the Add button.

If you don't have an application that can open a specific file type, you can also opt to search the App Store for an application you can purchase to open it — choose App Store from the Open With pop-up menu. (A sometimes pricey option, of course, but certainly convenient!)

5. **To globally update all the documents of the same type to launch the application that you chose, click the Change All button.**

   Mac OS X displays a confirmation dialog asking whether you're sure about making this drastic change. Click Continue to update the other files of the same type or click Cancel to return to the Info dialog.

6. **Close the Info dialog to save your changes.**

Locking files against evildoers

"Holy Item Insurance, Batman!" That's right, Boy Wonder: Before I leave the friendly land of the Info dialog, every Mac owner needs to know how to protect files and folders from accidental deletion or editing. By locking a file, you allow it to be opened and copied — but not changed, renamed, or sent to the Trash. Locked items appear in the Finder with a small padlock attached to the icon.

To lock or unlock a file, you have to have ownership of the file. I cover privileges in Book II, but on a Mac where you've configured only one administrator account, you should already have ownership.

If you're considering changing the ownership of a system-owned file, *don't do it.* You could throw a serious monkey wrench into your Lion system.

To lock a file, follow this procedure:

1. **Display the Info dialog for the item.**

2. **Select the Locked check box to enable it.**

   The Locked check box is in the General section of the dialog.

3. **Close the Info dialog to save your changes.**

Creating an Alias

I mention aliases in Book I, Chapter 2. As I discuss in that chapter, an *alias* acts as a link to an application or document that actually exists elsewhere on your system (a handy trick to use when organizing items on your hard drive). You have a number of different ways to conjure an alias after you select an item:

✦ Choose File from the Finder menu and choose the Make Alias menu item. (You have to move the alias yourself.)

✦ Press the ⌘+L keyboard shortcut. (Again, you have to move the new alias to its new location.)

✦ Click the Action button on the Finder toolbar and then click Make Alias.

✦ Right-click the selected item and then choose Make Alias from the contextual menu that appears.

In addition, you can hold down the ⌘+Option key combination and drag the item to the location where you want the alias.

Although Mac OS X does a great job in tracking the movements of an original and updating an alias, some actions can break the link. For example, if you delete the original, the alias is left wandering in search of a home. However, all is not lost — when you double-click a broken alias, Mac OS X offers to help you fix the alias. This involves browsing through your system to locate a new original.

Using the Apple Menu

The Apple menu is a familiar sight to any Mac owner. Although Apple contemplated removing it during the original development and beta cycle for Mac OS X version 10.0, the ruckus and cry from beta-testers ensured that it remains today. It's amazing how reassuring that little fellow can be when you boot the Big X for the first time.

In this section, I cover the important things that are parked under the Apple menu.

Using Recent Items

If you're like most of us — and I think I'm safe in assuming that you are — you tend to work on the same set of applications and files (and use the same network servers) during the day. Even with features like Mission Control, Launchpad, and Stacks, you'll sometimes find yourself drilling down through at least one layer of folders to actually reach the stuff that you need. To make things easier on yourself, you could create a set of aliases on your

Desktop that link to those servers, files, and applications . . . but as you moved from project to project, you'd find yourself constantly updating the aliases. As Blackbeard the Pirate was wont to exclaim, "Arrgh!"

Ah, but Mac OS X is a right-smart operating system, and several years ago, Apple created the Recent Items menu to save you the trouble of drilling for applications and files (and even network servers as well). Figure 3-4 illustrates the Recent Items menu from my system. Note that the menu is thoughtfully divided into Applications, Documents, and Servers. When you open documents or launch applications, they're added to the list. (Accountants will revel in this First In, First Out technology.) To launch an application or document from the Recent Items menu — or connect to a network server — just click it.

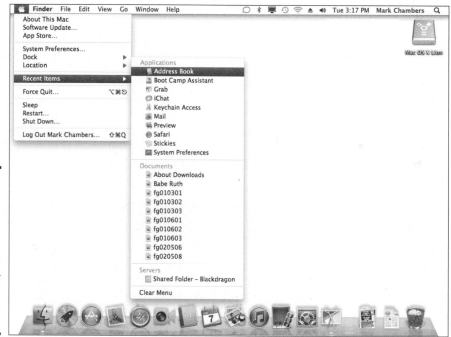

Figure 3-4:
Use the
Recent
Items
menu to
access files,
applications,
and servers
you've been
using.

To wipe the contents of the Recent Items menu — for example, if you've just finished a project and want to turn over a new digital leaf — click Recent Items and choose the Clear Menu item.

You can specify the number of recent items that will appear in the menu from System Preferences; display the Appearance pane and click the Applications, Documents, and Servers list boxes in the Number of Recent Items field. (More on this in Book II, Chapter 3.)

Also, remember the trick that I mention earlier: You can drag any folder or server into the Sidebar column at the left of a Finder window, adding it to that exclusive club that includes your Home folder, Applications folder, and media folders.

Playing with the Dock

You know how Air Force One acts as the mobile nerve center for the president? And how The Chief can jet all around the world and take all his stuff along with him? Well, the Dock is kind of like that. Sort of.

If you want your Dock to go mobile as well, click the Apple menu and choose the Dock item to display the submenu. Here's a rundown of the options that you'll find:

✦ **Hiding:** Click Turn Hiding On/Off to toggle the automatic hiding of the Dock. With hiding on, the Dock disappears off the edge of the screen until you move the mouse pointer to that edge. (This is great for those who want to make use of as much Desktop territory as possible for their applications.)

You can press ⌘+Option+D to toggle Dock hiding on and off from the keyboard.

✦ **Magnification:** Click Turn Magnification On/Off to toggle icon magnification when your pointer is selecting an icon from the Dock. With magnification on, the icons in the Dock get really, *really* big . . . a good thing for Mr. Magoo or those with grandiose schemes to take over the world. Check out the rather oversized icons in Figure 3-5. (The amount of magnification can be controlled from the System Preferences Dock settings, which I explain in Book II, Chapter 3.)

✦ **Position:** Click one of three choices (Position on Left, Bottom, or Right) to make the Dock appear on the left, bottom, or right of the screen, respectively.

✦ **Dock Preferences:** Click this to display the System Preferences Dock settings, which I explain in Book II, Chapter 3.

Bad program! Quit!

Once in a while, you'll encounter a stubborn application that locks up, slows to a crawl, or gets stuck in an endless loop. Although Mac OS X is a highly advanced operating system, it can still fall prey to bad programming or corrupted data.

Luckily, you can easily shut down these troublemakers from the Apple menu. Just choose Force Quit to display the Force Quit Applications dialog that you see in Figure 3-6. (Keyboard types can press ⌘+Option+Esc.) Select the application that you want to banish and then click the Force Quit button; Mac OS X requests confirmation, after which you click the Force Quit button again.

Figure 3-5:
Now those,
my friend,
are some
pumped-up
icons.

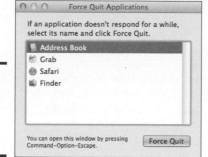

Figure 3-6:
Forcing an
application
to take a
hike.

If you select Finder in the Force Quit Applications dialog, the button changes
to Relaunch. This allows you to restart the Finder, which comes in handy
if your system appears to be unstable. (This is much faster than actually
restarting your Mac.)

Forcing an application to quit will also close any open documents that you
were working with in that application, so *save your work* (if the program
will allow you to save anything). If you relaunch the Finder, some programs
might restart as well.

Tracking down your version

This isn't a big deal, but if you choose About This Mac from the Apple menu, Mac OS X displays the About This Mac dialog that you see in Figure 3-7. In case you need to check the amount of memory or the processor in an unfamiliar Mac, the About This Mac dialog can display these facts in a twinkling. However, I primarily use it to check the Mac OS X version and build number as well as to launch the Apple System Information utility (which I discuss in full in Chapter 7 of this minibook). Click the More Info button to launch System Information.

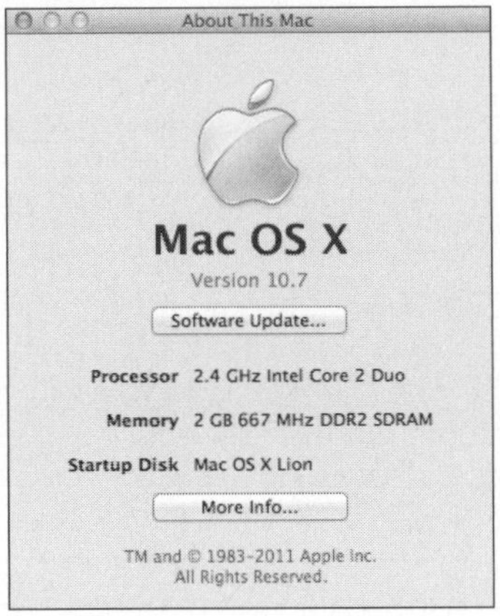

Figure 3-7:
Display
your Mac's
memory,
processor,
startup disk,
and Big X
version.

About This Mac

Mac OS X

Version 10.7

Software Update...

Processor   2.4 GHz Intel Core 2 Duo

Memory   2 GB 667 MHz DDR2 SDRAM

Startup Disk   Mac OS X Lion

More Info...

TM and © 1983–2011 Apple Inc.
All Rights Reserved.

Apple allows you to launch Software Update from three spots: the About This Mac dialog, the System Preferences window, and the Apple menu . . . sheesh, they must really want you to keep your Big X up to date, I guess.

Visiting the App Store

If you haven't jumped into Apple's virtual storefront for Mac software, click the Apple menu and choose App Store, or click that handy App Store icon in the Dock. The App Store is a slick way to take care of the Big Three Points when shopping for software: finding the right application, installing the application, and keeping it updated. You can shop by categories, view the latest software additions to the App Store, or click in the App Store search box (at the upper right corner of the window) to find a specific title or type of application. Click the thumbnail for an application to view detailed information, including screenshots and user reviews. Click the Back arrow at the top left corner of the App Store window to return to the previous screen.

Along the top of the App Store window, you'll see a number of toolbar buttons that let you jump directly to Apple's featured titles, as well as lists of the applications you've already purchased and a list of the software you've bought that needs updating.

When you've located the perfect application for your needs, click on the price button to purchase it. You'll need an Apple ID — if you haven't set up an Apple ID account yet, click Create Apple ID and the App Store will be happy to lead you through the (relatively) painless process.

After you've purchased the application, it's automatically downloaded to your Mac, and the App Store even adds an icon to your LaunchPad so that you can try out your new software! In fact, you can install your App Store purchases on all of your Macs, without having to buy additional copies or licenses. Leave it to Apple to Do Things the Right Way.

Specifying a location

Mac OS X allows you to create multiple network locations. Think of a location as a separate configuration that you use when you connect to a different network from a different locale. For instance, if you travel to a branch office, you'd assign a location for your desk and a location for the remote branch. A student might assign one location for her home network and another for the college computer lab network.

A location saves all the specific values that you've entered in the System Preferences Network settings, including IP address, DNS servers, proxy servers, and the like. If all this means diddly squat to you, don't worry — I explain this in Book VI, Chapter 1. For now, just remember that you can switch between locations by choosing Location from the Apple menu, which displays a submenu of locations that you can choose among. (You must create at least a second location for the Location menu item to appear in the Apple menu.)

Availing Yourself of Mac OS X Services

In Mac OS X, Services allow you to merge information from one application with another. To Mac old-timers, that might sound suspiciously like the Clipboard; however, Services can also include functionality from an application, so you can create new documents or complete tasks without running another program! Services can be used in both the Finder and Mac OS X applications.

To illustrate, here's a fun example:

1. **Launch TextEdit (you'll find it in your Applications folder) and type your name.**

2. **Highlight your name.**

3. **Click the TextEdit menu — don't switch to the Finder; use the TextEdit Application menu — and choose Services.**

4. **From the Services submenu, choose Search with Google.**

After you've shaken your head at all the sites devoted to people with the same name, consider what you just did — you ran the Safari application from within TextEdit, using selected words! Pretty slick, eh?

A glance at the other Services that show up from within most applications gives you an idea of just how convenient and powerful Mac OS X Services can be. I often use Services to take care of things such as

✦ Sending an e-mail message from an e-mail address in a text file or the Address Book (via the Mail Service)

✦ Capturing a screen snapshot within an application (using the Capture Selection from Screen Service)

✦ Sending a file to a Bluetooth-equipped PDA or cell phone within an application (using the Send File to Bluetooth Device service)

Remember, you can access the Services menu from a Mac OS X application by picking that program's Application menu (sometimes called the *named menu*). For instance, in the demonstration earlier, I use the TextEdit menu that appears on the TextEdit menu bar. In Microsoft Word, I would click the Word menu.

Geez, I think the computing world needs another word for *menu* — don't you?

Many third-party applications that you install under Mac OS X can add their own commands under the Services menu, so be sure to read the documentation for a new application to see what Service functionality it adds.

You can enable or disable menu items from the Services menu — for example, the Send File to Bluetooth Device service that I mentioned earlier is turned off by default. To make changes to your Services, display the Services menu from the Finder menu bar and choose Services Preferences. Lion displays the Services list in the Keyboard pane of System Preferences, and you can toggle the display of a service by clicking the check box next to it.

Get Thee Hence: Using the Go Menu

Remember the transporter from *Star Trek*? Step on the little platform, assume a brave pose, and whoosh! — you're transported instantaneously to another ship or (more likely) to a badly designed planet exterior built inside a soundstage. Talk about convenience . . . that is, as long as the doggone thing didn't malfunction.

The Finder's Go menu gives you the chance to play Captain Kirk: You can jump immediately to specific spots, both within the confines of your own system as well as external environments, such as your network or the Internet. (You can leave your phaser and tricorder in your cabin.)

The destinations that you can travel to using the Go menu and the iDisk submenu include the following:

✦ **Back/Forward/Enclosing Folder:** I lump these three commands together because they're all basic navigation commands. For example, Back and Forward operate just as they do in Safari or your favorite web browser. If you're currently inside a folder, you can return to the parent folder by clicking Enclosing Folder.

✦ **All My Files:** This window displays all of the documents you've created or added, like word processing documents, images, and movies.

✦ **Documents:** Yep, you guessed it: This window displays the contents of your Documents folder.

✦ **Desktop:** This window displays the files and folders that you've stored on your Leopard desktop.

✦ **Downloads:** Here you'll find the contents of your Downloads folder.

✦ **Home:** This window displays the home directory for the user currently logged in.

✦ **Library:** This window displays the contents of the Library folder for the user currently logged in (the Library folder is located within the user's home directory). Note that the Library entry in the Go menu appears only when you hold down the Option key.

✦ **Computer:** This window includes your hard drives, CD and DVD drives, and your network — the same places that appear when you open a new Finder window with the ⌘+N key shortcut.

✦ **Network:** Did you guess that this displays a window with all your network's servers? Dead giveaway, that.

✦ **iDisk:** This window displays the contents of your Internet iDisk storage (or someone else's). (More on the coolness that is iDisk in Book V, Chapter 4.)

✦ **Applications:** This window includes all the applications that appear in your Mac OS X Applications folder (a neat *Just the programs, ma'am* arrangement that really comes in handy).

✦ **Utilities:** This window displays the contents of your Mac OS X Utilities folder.

✦ **Recent Folders:** This window displays a submenu that allows you to choose among the folders that you've recently opened.

You can also type the path for a specific folder (use the Go to Folder command) or connect to a specific network server (use the Connect to Server command).

Note that most of the Go menu commands include keyboard shortcuts, proving once again that the fingers are quicker than the mouse.

Monkeying with the Menu Bar

Ever stared at a menu bar for inspiration? Fortunately for Mac owners like you and me, people in Cupertino are paid to do just that, and these designers get the big bucks to make the Mac OS X menu bar the best that it can be. Thus were born menu bar icons, which add useful controls in what would otherwise be a wasted expanse of white.

Using menu bar icons

Depending on your hardware, Mac OS X might install several menu bar icons. The Volume icon is always there by default, along with the Clock display, which is actually an icon in disguise. Figure 3-8 illustrates these standard icons, along with a couple of others.

Figure 3-8:
Adjust your
Mac with
a click of
these menu
icons.

Some icons won't appear unless you turn them on. For instance, the Displays icon won't appear unless you enable the Show Displays in Menu Bar check box within the Displays pane in System Preferences. The Displays menu bar icon, which looks like a monitor, allows you to choose from the recommended resolutions and color depth settings for your graphics card and monitor. For example, the recommended settings for my MacBook Pro, which has an LCD monitor, include 1024 x 768, 1280 x 800, and 1440 x 900 resolutions, and my display can be set to thousands or millions of colors.

Typically, it's a good idea to choose the highest resolution and the highest color depth. You can also jump directly to the System Preferences Display settings by clicking Open Displays Preferences in the menu.

To quickly change the audio volume level within Mac OS X, click the Sound Volume icon (it looks like a speaker with emanating sound waves) once to display its slider control; then click and drag the slider to adjust the level up or down. After you select a level by releasing the mouse button, your Mac thoughtfully plays the default system sound to help you gauge the new volume level.

Depending on the functionality that you're using with Mac OS X, these other menu bar icons might also appear:

✦ **Modem status:** You can turn on the display of the Modem status icon from the corresponding modem panel on the Network pane in System Preferences, which I discuss in Book II, Chapter 3. The icon can be set to show the time that you've been connected to the Internet as well as the status of the connection procedure. (Naturally, your Mac will need an external USB modem to use this status icon.)

✦ **Wi-Fi:** If your Mac is equipped with an AirPort or AirPort Extreme card, you can enable the Show Wi-Fi Status in Menu Bar check box within System Preferences. To do so, click the Network icon and then choose your Wi-Fi connection in the column at the left. The Wi-Fi status icon displays the status of the connection; click the Wi-Fi icon to toggle your wireless hardware on or off. The icon displays the relative strength of your Wi-Fi signal, whether you're connected to a Base Station or a peer-to-peer computer network, or whether Wi-Fi is turned off. You can also switch between multiple Wi-Fi networks from the menu.

✦ **Bluetooth:** For those Macs with Bluetooth hardware, you can toggle Bluetooth networking on or off. You can also make your Mac discoverable or hidden to other Bluetooth devices, send a file to a Bluetooth device, or browse for new Bluetooth devices in your vicinity. Additionally, you can set up a Bluetooth device that's already recognized or open the Bluetooth pane within System Preferences. (If you don't see the angular Bluetooth icon in your menu bar, display the Bluetooth pane within System Preferences and make sure the Show Bluetooth Status in the Menu Bar check box is enabled.)

✦ **Time Machine:** If you're using Time Machine to back up your Mac automatically, this icon displays the date of your last backup. You can also manually start a backup from the menu bar icon. To display the icon, open System Preferences and click the Time Machine icon; click the Show Time Machine Status in the Menu Bar check box to select it.

✦ **PPoE:** The display of this icon is controlled from the PPoE settings on the Network pane within System Preferences. Click this icon to connect to or disconnect from the Internet using *Point-to-Point over Ethernet* (PPoE), which is a type of Internet connection offered by some digital subscriber line (DSL) providers.

Doing timely things with the Clock

Even the Clock itself isn't static eye candy on the Mac OS X menu bar. (I told you this was a hardworking operating system, didn't I?) Click the Clock display to toggle the icon between the default text display and a miniature analog clock. You'll also find the complete day and date at the top of the menu.

In fact, you can even open the System Preferences Date & Time settings from the icon. From within the Date & Time settings, you can choose whether the seconds or day of the week are included, whether the separators should flash, or whether Mac OS X should display the time in 24-hour (military) format. More on this in Book II, Chapter 3.

Eject, Tex, Eject!

Mac OS X makes use of both static volumes (your Mac's hard drive, which remains mummified inside your computer's case) and removable volumes (such as USB Flash drives, your iPod, and CDs/DVD-ROMs). Mac OS X calls the process of loading and unloading a removable volume by old-fashioned terms — *mounting* and *unmounting* — but you and I call the procedure *loading* and *ejecting*.

Mark's totally unnecessary Computer Trivia 1.0

"Where the heck did *mounting* come from, anyway? Sounds like a line from a John Wayne western!" Well, pardner, the term dates back to the heyday of Big Iron — the Mainframe Age, when giant IBM dinosaurs populated the computing world. Sherman, set the WayBack Machine . . . .

At the time, disks were big, heavy, removable cartridges about two feet in diameter (and about as tall as a 100-count spindle of CD-Rs). The acolytes of the mainframe, called computer *operators,* would have to trudge over to a cabinet and *mount* (or swap) disk cartridges whenever the program stopped and asked for them. That's right, those mainframes would

actually stop calculating and print, "I need you to mount cartridge 12-A-34, or I can't go any further. Have a nice day." (Can you imagine what it'd be like loading and unloading a hard drive every time you needed to open a folder?)

Anyway, even though eons passed and minicomputers appeared — which were only the size of a washing machine — the terms *mounting* and *unmounting* still commonly appeared in programs. This time, the removable volumes were 8-inch floppy disks and tape cartridges. Because UNIX (and its offspring Linux) date from the Minicomputer Age, these operating systems still use the terms.

Just to keep things clear, I should point out that we're talking hardware devices here, so static and removable volumes have nothing to do with the *sound* volume control on your menu bar.

I won't discuss loading/mounting a removable volume — the process differs depending on the computer because some Macs need a button pushed on the keyboard, others have buttons on the drive itself, and some drives have just a slot, with no button at all. However, there are a number of standard ways of unloading/unmounting/ejecting a removable volume:

✦ **Drag the Volume's icon from the Desktop to the Trash,** which displays an Eject pop-up label to help underline the fact that you are *not* deleting the contents of the drive. Let me underline that with a Mark's Maxim because Switchers from the Windows world are usually scared to death by the concept of dragging a volume to the Trash.

> **Have no fear — in the Apple universe, you *can* drag removable volumes to the Trash with aplomb.**

✦ **Click the Volume's icon and use the ⌘+E keyboard shortcut.**

✦ **With the volume open in a Finder window, click the Action button and choose Eject from the pop-up menu.**

✦ **Click the File menu and choose Eject.**

✦ **Click the Eject button next to the device in the Finder window sidebar.**

✦ **Right-click the Volume's icon to display the contextual menu; then choose Eject.**

✦ **Press your keyboard Eject key (if it has one) to eject a CD or DVD from your built-in optical drive. (If you're using a keyboard without a Media Eject key, press and hold F12 instead.)**

You can't unmount a static volume from the Desktop — you have to use the Disk Utility application — so your internal hard drive icon will stay where it is.

Common Tasks Aplenty

Okay, I admit it — this section is kind of a grab bag of three very common tasks. However, I want to walk you through these three procedures early in the book. Most Mac owners will want to listen to and record CDs as soon as they start using Lion, and you'd be amazed how much information still flows across the Internet in plain, simple text.

Therefore, hang around and take care of business.

Opening and editing text files

Text files would seem to be another anachronism in this age of formatted web pages, rich text format (RTF) documents, and word processors galore. However, virtually every computer ever built can read and write in standard text, so text files are often used for

✦ **Information files on the Internet,** such as FAQs (Frequently Asked Questions files)

✦ **README and update** information by software developers

✦ **Swapping data between programs,** such as comma- and tab-delimited database files

Here's the quick skinny on opening, editing, and saving an existing text file:

1. **Navigate to your Applications folder and launch TextEdit.**

2. **Press ⌘+O to display the Open dialog.**

3. **Navigate to the desired text file and double-click the filename to load it.**

You can also open an existing text file by dragging its icon from the Finder window to the TextEdit icon.

4. **Click the insertion cursor anywhere in the file and begin typing. Or, to edit existing text, drag the insertion cursor across the characters to highlight them and type the replacement text.**

TextEdit automatically replaces the existing characters with those that you type. To simply delete text, highlight the characters and press Delete.

5. **After you finish editing the document, you can overwrite the original by pressing ⌘+S (which is the same as choosing File⇨Save), or you can save a new version by choosing File⇨Save As and typing a new, unique filename.**

6. **To exit TextEdit, press ⌘+Q.**

Listening to an audio CD

By default, Lion uses iTunes to play an audio CD. Although I cover iTunes in complete detail in Book III, Chapter 2, take a moment to see how to master the common task of playing an audio CD (just in case you want to jam while reading these early chapters). Follow these steps:

1. **Load the audio CD into your Mac's optical drive.**

A CD volume icon appears on your Desktop.

2. **Mac OS X automatically loads iTunes and displays its spiffy window.**

3. **By default, iTunes automatically begins playing the disc — however, if you have to manually start the music, click the Play button at the upper left of the iTunes window to begin playing the disc at the beginning. To play an individual track, double-click the track name in the iTunes window.**

   iTunes may also ask if you'd like the music from the CD added (or *imported*) into your iTunes music library. If you'd like to listen to the contents of the CD without having to load the physical disc in the future, feel free to import the CD tracks to your library!

4. **To adjust the volume from within iTunes, drag the Volume slider to the left or right — it's to the right of the Play and Fast Forward buttons.**

5. **To eject the disc and load another audio CD, press ⌘+E, click the Eject icon next to the CD entry in the Source list, or click Controls⇨Eject Disc.**

6. **To exit iTunes, press ⌘+Q.**

The first time that you run iTunes, you're asked to configure the program and specify whether Mac OS X should automatically connect to the Internet to download the track titles for the disc you've loaded. I recommend that you accept all the default settings and that you allow automatic connection. Is simple, no?

Recording — nay, burning — a data CD

Mac OS X offers a built-in CD recording feature that allows you to burn the simplest form of CD: a standard data CD-ROM that can hold up to approximately 700MB of files and folders and can be read on both Macs and PCs running Windows, UNIX, and Linux. (To burn an audio CD, use iTunes, as I show you in Book III, Chapter 2.) Naturally, you'll need a Mac with a CD or DVD recorder.

Adding the perfect font with Font Book

Need to install a font in Mac OS X, or perhaps you'd like to organize your fonts into collections based on their theme or their designer? If so, you're talking about *Font Book,* which is the font organizer that ships with Lion. To open Font Book, visit your Applications folder and double-click the Font Book icon.

Press ⌘+O (or choose File⇨Add Fonts) to import a new font into your system, or simply drag the font file from a Finder window into the Font Book window. Lion can accept TrueType,

OpenType, and PostScript Type 1 fonts. When it's been added, your new font can be categorized by dragging it into one of your *collections,* thus making that font easier to locate and display. Individual fonts and entire collections can be enabled or disabled (by using the Enable and Disable items on the Edit menu) so that you can "turn on" only those fonts that you need for a specific application or project. The Font Book window also comes fully equipped with a Search box, so you can find any font by name.

Back to the story! To record a disc, follow these steps:

1. **Load a blank CD-R, CD-RW, DVD-R, or DVD-RW into your drive.**

   I assume for this demonstration that you're using a write-once CD-R.

2. **A dialog appears and prompts you for an action to take. Choose the default, Open Finder, for this demonstration.**

   Mac OS X displays an Untitled CD volume icon on your Desktop. (It's marked with the letters CDR so you know that the disc is recordable.)

3. **Double-click the Untitled CD icon to display the contents — it'll be empty, naturally.**

4. **Click and drag files and folders to the CD window as you normally do.**

5. **Rename any files or folders as necessary — remember, after you've started recording, this stuff is etched in stone, so your disc window should look just like the volume window should look on the finished CD-ROM.**

6. **Click the Burn button next to the disc heading in the Finder window sidebar, or click the Burn button in the CD window.**

   The Big X displays a confirmation dialog.

7. **If you've forgotten something, you can click the Cancel or Eject button. Otherwise, click the Burn button and sit back and watch the fun.**

Unfortunately, Mac OS X doesn't support recording from the Finder for some external and third-party drives available for the Macintosh. If you can't burn from the Finder (or you're willing to pay for extra features), I recommend that you buy a copy of Roxio Toast Titanium recording software (www.roxio.com).

All You Really Need to Know about Printing

To close out this chapter, I turn your attention to another task that most Mac owners need to tackle soon after buying a Mac or installing Lion: printing documents. Because basic printing is so important (and in most cases, so simple), allow me to use this final section to demonstrate how to print a document.

Most of us have a Universal Serial Bus (USB) printer — the USB being the favored hardware connection within Mac OS X — so as long as your printer is supported by Mac OS X, setting it up is as easy as plugging it into one of your Mac's USB ports. The Big X does the rest of the work, selecting the proper printer software driver from the Library/Printers folder and setting your printer as the default power of the universe.

Before you print, *preview!* Would you jump from an airplane without a parachute? Then why would you print a document without double-checking it first? Click Preview, and Mac OS X opens the Preview application to show you what the printed document will look like. (Once again, some upstart programs have their own built-in Print Preview mode thumbnails within the Print dialog.) When you're done examining your handiwork, close the Preview application to return to your document.

To print from within any application using the default page characteristics — standard 8½-x-11 inch paper, portrait mode, no scaling — follow these steps:

1. **Within your application, click File and choose Print — or press the ⌘+P keyboard shortcut.**

Within most applications, Mac OS X displays the simple version of the Print dialog. (To display all the fields that you see in Figure 3-9, click the Show Details button at the bottom of the sheet.)

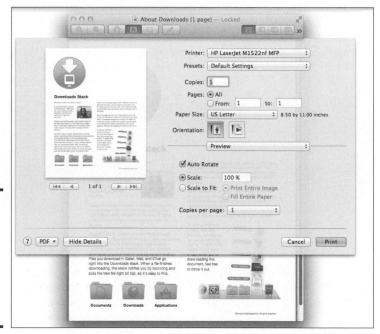

Figure 3-9:
The Print dialog is available from any application with any real guts.

Some applications use their own custom Print dialogs, but you should see the same general settings.

2. **Click in the Copies field and enter the number of copies that you need.**

You can also enable or disable collation, just as you can with those oh-so-fancy copiers.

3. **Decide what you want to print.**

- *The whole shootin' match:* To print the entire document, use the default Pages radio button setting of All.

- *Anything less:* To print a range of selected pages, select the From radio button and enter the starting and ending pages.

4. **(Optional) Choose application-specific printing parameters.**

Each Mac OS X application provides different panes so that you can configure settings specific to that application. You don't have to display any of these extra settings to print a default document, but the power is there to change the look dramatically when necessary. To display these settings, click the pop-up menu in the center of the Print dialog and choose one of these panes. For example, if you're printing from the Address Book, you can choose the Address Book entry from the pop-up menu and elect to print a phone list, envelope, mailing labels, or an e-mail list.

5. **When everything is go for launch, click the Print button.**

Of course, there are more settings and more functionality to the printing system within Mac OS X, and I cover more complex printing topics in much more detail in Book VII, Chapter 4. However, I can tell you from my experiences as a consultant and hardware technician that this short introduction to printing will likely suffice for 90 percent of the Mac owners on Earth. 'Nuff said.

Chapter 4: Searching Everything with Spotlight

In This Chapter

✔ Mastering basic Spotlight searching skills

✔ Selecting text and keywords for best results

✔ Displaying results in the Spotlight window

✔ Customizing Spotlight settings in System Preferences

Spotlight is Apple's desktop search technology that you can use to find anything on your computer as quickly as you can type. (Yep, that includes all the documents, Address Book contacts, Mail messages, folders, and drives that your Mac can access.) In fact, the version of Spotlight included with Lion can even search other Macs across your network! Yes, you read right: If the information is on a Mac's hard drive, a CD, your network, or even *another Mac* in your network, consider it located.

This chapter is your ticket to using this new search technology like a professional techno-wizard from day one. I discuss how Spotlight works and how you can use it to locate exactly what you want (and present those results as proudly as a wine steward showing off a fine vintage).

Doing a Basic Search

Figure 4-1 illustrates the Spotlight search field, which is always available from the Finder menu bar. Click the magnifying glass icon once (or press ⌘+Spacebar), and the Spotlight search box appears.

To run a search, simply click in the Spotlight box and begin typing. You see matching items appear as soon as you type, and the search results are continually refined while you type the rest of your search criteria. As with the Search box in earlier Finder window toolbars, you don't need to press Return to begin the search.

Figure 4-1:
A lot of power is behind this single Spotlight search box.

The results of your Spotlight search appear in the Spotlight menu, which is updated automatically in real time while you continue to type. The top 20 most-relevant items are grouped into categories right on the Spotlight menu, including Messages, Definitions, Documents, Folders, Images, Contacts, and so on. Spotlight takes a guess at the item that's most likely the match you're looking for (based on your Search Results list in System Preferences, which I cover later in the chapter) and presents it in the special Top Hit category that always appears first.

To open the Top Hit item like a true Lion power user, just press Return. (My brothers and sisters, it just doesn't get any easier than that.)

Literally any text string is acceptable as a Spotlight search. However, here's a short list of the common search criteria I use every day:

✦ **Names and addresses:** Because Spotlight has access to Lion's Address Book, you can immediately display contact information using any portion of a name or address.

✦ **E-mail message text:** Need to open a specific e-mail message, but you'd rather not launch Mail and spend time digging through the message list? Enter the person's e-mail address or any text string contained in the message you're looking for.

✦ **File and folder names:** This is the classic search favorite. Spotlight searches your entire system for that one file or folder in the blink of an eye.

✦ **Events & To Do items:** Yep, Spotlight gives you access to your iCal calendars and those all-important To Do lists you've created.

✦ **System Preferences:** Now things start to get *really* interesting! Try typing the word **background** in the Spotlight field. Some of the results will actually be System Preference panes! That's right: Every setting in System Preferences is referenced in Spotlight. (For example, the desktop background setting is on the Desktop & Screen Saver pane in System Preferences.)

✦ **Web pages:** *Whoa.* Stand back, Google. You can use Spotlight to search the Web pages you've recently displayed in Safari! (Note, however, that this feature doesn't let you search through all the Internet as Google does . . . only the pages stored in your Safari Web cache and any HTML files you've saved to your Mac's hard drive.)

✦ **Metadata:** That's a pretty broad category, but it fits. If you're not familiar with the term *metadata*, think of the information stored by your digital camera each time you take a photo — things like the exposure setting, time and date, and even the location where the photo was taken, which are also transferred to iPhoto when you import. Here's another example: I like to locate Word documents on my system using the same metadata that's stored in the file, such as the contents of the Comments field in a Word document. Other supported applications include Adobe Photoshop images, Microsoft Excel spreadsheets, Keynote presentations, iTunes media, and other third-party applications that offer a Spotlight plug-in.

To reset the Spotlight search and try another text string, click the X icon that appears at the right side of the Spotlight box. (Of course, you can also backspace to the beginning of the field, but that's a little less elegant.)

After you find the item that you're looking for, you can click it once to

✦ Launch it (if the item is an application)

✦ Open it in System Preferences (if it's a setting or description on a Preferences pane)

✦ Open it within the associated application (if the item is a document or a data item)

✦ Display it within a Finder window (if the item is a folder)

Here's another favorite timesaver: You can display all the files of a particular type on your system by using the file type as the keyword. For example, to provide a list of all images on your system, just use *images* as your keyword — the same goes for *movies* and *audio,* too.

How Cool Is That: Discovering What Spotlight Can Do

Don't get fooled into simply using Spotlight as another file-'n-folder-name search tool. Sure, it can do that, but Spotlight can also search **inside** PDF, Pages and Word documents, and HTML files, finding matching text that doesn't appear in the name of the file! To wit: A search for *Lion* on my system pulls up all sorts of items with Lion in their names, but also files with Lion *in* them:

✦ Apple Store SF.ppt: A PowerPoint presentation that contains several slides containing the text *Lion*

✦ bk01ch03.doc: A rather cryptically named Microsoft Word file chapter of this book that mentions Lion in several spots

✦ Conference Call with Bob: An iCal event pointing to a conference call with my editor about upcoming Lion book projects

Notice that not one of these three examples actually has the words *Lion* occurring anywhere in the title or filename, yet Spotlight found them because they all contain the text *Lion* therein. That, dear reader, is the true power of Spotlight, and how it can literally guarantee you that you'll never lose another piece of information that Spotlight can locate in the hundreds of thousands of files and folders on your hard drive!

Heck, suppose that all you remember about a file is that you received it in your mail last week or last month. To find it, you can actually type in time periods, such as *yesterday, last week,* or *last month,* to see every item that you saved or received within that period. (Boy, howdy, I *love* writing about TGIs — that's short for Truly Good Ideas.)

Be careful, however, when you're considering a search string. Don't forget that (by default) Spotlight matches only those items that have *all* the words you enter in the Spotlight box. To return the highest number of possible matches, use the fewest number of words that will identify the item; for example, use *horse* rather than *horse image,* and you're certain to be rewarded with more hits. (On the other hand, if you're looking specifically for a picture of a knight on horseback, a series of keywords, such as *horse knight image,* shortens your search considerably. It all depends on what you're looking for and how widely you want to cast your Spotlight net.)

To allow greater flexibility in searches, Apple also includes those helpful Boolean friends that you may already be familiar with: AND, OR, and NOT. For example, you can perform Spotlight searches, such as

✦ *Horse* AND *cow* (which collects all references to both those barnyard animals into one search)

✦ *Batman* OR *Robin* (which returns all references to either Batman or Robin, but not both)

✦ *Apple* NOT *PC* (which displays all references to Apple that don't include any information on dastardly PCs)

Because Spotlight functions are a core technology of Mac OS X Lion — in other words, all sorts of applications can make use of Spotlight throughout the operating system, including the Finder — the Finder window's Search box now shares many of the capabilities of Spotlight. In fact, you can use the time period trick that I mention earlier (entering *yesterday* as a keyword) in the Finder window Search box.

Is Spotlight secure?

So how about all those files, folders, contacts, and events that you *don't* want to appear in Spotlight? What if you're sharing your Mac as a multiuser computer or accessing other Macs remotely? Can others search for and access your personal information through Spotlight?

Definitely not! The results displayed by Spotlight are controlled by file and folder permissions as well as your account login, just as the applications that create and display your personal data are. For example, you can't access other users' calendars using iCal, and they can't see your Mail messages. Only

you have access to your data, and only after you've logged in with your username and password. Spotlight works the same way. If a user doesn't normally have access to an item, the item simply doesn't appear when that user performs a Spotlight search. (In other words, only you get to see your stuff.)

However, you can even hide certain folders and disks from your own Spotlight searches if necessary. Check out the final section of this chapter for details on setting private locations on your system.

Okay, parents, listen closely: Here's a (somewhat sneaky) tip that might help you monitor your kid's computer time as well as what your kids are typing/reading in iChat:

1. **Enable the iChat transcript feature.**

   a. From within iChat, choose iChat➪Preferences.

   b. Click Messages.

   c. Select the Save Chat Transcripts To check box and choose a destination folder in a location you can access.

2. **Click the Close button to return to iChat.**

   Now you can use Spotlight to search for questionable words, phrases, and names within those iChat transcripts. (For more on iChat, turn to Book V, Chapter 3.)

Expanding Your Search Horizons

I can just hear the announcer's voice now: "But wait, there's more! If you click the Show in Finder menu item at the beginning of your search results, we'll expand your Spotlight menu into the Spotlight window!" (Fortunately, you don't have to buy some ridiculous household doodad.)

Keyboard mavens will appreciate the Spotlight window shortcut key, and I show you where to specify this shortcut in the final section of this chapter.

Figure 4-2 illustrates the Spotlight window (which is actually a Finder window with extras). To further filter the search, click one of the buttons on the Spotlight window toolbar or create your own custom filter. Click the button with the plus sign to display the search criteria bar and then click the pop-up menus to choose from criteria, such as the type of file, the text content, or the location on your system (for example, your hard drive, your Home folder, or a network server). You can also filter your results listing by the date the items were created or last saved. To add or delete criteria, click the plus and minus buttons at the right side of the search criteria bar. To save a custom filter that you've created, click the Save button.

Figure 4-2: The spacious borders of the Spotlight window.

Images appear as thumbnail icons, so you can use that most sophisticated search tool — the human eye — to find the picture you're looking for. (If you don't see thumbnail images, click the Icon view button on the toolbar.) Don't forget that you can increase or decrease the size of the icons by dragging the slider at the bottom right of the window.

To display the contents of an item in the list (without leaving the comfortable confines of the Spotlight window), click the icon to select it and click the Quick Look icon in the toolbar (or press the spacebar) for a better view.

Again, when you're ready to open an item, just double-click it in the Spotlight window.

As I mention earlier, Spotlight can look for matching items on other Macs on your network — but only if those remote Macs are configured correctly. To allow another Mac running Mac OS X Tiger, Leopard, Snow Leopard, or Lion to be visible to Spotlight on your system, enable File Sharing on the other Mac. (Oh, and remember that you need an admin-level account on that Mac — or access to a good friend who has an admin-level account on that Mac.)

Follow these steps to enable File Sharing on the other Mac:

1. **Click the System Preferences icon in the Dock.**

2. **Click the Sharing pane.**

3. **Select the On check box next to the File Sharing item in the service list to enable it.**

4. **Click the Close button on the System Preferences window.**

Remember, you can search only items that you have rights and permissions to view on the remote Mac (such as the contents of the Public folders on that computer). I discuss more about these limitations earlier in this chapter, in the "Is Spotlight secure?" sidebar.

Customizing Spotlight to Your Taste

You might wonder whether such an awesome Mac OS X feature has its own pane within System Preferences — and you'd be right again. Figure 4-3 shows off the Spotlight pane within System Preferences: Click the System Preferences icon (look for the gears) in the Dock and then click the Spotlight icon (under Personal) to display these settings.

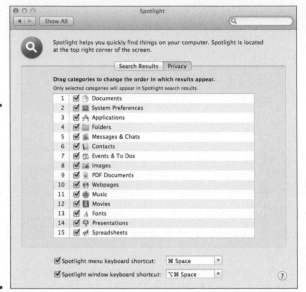

Figure 4-3:
Fine-tune your Spotlight menu and Results window from within System Preferences.

Click the Search Results tab to

✦ **Determine which categories appear in the Spotlight menu and Results window.** For example, if you don't use any presentation software on your Mac, you can clear the check box next to Presentations to disable this category (thereby making more room for other categories that you will use).

✦ **Determine the order that categories appear in the Spotlight menu and Results window.** Drag the categories to the order in which you want them to appear in the Spotlight menu and window. For example, I like the Documents and System Preferences categories to appear higher in the list because I use them most often.

✦ **Specify the Spotlight menu and Spotlight Results window keyboard shortcuts.** You can enable or disable either keyboard shortcut and choose the key combination from the pop-up menu.

Click the Privacy tab (as shown in Figure 4-4) to specify disks and folders that should never be listed as results in a Spotlight search. I know, I know, I said earlier that Spotlight respected your security, and it does. However, the disks and folders that you add on this list won't appear even if *you* are the one performing the search. (This is a great idea for folders and removable hard drives that you use to store sensitive information, such as medical records.)

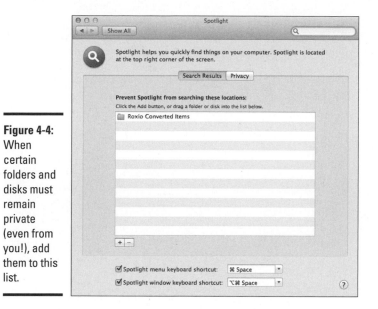

Figure 4-4:
When certain folders and disks must remain private (even from you!), add them to this list.

To add locations that you want to keep private, click the Add button (bearing a plus sign) and navigate to the desired location. Click the location to select it and then click Choose. (Alternatively, you can drag folders or disks directly from a Finder window and drop them into the pane.)

Chapter 5: Fun with Photo Booth

In This Chapter

✔ **Using Photo Booth to take photos**

✔ **Adding effects to images and movie clips**

✔ **Capturing video with iMovie**

Many Apple switchers and first-time owners quickly notice the webcam that accompanies their iMacs and MacBooks: a tiny square lens and LED light at the top of the Mac screen. That square is the lens of your Mac's built-in FaceTime camera, which allows video chatting in iChat, video chatting in FaceTime or a quick, fun series of photos or video clips via Lion's Photo Booth and iMovie applications — you can even take your user account photo with your FaceTime camera (in the System Preferences window)!

What's that you say? Your last computer didn't have a video camera? Well then, good reader, you've come to the right place! In this chapter, I show you how easy it is to produce photos and video with your FaceTime camera. *Sassy!*

Capturing the Moment with FaceTime and Photo Booth

As I mentioned earlier, every MacBook and iMac running Lion is ready to capture video, so pat yourself on the back and do the Technology dance.

If you're using a Mac mini or Mac Pro, you're not stuck out in the cold! You can still add your own FaceTime external camera — check eBay or craigslist to pick up a used FaceTime camera — or connect a FireWire DV camcorder for your Photo Booth input. (Many external USB and FireWire web cameras support Mac OS X as well.) Lion automatically recognizes any supported external video camera.

Figure 5-1 illustrates a typical MacBook FaceTime camera. What can you do with your camera? Here's the rundown:

✦ With iChat, you can videoconference in style — you'll find everything you need to join the ranks of the iChat elite in Book V, Chapter 3.

✦ Book V, Chapter 3 also includes coverage of FaceTime, the video chat application that lets you talk to owners of Mac computers (as well as devices like the iPhone 4, iPad 2, and iPod touch).

✦ You can capture video clips using iMovie and use the footage in all of your iLife applications.

✦ Finally, Photo Booth allows you to snap digital pictures just as you did in the old automatic photo booth at your local arcade, but Photo Book comes complete with visual effects to add pizzazz and punch to your photos. (Oh, did I mention you can shoot video as well?) If you've used the Photo Booth application on an iPad 2, you're already familiar with how much fun you can have with your images and video clips!

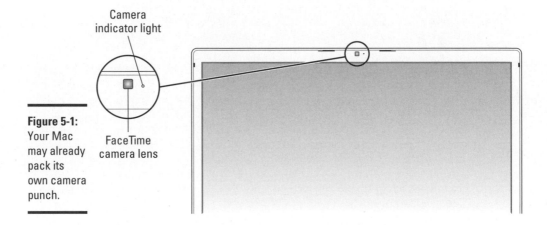

Camera indicator light

FaceTime camera lens

Figure 5-1: Your Mac may already pack its own camera punch.

The FaceTime camera's indicator light glows green whenever you're taking a snapshot or recording video . . . which, when you think about it, is A Good Thing (especially if you prefer chatting at home in Leisure Mode).

Need to quickly get a picture of yourself for use on your web page? Or perhaps your iChat icon needs an update to show off your new haircut? Photo Booth can capture images at 640 x 480 resolution and 32-bit color — and although today's digital cameras produce a much higher-quality photo, you can't beat the built-in convenience of Photo Booth for that quick snapshot! To snap an image in Photo Booth, follow these steps:

1. **Launch Photo Booth from the Applications folder.**

Figure 5-2 illustrates the application window that appears. (Ignore the rather silly gentleman who wandered into the frame. I doubt he'll be in your Photo Booth window!)

Photo Booth features a very different appearance in full-screen mode, complete with a fancy wooden stage and curtain! To try things out fullscreen, click View➪Enter Full Screen.

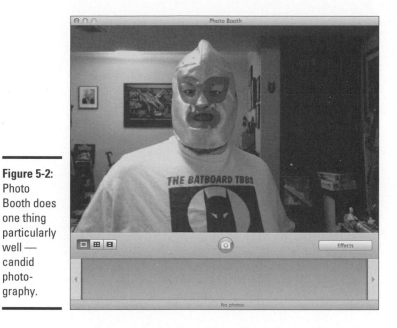

Figure 5-2:
Photo
Booth does
one thing
particularly
well —
candid
photo-
graphy.

2. **(Optional) Choose to take one image, four quick photos as a group, or digital video.**

   The three buttons at the lower left side of the Photo Booth window allow you to switch between taking one photo, four photos in a row (arranged as a group, like an arcade photo booth), or a movie clip.

3. **(Optional) Click the Effects button to choose an effect you'd like to apply to your image.**

   Photo Booth displays a screen of thumbnail preview images so that you can see how each effect changes the photo. You can produce some of the simple effects you may be familiar with from Photoshop, such as a black-and-white image or a fancy color-pencil filter . . . but it can also deliver some mind-blowing distortion effects, and even an Andy Warhol–style pop-art image!

   To return the display to normal without choosing an effect, click the Normal thumbnail, which appears in the center. (Paul Lynde's spot, for those of you old enough to remember "Hollywood Squares.")

   Of course, you can always launch your favorite image editor afterward to use a filter or effect on a photo — for example, the effects available in iPhoto. However, Photo Booth can apply these effects automatically as soon as you take the picture.

4. **(Optional) Click a thumbnail to select the desired effect.**

   When you choose an effect, Photo Booth automatically closes the Effects display.

5. **Click the Camera button.**

You'll notice that the image (or video clip) appears in the film strip at the bottom of the window. Photo Booth keeps a copy of all the images and clips you take in the film strip so that you can use them later. After you click a photo or film clip in the filmstrip, a series of buttons appears, including

✦ Sending the photo in an e-mail message

✦ Saving the photo directly to iPhoto

✦ Using the image as your Lion user account icon

✦ Using the image as your iChat Buddy icon

To delete an image or clip from the Photo Booth filmstrip, click the offending thumbnail and then click the X button that appears underneath.

Producing Video on the Spot with iMovie

"Mark, am I limited to capturing stuff with Photo Booth?" Oh, pshaw on limitations . . . you're a Mac owner, after all! You can also use your FaceTime camera to snag video clips (complete with audio) in iMovie.

You don't need an expensive digital camcorder to produce video clips for use in iMovie! Your Mac's camera can capture those clips for you — think of the party possibilities! (Or the opportunity for practical jokes. But then again, you're not that kind of person, now, *are* you?) To capture video directly from your FaceTime camera into iMovie, follow these steps:

1. **Launch iMovie from the Dock or from the Applications folder.**

2. **Click the Open Camera Import Window button to switch to Import Video mode.**

   In case you haven't used it yet, the button is located at the far left of the toolbar running across the center of the iMovie window, and it sports a camera icon.

3. **Click the Camera pop-up menu at the bottom of the Import window and click Built-in FaceTime.**

4. **When you're ready to start recording video, click the Capture button.**

   iMovie displays a sheet allowing you to select the location for the movie clip (including the approximate amount of time you can record). You can also choose to add the video to an existing iMovie Event or a brand-new Event. To help keep things steady in your clip, click the Analyze for Stabilization after Import check box to enable it — but note that the stabilization process will significantly add to the time it takes for iMovie to save your clip to disk.

5. **When you're ready to start recording video, click the Capture button.**

   iMovie automatically displays the incoming video in the monitor window while it's recorded. (As you might expect, the goofy behavior on the part of the distinguished cast usually starts at about this moment.)

6. **Click the Stop button to stop recording.**

   After you've ended the recording, iMovie creates the video clip and adds it to your Clips pane.

I go into much more detail on iMovie in Chapter 4 of Book III, but that's the gist of recording video clips.

Chapter 6: Keeping Track with the Address Book

In This Chapter

↙ **Adding contact cards**

↙ **Editing contacts**

↙ **Using contact information throughout Mac OS X**

↙ **Creating and e-mailing groups**

↙ **Printing contacts**

↙ **Importing and exporting vCards**

Do you have a well-thumbed address book stuck in a drawer of your office desk? Or do you have a wallet or purse stuffed with sticky notes and odd scraps of paper, each of which bears an invaluable e-mail address or phone number? If so, you can finally set yourself free and enjoy the "Paperless Lifestyle" of the new millennium with the revolutionary new Rauncho Digital Address Book! As seen on TV! Only $29.95 — and it doubles as an indestructible garden hose! But wait! If you order now, we'll also send you . . .

Of course, you and I would tune that stuff out as soon as we heard, "As seen on TV" — but, believe it or not, the Rauncho Digital Address Book does exist (after a fashion), and you already have one on your Mac. It's called the *Address Book,* and in this chapter, I show you how to store and retrieve all your contact data, including iChat information, photographs, and much more.

(And before you ask, operators are *not* standing by.)

Hey, Isn't the Address Book Just a Part of Mail?

It's true that in early versions of Mac OS X, Address Book was relegated to the minor leagues and usually appeared only when you asked for it within Mail. Although it could be run as a separate application, there was no convenient route to the Address Book from the Desktop, so most Mac owners never launched it as a standalone.

Now, however, the Address Book appears in the limelight, earning a default location in the Dock and available whenever you need it. Although the Address Book can still walk through a meadow hand-in-hand with Mail, it also flirts with other Mac OS X applications and can even handle some basic telephony chores all by itself through the use of Services.

Figure 6-1 illustrates the default face of the Address Book, complete with a personal address card: your own contact information, which you enter within the Setup Assistant that I mention in Book I, Chapter 1. This card carries a special me tag on your thumbnail image (indicating that it's your personal card) as well as a suave-looking silhouette next to your name in the Name column. Other Mac OS X applications use the data in your card to automatically fill out your personal information in all sorts of documents. (In Figure 6-1, I added a number of well-known friends as well . . . a few TV characters, a composer or two. You know the drill.)

Figure 6-1:
Greetings
from the
Mac OS X
Address
Book!

TIP

Address Book features an entirely new appearance in Mac OS X Lion. You'll notice two icons at the lower left corner of the Address Book window: These two buttons set the application's display mode. By default, Address Book uses a two-pane display mode that's similar to a printed book, but you can click on the button bearing the square icon to switch to a single-pane display. The single-pane display takes up less room, but sometimes requires an extra mouse click or two while you're using Address Book.

Entering Contact Information

Unless you actually meet and hire a group of DataElves — see the sidebar, "I gotta type (or retype) that stuff?" — you have to add contacts to your Address Book manually. Allow me to demonstrate here how to create a new contact within your Address Book:

1. **Launch Address Book from the Dock by clicking its icon.**

The icon looks like an old-fashioned paper Address Book with an @ symbol on the cover.

2. **Press the ⌘+N shortcut to create a new contact. Alternatively, choose File⇨New Card or click the Add a New Person button at the bottom of the Name column.**

Address Book displays the template that you see in Figure 6-2, with the First Name field highlighted and ready for you to type.

3. **Enter the contact's first name and press Tab to move to the Last name field.**

4. **Continue entering the corresponding information in each field, pressing Tab to move through the fields.**

If a field isn't applicable (for example, if a person has no home page), just press Tab again to skip it. You can press Return to add extra lines to the Address field.

Figure 6-2:
"Hey, I don't know anyone named *First Last!*"

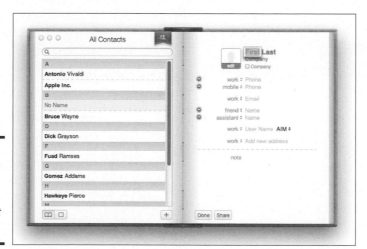

Notice those icons next to each field — the ones that look like up and down arrows? That's the Address Book telling you that there are additional versions of the field that you can enter as well. (Think home and work addresses.) Click the up/down icon and a pop-up menu appears, allowing you to choose which version of the field will be displayed. Depending on the field, Address Book may automatically display an additional version — for example, if you enter a work address for the contact, another field for the contact's home address appears. Click this new field and then you can enter the contact's home address, too.

You can also add new fields to a card, such as web addresses (also called URLs), birthdays, maiden names, and the like. To add a new field, click Card⇨Add Field and choose the field you want to add from the menu that appears.

5. To add a photograph to the card, click Card⇨Choose Custom Image (or drag an image from a Finder window on top of the thumbnail square).

Address Book displays a sheet that you can use to select the image. Click Choose to display our old friend the Open dialog.

If your Mac has an iSight camera, you can click the Capture a picture from a video camera button (which bears a snazzy camera icon). You can also choose one of the faces you've tagged in iPhoto!

6. When you're done, click the Done button at the bottom of the Address Book window to save the card.

You can edit the contents of a card at any time by displaying it and clicking the Edit button at the bottom (or by pressing ⌘+L, or even by clicking Edit and choosing the Edit Card menu item).

No need to edit a card to add information to the Note field — just click and type.

You can also add contact cards directly to your Address Book from the Mac OS X Mail application — go figure. Within Mail, click the message (to highlight it) from the person whom you want to add, click the friendly Message menu, and then click Add Sender to Address Book, or press ⌘+Shift+Y. Naturally, adding people this way doesn't add their supporting information — just their name and e-mail address (and, if they used Mail on their end to send the message and they have a photo attached to their personal card, their photo gets imported as well). Once again, your nimble fingers have to manually enter the rest. For more on Mail, see Book V, Chapter 2.

TIP

"Mark, I never use the Assistant field when I add a contact. Can't I get rid of it completely?" Indeed you can, good reader! To customize the default fields that appear when you create a new contact card, click the Address Book menu and choose Preferences, and then click the Template tab. Each field has a Delete icon (the red minus sign) and some have an Add icon (the green plus sign). To remove a field from your template, click the Delete icon. To add a new version of a field (for example, a home email address), click the Add icon next to the existing field of the same type, and then click the up/down arrow icon to select the field name. To add a completely new field (like Middle or Maiden Name), click the Add Field drop-down menu.

Don't forget to add those fax numbers! If you have an external analog modem, Lion can fax from any application — just click File and choose Print (or press ⌘+P) as you always have, and then click the PDF button at the bottom of the Print dialog and choose Fax PDF. Mac OS X automatically fills in the address for you, but only if the contact has a fax number entered as part of the contact card.

"I gotta type (or retype) that stuff?"

In my three decades of travel through the personal computing world, I've noticed one lovely recurring fantasy shared by computer owners that keeps cropping up over and over: I call it the *DataElf Phenomenon*. You see, *DataElves* are the hard-working, silicon-based gnomes in tiny green suspenders who magically enter all the information that you want to track into your database (or Address Book, or Quicken, or whatever). They burrow into your papers and presto! — out pops all that data, neatly typed and . . . whoa, Nellie! Let's stop there.

For some reason, computer users seem to forget that *there are no DataElves*. I wish I had a dime for every time I've heard a heartbroken computer owner say, "You mean I have to *type* all that stuff *in?*" (My usual retort is, "Affirmative . . . unless you want to pay me a hideous amount to do it for you.") Make no mistake — adding a lifetime's worth of contact information into your Address Book can be several hours of monotonous and mind-bendingly boring work, which is another reason that

many computer owners still depend on paper to store all those addresses. But take my word for it, dear reader, your effort is worth it — the next time that you sit down to prepare a batch of Christmas cards or you have to find Uncle Milton's telephone number in a hurry, you *will* appreciate the effort that you made to enter contact information into your Address Book. (Just make sure that you — say it with me — *back up your hard drive.)*

By the way, if you've already entered contact information into another PIM (short for Personal Information Manager), you can reuse that data without retyping everything — that is, as long as your old program can export contacts in vCard format. After you export the records, just drag the vCards into the Address Book window to add them, or import them by pressing ⌘+I. (More on this at the end of this chapter.) You can also export contact information in tab-delimited format with most PIMs, and import the file using Address Book from the File➪Import menu item.

If someone sends you a vCard (look for an attachment with a `.vcf` extension), consider yourself lucky. Just drag the vCard from the attachment window in Mail and drop it in your Address Book; any information that the person wants you to have is added automatically!

To delete a card, click the unlucky name to display the card, click Edit, and then choose Delete Card.

Using Contact Information

Okay, after you have your contact information in Address Book, what can you actually *do* with it? Often, all you really need is a quick glance at an address. To display the card for any contact within Address Book, just click the desired entry in the Name column. You can move to the next and previous cards by using the up- and down-arrow keys on your keyboard. (Oh, and don't forget that you can right-click many items within a card to display menu commands specific to those items.)

But wait, there's more! You can also

+ **Copy and paste.** The old favorites are still around. You can copy any data from a card (press ⌘+C) and paste it into another open application (press ⌘+V).

+ **Visit a contact's home page**. Click the contact entry to select it, and click the page link displayed within the card. Safari dutifully answers the call, and next thing you know, you're online and at the home page specified in the entry.

+ **Send an e-mail message.** If you've already read through Chapter 3 of this minibook, you'll remember the Mac OS X Services feature that I tell you about. Click and drag to select any e-mail address on a card; then click the Address Book menu, click the Services menu, and choose New Email to Address. Bingo! Depending on the information that you select, other services might also be available.

+ **Add an iChat buddy.** From within iChat, click the Buddies menu and then click Add a Buddy. From the dialog that appears, you can select a contact card that has an Instant Messenger address and add it to your Buddy List.

+ **Export contacts.** From within the Address Book, select the contacts that you want to export, click File, and then choose Export vCards from the Export submenu. Address Book displays a Save sheet. Navigate to the location where you want to save the cards and click Save.

✦ **Search amongst your contacts.** If you're searching for a specific person and all you have is a phone number or a fragment of an address, click in the Search field (which bears a magnifying glass icon) and type the text. While you continue to enter characters, Address Book shows you how many contacts contain matching characters and displays just those entries in the Name column. Now that's *sassy!* (And convenient. And fast as all get-out.) Check out Figure 6-3 — note that a couple of very familiar folks share the same address in Gotham City, and I found them by using the Search field.

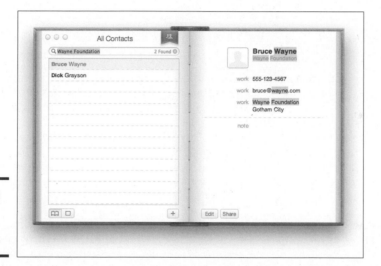

Figure 6-3:
Holy Text
Match,
Batman!

Speaking of searching using a contact in the Address Book, Spotlight is also at your beck and call — click a contact to select it, then click the Edit menu and choose Spotlight. *Whoosh!* Lion searches your entire system for everything related to that contact and displays it in the familiar Spotlight window.

Arranging Your Contact Cards

Address Book also provides you with a method of organizing your cards into groups. A *group* usually consists of folks with a common link, such as your family, friends, co-workers, and others who enjoy yodeling. For example, you could set up a Cell Phone group that you can use when syncing data with your Bluetooth cell phone. You can switch to the *groups display* within Address Book by clicking on the red bookmark at the top of the window — if the icon shows a single profile, you've switched to the group display.

To create a group, choose File⇨New Group or press ⌘+Shift+N. (Using the Hollywood method, click the plus-sign button at the bottom left of the group display.) Address Book adds a highlighted text box so that you can type the group name. After you type the group name, press Return to save it.

If you already selected the entries for those contacts that you want to add to the group, choose File⇨New Group from Selection instead. This saves you a step because the group is created and the members are added automatically.

If you've created an empty group, it's easy to add folks manually. From the group display, click the All Contacts link to see a list of everyone in your Address Book, and then click and drag the entries that you want to add to the desired group name.

After you create a New Group, you can instantly display members of that group by clicking its name in the group display. To return to the display of all your contacts, click the All Contacts link, or click the bookmark to switch back to individual display.

To further organize your groups, you can drag and drop a group on top of another group. It becomes a subgroup, which is handy for things like branch offices within your company or perhaps relatives to whom you're not speaking at the moment.

Need an even harder-working group? Create a *Smart Group,* which — get this — automatically adds new contacts you create to the proper group or removes them from the group, depending on the criteria you specify! To create a Smart Group, follow these steps:

1. **Click File and click New Smart Group.**

2. **Type a name for the new Smart Group.**

3. **Click the Card pop-up menu and choose the item that will trigger the action.**

   For example, you can choose to automate a Smart Group according to the contents of each new card, a company name, or a particular city or state.

4. **Click the Contains pop-up menu and choose the criteria for the item.**

   An item might contain (or not contain) a specific string of characters, or it might have changed in a certain amount of time. To illustrate, one of my hardest-working Smart Groups automatically checks the Company field in every new card for my publisher's company name and adds that contact card to my Wiley Publishing group if a match occurs.

5. **To add another criteria line, click the button with the plus sign at the end of the first text field.**

   If you decide you have one criteria line too many, click the button with the minus sign next to the offending rule.

6. **After your Smart Group criteria are correct, click OK.**

   The Smart Group name appears in your group list. *Voilà!*

Here's another handy feature of an Address Book group: You can send all the members of a group the same e-mail message at one time. Within Mail, simply enter the Group name in the To field in the Compose window, and the same message is sent to everyone. Even Gandalf couldn't do that (but my copy editor bets that Dumbledore could).

Using Network Directories

I know, I know, I said earlier that you'd have to enter all your contacts yourself — but I was talking about your personal contacts! You can also access five types of external directories from within Address Book:

✦ Mac users working in a Windows network environment can use Exchange 2007 (or later) network directories.

✦ If you're a member of a company NetInfo network — and if you don't know, ask your wizened network administrator — you can search network directory servers from within Address Book. These servers are available automatically, so no configuration is necessary. *Sweet.*

✦ Mac OS X Lion Server offers an Address Book server feature for sharing directories across your network, using the CardDAV standard.

✦ Address Book can share contact information using your Yahoo! account.

✦ You can search Internet-based LDAP directories. Sorry, folks, I know that's pretty cryptic, but others have written entire books on this technology. Again, suffice it to say that your network guru can tell you whether LDAP servers are available to you. (In another blazing display of techno-nerd acronym addiction, LDAP stands for *Lightweight Directory Access Protocol.*) With LDAP, you can search a central company directory from anywhere in the world as long as you have an Internet connection. To configure this feature, click Address Book from the menu and choose Preferences; click the Accounts tab and then click the + (plus sign) button at the bottom of the Accounts list to enter the specific settings for the server that you want to access. Your network administrator or the LDAP server administrator can supply you with these settings.

To search any network directory, you need to create a corresponding directory account. Follow these steps to add a directory account:

1. **Click Address Book⇨Preferences to display the Preferences window.**

2. **Click the Accounts tab.**

3. **Click the Add button at the bottom of the Accounts list to launch the Add Account assistant.**

4. **Click the Account Type pop-up menu to choose the desired species of network directory.**

Type the required information in the fields that appear. (Your network administrator should be able to provide you with the necessary values.)

5. **Click Create.**

You'll see the blue network directory entry appear in the Group column.

The rest is easy! Click the desired directory link in the group display and use the Search field as you normally would. Matching entries display the person's name, e-mail address, and phone number.

"But hey, Mark, what if I'm not online? My company's LDAP directory isn't much good then, right?" Normally, that's true. If you're a mobile user, LDAP information is available to you only when you're online and the LDAP server is available. Ah, but here's a rocking power user tip that'll do the trick for MacBook owners: To make a person's information always available, search the LDAP database and drag the resulting entry from the contacts list to the desired group (or the All Contacts link) on the group display. You'll import the information to your local Address Book — and you'll see it even when you're not online!

Printing Contacts with Flair

Consider how to print your contacts (for those moments when you need an archaic hard copy). Address Book offers a whopping four different formats: mailing labels, envelopes, lists, and even a snappy pocket address book!

By default, Address Book prints on standard U.S. letter-size paper (8½ x 11 inches) in portrait orientation. You can change these settings right from the Print dialog: Choose File and click Print or press ⌘+P. From the Print dialog, you can choose exotic settings, such as legal-size paper or landscape orientation.

Follow these steps to print your contacts:

1. **Press ⌘+P.**

Address Book displays the Print dialog. To show all the settings, click the Show Details button at the bottom of the sheet.

If you need more than one copy, click in the Copies field to specify the desired number.

Need labels? We've got 'em! Click the Style pop-up menu and choose Mailing Labels to specify what type of label stock you're using on the Layout pane. Click the Label button to sort your labels by name or postal code, choose a font, select a text color, and add an icon or image to your labels. To switch to a standard contact list, click Style again and then click Lists. (You can also print envelopes and pocket address book pages in a similar manner — just choose the desired entry from the Style pop-up menu.)

2. **Select the desired Attributes check boxes to specify which contact card fields you want to appear in your list.**

The Attributes list appears only if you're printing contacts in either the Lists style or the pocket address book style.

3. **Click the Print button to send the job to the selected printer.**

Alternatively, you can create a PDF file in a specified location — a handy trick to use if you'd rather not be burdened with paper, but you still need to consult the list or give it to others. (*PDF files* are a special document display format developed by Adobe; they display like a printed document but take up minimal space.) To display the contents of a PDF file in Mac OS X, you need only double-click it in the Finder window, and the built-in Preview application is happy to oblige — even faster, select the PDF file in the Finder window and press the space bar for a Quick Look.

Swapping Bytes with vCards

A *vCard* is a standard file format for exchanging contacts between programs such as Address Book, Microsoft Entourage and Outlook, Eudora, and the Android operating system. (Heck, if you're lucky enough to have an iPod, iPhone, or iPad, you can even store vCard data there.) Think of a vCard as an electronic business card that you can attach to an e-mail message, send via File Transfer Protocol (FTP), or exchange with others by using your cellular phone and palmtop computer. vCard files end with the extension .vcf.

In Address Book, you can create a single vCard containing one or more selected entries by choosing File⇨Export and choosing Export vCard. Then, as with any other Mac OS X Save dialog, just navigate to the spot where you want the file saved, give it a name, and click Save.

To import vCards into Address Book

✦ Drag the vCard files that you've received to Address Book and drop them in the application window.

✦ Alternatively, choose File⇨Import (or press ⌘+O). From the Open dialog, navigate to the location of the vCard files that you want to add, select them, and then click Open.

The vCard tab in the Address Book Preferences window allows you to choose the format of your exported vCard files (older devices only work with vCard 2.1 format, while newer applications recognize the improved vCard 3 format). You can also specify whether your exported vCard files will contain the contents of the Notes field, and whether they will include any photos you've attached.

Chapter 7: The Joys of Maintenance

In This Chapter

- ✔ Deleting applications
- ✔ Using Apple System Profiler
- ✔ Using Activity Monitor and Disk Utility
- ✔ Updating Mac OS X and your drivers
- ✔ Backing up your system
- ✔ Using a disk defragmenter and start-up keys

*T*he title of this chapter really sounds like a contradiction in terms, doesn't it? The concepts of *joy* and *maintenance* are likely mutually exclusive to you — and it's true that most Mac OS X owners would rather work or play than spend time under the hood, getting all grimy. I understand completely; maintenance is far less sexy than a game like Call of Duty: Black Ops or even an exciting productivity application like Pages.

However, if you do want to work or play uninterrupted by lockups and crashes — yes, believe it or not, the Big X can indeed take a dive if it's not cared for — and you'd like your Mac to perform like Lance Armstrong, you have to get your hands dirty. That means performing regular maintenance on your hardware, Mac OS X, and your all-important applications, documents, and folders.

Like most techno-types, I actually *enjoy* pushing my system to the limit and keeping it running in top form. And who knows — after you become a Lion power user, you could find yourself bitten by the maintenance bug as well. In this chapter, I cover how to take care of necessary tune-up chores, step by step.

Deleting Applications the Common Sense Way

Nothing lasts forever, and that includes your applications. You might no longer need an application, or maybe you need to remove it to upgrade to a new version or to reinstall it. In contrast to Windows XP and Vista (which have the Add or Remove Programs utility within Control Panel) or Windows 7 (which has the Programs and Features utility), Mac OS X doesn't have a stand-alone utility for uninstalling software — nor does it need one because virtually all Macintosh applications are self-contained in a single folder or series of nested folders. (And not by accident . . . keeping everything related to an application within a single folder has always been a rule for Apple software developers since the first days of the Macintosh.) Therefore, removing an application is usually as easy as deleting the contents of the installation folder from your hard drive (for example, removing the Quicken folder to uninstall Quicken). If an application does indeed sport an uninstall utility, that utility almost always appears in the same folder as well.

Always check the application's README file and documentation for any special instructions before you delete any application's folder! If you've created any documents in that folder that you want to keep, don't forget to move them before you trash the folder and its contents. In fact, some applications may come complete with their own uninstall utility, so checking the README and documentation may save you unnecessary steps.

Some applications can leave preference files, start-up applications, or driver files in other spots on your disk besides their home folder. When you're uninstalling a program that has support files in other areas, use the Search box in the Finder toolbar to locate other files that might have been created by the application. (I cover this feature in Book II, Chapter 1.) Again, don't forget to check whether an application has an uninstall utility (or an uninstall option available through the original setup application).

For example, Figure 7-1 illustrates a Spotlight search that I've run on my Adobe software. By searching for the word *Adobe,* I found a number of files created in other folders, such as the font files that appear in my Fonts folder. Typically, you want to delete the main application folder and then remove these orphans.

Spring Cleaning Deluxe, from Smith Micro ($50; my.smithmicro.com), also has the ability to uninstall a program, as well as a feature that can find and remove orphaned files left from past applications.

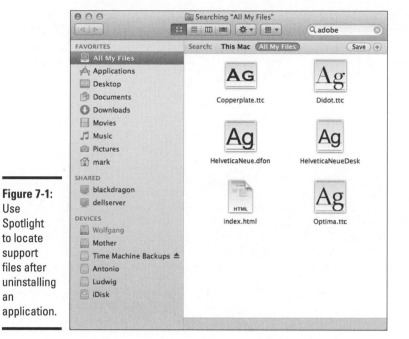

Figure 7-1:
Use
Spotlight
to locate
support
files after
uninstalling
an
application.

Popping the Hood: Using the System Information Utility

Need hard information about your hardware? You might need to determine precisely what hardware is installed in your Mac for the following reasons:

✦ **If you're working with a technical support person to solve a problem:**
This person will usually request information about your system, such as what processor you're running and how much memory you have.

✦ **If you're evaluating an application before you buy it:** You'll want to check its minimum system requirements against the hardware on your Mac.

✦ **If you're considering an upgrade to your Mac:** You'll likely need to determine how much memory you have, what type it is, and which memory slots are filled. (The same goes for your hard drive and your video card, for those Macs with video card slots.) For more on upgrading your Mac, thumb through Book VII, Chapter 2.

Apple provides Mac OS X with an all-in-one hardware and software display tool, aptly named *System Information,* which you can find in the Utilities folder within your Applications folder. You can also reach the Profiler through the Apple menu (). Just click About This Mac, click the More Info button, and then click System Report.

As with the folders in a Finder window in List View mode, you can expand or collapse each major heading that appears in an Information screen. Just click the triangle that appears to the left of each Contents heading to expand or collapse that heading.

The System Information major headings include

✦ **Hardware:** This heading tells you volumes about your hard drives — forgive me, I couldn't help that — as well as specifics concerning your memory; optical drives; modem; AirPort and Bluetooth hardware; printers; graphics and audio hardware; AC power settings; and any FireWire, Thunderbolt, eSATA, and USB devices connected to your system. Figure 7-2 illustrates the information from my USB screen, with many of the devices expanded so that you can see them. (The text you see at the bottom half of the window is the detailed information on the item that's selected.)

Figure 7-2:
Display information about your Mac's ports and connections.

✦ **Network:** This heading shows a listing of your network configuration, active network connections, and other assorted network paraphernalia. You'll probably need this screen only when asked by a technical support person for the network protocols that you're using, but it's handy nonetheless. (You'll find details on your network connection here that you can't find anywhere else in Lion.)

✦ **Software:** Okay, this heading shows something useful to the average human being! This screen lists all the applications, fonts, and preferences recognized on your start-up volume, along with their version numbers. If you're wondering whether you need to update an application with a *patch file* (to fix bugs in the software) or update a file from the developer, you can look here to check the current version number for the application. You also get a rather boring list of the *extensions* (or drivers) used by Mac OS X applications. Logs are usually valuable only to tech support personnel; they document recent lockups, application crashes, and even system crashes.

Tracking Performance with Activity Monitor

Our next stop in Maintenance City is a useful little application dubbed *Activity Monitor,* which is specially designed to show you just how hard your CPU, hard drives, network equipment, and memory modules are working behind the scenes. To run Activity Monitor, open the Utilities folder in your Applications folder.

Processes for dummies

"Mark, what's that arcane-looking list doing in the middle of the Activity Monitor window in Figure 7-3?" I'm glad you asked. Those are processes. A *process* is a discrete task (either visible or invisible) that Lion performs in order to run your applications. (Some processes are executed by Lion just to keep itself running.) For example, the Dock and Finder are actually processes, as are Adobe Acrobat and iPhoto.

You can quit a specific process within Activity Monitor. Just click the offending process in the list and then click the Quit Process button on the Activity Monitor toolbar. But tread carefully, Mr. Holmes, for there's danger afoot. For example, deleting a system process (such as the Dock or Finder) can result in *all* of Mac OS X locking up! Therefore, delete a process **only** *if instructed to do so by a support technician.* If you need to terminate a misbehaving application, click the Apple menu and choose Force Quit instead.

To display each different type of usage, click the buttons in the lower half of the window; the lower pane changes to reflect the desired type (see Figure 7-3). For example, if you click System Memory, you see the amount of unused memory; click CPU or Network to display real-time usage of your Mac's CPU and network connections.

Figure 7-3: Keep tabs on Lion and what you're running.

You can also display a separate window with your CPU usage; choose Window⇨CPU Usage or press ⌘+2. There are three different types of central processing unit (CPU, which is commonly called the "brain" of your Macintosh) displays available from Activity Monitor:

✦ **Floating CPU window:** This is the smallest display of CPU usage; the higher the CPU usage, the higher the reading on the monitor. You can arrange the floating window in horizontal or vertical mode from the Window menu.

✦ **CPU Usage window:** This is the standard CPU monitoring window, which uses a blue thermometer-like display. The display works the same as the floating window.

✦ **CPU History window:** This scrolling display uses different colors to help indicate the percentage of CPU time being used by your applications (green) and what percentage is being used by Lion to keep things running (red). You can use the History window to view CPU usage over time.

Do you have two (or more) bars in your CPU usage monitor? That's because you're running one of Apple's multiple-core Intel processors. More than one engine is under the hood!

Whichever type of display you choose, you can drag the window anywhere that you like on your Mac OS X Desktop. Use the real-time feedback to determine how well your system CPU is performing when you're running applications or performing tasks in Mac OS X. If this meter stays peaked for long periods of time while you're using a range of applications, your processor(s) are running at full capacity.

You can even monitor CPU, network, hard drive, or memory usage right from the Dock! Choose View➪Dock Icon; then choose what type of real-time graph you want to display in your Dock. (Feeling like a Lion power user yet? I thought so.) When you're monitoring CPU usage from the Dock, the green portion of the bar indicates the amount of processor time used by application software, and the red portion of the bar indicates the CPU time given to the Mac OS X operating system (same as how this works in the CPU History window).

Note, however, that seeing your CPU capacity at its max doesn't necessarily mean that you need a faster CPU or a new computer. For example, when I'm running memory-ravenous applications, such as Photoshop or Word, the Activity Monitor on my MacBook Pro is often pegged (indicating maximum use) for several seconds at a time. The rest of the time, it barely moves. Whether a computer is actually fast enough for you and the applications that you run is more of a subjective call on your part.

Fixing Things with the Disk Utility

Another important application in your maintenance toolbox is Disk Utility, which you find — no surprise here — in the Utilities folder within your Applications folder. When you first run this program, it looks something like Figure 7-4, displaying all the physical disks and volumes on your system.

The Disk Utility application has its own toolbar that you can toggle on and off. Click Window➪Hide/Show Toolbar to display or hide the toolbar, or Window➪Customize Toolbar to select which icons inhabit the Disk Utility toolbar.

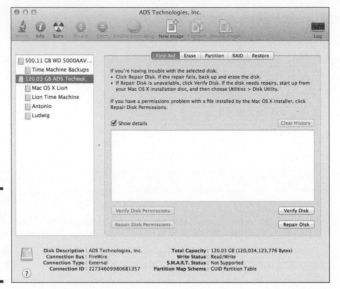

Figure 7-4:
The familiar face of Lion's Disk Utility.

Displaying the goods on your disks

The volume tree structure on the left of the Disk Utility window lists both the physical disks and the partitions that you've set up. A *partition* is nothing more than another word for *volume,* which is the formatted section of a disk that contains data. A single physical hard drive can contain several partitions. The information display at the bottom of the Disk Utility window contains data about both the volumes and the partitions on your hard drive.

To illustrate: On my system, clicking the drive labeled 500.11 GB (the physical external FireWire hard drive at the top of the tree) displays a description of the drive itself, including its total capacity, connection bus (the interface it uses), and whether the drive is internal or external (connection type). (See Figure 7-5.)

Clicking the tree entry for Time Machine Backups, however — that's the name of the partition that I created when I formatted the drive — displays information about the type of formatting, the total capacity of the partition and how much of that is used, and the number of files and folders stored on the partition (as shown at the bottom of Figure 7-6).

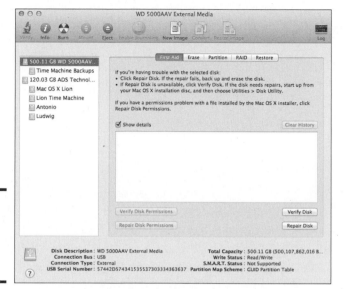

Figure 7-5:
Display
data on a
physical
drive.

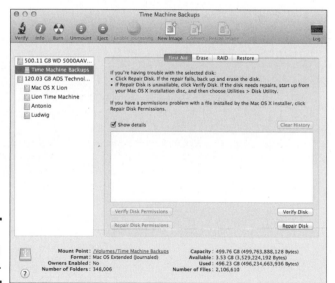

Figure 7-6:
Display data
on a volume.

So what's a disk image?

You might have noticed the New Image button on the Disk Utility toolbar (or the image creation commands on the File⇨New submenu). If you're wondering what a *disk image* is, you've come to the right place. Think of a disk image as a file that looks (and acts) like an external storage device within Lion; for example, a mounted disk image operates much like a CD or DVD, and it can be ejected just as a disc can. Images can be read-only (same as a standard CD-ROM or DVD-ROM) or they can be created blank (same as an empty hard drive), ready to accept files and folders that you copy using the Finder.

So what are images used for? They're great for storing data that would normally have to be loaded from a CD or DVD (a great convenience if you don't want to lug optical media along with you during a vacation). Remember, a disk image acts just the same as removable storage media as far as Lion's concerned. Many Mac Web sites also offer images as download files because a simple double-click is all that's necessary to automatically mount a disk image. (Software developers like words such as *fast*

and *simple* when offering their shareware and demo applications to the public.)

Finally, images are often used to create simple archives of little-used data: The images can be burned to CD/DVD or even copied to other hard drives. Oh, and don't forget the security aspect — you can choose to encrypt the data stored in an image, protecting it from prying eyes. (However, I don't recommend using disk images to create full backups of your Mac's hard drives; more on this in the section "Hitching a ride on the Time Machine," later in the chapter.) To restore a disk image, you can use the Restore tab in Disk Utility.

If you're intrigued, I encourage you to click New Image on the Disk Utility toolbar (see Figure 7-5) and create a simple, unencrypted blank disk image on your Desktop. Then you can experiment with it. A disk image can be ejected to unmount it (same as with a CD/DVD, an iPod, or a USB Flash drive), and you can delete the image file at any time. (Just remember not to delete it if it contains anything you want to keep, of course . . . but you knew that already.)

Playing doctor with First Aid

From the First Aid pane, you can use Disk Utility to *verify* (or check) any disk (well, *almost* any disk) for errors, as well as repair any errors that it finds. Here are the two exceptions when the buttons are disabled:

✦ **The start-up disk:** Disk Utility can't repair the *start-up disk* — that's Mac talk for the boot drive that contains the Mac OS X Lion system you're using at the moment — which makes sense if you think about it, because that drive is currently being used!

If you have multiple operating systems on multiple disks, you can boot from another Mac OS X installation on another drive to check your current start-up disk. Or you can boot your system from the original Mac OS X installation DVD and run Disk Utility from the Installation menu.

✦ **Write-protected disks:** Although you can use the Disk Utility to verify CDs and DVDs, Disk Utility can't repair them. (Sound of my palm slapping my forehead.)

You usually can't repair a disk that has *open* files that are currently being used. If you're running an application from a drive or you've opened a document that's stored on that drive, you probably can't repair that drive.

You can also elect to verify and repair *permissions* (or *privileges*) on a disk; these are the read/write permissions that I discuss in detail in Book II, Chapter 6. If you can't save or move a file that you should be able to access, I recommend checking that drive for permissions problems. Although you can't fix disk errors on a boot drive, you can verify and repair permissions on any volume that contains a Mac OS X installation (whether it was used to boot your Mac or not).

In order to verify or repair, you must be logged in as an admin-level user.

To verify or repair a drive, first select the target volume/partition in the list at the left. To check the contents of the drive and display any errors, click the Verify Disk button. Or, to verify the contents of the drive and fix any problems, click the Repair Disk button. (I usually just click Repair Disk because an error-free disk needs no repairs.) Disk Utility displays any status or error messages in the scrolling list; if you have eagle eyes, you'll note that the window can be resized so that you can expand it to display more messages. (You can also drag the dot between the left and right panes to expand the list.)

I generally check my disks once every two or three days. If your Mac is caught by a power failure or Mac OS X locks up, however, it's a good idea to immediately check disks after you restart your Mac. (Don't forget that the start-up volume is automatically checked and repaired, if necessary.)

A number of very good commercial disk repair utilities are on the market. My favorite is Drive Genius 3 from Prosoft Engineering ($99; `www.prosofteng.com`) — however, Disk Utility does a good job on its own, and it's free.

Erasing without seriously screwing up

"Danger, Will Robinson! Danger!" That's right, Robot, it is indeed very easy to seriously screw up and get "Lost in Erase." (Man, I can't believe I actually typed such a bad pun. I have no shame.) Anyway, it's time for another of Mark's Maxims. To paraphrase the rules for handling a firearm responsibly:

Never — and I do mean *never* — click the Erase tab unless you mean to use it.

Figure 7-7 illustrates the Erase controls within Disk Utility. You need to erase a disk or volume only when you want to *completely wipe* the contents of that existing disk or volume. You can also erase a rewritable CD (CD-RW) or DVD (DVD-RW, DVD+RW, or DVD-RAM) from this pane.

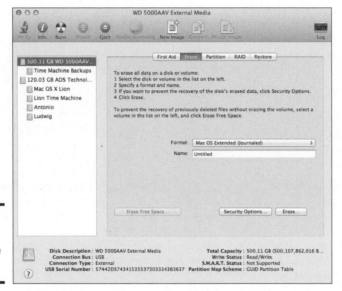

Figure 7-7:
The Disk Utility Erase controls.

✦ Erasing an *entire disk* deletes *all volumes* on the disk and creates a single new, empty volume.

✦ Erasing a *volume* wipes only the *contents of that specific volume,* leaving all other volumes on the physical disk untouched.

To erase, follow these steps:

1. **Click the disk or volume icon that you want to erase from the list on the left side of the screen.**

2. **Click the Erase tab.**

3. **Click the format that you want to use from the Format pop-up menu.**

Always choose Mac OS Extended (Journaled) entry from the Format list unless you have a specific reason to use the MS-DOS File System (for compatibility with PCs running Windows) or the ExFAT File System (for compatibility with high-capacity USB flash drives). In some cases, Disk Utility will force you to choose the Mac OS Extended entry instead, but the end result is the same. Note that you do not need to format a disk or volume with the MS-DOS File System just to read a file from a PC system — Mac OS X recognizes MS-DOS removable media (such as a USB drive formatted under Windows) without a problem. You can also choose to encrypt a volume when formatting it — not a necessity (in most cases) for a personal Mac, but often a requirement in business and government offices.

4. **In the Name field, type the name for the volume.**

   If you're erasing an existing volume, the default is the existing name.

5. **If you're worried about security, click Security Options and specify the Secure Erase method you want to use.**

   By default, this is set to Fastest, so Disk Utility doesn't actually overwrite any data while formatting; instead, it simply trashes the existing directory, rendering that data unreachable. *Or is it?* With some third-party disk utilities, an unscrupulous bum could actually recover your files after a simple Fast format, so you can specify alternative, more secure methods of erasing a disk or volume. Unfortunately, these more secure erasure methods can take a horrendous amount of time.

   Therefore, it's okay to use the Fast option unless you want to make sure that nothing can be recovered, or use the Zero Out Data to take a more secure route with the least amount of extra waiting. For example, you'd want to use the next-slowest option (which writes a single pass of all zeros over the entire disk) if you're selling your Mac on eBay and you're formatting the drive for the new owner. If you're really set on the tightest, government-quality security, select Most Secure . . . but make sure you have plenty of time to spare!

   You can even click Erase Free Space to wipe the supposedly "clean" areas of your drive *before* you format. Man, talk about airtight security! Again, the Zero Out method is the fastest.

6. **Click the Erase button.**

   In the sheet that appears, click Erase to confirm that you do actually want to do the deleterious deed.

Partitioning the right way

From time to time, just about everyone wishes he or she had additional volumes handy for organizing files and folders, or at least a little extra space on a particular partition. If you find yourself needing another volume on a disk — or if you need to resize the total space on existing volumes on a disk — click the Partition tab within Disk Utility to display the controls that you see in Figure 7-8. (Make sure that you select a *disk* and not a volume.) From here, you can choose a volume scheme, creating anywhere from 1 to 16 volumes on a single disk.

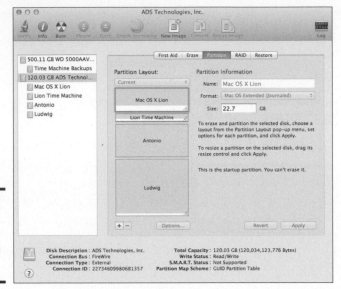

Figure 7-8:
The Disk
Utility
Partitioning
controls.

You can't monkey around with the partitions on a start-up disk because Mac OS X is currently running on that disk. (Think about removing your own appendix, and you get the idea.) Also, if you resize an existing volume, you may lose files and folders on that volume — Disk Utility prompts you for permission, but it's always a good idea to back up a partition before you resize it!

To set up the partitions on a disk, follow these steps:

1. **From the Partition panel within Disk Utility, click the disk icon (left side of the pane) that you want to partition.**

2. **Click the Partition Layout pop-up menu and choose the total number of volumes that you want on the selected disk.**

   To add a partition to an existing layout, click the Add button (which carries a plus sign).

3. **Click the first volume block in the partition list (under the Partition Layout pop-up menu) to select it.**

   I have three partitions set for this disk, as you can see.

4. **Click in the Name field and enter the name for the selected volume.**

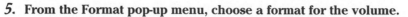

5. **From the Format pop-up menu, choose a format for the volume.**

   Always use Mac OS Extended or Mac OS Extended (Journaled) from the Format menu unless you have a specific reason to use the MS-DOS file system (for compatibility with PCs running Windows) or the ExFAT file system (for compatibility with high-capacity USB flash drives).

6. **Type a total size for this volume in the Size field.**

7. **If you're creating multiple volumes, click the next volume block to select it and repeat Steps 4–6.**

   Some folks create multiple volumes so that they can boot from multiple versions of Lion — like us author types.

8. **To delete a partition from your new scheme, click the unwanted volume and then click the Delete button (which carries a minus sign) to remove it.**

9. **After everything is set to your liking, click the Apply button to begin the process.**

   If you suddenly decide against a partition change, click the Revert button to return to the original existing partition scheme.

   The Revert button is available only before you click the Apply button!

If you have more than one partition, check out the handles separating the volumes in the partition list — they appear as dashed lines in the lower-right corner of the partition. You can click and drag these handles to dynamically resize the volumes. This makes it easy to adjust the individual volume sizes for the disk until you get precisely the arrangement you want.

RAID has nothing to do with insects

The next stop on the Disk Utility hayride isn't for everyone — as a matter of fact, only a Mac OS X power user with a roomful of hardware is likely to use it. RAID, *Redundant Array of Independent/Inexpensive Disks,* is actually what it says. In normal human English, a *RAID set* is a group of multiple separate disks, working together as a team. RAID can

✦ Improve the speed of your system

✦ Help prevent disk errors from compromising or corrupting your data

The RAID controls within Disk Utility are illustrated in Figure 7-9. You need at least two additional hard drives on your system besides the start-up disk, which I don't recommend that you use in a RAID set.

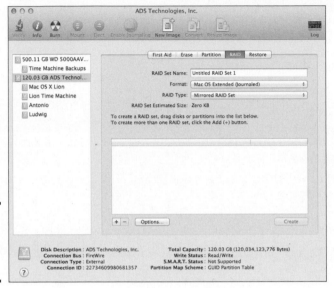

Figure 7-9:
The Disk Utility RAID controls.

To set up a RAID array in Mac OS X, follow these steps:

1. From the RAID tab of Disk Utility, click and drag the disks from the list at the left to the Disk box at the right.

2. Click the RAID Type pop-up menu to specify the type of RAID that you need.

- *Striped RAID Set:* Choosing this can speed up your hard drive performance by splitting data between multiple disks.

- *Concatenated RAID Set:* Choosing this allows several volumes (or even multiple disks) to appear as one volume within Lion.

- *Mirrored RAID Set:* Choosing this increases the reliability of your storage by creating a mirror backup of that data across multiple disks.

3. Click in the RAID Set Name field and type the name for your RAID set.

4. From the Volume Format pop-up menu, choose a format for the volumes.

Always use Mac OS Extended or Mac OS Extended (Journaled) from the Volume Format list unless you have a specific reason to use the MS-DOS File System (for compatibility with PCs running Windows). Journaling helps reduce the amount of disk fragmentation and also helps speed up your hard drive's performance.

5. **Click the Create button.**

Updating Mac OS X

As any good software developer should, Apple constantly releases improvements to Mac OS X in the form of software updates. These updates can include all sorts of fun stuff, like

✦ Bug fixes

✦ Improvements and new features

✦ Enhanced drivers

✦ Security upgrades

✦ Firmware upgrades

Apple makes it easy to keep Mac OS X up-to-date with the Software Update controls in System Preferences.

You don't even have to display the System Preferences window to check for new software updates manually. Click the Apple menu in the Finder menu bar and then choose Software Update to perform a manual check immediately.

To check for new updates periodically, display the Software Update pane in System Preferences and click the Scheduled Check tab. Select the Check for Updates check box and choose how often you want these updates from the pop-up menu. (I suggest at least weekly, if not daily.) For a manual check, make sure that you're connected to the Internet and then click the Check Now button.

To download updates automatically, mark the Download Updates Automatically check box to enable it; the Big X politely downloads the updates behind the scenes and then alerts you that they're ready to be installed. (With automatic downloading disabled, Mac OS X displays any available updates with short descriptions, and you can toggle the installation of a specific update by enabling or disabling the check boxes next to it.)

I recommend installing all updates, even for hardware that you don't have yet. For example, I always install AirPort updates even though I don't use an AirPort connection at home. The reason? Often, the functionality covered by an update may include system software that you *do* use, so you still benefit from installing it.

After you specify the updates that you want to install, click the Install button to begin the update process. You might have to reboot after everything has been installed.

To see which updates you've installed already, click the Installed Software tab on the Software Update pane in System Preferences.

I Demand That You Back Up Your Hard Drive

I know we're friends, but there's **no excuse** for not backing up your data. The more valuable and irreplaceable your documents are, the more heinous it is to risk losing them. (I don't get to use the word *heinous* in many of my books, but it fits *really* well here.)

Although Apple does include the ability to create disk images and restore them in the Disk Utility (see the "So what's a disk image?" sidebar, earlier in this chapter), I don't recommend that you use disk images as your comprehensive backup solution. (Insert sound of stunned silence here.) That's because the restore process can be confusing, and the disk image method doesn't offer the level of control that you need when it comes to backing up individual files and folders (or selectively backing up by date or recent use).

If you do create backup datasets using disk images, you can restore them from the Restore tab in Disk Utility. You can also restore from a volume — typically, a volume you want to restore would be saved on a DVD or an external hard drive.

"Okay, Mark, what do I use to back up my valuable data?" Well, good citizen, only a bona fide backup application gives you such flexibility and convenience . . . and that's why Lion power users turn to *Time Machine,* a feature that makes restoring files as easy as pointing and clicking!

Hitching a ride on the Time Machine

If you enable backups through Lion's Time Machine feature, you can literally move backward through the contents of your Mac's hard drive, selecting and restoring all sorts of data. Files and folders are ridiculously easy to restore — and I mean easier than *any* restore you've ever performed, no matter what the operating system or backup program. Time Machine can even handle things like deleted Address Book entries and photos you've sent to the Trash from iPhoto! To be blunt, Time Machine should be an important and integral part of every Mac owner's existence.

Before you can use Time Machine, it must be enabled within the Time Machine pane in System Preferences. I cover these settings in detail in Chapter 3 of Book II. I also recommend that you invest in an external USB, Thunderbolt, or FireWire hard drive to hold your Time Machine backups.

Here's how you can turn back time, step-by-step, to restore a file that you deleted or replaced in a folder:

1. **Open the folder that contained the file you want to restore.**

2. **In a separate window, open your Applications folder and launch the Time Machine application, or click the Time Machine icon in the menu bar and choose Enter Time Machine.**

The oh-so-ultra-cool Time Machine background appears behind your folder, complete with its own set of buttons at the bottom of the screen (as shown in Figure 7-10). On the right, you see a timeline that corresponds to the different days and months included in the backups that Lion has made.

Figure 7-10: Yes, Time Machine really *does* look like this!

3. **Click within the timeline to jump directly to a date (displaying the folder's contents on that date).**

   Alternatively, use the Forward and Back arrows at the right to move through the folder's contents through time. (You should see the faces of Windows users when you "riffle" through your folders to locate something you deleted several weeks ago!)

   The backup date of the items you're viewing appears in the button bar at the bottom of the screen.

4. **After you locate the file you want to restore, click it to select it.**

5. **Click the Restore button at the right side of the Time Machine button bar.**

   If you want to restore all the contents of the folder, click the Restore All button instead.

Time Machine returns you to the Finder, with the newly restored file now appearing in the folder. *OUTstanding!*

To restore specific data from your Address Book or images from iPhoto, launch the desired application first and then launch Time Machine. Instead of riffling a Finder window, you can move through time within the application window.

For simple backup and restore protection, Time Machine is all that a typical Mac owner at home is likely to ever need. Therefore, a very easy Mark's Maxim to predict:

Connect an external hard drive and turn on Time Machine. *Do it now.* Don't make a heinous mistake.™

How about that? I got to use *heinous* twice in one chapter.

Using other backup solutions

Time Machine is indeed awesome, but some Mac owners prefer a more traditional automated backup and restore process — one that doesn't involve running the Time Machine application and navigating through the files and folders on a drive. For example, a person backing up a Mac acting as a web server or iTunes media server would much rather restore the entire contents of a volume automatically, in bulk, or create a custom backup/restore schedule that safeguards only certain files and folders.

If you're dead-set against Time Machine, you can turn to a commercial backup application for your salvation — my personal recommendation is Roxio Retrospect Desktop 8 (www.roxio.com). This well-written "software bungee cord" has saved my posterior more than once.

Using Retrospect Desktop 8 is good security, but if you can't afford it at the moment, take a second to at least back up your most important documents by copying them to a rewriteable CD or a USB flash drive. With this poor man's backup, even if you lose your entire hard drive, you can still restore what matters the most.

I Further Demand That You Defragment

Defragmenting your hard drive can significantly improve its performance. Using a defragmenter scans for little chunks of a file that are spread out across the surface of your hard drive and then arranges them to form a contiguous file. After a file has been optimized in this way, it's far easier and faster for Mac OS X to read than reassembling a fragmented file.

However, Apple dropped the ball on this one and didn't include a defragmenter with Mac OS X. Luckily, many third-party disk utilities (such as the aforementioned Drive Genius 3 from Prosoft Engineering) also include a defragmenting feature. If you have a defragmenter, I recommend that you use it once a month.

Special Start-Up Keys for Those Special Times

Mac OS X includes a number of special keys that you can use during the boot process. These keys really come in handy when you need to force your operating system to do something that it normally wouldn't, such as boot from a CD instead of the hard drive.

✦ **To boot from a CD or DVD:** Restart your Mac while pressing the C key. This is a great way to free your startup volume when you want to test it or optimize it using a commercial utility.

✦ **To eject a recalcitrant disc that doesn't show up on the Desktop:** Restart Mac OS X and hold down the mouse button — or if you have a late-model Mac, press the Media Eject key as soon as you hear that magnificent startup chord.

✦ **To force your Mac to boot in Mac OS X:** Hold down the X key while restarting or booting the Mac.

✦ **To display a system boot menu:** Hold down the Option key while restarting or booting the Mac, and you can choose which operating system you want to use.

✦ **To prevent start-up applications from running during login:** Hold down the Shift key while you click the Login button on the Login screen. If you don't see the Login screen during startup, just hold down Shift while Mac OS X boots until the Finder menu appears.

Crave the Newest Drivers

No chapter on maintenance would be complete without a reminder to keep your hardware drivers current. *Drivers* are simply programs that allow your Mac to control hardware devices, such as a video card or an external SATA (eSATA) card that you've added to your Mac. The Mac OS X Software Update feature that I discuss earlier, in the section "Updating Mac OS X," provides most of the drivers you need for things like printers, USB, Thunderbolt, and FireWire peripherals, and digital cameras, but it's still very important to check those manufacturer web sites.

Like the software updates from Apple, updated drivers can fix bugs and even add new features to your existing hardware, which is my definition of getting something for nothing.

Chapter 8: Getting Help for the Big X

In This Chapter

✓ Using the Mac OS X Help Center

✓ Searching for specific help

✓ Getting help in applications

✓ Finding other help resources

*W*hether the voice echoes from a living room, home office, or college computer lab, it's all too familiar: a call for help. No matter how well written the application or how well designed the operating system, sooner or later, you're going to need support. That goes for everyone from the novice to the experienced Mac owner to the occasional e-mail user to the most talented software developer.

In this short but oh-so-important chapter, I lead you through the various help resources available within Mac OS X as well as native Mac OS X applications. I show you how to tap additional resources from Apple, and I also point you to other suppliers of high-quality (as well as even questionable) assistance on the Internet and in your local area.

Displaying the Help Center Window

Your first line of defense is the Mac OS X Help Center, as shown in Figure 8-1. To display the Help Center from the Finder menu, click Help and choose Help Center. This Help menu is context-sensitive, so it contains different menu items when you're working inside an application.

Quick Links

Toolbar

Figure 8-1:
The
reservoir
of Lion
assistance:
The Help
Center.

Featured help

As shown in Figure 8-1, the Help Center is divided into three sets of controls:

✦ **Toolbar:** The toolbar includes navigational controls (Back, Forward, and Home buttons), an Action button (where you can print a topic or change the text size), and the Ask a Question (or Search) text box.

✦ **Quick Clicks:** Clicking these links takes you directly to some of the most frequently asked Help topics for the Finder (or the application you're using), such as Personalize Your Mac and Set Up Accounts. To use a Quick Click, just click once on the question that you want to pursue.

✦ **Featured Help:** Click the Help for All Your Apps link, then click one of these icons to display specific help for a Mac OS X application. (To see the comprehensive list of application help icons, click Show All.)

I know that the Help Center looks a little sparse at first glance. However, when you realize how much information has to be covered to help someone with an operating system — check out the size of the book you're holding, for instance — you get an idea of why Mac OS X doesn't try to cover everything on one screen. Instead, you get the one tool that does it all: the Spotlight search box.

Searching for Specific Stuff

To search for the Help topic you need, here are two paths to righteousness:

✦ **From the Finder Help menu:** Wowzers! In Lion, you don't even have to open the Help Center to search for assistance on a specific topic . . . just choose Help from the Finder menu (or press the ⌘+Shift+/ shortcut). Click in the Search field right there in the menu, and type a keyword or two. (Although you can ask a full-sentence question, I find that the shorter and more concise your search criteria are, the more relevant your results are.) As with the Spotlight search box, you don't need to press Return; just click the topic that sounds the most helpful.

✦ **From the Help Center:** Click in the Search text box at the right side of the toolbar, type one or two words that sum up your question, and press Return. Figure 8-2 illustrates a typical set of topics concerning DVD movies.

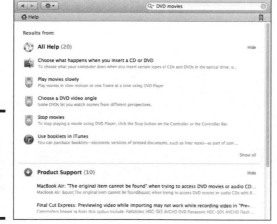

Figure 8-2:
The results
of a search
within
the Help
Viewer.

Within the Help Center window, articles taken from the AppleCare Support section of the Apple web site appear in the Support portion of the window. (Because web stuff is going on in the background, you don't see these articles unless your Mac has an active Internet connection.)

You can double-click any topic to display the topic text, which looks like the text that you see in Figure 8-3.

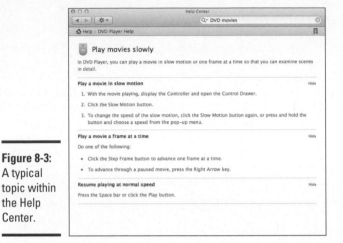

Figure 8-3:
A typical topic within the Help Center.

To move back to the previous topic that you chose, click the Back button on the Help Center toolbar.

Prodding Apple for the Latest Gossip

As I mention in the earlier section, "Displaying the Help Center Window," in this chapter, I heartily recommend that you visit the Apple web site at www.apple.com and surf wildly to and fro. You'll often pick up on news and reviews that you won't find anywhere else on the Internet.

From the opening web screen, click the Hot News Headlines link on the Apple tab and the Support tab during every visit to the Apple site. These pages give you

✦ Articles about the latest news from Cupertino

✦ Downloads of the latest Mac OS X freeware, shareware, and demoware

✦ The *Knowledge Base* (an online searchable troubleshooting reference)

✦ News about upcoming versions of Mac OS X and Apple applications galore

You'll also find Mac OS X product manuals in Adobe Acrobat PDF format and online discussion forums that cover Mac OS X.

Calling for Help Deep in the Heart of X

A number of different help avenues are available within Mac OS X applications as well. They include

✦ **The Help button:** A number of otherwise upstanding Mac OS X windows, dialogs, and System Preference panes include a Help button, as shown in the lower right of Figure 8-4. Click the button marked with a question mark (?) to display the text for the settings in that dialog or window.

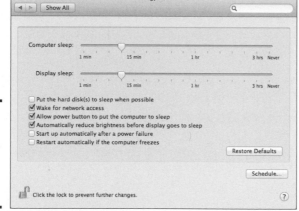

Figure 8-4:
Notice the not-so-well-camou-flaged Help button.

✦ **Pop-up help for fields and controls:** Most Mac OS X applications display a short line of help text when you hover the mouse pointer on top of a field or control. Sometimes it's just the name of the item; sometimes it's a full descriptive line. Them's the breaks.

✦ **Application-specific help:** Applications typically have their own Help system, which can use the Help Center window, a separate Help display program, or a HyperText Markup Language (HTML; read that *web-based*) Help system.

Other Resources to Chew On

Although the Help Center can take care of just about any question that you might have about the basic controls and features of Mac OS X, you might also want to turn to other forms of help when the going gets a little rougher. In this last section, I cover resources that you can call on when the Help Center just isn't enough.

Voice support

As of this writing, Apple provides voice technical support for Mac OS X. You can find the number to call in your Mac's printed manuals or online in the Support section of the Apple web site. However, exactly when you qualify for voice support and exactly how long it lasts depends on a number of different factors, such as whether you received Mac OS X when you bought a new machine or whether you purchased a support plan from Apple.

You can also try the general online support site at www.apple.com/support — it's a great starting point for obtaining Mac OS X help.

Mac publications and resource sites

You can refer to a number of great Mac-savvy publications and resources, both printed and online, for help. My favorites include

✦ **Macworld** (www.macworld.com), both in archaic hard copy and oh-so-slick online versions

✦ **MacGamer** (www.macgamer.com), the online gaming resource for the Macintosh

✦ **Download.com** (www.versiontracker.com), an online resource for the latest updates on all sorts of Macintosh third-party applications

✦ **MacFixIt** (www.macfixit.com), a well-respected troubleshooting site devoted to the Mac that offers downloads, news, and discussion areas (a subscription may be required for some of the more useful sections of the site)

In most of my books, I mention specific Internet newsgroups that cater to the topic I'm discussing; however, virtually all of the *alt.binaries* hierarchy Mac-specific newsgroups are devoted to illegally swapping pirated games and applications, so I don't cover them. (The *comp.sys.mac* hierarchy is usually far more helpful anyway.) Also, the help that you receive from individuals in newsgroups is sometimes misguided — and sometimes downright *wrong* — so take any claims with a grain of salt.

As a general rule, *never* identify yourself or provide your snail-mail or e-mail addresses in a newsgroup post! These messages are public, and they remain hanging around in cyberspace on newsgroup servers for years — you'll be a prime target for spam (or even worse).

Local Mac outlets and user groups

Finally, you can find local resources in any medium-size to large town or city: A shop that's authorized by Apple to sell and repair Macintosh computers can usually be counted upon to answer a quick question over the phone or provide more substantial support for a fee. (For example, my local Mac outlet sponsors inexpensive classes for new Mac owners, and if you can reach an Apple Store, the Genius Bar is a great resource.)

You might also be lucky enough to have a local Macintosh user group that you can join — members can be counted on for free answers to your support questions at meetings and demonstrations. To find a group near you, visit the Apple User Group Support site at www.apple.com/usergroups and click the Find a Group link.

Chapter 9: Troubleshooting the X

In This Chapter

✔ **Mastering the scientific approach**

✔ **Using troubleshooting techniques**

✔ **Performing the radical solutions**

✔ **Checking troubleshooting resources**

Mac OS X Lion is rugged, stable, and reliable — and as you can read in Chapter 7 of this minibook, practicing regular maintenance can help prevent problems caused by everything from power failures to faulty software drivers to cats on the keyboard. However, sooner or later you *will* encounter what I like to call *The Dark Moments* . . . a blank screen, a locked Mac, or an external device that sits there uselessly like an expensive paperweight.

How you handle The Dark Moments defines you as a true Mac OS X power user because most folks seem to fall into one of two categories: Either you panic and beat your head against the wall (which really has little effect on the computer, when you think about it), or you set your brow in grim determination and follow the troubleshooting models that I provide in this chapter to locate (and, I hope, fix) the source of the problem.

Don't Panic!

My friend, this is the first — and **most important** — rule of troubleshooting, and yet another of Mark's Maxims:

Whatever the problem, you *can* fix it (or get it fixed).

Most computer owners seem to forget the idea that a hardware or software error can be fixed because they panic — they simply see The Problem, and somehow they feel that they'll never be able to use their computer again.

Although the situation might look grim, don't ignore these facts:

✦ **You don't need to scrap your Mac.** As long as you haven't taken a hammer or a chainsaw to your Mac, the problem is only temporary. Sure, individual components do fail over time — heck, so do *people* — but the problem is certainly something that can be tracked down and fixed without scrapping your entire computer.

✦ **Don't beat yourself up.** As long as you haven't installed a virus on purpose or deleted half your system files to spite yourself, the problem *isn't* your fault. Sure, it's possible that you might have done something by accident, but don't blame yourself — accidents happen to everybody. (Trust me, I do mean *everybody*. Even Steve Jobs, I'm told.)

✦ **Trust your Apple dealer.** As long as an Apple dealer is in your area, you can usually get your computer repaired professionally if a component's gone south. (In some cases, professional help is a necessity: For example, I'd be a fool to try to fix a power supply or a monitor on my own because both can pack a heavy electrical punch.)

✦ **Rely on your backup.** As long as you've made a backup, you won't lose much (if any) work. (You *did* back up your hard drive, didn't you? I harp about backups further in Chapter 7 of this minibook.) I'm talking about a backup to an external hard drive here, using either an application such as Disk Utility or Lion's Time Machine feature. (Or even a "quickie" backup of your most important stuff to a recordable DVD.)

Commit these facts to head and heart, and you can rest easy while you track down and attack the *real* enemy — whatever's causing the problem.

The Troubleshooting Process

When I first conceived this chapter, I had originally decided to divide this section into separate hardware and software troubleshooting procedures. However, that turned out to be impractical because often you won't know whether a problem is caused by hardware or software until you're practically on top of it.

Therefore, here's the complete 12-step troubleshooting process that I designed while working as a consultant and Macintosh hardware technician for 20 years. Feel free to add your own embellishments in the margin or include reminders with sticky notes.

If you're not sure quite what's producing the error, this process is designed to be *linear* — meaning that it's meant to be followed in order — but if you already know that you're having a problem with one specific peripheral or one specific application, feel free to jump to the steps that concern only hardware or software.

 It's always a good idea to create a completely default user account for troubleshooting — techs call this a *vanilla* or *clean* account. You can use the vanilla account to test whether a problem occurs system-wide or is limited to a single user account. For example, this is a great way to determine whether an application is misbehaving because of a corrupted preference file: If the same problem doesn't appear when you use the application with the vanilla account, the culprit is likely the user's copy of the application's preference file or a corrupt font. (Follow the instructions provided by the application for resetting or deleting the preference file it creates.)

Step 1: Always try a simple shutdown

You'd be amazed at how often a *reboot* (the process of shutting down and restarting) can cure a temporary problem. For example, this can fix the occasional lockup in Mac OS X or a keyboard that's not responding because of a power failure. If possible, make sure that you first close any open documents; otherwise, you might lose unsaved work. When troubleshooting, always do a shutdown instead of simply restarting the computer because when Mac OS X shuts down, all the hardware components that make up your system are reset.

 If your Mac is locked tight and you can't use the Shut Down command from the Apple menu (), you have two choices. First, press and hold the Power button on your Mac for a few seconds (which turns your computer off). If this doesn't work — and, from time to time, it actually doesn't — you have to physically pull the power cord from the wall (or turn off the surge protector, if you're using one).

Step 2: Check all cable connections

Check all connections: the AC power cord and the keyboard cord, as well as any modem or network connections and all cable connections to external peripherals. Look for loose connectors — and if you have a cat or dog, don't forget to check for chew marks. (Yep, that's the voice of experience talking there.) If you've recently replaced a cable — especially a network, Universal Serial Bus (USB), or FireWire cable — replace it with a spare to see whether the problem still occurs.

Step 3: Retrace your steps

If the problem continues to occur, the next step is to consider what you've done in the immediate past that could have affected your Mac. Did you install any new software, or have you connected a new peripheral? If your Mac was working fine until you made the change to your system, the problem likely lies in the new hardware or software.

✦ **If you added an external device:** Turn off your Mac and disconnect the peripheral. Then turn on the computer to see whether all proceeds normally. If so, check the peripheral's documentation and make sure that you correctly installed the *driver* — the software provided by the device manufacturer — and that you connected it properly to the right port. (You can also use the System Information utility, which I discuss later in this chapter, to check to see whether your Mac recognizes the external device.) To verify that the cable works, substitute another cable of the same type or try the peripheral on another Mac.

Make it a practice to check the manufacturer's web site for the latest driver when you get new hardware. The software that ships in the box with your new toy could have been on the shelf for months before being sold, and the manufacturer has probably fine-tuned the driver in the interim. You should also run Software Update to verify that the drivers that Apple supplies are up-to-date.

✦ **If you installed new software or applied an update/patch:** Follow the guidelines in Chapter 7 of this minibook to uninstall the application and search for any files that it might have created elsewhere. (Searching by date created and date modified can help you locate files that were recently created.) If this fixes the problem, it's time to contact the developer and request technical support for the recalcitrant program; you can always re-install the program after the problem has been solved by the developer.

Not all versions of Mac OS X are created equal. If you've recently upgraded to a major or minor new release of Mac OS X, some of the applications that you've been using without trouble for months can suddenly go on the warpath and refuse to work (or exhibit quirky behavior). If this happens, visit the developer's web site often to look for a patch file that will update the application to work with the new version of Mac OS X.

✦ **If you recently made a change within System Preferences:** It's possible that you've inadvertently "bumped" something. For instance, you might have accidentally changed your modem or network settings or perhaps made a change to your login options. Verify the settings screens that you visited to make sure that everything looks okay.

Step 4: Run Disk Utility

Next, run Disk Utility (as shown in Figure 9-1) to check for disk errors and permissions errors — especially permissions errors, which can wreak absolute havoc on just about any application on your hard drive. (Click the Disk Utility icon in the Utilities folder inside your Applications folder. Chapter 7 of this minibook provides all the details.)

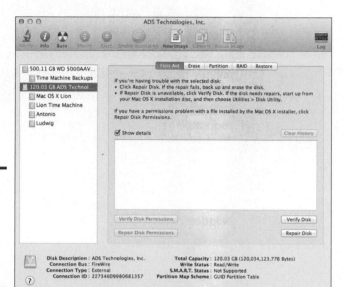

Figure 9-1:
Use Disk
Utility to
check the
integrity of
your drive
and files.

Step 5: Run antivirus software

Run your antivirus software and scan your entire system for viruses, including all system disks and removable disks. Although Mac OS X doesn't come with antivirus protection built in, the world-class program Intego VirusBarrier X6 (www.intego.com) constantly scans each file that you open or download for infections. You can also run the great freeware ClamXav 2 virus scanner (available for downloading at www.clamxav.com).

If you haven't already set your antivirus application to automatically update itself, download the latest virus update — usually called a *signature file* or *data file* — to keep your virus protection current.

Step 6: Check the Trash

Check the contents of your Trash to make sure that you haven't inadvertently tossed something important that could be causing trouble for an application. Click the Trash icon in the Dock to open the Trash window and peruse its contents. (To see the file types easier, switch to List mode.) To restore items to their rightful place, drag them from the Trash back to the correct folder on your hard drive.

Step 7: Check online connections

If you're connected to an Ethernet network, a cable modem, or a digital subscriber line (DSL), check your equipment to make sure that you're currently online and receiving packets normally. Your network system administrator will be happy to help you with this, especially if you're blood relatives.

Step 8: Disable troublesome Login Items

Disable any *Login Items* that might be causing trouble. As you can read in Book II, Chapter 3, Login Items are launched automatically as soon as you log in. For example, an older application that doesn't fully support Mac OS X Lion can cause problems if used as a Login Item. You can do this from the Login Items settings in the System Preferences Accounts pane (as shown in Figure 9-2); click the Apple menu, choose System Preferences, click Users & Groups, and then click the Login Items tab.

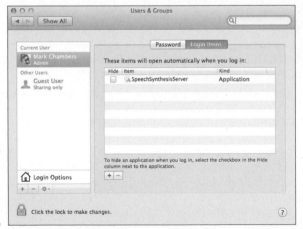

Figure 9-2:
A misbehaving Login Item can cause you a world of grief.

Unfortunately, if a Login Item doesn't display an error message, your old friend Trial-and-Error is just about the only sure-fire way to detect which item (if any) is causing the problem. Click an item to select it, click the Remove button (marked with a minus sign), and then press ⌘+Q to quit System Preferences. Log out to see whether the problem's solved. (If not, don't forget to add the item again to the Login Items list.)

You can also disable Login Items entirely when you reboot. If the login window appears when you reboot your computer, hold down the Shift key and then click the Login button. If you don't see the login window when you reboot, hold down the Shift key when you see the James Bond–style twirling progress indicator in the startup window and continue to hold down the key until the Finder appears.

Step 9: Turn off your screen saver

Another candidate for intermittent lockups is your screen saver, especially if you're running a shareware effort written by a 12-year-old with a limited attention span. Display your System Preferences, choose Desktop & Screen Saver, and click the Screen Saver tab. You can deactivate the saver entirely (by moving the Start Screen Saver slider to Never) or choose the Computer Name saver (which is provided by Apple) from the Screen Savers list.

Step 10: Check for write protection

If you're running a multiuser ship, check to make sure that another user with administrator access hasn't accidentally write-protected your documents, your application, or its support files. If possible, log in with an administrator account yourself (as I describe in Book II, Chapter 5) and then try running the application or opening the document that you were unable to access under your own ID.

Trying an application under the aforementioned "clean" account is also a great way to determine whether your user-specific preference file for that application has been corrupted. If you can run the application using your "clean" account, contact the software developer to see how you can repair or delete a preference file that's causing problems.

Step 11: Check your System Information

If you've reached this point in the troubleshooting process and haven't found the culprit, you've probably experienced a hardware failure in your Macintosh. If possible, display the Hardware category within the Apple System Information utility (see Figure 9-3) and make sure that it can recognize and use all the internal drives, ports, and external devices on your Mac. To start System Information, open your Utilities folder (inside the Applications folder) and double-click the System Information icon.

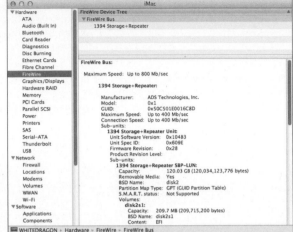

Figure 9-3:
Use System
Information
to check
the devices
and ports on
your system.

Step 12: Reboot with the Mac OS X Recovery HD volume

In case your Mac is in sad shape and won't even boot from its hard drive, here's a last step that you can take before you seek professional assistance: Reboot your Mac from the Mac OS X Recovery HD volume. Hold down the Option key immediately after you hear the startup chord (which displays a boot menu), choose the Recovery HD volume and then run Disk Utility from the window that appears. Because you've booted the system from the Recovery HD volume, you can verify and repair problems with your startup hard drive. (Some new Mac models also come with a diagnostic DVD that can help you pin down hardware problems.) After you're done, restart your system.

Booting from the Recovery HD volume also allows you to restore your system from your most recent Time Machine backup — a real life-saver if your Mac's internal drive was the victim of catastrophe. (Think "accidental format." No, wait, don't even *think* it.)

Do I Need to Reinstall Mac OS X?

To be honest, this is a difficult question to answer. Technically, you should never *need* to reinstall the Big X, but there's also no reason why you *can't*.

I can think of only two scenarios where reinstalling the operating system will **likely** solve a problem. One, if your system files have been so heavily corrupted — by a faulty hard drive or a rampaging virus, for example — that you can't boot Mac OS X at all. Two, if the operating system encounters the death-dealing kernel panic on a regular basis. A *kernel panic* displays a dialog that instructs you to restart your Mac (in multiple languages, no less), usually overwriting whatever's on the monitor at the time. (This is analogous to the infamous Windows Blue Screen of Death — I've grown to hate that shade of blue with a passion.)

If you receive kernel panics on an ongoing basis, something is really, *really* wrong. Make sure that your documents are copied to a rewriteable DVD or network drive, and don't overwrite any existing backup that you have with a new backup because the backup application is likely to lock up as well.

To reinstall, you can turn once again to Lion's Recovery HD volume. (That thing really comes in handy!) Hold down the Option key immediately after you hear your Mac's startup chord, and choose the Recovery HD volume from the boot menu. (Read the earlier section, "Step 12: Reboot with the Mac OS X Recovery HD volume.") Click the Reinstall Mac OS X option in the window that appears.

It's Still Not Moving: Troubleshooting Resources

As I mention earlier in this chapter, you can pursue other avenues to get help when you can't solve a troubleshooting problem on your own. Mind you, I'm talking about professional help from sources that you can trust. Although you can find quite a bit of free advice on the Internet (usually on privately run web sites and in the Internet newsgroups), most of it isn't worth your effort. In fact, some of it's downright wrong. That said, here are some sources that I *do* recommend.

The Mac OS X Help Center

Although most Mac OS X owners tend to blow off the Help Center when the troubleshooting gets tough, that's never the best course of action. Always take a few moments to search the contents of the Help Center — click Help on the Finder menu — to see whether any mention is made of the problem that you've encountered.

The Apple Mac OS X Support site

Home to all manner of support questions and answers, the Mac OS X Support section of the Apple web site (www.apple.com/support) should be your next stop in case of trouble that you can't fix yourself. Topics include

✦ Startup issues

✦ Internet and networking problems

✦ Printing problems

You can search the Apple Knowledge Base, download the latest updates and electronic manuals, and participate in Apple-moderated discussion boards from this one central location.

Your local Apple dealer

Naturally, an Apple dealer can provide just about any support that you're likely to need — for a price — but you can usually get the answers to important questions without any coinage changing hands. Your dealer is also well versed in the latest updates and patches that can fix those software incompatibility problems. Check your telephone book for your local dealer.

Chapter 10: Running Windows on Your Mac

In This Chapter

- ✔ Introducing Boot Camp
- ✔ Comparing Boot Camp to software emulation
- ✔ Creating your Windows partition
- ✔ Switching to your Windows system
- ✔ Updating Apple software in Windows

Do you sometimes miss that *other* operating system? Are there legacy Windows programs you'd like to run on your Mac? Do you miss the familiar confines of the Microsoft world?

No need to be furtive about your Windows yearnings — although I'm an enthusiastic Mac owner, I also own two smooth-running PCs, and they cohabitate quite well in my office. I use Windows 7 every day for a number of tasks. So, dear reader, what if I told you that both Mac OS X Lion and Windows XP, Vista, or 7 can live together in peace and harmony, *all on the same hard drive inside your Mac?*

In this chapter, I discuss the wonder that is Boot Camp — the free utility included with Lion that allows you to install and run Windows on your Mac's hard drive. I explain why Boot Camp is superior to Windows emulator software, and how to switch between operating systems with a simple reboot.

Hold on to your hat, Mac owners: You're about to take a wild trip that proves you can indeed have the best of both worlds!

Figuring Out How Boot Camp Works

First, a bit of technobabble — but I promise it'll be over soon, and I'll try to keep things from getting too boring. In years past, you may have heard that a Mac computer couldn't run Windows out of the box (without expensive hardware or software), and Mac software was off-limits to PCs . . . and you'd have been correct, at least for all but the most recent history of the Macintosh computer. Why the incompatibility? It was because Apple used a series of Motorola processors (or CPUs) that didn't "talk the same language" as the Intel CPUs used in PCs. Consider a person speaking Korean trying to read a book in Arabic, and you get the general idea.

Then Apple began using Intel processors in Macs, and the ground rules changed. Now Apple hardware was suddenly compatible with Windows. All that was needed was a "bridge" to help keep both operating systems separate on the same hard drive — and Apple developed Boot Camp. Of course, that bridge only works in one direction because you still can't run Macintosh software on a PC. (Go figure.)

Boot Camp accomplishes this magic by creating a separate Windows partition on your Mac's hard drive. The partition holds all of your Windows data, including the operating system, your program files, and the documents you create while running Windows. Consider this partition as completely separate from your Mac OS X data, even though both partitions exist on the same physical hard drive.

When you reboot your Mac using Boot Camp, it's similar to changing the station on your FM radio: the hardware is the same, but you've switched to a different DJ (Windows instead of Mac OS X) and you're listening to different music (country instead of rock). How's *that* for a comparison, Dr. Science?

Naturally, you'll need free space on your Mac's hard drive to install Boot Camp — Apple recommends 10GB of free space for a Windows 7 installation, but I'd bump that up to 40GB. Both the 32-bit and 64-bit versions of Vista and Windows 7 are compatible with most Macs capable of running Mac OS X Lion, and any Intel-based Mac can run 32-bit Windows XP or Vista.

When your Mac is running Windows, it's as susceptible to virus and spyware attack as any other Windows PC. Make sure that you invest in quality anti-virus and anti-spyware protection for your Windows side!

Comparing Boot Camp to Windows Emulators

"But Mark, what about Windows emulators?" you ask. Ah, that's a good point: A number of excellent Mac applications let you run Windows within what's called a *virtual machine*. Although your Mac is still running Mac OS X, these emulators create an environment where Windows can share system resources like hard drives, RAM, and even peripherals. I discuss my favorite, Parallels Desktop, in Book VII, Chapter 5.

These Windows emulators have three big advantages over Boot Camp:

✦ **Versatility:** Unlike Boot Camp, where you're restricted to creating one Windows partition, Parallels Desktop allows you to create as many virtual machines as you have hard drive space. Plus, you can run multiple versions of Windows, or even other operating systems like UNIX, Linux, and DOS.

✦ **Shared data:** If you have Windows and Mac OS X applications that you must run concurrently (or you must access the same data with both Lion and Windows), an emulator is your only option.

✦ **No need to reboot:** With Boot Camp, you must reboot to run your Mac under Windows. Software Windows emulators don't need a reboot.

"OK then, Mark, why are you such a fan of Boot Camp?" I'm glad you asked! Here are two major reasons why you would choose Boot Camp over a Windows emulator:

✦ **Performance:** One word, dear reader: *speed*. No software Windows emulator will ever run as fast or perform as trouble-free as Boot Camp! That's because a Mac running Boot Camp is *actually running as a true Windows PC*, able to access all the system resources Windows demands without an emulator slowing things down. It makes sense when you think about it — because you're running Parallels Desktop "on top" of Lion, your Mac has to devote a significant amount of computing time to just keeping Mac OS X running. In fact, there are some Windows applications that simply won't run well at all under emulation, like today's memory- and processor-hungry 3D games.

✦ **Peripheral control:** If you're running a software Windows emulator and you plug a USB flash drive into your Mac, which operating system gets to use it? How about your digital camera, or that external Blu-Ray recorder? Although Parallels Desktop has all sorts of automatic and manual controls you can set to determine which operating system gets to use what, a Mac running Boot Camp owns everything you plug into it free and clear, with no troublesome conflicts between operating systems arguing over peripherals.

Oh, and don't let me forget what many Mac owners consider the most important advantage for Boot Camp: It's free. You need a licensed copy of the version of Windows you want to run, but there's nothing else to buy!

 Remember what I said about Boot Camp modifying your hard drive? **Do not install Boot Camp without backing up your existing data on your Mac's hard drive!** I personally have never had a problem with Boot Camp, but there's always a first time. In case of catastrophe, you can always use your Time Machine backup to restore your Mac's operating system and all your data.

Configuring Boot Camp

Ready to install Boot Camp? The process is surprisingly easy, and takes far less time than it takes to install Windows afterwards. Follow these steps:

1. **Launch the Boot Camp Assistant.**

The Assistant resides in your Utilities folder inside your Applications folder. I use Launchpad to reach it quickly: click the Launchpad icon in the Dock, click the Utilities folder icon, and then click the Boot Camp Assistant icon.

It's a good idea to click the Print Installation & Setup Guide button on the Introduction screen. Keep this additional documentation handy just in case you have questions about running Windows that aren't covered within the confines of this chapter!

2. **Click Continue at the Introduction screen.**

Figure 10-1 illustrates the Boot Camp Assistant Support Software screen that appears.

3. **Click the Download the Windows Support Software for This Mac radio button and click Continue.**

Boot Camp Assistant can copy these drivers to a blank CD, blank DVD, or to an external drive. I think the CD is the easiest choice. You load this disc after your Windows installation is complete, and it provides all the drivers that Windows needs for your Mac's hardware.

4. **Choose the size of your Windows partition and click Create.**

Again, you can devote more hard drive space to your Windows partition than the amount recommended by the Assistant, but don't forget this important fact: what you reserve for use in Windows cannot be used by Mac OS X Lion! Therefore, I always suggest a conservative amount. (In other words, don't devote 300GB of your 500GB drive to your Windows partition because you'll cramp your style within Mac OS X.)

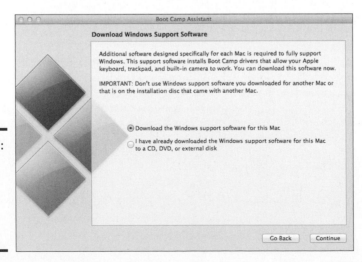

Figure 10-1:
Yes, you want the Windows support software. Trust me.

5. **Reboot if required.**

You may be prompted to launch the Assistant again.

6. **Click Start the Windows Installer and click Continue.**

From this point on, you're running the Windows installation program, just as you would if you were using a PC. (Well, actually you *are* using a PC now.) Follow the on-screen prompts, which differ for each version of Windows.

When prompted by the Windows Installer to choose the partition to format, choose the partition named BOOTCAMP. Formatting any other partition will likely result in the loss of all of your Mac OS X files and data. (Again, this is why you should always back up your existing system before putting Boot Camp to work.)

After Windows has been installed, load the CD you burned with the drivers and support software. Windows should automatically run the Boot Camp driver installation program for you. After the drivers are in place, you're ready to do the Microsoft Dance.

Are you moving your stuff from Windows (running on your old PC) to . . . well, Windows (running on your Mac)? Brings an entirely new meaning to the term *Switcher*, doesn't it? If so, the files and folders on your existing PC can be copied directly to Windows running on your Mac by using the Files and Settings Transfer Wizard (in Windows XP) or the Windows Easy Transfer utility (in Windows Vista and 7).

Switching to Windows

There are three methods of switching back and forth between your Mac OS X partition and your Windows partition:

✦ **From within Mac OS X Lion:** To restart your Mac in Windows, click System Preferences in the Dock and click the Startup Disk icon to display the settings you see in Figure 10-2. Click the Windows partition you created in the list to select it (the folder icon will bear the Windows logo, and it will be labeled *Windows* as well). Click Restart, and then click Restart again when asked for confirmation. Your Mac reboots and loads Windows, and continues to run Windows when started or rebooted until you follow one of the next two methods of returning to Mac OS X.

✦ **From within Windows:** Right-click on the Boot Camp icon in the notification area at the right side of your Windows task bar — it looks like a slanted square — and choose Restart in Mac OS X. Again, you'll be asked to confirm your choice. After you click OK, your Mac reboots and returns to Lion.

✦ **During the boot process:** Need a temporary fix from your other operating system? You can reboot from within either Lion or Windows and hold down the Option key when you see the Apple logo appear. Your Mac displays a nifty row of icons, each of which represents a bootable operating system your Mac can use. To boot Mac OS X, click the Lion partition icon. To choose Windows, click the Windows partition icon. Note that when you turn on or reboot your Mac, it returns to the operating system you were using previously.

Figure 10-2:
Preparing to
jump ship to
Windows.

Checking for Apple Updates

Apple sometimes releases updates for Boot Camp software and drivers. If you have an active Internet connection, you can easily check for updates within Windows using the Apple Software Update program.

To run Update, click the Start button and click Apple Software Update. The program automatically connects to Apple's servers and displays any updates (including those for the Windows versions of programs like Safari and iTunes). Click the check box next to each update you want to apply to enable it, and then click the Install button to start the ball rolling.

Although it's a shameless plug, it fits very well at the end of a chapter dedicated to Windows: If you'd like a handy companion guide to Windows 7, Microsoft Office 2010 and the world of PCs, I can highly recommend the book *PCs All-in-One For Dummies, 5th Edition*, also written by yours truly and published by John Wiley & Sons, Inc.! (As I said at the beginning of this chapter, I draw no favorites between PC and Mac.)

Using the Boot Camp Control Panel

Besides the ability to restart your Mac in Mac OS X Lion, the Windows Boot Camp notification icon also includes a number of other features. Right-click the icon and choose Boot Camp Control Panel from the contextual menu to display the settings, which vary depending on the version of Windows you're using and the type of Mac you're running.

The Startup Disk tab is essentially a Windows version of Lion's Startup Disk pane in System Preferences. From here, you can choose to reboot in Mac OS X Lion by clicking the Mac OS X folder and clicking Restart.

Click the Brightness tab to display the Brightness slider, which you can drag to dim or brighten your display.

Click the Remote tab to enable or disable remote control by an Apple Remote.

Click the Power tab to specify whether your Mac should restart automatically after a power failure.

After you've made any changes within the Boot Camp Control Panel, click OK to save your changes and return to Windows.

Book II

Customizing and Sharing

The 5th Wave   By Rich Tennant

"Oh, Anthony loves working with Applescript. He customized all our Word documents with a sound file so they all close with out with a 'Bada Bing!'"

Contents at a Glance

Chapter 1: Building the Finder of Your Dreams

In This Chapter

↙ **Choosing a view mode**

↙ **Modifying the toolbar**

↙ **Searching for files from the toolbar**

↙ **Searching for files with the Find command**

↙ **Changing view options**

↙ **Changing Finder preferences**

T he Finder is the heart of Mac OS X, and as you might expect, it's highly configurable. You can customize the Finder to present icons, or you can peruse folders with a column view that can pack much more information on-screen at one time. Some folks prefer the default Finder toolbar, and others like to customize it with the applications and features that they use most often.

Decisions like these can help you transform Lion into *Your Personal Operating System* — and every Mac OS X power user worth the title will take the time to apply these changes because an operating system that presents visual information the way that you want to see it is easier and more efficient to use.

No need for a hammer or saw — when you're building the Finder of your dreams, the only tools that you need are your mouse and keyboard!

Will That Be Icons or Lists or Columns . . . or Even a Flow?

The default appearance of a window in Mac OS X uses the familiar large-format icons that have been a hallmark of the Macintosh operating system since Day One — but there's no reason you *have* to use them. (In fact, most Mac OS X power users I know consider the icon view mode rather inefficient and slow.) Besides the icon view, as shown in Figure 1-1, Mac OS X offers three other window view modes: *list, column,* and *flow.*

Figure 1-1:
A Finder
window in
icon view
mode.

Mac OS X old-timers will thrill to the slider control at the bottom-right corner of Finder windows in icon view mode. Why? Drag this control to the right to expand the size of the icons within the window, and drag the control to the left to reduce the icon size! (This is A Big Thing for those who prefer icon view — and it makes quite a difference for those with less-than-perfect eyesight.) However, the Finder window Status bar must be displayed to see the slider control — if the Status bar is currently hidden, click View➪Show Status Bar.

✦ **List view:** Another feature familiar to long-time Mac owners, *List view* displays the folders on the volume in a hierarchical fashion. To display the contents of a folder, you can click the right-facing small triangle next to the folder name (called a *disclosure triangle*, believe it or not) — it rotates downward to indicate that you've expanded the folder. Alternately, you can double-click the folder icon to display the contents in a Finder window. To collapse the contents of the folder, click the disclosure triangle again; it rotates back to face the right. Figure 1-2 illustrates the same Finder window in list view.

You can resize a column by dragging the right edge of the column heading.

✦ **Column view:** Figure 1-3 shows the same window in column view, in which the volumes on your Mac OS X system are displayed on the left. Each column on the right represents a lower level of subfolders. Click the volume in the Devices list and then click the desired folder in the first column on the right to display its contents, and so forth. (Personally, this is my favorite view — thanks, Apple! It's efficient and fast as all get-out.) When you drill deeper, the columns shift automatically to the left. When you click an item (instead of a folder), the Finder displays a preview and a quick summary of the selected item in the rightmost column.

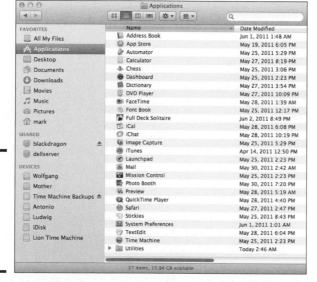

Figure 1-2: The contents of a Finder window in list view mode.

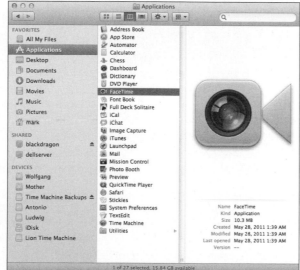

Figure 1-3: Lion's column view requires very little scrolling.

Each column has its own scroll bar (for those really, really big folders), and you can drag the column handle at the bottom of the separators to resize the column width to the left. When you hold down Option and drag a column handle, all the columns are adjusted at once.

✦ **Flow view:** When a new software feature or function turns out to be incredibly popular, a developer tries to use it wherever possible — hence the Flow view shown in Figure 1-4, which Apple took directly from the Cover Flow view that proved so successful in iTunes (as well as on the iPhone and iPod touch). Flow view still displays the sidebar, but each document or item is showcased in a preview pane (and with an accurate thumbnail, if possible). You can resize the preview pane by dragging the three-line handle on the bottom edge of the pane. The remainder of the Finder window in Flow view works very similarly to list view, complete with the rotating triangles. However, if you like, you can click the scroll buttons or drag the scroll bar under the preview pane to move through the contents of your drive in a very classy visual display!

Figure 1-4:
Wowzers!
Check out
the Flow
view for
Lion's Finder
windows!

Another of my pet peeves is cluttered disks. If you're continually having problems locating files and folders, ask yourself, "Self, do I need to organize? Am I — gasp — *cluttered*?" If your answer is yes, take an hour and organize your files logically into new folders. (Remember, I'm talking your documents and such — not your applications, which are usually where they need to be —

in your Applications folder, and easily displayed using Launchpad.) Often, documents that you create end up as stragglers, usually located in the root folder of your hard drive, which sooner or later ends up looking like a biker bar after Ladies' Night. (The same can be said of many Mac OS X Desktops, too.) By keeping your root folder and Desktop clean and saving your files in organized folders, you waste less time searching for files and more time actually *using* them.

To switch between the four modes, click one of the four view mode buttons on the Finder window toolbar (the current view is highlighted) or click the View menu and choose As Icons, As List, As Columns, or As Cover Flow. Mac OS X places a helpful check mark next to the current view mode. (Keyboard lovers can hold down ⌘ and press the 1, 2, 3, or 4 keys to switch views.)

Doing the Toolbar Dance

You can work your customization magic on the Finder toolbar as well! In this section, I show you how to customize that strip of icons across the top of the Finder window that's affectionately called the *toolbar*. Or, if you like, you'll discover how to dismiss it entirely to gain additional real estate for the contents of your Finder window.

Hiding and showing the toolbar

You can toggle the display of the toolbar in an active Finder window in one of three ways:

✦ By right-clicking the toolbar and choosing Hide Toolbar

✦ By pressing ⌘+Option+T

✦ By choosing View from the Finder menu and then choosing Hide (or Show) Toolbar

Hiding the toolbar also hides the Sidebar.

Hiding and showing the status bar

The status bar appears either at the bottom or top of the Finder window, depending on whether the toolbar has been hidden, and it displays a number of helpful informational-type tidbits about the window's contents. Depending on what you've opened, the status bar can include

✦ **Statistics:** See the number of items in the window and the amount of free space remaining on the volume.

✦ **A write-protect icon:** This icon looks like a pencil with a line running through it, as shown in the lower left of Figure 1-5. This indicates that you don't have write permissions for the contents of the window — or the volume where the contents reside. (Note that this doesn't necessarily mean that folders at a lower level are write-protected as well.) You'll typically see this icon when you're viewing the contents of a CD or DVD, where everything is write-protected.

Back and Forward buttons

Action button   Search box

View icons   Arrange button

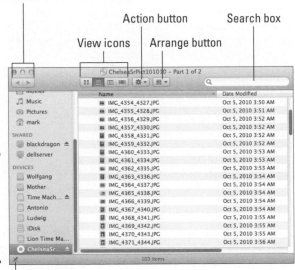

Figure 1-5:
Check the
status bar
to scope out
your write
permissions.

Write-protect icon

To toggle the display of the status bar, choose View from the Finder menu and then choose Show/Hide Status Bar, or press ⌘+/.

The *path bar* is a close relative of the status bar — if you turn it on, the path bar also resides at the bottom of every Finder window, and it shows the *system path* that leads to the selected file or folder (starting with the volume where the file resides, and following each enclosing folder). For example, if you select your Home folder in the Finder window Sidebar, the path might read *Hard Drive > Users > mark*. I like this feature because it identifies the location of files and folders that I'm using. To view the path bar, click View ➪ Show Path Bar.

Hey, where's my Quick Look icon?

New accounts you create in Lion are missing a good friend on the default toolbar: the Quick Look button, which was standard equipment on the Finder window toolbar in Snow Leopard. Luckily, the user can easily add the Quick Look icon back to the toolbar using the instructions on customizing the toolbar in this section.

After you've added Quick Look to your toolbar, click the icon to display a window with the contents of the selected file or document without launching the corresponding application. Quick Look works with all sorts of images, video, and documents, allowing you to efficiently peruse files on your system without the hassle of constantly launching and quitting applications. Quick Look works in any Finder window

view mode, too. To activate Quick Look for a selected file from the keyboard, press the spacebar. To switch to a full-screen display, click the diagonal arrow icon at the upper right of the Quick Look window.

While Quick Look is active (and in full-screen mode), a number of format-specific buttons appear in the Quick Look window. For example, displaying an image file in Quick Look adds a button that can automatically import the image into iPhoto. These buttons vary with the format or type of document, but you'll always see a full-screen/exit full-screen button that toggles the Quick Look window between full-screen and regular size.

Giving your toolbar big tires and a loud exhaust

The default icons on the toolbar include

✦ **Back and Forward:** As with a web browser, clicking the Back button moves you to the previous window's contents. If you use the Back button, the Forward button becomes enabled. Click this to return to the contents that you had before clicking the Back button.

✦ **View:** Click this control to toggle between the four view modes (icon, list, column, or flow).

Pssst. Selecting a folder and pressing the spacebar displays a summary of its size and last modification date. Pass it on.

✦ **Action:** Click this pop-up menu to display context-sensitive commands for the selected items. In plain English, you'll see the commands that you'd see if you right-clicked on the selection.

✦ **Arrange:** The items on this pop-up menu allow you to sort the items in the Finder window by a number of different criteria, including everything from the file name to the size and the date it was last opened or modified.

✦ **Search:** Okay, I know it's not technically an icon, but the Search box is a member of the default toolbar family nonetheless. You can search for a file or folder using this box. More on this in the section "Searching for Files from the Toolbar," later in this chapter.

But, as one of my favorite bumper stickers so invitingly asks, "Why be normal?" Adding or deleting items from the toolbar is a great way to customize Mac OS X. Follow these steps:

1. **From the active Finder window menu, choose View↷Customize Toolbar to display the sheet that you see in Figure 1-6.**

Along with controls such as Back, Forward, and View, you find a number of system functions, such as Eject and Burn, and features you'd normally see on a contextual (right-click) menu, like Get Info, Delete, and Quick Look.

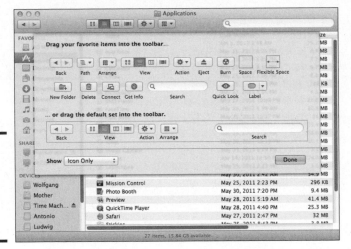

Figure 1-6:
Changing
the toolbar
status
quo in
Mac OS X.

2. **To add items to the toolbar, drag them from the Customize Toolbar dialog up to the toolbar at the top of the window.**

To add an item between existing buttons, drop it between the buttons, and they obligingly move aside. If you get exuberant about your toolbar and you add more icons than it can hold, a double-right arrow appears at the right side of the toolbar. A click of the arrow displays a pop-up menu with the icons that won't fit.

In fact, the Customize Toolbar dialog isn't necessary for some toolbar modifications: You can also drag files, folders, and disk volumes directly from the Desktop or other Finder windows and add them to your toolbar

at any time. To remove a file, folder, or disk volume from the toolbar, right-click the icon on the toolbar and choose Customize Toolbar, and then drag the icon off the toolbar — it vanishes like a CEO's ethics.

You can also hold down ⌘ and drag any item off the toolbar, or hold down ⌘ and drag toolbar items to reorder them.

You can always drag a file or folder into the Sidebar column at the left of the Finder window. (The Sidebar column is a separate entity entirely from the toolbar.)

3. **To remove an item from the toolbar, drag it off to the center of the window, amongst the other icons.**

4. **Naturally, you can swap item positions. Just click an item, drag it to its new spot, and then release the mouse button.**

5. **To choose the default toolbar configuration or to start over, drag the default bar at the bottom of the dialog to the toolbar at the top.**

   This is the toolbar equivalent of tapping your ruby slippers together three times and repeating, "There's no place like home."

6. **To toggle between displaying the icons with accompanying text (the default), the icon only, or a text button only, click the Show pop-up menu at the bottom of the Customize Toolbar dialog.**

   You can also right-click on the toolbar and make the same changes.

7. **After you arrange your toolbar as you like, click the Done button.**

Book II
Chapter 1

Building the Finder
of Your Dreams

It's All My Files in one place

Time to welcome another new feature within Lion: the All My Files view, which appears in the Finder window sidebar under the Favorites heading. Click All My Files to display just your documents, grouped by category — images, PDF documents, music tracks, movies, and more. (No applications are included in All My Files, which avoids clutter and speeds things up.) While you're checking out the contents of All My Files, don't forget that you can use the Search box to locate specific files quickly, just like any other Finder window.

If you need different information in the All My Files view, just right-click on any of the major headings to display a menu of column choices. To add a column, click the desired data, and a checkmark appears — for example, I like to see the size of each file in my All My Files view. To hide a column, right-click on a major heading, and click the item to remove the checkmark.

Searching for Files from the Toolbar

Need to find a file fast? The default toolbar has just what you need: the *Search field,* which offers the ability to perform a Spotlight search for a string of text within your files (including both filenames and contents). To locate a file with the Search field, follow these steps:

1. **Click in the Search box on the toolbar and type the text that you want to find.**

It's the text box on the right with the magnifying glass. (The folks at Apple are really, really into Sherlock Holmes . . . so am I!) If you need to clear the field and start over again, click the circular X button, which appears only when text is in the Search field.

Hey, who needs to press Return? The Finder immediately displays the files with names (or contents) that include the text, as shown in Figure 1-7. Depending on what you entered, you may also see a pop-up menu option to display only those files with names that contain the text you specified, or even specific file types that are related to the search text.

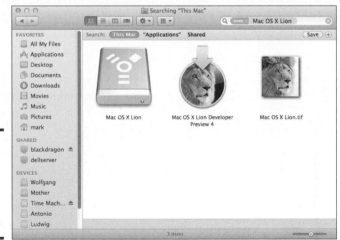

Figure 1-7: Locating a file or folder with the toolbar Search box.

2. **To display the location of a file, click it once. To launch it, double-click the entry.**

Files can also be moved or copied from the Search results list with the standard drag and Option+drag methods.

3. **To perform a new search, click the circular X button and type new text in the Search field.**

   To return to your original location in the Finder window, click the Back button on the toolbar.

Searching for Files from the Find Dialog

Although the Search box on the toolbar is all you usually need to find most files and folders, sometimes you need a little more flexibility and power to locate what you need on your system. To do so, add the Find controls, which you can use to create custom searches with more complex criteria. To locate a file by using the Find controls, follow these steps:

1. **With the Finder active, display the Find controls by pressing ⌘+F (or choose File from the Finder menu and then choose Find).**

   Mac OS X displays the controls that you see in Figure 1-8.

2. **Click the buttons at the top of the list to specify where you want to search.**

   You can choose This Mac (your entire system, including network volumes) or a local volume.

Figure 1-8:
The Find controls add a bit of extra power to a search.

3. **To search for a specific filename, click the first pop-up menu in the Search Criteria strip at the top of the window and choose Name; type all or part of the filename in the Contains box.**

   Lion automatically begins searching as soon as you type at least one character.

   After you locate the file or folder that you need, click the entry name to reveal the location of the matching file or folder in the path bar at the bottom of the window. You can also double-click it to launch (or display) it.

4. **If you want to search for a text string within the document itself, click the first pop-up menu in a row, choose Contents, and then type the string to match in the box.**

   The text must appear just as you've typed it, so it's always a good idea to restrict what you're searching for to a minimum of words that you're fairly sure will cause a match. (Content searching is not case-sensitive, though.) Content searching works only when you've generated an index, which I explain later in this section.

5. **To include additional search criteria lines, click the button with the plus sign next to the last criterion line.**

   You can limit your results based on all sorts of rules, including the date that the file or folder was last modified, when it was created, the file type, the size, the extension, or whether the file or folder is marked visible or hidden (such as a system file).

   You can also remove a search criterion line by clicking the button with the minus sign.

6. **To save the search criteria that you selected, click Save.**

   This creates a *Smart Folder*, which (you're gonna *love* this) Lion automatically updates (in real time) to contain whatever items match the criteria you've saved! You can specify the location for your Smart Folder, and you can choose to add it to your Finder sidebar for the ultimate convenience. *Sweet.*

7. **When you're done canvassing your computer, click the Back button in the Find dialog to return to the Finder.**

Configuring the View Options

As I discuss at the beginning of the chapter, you have a lot of control over how Mac OS X presents files and folders in the Finder. In this section, I cover how you can make further adjustments to the view from your windows. (Pardon me for the ghastly cliché posing as a pun.)

Setting icon view options

First, allow me to provide a little detail on housekeeping in the Big X. After a few hours of work, a Finder window in icon mode can look something like a teenager's room: stuff strewn all over the place, as I demonstrate with my Applications folder in Figure 1-9. To restore order to your Desktop, right-click in any open area of the active window, choose Clean Up By and click Name. This command snaps the icons to an invisible grid so that they're aligned and sorted by name, as shown in Figure 1-10.

**Book II
Chapter 1**

**Building the Finder
of Your Dreams**

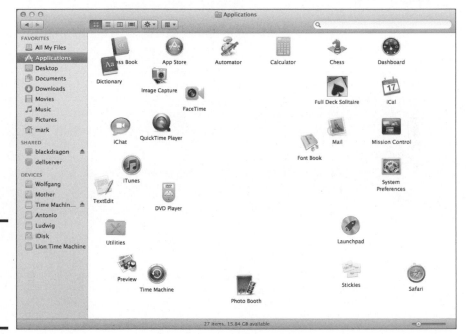

Figure 1-9:
Will someone please clean up this mess?

Figure 1-10:
Tidying up is
no problem
with the
Clean Up
and Clean
Up By menu
commands.

After things are in alignment, work with the icon view options. (Naturally, you'll want the active Finder window in icon view first, so choose View⇨ As Icons or press ⌘+1.) From the Finder menu, choose View⇨Show View Options — or press that swingin' ⌘+J shortcut — to display the View Options dialog that you see in Figure 1-11. (Remember that these are the options available for icon view; I discuss the options for list, column, and Cover Flow view later in this chapter.)

Of course, Mac OS X remembers the changes that you make within the View Options dialog, no matter which view mode you're configuring. Now, the changes that you can make from this dialog include

✦ **Always Open in Icon View:** When you select this check box, each Finder window that you open automatically uses icon view. (If deselected, the new window uses the last view mode you used.)

✦ **Arrange By:** From this pop-up menu, you can automatically separate items within the window with dividers, sorted by one of the following criteria from its pop-up menu: by name, kind (item type), application (the default application that opens each file type), date last opened, date added, date modified, date created, size, or the icon label you've assigned.

Figure 1-11:
The settings available for icon view.

Book II
Chapter 1

Building the Finder of Your Dreams

✦ **Sort By:** If the Arrange By pop-up menu is set to None, you can click this pop-up menu and automatically align icons to a grid within the window, just as if you had used the Clean Up menu command. You can also sort the display of icons in a window by choosing one of the following criteria: by name, kind (item type), application (the default application that opens each file type), date last opened, date added, date modified, date created, size, or icon label.

✦ **Resizing your icons:** Click and drag the Icon Size slider to shrink or expand the icons within the window. The icon size is displayed in pixels above the slider. (Remember, however, that Lion offers an icon resizing slider at the right side of the status bar of any Finder window in icon view mode; it's much easier and more convenient just to drag the slider to expand or reduce the size of icons in a window.)

✦ **Specifying grid spacing:** Click and drag the Grid Spacing slider to shrink or expand the size of the grid used to align icons within the window. The larger the grid, the more white space between icons.

✦ **Resizing icon label text:** Click the up and down arrows to the right of the Text Size pop-up menu to choose the font size (in points) for icon labels.

✦ **Moving icon label text:** Select either the Bottom (default) or the Right radio button to choose between displaying the text under your Desktop icons or to the right of the icons.

✦ **Show Item Info:** With this check box selected, Mac OS X displays the number of items within each folder in the window.

✦ **Show Icon Preview:** If you select this check box, the Finder displays icons for image files using a miniature of the actual picture. (A cool feature for those with digital cameras; however, this does take extra processing time because Mac OS X has to load each image file and shrink it down to create the icon.)

✦ **Choosing a background:** To select a background for the window, select one of three radio buttons here:

• *White:* This is the default.

• *Color:* Click a color choice from the color block that appears if you make this selection.

• *Picture:* Select this radio button and then click the Select button to display a standard Open dialog. Navigate to the location where the desired image is stored, click it once to select it, and then click Open.

✦ **Use as Defaults:** When you first open the View Options dialog, the changes you're making apply only to the Finder window that opens when you open the selected item — in other words, the item that appears in the window's title bar, such as a folder or drive.

For example, any changes made to the settings in Figure 1-11 will affect only my Applications folder because it was the active Finder window when I pressed ⌘+J. (You might have noticed that the window name also appears as the title of the View Options dialog.)

However, you can decide to apply the changes that you make to *all* Finder windows that you view in your current mode. Simply click the Use as Defaults button.

After all your changes are made and you're ready to return to work, click the dialog's Close button to save your settings.

Setting list view options

If you're viewing the active window in list view, choose View⇨Show View Options to display the View Options dialog that you see in Figure 1-12.

Figure 1-12:
Here
are your
list view
settings.

As in icon view, changes you make in this dialog normally apply only to this window, but you can click Use as Defaults to assign these settings to all windows that you view in list mode. The other list view settings include

✦ **Always Open in List View:** Select this check box and Lion will open all Finder windows in list view. (If deselected, new windows use the last view mode you used.)

✦ **Arrange By:** Click this pop-up menu to automatically separate items within the window with dividers, sorted by one of the following criteria from its pop-up menu: by name, kind (item type), application (the default application that opens each file type), date last opened, date added, date modified, date created, size, or the icon label you've assigned.

✦ **Sort By:** If the Arrange By pop-up menu is set to None, click this pop-up menu to automatically sort the display of icons in a window by choosing one of the following criteria: by name, kind (item type), application (the default application that opens each file type), date last opened, date added, date modified, date created, size, or icon label.

✦ **Resizing your icons:** You can choose between two icon sizes.

✦ **Resizing icon label text:** Click the up and down arrows to the right of the Text Size pop-up menu to choose the font size (in points) for icon labels.

✦ **Show Columns:** Select the check boxes under this heading to display additional columns in list view, including the date that the item was modified, the creation date, the date the file was last opened, the date the file was added to your system, the size, the item type, the version (supplied by most applications), the label color, and any comments you've added in the Info dialog for that item. (In my personal opinion, the more columns you add, the more unwieldy the Finder gets, so I advise disabling the display of columns that you won't use.)

✦ **Use Relative Dates:** Select this check box to display modification dates and creation dates with relative terms, such as *Today* or *Yesterday*. If this freaks you out, deselect this check box to force all dates to act like adults.

✦ **Calculate All Sizes:** Select this check box to have Mac OS X display the actual sizes of folders, including all the files and subfolders they contain. (Handy for figuring out where all your disk space went, no?) ***Note:*** Using this option takes processing time, so I recommend that you avoid using it unless you really need to see the size.

✦ **Show Icon Preview:** Select this check box to display preview icons for image files. (Again, this takes extra processing time, and the image preview icons are pretty doggone small in list view, so this feature may be of limited value to you.)

To save your settings, click the dialog's Close button (or press ⌘+J).

Setting column view options

To make changes to view options in any Finder window displaying items in column view mode, choose View⇨Show View Options to display the View Options dialog that you see in Figure 1-13.

Any changes that you make to this dialog are *always* reflected in *every* column view:

✦ **Always Open in Column View:** If this check box is selected, all Finder windows open in column view. (If deselected, new windows use the last view mode you used.)

✦ **Arrange By:** Click this pop-up menu to automatically separate items, sorted by one of the following criteria from its pop-up menu: by name, kind (item type), application (the default application that opens each file type), date last opened, date added, date modified, date created, size, or the icon label you've assigned.

Figure 1-13:
Lion's
glamorous
column view
settings.

✦ **Sort By:** If the Arrange By pop-up menu is set to None, click this pop-up
menu to automatically sort the display of icons in a window by choosing one of the following criteria: by name, kind (item type), application
(the default application that opens each file type), date last opened, date
added, date modified, date created, size, or icon label.

✦ **Resizing icon label text:** Click the Text Size pop-up menu to choose the
font size (in points) for icon labels.

✦ **Show Icons:** Select this check box to display icons in the columns. If this
option is deselected, the icons don't appear and you'll gain a little space.

✦ **Show icon preview:** Click this check box to select it, and Lion displays
preview icons for image files — taking a little extra time to perform this
service, naturally. (As you find out in the next bullet, column mode can be
set to automatically display a preview thumbnail in the last column when
you click an image or video file, and even some documents to boot . . . .
Therefore, the usefulness of tiny icon previews in column mode may be
limited for you.)

✦ **Show Preview Column:** If this check box is selected, clicking a file in
column mode displays a *thumbnail* (reduced image) and preview information in the right-most column, as shown in Figure 1-14.

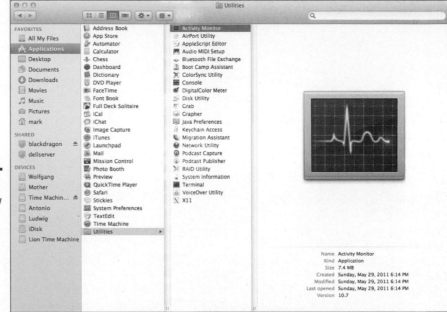

Figure 1-14: The Preview column provides more information on the selected file.

If you store a slew of smaller QuickTime movies and digital images on your drive, the Preview column is great. (You can even play a QuickTime movie from the Preview column.) Of course, longer movies and larger photos take more time to load!

Click the dialog's Close button to save your settings and return to the Finder.

Setting Cover Flow view options

The View options for Cover Flow view are the same as those for list view that I covered earlier in this section, except for the Always Open in Cover Flow check box. Enabling this check box opens all new Finder windows in Cover Flow view. (If deselected, new windows use the last view mode you used.)

Setting Finder Preferences

Finally, you can change a number of settings to customize the Finder itself. From the Finder menu, click Finder and choose the Preferences menu item to display the Finder Preferences dialog that you see in Figure 1-15.

Figure 1-15:
You can configure your Finder preferences here.

In the General section, the preference settings include

✦ **Show These Items on the Desktop:** Select these check boxes to display your internal hard disks, external hard drives, removable volumes (including CDs, DVDs, and iPods), and connected network servers.

✦ **New Finder Windows Show:** Click the pop-up menu to specify the spot where a new Finder window should open. By default, a new window displays the contents of the All My Files location.

✦ **Always Open Folders in a New Window:** When this check box is selected, double-clicking a folder will open it in a new Finder window, as did earlier versions of Mac OS. (If deselected, the contents of the folder appear in the same Finder window, which makes it easier to focus on just the folder you need at the moment.)

✦ **Spring-Loaded Folders and Windows:** It sounds a little wacky, but using this feature can definitely speed up file copying! If this check box is selected, you can drag an item on top of a folder — *without* releasing the mouse button — and after a preset time (controlled by the Delay slider), a spring-loaded window appears to show you the folder's contents. At that point, you can either release the mouse button to drop the file inside the folder (upon which the window disappears), or you can drag the icon on top of another subfolder to spring it forth and drill even deeper.

The Labels preference pane is a simple one — just click next to each label color to type your own text for that label. (I've gotta recommend red for deadlines and green for contracts . . . call me sentimental.)

From the Sidebar preferences pane, you can choose which default items should appear in the Finder window Sidebar column. Your choices include locations (such as your Home and Applications folders), network servers, removable media, the Desktop itself, and — naturally — your hard drives. To add a default item to the Sidebar column, click the corresponding check box to select it, or deselect the check box to banish that item forthwith.

The Advanced preference settings include

✦ **Show All Filename Extensions:** If this check box is selected, the Finder displays the file extensions at the end of filenames. This comes in handy for some applications, where everything from a document to a preference file to the application itself all share the same icon. However, I find extensions distasteful and leave things set with the default of extensions off.

✦ **Show Warning before Changing an Extension:** Also on by default, this setting forces Lion to display a confirmation dialog before allowing you to change the extension on a filename. Why? Well, changing an extension usually results in a "broken" file association, so the file's corresponding application may not launch automatically any longer when you double-click the item. Double-clicking a Word document, for example, might not launch Word automatically as it used to do. If you show file extensions and you often change them, click this check box to disable the warning.

✦ **Show Warning before Emptying the Trash:** By default, this check box is selected, and Mac OS X displays a confirmation dialog before allowing you to — in the words of Mac OS X patrons around the world — *toss the Bit Bucket.* If you're interested in speed and trust your judgment (and your mouse finger), you can disable this setting.

✦ **Empty Trash Securely:** If you'd prefer to use the more secure method of emptying your Trash — where deleted items are far harder for anyone to recover — select this check box.

✦ **When Performing a Search:** Click this pop-up menu to specify whether the text you enter in the Finder window Search box should match everything on your Mac or whether the search should be limited to the current folder only. Choose Use the Previous Search Scope to use the scope setting you used during your last search.

After you make the desired changes to the Finder Preferences, click the dialog's Close button to save your settings and return to the Finder.

**Book II
Chapter 1**

**Building the Finder
of Your Dreams**

Chapter 2: Giving Your Desktop the Personal Touch

In This Chapter

- ✓ Picking your own background
- ✓ Adding and selecting a screen saver
- ✓ Choosing menu colors and highlights
- ✓ Keeping track of things with Stickies
- ✓ Customizing the Dock and using Dashboard
- ✓ Cleaning and sorting the Mac OS X Desktop

"Tweak! Tweak!" It's not the cry of some exotic bird — that's the call of the wild Mac Power User. Power users like to tweak their Mac OS X Desktops just so, with *that* menu color, *this* background, and *those* applications in the Dock. Noncomputer types just can't understand the importance of the proper arrangement of your virtual workplace: When things are familiar and customized to your needs, you're more productive and things get done faster — just like the layout of your physical desktop in your home or office. In fact, if you've set up multiple users on your computer under Mac OS X, the Big X automatically keeps track of each user's Desktop and restores it when that person logs in. (For example, when you use the Mac, you get that background photo of Farrah Fawcett from the '70s, whereas your daughter gets Justin Bieber.)

In this chapter, I show you what you can do to produce a Desktop that's uniquely your own, including tweaks that you can make to the background and your Desktop icons. I also show you how to use Desktop Stickies instead of a forest of paper slips covering your monitor.

With your Mac OS X Desktop clad in the proper harmonious colors — yes, that can be your favorite photo of Elvis himself — and your new Dock icons ready for action, you're indeed prepared for whatever lies ahead in your computing world!

Changing the Background

You might be asking, "Mark, do I really need a custom background?" That depends completely on your personal tastes, but I've yet to meet a computer owner who didn't change his or her background when presented with the opportunity. Favorite backgrounds usually include

✦ Humorous cartoons and photos that can bring a smile to your face (even during the worst workday)

✦ Scenic beauty

✦ Solid colors (relaxing and distraction-free)

✦ Photos of family and friends (or the latest Hollywood heartthrob)

✦ The company logo (not sure it does much for morale, but it does impress the boss)

If you do decide to spruce up your background, you have three choices: You can select one of the excellent default Mac OS X background images, choose a solid color, or specify your own image. All three backgrounds are chosen from the Desktop & Screen Saver pane, located within System Preferences (as illustrated in Figure 2-1).

Figure 2-1:
To select a background, get thee hence to System Pref-erences.

Picking something Apple

To choose a background from one of the collections provided by Apple, click one of these groups from the list at the left:

+ **Desktop Pictures:** These backgrounds feature scenic beauty, such as blades of grass, sand dunes, snowy hills . . . that sort of thing. You also get close-up backgrounds of plant life — I especially recommend the green grass.

+ **Solid Colors:** This is for those who desire a soothing solid shade. More on this in the following section.

+ **iPhoto:** Choose an image from your iPhoto Library.

+ **Pictures:** This displays the images saved in the active user's Pictures folder.

+ **Choose Folder:** You can open a folder containing images and display them instead. (I discuss this in more detail in a page or two.)

If you see something you like, click the thumbnail, and Mac OS X displays it in the well and automatically refreshes your background so that you can see what it looks like. (By the way, in the Apple universe, a *well* is a sunken square area that displays an image, color swatch or even a sound file icon — in this case, the background image that you select.)

Notice your iPhoto albums in the list? That's no accident — Lion automatically offers your iPhoto Photo Library so that you can choose images from your iPhoto collection!

Mac OS X automatically manipulates how the background appears on your Desktop. If an image conforms to your screen resolution, fine — otherwise, click the pop-up menu next to the well and you can choose to

+ **Tile the background.** This repeats the image to cover the Desktop. (This is usually done with pattern images to produce a smooth, creamy, seamless look.)

+ **Fill the screen.** This can be used with a solid color to get uniform coverage. The original aspect ratio of the image is preserved, so it's not stretched.

+ **Fit to screen.** Choose this option to resize the height or width of the image to fit your screen, keeping the original aspect ratio.

✦ **Stretch the background to fit the screen.** If your Desktop image is smaller than the Desktop acreage, this works, but be warned — if you try to stretch too small of an image over too large a Desktop, the pixilated result can be pretty frightening. (Think of enlarging an old Kodak Instamatic negative to a 16 x 20 poster. Dots, dots, dots.) The original aspect ratio of the image isn't preserved, so you might end up with results that look like the funhouse mirrors at a carnival.

✦ **Center the image on the screen.** This is my favorite solution for Desktop images that are smaller than your resolution.

Note that this pop-up menu appears only if the Desktop picture that you select isn't one of the standard Apple images. All the pictures in the Apple Desktop Pictures and Solid Colors categories are scaled automatically to the size of your screen.

To change your Desktop background automatically on a regular basis, select the Change Picture check box and then choose the delay period from the corresponding pop-up menu. To display the images in random order, select the Random Order check box; otherwise, Mac OS X displays them in the order that they appear in the folder. You can also select a translucent Finder menu bar, which (almost) blends in with your background. If you prefer a solid-color, matter-of-fact workman's menu bar, click the Translucent Menu Bar check box to deselect it.

I just gotta have lavender

As I mention earlier, for those who want their favorite color without the distraction of an image, you can choose from a selection of solid colors. You can choose from these colors the same way that you'd pick a default Mac OS X background image (as I describe in the preceding section).

How to annoy friends and confuse co-workers

Never let it be said that I can't dish out revenge when necessary. I don't know whether I should call this a *Tip* or a *Devilish Practical Joke That Will Drive People Nuts* — anyway, it's fun as all get-out. Right before you go to lunch, use the Grab utility in your Applications/Utilities folder to take a snapshot of your Desktop with a number of windows open (or an error dialog with an OK or a Close button) and then save the image to your Pictures folder. Select the image as your Desktop background and then watch others go crazy trying to click those faux windows, buttons, and icons. For an archenemy, try the same trick on *his* Mac! Arrange a slightly embarrassing Desktop on his computer, specify it as the background, and sit back while the fun begins. (Perhaps a web browser that's open to a somewhat unusual website?)

To choose the exact color you're looking for, click the Custom Color button, then use the Colors dialog to find just the right match.

Selecting your own photo

Finally, you can drag your own image into the well from a Finder window to add your own work of art. To view thumbnails of an entire folder, click the Pictures Folder (to display the contents of your personal Pictures folder) or click the Add button (bearing the plus sign) at the lower left of the Desktop & Screen Saver pane to specify any folder on your system. Click the desired thumbnail to embellish your Desktop.

Changing the Screen Saver

Screen savers are another popular item. Because I cover the Screen Saver preferences in Chapter 3 of this minibook, I simply illustrate here how to choose one. Open System Preferences and click the Desktop & Screen Saver icon; then click the Screen Saver tab to display the settings that you see in Figure 2-2.

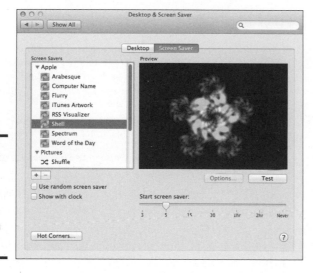

Figure 2-2:
A good screen saver can cancel the effects of a bad boss.

To add a third-party screen saver module so that everyone can use it on a multiuser system, copy it into the Screen Savers folder within the top-level Library folder. To selfishly keep that saver all to yourself, copy it into your user account's Screen Savers folder (which is located within the Library folder in your Home folder). To access your Library folder, hold down the Option key while clicking the Go menu on the Finder menu bar, and then click the Library menu item that appears.

Click one of the entries in the Screen Savers column to display a thumbnail of the effect. Selecting the Use Random Screen Saver check box runs through 'em all, naturally. You can also test the appearance of the saver module by clicking the Test button; the screen saver runs until you move the mouse or press a key.

To keep tabs on the current time, click the Show with Clock check box to select it. Lion adds a clock display to any screen saver.

Many screen savers allow you to monkey with their settings. If the Options button is enabled (not grayed out), click it to see how you can change the effects.

Changing Colors in Mac OS X

I can't understand it, but some people just don't appreciate menus with purple highlights! (You can tell a Louisiana State University graduate a mile away.) To specify your own colors for buttons, menus, and windows, follow these steps:

1. **Open System Preferences and click the Appearance icon to display the settings, as shown in Figure 2-3.**

2. **Click the Appearance pop-up menu and choose the main color choice for your buttons and menus.**

3. **Click the Highlight Color pop-up menu and pick the highlight color that appears when you select text in an application or select an item from a list.**

4. **Press ⌘+Q to exit System Preferences and save your changes.**

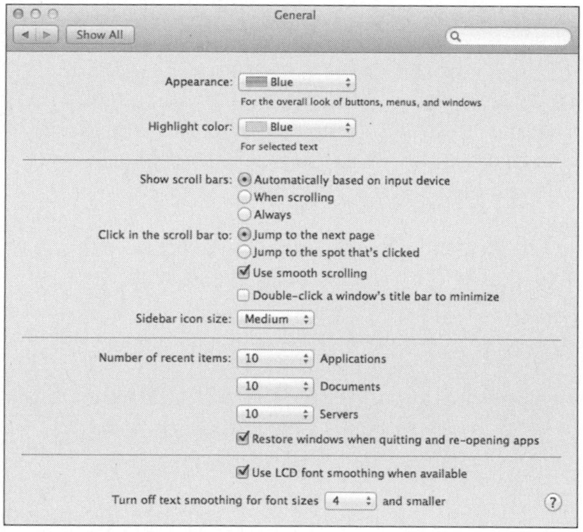

Book II Chapter 2

Giving Your Desktop the Personal Touch

Figure 2-3: Okay, then, set up your own school colors with the Appearance settings!

Adding Stickies

Stickies are interesting little beasts — I don't know their genus or phyla, but they're certainly handy to have around. To be technical for a moment, a *Sticky* is actually nothing more than a special type of document window, but these windows remain on your Desktop as long as the Stickies application is running.

I use Stickies for anything that a real-world sticky note can handle, including

✦ Reminders that you don't want to misplace

✦ Snippets of text that you want to temporarily store while your Mac is turned off (without launching a behemoth like Word or digging for TextEdit)

✦ Boilerplate (repeated and standard) text that you're constantly including in your documents, such as your address

✦ A quick note that includes someone's e-mail address or phone number

✦ Today's Dilbert cartoon from www.dilbert.com

A Sticky can contain data pasted from the Clipboard, or you can simply type directly into the active Stickies document window. Sticky windows can include graphics and different fonts and colors. You can even locate specific text from somewhere in your vast collection of Stickies by using the Find command within the Stickies application. Just press ⌘+F while the Stickies menu is active to display the Stickies Find dialog. (And you don't use up our bark-covered friends of the forest, either.)

In Book I, I discuss the Mac OS X Services menu. You can make a Sticky note from the Services menu in many applications as well.

Follow these steps to stick your way to success:

1. **Open your Applications folder and run the Stickies application to display the new window that you see in Figure 2-4.**

   The text cursor is already idling in the new window.

2. **Type text in the window or press ⌘+V to paste the contents of the Clipboard into the window.**

   You can also import the contents of an existing file into a Sticky. Just click File and then choose Import Text to display a standard Open dialog.

3. **(Optional) Add text formatting, change the text font, and change font color from the Font menu.**

   From the Note menu, you can also choose to make the Sticky translucent. (No pressing reason; they just look cool.)

4. **To change the Sticky color, click the Color menu and choose the appropriate hue.**

5. **Resize and drag the Sticky window to the desired location.**

   Press ⌘+M to toggle between a *miniaturized* view (showing only the title bar) and the expanded view.

To automatically run the Stickies application each time you log on, open the Users & Groups settings in System Preferences and click your account in the list. Click the Login Items button and add Stickies to the list by clicking the plus button.

To delete a Sticky, simply click the Close button at the upper-left corner of the Sticky window. Or click the Sticky to make it the active note and then click Close. Stickies display a dialog to confirm that you want to close the note; click Save to save the contents in a file or click the Don't Save button to close the note and discard its contents.

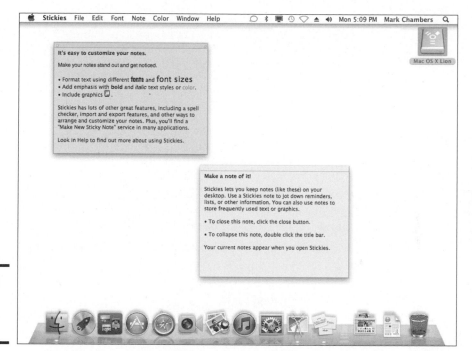

Figure 2-4:
"Look, Ma, it's a Sticky!"

To close the Stickies application completely, click any note and press ⌘+Q. The application remembers the position and contents of each note for when you launch it again.

Customizing the Dock

In terms of importance, the *Dock* — the quick-access strip for applications and documents that appears on your Desktop — ranks right up there with the command center of a modern nuclear submarine. As such, it had better be easy to customize, and naturally, Mac OS X doesn't let you down.

Adding applications and extras to the Dock

Why be satisfied with just the icons that Apple places in the Dock? You can add your own applications, files, and folders to the Dock as well.

✦ **Adding applications:** You can add any application to your Dock by simply dragging its icon into the area to the *left* side of the Dock (that's to the left side of the vertical dotted line that's visible in the Dock). You'll know when you're in the proper territory because the existing Dock icons obligingly move aside to make a space for it.

Attempting to place an application directly on the right side of the Dock sends it to the Trash (if the Trash icon is highlighted when you release the button), so beware. Note, however, that you can drop an application icon inside a Stack or a folder that already exists at the right side of the Dock.

✦ **Adding individual files and volumes:** Individual files and volume icons can be added to the Dock by dragging the icon into the area to the *right* side of the Dock. (Attempting to place these to the left side of the Dock opens the application associated with the contents, which usually doesn't work.) Again, the existing Dock icons will move aside to create a space when you're in the right area.

To open the Dock item you've added in a Finder window, right-click the icon to display a Dock menu, where you can open documents, run applications, and have other assorted fun, depending on the item you choose.

✦ **Adding several files or a folder:** Lion uses a feature called Stacks, which I discuss in a few paragraphs, to handle multiple files or add an entire folder to the Dock.

✦ **Adding websites:** You can drag any URL from Safari directly into the area at the right of the Dock. Clicking that icon automatically opens your browser and displays that page. (Safari gets the treatment in Book V, Chapter 5.) Now that, my friends, is genuine *sassy!*

To remove an icon from the Dock, just click and drag it off the Dock. You get a rather silly (but somehow, strangely satisfying) animated cloud of debris, and the icon is no more. Note, however, that the original application, folder, or volume is not deleted — just the Dock icon itself is permanently excused. If you like, you can delete almost any of the default icons that Mac OS X installs in the Dock; only the Finder and Trash icons must remain in the Dock.

To set up a Dock icon as a Login Item — without the hassle of opening the Users & Groups pane in System Preferences — just click a Dock icon and hold the mouse button down until the pop-up menu appears. Select Options, and then select the Open at Login item from the submenu.

If you can't delete items from the Dock, you're using a *managed* account — your account is configured with Parental Controls turned on, and your administrator has deselected the Can Modify the Dock check box in your account. In order to delete Dock items, you'll need an admin-level user to log in; then visit the Users & Groups pane in System Preferences, click your account, and deselect the check box. For more information on user accounts, see Chapter 5 of this minibook.

Keeping track (s) with Stacks

I know, it's a horrible play on words, but my editors are doing me a favor.

Lion offers *Stacks,* which are groups of items (documents, applications, and folders) that you want to place in the Dock for convenience — perhaps the files needed for a project you're working on, or your favorite game applications. For example, I have a Stack named Wiley on my Dock that holds all the project files I need for the book I'm currently writing.

To create a Stack, just select and drag the items you want to include to the right side of the Dock. As always, the Dock opens a spot on the right side of the Dock to indicate you're in the zone.

To display the items in a Stack, just click it:

✦ **If the Stack holds relatively few items,** they're displayed in a really cool-looking arc that Apple calls a *fan* (as shown in Figure 2-5), and you can click the item you want to open or launch.

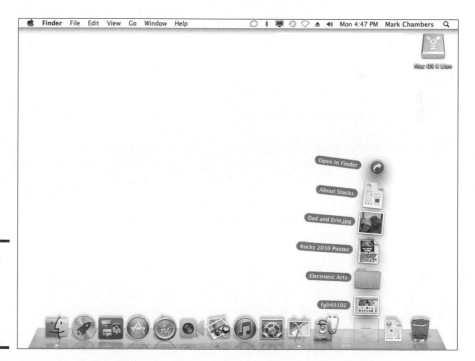

Figure 2-5: Click a Stack in the Dock to view its contents.

✦ **If the Stack is stuffed full of many items,** the Stack opens in a grid display, allowing you to scroll through the contents to find what you need.

Lion provides a number of new display and sorting options for a Stack — right-click the Stack icon, and you can choose to sort the contents by name, date created or added, date modified, or file type. If you'd prefer a grid display (no matter how many items the Stack contains), you can choose your view mode for the Stack as well.

You can remove a Stack from the Dock by right-clicking the Stack icon and selecting Options. Choose Remove from Dock from the submenu that appears. Alternatively, just drag that sucker right off the Dock.

You can also display the contents of a Stack in a Finder window. Right-click the Stack icon and choose the Open item at the bottom of the pop-up menu.

If you add a folder full of items, the Stack is named after the folder; otherwise, Lion does the best job it can in figuring out what to name the Stack.

Apple provides two Stacks already set up for you. One, the Download folder, situated next to the Trash, is the default location for any new files that you download using Safari or receive in your e-mail. Lion bounces the Download Stack icon to indicate that you've received a new item. Next to the Download Stack is the Documents Stack, which conveniently displays the contents of your Documents folder.

Resizing the Dock

You can change the size of the Dock from the Dock settings in System Preferences — I explain this in more detail in Book II, Chapter 3 — but here's a simpler way to resize the Dock, right from the Desktop.

Move your mouse cursor over the vertical dashed line that separates the left side of the Dock from the right side; the cursor turns into a funky line with arrows pointing up and down. This is your cue to click and drag while moving the mouse up and down, which expands and shrinks the Dock, respectively.

You can also right-click when the funky line cursor is visible to display a menu of Dock preferences. This allows you to change your Dock preferences without the hassle of opening System Preferences and displaying the Dock settings.

Stick It on the Dashboard

One of Lion's most popular features is *Dashboard,* which you can use to hold widgets and display them with the press of a button. (Okay, I know that sounds a little wacky, but bear with me.) *Widgets* are small applications — dubbed by some as *applets* — that typically provide only one function. For example, Dashboard comes complete with a calculator, a dictionary, a clock, a weather display, and a quick-and-simple calendar. You can display and use these widgets at any time by pressing the Dashboard key; by default, that's F12 on older and non-Apple keyboards (and F4 on current Apple keyboard models), but you can modify the key on the Mission Control pane within System Preferences. Dashboard appears as a desktop within the Spaces strip on the Mission Control screen, and Lion also includes a thoughtful Dashboard application icon in your Applications folder, which you can launch to display your widgets. (Geez, that sounds kind of racy. Best not to pursue it.)

Figure 2-6 illustrates Dashboard in action. Press the Dashboard key, and the widgets appear, ready for you to use. You can add widgets to or delete them from your Dashboard by clicking the Add button (which bears a plus sign, naturally) at the lower-left corner of the Dashboard screen. When you click the Add button, a scrolling menu strip appears at the bottom of the Dashboard display, and you can drag new widgets directly onto your Dashboard from this menu. It's also easy to rearrange the widgets that are already populating Dashboard by dragging them to the desired spot. After you've finished customizing your Dashboard display, click the Close button above the menu strip (which bears an X icon) to return to your Dashboard. When it's time to go back to work (or play), press the Dashboard key again to return to your Lion Desktop, or click the button with the right arrow at the lower right side of the screen.

Most widgets have an option button that allows you to change things, such as borders, ZIP codes, display columns, and the like; look for a tiny circle with a lowercase letter *i*. Click this information icon and you can tweak whatever options are available for that widget.

To remove a widget, just click the Add button to display the menu strip, and you'll notice a tiny X button appears next to each widget on your Dashboard. Click the X button next to the widget you want to remove, and it vanishes from the display. You can add it back again at any time from the strip.

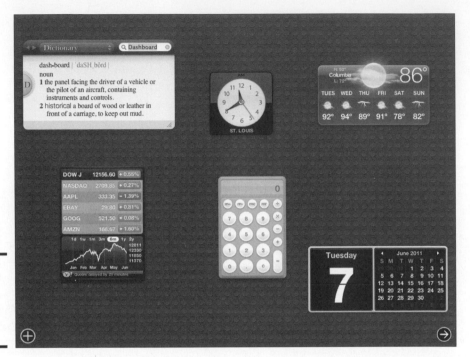

Figure 2-6:
Dashboard proudly displays its widgets.

While you're adding or deleting widgets, you can also click Manage Widgets, which displays a dialog where you can sort your widgets in a list by name or date added, disable any widget, and delete a widget (click the red minus icon next to the offending widget in the list). Click the More Widgets button to jump directly to the widget download area on the Apple website.

If you need to use a widget for only a second or two, press the Dashboard key and hold it. When you release the key, you're back to your Desktop.

Apple offers additional widgets that you can download on the Mac OS X download site (www.apple.com/macosx). Third-party software developers also provide both freeware and shareware widgets.

You can also modify the Dashboard key by turning it into a key sequence or mouse button action, which is a good thing if you're already using an application that thrives on F12 (or F4, depending on your keyboard). Visit the Mission Control pane in System Preferences, and use the Shift, Control, Option, and ⌘ keys in conjunction with the Dashboard key to specify a modifier, or choose a mouse button to activate Dashboard.

Oh, did I mention that Lion allows you to create your own Dashboard widgets? That's right, this feature is sure to be a winner amongst the In Crowd. Follow these steps to create a new *WebClip* Dashboard widget from your favorite website:

1. **Run Safari and navigate to the site you want to view as a widget.**

2. **Click File⇨Open in Dashboard.**

3. **Select the portion of the page you want to include in your widget and click Add.**

Most web pages use frames to organize and separate sections of a page, so this step allows you to choose the frame with the desired content.

4. **Drag the handles at the edges of the selection border to resize your widget frame to the right size and then click Add.**

Bam! Lion displays your new WebClip widget within Dashboard.

A WebClip widget can include text, graphics, and links, which Dashboard updates every time you display your widgets. Think about that for a second: Dynamic displays, such as weather maps, cartoons, even the Free Music Download image from the iTunes Store, are all good sources of WebClip widgets! (That last one is a real timesaver.)

If you click a link in a WebClip widget, Dashboard loads the full web page in Safari, so you can even use WebClips for surfing chores with sites you visit often.

Arranging Your Precious Desktop

Consider the layout of the Desktop itself. You can set the options for icon placement from the Finder View menu — click View⇨Show View Options, or press ⌘+J. Just as you can with the options for Finder windows that I cover in Chapter 1 of this minibook, you can clean up and arrange your Desktop by name, date, size, or kind.

The View Options for the Desktop are different in two ways from the View Options for a Finder window in icon view (which I discuss in Chapter 1 of this minibook):

✦ You choose a background for the Finder from System Preferences.

✦ There's no Always Open check box. Your Desktop always opens in Icon view!

Chapter 3: Delving under the Hood with System Preferences

In This Chapter

- ✓ Displaying and customizing settings in System Preferences
- ✓ Saving your changes
- ✓ Changing settings

The System Preferences window is the place to practice behavior modification in Mac OS X. The settings that you specify in System Preferences affect the majority of the applications that you use as well as the hardware that you connect to your MacBook; your Internet and network traffic; the appearance and activity on your Desktop; and how Lion handles money, dates, and languages. Oh, and don't forget your screen saver — important stuff!

In this chapter, I discuss the many settings in System Preferences. You discover what does what and how you can customize the appearance and operation of Mac OS X.

The Preferred Way to Display the Preferences

Apple has made it easy to open the System Preferences window. Just click the System Preferences icon (which looks like a number of gears) in the Dock, and the window shown in Figure 3-1 appears. You can also open the window by clicking the Apple menu and choosing the System Preferences item, or by clicking the System Preferences icon within Launchpad.

To display all the System Preferences icons at any time, click the Show All button. You can also use the Back and Forward buttons (in the toolbar's upper-left corner) to move backward and forward through the different panes you've accessed in System Preferences, just as you use the similar buttons in a Web browser (yes, just like Safari!).

Figure 3-1:
The System Preferences window is a familiar face to any Lion user.

Although the System Preferences panes are arranged by category when you first install Lion, you can also display the panes in alphabetical order — making it easier to choose a pane if you're unsure what group it's in. To do so, choose View➪Organize Alphabetically. (Note that you can also select any pane directly from the View menu.) Click View➪Customize, and you can hide specific icons from the System Preferences window — disable the check box next to each icon that you want hidden and then click Done. (You can still reach hidden icons from the System Preferences View menu, so they're not banished forever!)

In fact, you can right-click the System Preferences icon in the Dock to jump to any pane from the contextual menu. *Wowzers!*

If a System Preference pane is *locked*, you won't be able to modify any of the settings on that pane unless you unlock the pane. Click the padlock icon (and, if prompted, type your Admin-level account password) to unlock the pane. After you've finished your tweaking, you can protect the settings from inadvertent changes by clicking the padlock icon again to close it.

Saving Your Preferences

Note that the System Preferences window has no Save or Apply button. Illustrating the elegant design of Mac OS X, simply quitting System Preferences automatically saves all the changes that you make. (However, some panes in System Preferences have an Apply button that you can click to apply your changes immediately.) As with any other Mac OS X application, you can quit the System Preferences window by pressing ⌘+Q or by choosing System Preferences➪Quit System Preferences.

Hey, I got bonus icons in my window!

Some third-party applications and media plug-ins can actually install their own groups within your once-pristine System Preferences window; you'll see them at the bottom of the window, in the Other section. (A good example is Perian, the great freeware QuickTime plug-in from `perian.org`. It allows QuickTime Player to open all sorts of video formats that would otherwise be unplayable.) Naturally, I can't document these invited guests in this chapter, but they work the same way as any other group within System Preferences. Click the icon, adjust any settings as necessary, and then close the System Preferences window to save your changes.

Searching for Specific Settings

Searching for a single button or check box amidst all the settings in System Preferences might seem like hunting for the proverbial needle in a haystack, but your friends at Apple have added a Search box to the right side of the window toolbar. Click in this Search box (or press ⌘+F) and type the setting name, like **screen saver** (or even a word that's generally associated with a setting, like **power** for the Energy Saver settings). Lion highlights all the icons in System Preferences that have anything to do with the search keywords you entered, as shown in Figure 3-2. You don't even have to press Return!

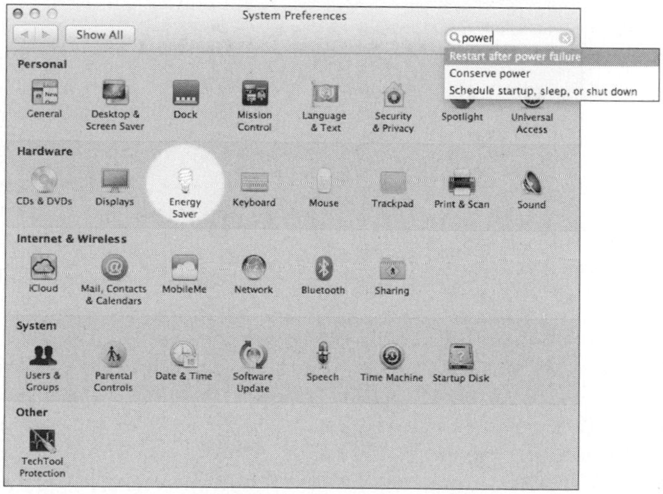

Figure 3-2: System Preferences highlights the panes that contain your search keywords.

To reset the Search field for a different keyword, click the X button that appears at the right of the Search box.

Getting Personal

The first stop on your tour of the System Preferences window is the Personal section. No singles ads here — this section is devoted to settings that you make to customize the appearance and operation of your Desktop and login account.

Appearance preferences

The Appearance group appears in Figure 3-3.

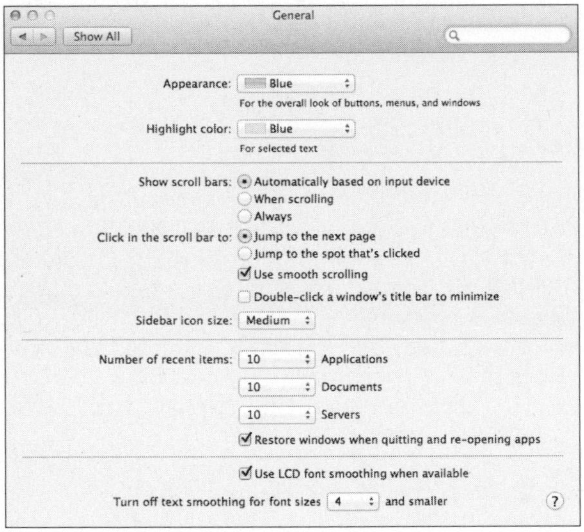

Figure 3-3: The Appearance pane.

These settings are

✦ **Appearance:** From this pop-up menu, choose a color to be used for buttons, menus, and windows.

✦ **Highlight Color:** From this pop-up menu, choose a color to be used to highlight selected text in fields and pop-up menus.

✦ **Show Scroll Bars:** Use these radio buttons to specify when Lion should display scroll bars within a window. By default, they're placed automatically when necessary, but you can choose to display scroll bars always, or only when you're actually scrolling through a document. (If you've used Mac OS X before, note that the familiar scroll arrows from past versions of the operating system no longer appear within Lion.)

✦ **Click in the Scroll Bar To:** By default, Mac OS X jumps to the next or previous page when you click in an empty portion of the scroll bar. Select the Jump to the Spot That's Clicked radio button to scroll the document to the approximate position in relation to where you click. (You can also choose smooth scrolling, which looks cool, but many folks think that it's too slow compared with the default scrolling speed.) If you select the Double-Click a Window's Title Bar to Minimize check box, you can minimize a Finder or application window by simply double-clicking the window's title bar. You can also set the size for the icons in the Finder window toolbar.

✦ **Number of Recent Items:** The default number of recent applications, documents, and servers (available from the Recent Items item in the Apple menu, which you can read more about in Book II, Chapter 3) is 10. To change the default, click any of the pop-up menus here and choose up to 50. (Personally, I like 20 or 30 for each.)

✦ **Restore Windows When Quitting and Re-Opening Apps:** If this check box is enabled, Lion's Resume feature automatically saves the state of an application when you quit. When you launch the application again, Lion restores all of the application windows and opens the documents you were working on when you quit — in effect, you can continue using the application just as if you had never quit. If you disable the check box, Lion will not restore your work, and you'll have to load your document again; this is the same action taken by earlier versions of Mac OS X.

✦ **Use LCD Font Smoothing:** By default, this check box is enabled, making the text on your MacBook's LCD display appear more like the printed page.

✦ **Turn Off Text Smoothing for Font Sizes:** Below a certain point size, text smoothing isn't much good for most on-screen fonts. By default, any font displayed at 8 point or smaller isn't smoothed, which is suitable for a high-end video card and monitor. You can speed up the display of text by turning off text smoothing for fonts up to 12 point.

Desktop and screen saver preferences

Figure 3-4 illustrates the settings in the Desktop & Screen Saver group.

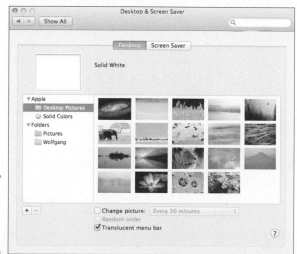

Figure 3-4:
The Desktop & Screen Saver pane.

The settings on the Desktop tab are

✦ **Current Desktop Picture:** You can click a picture in the thumbnail list
at the right half of the screen to use it as your Desktop background. The
Desktop is immediately updated, and the thumbnail appears in the *well*
(the square box in Figure 3-4). To display a different image collection
or open a folder of your own images, click the Add Folder button at the
lower left of the window (which carries a plus sign) and browse for your
heart's desire; click Choose to select a folder and display the images it
contains.

✦ **Layout:** As I explain in Chapter 2 of this minibook, you can tile your
background image, center it, fill the screen with it, and stretch it to fill
the screen. (Note that filling the screen may distort the image.) The
layout pop-up menu appears only when you're using your own pictures,
so you won't see it if you're using a Desktop image supplied by Apple.

✦ **Change Picture:** Select this check box to change the Desktop background automatically after the delay period that you set, including each
time you log in and each time your Mac wakes up from sleep mode.

✦ **Random Order:** To display screens randomly, enable the Random Order
check box. Otherwise, the backgrounds are displayed in the sequence in
which they appear in the thumbnail strip.

✦ **Translucent Menu Bar:** When enabled, this feature turns your Finder
and application menu bars semi-opaque, allowing them to blend in
somewhat with your Desktop background. If you'd rather have a solid-
color menu bar, deselect this check box.

Click the Screen Saver tab to see the following settings:

✦ **Screen Savers:** In the Screen Savers list at the left, click the screen saver
that you want to display an animated Preview of on the right. To try out
the screen saver in full-screen mode, click the Test button. (You can end
the test by moving your finger across the trackpad.) If the screen saver
module that you select has any configurable settings, click the Options
button to display them. (A screen saver is configurable if the Options
button is enabled.)

✦ **Start Screen Saver:** Click and drag the slider here to specify the period
of inactivity that triggers the screen saver. To disable the screen saver,
choose the Never setting at the far right of the slider.

✦ **Use Random Screen Saver:** Just what it says: If this check box is
enabled, a different screen saver module is used each time the screen
saver is activated.

✦ **Show with Clock:** If you want your selected screen saver to display the
time as well, click this check box to enable it.

✦ **Hot Corners:** Click any of the four pop-up menus at the four corners
of the screen to specify that corner as an *activation hot corner* (which

immediately activates the screen saver) or as a *disabling hot corner* (which prevents the screen saver from activating). As long as the pointer stays in the disabling hot corner, the screen saver doesn't kick in no matter how long a period of inactivity passes. Note that you can also set the Sleep, Mission Control, Launchpad, and Dashboard activation corners from here. (For the scoop on Mission Control, see the upcoming section "Mission Control preferences.")

Dock preferences

The Dock group is shown in Figure 3-5.

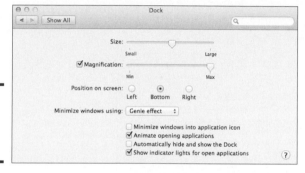

Figure 3-5:
The Dock preference pane.

Settings here are

✦ **Size:** Move this slider to change the overall size of the Dock.

✦ **Magnification:** With this check box selected, a Dock icon magically expands, like the national deficit, when you move your pointer over it. You can move the Magnification slider to specify just how much magnification is right for you.

This feature is useful for helping you click a particular Dock icon if you've resized the Dock smaller than its default dimensions or if you have a large number of items in the Dock.

✦ **Position on Screen:** Choose from three radio buttons to make that crazy Dock appear at the left, bottom, or right edge of your Desktop.

✦ **Minimize Windows Using:** By default, Mac OS X animates a window when it's shrunk into the Dock (and when it's expanded back into a full window). From the Minimize Using pop-up menu, you can choose from a genie-in-a-bottle effect or a scale-up-or-down-incrementally effect. To demonstrate, choose an effect and then click the Minimize button (the yellow button in the upper-left corner) on the System Preferences window.

✦ **Minimize windows into application icon:** If this check box is not selected, minimized application windows appear as thumbnail icons in the Dock. To minimize application windows into the application icon in the Dock — which can save space on your Dock — click this check box to select it.

✦ **Animate Opening Applications:** By default, Mac OS X has that happy, slam-dancing feeling when you launch an application: The application's icon bounces up and down in the Dock two or three times to draw your attention and indicate that the application is loading. If you find this effervescence overly buoyant or distracting, deselect this check box.

✦ **Automatically Hide and Show the Dock:** If you like, the Dock can stay hidden until you need it, thus reclaiming a significant amount of Desktop space for your application windows. Select this check box to hide the Dock whenever you're not using it.

To display a hidden Dock, move your pointer over the edge of the Desktop where it's hiding.

✦ **Show Indicator Lights for Open Applications:** Mac OS X indicates which applications are running in the Dock with a small blue dot in front of the icon. To disable these indicators, deselect this check box.

You can also change most of these Dock preference settings from the Apple menu.

Language & Text preferences

The Language & Text group appears in Figure 3-6 with the following tabs:

Figure 3-6:
The Language & Text pane in System Preferences.

✦ **Language:** Choose the preferred order for language use in menus and dialogs as well as the standards that Mac OS X will use for sorted lists.

✦ **Text:** Specify character combinations that will be automatically replaced with special characters. For example, Lion will automatically replace the combination **TM** with the special character ™. You can also choose a language for spell-checking and turn on "smart" quotes (where Lion chooses double or single quotation marks for you). Note that these settings can be overridden by preferences set within applications — for example, Microsoft Word.

✦ **Formats:** Find the following settings here:

- *Dates:* You can select a region and use its date conventions (for example, month-day-year versus day-month-year) or you can click the Customize button to build a custom format for the full date (Saturday, September 24, 2011), long date (September 24, 2011), medium date (Sep 24, 2011), and short date (9/24/2011) used throughout Mac OS X.

- *Times:* Click Customize to configure the appearance of the full time (7:18:30 PM Central Standard), long time (7:18:30 PM CST), medium time (7:18:30 PM), and short time (7:18 PM) displayed within Lion. You can also specify different suffixes for morning (a.m.) and evening (p.m.).

- *Numbers:* These convention settings determine the separators used for large numbers or numbers with decimals, as well as the currency symbol that you want to use and where it appears in a number. You can also choose between standard (U.S.) and metric measurement systems.

✦ **Input Sources:** Each check box toggles the keyboard layouts available from the Input menu. (To display the Input menu on the Finder menu bar, click the Show Input Menu in Menu Bar check box to select it.) Click the Keyboard Shortcuts button to toggle the shortcuts for switching layouts and input methods.

Mission Control preferences

Figure 3-7 illustrates the Mission Control, Spaces, and Dashboard settings that you can configure in this group. You can use Mission Control to view all the application windows that you're using at one time so that you can select a new active window. Or, you can move all windows aside so that you can see your Desktop. Dashboard presents a number of mini-applications (or *widgets*), which you can summon and hide with a single key.

**Book II
Chapter 3**

**Delving Under the
Hood with System
Preferences**

Figure 3-7:
Set your
Mission
Control
preferences
here.

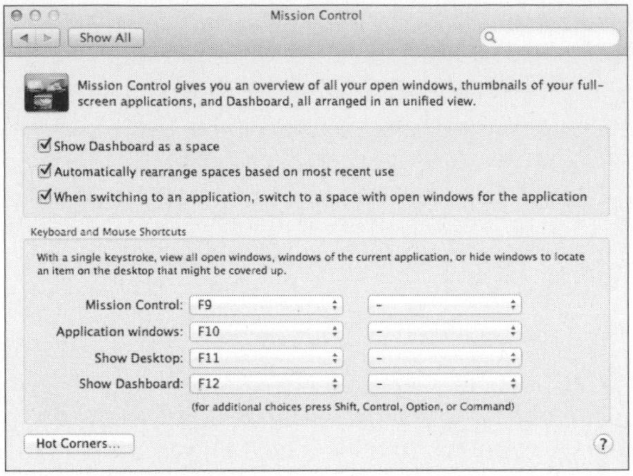

The settings are

✦ **Active Screen Corners:** These four pop-up menus operate just like the
Hot Corners/Active Screen Corners in the Desktop & Screen Savers
pane, but they control the operation of Lion's screen management
features. Click one to specify that corner as one of the following: an
All Windows corner (which displays all windows on your Desktop); an
Application Windows corner (which displays only the windows from the
active application); a Desktop corner (which moves all windows to the
outside of the screen to uncover your Desktop); or a Dashboard corner
(which displays your Dashboard widgets). Choose Launchpad to activate the Launchpad screen. Note that you can also set the Screen Saver
Start and Disable corners from here, as well as put your display to sleep.

✦ **Keyboard and Mouse Shortcuts:** Click each pop-up menu to set the key
sequences (and mouse button settings) for Mission Control, Application
windows, Show Desktop, and the Dashboard.

You're not limited to just the keyboard and mouse shortcuts on the
pop-up menus. Press Shift, Control, Option, and Command keys while
a pop-up menu is open, and you see these modifiers appear as menu
choices! (Heck, you can even combine modifiers, such as ⌘+Shift+F9
instead of just F9.)

To display your Dashboard as a Space within the Mission Control
screen, select the Show Dashboard As a Space check box. If you prefer
your Dashboard widgets to appear as an overlay (as they did in previous
versions of Mac OS X), disable this check box.

✦ **Automatically Rearrange Spaces Based on Most Recent Use:** If this
check box is enabled, Mission Control presents your most recently used
Spaces first within the thumbnails at the top of the screen.

✦ **When Switching to an Application:** When selected, this check box allows you to switch applications between Spaces desktops using the ⌘+Tab shortcut. Lion jumps to the desktop that has an open window for the application you choose, even if that desktop is not currently active.

Security & Privacy preferences

The Security & Privacy group is shown in Figure 3-8.

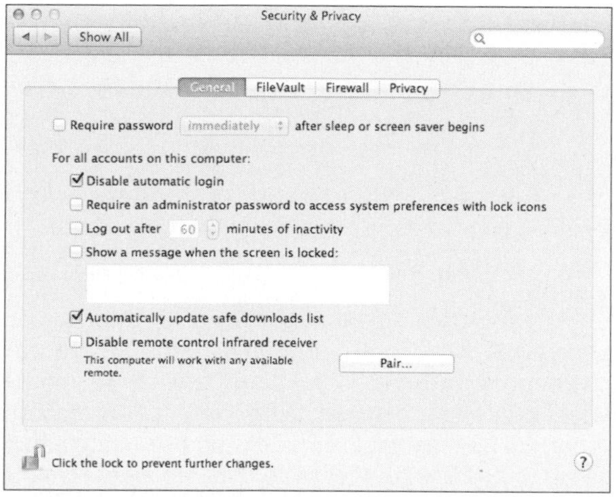

Figure 3-8:
Set Security preferences here.

Book II
Chapter 3

Delving Under the Hood with System Preferences

Settings here are divided into three tabs:

✦ **General:** To add an extra layer of password security for your MacBook, select the Require Password After Sleep or Screen Saver Begins check box. Mac OS X then requires that you enter your login password before the system returns from a sleep state or exits a screen saver. Click the pop-up delay menu to specify when the password requirement will kick in (it's immediate by default). If you're an admin-level user, you can set the global security features in the For All Accounts on This Computer section, which affect all user accounts. You can choose to do the following: disable the automatic login feature; force Mac OS X to require a login password each time that a System Preference pane is opened; automatically log off any user after a certain amount of inactivity; and display a message when the screen is locked. You can also specify whether Lion should update Safari's safe download list automatically. (Safari uses this list to determine what files should be opened after downloading, which helps you prevent attacks by viruses and malware.)

Don't want small fingers accidentally controlling your MacBook with the Apple Remote? If you don't need the Remote on a regular basis, click the Disable Remote Control Infrared Receiver check box to select it. (But don't forget to turn your IR receiver back on for your next movie night!)

✦ **FileVault:** These controls allow you to turn on FileVault hard drive encryption, which makes it virtually impossible for others to access files on your Mac. Click the Turn On FileVault button to enter the passwords for each user, because even if you're using an Admin account, each user on your Mac must enter her password to enable her account for use with FileVault, which allows her access to data on the hard drive. Click Continue to display the recovery key — go ahead and write that key down and store it in a **very** safe place — and then click Continue to enable FileVault encryption for the user who's currently logged in; the user's Login password becomes his FileVault password as well.

If you forget both your login password and the recovery key, not even the technical experts at Apple can retrieve your data!

✦ **Firewall:** As I discuss in Book VI, Chapter 6, Mac OS X includes a built-in firewall, which you can enable from this pane.

To turn the firewall off entirely, simply click the Stop button. This is the very definition of Not a Good Thing, and I **always** recommend that any MacBook hooked up to a network or the Internet have the system firewall turned **on.** (The only exception is if you're using a network that you *know* to be secure and your access to the Internet is through a router or sharing device with its own built-in firewall.)

When the firewall is enabled, click the Advanced button to set firewall options.

- *To turn the firewall on with only Mac OS X application exclusions,* click Block All Incoming Connections — only the sharing services you select on the Sharing pane in System Preferences are allowed through your firewall.) This is a good choice for the most security-conscious MacBook owner, but your firewall will block third-party applications that try to access your network or the Internet.

- *To turn the firewall on with exclusions,* click Automatically Allow Signed Software to Receive Incoming Connections. (Yep, this is the correct option for just about every MacBook owner.) Any connection to a service (such as Web Sharing) or an application (such as iChat) that isn't listed is blocked, but you can enable access for third-party applications on an as-needed basis.

In firewall-speak, these entries are *rules* because they determine what's allowed to pass through to your MacBook.

It's easy to enable communications with a Mac OS X service: Just use the Sharing pane within System Preferences to turn on a service, and Lion automatically configures your firewall to allow communications. I describe the Sharing pane in detail later in this chapter.

To add a third-party application, click the Advanced button at the bottom of the Firewall pane, then click the button with the plus sign. Navigate to the application that needs to communicate with the outside world. Click the application to select it and then click Add. To delete an application, select it in the list and click the button with the minus sign. Remember, you don't have to add any of the applications provided by Apple with Lion, such as Apple Mail, iChat, or Safari; only third-party applications that you install yourself need a firewall rule.

You can edit the rule for a specific service or application by clicking the rule at the right side of the entry. By default, the rule reads Allow Incoming Connections (including both your local network and the Internet); however, when you click the rule, you can also choose Block Incoming Connections to temporarily deny access to that application.

For heightened security, click the Enable Stealth Mode check box, which prevents your Mac from responding to attempts to identify it across your network and the Internet.

If you suddenly can't connect to other computers or share files that you originally could share, review the rules that you've enabled from this pane. You can also verify that everything's shipshape in the Sharing pane in System Preferences, which I cover later in this chapter.

Spotlight preferences

The Spotlight group is shown in Figure 3-9.

Settings here are

✦ **Search Results tab:** You can enable or disable the check boxes next to each of the categories to display or hide each category in the Spotlight search menu and dialog. Click and drag the categories to the order that you prefer. For example, I like to see matching documents immediately after matching applications in the Spotlight dialog, so I dragged Documents to the second position in the list. You can also specify a different keyboard shortcut for the Spotlight menu and window.

✦ **Privacy tab:** If you don't want to display the contents of certain folders in the Spotlight — for instance, if you work in a hospital setting and you can't allow access to patient information and medical records — click the Add button (which carries a plus sign) and specify the folder or disk you want to exclude from Spotlight searches. Alternatively, just drag the folders or disks to exclude into the list from a Finder window.

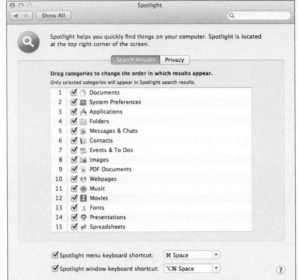

Figure 3-9:
Fine-tune
your
Spotlight
search
results here.

Universal Access preferences

The Universal Access pane is shown in Figure 3-10. These settings modify
the display and sound functions within Mac OS X to make them friendlier to
physically challenged users. Note that if you select the VoiceOver On radio
button, Mac OS X speaks the text for all text and buttons onscreen.

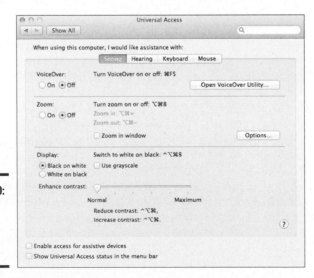

Figure 3-10:
The
Universal
Access
pane.

If you have an assistive device that's recognized by Mac OS X, select the Enable Access for Assistive Devices check box to allow it to be used throughout the operating system. You can also elect to display the Universal Access status icon in the Finder menu bar.

The four tabs here are

✦ **Seeing:** These settings make it easier for those with limited vision to use Mac OS X. You can toggle VoiceOver on and off from here; I discuss this feature and these settings more in Book VIII, Chapter 3. To turn on the display Zoom feature, select the Zoom On radio button or press ⌘+Option+8.

   To specify how much magnification is used, click the Options button. From the sheet that appears, you can set the minimum and maximum Zoom magnification increments. From the keyboard, use ⌘+Option+= (equal sign) to zoom in and ⌘+Option+− (minus sign) to zoom out. Optionally, you can display a preview rectangle of the area that's included when you zoom. Mac OS X can smooth images to make them look better when zoomed; click the Options button in the Zoom section of the pane and select the Smooth Images check box.

   You can also determine how the screen moves in relation to the track-pad pointer from the Zoom Options sheet: By default, the zoomed screen moves with the pointer, but you can set it to move only when the pointer reaches the edge of the screen or maintain the pointer near the center of the zoomed image automatically. If you're using a mouse that has a scroll wheel or ball, you can specify a modifier key to activate the Zoom feature.

   If you prefer white text on a black background, select the White on Black radio button (or press the ⌘+Option+Control+8 keyboard shortcut). Note that depending on your display settings, it'll probably be easier on the eyes to use grayscale display mode by selecting the Use Grayscale check box. Drag the Enhance Contrast slider to increase the contrast between text and background.

✦ **Hearing:** If you need additional visual cues to supplement the spoken and audio alerts in Mac OS X, click this tab and select the Flash the Screen When an Alert Sound Occurs check box. Two-channel stereo audio can be combined to single-channel mono audio with the Play Stereo Audio as Mono check box. To raise the overall sound volume in Mac OS X, you can click the Adjust Volume button to display the Sound System Preferences settings, where you can drag the Volume slider to the right.

✦ **Keyboard:** These settings help those who have trouble pressing keyboard shortcuts or those who often trigger keyboard repeats (repetition of the same character) accidentally. If you mark the Sticky Keys On radio button, you can use *modifier keys* individually that are grouped together automatically as a single keyboard shortcut. In other words, you can press the modifier keys in a key sequence one after another instead of all together. Sticky Keys can be toggled on and off from the keyboard by pressing the Shift key five times. (You can optionally specify that Mac OS X sound a beep tone when a modifier key is pressed and whether the modifier keys are displayed onscreen.)

Turn Slow Keys on to add a pause (of the length that you specify) between when a key is pressed and when it's actually acted upon within Mac OS X. You can optionally add a key-click sound each time you press a key. To turn keyboard repeat off entirely, click the Set Key Repeat button, which opens the Keyboard preference settings that I discuss earlier.

✦ **Mouse & Trackpad:** With Mouse Keys active, you can use the numeric keypad to move the pointer across your screen. Mouse Keys can be toggled on and off by pressing the Option key five times. Drag the Initial Delay and Maximum Speed sliders to specify how long you must hold down a keypad key before the pointer starts to move as well as how fast the pointer should move across the screen. You can also disable the trackpad on your MacBook when using Mouse Keys. Click the Options button to configure device-specific speed settings (such as the double-click speed for a mouse).

If you prefer a larger pointer, the cursor can be resized to make it easier to spot onscreen. You can also click the Open Keyboard Preferences button to turn on Full Keyboard Access or to remap keyboard shortcuts for both the Finder and many applications.

It's All about the Hardware

The next category, Hardware, allows you to specify settings that affect your laptop's hardware.

CDs and DVDs preferences

The CDs & DVDs group is shown in Figure 3-11.

Figure 3-11: The CD & DVD preferences.

Choices here are

✦ **When You Insert a Blank CD:** Click this pop-up menu to specify the action that Mac OS X takes when you load a blank CD-R or CD-RW. You can choose to be prompted or to open the Finder, iTunes, or Disk Copy. Additionally, you can open another application that you select, run an AppleScript that you select, or ignore the disc.

✦ **When You Insert a Blank DVD:** Use this feature to specify the action that your MacBook takes when you load a recordable DVD.

✦ **When You Insert a Music CD:** Choices from this pop-up menu specify what action Mac OS X takes when you load an audio CD. By default, iTunes launches.

✦ **When You Insert a Picture CD:** Choices from this pop-up menu specify what action Mac OS X takes when you load a picture CD.

✦ **When You Insert a Video DVD:** Choices from this pop-up menu specify what action Mac OS X takes when you load a DVD movie. By default, DVD Player launches.

Displays preferences

The Displays group is shown in Figure 3-12.

Book II
Chapter 3

Delving Under the
Hood with System
Preferences

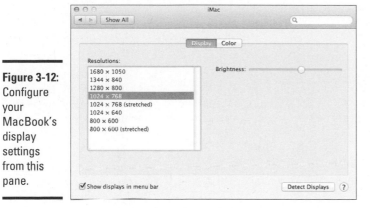

Figure 3-12: Configure your MacBook's display settings from this pane.

The two tabs here are

✦ **Display:** Click the resolution that you want to use from the Resolutions list on the left and then choose the number of colors (from the Colors pop-up menu) to display. In most cases, you want to use the highest resolution and the highest number of colors. You can also choose a refresh rate (from the, ahem, Refresh Rate pop-up menu). Again, generally, the higher the refresh rate, the better. Move the Brightness slider to adjust the brightness level of your display. If you've connected an external monitor or flat-screen TV to your MacBook, click the Detect Displays button and Lion will add them to the list of available displays, allowing you to redirect your MacBook's video signal.

Enable the Show Displays in Menu Bar check box if you'll be switching resolutions and color levels often — this means you, Ms. Image Editor and Mr. Web Designer!

✦ **Color:** Click a display color profile that will control the colors on your monitor. To load a profile, click the Open Profile button. To create a custom ColorSync profile and calibrate the colors that you see on your monitor, click the Calibrate button to launch the Display Calibrator. (You can also launch it from your Utilities folder within your Applications folder.) This easy-to-use assistant walks you step-by-step through the process of creating a ColorSync profile matched to your monitor's gamma and white-point values.

Energy Saver preferences

The Energy Saver group is shown in Figure 3-13.

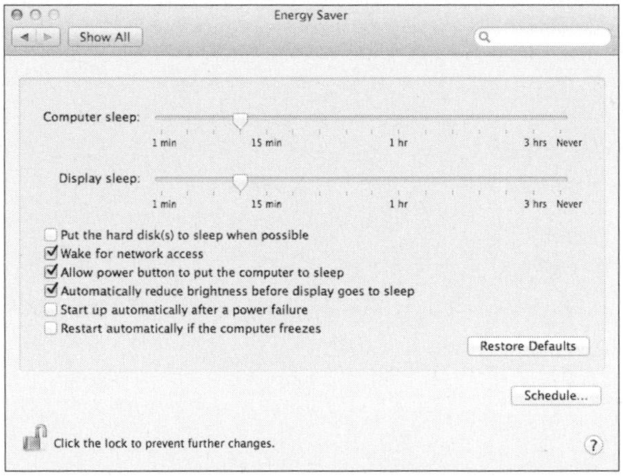

Figure 3-13:
The Energy
Saver pane.

Move the Computer Sleep slider to specify when Mac OS X should switch to sleep mode. The Never setting here disables sleep mode entirely. To choose a separate delay period for blanking your monitor, drag the Display Sleep delay slider to the desired period. You can also power down the hard drive to conserve energy and prevent wear and tear (an especially good feature for laptop owners).

If you want to start or shut down your laptop at a scheduled time, click the Schedule button. Mark the desired schedule (the Start Up or Wake check box and the Shut Down/Sleep check box) to enable them; then click the up and down arrows next to the time display to set the trigger time. Click OK to return to the Energy Saver pane.

Some of the settings can toggle events that control Lion's sleep mode, including a network connection by the network administrator (Wake for Network Access). If you want the display to dim before your Mac goes to sleep, enable the Automatically Reduce Brightness before Display Goes to Sleep check box. You can also set Mac OS X to restart automatically after a power failure, which is a good idea if you're sharing music or files with others. By default, the Battery Status icon is shown in the Finder menu bar — however, you can click the Show Battery Status in the Menu Bar check box to deselect it and hide the Battery Status icon if desired.

Mac laptop owners can set two separate Energy Saver configurations by clicking one of the two tabs at the top of the pane:

✦ **Battery Power:** Applies when their MacBook is running on battery power)

✦ **Power Adapter:** Kicks in when the laptop is connected to an AC outlet

Your MacBook will automatically switch to the proper configuration when you plug or unplug your laptop.

Keyboard preferences

The Keyboard group is shown in Figure 3-14.

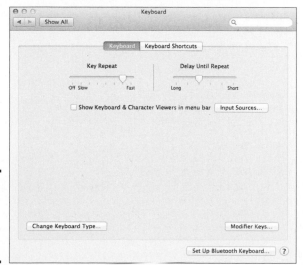

Figure 3-14:
The Keyboard preferences pane.

The two tabs include

- ✦ **Keyboard:** Move the Key Repeat Rate slider to alter the rate at which a keystroke repeats. You can also adjust the Delay until Repeat slider to alter how long a key must be held down before it repeats. You can also set up a wireless Bluetooth keyboard from this pane.

   MacBook owners can set the F1–F12 keys as standard function keys within applications by enabling the Use All F1, F2, Etc. Keys as Standard Function Keys check box. If you enable this feature, you have to hold down the Function (or Fn) key while pressing the F1 through F12 keys to use the regular hardware keys.

   If you have a MacBook Pro, you can choose to turn the ambient keyboard lighting on and off from this pane, or turn off keyboard lighting after an inactivity delay that you set.

- ✦ **Keyboard Shortcuts:** If you're a power user who appreciates the lure of the keyboard shortcut, you can edit your shortcuts here.

   Looking for even more keyboard customizing possibilities? Select the All Controls radio button on the Keyboard Shortcuts pane to see additional keys to use.

Mouse preferences

Figure 3-15 illustrates the Mouse preferences pane.

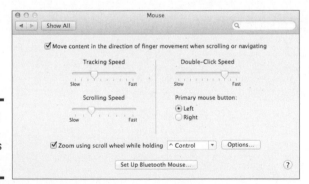

Figure 3-15: The Mouse preferences pane.

The contents of this pane depend on whether your MacBook has a USB or wireless Bluetooth mouse installed. If you haven't installed a mouse yet, you see a Waiting screen that leads you through the installation process. After you add a mouse, trackball, or other pointing device to your system, you see the settings shown in Figure 3-15.

✦ **Mouse:** Drag the Tracking Speed slider to determine how fast the mouse tracks across your Desktop. You can also drag the Double-Click Speed slider to determine how fast you must click your mouse to cause a double-click. Drag the Scrolling Speed slider to specify the rate at which the contents of windows will scroll. Lefties might want to change the primary mouse button for aftermarket pointing devices. You can also zoom the display with your Mighty Mouse scroll ball while holding down the key of your choice — a great option for image editing. To install a wireless Bluetooth mouse from this pane, click the Set Up Bluetooth Mouse button, which runs the Bluetooth device Set Up assistant.

✦ **(Optional) Bluetooth:** If you're using a wireless Bluetooth mouse or keyboard, you can check the battery level on these devices from this pane. You can also specify whether your Bluetooth keyboard or mouse wakes your Mac from sleep mode. If you don't have a Bluetooth keyboard or mouse, this tab doesn't appear.

Trackpad preferences

Figure 3-16 illustrates the Trackpad preferences pane.

Figure 3-16: The Trackpad preferences pane.

This pane allows the elite MacBook crowd to customize their pointing contraption. Note that the settings you see here depend on the specific type of trackpad you're using, so don't worry if your TrackPad preferences pane looks different. Each pane allows you to turn a gesture on or off with the corresponding check box, so you can disable those gestures you don't use to prevent spurious actions.

Due to differences in the actual trackpad hardware, older MacBook models that are upgraded to Lion may not support the Multi-Touch gestures available on newer models.

It pays to watch the neat animated preview pane shown in Figure 3-16, since it ably demonstrates both the gesture for the selected setting and the resulting action performed by your MacBook.

On the Point & Click pane, you can configure a single tap on the trackpad as a click. Click the down arrow next to the Secondary Click item to configure the two-finger secondary click action. (I think I'm going a bit click-crazy.) Your MacBook can recognize two separate three-finger gestures as well — *Look Up* and *Drag*. At the bottom of the pane, the Tracking Speed slider allows you to fine-tune the movement speed of your cursor.

On the Scroll & Zoom pane, you can set your MacBook's trackpad for *scrolling*, *zooming* and *rotating* using two fingers. (I imagine all three will someday become Olympic events.)

On the More Gestures pane, you'll find the settings for *swiping* (both between pages using two fingers and between entire applications in full-screen mode using three fingers), activating Mission Control, Spaces, and Launchpad, and displaying the desktop.

Print & Scan preferences

Figure 3-17 illustrates the Print & Scan preferences, where Apple recognizes the ascendancy of multifunction printers with scanning and faxing features built-in.

Figure 3-17: Configure faxing, scanning and printing with these settings.

Click the Options & Supplies button to configure the selected printer's features, and click the Open Print Queue button to display the Print Queue window (no great shockers there). To add a new printer, scanner or fax connection, click the Add button, which bears a plus sign. Lion launches the Browser. You can read more about printer, scanner and fax setup in Book VIII, Chapter 4.

The other settings here are

✦ **Share This Printer/Fax/Scanner on the Network:** Click this check box to share the selected device with other computers on your network. To specify who can use your shared device, click the Set Permissions button. System Preferences switches to the Sharing pane, where you can add or remove users from the permission list. (Note that there are separate Printer Sharing and Scanner Sharing services. Sharing a fax device is configured through the Printer Sharing service.)

✦ **Default Printer:** Click this pop-up menu to select the installed printer that acts as the default printer throughout your system. If you choose Last Printer Used, Mac OS X uses the printer that received the last print job.

✦ **Default Paper Size:** Will that be US Letter or Tabloid? Click this pop-up menu to specify the default paper size for future print jobs.

If you've added a fax entry to the list, click the entry to set up the fax send/receive functions built into Lion. To receive faxes on your MacBook, you must first set up a fax connection; then, click the Receive Options button and select the Receive Faxes on This Computer check box.

After faxing is turned on, you can configure the other settings from the Print & Scan pane and the Receive Options sheet. These settings include

✦ **Fax Number:** Enter the phone number that others call to reach your MacBook.

✦ **When a Fax Arrives:** You can determine how many times the phone rings before your laptop's external modem answers the incoming call. By default, Mac OS X saves the incoming fax to your Shared Faxes folder, but you can change that location, or you can choose to print the incoming fax on the printer that you specify. Heck, if you like, you can send your fax to both destinations (a disk folder and a printer) or even mail the fax to the e-mail address you specify.

If you send and receive a large number of faxes, make sure you enable the Show Fax Status in Menu Bar check box.

Book II
Chapter 3

Delving Under the Hood with System Preferences

You can also allow other computer users on your local network to send faxes through your MacBook. Enable the Share This Fax on the Network check box, and your laptop's external fax modem appears when the other users add a fax connection.

Sound preferences

The Sound group is shown in Figure 3-18. To set the overall system audio volume, drag the Output Volume slider. To mute all sound from your MacBook, select the Mute check box. I recommend that you select the Show Volume in Menu Bar check box, which displays a convenient volume slider menu bar icon.

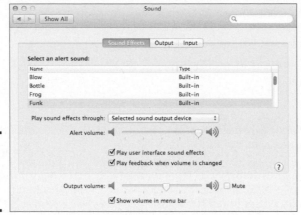

Figure 3-18: The Sound preferences pane.

The three tabs here are

✦ **Sound Effects:** From this pane, you can choose the system alert sound and the volume for alerts. You can also choose to mute application and Finder menu sound effects, as well as toggle the sample sound effect when the volume keys are pressed on your MacBook's keyboard (or from the Volume slider).

✦ **Output:** Use these settings to choose which audio controller your MacBook uses for playing sound. Unless you've installed additional audio hardware, this remains set to Built-in Audio or Internal Speakers. You can adjust the balance between the left and right channels for the selected output controller.

✦ **Input:** These settings allow you to specify an input source. Unless your MacBook includes a Line In input source, leave this set to your Internal Microphone. Drag the Input Volume slider to increase or decrease the input signal volume; the input level display provides you with real-time sound levels. If your MacBook is in a location with a large amount of background noise, click the Use Ambient Noise Reduction check box to improve the quality of your audio input.

Sharing the Joy: Internet & Wireless

Your Internet & Wireless connections are controlled from the settings in this category.

iCloud preferences

Lion's new iCloud Preference pane allows you to specify which types of data will be automatically pushed to your MacBook and iOS devices. If you haven't created an iCloud account yet — or if you signed out of an existing account earlier — System Preferences will prompt you to enter your Apple ID and password. Click Sign In to display the contents of the iCloud pane.

The check boxes for each category are

✦ **Mail & Notes:** Synchronizes your Mail messages and Notes between devices.

✦ **Contacts:** Enable this check box to push your Address Book contacts.

✦ **Calendars:** Pushes your iCal calendars to your iOS devices.

✦ **Bookmarks:** Synchronizes your Safari bookmarks.

✦ **Photo Stream:** Pushes the latest photos and video clips you've added in iPhoto to other devices, and updates your iPhoto library with photos and video clips pushed from your iOS devices.

✦ **Documents & Data:** Enable this check box to automatically synchronize the documents you create and your personal settings between your MacBook and other iOS devices.

✦ **Back to My Mac:** Controls file and screen sharing across all the Macs sharing this iCloud account. Back to My Mac must be enabled on all computers that will use this feature.

✦ **Find My Mac:** Enable this check box and you can locate your MacBook from a Web browser or your iOS device; also, you can choose to remotely lock your laptop — or even *wipe your MacBook's hard drive completely* to prevent someone from stealing your data!

Locking or wiping your MacBook remotely will prevent it from being located in the future. These are dire steps indeed!

To display the storage currently being used by your Mail, Backups, and Documents, click the Manage button at the lower-right corner of the pane. Apple provides each iCloud account 5GB of space for free, but you can also elect to buy additional storage from this sheet.

**Book II
Chapter 3**

Delving Under the
Hood with System
Preferences

MobileMe preferences

The MobileMe group is illustrated in Figure 3-19.

At the time of this writing, Apple is not accepting any new subscribers to MobileMe, and the company has announced that the MobileMe service is being discontinued in June of 2012.

Figure 3-19: Your MobileMe account is controlled and configured using these settings.

The four tabs are

✦ **Account:** In the MobileMe Member Name and the Password text boxes, respectively, type your MobileMe member name and password to display the Account tab. If you want to subscribe, click the Learn More button to launch your Web browser and you're whisked to the MobileMe sign-up page. For more information about joining Apple's MobileMe service, see Book VI, Chapter 4.

✦ **Sync:** If you want to synchronize your MacBook (or multiple Macintosh computers) with the personal information and data stored online in your MobileMe account, select the Synchronize with MobileMe check box and click the pop-up menu to specify manual or automatic synchronization. (To manually sync, click Sync Now.) You can also specify which categories of data you want to sync. Naturally, the fewer categories you choose, the less time it takes to sync. To register a computer so that you can sync with it, click the Advanced button and then click Register Computer. Lion can display your Sync status in the Finder menu bar.

✦ **iDisk:** This pane displays your current iDisk usage and allows you to subscribe for additional space with the Upgrade button. You can set your access privileges for your public folder by selecting or deselecting the Allow Others to Write Files in Your Public Folder check box, and you can add a password that others have to enter before they can access your public folder. For a complete description of iDisk, see Book VI, Chapter 4.

I recommend that you click the iDisk Sync Start button on the iDisk tab to enable the Lion iDisk syncing function (which creates a local copy of your iDisk on your MacBook). Select the Update Automatically option; this option allows iDisk to run much faster because Mac OS X can read and write by using your local iDisk copy on your hard drive. Your MacBook regularly synchronizes the data on your local hard drive across the Internet with the iDisk on the Apple server. To make sure that you're always using the most recent copy of a file on your iDisk, select the Always Keep the Most Recent Version of a File check box.

✦ **Back to My Mac:** From this list, you can control file and screen sharing across all the computers you use with your MobileMe account. To begin using the Back to My Mac features, click the Start button. (Remember, you'll have to turn on Back to My Mac on all computers that will use this service.)

Mail, Contacts & Calendars preferences

The Mail, Contacts & Calendars group is shown in Figure 3-20.

**Book II
Chapter 3**

**Delving Under the
Hood with System
Preferences**

Figure 3-20:
Keep track
of all your
accounts
from this
pane.

This pane is a central location for adding, editing, and configuring your Internet, iCloud, and local network accounts for e-mail, Address Book contacts, and calendar information. Note that accounts appear automatically in this pane when you create them in many applications. For example, creating a mail account within Apple Mail also automatically adds that account to the list in the Mail, Contacts & Calendars pane.

To add a new account, click the New Account button and then click the account type in the list at the right side of the pane. System Preferences displays a custom assistant that will lead you through the setup process for that specific account.

After you've configured an account, it appears in the list at the left. Click an account in the list and you can specify whether that account will be used with Apple Mail, iCal, FaceTime, and iChat. You can also change account information by clicking in the desired field and typing the new information, or delete the selected account entirely by clicking the Delete Account button.

Network preferences

The Network group is shown in Figure 3-21.

Figure 3-21:
The Network pane, showing the Wi-Fi status information.

You can choose an existing Location by clicking the Location pop-up menu at the top of the dialog, or you can create and edit your Locations by choosing Edit Locations from this pop-up menu. (Automatic is the default, and it does a pretty good job of figuring out what settings you need.) As I mention in Book II, Chapter 3, creating Locations makes it easy to completely recon-figure your Network preferences when you connect your computer to other networks — for example, when you take your laptop to a branch office. You can also set up Locations to accommodate different ISP dial-up telephone numbers in different towns.

If you need to create a new Location that's very similar to an existing Location, click the Location pop-up menu and choose Edit Locations. Then select the Location that you want to copy, click the Action button (bearing the gear symbol), and choose Duplicate Location from the pop-up menu. The new Location that you create contains all the same settings (without sev-eral minutes of retyping), so you can easily edit it and make minor changes quickly.

You can choose locations from the Apple menu — a useful trick for laptop road warriors.

Ethernet network settings

When you select Ethernet from the list of connection types, the Status pane shows your connection information. Because most networks have a DHCP server to provide automatic settings, you probably don't have to change anything; Lion does a good job at making introductions automatic between your MacBook and both a local network and the Internet.

Notice the very attractive Assist Me . . . button at the bottom of the Network pane? It's there for a very good reason: Click it, and Lion launches a network connection and troubleshooting assistant that guides you step-by-step. If your ISP doesn't provide you with instructions on setting up your Internet connection — or that oh-so-smart Mr. Network Administrator is too busy to help connect your MacBook to your office network — use both this book and the network assistant to do the job yourself!

Need to make manual changes to your network settings? Click the Advanced button (it's like opening the hood on your car). The tabs on the Advanced sheet include

+ **TCP/IP:** These settings are provided either automatically (by using Dynamic Host Configuration Protocol [DHCP]) or manually (by using settings provided by your network administrator). For more details on TCP/IP settings, see Book VII, Chapter 1.

+ **DNS:** The settings that you enter here specify the DNS servers and search domains used by your ISP. Typically, any changes you make here are requested by your ISP or your network administrator. Click the Add

**Book II
Chapter 3**

**Delving Under the
Hood with System
Preferences**

buttons (with the plus signs) to add a new DNS server address or search domain.

✦ **WINS:** Dating back a few years, WINS is a name server required for computers running NetBIOS (practically dinosaurs in the computer timeline), and likely only those computers running a version of Windows older than Windows 2000. If that sounds like gobbledygook to you, you need to enter something on this tab only if instructed to do so by your network administrator.

✦ **802.1X:** This tab controls which wireless networking security protocols that you may need to connect to a third-party wireless base station or access point. Click the Enable Automatic Connection check box when making a wireless connection with an Apple Airport Extreme base station or Time Capsule backup unit.

✦ **Proxies:** Network proxy servers are used as part of a firewall configuration to help keep your network secure, but in most cases, changing them can cause you to lose Internet functionality if you enter the wrong settings.

Most folks using a telephone modem, cable modem, or digital subscriber line (DSL) connection should leave these settings alone. Enable and change these settings only at the request of your network administrator, who should supply you the location of a PAC file to automate the process.

If you've enabled your Mac OS X firewall and you use FTP to transfer files, enable the Passive FTP Mode check box on the Proxies pane. I recommend that you enable this setting to allow downloading from some Web pages as well.

✦ **Hardware:** From this pane, you can configure the settings for your Ethernet network interface card. I *strongly* recommend that you leave the Configure pop-up menu set to Automatically (unless specifically told to set things manually by your system administrator or that nice person from Apple tech support).

Modem network settings

When you select Modem from the list of connection types, you can enter the telephone number, account name, and password provided by your ISP. In most cases, that's all the information you need. But if you need to make a manual change, click the Advanced button to display these tabs:

✦ **Modem:** Click the Modem pop-up menu and choose the brand and model of your external modem.

I strongly recommend that you enable the Enable Error Correction and Compression in Modem check box; also select Wait for Dial Tone before

Dialing from the Dial Mode pop-up menu. These settings provide you with the best performance and the fastest speeds.

You can also select tone or pulse dialing and whether you want to hear the two modems conversing. (If the caterwauling bothers you, turn off the Sound option.)

✦ **DNS:** These settings are the same as those I cover earlier, in the section "Ethernet network settings."

✦ **WINS:** Again, you're likely to never need these WINS settings, so make changes on this tab only if instructed to do so by your network administrator.

✦ **Proxies:** Some ISPs use proxy servers for their dial-up accounts to maintain security, but changing these settings willy-nilly is inviting disaster. Leave them disabled unless given specific instructions on what to set by your ISP.

✦ **PPP:** These settings are used for a Point-to-Point Protocol connection over a telephone modem. Again, your ISP provides you with the right values to enter here.

If you're concerned about who's using your Internet connection — or you want to add an extra layer of security when you dial out — select the Prompt for Password after Dialing check box on the PPP tab, and Mac OS X prompts you each time for your Internet account password.

I recommend that you select the Show Modem Status in Menu Bar check box on the Modem status pane, which gives you a visual reference on your connection status.

FireWire and Wi-Fi network settings

The FireWire and AirPort settings on the Advanced sheet are the same as those for Ethernet that I cover earlier in this chapter. However, four settings are on the Wi-Fi status pane that I cover here:

✦ **Network Name:** Lion handles wireless connections automatically in most cases; if possible, it connects to the last wireless network you joined. If that network isn't available or there are others to choose from, Lion displays a dialog asking you which available network you want to join. If you want to join only one or more preferred networks (for security or convenience reasons), click the Advanced button and click the Add button (which bears a plus sign) to enter the wireless network name and password.

✦ **Ask to Join New Networks:** Lion will always automatically join known networks in range. A *known network* is a network you've connected

Book II
Chapter 3

Delving Under the
Hood with System
Preferences

to in the past. This check box, however, controls what happens if no networks in range are known; if the check is disabled, you must click the Wi-Fi icon in the Finder menu bar and select a network to use. If the check box is enabled, Lion automatically prompts you for confirmation before attempting to join a new network.

✦ **Turn Wi-Fi Off:** Okay, here's the honest truth — wireless networking is a significant drain on a laptop battery! If you're sure you're not going to use your MacBook's wireless network hardware in the near future, you can click this button to activate and deactivate your laptop's network hardware. (Alternatively, just click the Wi-Fi icon in the Finder Menu Bar and choose Turn Wi-Fi Off.) Turn off Wi-Fi if you don't need it, and your laptop will thank you. (Just turn it back on using this same button when you need it or use the Wi-Fi status menu in the Finder menu bar.)

✦ **Show Wi-Fi Status in Menu Bar:** Hey, speaking of the AirPort Status Menu in the Finder Menu Bar . . . select this check box to display it! You can immediately see the relative signal strength of your connection, switch among available wireless networks, and turn off your AirPort hardware to conserve your battery power (without digging deeply into System Preferences).

Bluetooth preferences

The Bluetooth group is shown in Figure 3-22.

Figure 3-22:
The
Bluetooth
pane.

The choices on this pane include

✦ **Device listing:** From this pane, you can opt to allow other Bluetooth devices to discover your MacBook (with the Discoverable check box). All recognized Bluetooth devices in range appear in the list, and you can configure or disconnect them. You can also set up a new Bluetooth device from here by clicking the Set Up New Device button. Also, if you like, Lion can display a Bluetooth status menu in the Finder menu bar.

MacBook owners who want to conserve power can disable Bluetooth entirely. Just click the On check box to disable it and you save a significant amount of battery time!

✦ **Advanced sheet:** Click the Advanced button to display another group of settings. The Open Bluetooth Setup Assistant check box determines whether Lion automatically launches the Bluetooth Setup Assistant when no Bluetooth devices are recognized. If you're using a Bluetooth mouse and keyboard, you can wake your MacBook using these devices. You can set Lion to alert you if an audio request is received from a Bluetooth device, and you can share an Internet connection with connected devices.

You can also edit your Bluetooth Serial Ports from the Advanced sheet, allowing you to use a Bluetooth connection as a virtual serial port. You can add or remove serial services from the Serial Port sheet as well.

Sharing preferences

Figure 3-23 illustrates the Sharing preferences.

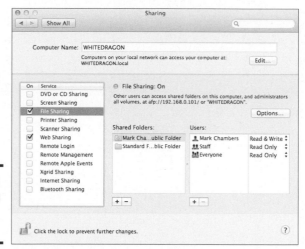

Figure 3-23:
The Sharing preference settings.

Book II
Chapter 3

Delving Under the
Hood with System
Preferences

Click the Edit button to change the default network name assigned to your MacBook during the installation process. Your current network name is listed in the Computer Name text field.

Each entry in the services list controls a specific type of sharing, including DVD or CD Sharing, File Sharing (with other Macs and PCs running Windows), Web Sharing, Screen Sharing, Remote Login, Remote Management (using Apple Remote Desktop), Remote Apple Events, Xgrid Sharing, Internet Sharing, Bluetooth Sharing, Scanner Sharing, and Printer Sharing. To turn on any of these services, select the On check box for that service. To turn off a service, click the corresponding On check box to deselect it.

From a security standpoint, I highly recommend that you enable only those services that you actually use. Each service you enable automatically opens your Lion firewall for that service. A Mark's Maxim to remember:

Poking too many holes in your firewall is *not* A Good Thing.

When you click one of the services in the list, the right side of the Sharing pane changes to display the settings you can specify for that particular service. Note that some services may be disabled, depending on the hardware connected to or installed in your MacBook.

Tweaking the System

The last section of the System Preferences window covers system-wide settings that affect all users and the overall operation of Mac OS X.

Date and time preferences

Click the System Preferences Date & Time icon to display the settings that you see in Figure 3-24.

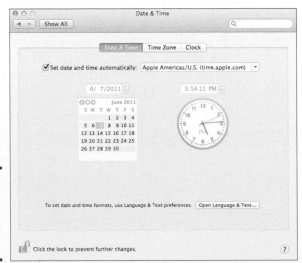

Figure 3-24:
The Date
& Time
preferences
panel.

The three tabs here are

+ **Date & Time:** To set the current date, click the date within the mini-calendar; to set the system time, click in the field above the clock and type the current time.

   You can't set these values manually if you use a network time server. To automatically set your MacBook's system time and date from a network time server, select the Set Date & Time Automatically check box and then choose a server from the pop-up menu that corresponds to your location. (Of course, you need an Internet connection to use a network time server.)

+ **Time Zone:** Click your approximate location on the world map to choose a time zone or click the Closest City pop-up menu and choose the city that's closest to you (and shares your same time zone). Alternatively, select the Set Time Zone Automatically Using Current Location check box — a real convenience for MacBook owners who are constantly traveling.

+ **Clock:** If you select the Show the Date and Time in Menu Bar check box, you can choose to view the time in text or icon format. You can also optionally display seconds, the date, AM/PM, and the day of the week; have the time separator characters flash; or use a clock based on 24 hours.

   Personally, I get a big kick out of my MacBook announcing the time on the hour . . . plus, it helps pull me back into the real world. (You have to eat sooner or later.) Anyway, if you'd like this helpful reminder as well, select the Announce the Time check box on the Clock pane, and click the pop-up menu to select an hour, half-hour, or quarter-hour announcement.

Parental Controls preferences

Click a standard level user account in the list to enable or configure Parental Controls for that user. Figure 3-25 shows the Parental Controls settings. (Parental Controls are disabled for administrator accounts and the Guest account.)

I discuss the Parental Control settings in detail in Chapter 5 of Book III. You can use these settings to restrict a user's access to certain applications, or limit Mail and iChat communications to specific individuals. An administrator can also switch a user account to the Simple Finder, making Lion much easier to navigate (and limiting the amount of damage a mischievous or malicious user can inflict on your system).

You can create a new, managed account directly from the Parental Controls pane by clicking the Add button (which bears a plus sign) at the bottom of the account list. This saves you a trip to the Users & Groups pane!

Book II
Chapter 3

Delving Under the Hood with System Preferences

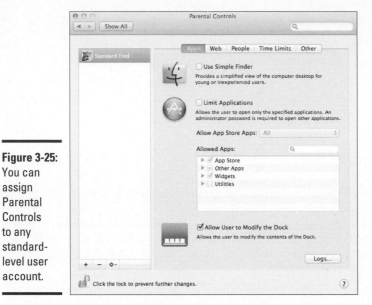

Figure 3-25:
You can
assign
Parental
Controls
to any
standard-
level user
account.

Software Update preferences

The Software Update settings are shown in Figure 3-26. (Oh, and don't forget
that you need an active Internet connection.)

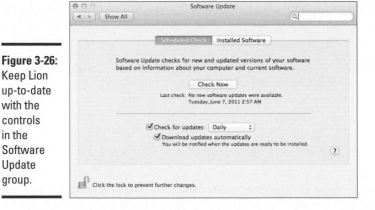

Figure 3-26:
Keep Lion
up-to-date
with the
controls
in the
Software
Update
group.

The two tabs here are

✦ **Scheduled Check:** I recommend selecting the Check for Updates check
box; I also recommend that you choose Daily or Weekly from the
pop-up menu. (You can also elect to download critical updates in the

background automatically while you continue working.) To check immediately, click the Check Now button.

✦ **Installed Software:** Click this tab to display a list of the applications you've installed and the updates you've already applied to Mac OS X and Apple applications.

Speech preferences

Figure 3-27 illustrates the Speech settings. For a discussion of how these settings are used, visit Book IX, Chapter 3.

Figure 3-27: Lion includes highly configurable Speech features.

The two tabs here are

✦ **Speech Recognition:** This pane has two tabs of its own: Settings and Commands. With Speakable Items toggled on, you can control Lion with spoken commands.

  • *Settings tab:* If you have more than one microphone, you can select which one you want to use as well as set the input volume with the Calibrate button. You can change the Listening key (Esc by default) and specify whether your MacBook should listen only while the key is pressed or whether the Listening Key toggles listening on and off. You can also change the name of your computer (using the Keyword box) and whether that name is required before a command. From the Play This Sound pop-up menu, you can indicate what sound effect Mac OS X plays when it recognizes a speech command. (Optionally, Lion can confirm the command by speaking it if you enable the Speak Command Acknowledgement check box.)

- *Commands tab:* Here, you can select which types of commands are available as well as whether exact wording of command names is required. Click the self-named button to open the Speakable Items Folder from this pane. Read more about these settings in Book IX, Chapter 3.

✦ **Text to Speech:** Here's a fun pane. Click a voice from the System Voice pop-up menu, and Mac OS X uses that voice to speak to you from dialogs and applications. You can set the Speaking Rate (from Slow to Fast) and play a sample by clicking the Play button. (Try Zarvox, Bubbles, and Pipe Organ.)

The Announce When Alerts are Displayed feature actually speaks the text within alert dialogs; to configure spoken alerts, click the Set Alert Options button. You can optionally add a phrase before the text, which you can choose from the Phrase pop-up menu. To add a phrase to the list, like *Don't Panic!,* choose Edit Phrase List from the list. Move the Delay slider to specify how much time your Mac waits before reading the dialog to you.

You can also optionally announce when an application wants your attention, and Lion can speak the text that's currently selected within an application when you press a key that you specify.

This pane also provides a couple of convenient shortcut buttons that take you to other "speech centers" within System Preferences — specifically, the Date & Time and Universal Access panes.

Startup Disk preferences

Figure 3-28 illustrates the Startup Disk settings.

Figure 3-28:
The Startup Disk pane within System Preferences.

To select a startup disk, click the desired startup drive from the scrolling icon list.

Mac OS X displays the version numbers of each system and the physical drives where each system resides. Select the Network Startup icon if you want to boot from a System folder on your local network; typically, such a folder is created by your network administrator. If you've set up a Windows partition on your hard drive using Boot Camp, the folder appears with a Windows logo.

If you're planning on rebooting with an external Universal Serial Bus (USB), Thunderbolt or FireWire startup disk, that disk must be connected already, powered on, and recognized by the system before you display these settings.

Click Target Disk Mode to restart your MacBook as a FireWire or Thunderbolt external hard drive connected to another computer. (This comes in especially handy when you're upgrading to a new Mac and you need to move files between the two computers. I've also used it when the video card in one of my Macs decided to stop working. This allowed me to make an updated backup copy of the ailing Mac's hard drive before I sent it off for repair.) You can also restart your MacBook and hold down the T key to invoke Target Disk Mode.

After you click a disk to select it, click the Restart button. Mac OS X confirms your choice, and your MacBook reboots.

Time Machine preferences

The Preferences pane shown in Figure 3-29 controls the automatic backups performed by Lion's Time Machine feature.

Figure 3-29: Configure your backups with these Time Machine settings.

To enable Time Machine, click the On toggle switch and then select a disk that will hold your Time Machine backup data on the sheet that appears; click Use for Backup to confirm your choice. If you have an external Time Capsule wireless unit, click Set Up Time Capsule.

By default, Time Machine backs up all the hard drives on your system; however, you may not need to back up some hard drives or folders on your MacBook. To save time and hard drive space, Time Machine allows you to exclude specific drives and folders from the backup process. Click Options and then click the Add button (with the plus sign) to select the drives or folders you want to exclude, and they'll appear in the Do Not Back Up list.

To remove an exclusion, select it in the list and click the Delete button (with the minus sign). Note the Estimated Size of Full Backup figure increases, and Time Machine adds the item you deleted from the list to the next backup.

By default, Lion warns you when deleting older backup files, but you can turn this off from the Options sheet as well.

You can elect to back up your MacBook immediately by clicking the Time Machine icon in the Finder menu bar and choosing Back Up Now.

Users & Groups preferences

The Users & Groups pane is illustrated in Figure 3-30.

Figure 3-30: Configuring accounts is easy from System Preferences.

Each user on your system has an entry in this list. The panes and settings here change, depending on the access level of the selected account. They can include

✦ **Password pane:** Click in these text fields to enter or edit the account name, password, and password hint for the selected user.

Click the Address Book Card Open button to edit the card that you mark in the Address Book as My Card. Mac OS X launches the Address Book, and you can edit your card to your heart's content. (For the complete scoop on the Mac OS X Address Book, see Book I, Chapter 6.)

You can change the corresponding Apple ID for each user account from this pane as well. If you're sharing your Mac with a number of other users, each person can set up his or her own Apple ID account!

If you have administrator access, you can enable Parental Controls for the selected user account or open the Parental Controls pane. (You'll find more on Parental Controls in Chapter 5 of Book II.)

✦ **Picture well:** From the *Picture well* — the square area to the right of the Account list — you can choose one of the thumbnail images provided by Apple to represent you, or drag a photo in from iPhoto. Click the well to display the thumbnails. Click Edit Picture to drag a new image from the Finder or take a video snapshot using your Mac's iSight camera.

✦ **Login Items pane:** The applications and documents that you add to this list launch automatically each time that the current user logs in to Mac OS X. To add an application or document, click the Add button (which carries a plus sign), navigate to the desired item and select it, and then click the Add button. (Alternatively, you can simply drag an item from a Finder window into the Login Items list.) To remove an application from the list, click to select it and then click the Remove button (which has a minus sign). Each application can be launched in a *hidden state* — its window doesn't appear on the Desktop. To toggle an item as hidden or visible, enable the Hide check box next to the desired application. The order that Login Items are launched can be changed by dragging entries in the list into the desired sequence.

Note that a user must be logged in to view and change the items on the Login Items pane — even an Administrator-level user can't access another user account's Login items!

You can even set up Login Items directly from the Dock! Right-click the desired Dock icon to display the Options pop-up menu and then click Open at Login.

✦ **Login Options pane:** Look for the button with the little house icon at the lower left. Click it to set a number of global options that control how users log in. For example, you can choose to display either a Name and Password field on the Login screen (which means that the user must actually type in the correct username) or a list of users, from which a person can select a user ID. (If security is a consideration, use the Name and Password option.) You can also add VoiceOver spoken interface support at the Login screen, making it easier for physically challenged users to log in to this Mac.

If you choose, you can log in automatically as the selected user by clicking the Automatically Login <*Username*> pop-up menu and choosing your account. (**Definitely** not a secure feature — especially for MacBook owners — but convenient as all get-out.)

The Login Options pane also allows you to enable or disable Fast User Switching (which I discuss in Book II, Chapter 5), and you can prevent anyone from restarting or shutting down the Mac from the Login screen by disabling the Show the Sleep, Restart, and Shut Down Buttons check box.

Chapter 4: You Mean Others Can Use My Mac, Too?

In This Chapter

↙ **Understanding how multiuser systems work**

↙ **Configuring login settings**

↙ **Changing the appearance of the login screen**

↙ **Tightening security during login**

↙ **Starting applications automatically when you log in**

*W*hether you're setting up Mac OS X for use in a public library or simply allowing your 12-year-old to use your Mac in your home office, configuring Lion for multiple users is a simple task. However, you must also consider the possible downsides of a mismanaged multiuser system: files and folders being shared that you didn't want in the public domain, users logging in as one another, and the very real possibility of accidental file deletion (and worse).

Therefore, in this chapter, I show you how to take those first steps before you open Pandora's Box — setting login options, configuring the personal account that you created when you first installed the operating system, and protecting your stuff. (Network administrators call this security check-up *locking things down*. Better start using the terminology now, even before you buy your suspenders and pocket protector.)

How Multiuser Works on Mac OS X

When you create multiple users in Mac OS X, each person who uses your Macintosh — hence the term *user* — has a separate account (much like an account that you might open at a bank). Mac OS X creates a Home folder for each user and saves that user's preferences independently from those of other users. When you log in to Mac OS X, you provide a username and a password, which identify you. The username/password combination tells Mac OS X which user has logged in — and therefore which preferences and Home folder to use.

Each account also carries a specific level, which determines how much control the user has over Mac OS X and the computer itself. Without an account with the proper access level, for example, a user might not be able to display many of the panes in System Preferences.

The three most common account levels are

✦ **Root:** Also called *System Administrator,* this uber-account can change *anything* within Mac OS X — and that's usually A *Very* Bad Thing, so it's actually disabled as a default. (This alone should tell you that the Root account shouldn't be toyed with.) For instance, the Root account can seriously screw up the UNIX subsystem within Mac OS X, or a Root user can delete files within the Mac OS X System Folder.

Enable the System Administrator account and use it only if told to do so by an Apple technical support technician.

✦ **Administrator:** (Or *admin* for short.) This is the account level that you're assigned when you install Mac OS X. The administrator account should *not* be confused with the System Administrator account!

It's perfectly okay for you or anyone you assign to use an administrator account. An administrator can install applications anywhere on the system, create/edit/delete user accounts, and make changes to all the settings in System Preferences. However, an administrator can't move or delete items from any other user's Home folder, and administrators are barred from modifying or deleting files in the Mac OS X System Folder. (There are UNIX commands you can use from the Terminal application that can work around these restrictions. However, I agree with Apple's thinking — these locations on your system are off-limits for good reason.)

A typical multiuser Mac OS X computer has only one administrator — like a teacher in a classroom — but technically, you can create as many administrator accounts as you like. If you do need to give someone else this access level, assign it only to a competent, experienced user whom you trust.

✦ **Standard:** A standard user account is the default in Mac OS X. Standard users can install software and save documents only in their Home folders and the Shared folder (which resides in the Users folder), and they can change only certain settings in System Preferences. Thus, they can do little damage to the system as a whole. For example, each of the students in a classroom should be given a standard-level account for the Mac OS X system that they share.

If Parental Controls are applied to a standard account, it becomes a *managed* account, allowing you to fine-tune what a standard account user can do. (I discuss Parental Controls at length in Book II, Chapter 5.)

Chapter 5 of this minibook covers the entire process of creating and editing a user account.

Working with the Guest account

The *Guest* account is a convenient method of granting someone temporary access to your Mac — in fact, your guest doesn't even need a password to log in! Your Guest account has all the attributes of a standard account, so the visitor has little chance of accidentally (or purposefully) damaging your system. However, after the guest user logs out, the Guest account is "flushed" and all the data and files that person created using the account are deleted automatically. (This allows the next guest to start with a clean slate.)

By default, the Guest account is disabled. To turn on this feature, open System Preferences,

click Users & Groups, and then click the Guest User entry in the list. (You may have to click the Lock icon in the lower-left corner of the Users & Groups pane and provide your admin password before you can continue.) Click the Allow Guests to Log In to This Computer check box to enable it.

Oh, and don't forget that you can enable specific Parental Controls for the Guest account, just as you can for any other account. That should come in handy if your daughter has a slumber party coming up this weekend . . .

Configuring Your Login Screen

Take a look at the changes you can make to the login process. First, Mac OS X provides two methods of displaying the login screen, as well as one automatic method that doesn't display the login screen at all:

✦ **Logging in with a list:** To log in, click your account username in the list, and the login screen displays the password prompt. Type your password — Mac OS X displays bullet characters to ensure security — and press Return (or click the Log In button).

✦ **Logging in with username and password:** Type your account username in the Name field and press Tab. Then type your password and press Return (or click the Log In button).

✦ **Automatic Login:** With Automatic Login set, Mac OS X automatically logs in the specified account when you reboot. In effect, you never see the login screen unless you click Log Out from the Apple menu, or you've enabled fast user switching. (Naturally, this is an attractive option to use if your computer is in a secure location — such as your office — and you'll be the only one using your Mac.)

To specify which type of login screen you see — if you see one at all — head to System Preferences, click Users & Groups, and then click the Login Options button.

✦ To set Automatic Login, display the Login Options settings, and click the Automatic Login pop-up menu. Choose the account that automatically logs in from the list. When Mac OS X displays the Password sheet that you see in Figure 4-1, type the corresponding password and then click OK.

Figure 4-1:
Configuring
Automatic
Login
from the
Accounts
panel.

Never set the Automatic Login feature to an admin-level account unless you're sure to be the only one using your Mac. If the computer is rebooted, you're opening the door for anyone to simply sashay in and wreak havoc!

✦ To determine whether Mac OS X uses a list login screen, you must again visit the Login Options settings pane (see Figure 4-2). Select the List of Users radio button for a list login screen or select the Name and Password radio button for a simple login screen where you must type your username and password.

Figure 4-2:
Will that be
a simple or
a list login
screen?

To change settings specific to your account — no matter what your access level — log in with your account, open System Preferences, and click Users & Groups. From here, you can change your account password and picture, the card marked as yours within the Address Book, the Apple ID associated with your account and whether Parental Controls are set. You can also specify the Login Items that will be launched automatically when you log in. (Peruse more information on the Address Book in Book I, Chapter 6.)

To log out of Mac OS X without restarting or shutting down the computer, choose the Apple menu and then choose Log Out or just press ⌘+Shift+Q. You see the confirmation dialog, as shown in Figure 4-3. Although Mac OS X displays the login screen after one minute, someone can still saunter up and click the Cancel button, thereby gaining access to your stuff. Therefore, make it a practice to always click the Log Out button on this screen before your hand leaves the mouse, or bypass the confirmation dialog altogether by holding down the Option key as you click Log Out from the menu!

Figure 4-3: Always click Log Out before you leave your Mac!

You can also enable *Fast User Switching* from the Login Options panel. This feature allows another user to sit down and log in while the previous user's applications are still running in the background. When you enable switching, Lion displays the currently active user's name or account icon at the right side of the Finder menu bar. Click the name, and a menu appears; click Login Window, and another user can then log in as usual. (From the Login Options pane, you can also choose to display the current user by the account's short name or the account icon.)

Even though you're playing musical chairs, the Big X remembers what's running and the state of your Desktop when you last left it. (When you decide to switch back, Lion prompts you for that account's login password for security . . . just in case, you understand.)

Locking Your Mac Down

If security is a potential problem and you still need to share a Mac between multiple users, lock things down. To protect Mac OS X from unauthorized use, take care of these potential security holes immediately:

✦ **Disable the Sleep and Shut Down buttons.** Any computer can be hacked when it's restarted or turned on, so disable the Sleep and Shut Down buttons on the login screen. (After a user has successfully logged in, Mac OS X can be shut down normally by using the menu item or the keyboard shortcuts that I cover earlier.) Open the Users & Groups pane in System Preferences, click the Login Options button, and deselect the Show the Sleep and Shut Down Buttons check box. Press ⌘+Q to quit and save your changes. (You can find more about restarting and shutting down in Book I, Chapter 2.)

✦ **Disable list logins.** With a list login, any potential hacker already knows half the information necessary to gain entry to your system — and often the password is easy to guess. Therefore, set Mac OS X to ask for the username and password on the Login screen, as I describe earlier. This way, someone has to guess both the username and the password, which is a much harder proposition.

✦ **Disable Automatic Login.** A true no-brainer. As I mention earlier in the chapter, Automatic Login is indeed very convenient. However, all someone has to do is reboot your Mac, and the machine automatically logs in one lucky user! To disable Automatic Login, display the Users & Groups pane in System Preferences and click the Login Options button. Then, click the Automatic Login pop-up menu and click the Off entry.

✦ **Disable the password hint.** By default, Mac OS X obligingly displays the password hint for an account after three unsuccessful attempts at entering a password. Where security is an issue, this is like serving a hacker a piece of apple pie. Therefore, head to System Preferences, display the Users & Groups settings, click the Login Options button, and make sure that the Show Password Hints check box is clear.

✦ **Select passwords intelligently.** Although using your mother's maiden name for a password might seem like a great idea, the best method of selecting a password is to use a completely random group of mixed letters and numbers. If you find a random password too hard to remember, at least add a number after your password, like *dietcoke1* — and no, that isn't one of my passwords. (Nice try.) My editor suggests a favorite location spelled backwards, with a number mixed in — easier to remember than a completely random sequence of characters!

TIP

For even greater security, make at least one password character upper-case, and use a number at the beginning and ending of the password. Or, do the "c001" thing and replace characters with numbers, like the zero that you insert in dietc0ke.

Starting Applications Automatically after Login

Here's one other advantage to logins: Each account can have its own selection of applications that run automatically when that user logs in. These applications are *Login Items,* and they appear as a list in the Users & Groups pane (shown in Figure 4-4). A caveat or two:

✦ **The users setting their Login Items must be logged in.** Only the user can modify his or her own Login Items.

✦ **Users must have access to System Preferences.** If the person is using a standard-level account, it must allow access to System Preferences.

Ready? Let's begin. Open System Preferences and click Users & Groups, click your account to select it, and then click Login Items (see Figure 4-4).

Book II
Chapter 4

You Mean Others
Can Use My
Mac, Too?

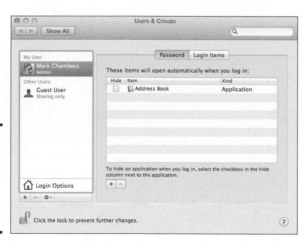

Figure 4-4:
Preparing
to launch
Address
Book every
time I log in.

Including an application in your Login Items list is easy: Click the button with the plus sign to navigate to the desired application, select it, and then click Add. (Alternatively, you can just drag items from a Finder window and drop them directly into the list.) Note that items in the list are launched in order. If something needs to run before something else, you can drag the item entries into any sequence.

To launch the application in hidden mode — which might or might not display it in the Dock, depending on the application itself — click the list entry for the desired item and enable its Hide check box.

Chapter 5: Setting Up Multiuser Accounts

In This Chapter

✓ **Adding, modifying, and deleting users**

✓ **Establishing Parental Controls**

✓ **Configuring FileVault**

✓ **Avoiding keychains**

In Chapter 4 of this minibook, I introduce you to the different Mac OS X multiuser account levels and the login process. If you're ready to share your Mac with others, you discover how to add new accounts and edit existing accounts in this chapter. Oh, and yes, I also show you how to *frag* — that's multiplayer game-speak for *delete* — accounts that you no longer need. I also demonstrate how to add optional limitations to an individual user account and how to avoid using a *keychain* (which is supposed to make it easier to store that pocketful of passwords that you've created on the Internet).

Yes, you read correctly. By all that's good and righteous, Mac OS X actually has a feature that I *don't* want you to use. Read on to find out more.

Adding, Editing, and Deleting Users

Most of the multiuser account chores you'll encounter take place in a single System Preferences pane. (Cue James Bond theme song.) The Users & Groups pane is the star of this chapter, so open System Preferences and click the Users & Groups icon.

If you haven't added any users to your system yet, the Users list should look like Figure 5-1. You should see your account, which you set up when you installed Mac OS X, set to administrator (admin) level.

TIP

You also have an entry for a *Guest* account, which anyone can use on an as-needed basis. To enable the Guest account, click the Guest entry in the list and click the Allow Guests to Log In to This Computer check box to select it. Note that any files created or settings changed by the Guest user are automatically deleted when the Guest user logs out (or you restart or reboot your Mac). If you like, you can also choose to apply Parental Controls to the Guest account — I'll discuss Parental Controls later in this chapter.

If you can't click the Guest User entry because it's grayed out, you need to *unlock* the Users & Groups pane first. Click the padlock icon in the lower left corner and type your Admin user account password, and then click Unlock. Most panes in System Preferences have this lock feature, which prevents accidental changes to your Lion settings — however, it can be frustrating the first time you encounter a locked pane!

Figure 5-1:
A typical
first look at
the Users
& Groups
pane.

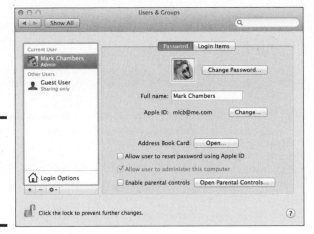

Adding a new user account

To add a new user account, follow these steps:

1. **In the Users & Groups pane in System Preferences, click the New User button at the bottom of the accounts list — which carries a plus sign — to display an empty user record sheet that you see in Figure 5-2.**

REMEMBER

   If the New User button is disabled and you can't click it, click the padlock at the bottom left of the System Preferences pane and provide your password to unlock the Users & Groups pane.

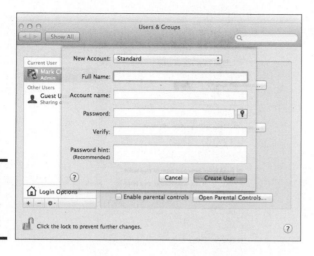

Figure 5-2:
Setting up
a new user
account.

2. **Select the access level for this user from the New Account pop-up menu.**

   By default, the user receives a standard level account. You can also choose an Administrator account, a Managed standard account with Parental Controls already enabled or a sharing-only account.

   The sharing-only account allows the user to copy or open shared files from your Mac remotely (from another computer), but that user can't directly log in to your Mac.

3. **In the Full Name text box, type the name that you want to display for this account (both in the Current User list and on the Login screen) and then press Tab to move to the next field.**

   Mac OS X automatically generates a *short name* in the Account Name field for use as your screen and Buddy name in iChat and various network applications. The short name is also the name of the folder that Mac OS X creates on the computer's hard drive for this user. You can keep the default short name or type a new one, but it must not contain any spaces. For more on iChat, jump to Book V, Chapter 3. (I'll wait for you here.)

4. **Press Tab again.**

5. **In the Password text box, type the password for the new account.**

   Click the button with the key icon next to the Password field, and Lion is happy to display the Password Assistant, complete with a suggestion. Click the Suggestion pop-up menu to see additional suggestions. You can choose the length of the password and select among several types: letters and numbers, numbers only, memorable, completely random, or even government-quality. The Assistant automatically copies the current password you're considering to the Password text box.

As always, when you enter a password or its verification, Mac OS X displays bullet characters for security.

6. **Press Tab, type the password in the Verify text box, and press Tab again.**

7. **(Optional) If you decide to use the password hint feature that I describe in Book II, Chapter 4, you can enter a short sentence or question in the Password Hint text box.**

   The hint is displayed after three unsuccessful attempts at entering the account password.

   I recommend that you *do not* *use this option.* Think about it: Any hack could type in anything three times to get your hint to pop up! If you do use this option, at least make sure that the hint is sufficiently vague!

   Press Tab to continue.

8. **Click the Create User button to finish and create the account.**

   The new account shows up in the Current User list and in the Login screen.

Editing an existing account

If you have administrator access, it's a cinch to make changes to an existing account from the Users & Groups pane in System Preferences. (Often, this is to assign a personalized account picture, so I demonstrate that here.) Follow these steps:

1. **Click the account that you want to change in the Current User list.**

   Don't forget, if the accounts in the list are disabled and you can't select one, you must unlock the Users & Groups pane. Click the lock at the bottom left of the System Preferences pane and type your password.

2. **Edit the settings that you need to change.**

3. **Click the square Picture well to specify the thumbnail image that appears in the Login list next to the account name.**

   Apple provides a number of good images in the preview collection — just click a thumbnail to select it.

4. **To add your own picture, click the Picture Well and click Edit Picture. You can drag a new image from the Finder or from the iPhoto window into the icon placeholder or click Choose to select one from an Open File dialog; then click Set.**

   Alternatively, you can click the Take a Video Snapshot button to grab a picture from your iSight or other video camera connected to your Mac. *Most* cool.

5. **After you make the changes (and you select just the right image to capture the user's personality — a more difficult task than you might think), press ⌘+Q to save them and close the System Preferences window.**

Deleting an existing account

To wipe an account from the face of the Earth, follow these steps:

1. **Click the account that you want to delete in the Current User list.**

2. **Click the Delete User button (which is smartly marked with a minus sign).**

   Mac OS X displays the confirmation sheet that you see in Figure 5-3.

So you like your privacy . . .

These days, everyone's interested in securing his or her personal files from prying eyes. Granted, this isn't a problem if you're the only one using your Mac. However, if you're sharing a computer in a multiuser environment, you might want a little more protection than just user permissions for those all-important Fantasy Football formations that you'll unleash next season.

Never fear, Lion offers a feature called *FileVault,* which provides disk encryption that prevents just about anyone except the NSA or FBI from gaining access to the files in your Home folder. (You'll notice that things slow down just a bit when logging in and out or working with files that are several gigabytes in size, but for those of us who need the peace of mind, this minimal performance hit is worth it.) You can enable the FileVault feature from the Security & Privacy pane in System Preferences. Two passwords control access to your drive when FileVault is active:

✔ The *Recovery Key* can unlock your drive if you forget your login password. Lion provides you with this key when you turn on the FileVault feature. **I highly recommend that you write down this key and store your copy in a safe place, away from your Mac.**

✔ Your *Login Password* unlocks the drive and provides access to your Home folder automatically when you log in.

Personally, I love this feature, and I use it on all my Macs running Lion. Yet a risk is involved (insert ominous chord here). To wit: **DO NOT forget your Login Password, and make doggone sure that your Admin user has access to a copy of that all-important Recovery Key!** Mac OS X displays a dire warning for anyone who's considering using FileVault: If you forget these passwords, you can't retrieve any data from your Mac's drive. *Period.* As Jerry Reed used to say, "It's a gone pecan."

Figure 5-3:
Are you *quite* sure that you want to delete this user?

Note that the contents of the user's Home folder can be saved in a disk image in the Deleted Users folder (just in case you need to retrieve something). Alternatively, you can choose to leave the deleted user's home folder as is, without removing it.

If you're absolutely sure you won't be dating that person again, click the Delete the Home Folder option (which doesn't save anything in the Deleted Users folder). You regain all the hard drive space that was being occupied by the contents of the deleted user's home folder. As an extra measure of protection, you can also choose to securely erase the contents of the deleted user's Home folder.

3. **Click OK to verify and delete the account. Click the Cancel button to abort and return to the Accounts list.**

Tightening Your Security Belt

Administrators are special people. Just ask one; you'll see. Anyway, when an administrator creates or edits the account for a standard-level user, Mac OS X offers a number of levels of specific rights — *Parental Controls* — that can be assigned on an individual account basis. When an account has Parental Controls assigned, it becomes a managed account.

Parental Controls are available only for standard-level users; administrators aren't affected by them because an administrator-level account already has access to everything covered by controls.

When do you need Parental Controls? Here are three likely scenarios:

✦ You're creating accounts for corporate or educational users, and you want to disable certain features of Mac OS X to prevent those folks from doing something dumb. Just tell 'em you're *streamlining the operating system.* (Yeah, that's it.) For example, you might not want that one particular kid making CD copies of *The Illustrated Anarchist's Cookbook* in the classroom while you're gone. Therefore, you disable the ability for that account to burn CDs or DVDs.

✦ In the same environment, you might want to give a specific standard-level account the ability to administer printers. If Roger in Accounting is both helpful and knowledgeable — oh, and add *trustworthy* in there, too — you might want to give him this capability so that he can handle the print queues while you're on vacation.

✦ You want one or more users to access one — and only one — application on the system, or perhaps just two or three applications. To illustrate: In my years as a hospital hardware technician, we had a number of computers that were used solely to display patient records. No Word, no e-mail, nothing but the one program that accessed the medical records database. We called these machines dumb terminals although they were actually personal computers. (This trick also works well if you're a parent and you want to give your kids access without endangering your valuable files. Just don't call your computer a dumb terminal lest your kids take offense. That's experience talking there.) If you want to allow access to a *specified* selection of applications, you can set them in that account's controls.

Setting Parental Controls

Time to review what each of the settings does. To display the controls for a standard account, click the account in the list and then click the Open Parental Controls button. Click the Enable Parental Controls button, and click the Lock icon in the lower-left corner to confirm your access (if necessary). Lion includes five different categories of controls, as shown in Figure 5-4:

✦ **Apps:** These settings (which I discuss in more detail in a second) affect what the user can do within Lion as well as what the Finder itself looks like to that user.

Figure 5-4:
You can
restrict
access
to many
functions
within a
Standard
account.

✦ **Web:** Lion offers three levels of control for Web sites:

• *Allow Unrestricted Access:* Select this radio button to allow unfettered access for this user.

• *Try to Limit Access:* You can allow Safari to automatically block Web sites it deems adult. To specify particular sites that the automatic adult figure should allow or deny, click the Customize button.

• *Allow Access to Only These Websites:* Choose this radio button to specify which Web sites the user can view. To add a Web site, click the Add button (which bears a plus sign) — Lion prompts you for a title and the Web site address.

✦ **People:** Click the Limit Mail and Limit iChat check boxes to specify the e-mail and instant messaging addresses that this user can communicate with. (Note that this affects only Apple Mail and iChat, so other mail clients, Web-based mail, and instant messaging applications aren't controlled.) To add an address that the user can e-mail or chat with, click the Add button, which bears the familiar plus sign.

Do you want a notification if the user is attempting to send an e-mail to someone not in the list? Click the Send Permission Requests To check box to select it and then type your e-mail address in the text box.

✦ **Time Limits:** Parents, click the Time Limits button, and you'll shout with pure joy — check out the options on this pane in Figure 5-5! You can limit an account to a certain number of hours of usage per weekday (Weekday Time Limits), limit to a specified number of hours of usage per weekend day (Weekend Time Limits), and set a bedtime computer curfew time for both weekdays and weekend days.

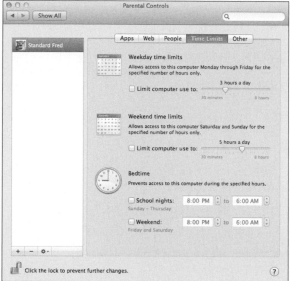

Figure 5-5: Lion keeps track of your kid's computer usage so that you don't have to.

Book II Chapter 5

Setting Up Multiuser Accounts

✦ **Other:** These settings control the Dictionary and hardware devices like your printer and DVD burner. They include

• *Hide Profanity in Dictionary:* With this check box selected, profane terms are hidden within the Dictionary for this user.

• *Limit Printer Administration:* With this check box selected, the user cannot modify the printers and printer queues within the Print & Scan pane in System Preferences. If this option is enabled, the user can still print to the default printer and switch to other assigned printers but can't add or delete printers or manage the Mac OS X print queue.

• *Limit CD and DVD Burning:* Select this check box to prevent the user from recording CDs or DVDs via the built-in disc recording features in Mac OS X. (Note, however, that if you load a third-party recording program, such as Toast, the user can still record discs with it.)

• *Disable Changing the Password:* Select this check box to prevent the user from changing the account password.

If you're creating a single standard-level account for an entire group of people to use — for example, if you want to leave the machine in kiosk mode in one corner of the office or if everyone in a classroom will use the same account on the machine — I recommend disabling the ability to change the account password. (Oh, and please do me a favor . . . *don't* create a system with just one admin-level account that everyone is supposed to use! Instead, keep your one admin-level account close to your bosom and create a standard-level account for the Unwashed Horde.)

Lion keeps a number of different types of *text log files* (which track where the user goes on the Internet, which applications are launched by the account, and the contents of any iChat conversations where the user was a participant). Click the Logs button on any Parental Control screen to monitor all the logs for a particular account.

You can always tell whether an account has been assigned Parental Controls because the account description changes from Standard to Managed in the Current User list.

Of particular importance are the Finder and applications controls. Click the Apps tab to modify these settings:

✦ **Use Simple Finder:** I discuss the Simple Finder in the following section because it's a great idea for families and classrooms with smaller children.

✦ **Limit Applications:** When this option is selected, you can select the specific applications that appear to the user. These restrictions are in effect whether the user has access to the Full Finder or just the Simple Finder.

From the Allow App Store Apps pop-up menu, you can choose to block the account from launching any applications purchased from the Apple App Store, or limit the user to installed App Store apps rated for specific ages.

To allow access to all the applications of a specific type — App Store, Other Apps (like the iLife and iWork suites), Widgets, and Utilities — click the check box next to the desired group heading to select it. To restrict access to all applications within a group, click the check box next to the heading to deselect it. You can also toggle the restriction on and off for specific applications in these groups; click the triangle icon next to each group heading to expand the list and then either mark or clear the check box next to the desired applications. To locate a specific application, click in the Search box and type the application name.

To add a new application to the Allowed list, drag its icon from the Finder and drop it in the list within the Other Apps group. After you add an application, it appears in the Other Apps group, and you can toggle access to it on and off like the applications in the named groups.

✦ **Allow User to Modify the Dock:** Select this check box, and the user can remove applications, documents, and folders from the Dock in the Full Finder. (If you don't want the contents of the Dock changing according to the whims of other users, it's a good idea to deselect this check box.)

Assigning the Simple Finder

You can restrict your standard-level users even further by assigning them the Simple Finder set of limitations. The default Simple Finder, as shown in Figure 5-6, is a highly simplified version of the regular Mac OS X Finder. The simplified Dock contains only the following: the Finder icon; the Trash; and the folders for the user's approved applications, documents, and shared files.

Figure 5-6:
Whoa! It's the Simple Finder — less filling; still runs great!

This is the network administrator's idea of a foolproof interface for Mac OS X: A user can access only those system files and resources needed to do a job, with no room for tinkering or goofing off.

A Simple Finder user can still make the jump to the full version of the Finder by clicking the Finder menu and choosing Run Full Finder. The user has to enter a correct admin-level username and password.

Planning on setting up a public access Mac? You can also change the Automatic Login account from the Users & Groups pane. Click the Login Options button under the Current User list and then click the Automatic Login pop-up menu to choose the account that automatically logs in when Mac OS X starts up. Enter the account password on the confirmation sheet that appears and click OK. Although I've made it clear elsewhere that Automatic Login is not a good security feature in many cases (as with a laptop on the road), it can be a good feature for those preparing a Mac for public use — if you set the Automatic Login to your public standard-access account, Mac OS X automatically uses the right account if the Mac is rebooted or restarted.

Don't forget, you can always choose Log Out from the Apple menu to log in under your own account.

Using Keychains — NOT

Before I leave this chapter, I want to discuss a Mac OS X feature that's been around for decades now: the *keychain*. Your account keychain stores all the username/password combinations for Web sites, file servers, File Transfer Protocol (FTP) servers, and the like, allowing you to simply waltz in and start using the service (whatever it is). Sounds downright convenient, doesn't it? And it can be, but you better watch your step.

I'm perfectly honest here: I **hate** account keychains. With a passion, mind you. As a consultant, webmaster, and the SYSOP (an ancient Bulletin Board Service abbreviation meaning *System Operator*) of an Internet-based online system, I know what a hassle it is for users to remember separate passwords, and I feel that pain. (I use separate passwords for everything.) However, three massively big problems are inherent with using keychains:

✦ **Anyone can log on as you.** If your keychain is unlocked, which happens automatically when you log in, all someone has to do is sit at your desk, visit a site or connect with a server, and *bam!* They're on. As *you.* **Think about that.** And then think how many times you get up from your desk, just for a second, to grab another Diet Coke or a doughnut.

✦ **You'll forget your passwords.** If the keychain file is corrupted — and it can happen — your passwords have gone to Detroit without you. Either you've got them on paper hidden somewhere, they're on your recent Time Machine backup, or it's time to change your online persona.

✦ **Keychains need yet another stinkin' password.** Yep, that's right — your keychain can be locked (either manually or, with the right settings, automatically), and you have to remember yet another password/passphrase to unlock your keychain. "When, oh, when will the madness end?"

From a security standpoint, keychains should be **completely off-limits** for anyone who's interested in maintaining a well-locked-down machine (whether it's a Mac used in a company office, or a Mac shared by a classroom).Unfortunately, Lion creates a keychain automatically for every user, so you have to monitor (and delete) your keychain data manually. (Sigh.)

However, if you're the only person using your Mac and it resides in your home — personally, I'd prefer a bank vault — and you absolutely *must* use keychains, you can display them all for the current account from the Keychain Access application (see Figure 5-7), conveniently located in Utilities within your Applications folder. Click the desired category, and then click an item in the keychain list to display or edit all its information.

Book II
Chapter 5

Setting Up
Multiuser
Accounts

Figure 5-7:
Take my
advice —
stay away
from the
allure of the
keychain.

Heck, just think about what I just wrote — anyone can display and *edit* server and site information just by launching this application! That includes your nephew Damien — you know, the one who considers himself the hacker extraordinaire. (While I'm at it, I should mention that it's just as bad to set the Automatic Login feature — which I discuss earlier in this chapter — to an admin-level account. One reboot, and you're rolling out the red carpet for the little rascal. For the inside information on Automatic Login, visit Chapter 4 in this very minibook.)

To help lock things down — at least when it comes to your Internet communications — follow this path:

1. **To display your Internet passwords, click the Passwords category.**

2. **Click each Internet password to select it in the list and then click the lowercase *i* button at the bottom of the window to display the information on that password.**

3. **Click the Access Control tab to display the settings that you see in Figure 5-8, one of which I strongly recommend.**

Figure 5-8:
Safe-
guarding a
keychain
rather
dilutes its
usefulness,
but I'm
security
conscious.

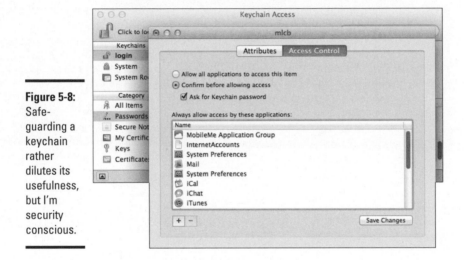

To minimize the damage that someone can do with this password, you can select the Confirm before Allowing Access radio button. And for yet another level of security, select the Ask for Keychain Password check box.

Of course, you're probably thinking, "Well, Mark, that pretty much eliminates the purpose of quick, convenient access without passwords, doesn't it?" Yes, indeed it does, but at least your online identity is somewhat safeguarded.

Click the plus sign button at the bottom of the Keychain Access window to add a new password. Type a name for the item, the username that you typically type to gain access, and the password for that server or site. Then click Add and cross your fingers.

To display all the keychains you can access, choose Edit⇨Keychain List. To create a brand-new keychain, choose File⇨New Keychain. Mac OS X prompts you for the filename for your new keychain file. In the New Keychain dialog that appears, enter a catchy name in the Save As text box. By default, the keychain file is created in the Keychains folder — a good idea — but if you want to store it elsewhere, click the down-arrow button next to the Save As text box and navigate to the desired folder. When you're ready, click the Create button. Now you need to enter yet another password, type it again to verify it, and click OK.

To lock or unlock your login keychain, click the Lock icon at the top-left of the Keychain Access window. (Unlocking your keychain requires you to enter your login password. Go figure.)

You might be saying to yourself, "Geez, this guy is more than a little paranoid." And yes, dear reader, I suppose I am. But then again, who's been uploading all those questionable images and MP3 files to the company server . . . using your account?

Chapter 6: Sharing Documents for Fun and Profit

In This Chapter

✔ Comparing network sharing with multiuser sharing

✔ Setting and changing permissions

✔ Sharing documents in Microsoft Office 2011 for the Mac

*N*ow here's a topic that any Mac OS X power user can sink his fangs into — the idea that a document on a multiuser system can be *everyone's* property, allowing anyone in your family, workgroup, or highly competitive mob to make whatever changes are necessary, whenever they like.

Of course, potential pitfalls lurk — even in the Apple world, there's no such thing as an operating system that's both powerful *and* perfectly simple. However, I think you'll find that our dear friends from Cupertino have done just about as well as can be expected and that the settings that you use to share documents are fairly easy to understand.

Prepare to share!

Sharing over a Network versus Sharing on a Single Mac

First, allow me to clear up what I've found to be a common misconception by using another of Mark's Maxims.

Sharing documents on a single computer is fundamentally different from the file sharing that you've used on a network.

True, multiple users can share a document over a network, which is a topic that I cover in Book VI. But although the results are the same, the way that you share that same document on a single machine betwixt multiple users is a completely different turn of the screw. In this section, I discuss the factoids behind the matter.

I'd be remiss if I didn't mention Lion's new *AirDrop* feature, which allows folks with Macs running Lion to transfer file wirelessly between their computers. AirDrop is easy and convenient to use, and I cover it in Book VI, Chapter 2.

No network is required

Although reiterating that no network is required is seemingly the most obvious of statements, many otherwise knowledgeable Mac OS X power users seem to forget that sharing a document over a network requires an active network connection. (Note the word *active* there.) Unless you physically copy the document to your hard drive — which defeats the purpose of document sharing — any loss of network connectivity or any problem with your network account will result in a brick wall and a brightly painted sign reading, "No luck, Jack." (Or perhaps it's flashing neon.)

On the other hand, a document shared on a multiuser Mac in the home or classroom is available whenever you need it. As long as the file is located in the Shared folder, the file privileges are set correctly, and you know the password (if one is required by the application, such as a password-protected Word document), then — as they say on "Star Trek" — "You have the conn" whether your network connection is active or not.

Relying on a guaranteed lock

Sharing documents over a network can get a tad hairy when multiple users open and edit the document simultaneously. Applications, such as Office 2011 for the Mac, have methods of *locking* the document (giving one person exclusive access) when someone opens it or saves it. However, you always face the possibility that what you're seeing in a shared network document isn't exactly what's in the document at that moment.

A multiuser system doesn't need such exquisite complexity. *You're* the one sitting at the keyboard, and *you* have control: This is what network administrators call a *guaranteed lock* on that document file. Refreshing, isn't it?

But wait! Mac OS X Lion includes a feature called *Fast User Switching* — I discuss it in Book I, Chapter 2 — that allows other users to remain logged in behind the scenes while another user is at the keyboard. Therefore, if you enable Fast User Switching, two users could have the same document open at the same time. To prevent this, you can simply turn off Fast User Switching from the Accounts panel in System Preferences. (Click Accounts, click Login Options, and clear the Enable Fast User Switching check box.)

It's also possible for someone to use Lion's Remote Login feature to login to their account across the Internet. You can disable this feature by opening the System Preferences window, clicking the Share icon, and deselecting the Remote Login check box.

Most places are off-limits

Network users are often confident that they can blithely copy and move a document from one place to another with the greatest of ease, and that's true. Most shared network documents created by an application — such as a project outline created in Word, for example — carry their own sharing information and document settings internally. Thus, you can move that same file to another folder on your hard drive, and the rest of the network team can still open it. (If they have the network rights to access the new folder, of course.)

This isn't the case when it comes to multiuser documents. As you can read in Chapters 4 and 5 of this minibook, Mac OS X places a rather tight fence around a standard-level user, allowing that person to access only the contents of certain folders. In this case, your document must be placed in the Shared folder for every standard-level user to be able to open it. If everyone using the document has administrator access, you can store the file in other spots on your system; as long as the permissions are set, you're set. And speaking of permissions . . .

Permissions: Law Enforcement for Your Files

Files are shared in Mac OS X according to a set of rules called *permissions,* the *ownership* of the file (typically the person who saved the document the first time), and an access level shared by multiple users who are specified as a *group.* The combination of privileges, ownership, and group determines who can do what with the file.

When you (or the person with the administrator account on your Mac) created your user account, you were automatically granted ownership of your Home folder and everything that it contains, as well as any files or folders that you store in the Shared folder or another user's Public folder.

Four possible actions are allowed through permissions:

✦ **Read Only:** This action allows the user to open and read the file, which includes copying it to another location.

✦ **Read & Write:** This permission grants full access to the file, including opening, reading, editing, saving, and deleting. Read & Write permission also allows the user to copy or move the file to another location.

✦ **Write Only (Drop Box):** A neat permission setting that appears only with a folder — it allows access to copy an item to the folder, but not to see any files it contains. (Hence the informal name *Drop Box*, and the + [plus sign] icon added to the folder's icon to identify it.) For example, a drop box is made to order for teachers: Students can submit homework by dragging their work to the teacher's drop box.

✦ **No Access:** This is just what it sounds like — the user can't open the file, copy it, or move it.

No matter what permissions you've set, only the System Administrator (or root user) can copy items into another user's Home folder. Take my word for it on this one: Simply consider that this can't be done, and **stay as far away from the Root/System Administrator account as possible.** (Trust me on this.) Read all about the perils of enabling the System Administrator account in Chapter 4 of this minibook.

These permissions are set in the Info dialog for a file or folder (always accessible by pressing ⌘+I). If you're setting the permissions for a folder, you can also elect to apply those same settings to all the enclosed items within the folder.

To set permissions, follow these steps:

1. **Click the item to select it, press ⌘ +I (or choose Finder⇨File), and then choose the Get Info menu item.**

You can right-click the item and choose Get Info instead. Either way, Mac OS X displays the Info dialog.

2. **Click the right-facing arrow next to the Sharing & Permissions heading to expand it, as shown in Figure 6-1.**

3. **To change your own permissions on the item, click the Privileges pop-up list next to your name — handily marked "(Me)" as well — and choose a new Ownership permissions level.**

This is likely set to Read & Write, and it's a good idea to leave it alone. If you're the file's owner, you're likely not a security risk.

Perhaps I should be a little less tactful here: *Never* choose an access level for yourself other than Read & Write without being absolutely sure of what you're doing because you can potentially prevent yourself from accessing or deleting the file in the future! For example, if you simply want to lock an item to prevent changes being made, **don't** set your Ownership permission to Read Only. (Instead, select the Locked check box in the General section of the Info dialog instead . . . you can easily clear the Locked check box later to make changes to the item.)

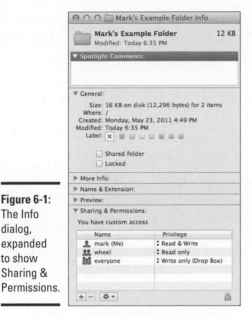

Figure 6-1:
The Info dialog, expanded to show Sharing & Permissions.

4. **To change permissions for someone else or a group, click the Privilege value for that user or group and then choose the appropriate value from the pop-up menu.**

   Assigning permissions for an entire group is a good idea for limiting specific files and folders to only Administrator access. (Note, however, that Lion reserves the group name *wheel* for internal tasks, so ***never*** alter any permissions for the *wheel* group.)

5. **If necessary, set the permission for the Everyone pop-up menu (otherwise known as "I'm going to lump everyone else into this category").**

   If a user isn't the owner of an item and doesn't fit into any group that you've selected, this access permission setting for this file applies to that user.

   Need to apply the same permissions to all the contents of a folder — including subfolders within it? If you selected a folder, you can click the Action button at the bottom of the Info dialog (which carries a gear icon) and choose Apply To Enclosed Items from the pop-up menu that appears. After you confirm the action, Lion automatically changes the permissions for all the items contained in the folder to the same settings.

   Generally, it's a good idea *not* to override the permissions for all the items in a folder, so use the Apply To Enclosed Items action only when necessary.

6. **After all the permissions are correct, click the Close button to save your changes and return to your friendly Finder.**

If a specific user or group doesn't appear already in the Privilege list, click the Add button (bearing the plus sign) and you can add a specific privilege level for that user or group. You can also delete a privilege level: Click the desired entry to select it and click the Delete button (which bears a minus sign).

Permission and Sharing Do's and Don'ts

After you get the basics of sharing files and assigning permissions under your belt, you need to master when to change permissions and why you should (and shouldn't) modify them. Follow these common-sense guidelines when saving documents, assigning permissions, and choosing access levels:

✦ *Do* **use your Shared folder.** The Shared folder is the center of proper document sharing. I know there's a strong urge to create a new document in your Home folder, but you're just making more work for yourself because you'll end up copying that document from your Home folder to the Shared folder. Instead of an extra step, store a document that's intended to be shared in the Shared folder — where it belongs in the first place.

✦ *Don't* **assign permissions just to protect a file from deletion.** Remember, if all you need to do is prevent anyone (including yourself) from deleting an item, you don't need to go to all the trouble of changing permissions. Instead, just display the Info dialog for the item and select the Locked check box to enable it, which prevents the item from being deleted from the Trash until the Lock status is disabled (or you specifically click Remove All Items when emptying the Trash).

✦ *Do* **review the contents of a folder before changing permissions for enclosed items.** That confirmation dialog doesn't appear just for kicks. For example, if you set a highly sensitive, private document with permissions of No Access for everyone but yourself and then you apply less-restrictive permissions globally to the folder that contains the document, you've just removed the No Access permissions, and anyone can open your dirty laundry. (Ouch.) Therefore, make sure that you open the folder and double-check its contents first before applying global permissions to the items it contains.

✦ *Don't* **change permissions in the Applications or Utilities folders.** If you have Administrator-level access, you can actually change the permissions for important applications such as Mail, Address Book, iTunes, and Safari, as well as their support files. This spells havoc for all users assigned to the standard-access level. Be polite and leave the permissions for these files alone.

✦ *Definitely don't* **change System ownership.** Mac OS X is stable and reliable. Part of that stability comes from the protected state of the System folder, as well as a number of other folders on your hard drive. If you displayed the Info dialog for the System folder, you'll see that the Owner is set to *system,* and the Group is set to *wheel* (a term from the UNIX world that encompasses all administrator accounts). Now, promptly close that Info dialog, **without making any changes!**

✦ *Never, never, never* **change any permissions for any files owned by the System unless specifically told to do so by an Apple support technician.** *Do not* **monkey with System-owned items.**

This last one is quite striking for a reason, so heed the warning.

Sharing Stuff in Office 2011

Many Mac OS X applications offer their own built-in document-sharing features. For example, Microsoft Office 2011 for the Mac includes both file-level and document-sharing features. Because Office 2011 is the most popular productivity suite available for Mac OS X, I discuss these commands in this final section.

Document-sharing features

You'll find a number of commands that help multiple users keep track of changes that have been made in a shared Office document. Probably the most familiar is the Word revision tracking features (heavily used during the development of this book), but there are others as well:

✦ **Revision marks:** If several users edit a document, how can you tell who did what? By using *revision marks,* which apply different colors to changes made by different editors, those additions and deletions can be accepted or rejected individually at a later date. If Johnson in Marketing adds incorrect material, you can easily remove just his changes. In a worst-case scenario, you can actually reject all changes and return the document to its pristine condition.

✦ **Compare Documents:** Using this feature allows you to compare a revised document with the original (if, of course, you still have the original file handy). I use Compare Documents only if revision marks weren't turned on before editing began.

✦ **Comments:** Editors can also converse within a document by using embedded Comments. These don't change the contents of the Word file the way revision marks do, but store commentary and notes in a behind-the-scenes kind of way. (Think of a Mac OS X Sticky that appears within a document.) Again, the author of each comment is listed, allowing for (sometimes heated) communication within the body of a document.

✦ **Highlighting:** You've heard the old joke about . . . Well, anyway, a traditional highlighter marker is pretty useless on a computer monitor (leaving a nasty mess for the next user to clean), but Word allows multiple highlighting colors for identifying text. (And for the occasional practical joke — nothing like adding eight different highlighting colors to that important proposal. Just make sure that your résumé is up-to-date.)

File-level sharing features

Along with the document-level sharing commands, you'll find that Office 2011 applications also offer sharing features that control access to the document file itself.

Password protection

You can add password protection to any Office 2011 document. Follow these steps with a document created within Word, Excel, or PowerPoint:

1. **Choose File⇨Save As.**

2. **In the Save As dialog that appears, click Options to display the Save Preferences pane.**

3. **Click the Show All toolbar button.**

4. **Click Security to display the Preferences pane that you see in Figure 6-2.**

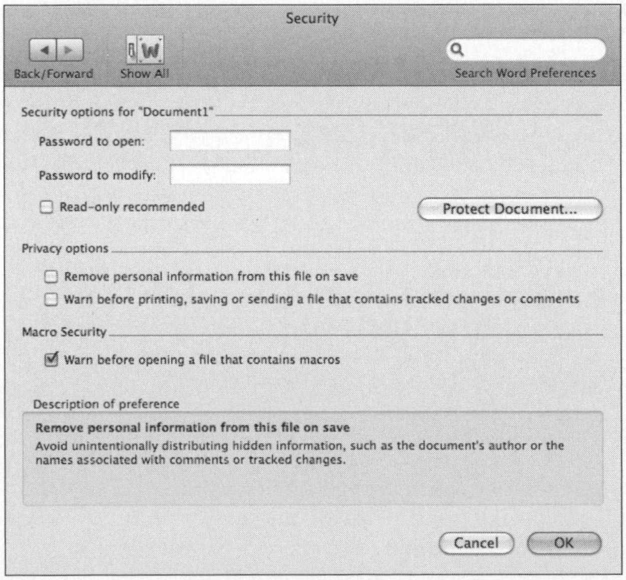

Figure 6-2: Office 2011 offers two types of document passwords.

5. **To password-protect the document, enter a password in the Password to Open field.**

This password must be provided when opening the document.

If you like, you can enter another password in the Password to Modify field. This second password would then also be required to modify the document.

Both passwords are case-sensitive.

6. **Click OK to save the preference changes and return to your document.**

Document protection

Think of the Protect Document dialog in Word, from which you can effectively write-protect certain elements, as an extra level of security in a multiuser environment. In this Office application, you can protect revision marks, comments, and sections of a document containing forms. A password can be added if desired. To display the Protect Document dialog, click Tools in any of the Office 2011 applications and choose Protect Document from the menu.

Book III

The Digital Hub

The 5th Wave   By Rich Tennant

HELP DESK

TECHNICAL   ETHICAL

Contents at a Glance

Chapter 1: The World According to Apple

In This Chapter

- Doing things the hub way
- Digitizing your life
- Making your digital devices work together

Huzzah! After years of empty promises of professional-quality media features for home and school — most of them coming from those Windows people in Redmond — Apple has developed a recipe for digital success.

By using tightly integrated hardware and software (where everything works smoothly together), Apple gives you the ability to easily organize and produce your own multimedia with the iLife suite of digital tools, which includes iMovie, iDVD, iPhoto, GarageBand, iWeb, and iTunes. That same software also provides fantastic editing capabilities. Finally (and this is very important) — to paraphrase Will Smith in the movie *Men in Black,* "Apple makes these programs look *good.*"

First, Sliced Bread . . . and Now, the Digital Hub

In today's overloaded world of personal electronic devices, people can try to juggle as many as five or six electronic wonders. Each device typically comes with its own software, power adapter, and connectors to the outside world. Although managing one or two devices isn't terribly difficult, as the number of devices increases, so do the headaches. When you have a half-dozen cables, power adapters, and software to cart around, the digital life can become pretty bleak. (And quite heavy. You'll need more than a backpack to lug all that gear around.)

To combat this confusion, Apple came up with the idea of a *digital hub,* whereby your Macintosh acts as the center of an array of electronic devices. By using standardized cables, power requirements, built-in software, and even wireless connections via *Bluetooth* (the standard for short-range wireless communications between devices) and 802.11x wireless (for connections to your Ethernet network and your Apple TV unit), the Macintosh — along with its operating system, Mac OS X — goes a long way toward simplifying your interaction with all the electronic gadgets that you use.

Given the hub terminology, think of the digital hub as a wagon wheel. (See Figure 1-1.) At the center of the wheel is your Macintosh. At the end of each spoke is a digital device. Throughout the rest of Book III, I give you the skinny on each device, but this chapter gives you the overview and tells you how they all work together.

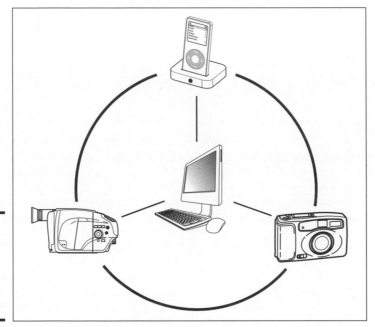

Figure 1-1: Hey, look what's in the center of your digital hub!

What Does Digital Mean, Anyway?

Computers are handy machines. They can process information very quickly and never get bored when asked to do the same task millions of times. The problem is that despite their propensity for reliability and speed, they aren't so hot in the intuition department. You have to tell them how to *do* everything (and most of them talk only to application developers and programmers). Computers know only one thing — numbers — although they do know numbers very, very well.

In fact, *binary* (the language of computers) has only two values — one and zero, which represent *on* and *off,* respectively. (Think of a light switch that toggles: The earliest computers were simply banks of switches that filled up an entire room.) To work with a computer in meaningful ways, you have to describe everything to a computer with numbers — or, if you prefer, *digits.*

By describing audio in numerical digits, you suddenly have something that a computer can work with. Toss a computer as many numbers as you want, and it can handle them. The scientists who figured this out knew that they had a good thing going, so they proceeded to convert anything that they could get their hands on into . . . well, digits. (Sorry about the atrocious pun.) Anyway, this resulted in some interesting technologies, most of which you'll surely recognize:

✦ **Audio CDs:** The music is represented as numbers and is stored on a plastic disc.

✦ **Digital video:** Images and sound are stored together on your hard drive or a DVD as one really, *really* long string of numbers.

✦ **Digital fingerprints:** (No pun intended this time.) Your fingerprint is converted into numerical data, which a computer can use to compare against fingerprint data from other people.

✦ **Automated telephone operators:** When you call a phone operator these days, you often aren't speaking to a real person. Rather, the computer on the other end of the line converts your voice into digits, which it uses to interpret your words. (At times, I think I'm talking to a real person, but it's hard to tell.)

What Can I Digitize?

As you've probably guessed by now, practically anything can be digitized. As long as you can represent something as numbers, you can digitize that data. Whether it's photographs, video, or audio, your Mac is adept at digitizing data and processing it.

Photographs

Perhaps the most popular of digital devices, the digital camera has transformed photography forever. By using sophisticated electronics, digital cameras convert the image that you see through the camera viewfinder into an image made purely of numbers.

After this numeric information is transferred to your Macintosh, your computer can cut, twist, fade, label, and paint your digital images. Because numbers are the only materials involved, you won't need scissors, paint, or adhesive tape to edit images. (Advertising photographers can say good-bye to the old-fashioned airbrush.) Your Macintosh does it all by manipulating those numbers. It cuts down on the messy art supplies and gives you the comfort of being able to go back in time — something that anyone who's not so handy with scissors can appreciate.

Music

As I mention earlier in this chapter, audio CDs are one application of music represented as digital data. The physical CD is just a piece of plastic with a metal coating, but you don't even really need CDs any longer. Your Macintosh can digitize audio for storage on your internal drive, too, which brings up another important point. Not only is digital information palatable to a computer, it's also very portable. You can store it on any number of storage devices, such as an iPod, an iPad, a USB flash drive, or an external hard drive. (By the way, if you're a musician, you can use GarageBand and external instruments that will turn your Mac into a combination of synthesizer, amplifier, and backup band. Mozart would've loved this stuff.)

Video

When you photograph a scene multiple times per second and then replay the sequence, you get (tah-dah!) moving pictures. In the analog (as opposed to digital) world, this would be a strip of celluloid film or magnetic tape. In the digital world, such a sequence of photographs is called *DV,* or *digital video.* After you take your digital video, you can transfer that data to your Macintosh to further manipulate it: You can edit it and add transitions, text, and other effects.

DVD

As is a CD-ROM or a hard drive, a *DVD* is simply a means of storing digital data. Although you can use it to save many different kinds of data, its most common use is for presenting video content. The Macintosh digital hub can produce DVDs by using any digital information you give it.

The Software That Drives the Hub

At the heart of your digital hub is your Macintosh. To use and manipulate all the data that arrives at your Mac, your computer needs software, which provides instructions on what to do with the information that you send. Fortunately, Apple has fashioned some of the most attractive and easy-to-use software ever written to help you manipulate and manage your digital lifestyle. The list of software that belongs to the digital hub includes

✦ **iPhoto:** Use iPhoto to download, manipulate, and organize your favorite digital photographs. After everything is just so, iPhoto can print them, burn them to disc, or even help you design and order a hardbound album! (For way more on iPhoto, go to Book III, Chapter 3.)

✦ **iTunes:** iTunes offers the ability to manage your music and movie collections, along with sundry other media such as podcasts, Internet radio, audiobooks, and music videos. You can also purchase and download audio tracks and video from Apple's iTunes Store. iTunes can even burn CDs! (Head to Book III, Chapter 2 for more.)

✦ **iMovie:** Every film director needs a movie-editing suite. iMovie gives you the chance to set up Hollywood in your living room with outstanding results. (For more, see Book III, Chapter 4.)

✦ **iDVD:** As home video moves toward the digital realm, iDVD becomes an essential tool for authoring your own DVD media. Home movies will never be the same! (iDVD is covered in Book III, Chapter 5.)

✦ **GarageBand:** Call it a "music-building" application! Even if you can't play a note, GarageBand makes it easy to create your own original songs — and if you *are* a musician, you can turn your Mac into a production studio. The latest version can even help you learn how to play an instrument. (Turn to Book III, Chapter 6 for more.)

✦ **iWeb:** Interested in producing a professional-quality web site, but afraid that you'll have to give up your personal life to build and maintain it? Never fear; with iWeb you can join the web publishing crowd the easy Apple way. (I cover iWeb like a blanket in Book III, Chapter 7.)

✦ **iCal:** To help keep your hectic digital lifestyle in order, iCal (which is included with Lion) offers complete calendar features. Besides tracking your dates and appointments on your Mac, you can publish calendars on the web or share them with different parts of the digital hub. (Or, if you have an iPod, you can even download your appointments and carry 'em with you.)

✦ **iSync:** With so many digital devices at your disposal, it gets hard to keep them all straight. *iSync* is software for automatically synchronizing contact and calendar information between cellphones, your personal digital assistant (PDA), an iPod, the Mac OS X Address Book, and iCal. iSync is included with Lion.

iPhoto

What good is a camera without a photo album? *iPhoto,* Apple's photography software, serves as a digital photo album. Use it to help you arrange and manage your digital photos. Beyond its functions as a photo album, iPhoto also gives you the ability to touch up your images through cropping, retouching, scaling, rotating, and red-eye reduction (photographically speaking, not morning-after speaking).

Besides offering editing features, iPhoto also works automatically with your digital camera. Simply plug in the camera to your Mac's Universal Serial Bus (USB) port, and iPhoto knows it's there. Need to transfer photos from the camera to your photo album? iPhoto can do that, too.

When you complete a collection of photographs that you find interesting, use iPhoto to help you publish them on the Internet or even to create your very own coffee-table book. (The latest in high-tech: a paper book.) And for those of you who still want that nifty wallet print to show off at work or a poster to hang on your wall, you can print them with your own printer or order them online through iPhoto. Orders made with iPhoto show up in your mailbox — the U.S. Postal Service physical one outside your domicile — a few days later.

iTunes

To help you wrangle your enormous digital music and movie collection, Apple offers iTunes (see Figure 1-2). For starters, iTunes is a sophisticated audio player for all your digital audio files. But iTunes is also handy for converting audio tracks from audio CDs to a number of popular digital audio file formats, such as AAC, and MP3. After you import or convert your music into computer files, iTunes helps you manage and maintain your music collection. You can even listen to streaming online "radio stations" 24 hours a day. The latest version of iTunes even allows you to rent or buy videos, TV shows, and movies, either on your Mac or on your video-capable iPod.

Figure 1-2: With iTunes, you can buy music and video from the iTunes Store.

Plus, Apple throws in the iTunes Store, where you can preview hundreds of thousands of songs, TV shows, movies, and videos for up to 90 seconds each without spending a dime. (Podcast subscriptions are usually free, bucko.) If you latch onto something that you'd like to buy, you can use your credit card to purchase and download your media (either as individual tracks, or as a complete album or movie for a package price). After the media that you've bought is comfortably nestled in iTunes, you can play it on your Mac, burn music to an audio CD, or download it to your iPod or iPad.

You'll also find college-level multimedia courseware in the iTunes U section of the iTunes Store — that's content that's educational and free for the asking!

Why do I keep harping on the iPod? Well, as a proud owner of one, I'm glad you asked: Apple's *iPod* is a versatile, lightweight audio and video player with hidden extras that James Bond would covet. It has enough capacity to store your entire collection of music and several movies, but it's small enough to fit into your shirt pocket. With iTunes, you can instantly exchange media between your Macintosh and your iPod. You can also use iTunes to create audio and MP3 CDs for playback elsewhere. And the iPod even works as honest-to-goodness, back-up storage . . . you see, it also functions as a standard external USB 2.0 hard drive. An iPod can display text files and play games; you can carry even your Address Book contacts and iCal appointments with you with aplomb. (For the lowdown on iPod, peruse Book III, Chapter 2.)

iMovie

You needn't restrict yourself to still images: Hook up your digital camcorder to your Mac as well. Use *iMovie,* the easy-to-use video editing application shown in Figure 1-3, to create and edit digital movies.

Figure 1-3:
iMovie can turn you into Hollywood material — let's do lunch.

With stunning video-editing candy such as transitions, sound effects, and video effects, iMovie turns your home movies into professional productions that you'll be proud to share with friends and family. Finally, you can have a home-movie night without putting everyone to sleep.

iDVD

Of course, after you create a video masterpiece, you probably want to save it on a DVD for preservation and future viewing. To help you in your endeavors, use iDVD to create — or, as video professionals call it, *author* — DVD movies. With the preset templates, iDVD will have you cranking out stunning DVDs with interactive menus in no time, ready to use with just about any DVD player.

GarageBand

Imagine the freedom to create your own original music by simply dragging "digital instruments" onto a canvas . . . and then adding your own voice or the lead instrument! After the basic melody is in place, you'd want to be able to edit whatever you like, or even choose different instruments with the click of a mouse. As recently as ten years ago, dear reader, that concept was indeed just a dream. Then, software-based synthesizers and mixing applications brought musicians into the digital age. (The problem was that normal human beings couldn't afford the expensive software or the sample libraries of literally thousands of different instruments.) With the addition of GarageBand, however, the iLife suite provides everything that you need to start making your own music (inexpensively) and then create MP3 files or burn your own audio CDs. And believe me, if I can create a techno track that actually hit the speakers at a local dance club, *you* can, too!

iWeb

In the days of old — I'm talking five or six years ago here — putting a web site online meant hours of drudgery, usually with a so-called "what you see is what you get" page creation application. Problem was, "what you saw" was very rarely easy to create, and if you were actually successful in getting the results you wanted, you still had to get all that stuff to appear on a web server somewhere so that visitors could actually *see* it. With iWeb, the creation of a web site is intuitive, easy, and downright fun! Click and drag your way to the web site you want, starting with a number of truly outstanding predesigned templates. Add all sorts of cool pages, such as blogs and automated online photo albums. And the best part? Click a couple of buttons, and your new work of online art appears automatically on your MobileMe web site, or as a group of files that's ready for uploading to your web server. Voilà!

Can I Use All This Stuff at One Time?

What makes the digital hub idea even juicier is that it's an *interoperable* model. Let's pause to appreciate that. (What, you don't speak *engineer?* No problem!) In plain English, the digital hub allows you to use digital media from one part of the hub with another part of the hub. Thus, the individual parts of the digital hub can work together to complement each other. To illustrate, consider some digital-sharing scenarios:

✦ **You shoot a great photograph of your kids.** It's so great, in fact, that you'd like to use it as the title screen of your family's home movie. With the digital hub, you can use that same photograph in iMovie to create your home flick. When you're done with that, transfer the whole thing to a DVD by using iDVD, and your masterpiece is safe for decades of viewing. One image just worked its way through three parts of the digital hub.

✦ **You just recorded a catchy song with GarageBand.** You add the song to the soundtrack of the music video that you're creating with iMovie. Then you create a fancy opening menu and burn the finished project to DVD with iDVD to show prospective agents. Again, one piece of media has traveled through three parts of the digital hub!

✦ **Your band becomes popular and starts to play some impressive gigs.** To document your band's rise to stardom, your friend films a concert with a DV camcorder. You use iMovie to transfer the video to your Macintosh and create clips of your favorite performances of the concert. The clips are transferred over to the primo web site you've created with iWeb, and your band's Internet image takes off! After that, it's a simple matter to author to DVD with iDVD, extract the audio from the video for use as an MP3 with iTunes, and grab an image from the video for a band scrapbook that you're creating with iPhoto. Now you've attained honest-to-goodness DHH (shorthand for *Digital Hub Heaven*). You've traversed the entire hub, easily sharing the media along the way.

Lest I forget, I should mention the other advantage of the digital hub: The media that you swap between all your "iApplications" remains in digital form, which is A Good Thing! In the previous example of shooting a concert, for instance, that concert footage remained practically pristine while it was being transferred to DVD, converted to MP3, pasted into your iPhoto album, or uploaded to your iWeb site. (Because some audio and video formats are *compressed* to save space, such as MP3, a purist will argue that you lost a little something. It ain't much.) Unlike with archaic analog VHS tape, you don't have to worry about whether your source is second generation — and you can forget degradation and that silly tracking control.

Chapter 2: Jamming with iTunes and iPod

In This Chapter

- Playing music with your Mac
- Arranging and organizing your music collection
- Tuning into the world with Internet radio
- Sharing your songs across a network
- Creating eye candy with the Visualizer
- Buying the good stuff from the iTunes Store

Good news! Every installation of Mac OS X comes with the finest stereophonic gadget in town: a great audio application called *iTunes*. With iTunes, you can listen to your favorite songs and podcasts, organize your music collection, watch video or a full-length movie, listen to radio stations from around the world, buy music and video online, burn CDs and DVDs, and much more! In no time, you'll be pondering how much new speakers with a subwoofer will cost for your Mac.

In this chapter, I show you how to play audio CDs, podcasts, videos, and Internet radio, but that's just the beginning. You discover how to use iTunes' Library to get one-click access to any song in your collection. I even show you how to tune into Internet radio (and share your favorite songs with others on your network), burn audio CDs, join in the Ping online community, plug in your iPod, and buy the latest hits from the iTunes Store. Heck, iTunes can even suggest new music for your library based on what you're listening to now. (And I demonstrate how to make your iTunes window look just as good as your music sounds, with visualizations.)

Just in case, though, keep your dad's hi-fi . . . it might fetch a hefty sum as an antique on eBay.

What Can I Play on iTunes?

Simply put, iTunes is a media player; it plays audio and video files. These files can be in any of many different formats. Some of the more common audio formats that iTunes supports are

✦ **MP3:** The small size of MP3 files has made them popular for file trading on the Internet. You can reduce MP3 files to a ridiculously small size (at the expense of audio fidelity), but a typical CD-quality, three-minute pop song in MP3 format has a size of 3–5MB.

✦ **AAC:** *AAC* (short for Advanced Audio Coding) is an audio format that's very similar to MP3; in fact, AAC files offer better recording quality at the same file sizes. However, this format originally supported a built-in copy protection scheme that prevented AAC music from being widely distributed on Macs. (Luckily, this copy protection is no longer applied to iTunes tracks, and you can still burn protected AAC tracks to an audio CD, just as you can MP3 tracks.) The tracks that you download from the iTunes Store are in AAC format.

The iTunes Store's *iTunes Plus* tracks are also in AAC format, but these tracks are not copy-protected, and they're encoded at a higher-quality 256 Kbps rate — hence their higher price.

✦ **Apple Lossless:** Another format direct from Apple, *Apple Lossless* format provides the best compromise between file size and sound quality: These tracks are encoded without loss of quality. However, Apple Lossless tracks are somewhat larger than AAC, so it's generally the favorite of the most discerning audiophile for his or her entire music library.

✦ **AIFF:** The standard Macintosh audio format produces sound of the absolute highest quality. This high quality, however, also means that the files are pretty doggone huge. A typical pop song in AIFF format has a size of 30–50MB.

✦ **WAV:** Not to be outdone, Microsoft created its own audio file format (WAV) that works much like AIFF. It can reproduce sound at higher quality than MP3, but the file sizes are very large, very similar in size to AIFF files. (Think 10MB per minute of audio.)

✦ **CD audio:** iTunes can play audio CDs. Because you don't usually store CD audio anywhere but on an audio CD, file size is no big whoop.

✦ **Movies and video:** You can buy and download full-length movies, TV shows, music videos, and movie trailers from the iTunes Store . . . and, with an Apple TV unit connected to your home theater system, you can watch those movies and videos from the comfort of your sofa on the other side of your house.

✦ **Podcasts:** These audio downloads are like radio programs for your iPod — but iTunes can play and organize them, too. Some podcasts also include video and photos to boot.

✦ **Ringtones:** iPhone owners, rejoice! iTunes automatically offers to create ringtones for your iPhone from the tracks you've bought from the iTunes Store.

✦ **Audiobooks:** No longer do you need cassettes or audio CDs to enjoy your spoken books — iTunes can play them for you, or you can send them to your iPod for listening on the go.

✦ **Streaming Internet radio:** You can listen to a continuous broadcast of songs from one of tens of thousands of Internet radio stations, with quality levels ranging from what you'd expect from FM radio to the full quality of an audio CD. You can't save the music in iTunes, but it's still great fun. (In fact, I run my own station . . . more on MLC Radio later in the chapter.)

Playing an Audio CD

Playing an audio CD in iTunes is simple. Just insert the CD in your computer's disc tray or disc slot, start iTunes by clicking its icon in the Dock, and click the Play button. (Note that your Mac might be set to automatically launch iTunes when you insert an audio CD.) The iTunes interface resembles that of a traditional cassette or CD player. The main playback controls of the iTunes are Play, Previous Song, Next Song, and the volume slider, as shown in Figure 2-1.

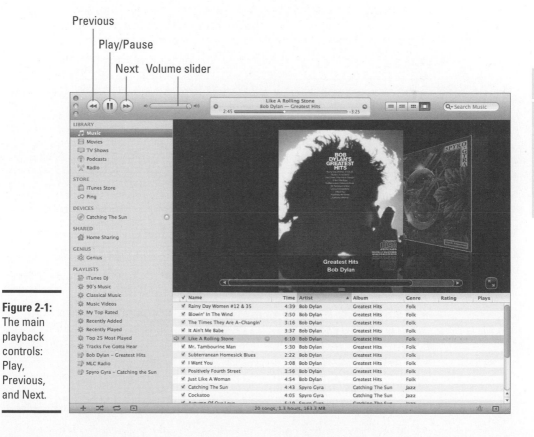

Previous

Play/Pause

Next Volume slider

Figure 2-1:
The main playback controls:
Play,
Previous,
and Next.

Click the Play button to begin listening to a song. While a song is playing, the Play button toggles to a Pause button. As you might imagine, clicking that button again pauses the music. If you don't feel like messing around with a mouse, you can always use the keyboard. The spacebar acts as the Play and Pause buttons. Press the spacebar to begin playback; press it again to stop.

Click the Next Song button to advance to the next song on the CD. The Previous Song button works like the Next Song button but with a slight twist: If a song is currently playing and you click the Previous Song button, iTunes first returns to the beginning of the current song (just like an audio CD player). To advance to the previous song, double-click the Previous Song button. To change the volume of your music, click and drag the volume slider.

As with other Macintosh applications, you can control much of iTunes with the keyboard. Table 2-1 lists some of the more common iTunes keyboard shortcuts.

Table 2-1	Common iTunes Keyboard Shortcuts
Press This Key Combination	*To Do This*
Spacebar	Play the currently selected song if iTunes is idle.
Spacebar	Pause the music if a song is playing.
Right-arrow key	Advance to the next song.
Left-arrow key	Go back to the beginning of a song. Press a second time to return to the previous song.
⌘+up-arrow key	Increase the volume of the music.
⌘+down-arrow key	Decrease the volume of the music.
⌘+Option+down-arrow key	Mute the audio if any is playing. Press again to play the audio.

Playing Digital Audio and Video

In addition to playing audio CDs, iTunes can play the digital audio files that you download from the Internet or obtain from other sources in the WAV, AAC, Apple Lossless, AIFF, and MP3 file formats. Enjoying a digital audio file is just slightly more complicated than playing a CD. After downloading or saving your audio files to your Mac, open the Finder and navigate to wherever you stored the files. Then simply drag the music files (or an entire folder of music) from the Finder into the Music entry in the iTunes Source list. (The added files appear in the Music section of your iTunes Library. Think of the Library as a master list of your digital media. To view the Music Library, select the Music entry in the left-hand column of the iTunes player, as shown in Figure 2-2. Go figure.) Heck, you can also drag a song file from a Finder window and drop it on the iTunes icon in the Dock, which adds it to your Music Library as well.

Source list

Music Entry

Figure 2-2: The Music Library keeps track of all your audio files.

Playlist

Book III Chapter 2

Jamming with iTunes and iPod

If you drop the file on top of a playlist name in the Source list, iTunes adds it to that particular *playlist* as well as the main Library. (More about playlists in a bit.)

To play a song, just double-click it in the Music list. Alternatively, you can use the playback controls (Play, Previous Song, and Next Song) that I discuss earlier in this chapter (refer to Figure 2-1).

The Source list of iTunes can list up to seven possible sources for music:

✦ **Library:** This section includes Music, Movies, TV Shows, Podcasts, Books, iTunes U, Apps (for iPhone and iPad), Ringtones (for iPhone), iPod Games, and Radio. (Think *Internet radio,* which I discuss further in the section "iTunes Radio.")

✦ **Store:** I discuss this later, in the section "Buying Digital Media the Apple Way."

✦ **Shared:** If another Mac on your local network is running iTunes and is set to share part or all of its library, you can connect to the other computer for your music. (Shared music on another Mac appears as a separate named folder in the Source list.)

✦ **Devices:** If an iPod is connected, it appears in the list. (And yes, Virginia, other models of MP3 players from other companies will also appear in the list if they support iTunes.) If you connect an iPhone or iPad to your Mac, it'll show up here as well.

✦ **Audio CD:** A standard audio CD . . . anything from the Bee Gees to Death Cab for Cutie.

✦ **Home Sharing:** You can turn on Home Sharing to share your Mac's media library across your wireless network with up to five other devices, including other Mac computers, iPhones, iPads and the iPhone touch. (More on Home Sharing later in the chapter.)

✦ **Playlists:** Think of playlists as folders you use to organize your music. (More on playlists later in this chapter.)

If you've invested in an Apple TV, it appears in the list as well, allowing iTunes to share media with your Apple TV, which in turn sends it to your ED- or HD-TV.

Notice also that the Library lists information for each song that you add to it, such as

✦ **Song Name:** The title of the song

✦ **Time:** The length of the song

✦ **Artist:** The artist who performs the song

✦ **Album:** The album on which the song appears

If some of the songs that you're adding don't display anything for the title, album, or artist information, don't panic; most MP3 files have embedded data that iTunes can read. If a song doesn't include any data, you can always add the information to these fields manually. I show you how later, in the section "Setting or changing the song information manually."

Clicking any of the column headings in the Library list causes iTunes to reorder the Library according to that category. For example, clicking the Song Name column heading alphabetizes your Library by song title. I click the Time heading often to sort my Library according to the length of the songs. Oh, and you can drag column titles to reorder them any way you like (as long as the Name column remains at the far left).

iTunes can display your Music Library in four ways: By default, the application uses the *list view* you see in Figure 2-1, where each song is one entry. A click on the second View button sorts your library into tracks by *album.* Click the third View button (at the top of the iTunes window) to group tracks together by album artwork in *grid view.* Click the fourth View button, and you're browsing by album cover in *cover flow view,* complete with reflective surface!

Browsing the Library

After you add a few dozen songs to iTunes, viewing the Library can become a task. Although a master list is nice for some purposes, it becomes as cumbersome as an elephant in a subway tunnel if the list is very long. To help out, iTunes can display your Library in another format, too: namely, browsing mode. To view the Library in browsing mode, click the View menu and click the Show Browser item, or press the ⌘+B keyboard shortcut.

The Browse mode of iTunes displays your library in a compact fashion, organizing your tunes into four sections:

✦ Genre

✦ Artist

✦ Album

✦ Song Name

Selecting an artist from the Artist list causes iTunes to display that artist's albums in the Album list. Select an album from the Album list, and iTunes displays that album's songs in the bottom section of the Browse window. (Those Apple software designers . . . always thinking of you and me.) You can also switch between sort fields for the Browse window from the View⇨Column Browser menu item.

Will I trash my Count Basie?

Novice iTunes users, take note: iTunes watches your back when you trash tracks.

To illustrate: Suppose you delete a song from the Library that's located only in the iTunes music folder (which you didn't copy into iTunes from another location on your hard drive). That means you're about to delete the song entirely, and there'll be no copy remaining on your Mac at all. Rest assured, though, that iTunes prompts you to make sure that you really want to move the file to the Trash. (I get fearful e-mail messages all the time from readers who are loath to delete anything from iTunes because they're afraid they'll trash their digital music files completely.)

Remember: If you delete a song from the Library that *also* exists elsewhere on your hard drive (outside the reach of the iTunes music folder), it isn't deleted from your hard drive. In fact, if you mistakenly remove a song that you meant to keep, just drag it back into iTunes from the Finder, or even from the Trash. 'Nuff said.

Finding songs in your Music Library

After your collection of audio files grows large, you might have trouble locating that Swedish remix version of "I'm Your Boogie Man." To help you out, iTunes has a built-in Search function. To find a song, type some text into the search field of the main iTunes window. While you type, iTunes tries to find a selection that matches your search text. The search is quite thorough, showing any matching text from the artist, album, song title, and genre fields in the results. For example, if you type **Electronic** into the field, iTunes might return results for the band named *Electronic* or other tunes that you classified as *electronic* in the Genre field. (The section "Know Your Songs," later in this chapter, tells you how to classify your songs by genre, among other options.) Click the magnifying glass at the left side of the Search field to restrict the search even more: by Artists, Albums, Composers, and Songs.

Removing old music from the Library

After you spend some time playing songs with iTunes, you might decide that you didn't *really* want to add 40 different versions of "Louie Louie" to your Library. (Personally, I prefer either the original or the cast from the movie *Animal House*.) To remove a song from the Library, click the song to select it and then press the Delete key on your keyboard.

You can also remove a song from the Library by dragging it to the Trash in your Dock.

Watching video

Watching video in iTunes is similar to listening to your music. To view your video collection, click one of these entries in the Source list:

✦ Movies

✦ TV Shows

If you select Movies or TV Shows, iTunes displays your videos as thumbnails or in cover flow view. Music videos appear as a smart playlist.

From your collection, you can

✦ Double-click a video thumbnail or an entry in the list.

✦ Drag a QuickTime–compatible video clip from the Finder window to the iTunes window. (These typically include video files ending in .mov or .mp4.)

iTunes plays video in the box below the Source list or in full-screen mode, depending on the settings you've chosen on the Playback pane in the iTunes Preferences window. In full-screen mode, move your mouse to display a control strip at the bottom of the screen, sporting the standard slider bar that you can drag to move through the video (as well as a volume control and Fast Forward/Reverse buttons). You can also pause the video by clicking the Pause button.

Keeping Slim Whitman and Slim Shady Apart: Organizing with Playlists

As I mention earlier, the iTunes Music Library can quickly become a fearsomely huge beastie. Each Library can contain thousands upon thousands of songs: If your Library grows anywhere near that large, finding all the songs in your lifelong collection of Paul Simon albums is *not* a fun task. Furthermore, with the Library, you're stuck playing songs in the order that iTunes lists them.

To help you organize your music into groups, use the iTunes playlist feature. A *playlist* is a collection of some of your favorite songs from the Library. You can create as many playlists as you want, and each playlist can contain any number of songs. Whereas the Library lists all available songs, a playlist displays only the songs that you add to it. Further, any changes that you make to a playlist affect only that playlist, leaving the Library intact.

To create a playlist, you can do any of the following:

✦ **Choose File⇨New Playlist.**

✦ **Press ⌘+N.**

✦ **Choose File⇨New Playlist from Selection.** This creates a new playlist and automatically adds any tracks that are currently selected.

✦ **Click a song to select it; click the Genius button at the lower-right corner of the window.** (The Genius button bears a striking "atom" symbol.) iTunes builds a playlist of songs that are similar in some way (typically by matching the genre of the selection or the beats per minute, but also based on recommendations from other iTunes members). Note that your Mac needs an Internet connection to create a Genius playlist, and the larger your music library the longer it will take iTunes to build your playlist.

✦ **Click the iTunes DJ entry in the Playlist section at the left side of the window.** iTunes delivers a random selection of songs taken from your iTunes Music Library — perfect for your next spontaneous party! You can change the order of the songs in the iTunes DJ playlist (known as Party Shuffle in older versions of iTunes), add songs from your Library, or delete songs that don't fit the scintillating ambience of your gathering. Enjoy!

✦ **Click the New Playlist button in the iTunes window** (the plus sign button in the lower-left corner). You get a newly created empty playlist (the toe-tappin' *untitled playlist*).

All playlists appear in the Source list. To help organize your playlists, it's a good idea to . . . well, *name* them. (Aren't you glad now that you have this book?) For example, suppose that you want to plan a party for your polka-loving friends. Instead of running to your computer after each song to change the music, you could create a polka-only playlist. Select and start the playlist at the beginning of the party, and you won't have to worry about changing the music the whole night. (You can concentrate on the accordion.) To load a playlist, select it in the Source list; iTunes displays the songs for that playlist.

The same song can appear in any number of playlists because the songs in a playlist are simply pointers to songs in your Music Library — not the songs themselves. Add and remove them at will to or from any playlist, secure in the knowledge that the songs remain safe in the Library. Removing a playlist is simple: Select the playlist in the Source list and then press Delete.

Removing a playlist doesn't actually delete any songs from your Library.

Some playlists are smarter than others

Click the File menu and you'll see the New Smart Playlist menu command. The contents of a *smart* playlist are automatically created from a specific condition or set of conditions that you set via the Smart Playlist dialog: You can limit the track selection by mundane things, such as album, genre, or artist; or you can get funky and specify songs that were played last, or by the date you added tracks, or even by the sampling rate or total length of the song. For example, iTunes can create a playlist packed with songs that are shorter than three minutes, so you can fill your iPod Shuffle with more stuff! Ah, but wait, you're not limited to a single criterion. If you want to add another criterion, click the plus sign at the right side of the dialog and you get another condition field to refine your selection even further.

You can choose the maximum songs to add to the smart playlist, or limit the size of the playlist by the minutes or hours of play or the number of megabytes or gigabytes the playlist will occupy. (Again, great for automatically gathering as much from your KISS collection that will fit into a specific amount of space on a CD or your iPod.) Mark the Live Updating check box for the ultimate in convenience. iTunes automatically maintains the contents of the smart playlist to keep it current with your conditions at all times in the future. (If you remove tracks manually from a smart playlist, iTunes adds other tracks that match your conditions.)

Now think about what all these settings mean when combined . . . *whoa.* Here's an example yanked directly from my own iTunes library. I created a smart playlist that selects only those songs in the Rock genre. It's limited to 25 songs, selected by least often played, and live updating is turned on. The playlist is named Tracks I've Gotta Hear because it finds the 25 rock songs (from my collection of over 5,000 songs) that I've heard least often! After I listen to a song from this smart playlist, iTunes automatically "freshens" it with another song, allowing me to catch up on the tracks I've been ignoring. Completely, unbelievably *sweet*— and another reason that iTunes is the best music player on Planet Earth!

Know Your Songs

Besides organizing your music into Elvis and non-Elvis playlists, iTunes gives you the option to track your music at the song level. Each song that you add to the Music Library has a complete set of information associated with it. iTunes displays this information in the Info dialog, including

+ **Name:** The name of the song

+ **Artist:** The name of the artist who performed the song

+ **Composer:** The name of the astute individual who actually *wrote* the song

+ **Album Artist:** The name of the artist responsible for a compilation or tribute album

+ **Album:** The album where the song appears

✦ **Grouping:** A group type that you assign

✦ **Year:** The year the artist recorded the song

✦ **BPM:** The beats per minute (which indicates the song's tempo)

✦ **Track Number:** The position of the song on the original album

✦ **Disc Number:** The original disc number in a multi-CD set

✦ **Comments:** A text field that can contain any comments on the song

✦ **Genre:** The classification of the song (such as rock, jazz, or pop)

You can display this information by clicking a song name and pressing ⌘+I — the fields appear on the Info tab.

Setting the song information automatically

Each song that you add to the iTunes Music Library might have song information included with it. If you add music from a commercial audio CD, iTunes connects to a server on the Internet and attempts to find the information for each song on the CD. If you download a song from the Internet, it often comes with some information embedded in the file already; the amount of included information depends on what the creator supplied. (And believe me, it's often misspelled as well — think *Leenard Skeenard.*) If you don't have an Internet connection, iTunes can't access the information and displays generic titles instead.

Setting or changing the song information manually

If iTunes can't find your CD in the online database or someone gives you an MP3 with incomplete or inaccurate information, you can change the information yourself — believe me, you want at least the artist and song name! To view and change the information for a song, perform the following steps:

1. **Select the song in either the Music Library list or a Playlist.**

2. **Press ⌘+I or choose File⇨Get Info.**

3. **Edit the song's information on the Info tab, as shown in Figure 2-3.**

Keep in mind that the more work you put into setting the information of the songs in your Music Library, the easier it is to browse and use iTunes. Incomplete song information can make it more difficult to find your songs in a hurry. If you prefer, you don't have to change all information about a song (it just makes life easier later if you do). Normally, you can get away with setting only a song's title, artist, and genre. The more information you put in, however, the faster you can locate songs and the easier they are to arrange. iTunes tries to help by automatically retrieving known song information, but sometimes you have to roll up your sleeves and do a little work. (Sorry, but the DataElves are out to lunch.)

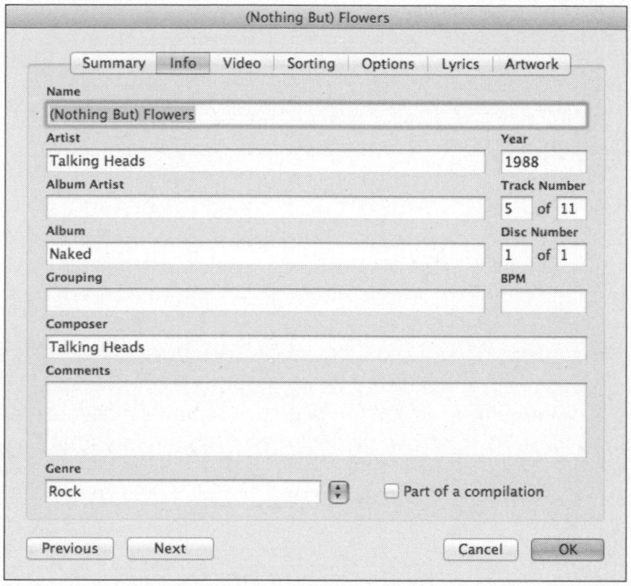

Figure 2-3:
View and
edit song
information
here.

(Nothing But) Flowers

| Summary | Info | Video | Sorting | Options | Lyrics | Artwork |

Name
(Nothing But) Flowers

Artist
Talking Heads

Year
1988

Album Artist

Track Number
5 of 11

Album
Naked

Disc Number
1 of 1

Grouping

BPM

Composer
Talking Heads

Comments

Genre
Rock

☐ Part of a compilation

[Previous] [Next]   [Cancel] [OK]

"What about cover art, Mark?" Well, I'm overjoyed that you asked! iTunes
can try to locate artwork automatically for the tracks you select. (Note that
embedding large images can significantly increase the size of the song file.)
Follow these steps:

1. **Select the desired songs from the track list.**

2. **Click Advanced⇨Get Album Artwork.**

You can set iTunes to automatically attempt the addition of album artwork
every time you rip tracks from an audio CD, or when you add songs without
artwork to your Music Library. Click iTunes and choose Preferences; then
click the Store button and click the Automatically Download Missing Album
Artwork check box to enable it.

Want to manually add album covers to your song info? Select one (or all) of
the songs from a single album in the track list, display the Info dialog, and
click the Artwork tab. Now launch Safari, visit Amazon.com, and do a search
on the same album. Drag the cover image from the Web page right into the
Info dialog, and drop it on top of the "sunken square" image well. When you
click OK, the image appears in the Summary pane, and you can display it
while your music is playing by pressing ⌘+G, or by pressing the Show or
Hide Song Artwork button at the lower left of the iTunes window!

By the way, if you buy tracks or an album from the iTunes Store, Apple always includes album covers automatically.

Ripping Audio Files

You don't have to rely on Internet downloads to get audio files: You can create your own MP3, AAC, Apple Lossless, AIFF, and WAV files from your audio CDs with iTunes. The process of converting audio files to different formats is called *ripping.* (Audiophiles with technical teeth also call this process *digital extraction,* but they're usually ignored at parties by the popular crowd.) Depending on what hardware or software you use, each has its own unique format preferences. For example, most iPod owners prefer MP3 or AAC files, but your audio CDs aren't in that format. Being able to convert files from one format to another is like having a personal translator in the digital world. You don't need to worry if you have the wrong format: You can simply convert it to the format that you need.

The most common type of ripping is to convert CD audio to MP3 (or AAC) format. To rip MP3s from an audio CD, follow these simple steps:

1. Launch iTunes by clicking its icon in the Dock.

Alternatively, you can locate it in your Applications folder.

2. Choose iTunes⇨Preferences.

3. In the Preferences window that appears, click the General toolbar button.

4. Click the Import Settings button.

5. Choose MP3 Encoder from the Import Using pop-up menu.

6. Choose High Quality (160 Kbps) from the Setting pop-up menu and then click OK.

This bit rate setting provides the best compromise between quality (it gives you better than CD quality, which is 128 Kbps) and file size (tracks you rip will be significantly smaller than "audiophile" bit rates such as 192 Kbps or higher).

7. Load an audio CD into your Mac.

The CD title shows up in the iTunes Source list (under the Devices heading), which is on the left side of the iTunes window. The CD track listing appears on the right side of the window.

If iTunes asks you whether you want to import the contents of the CD into your Music Library, you can click Yes and skip the rest of the steps; however, if you've disabled this prompt, just continue with the remaining two steps.

8. **Clear the check box of any song that you don't want to import from the CD.**

   All songs on the CD have a check box next to their title by default. Unmarked songs aren't imported.

   Notice that the Browse button changes to Import CD.

9. **After you select the songs that you want added to the Library, click the Import CD button.**

There's also another form of ripping: If you have a USB turntable or cassette deck connected to your Mac, you can digitize your old analog recordings on albums and cassettes into shiny digital audio files. Often it's simpler to just buy the same music from the iTunes Store, but if your treasured music isn't available on the Store or on audio CD, it's the next best thing!

Tweaking the Audio for Your Ears

Besides the standard volume controls that I mention earlier in this chapter, iTunes offers a full equalizer. An *equalizer* permits you to alter the volume of various frequencies in your music, allowing you to boost low sounds, lower high sounds, or anything in between. Now you can customize the way your music sounds and adjust it to your liking.

To open the Equalizer (as shown in Figure 2-4), do one of the following:

Figure 2-4: Use the Equalizer sliders to tweak the sound of your music.

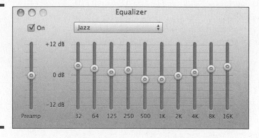

Book III
Chapter 2

Jamming with iTunes and iPod

✦ Choose Window➪Equalizer.

✦ Press ⌘+Option+2.

What's with the numbers next to the station names?

When choosing an Internet radio station, keep your Internet connection speed in mind. If you're using a broadband DSL or cable connection — or if you're listening at work over your company's high-speed network — you can listen to stations broadcasting at 128 Kbps (or even higher). The higher the bit rate, the better the music sounds. At 128 Kbps, for example, you're listening to sound that's as good as an audio CD.

However, if you're listening over a dial-up modem connection, iTunes can't keep up with audio streaming at higher bit rates, so you're limited to stations broadcasting at 56 Kbps or lower.

The Equalizer window has an impressive array of 11 sliders. Use the leftmost slider (Preamp) to set the overall level of the Equalizer. The remaining sliders represent various frequencies that the human ear can perceive. Setting a slider to a position in the middle of its travel causes that frequency to play back with no change. Move the slider above the midpoint to boost that frequency; conversely, move the slider below the midpoint to reduce the volume of that frequency.

Continue adjusting the equalizer sliders until your music sounds the way you like it. When you close the Equalizer window, iTunes remembers your settings until you change them again. In case you prefer to leave frequencies to the experts, the iTunes Equalizer has several predefined settings to match most musical styles. Click the pop-up menu at the top of the Equalizer window to select a genre.

After you adjust the sound to your satisfaction, close the Equalizer window to return to the iTunes interface and relax with those funky custom notes from James Brown.

A New Kind of Radio Station

Besides playing back your favorite audio files, iTunes can also tune in Internet radio stations from around the globe. You can listen to any of a large number of preset stations, seek out lesser-known stations not recognized by iTunes, or even add your favorite stations to your playlists. This section shows you how to do it all.

iTunes Radio

Although it's not a radio tuner in the strictest sense, iTunes Radio can locate virtual radio stations all over the world that send audio over the Internet — a process usually dubbed *streaming* amongst the "in" Internet crowd. iTunes can track down hundreds of Internet radio stations in a variety of styles with only a few mouse clicks.

To begin listening to Internet radio with iTunes, click the Radio icon located beneath the Library icon in the Source list. The result is a list of more than 20 types of radio stations, organized by genre.

When you expand a Radio category by clicking its disclosure triangle, iTunes queries a tuning server and locates the name and address of dozens of radio stations for that category. Whether you like Elvis or not-Elvis (those passing fads, like new wave, classical, or alternative), something's here for everyone. The Radio also offers news, sports, and talk radio.

After iTunes fetches the names and descriptions of radio stations, double-click one that you want to hear. iTunes immediately jumps into action, loads the station, and begins to play it.

Tuning in your own stations

Although iTunes offers you a large list of popular radio stations on the web, it's by no means comprehensive. Eventually, you might run across a radio station that you'd like to hear, but it's not listed in iTunes. Luckily, iTunes permits you to listen to other stations, too. To listen to a radio station that iTunes doesn't list, you need the station's web address.

In iTunes, choose Advanced⇨Open Audio Stream (or press ⌘+U). In the Open Stream dialog that appears (as shown in Figure 2-5), enter the URL of your desired radio station and then click OK. Within seconds, iTunes tunes in your station.

Figure 2-5:
Tuning into MLC Radio, my Internet radio station.

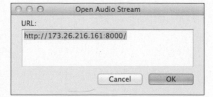

"I have an itch to hear 'Kung Fu Fighting'!"

This particular technology author has a preference for a certain hot Net jam spot: *MLC Radio,* the Internet radio station I've been running for several years now. I call my station a '70s Time Machine because it includes hundreds of classic hits from 1970–1979, inclusive. You hear everything from "Rock and Roll Hoochie Koo" by Rick Derringer to "Moonlight Feels Right" by Starbuck. (Hey, I'm summing up a decade here, so be prepared for both Rush and the Captain and Tennille, too.) The station broadcasts at 128 Kbps (audio CD quality), so you need a broadband connection to listen. For the radio's Internet address or help connecting to MLC Radio, visit my web site at `www.mlcbooks.com` — and then follow the steps in the next section to add MLC Radio to your playlists!

Radio stations in your playlists

If you find yourself visiting an online radio station more than once, you'll be glad to know that iTunes supports radio stations in its playlists. To add a radio station to a playlist from the Radio list, do the following:

1. **Open the category that contains the station you want to add to your playlist.**

2. **Locate the station that you want to add to your playlist and drag it from the Radio list to the desired playlist on the left.**

   If you haven't created any playlists yet, see the section "Keeping Slim Whitman and Slim Shady Apart: Organizing with Playlists" earlier in this chapter to find out how.

Adding a radio station that doesn't appear in the Radio list is a bit trickier but possible nonetheless. Even though iTunes allows you to load a radio station URL manually by using the Open Stream command in the Advanced menu, it doesn't give you an easy way to add it to the playlist. Follow these steps to add a specific radio station to a playlist:

1. **Add any radio station from the Radio list to your desired playlist.**

   Any station in the list will do, as you'll immediately change both the station's URL and name to create your new station entry in the Playlist.

2. **Press ⌘+I or choose File⇨Get Info to bring up the information dialog for that station.**

3. **Click the Summary section and change the URL by clicking the Edit URL button.**

4. **Enter the desired URL and click OK.**

5. **Click the Info tab, type the new station name, and then click OK.**

iSending iStuff to iPod

If you're cool enough (like me) to own an iPod, you'll be happy to know that iTunes has features for your personal audio and video jukebox as well. *iPods,* Apple's multimedia players, comprise an entire family of portable devices (ranging from $49 to about $249) that can hold anywhere from about 300 songs to literally thousands of songs, as well as podcasts, photos, and video. This great gadget and those like it have become known world-wide as *the* preferred portable digital media player.

If you own an iPod touch, iPhone or iPad, you can also buy all sorts of applications for these devices on the iTunes Store, and iTunes even keeps track of these applications as part of your library.

You connect your iPod to any Macintosh or Windows PC with USB 2.0 ports with the included cable. After the iPod's connected, it automatically synchronizes to the playlists in iTunes. The iPod and the iTunes software communicate with each other and figure out what items are in your iTunes Library (as compared with the iPod Library). If they discover songs, podcasts, and video in your iTunes Library that are missing from your iPod, the items automatically transfer to the iPod. Conversely, if the iPod contains stuff that's no longer in iTunes, the iPod automatically removes those files from its drive.

Go back and reread that last sentence about the iPod *automatically removing* files from its drive. (I'll wait here.) Apple added this feature in an effort to be attentive to copyright concerns. The reasoning is that if you connect your iPod to your friend's computer, you can't transfer songs from the iPod to that computer. Of course, you could always look at it from the marketing perspective as a feature that makes sure your Mac and iPod are always in total sync. Whatever the case, pay close attention and read all warning dialogs when connecting to a computer other than your own, or you might wipe out your iPod's library.

The best thing I can say about the iPod and iTunes combination is . . . well . . . that there *isn't* anything else to say about them. The auto-sync feature is so easy to use, you forget about it almost immediately.

This chapter — even as long as it is — just can't explain all the ins and outs of the iTunes/iPod relationship! For a complete look at both iTunes and the iPod, I can heartily recommend a fellow *For Dummies* book, *iPod & iTunes For Dummies,* 8th Edition, by Tony Bove (Wiley Publishing).

**Book III
Chapter 2**

**Jamming with
iTunes and iPod**

Sharing Your Media across Your Network

Ready to share your music, podcasts, and video — *legally,* mind you — with other folks on your local network? You can offer your digital media to other iTunes users across your home or office. Follow these steps:

1. **Choose iTunes⇨Preferences to open the Preferences dialog.**

2. **Click Sharing.**

3. **Select the Share My Library on My Local Network check box.**

4. **Specify whether you want to share your entire library or only selected playlists and files.**

   Sharing selected playlists is a good idea for those Meatmen and Sex Pistols fans who work at a cubicle farm in a big corporation.

5. **If you want to restrict access to just a few people, select the Require Password check box; then type a password in the text box.**

6. **Click OK.**

Your shared folder appears within the Source list for all iTunes users who enabled the Look for Shared Libraries check box on the same pane of their iTunes Preferences dialog. Note that the music you share with others can't be imported or copied, so everything stays legal.

Want to change that frumpy default name for your shared media library to something more exotic, like "Dan's Techno Beat Palace"? No problem — display the Preferences dialog again, but this time click the General button and click in the Library Name text box. Edit your network entertainment persona to your heart's content.

You can also share your media library using *Home Sharing*, which allows up to five devices to join in the fun — that includes both Mac computers and iOS devices (your iPad, iPhone and iPod touch, running iOS 4.3 or later). Home Sharing requires a wireless network connection for all of your devices, and you'll have to enter the same Apple ID information on each device. To turn on Home Sharing within iTunes, click Advanced on the iTunes menu and choose Turn On Home Sharing. (Don't forget to repeat this setup on each computer.) Once Home Sharing is enabled, shared libraries will appear in the Source list under the Shared heading.

Sending music elsewhere with AirPlay

If your Mac has an AirPort Extreme wireless card and you're using an AirPort Express portable wireless Base Station, you can ship your songs right to your Base Station from within iTunes, and from there to your home stereo or boom box! (I get into some serious discussion of AirPort Express in Book VI, Chapter 3.)

After your AirPort Express Base Station is plugged in and you connect your home stereo (or a boombox, or a pair of powered stereo speakers) to the stereo minijack on the Base Station, you see a Speakers pop-up list button

appear at the bottom of the iTunes window. (If the Speakers button doesn't appear, choose iTunes⇨Preferences to open the Preferences dialog and click the Devices button on the toolbar. Make sure that the Look for Remote Speakers Connected with AirPlay check box is enabled.)

Click the Speakers button, and you can choose to broadcast the music you're playing in iTunes across your wireless network. Ain't technology truly *grand?*

Joining the Ping People

Sure, it's a silly name, but don't let that fool you — the addition of Apple's new Ping social networking feature to iTunes has quickly built a formidable online community! When you enable Ping within iTunes, you can interact with both artists and other music lovers in a number of different ways:

✦ **Follow your favorite artists.** Are you a fan of Katy Perry? How about Rascal Flatts? With Ping, you can follow your favorite artists and bands online (without all that tiresome traveling from concert to concert and the repeated arguments with their bodyguards). When performers you follow add a new photo or video, recommend songs or post concert information to Ping, you'll receive those updates immediately!

✦ **Follow your friends:** You can also choose other Ping music fans to follow, creating your own miniature "music appreciation society"! Like Facebook, you can send messages — but Ping also makes it easy to share your music reviews (and comment on the reviews that others post), and you can recommend your favorite artists to others.

✦ **Share your playlists:** Of course, you've already created the perfect party mix playlist — why not share that playlist with the world? When you publish a playlist through the iTunes Store, it's easily shared on Ping as well, and your followers can comment on your choice of The Perfect Opening Song.

**Book III
Chapter 2**

**Jamming with
iTunes and iPod**

To turn Ping on within iTunes, follow these steps:

1. **Click the Ping item under the Store heading in the Source list.**

2. **Click the large friendly Turn On Ping button.**

   iTunes displays the Apple ID login dialog — if you've already purchased items through the iTunes Store, you're familiar with this dialog and you've already created an Apple ID. (If you need to create an Apple ID account, click on the Create Account button and enter the required information.)

3. **Type your Apple ID and password, and then click Sign In.**

   Before you can enter the fray, you need to create your Ping profile, which includes information that will be visible to other Ping users.

4. **Enter your profile information and click Continue.**

   You can add a photo of yourself from your hard drive (or take a quick snapshot using iPhoto) by clicking the Add Photo button.

   Whatever you type in the About Me box is visible to the general public, so don't include your e-mail address, telephone number, or other personal data in your comments!

5. **Choose how iTunes will display your favorite music and click Continue.**

   By default, any music you like or buy is displayed within Ping, as well as any music you rate or review. However, you can also choose to manually pick the music Ping displays, or turn off your music display entirely.

6. **Choose your privacy settings.**

   If you're familiar with my views on security, you've already guessed what I recommend here: If you do allow others to follow you on Ping, make sure you click the Require My Approval to Follow Me check box to enable it. (This way, you can choose who is able to follow you on Ping — I'm all about weeding out undesirables.) If you'd rather not be followed at all, click the Don't Allow People to Follow Me radio button.

7. **Click Done.**

The Ping pane within iTunes is similar to the display of recent activity within Facebook, but you can use the links at the right side of the pane to jump directly to your reviews, your favorite artists, or the folks who follow you. Naturally, Apple also allows you to purchase music, movies, and video at every turn, offering direct links from reviews and comments to corresponding items in the iTunes Store.

It's easy to search for a specific artist or personal profile. Click the People link at the right side of the pane, and then click in the Find People search box and type the desired name.

To invite specific people to join you within Ping, click the Invite Friends by Mail link.

Now here's where things get truly nifty: Choose a track from your iTunes music library that you bought from the iTunes Store and click on the track name in the list. See the Ping menu button that appears? Click it and choose Like or Post, and iTunes automatically updates your Ping profile with your recommendation or comment! Your followers can listen to a portion of the track, and then buy it if they like what they hear. It's this close integration between iTunes, the iTunes Store, and Ping that excites music fans — stay tuned as Apple continues to add functionality and new features to Ping.

Burning Music to Shiny Plastic Circles

Besides being a great audio player, iTunes is adept at creating CDs, too. iTunes makes the process of recording songs to a CD as simple as a few mouse clicks. Making the modern version of a compilation (or *mix*) tape is easier than getting a kid to eat ice cream. iTunes lets you burn CDs in one of three formats:

✦ **Audio CD:** This is the typical kind of commercial music CD that you buy at a store. Most typical music audio CDs store 700MB of data, which translates into about 80 minutes of music.

✦ **Data CD or DVD:** A standard CD-ROM or DVD-ROM is recorded with the audio files. This disc can't be played in any standard audio CD player (even if it supports MP3 CDs, which I discuss next). Therefore, you can listen to these songs only by using your Mac and an audio player, such as iTunes or a PC running Windows.

✦ **MP3 CD:** As does the ordinary computer CD-ROM that I describe, an MP3 CD holds MP3 files in data format. However, the files are arranged in such a way that they can be recognized by audio CD players that support the MP3 CD format (especially boomboxes, DVD players, personal CD players, and car stereos). Because MP3 files are so much smaller than the digital audio tracks found on traditional audio CDs, you can fit as many as 160 typical four-minute songs on one disc. These discs can also be played on your Mac via iTunes.

Backing up within iTunes

iTunes offers a built-in backup feature for your media library — I told you this was the best media player ever designed!

Choose File⇨Library⇨Back Up to Disc to start the process. You can choose to back up your entire iTunes library and all your playlists (which I recommend) or just the content you've purchased from the iTunes Store. Personally, if I lost everything in my collection except for what I've bought from the iTunes Store, I'd be just as crushed .... Back it all up, and you won't be sorry.

Click Back Up, and iTunes will prompt you for blank CDs or DVDs. If you need to restore from your completed backup, just launch iTunes and load the first backup disc into your drive.

How often is often enough when it comes to backing up your content? That depends completely on how often your media library changes. The idea is to back up often enough so that you always have a recent copy of your media files close by. (Note that if you're already backing up your Mac's hard drive using Time Machine, there's no reason to back up your library separately to disc.)

Keep in mind that MP3 CDs aren't the same as the standard audio CDs that you buy at the store, and you can't play them in older audio CD players that don't support the MP3 CD format. Rather, this is the kind of archival disc that you burn at home for your own collection.

To begin the process, build a playlist (or select an existing playlist that you want to record). If necessary, create a new Playlist and add to it whatever songs you would like to have on the CD. (See the earlier section, "Keeping Slim Whitman and Slim Shady Apart: Organizing with Playlists," if you need a refresher.) With the songs in the correct order, right-click the playlist and choose Burn Playlist to Disc to commence the disc burning process. Click the desired recording format (again, usually Audio CD) in the Burn Settings dialog that appears.

To save yourself from sonic shock, I always recommend that you enable the Sound Check check box before you burn. iTunes adjusts the volume on all the songs on your audio CD so that they play at the same volume level.

Ready to go? Click Burn and load the blank disc. iTunes lets you know when the recording is complete.

Feasting on iTunes Visuals

By now, you know that iTunes is a feast for the ears, but did you know that it can provide you with eye candy as well? With just a click or two, you can view mind-bending graphics that stretch, move, and pulse with your music, as shown in Figure 2-6.

Figure 2-6:
iTunes can
display
some
awesome
patterns!

To begin viewing iTunes visuals, choose View➪Show Visualizer (or press
⌘+T). Immediately, most of your iTunes interface disappears and begins
displaying groovy lava lamp-style animations (like, *sassy,* man). To stop the
visuals, choose View➪Hide Visualizer (or press ⌘+T again). The usual sunny
aluminum face of iTunes returns.

You can also change the viewing size of the iTunes visuals in the View menu.
From the View menu item, choose Full Screen (or press ⌘+F). To escape
from the Full Screen mode, click the mouse or press Esc.

You can still control iTunes with the keyboard while the visuals are zooming
around your screen. See Table 2-1 earlier in this chapter for a rundown on
common keyboard shortcuts.

The iTunes Visualizer has many hidden features. While viewing the
Visualizer, press ? to see a list of hidden Visualizer settings.

But wait, more Easter eggs are to be found! Again, while viewing the
Visualizer, press one of following keys:

✦ **M:** Changes the Visualizer pattern

✦ **P:** Changes the Visualizer color scheme

Press either of these keys repeatedly to cycle through the various patterns and color schemes lurking deep within the Visualizer. (Personally, I'm a random Visualizer guy . . . there are so many patterns and schemes, I just let my Mac do all the work.)

Additionally, you'll find third-party Visualizer plug-ins available for downloading on Apple's web site and other Mac-related download sites — heck, some even display lyrics, karaoke-style! Choose a different Visualizer plug-in from the View⇨Visualizer menu item. (Call me old-fashioned, but I like the default, iTunes Visualizer.)

Exercising Parental Authority

Do young children use your Mac? I'll be honest here: A large amount of content within the iTunes Store, including audio, movies, and even apps, is stuff that I don't consider suitable for kids. And what about the media that others in the family may decide to share? Such is the world we live in today — and the good folks at Apple recognize that you may not want to inadvertently allow your kids to have access to explicit content.

Luckily, you can use the Parental settings within iTunes to build a secure fence around content that's for "grown-ups only" — heck, you can even banish items from the Source list entirely. Figure 2-7 illustrates the Parental pane within the iTunes Preferences dialog.

You must log in with an Administrator account to change these settings, just like with the Parental Controls within Lion's System Preferences dialog. If the settings are *locked* — the padlock icon at the bottom of the dialog is closed — click on it and supply your administrator password to unlock them.

To enable parental control, follow these steps:

1. **Choose iTunes⇨Preferences.**

2. **Click the Parental tab.**

3. **Click any of the Disable check boxes to prevent access to those features.**

It's important to note that disabling features inside iTunes applies to *all* user accounts — no matter who is logged in! You'll notice that any features you disable disappear completely from the Source list at the left side of the iTunes window once you click OK at the end of these steps.

4. **Click the Ratings For pop-up menu and choose your country.**

Because Apple maintains separate iTunes Stores for different nations, you can choose which country's iTunes Store to monitor. If you like, you can disable the display of content ratings within your iTunes library by deselecting the Show Content Ratings in Library check box.

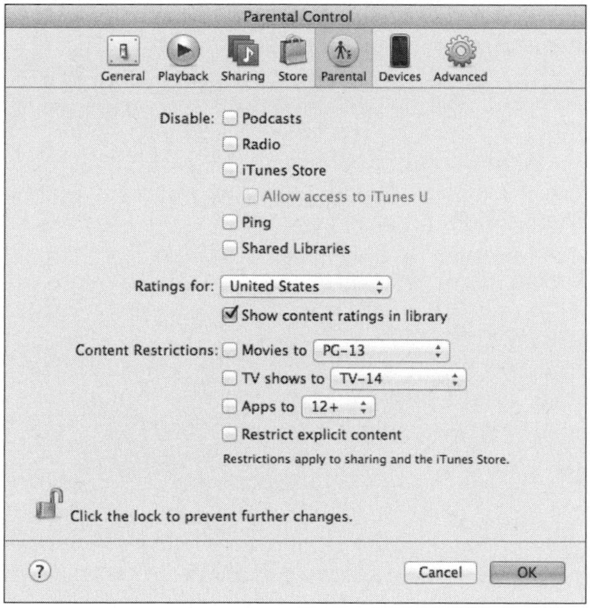

Figure 2-7:
You can protect your kids from explicit content using the Parental settings.

5. **To restrict specific content within the iTunes Store, click the check box next to the source, and then click the corresponding pop-up menu to choose the restriction level.**

    Note that these restrictions apply only to content on the iTunes Store and media shared with your Mac — content within your iTunes library is never restricted.

6. **Click the padlock icon at the bottom of the dialog to close it and prevent any changes.**

7. **Click OK.**

Buying Digital Media the Apple Way

Before we wave goodbye to the happy residents of iTunes iSland, I won't forget to mention the hottest spot on the Internet for buying music and video: the iTunes Store, which you can reach from the cozy confines of iTunes. (That is, as long as you have an Internet connection. If you don't, it's time to turn the page to a different chapter.)

Click the iTunes Store item in the Source list, and after a few moments you're presented with the latest offerings. Click a link in the store list to browse according to media type, or click the Power Search link to search by song title, artist, album, or composer. The Back/Forward buttons at the top of the iTunes Store window operate much the same as those in Safari, moving you backward or forward in sequence through pages you've already seen.

Clicking the Home button (which, through no great coincidence, looks like a miniature house) takes you back to the Store's main page.

To display the details on a specific album, track, video, podcast, or audiobook (whew), just click it. If you're interested in buying just certain tracks (for that perfect road warrior mix), you get to listen to 90 seconds of any track — for free, no less, and at full sound quality. To add an item to your iTunes Store shopping cart, click the Add Song/Movie/Album/Video/Podcast/Audiobook button (sheesh!). When you're ready to buy, click the Shopping Cart item in the Source list and then click the Buy Now button. (At the time of this writing, tracks are usually 99 cents a pop, and an entire album is typically $9.99 . . . what a bargain!

The iTunes Store creates an account for you based on your e-mail address, and it keeps secure track of your credit card information for future purchases. After you use the iTunes Store once, you rarely have to log in or retype your credit card information again.

The tracks and files that you download are saved to a separate playlist called Purchased. After the download is finished, you can play them, copy them to other playlists, burn them to CD or DVD, share 'em over your network, or ship them to your iPod, just as you can any other item in your iTunes Library.

You can also put the Genius button to work for you, in league with the iTunes store. Click the Show Genius Sidebar button at the lower-right corner of the iTunes window — it looks like an arrow inside a square — and iTunes displays the Genius Sidebar, where iTunes recommends music that you can buy from the iTunes Store that's similar to the albums in your Music Library. Click the button again to banish the sidebar.

Remember all those skeptics who claimed that buying digital audio and video could never work over the Internet because of piracy issues and high costs? Well, bunkie, hats off to Apple: Once again, our favorite technology leader has done something the *right* way!

Chapter 3: Focusing on iPhoto

In This Chapter

⤲ **Importing pictures from your hard drive or digital camera**

⤲ **Organizing images with iPhoto**

⤲ **Tweaking the appearance of photographs**

⤲ **Sharing photos with your friends**

For years, the Macintosh has been the choice of professional photographers for working with digital images — not surprising, considering the Mac's graphical nature. Apple continues this tradition with *iPhoto,* a photography tool for the home user that can help you organize, edit, and even publish your photographs. (It sports more features than a handful of Swiss army knives.) After you shoot your photos with a digital camera, you can import them into iPhoto, edit them, and publish them. You're not limited to photos that you take yourself, either; you can edit, publish, and organize all kinds of digital image files. You can even create a photo album and use the iPhoto interface to order a handsome soft- or hard-bound copy shipped to you, or create a slideshow that you can burn to a DVD.

In this chapter, I walk you through an overview of what iPhoto can do. After that, I give you a brief tour of the controls within iPhoto so that you can see what features are available to you, including features for managing, printing, and publishing your photos.

Delving into iPhoto

In Figure 3-1, you can see most of the major controls offered in iPhoto '11. (Other controls automatically appear when you enter different modes; I cover them in upcoming sections of this chapter.)

Although I cover these controls and sections of the window in more detail in the following sections, here's a quick rundown of what you're looking at when you first launch iPhoto:

✦ **Source list:** This list of image locations determines which photos iPhoto displays.

- You can choose to display either your entire image library or just the last set of digital images that you downloaded from your camera.

- You can create new *albums* of your own that appear in the Source list; albums make it much easier to organize your photos.

- Photos can be grouped by *Event* (when they were taken), *Faces* (who appears in the photos), and *Places* (where photos were taken).

- You can view the photos you've shared online using MobileMe, Facebook and Flickr.

- You can create books, calendars, cards, and slideshows.

✦ **Viewer:** This pane displays the images from the currently selected photo source.

You can drag or click to select photos in the Viewer for further tricks, such as assigning keywords and image editing.

✦ **Full Screen button:** Click this button to switch to a full-screen display of your photos. In full-screen mode, the Source list disappears, and both images and events appear as thumbnails. You can double-click on a thumbnail to view the image (or the contents, if it's an event) using your Mac's entire screen real estate. You can also use the same controls that I discuss later in this chapter for chores like sharing and editing images — the toolbar is still available at the bottom of the screen.

✦ **Search button:** Click the button next to the Search text box to locate photos by specific criteria, or just click in the box and start typing to search by description and title.

✦ **Zoom slider:** Drag this slider to the left to reduce the size of the thumbnails in the Viewer. This allows you to see more thumbnails at one time, which is a great boon for quick visual searches. Drag the slider to the right to expand the size of the thumbnails, which makes it easier to differentiate details between similar photos in the Viewer.

✦ **Play Slideshow:** Select an event, album, book, or slideshow in the Source list (or multiple images you've selected in the Viewer) and click this button to start a full-screen slideshow using those images.

✦ **Info button:** Click this button to display information on the currently selected photos (or the item selected in the Source list).

✦ **Edit button:** Click this button to edit the currently selected photos. (I cover editing in depth later in the chapter.)

✦ **Create button:** Click this button to add a new blank album, book, calendar, card, or slideshow to your Source list.

✦ **Add To button:** Click this button to add the currently selected photos to an existing album, slideshow, book, card, or calendar.

✦ **Share button:** Click this button to share the currently selected photos on MobileMe, Flickr, or Facebook — you can also order prints or e-mail the photos.

The toolbar buttons you see depend on which operation you're performing — for example, you see different toolbar buttons when you're editing a photo.

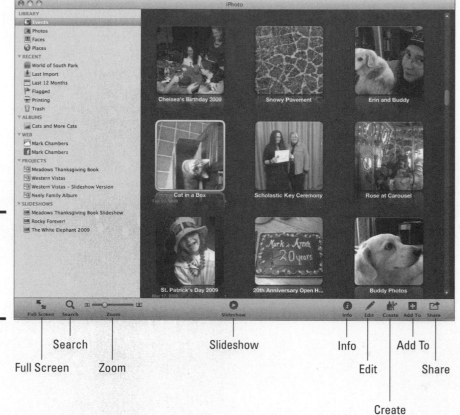

Figure 3-1:
iPhoto
greets you
with an
attractive
window.

Search   Slideshow   Info   Add To

Full Screen   Zoom   Edit   Share

Create

Working with Images in iPhoto

Even a superbly designed image display and editing application such as iPhoto '11 would look overwhelming if everything were jammed into one window. Thus, Apple's developers provide different operational modes (such as editing and book creation) that you can use in the one iPhoto window. Each mode allows you to perform different tasks, and you can switch modes at just about any time by clicking the corresponding toolbar button.

In this section, I discuss three of these modes — import, organize, and edit — and what you can do when you're in them. Then I conclude the chapter with sections on publishing and sharing your images.

Import Images 101

In *import* mode, you're ready to download images directly from your digital camera — as long as your specific camera model is supported in iPhoto.

You can find out which cameras are known to be supported by visiting the Apple iPhoto support page at www.apple.com/support/iphoto/. And you're not limited to cameras, of course: You can also import photos from a memory card reader (like the SDXC card slot sported by your MacBook Pro), or even a Kodak PhotoCD.

Follow these steps to import images:

1. **Connect your digital camera to your Mac.**

Plug one end of a USB cable into your camera and the other end into your Mac's USB port and prepare your camera to download images.

2. **Launch iPhoto.**

Your Mac will probably launch iPhoto automatically when your camera is detected, but you can always launch iPhoto manually by clicking its icon in the Dock (or in your Applications folder).

3. **Type an event name for the imported photos, such as** Birthday Party **or** Godzilla Ravages Tokyo.

4. **To allow iPhoto to automatically separate images into separate events based on the date they were taken, click the Split Events check box to select it.**

5. **Click the Import All button to import your photographs from the camera.**

The images are added to your Photo Library, where you can organize them as you wish.

To select specific images to import, hold down the ⌘ key and click each desired photo; click Import Selected instead of Import All.

6. **Specify whether the images you're importing should be deleted from the camera afterward.**

If you don't expect to download these images again to another computer or another device, you can choose to delete the photos from your camera automatically. This saves you a step, frees space for new photos, and helps eliminate the guilt that can crop up when you nix your pix. (Sorry, I couldn't resist.)

"What's that about an Event, Mark?" After you download the contents of your digital camera, those contents count as a virtual *Event* in iPhoto — based on either the date that you imported them or the date they were taken. For example, you can always display the last images you imported by clicking Last Import. If you want to see photos from your son's graduation, they appear as a separate Event. (Events and Last Import both appear in the Source list). Think about that . . . it's pretty tough to arrange old-fashioned film prints by the moment in time that they document, but iPhoto makes it easy for you to see just which photos are part of the same group! I explain more about Events in the next section.

Importing images from your hard drive

If you have a folder of images that you've collected already on your hard drive, a CD, a DVD, an external drive, or a USB flash drive, adding them to your library is easy. Just drag the folder from a Finder window and drop it into the Source list in the iPhoto window. iPhoto automatically creates a new album using the folder name, and you can sit back while the images are imported into that new album. iPhoto recognizes images in several formats: JPEG, GIF, RAW, PNG, PICT, PSD, PDF, and TIFF.

If you have individual images, you can drag them as well. Select the images in a Finder window and drag them into the desired album in the Source list. To add them to the album currently displayed in the Viewer, drag the selected photos and drop them in the Viewer instead.

If you'd rather import images by using a standard Mac Open dialog, choose File⇨Import to Library. Simplicity strikes again!

There are four methods of organizing photos: the *album*, which you may be familiar with from older versions of iPhoto, *Events*, *Faces,* and *Places*.

Organize mode: Organizing and sorting your images

In the days of film prints, you could always stuff another shoebox with your latest photos or buy another sticky album to expand your library. Your digital camera, though, stores images as files instead, and many folks don't print their digital photographs. Instead, you can keep your entire collection of digital photographs and scanned images well ordered and easily retrieved by using iPhoto's *organize* mode. Then you can display them as a slideshow, print them to your system printer, use them as Desktop backgrounds, or burn them to an archive disc.

A new kind of photo album

The most familiar method of organizing images in iPhoto is the *album.* Each album can represent any division you like, be it a year, a vacation, your daughter, or your daughter's ex-boyfriends. Follow these steps:

1. **Create a new album.**

   You can either choose File⇨New Album or press ⌘+N, as shown in Figure 3-2. iPhoto creates a new entry under the Albums heading in the Source list.

2. **Type the name for your new photo album.**

3. **Press Return.**

iPhoto also offers a special type of album called a *Smart Album,* which you can create from the File menu (or, from the keyboard by pressing Option+⌘+N). A Smart Album contains only photos that match certain criteria that you choose, including using the keywords and rating that you assign your images. Other criteria include text in the photo filenames, dates the images were added to iPhoto, and any comments you might have added (as well as camera-specific data like ISO and shutter speed). Now here's the really nifty angle: iPhoto *automatically* builds and maintains Smart Albums for you, adding new photos that match the criteria (and deleting those that you remove from your Photo Library)! Smart Albums icons carry a gear symbol in the Source list.

You can display information about the currently selected item in the information pane under the Source list. Just click the Info button at the bottom of the iPhoto window, which sports the familiar "*i*-in-a-circle" logo. You can also type a short note or description in the Description box that appears in the Infopane, or add keywords to help you organize your photos.

You can also change information on an image by selecting it in the Viewer and clicking the Info button. Click the Title heading in the pane to display a text edit box, and you can simply click in the box to type a new value.

You can drag images from the Viewer into any album you choose. For example, you can copy an image to another album by dragging it from the Viewer to the desired album in the Source list.

Figure 3-2:
Add a new album in iPhoto.

To remove a photo that has fallen out of favor, follow these steps:

1. **In the Source list, select the desired album.**

2. **In the Viewer, select the photo (click it) that you want to remove.**

3. **Press Delete.**

When you remove a photo from an album, you *don't* remove the photo from your collection (which is represented by the Photos entry under the Library heading in the Source list). That's because an album is just a group of links to the images in your collection. To completely remove the offending photo from iPhoto, click the Photos entry under the Library heading to display your entire collection of images and delete the picture there.

To remove an entire album from the Source list, just click it in the Source list to select it — in the Viewer, you can see the images that it contains — and then press Delete. (Alternatively, right-click or Control-click the offending album and choose Delete Album from the pop-up menu.)

To rename an album, click the entry under the Albums heading in the Source list to select it and then click again to display a text box. Type the new album name and press Return.

Change your mind? Daughter's ex is back in the picture, so to speak? iPhoto comes complete with a handy-dandy Undo feature. Just press ⌘+Z, and it's as though your last action never happened. (A great trick for those moments when you realize you just deleted your only image of your first car from your Library.)

Arranging stuff by Events

As I mention earlier, Events are essentially a group of images that you shot or downloaded at the same time — iPhoto figures that those images belong together (which is usually a pretty safe assumption). Figure 3-3 illustrates some of the Events I've created in my iPhoto collection.

An Event can be renamed, as can an album — you just use a different procedure. Click the Events entry under the Library heading in the Source list to display your Events in the Viewer; click the existing Event name in the caption underneath the thumbnail. A text box appears in which you can type a new name; click Return to update the Event.

Although a photo can appear in multiple albums, it can only appear in one Event.

Try moving your mouse cursor over an Event thumbnail in the Viewer and you'll see that iPhoto displays the date range when the images were taken, as well as the total number of images in the Event. Ah, but things get *really* cool when you move your mouse cursor back and forth over an Event with many images. The thumbnail animates and displays all the images in the Event, without your using old-fashioned scroll bars or silly arrows! (Why can't I think of this stuff? This is the future, dear readers.)

To display the contents of an Event in the Viewer, just double-click the Event thumbnail. To return to the Events thumbnails, click the All Events button at the top of the Viewer.

Decided to merge those Prom Event pictures with your daughter's Graduation Event? No problem! You could drag one Event thumbnail on top of another, but that's the easy way. Alternatively, click the Events entry under the Library heading in the Source list to display your Events and then hold down ⌘ while you click the Events that you want to merge. Heck, if the events you want to merge are selected, right-click on one of them and choose Merge Events from the menu that appears. Click Merge in the confirmation dialog that appears.

Whilst organizing, you can create a brand-new empty Event by clicking Events➪Create Event. Feel free to drag photos from albums, other Events, or your Photo library into your new Event.

Figure 3-3: Events help you organize by what happened, not just when it happened!

Working with Faces and Places

iPhoto '11 includes two organizational tools called Faces and Places. These two categories appear in the Library section of the Source list.

Putting names to faces:

First, tackle Faces. (Well, don't literally tackle anyone's face. That would hurt!) Faces is a sophisticated recognition system that automatically recognizes human faces within the photos that you add to your Library. (I don't know whether it works well with pets — but you can try, anyway.) Naturally, you have to identify faces first before iPhoto can recognize them, which it does through a process called *tagging*.

To tag a face, follow these steps:

1. **In the Source list, click the Photos item to display your image library.**

2. **In the Viewer, click the photo with a person you want to tag.**

The photo is selected, as indicated by the yellow border.

3. **Click the Info button in the iPhoto toolbar at the bottom of the window.**

iPhoto displays the Info pane you see in Figure 3-4.

4. **Click the Add a Face link in the Faces section of the Info pane.**

**Book III
Chapter 3**

Focusing on iPhoto

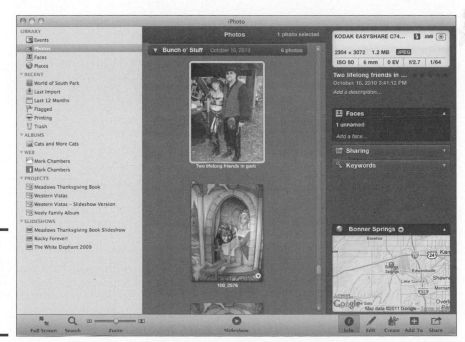

Figure 3-4:
Adding another mug to my collection of Faces.

5. If the face is unrecognized (labeled as Click to Name), click the label to open a text box and type the person's name.

If iPhoto recognizes the face correctly and the name matches the person, click the check mark to confirm the tag. If the face is incorrectly identified, click the X at the right of the text box and you can enter a new name.

If the name appears on an Address Book contact card — or is recognized as one of your Facebook friends — you can click the matching entry that appears to confirm the identity. Wowzers!

To delete a Face recognition box that isn't necessary, hover your mouse cursor over the box and click the X button that appears at the top left corner of the box.

If iPhoto doesn't recognize the face at all in the photo (which can happen if the person's face is turned at an angle to the camera, or is in a darker area of the photo), click the box border and drag the box over the person's face. If necessary, you can resize the box using the four handles at the corner of the box. Now you can click the label and type the person's name.

6. Click the Info button to hide the Info pane after you've identified all the faces in the photo.

After you've tagged an image, it appears in your Faces collection, which you can view by clicking the Faces entry in the Source list. You can double-click a portrait in your Faces collection to see all the images that contain that person.

Notice the Confirm Additional Faces button that appears next to the person's name? Click it, and iPhoto displays other photos that likely contain this person's face, allowing you to tag them there as well. If a face is a match, click on the thumbnail to confirm it.

As you might expect, the more tags you add for a specific person, the better iPhoto gets at recognizing that person!

Putting photos in their place:

Places makes it easy to track the location where photos were taken, but it requires a digital camera that includes GPS tracking information in the image metadata for iPhoto to do so without your help. (This is a relatively new feature for digital cameras, so older models aren't likely to support GPS tracking.) Places also requires an Internet connection because it uses Google Maps.

Click the Places entry in the Source list to display a global map, with pushpins indicating where your photos were taken. You can switch the Places map between terrain and satellite modes, or choose a hybrid display. If you're familiar with Google Maps, these settings are old friends of yours.

Alternatively, click the text Location buttons at the top of the map to display a character-based browser, where you can click on country, state, city, and place names.

No matter which view mode you choose, clicking a pushpin or location displays the images taken in that area.

Organizing with keywords

"Okay, Mark, albums, Events, Faces, and Places are great ideas, but there has to be a way to search my collection by category!" Never fear, good Mac owner. You can also assign descriptive *keywords* to images to help you organize your collection and locate certain pictures fast. iPhoto comes with a number of standard keywords, and you can create your own as well.

To illustrate, suppose you'd like to identify your images according to special events in your family. Birthday photos should have their own keyword, and anniversaries deserve another. By assigning keywords, you can search for Elsie's sixth birthday or your silver wedding anniversary (no matter what Event or album they're in), and all related photos with those keywords appear like magic! (Well, *almost* like magic. You need to choose View⇨Keywords, which toggles the Keyword display on and off in the Viewer.)iPhoto includes a number of keywords that are already available:

 ✦ Favorite

 ✦ Family

 ✦ Kids

 ✦ Vacation

 ✦ Birthday

 ✦ RAW

 ✦ Photo Booth

 ✦ Movie

 ✦ Checkmark

 What's the Checkmark all about, you ask? It's a special case: Adding this keyword displays a tiny check mark icon in the bottom-right corner of the image. The checkmark keyword comes in handy for temporarily identifying specific images because you can search for just your checkmarked photos.

To assign keywords to images (or remove keywords that have already been assigned), select one or more photos in the Viewer. Choose Window⇨Manage My Keywords or press ⌘+K to display the Keywords window, as shown in Figure 3-5.

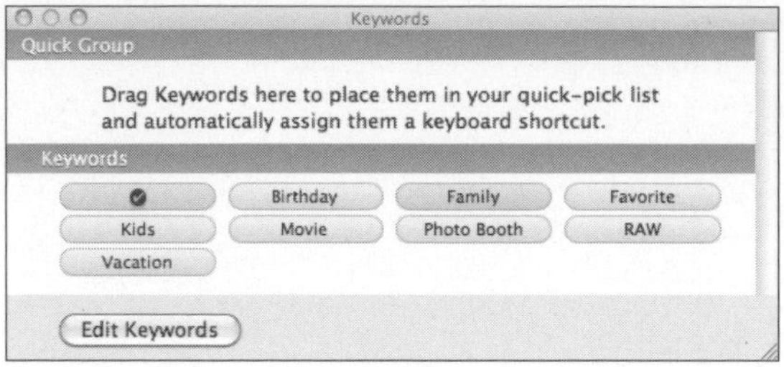

Figure 3-5: Time to add keywords to these selected images.

Click the keyword buttons that you want to attach to the selected images to mark them. Or click the highlighted keyword buttons that you want to remove from the selected images to disable them.

TIP

Drag the keyword buttons that you use the most to the Quick Group section of the Keywords window, and iPhoto automatically creates a keyboard shortcut for each keyword in the Quick Group. Now you don't even need to display the Keywords window to get business done!

Digging through your library with keywords

Behold the power of keywords! To sift through your entire collection of images by using keywords, click the Search button in the toolbar, and then click the magnifying glass button next to the Search box and choose Keyword from the pop-up menu. iPhoto displays a pop-up Keywords panel, and you can click one or more keyword buttons to display just the photos that carry those keywords.

You're gonna need your own keywords

I'll bet you take photos of other things besides just kids and vacations — and that's why iPhoto allows you to create your own keywords. Display the iPhoto Keywords window by pressing ⌘+K, click the Edit Keywords button, and then click Add (the button with the plus sign). iPhoto adds a new unnamed keyword to the list as an edit box, ready for you to type its name.

You can rename an existing keyword from this same window, too. Click a keyword to select it and then click Rename. Remember, however, that renaming a keyword affects *all the images that were tagged with that keyword.* That might be confusing when, for example, photos originally tagged as Family suddenly appear with the keyword Foodstuffs. (I recommend applying a new keyword and deleting the old one if this problem crops up.)

To change the keyboard shortcut assigned to a keyword, click the Shortcut button. To remove an existing keyword from the list, click the keyword to select it and then click the Delete button, which bears a minus sign.

The images that remain in the Viewer after a search must have *all* the keywords that you specified. If an image is identified, for example, by only three of four keywords you chose, it isn't a match and it doesn't appear in the Viewer. (You can create a Smart Album with specific keywords to get around this limitation.)

To search for a photo by words in its description, just click in the Search box and start typing. You can also click that same magnifying glass by the Search box to search through your images by date and rating as well.

Speaking of ratings . . .

Playing favorites by assigning ratings

Be your own critic! iPhoto allows you to assign any photo a rating of anywhere from zero to five stars. I use this system to help me keep track of the images that I feel are the best in my library. Select one image (or more) and then assign a rating using one of the following methods:

✦ Choose Photos⇨My Rating and then choose the desired rating from the pop-up submenu.

✦ Hover your mouse over the photo and click the More button in the lower right corner of the thumbnail, and then click on the desired star rating in the menu that appears.

✦ Use the ⌘+0 through ⌘+5 shortcuts.

Sorting your images just so

The View menu provides an easy way to arrange your images in the Viewer by a number of different criteria. Choose View⇨Sort Photos and then click the desired sort criteria from the pop-up submenu. You can arrange the display by date, keyword, title, or rating. If you select an album in the source list, you can also choose to arrange photos manually, which means that you can drag and drop thumbnails in the Viewer to place them in the precise order you want them.

Naturally, iPhoto allows you to print selected images, but you can also send photos directly to iWeb for use on your MobileMe Web site. Click Share⇨iWeb and then choose either Photo Page or Blog from the submenu. iPhoto automatically sends the selected images or album to iWeb and launches the application! You can also use iPhoto's MobileMe Gallery feature to get your photos on the web. (More on the MobileMe Gallery at the end of this chapter.)

Edit mode: Removing and fixing stuff the right way

Not every digital image is perfect — just look at my collection if you need proof. For those shots that need a pixel massage, iPhoto includes a number of editing tools that you can use to correct common problems.

The first step in any editing job is to select the image you want to fix in the Viewer. Then click the Edit button on the iPhoto toolbar to display the Edit mode controls at the right side of the window, as shown in Figure 3-6. Now you're ready to fix problems, using the tools that I discuss in the rest of this section. (If you're editing a photo that's part of an Event, album, Faces, or Places, note the spiffy scrolling photo strip at the bottom, which allows you to switch to another image to edit from the same grouping.)

If you'd prefer to edit images with more of your screen real estate, click the Full Screen button at the far left of the iPhoto toolbar. To switch back to the standard window arrangement, click the Full Screen button again.

When you're done with Edit mode, click the Edit button again to return to the Viewer.

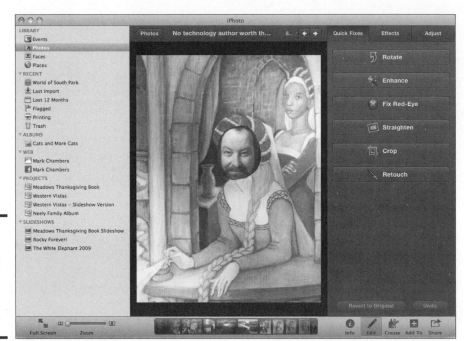

Figure 3-6: iPhoto is now in edit mode — watch out, image problems!

Rotating tipped-over shots

If an image is in the wrong orientation and needs to be turned to display correctly, click the Rotate button to turn it once in a counterclockwise direction. Hold down the Option key while you click the Rotate button to rotate in a clockwise direction.

Find yourself using that Option key often when rotating? Consider reversing the default direction! Click iPhoto⇨Preferences and click the General tab, then click the Rotate radio button to change the default direction.

Crop 'til you drop

Does that photo have an intruder hovering around the edges of the subject? You can remove some of the border by *cropping* an image, just as folks once did with film prints and a pair of scissors. (We've come a long way.) With iPhoto, you can remove unwanted portions from the edges of an image; it's a great way to get Uncle Milton's stray head (complete with toupee) out of an otherwise perfect holiday snapshot.

Follow these steps to crop an image:

1. **Click the Crop button in the Edit toolbar.**

2. **Select the portion of the image that you want to keep.**

    In the Viewer, click and drag the handles on the rectangle to outline the part of the image that you want. Remember, whatever's outside this rectangle disappears after the crop is completed.

    When you drag a corner or edge of the outline, a semi-opaque grid (familiar to amateur and professional photographers as the nine rectangles from the Rule of Three) appears to help you visualize what you're claiming. (Check it out in Figure 3-7.)

    You can expand the outline to the full dimensions of the image at any time — just click the Reset button.

3. **(Optional) Choose a preset aspect ratio.**

    If you want to force your cropped selection to a specific aspect ratio — such as 4 x 3 for an iDVD project — click the Constrain check box and select that ratio from the Constrain pop-up menu.

4. **Click the Done button.**

    Oh, and don't forget that you can use iPhoto's Undo feature if you mess up and need to try again. Just press ⌘+Z.

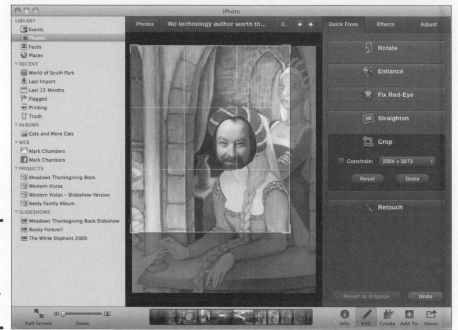

iPhoto features multiple Undo levels, so you can press ⌘+Z several times to travel back through your last several changes. Alternately, you can always return the image to its original form (before you did any editing at all) by clicking the Revert to Original button.

Straightening what's crooked

Was your camera slightly tilted when you took the perfect shot? Never fear! Click the Straighten button and then drag the Angle slider to tilt the image in the desired direction. Click the Done button to return to Edit mode.

Enhancing images to add pizzazz

If a photo looks washed out, click the Enhance button to increase (or decrease) the color saturation and improve the contrast. Enhance is automatic, so you don't have to set anything — but be prepared to use Undo if you're not satisfied with the changes.

Removing rampant red-eye

Unfortunately, today's digital cameras can still produce the same "zombies with red eyeballs" as traditional film cameras. *Red-eye* is caused by a camera's flash reflecting off the retinas of a subject's eyes, and it can occur with both humans and animals. (I'm told that pets get *green-eye*, actually, but iPhoto can handle that, too!)

iPhoto can remove that red- and green-eye and turn frightening zombies back into your family and friends! Click the Red-Eye button and then select a demonized eyeball by clicking in the center of it. (If the Red-Eye circular cursor is too small or too large, drag the Size slider to adjust the dimensions.) To complete the process, click the Done button.

Retouching like the stars

The iPhoto Retouch feature is perfect for removing minor flecks or lines in an image (especially those you've scanned from prints). Click Retouch and you'll notice that the mouse cursor turns into a circle; as with the Red-Eye tool, you can drag the Size slider to change the size of the Retouch cursor. Just drag the cursor across the imperfection and click Done when you're finished touching things up. Don't forget to take a moment and marvel at your editing skill!

When you first enter Editing mode, the Quick Fixes tab is selected, providing you with the tools I've already covered. (These are the changes you'll make most often, so that makes sense.) However, you can also choose to apply an effect from the Effects tab, or make specific changes to the appearance of an image from the Adjust tab.

Switching to black-and-white or sepia

Ever wonder whether a particular photo in your library would look better as a black-and-white (or *grayscale*) print? Or perhaps old-fashioned *sepia* tone in shades of copper and brown? Just click the Effects tab, which offers nine different effects you can apply to the photo. You can also make "one-click" changes to your photo from the Effects tab, including lightening and darkening an image or enhancing the contrast.

Adjusting photo properties manually

Click the Adjust tab to perform manual adjustments to brightness and contrast (the light levels in your image), as well as attributes like sharpness, shadow, and highlight levels. To adjust a value, make sure that nothing's selected in the image and then drag the corresponding slider until the image looks the way you want. Click the Close button to return to Edit mode.

While you're editing, you can use the Next and Previous buttons at the left of the tab buttons to move to the next image in the current group (or back to the previous image).

Book III
Chapter 3

Focusing on iPhoto

Producing Your Own Coffee-Table Masterpiece

Book mode unleashes what I think is probably the coolest feature of iPhoto: the chance to design and print a high-quality bound photo book! After you complete an album — all the images have been edited just the way you want, and the album contains all the photos you want to include in your book — iPhoto can send your images as data over the Internet to a company that prints and binds your finished book for you. (No, they don't publish *For Dummies* titles, but then again, I don't get high-resolution color plates in most of my books, either.)

At the time of this writing, you can order many different sizes and bindings, including an 8.5-by-11-inch soft-cover book with 20 double-sided pages for about $20 and a hardbound 8.5-by-11-inch keepsake album with 10 double-sided pages for about $30 (shipping included for both). Extra pages can be added at $0.70 and $1.00 a pop, respectively.

iPhoto '11 can also produce and automatically order calendars and greeting cards, using a process similar to the one I describe in this section for producing a book. Who needs that stationery store in the mall anymore? (You can even order old-fashioned prints from the Share toolbar menu.)

If you're going to create a photo book, make sure that the images have the highest quality and highest resolution. The higher the resolution, the better the photos look in the finished book. I personally always try to use images of over 1,000 pixels in both the vertical and horizontal dimensions.

To create a photo book, follow these steps:

1. **Click the desired album in the Source list to select it.**

   Make sure that no individual photos are selected in the Viewer — this way, iPhoto uses all the images in the chosen album.

2. **Click the Create toolbar button and click Book from the pop-up menu.**

3. **Select the type of book using the Binding buttons (Hardcover, Softcover, and Wire-bound) at the top of the window and the Size buttons (Large and Extra-Large) at the left side of the window.**

   Your choices determine the number of pages and the size of the book. iPhoto displays the approximate cost of your book as you browse the options.

4. **Choose a theme.**

   Use the left and right arrow keys to cycle through the theme selections. The theme you choose determines both the layout scheme and the background graphics for each page. To change the color scheme for a theme, click on one of the color swatches at the right side of the window.

5. **Click Create.**

   iPhoto adds your new book project under the Project heading in the Source list, and you'll see the controls shown in Figure 3-8.

   In Book mode, the Viewer displays a collection of thumbnail images, each of which represents a portion of your book — either the front cover, internal pages, or the back cover. To display the photos you selected, click the Photos button in the toolbar. You can drag any image thumbnail into one of the photo placeholders to add it to the page.

   It's easy to switch to another theme at any time by clicking the Change Theme button at the top of the window.

6. **Rearrange the page order to suit you by dragging the thumbnail of any page from one location to another.**

   If you'd prefer a book without page numbers, right-click on any page and choose Show Page Numbers to toggle it off (the check mark next to the menu item disappears).

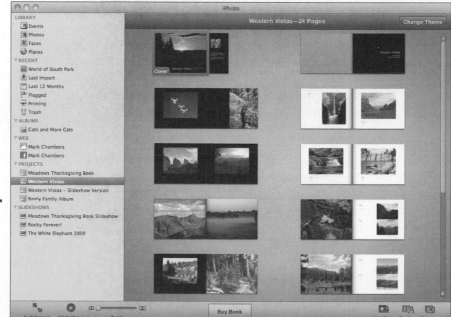

Figure 3-8: Preparing to publish my own coffee-table master-piece.

7. **Need to change the look of a single page? Click on either cover or a page to select it, then click the Design button in the toolbar to change the color and design layout for that element.**

   Clicking on a design thumbnail automatically updates the page display.

8. **Double-click on a page to edit captions and short descriptions.**

   Click any one of the text boxes in the page display and begin typing to add text to that page. Some themes do not have caption or description text boxes, but you can add them — display the Design pane and click on the desired photo placeholder, and then click on one of the Border thumbnails that includes a text box.

   After you're done editing, click the All Pages button at the top of the window to return to your full spread.

9. **To add pages to your book, click the Add Page button in the toolbar.**

   As I mentioned earlier, the price for additional pages varies according to the size and type of binding you choose.

10. **To view the book at any time, right-click on any page and choose Preview Book.**

   After a short wait, Lion's Preview application opens and you can scroll through the contents of your book (or even print a quick copy). To close the Preview window, choose Preview➪Quit Preview.

You can also right-click on any page and choose Save Book as PDF to create a snazzy electronic version of your book.

11. **When you're ready to publish your book, click the Buy Book button.**

12. **In a series of dialogs that appears, iPhoto guides you through the final steps to order a bound book.**

   Note that you'll be asked for credit card information, so have that plastic ready.

Why limit yourself to just paper copies of your publishing success? If you'd like to create a digital copy of your book, right-click on any page and choose Save Book as PDF.

I really need a slideshow

You can use iPhoto to create slideshows! Click the album or Event you want to display in the Source list, and then click the Create button and choose Slideshow. Notice that iPhoto adds a Slideshows item in the Source list. A scrolling thumbnail strip appears at the top of the Viewer — it displays the images in the album or Event. Click and drag the thumbnails so that they appear in the desired order.

Click the Themes button on the Slideshow toolbar to choose the theme for your slideshow. The theme you choose controls the animation, transition type, and screen layout iPhoto will use — everything from the classic Ken Burns "moving photo" animation to a really nifty Sliding Panels layout.

To choose background music for your slideshow, click the Music button in the Slideshow toolbar to display Apple's theme music, as well as the tracks from your iTunes library. To choose a standard theme, click the Source pop-up menu and choose Theme Music; select that perfect song and click Choose. To choose an iTunes song or playlist, click the Source pop-up menu and choose a playlist (or throw caution completely to the wind and choose one of your GarageBand compositions). You can also create a custom playlist by selecting the Custom Playlist for Slideshow check box. Then drag the individual songs you want to the song list at the bottom of the sheet. (You can drag them to rearrange their order in the list as well.) Click Choose to accept your song list.

To configure your slideshow, click the Settings button in the Slideshow toolbar and click the All Slides tab. In the dialog that appears, you can specify the amount of time that each slide remains on the screen, as well as an optional title slide. Widescreen Mac owners appreciate the Aspect Ratio pop-up menu, which allows you to choose a 16:9 widescreen display for your slideshow.

Click the This Slide tab to set the selected photo to display in black and white, sepia, or antique coloring.

To display a quick preview of your slideshow without leaving the iPhoto window, click Preview; this is a handy way of determining whether the theme and music you've selected are really what you want. When you're ready to play your slideshow, click the Play button, and iPhoto switches to full-screen mode. To create a movie file from your completed slideshow, click Export in the Slideshow toolbar.

**Book III
Chapter 3**

Focusing on iPhoto

You'll Love MobileMe Gallery!

iPhoto '11 includes a feature called MobileMe Gallery that does for images what podcasting does for audio: You can share your photos with friends, family, business clients, and anyone else with an Internet connection! (Your adoring public doesn't even require a Mac; it can use That Other Kind of Computer, or one of those crazy Linux systems.) iPhoto automatically uploads the selected images and leads you through the process of creating a new web page to proudly display your photos. However, you *must* be a MobileMe subscriber to use the MobileMe Gallery feature. If you haven't heard the news on Apple's MobileMe service yet, see Chapter 4 of Book V for the details.

To create a MobileMe Gallery, you must first designate one or more photos in the Viewer (or even select entire albums or Events in the Source list). Click the Share button, and then choose MobileMe Gallery from the pop-up menu. To create a new album, select (you guessed it) New Album — alternately, you can add new photos to an existing Gallery by clicking on the corresponding thumbnail.

Is that Facebook and Flickr I spy?

Indeed it is! iPhoto '11 includes a direct connection to both your Facebook social networking account (at `www.facebook.com`) and your Flickr online gallery account (at `www.flickr.com`), allowing you to simply select one or more photos and send them automatically to either service! Click the Share button on the toolbar to select either type of account.

The first time you select photos in the Viewer (or an album or Event in the Source list) and choose either option, iPhoto prompts you for permission to set up your connection. (Of course, this will require you to enter your Facebook and Flickr account information — hence the confirmation request.) Click Set Up and provide the data that each site requires.

After you've set up your accounts, simply select your photos, albums, or Events and click the Share toolbar button, and then choose the menu item for the desired service. Apple, you absolutely *rock*!

If you're creating a new Gallery, iPhoto prompts you for a name. You can elect to show the title of each photo, allow your visitors to download your images or upload their own, and even allow photos to be uploaded by other computer owners using an e-mail client or a web browser!

By default, any visitor to your MobileMe web site can see your gallery. But what if you prefer a little security for those images? In that case, click the Album Viewable By pop-up menu, where you can limit your viewing audience (you can even require that your visitors enter a login name and password before they can receive your photos).

Click Publish, and you'll see that iPhoto indicates that your images are being uploaded with a cool twirling progress icon to the right of the album in the Source list. When the process is complete, iPhoto indicates that the photos appear in a MobileMe Gallery with a new heading in the Source list. You're on the air! Any changes you make to the contents of your MobileMe Gallery are updated automatically on your MobileMe account, and, in turn, are updated automatically to everyone who receives your images.

Now for the other side of the coin: By selecting your MobileMe Gallery in the Source list and clicking the Info button on the toolbar, you can choose to Tell a Friend about your new additions! iPhoto automatically prepares an e-mail message in Apple Mail that announces your new Gallery! Just add the recipient names and click Send. This spiffy message includes instructions for

✦ **Folks using iPhoto '09 or '11 on a Mac:** As you can imagine, this is the easiest receive option to configure. After these folks are subscribed, they get an automatically updated album of the same name that appears in their Source list, and they can use those images in their own iPhoto projects! From within iPhoto, your visitors can subscribe to your MobileMe Gallery by clicking File⇨Subscribe to Photo Feed and entering the subscription URL.

✦ **Folks using Windows or an older version of iPhoto:** These subscribers can use any web browser with RSS support (such as the Safari browser that comes with Lion and is available from Apple for Windows XP, Vista, and 7) or any RSS reader. (In effect, your MobileMe Gallery becomes an RSS feed for those with a version of iPhoto previous to iLife '09.)

E-Mailing Photos to Aunt Mildred

iPhoto can help you send your images through e-mail by automating the process. The application can prepare your image and embed it automatically in a new message.

To send an image through e-mail, select it and click the Share button in the toolbar, and then click the Email menu item. The layout shown in Figure 3-9 appears, allowing you to choose a theme for your message (complete with a background image and matching font selection). You can also specify the size of the images from the Photo Size pop-up menu, which can save considerable downloading time for those recipients that are still using a dial-up connection. To add the images as attachments to the message, click the Attach Photos to Message check box to enable it.

Keep in mind that most ISP (Internet service provider) e-mail servers don't accept an e-mail message that's more than 3MB or 4MB, so watch that Size display at the bottom of the window. (In fact, the encoding necessary to send images as attachments can *double* the size of each image!) If you're trying to send a number of images and the size goes over 3MB, you might have to click the Photo Size pop-up menu and choose a smaller size (reducing the image resolution) to get them all in a single message.

When you're satisfied with the total file size and you're ready to create your message, click the Send button. iPhoto automatically launches Apple Mail (or whatever e-mail application you specify) and creates a new message containing the images, ready for you to click Send!

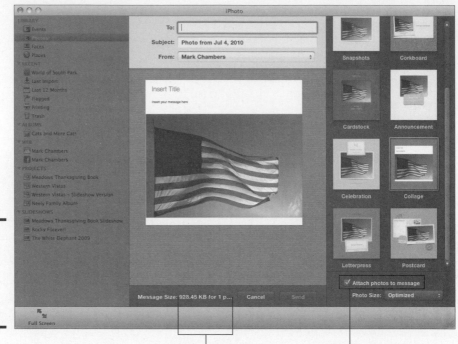

Figure 3-9:
Preparing
to send
an image
through
Apple Mail.

Message Size

Click to attach photos

Chapter 4: Making Magic with iMovie

In This Chapter

↙ **Taking stock of the iMovie window**

↙ **Importing and adding media content**

↙ **Using transitions in your movie**

↙ **Putting text titles to work**

↙ **Adding animated maps**

↙ **Creating a movie trailer**

↙ **Sharing your movie with others**

Alfred Hitchcock, Stanley Kubrick, George Lucas, and Ridley Scott — those guys are amateurs! Welcome to the exciting world of moviemaking on your Mac, where *you* call the shots. With iMovie, you can try your hand at all aspects of the movie-creating process, including editing and special effects. Built with ease-of-use in mind, iMovie lets you perform full-blown movie production on your Macintosh with a minimum of effort.

Don't let iMovie's fancy buttons and flashing lights fool you: This application is a feature-packed tool for serious movie production. The iMovie controls work the same as many top-notch, movie-editing tools that professionals use. From basic editing to audio and video effects, iMovie has everything that you need to get started creating high-quality movies.

The iMovie Window

If you've ever tried a professional-level video editing application, you probably felt as though you were suddenly dropped in the cockpit of a jumbo jet. In iMovie, though, all the controls you need are easy to use and logically placed.

To launch iMovie, click the iMovie icon in the Dock or in Launchpad. (It looks like a star from the Hollywood Walk of Fame.) You can also click the Application folder in any Finder window sidebar and then double-click the iMovie icon.

To follow the examples I show you here, follow these strenuous steps and create a new movie project:

1. **Click the File menu and choose New Project (or press ⌘+N).**

   iMovie displays the sheet you see in Figure 4-1.

2. **Type a name for your project.**

3. **Select the aspect ratio (or screen dimensions) for your movie.**

   You can select a widescreen display (16:9) or a standard display (4:3). If compatibility with the familiar SDTV format is important, I always recommend that you choose standard (4:3) ratio; choosing 16:9 for an SDTV set will result in those familiar black "letterbox" bars at the top and bottom of the screen. On the other hand, choosing standard ratio for an HDTV results in black bars on the left and right sides of the screen.

4. **Choose the frame rate.**

   The default frame rate is 30 frames per second (or *fps* for short), which is normal for the North American NTSC video standard. However, you can choose a slower frame rate if necessary.

Figure 4-1: Creating a new movie project within iMovie.

5. **Click a Project Theme thumbnail to select a theme to apply to your finished movie.**

If you choose a theme, iMovie automatically adds the transitions and titles that correspond to that theme. (Normally, this is what you want to do. However, if you want to add transitions and titles manually, click the Automatically Add Transitions and Titles check box to deselect it.)

If you decide not to use a theme (by selecting the No Theme thumbnail), iMovie can still add an automatic effect between clips. Click the Automatically Add check box and click the pop-up menu to choose the desired effect.

You can also create movie trailers within iMovie — I demonstrate how later in this chapter. Generally, however, it's a good idea to create your trailer project *after* your movie project is completed (unless, of course, you're specifically creating just a trailer project). Why? For the same reason that studios create trailers after the filming is finished: After you've completed your movie, you'll have all the clips imported already, and you'll have a better idea of what you want to include while "teasing" your audience!

6. **Click Create.**

iMovie adds the new project to the list in the Project Library pane, and you're on your way! Check out Figure 4-2: This is the whole enchilada, in one window.

The controls and displays that you'll use most often are

✦ **Monitor:** Think of this as being just like your TV or computer monitor. Your video clips, still images, and finished movie play here.

✦ **Media Browser toolbar:** This row of buttons allows you to add media content (video clips, photos, and audio). The selected items fill the right side of the browser pane below the monitor.

✦ **Event Library:** This list displays all of the video clips you can add to your project, including video clips you've created within iPhoto.

✦ **Event pane:** If you select a video clip in the Event Library list, iMovie displays a thumbnail of the content in the Event pane — if you decide you want to include it, you can add it to your project. I show you what each of the panes in the iMovie workspace looks like when you tackle different tasks in this chapter.

✦ **Project Library/Project/Trailer pane:** iMovie displays the movie projects that you've created in the *Project Library* pane. Note that when you double-click on a project in the Project Library pane, it turns into the *Project* pane, which displays the elements you've added to that specific project (such as video clips, still photos, and audio clips). If you drag an element into the Project Library pane, it turns into the Project pane for the selected project, and if you're working on a movie trailer, the Project Library pane turns into the Trailer pane.

✦ **Playhead:** The red vertical line that you see in the Event and Project Library panes is the *playhead,* which indicates the current editing point while you're creating your movie. When you're playing your movie, the playhead moves to follow your progress through the movie.

✦ **Editing toolbar:** This strip of buttons allows you to control editing functions such as cropping, audio and video adjustments, voiceovers, and selecting items.

✦ **Camera Import window:** Click this switch to import DV clips from your DV camcorder or iSight camera.

Those are the major highlights of the iMovie window. A director's chair and megaphone are optional, of course, but they do add to the mood.

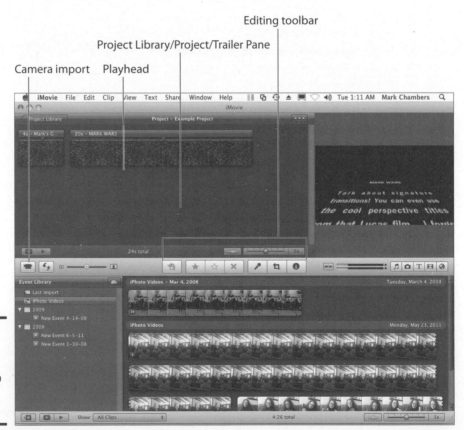

Camera import   Playhead   Project Library/Project/Trailer Pane   Editing toolbar

Figure 4-2:
iMovie is a lean, mean video producing machine.

A Bird's-Eye View of Moviemaking

I don't want to box in your creative skills here — after all, you can attack the moviemaking process from a number of angles. (Pun unfortunately intended.) However, I've found that my movies turn out the best when I follow a linear process, so before I dive into specifics, allow me to provide you with an overview of moviemaking with iMovie.

Here's my take on the process, reduced to seven steps:

1. **Import your video clips either directly from your DV camcorder, iSight camera, or your hard drive.**

2. **Drag your new selection of clips from the Event pane to the Project pane and arrange them in the desired order.**

3. **Import or record audio clips (from iTunes, GarageBand, or external sources, such as audio CDs or audio files that you've recorded yourself) and add them to your movie.**

4. **Import your photos (directly from iPhoto or from your hard drive) and place them where needed in your movie.**

5. **Add professional niceties, such as voiceovers, transitions, effects, and text to the project.**

6. **Preview your film and edit it further if necessary.**

7. **Share your finished film with others through the web, e-mail, or a DVD that you create and burn with iDVD.**

That's the first step-by-step procedure in this chapter. I doubt that you'll even need to refer back to it, however, because you'll soon see just how easy it is to use iMovie.

As you might imagine, this chapter simply can't hold a description of all the settings and procedures within iMovie '11 — but luckily, Tony Bove has done exactly that in his book *iLife '11 For Dummies* (Wiley Publishing). Tony will take you from basics to all the in-depth features of each of the iLife applications!

Importing the Building Blocks

Sure, you need video clips to create a movie of your own, but don't panic if you have but a short supply. You can certainly turn to the other iLife applications for additional raw material. (See, I told you that integration thing would come in handy.)

Along with video clips you import from your DV camcorder, iSight camera, and hard drive, you can also call on iPhoto for still images (think credits) and iTunes for background audio and effects. In this section, I show you how.

Pulling in video clips

Your Mac is probably equipped already with the two extras that come in handy for video editing — namely, a large hard drive and a FireWire port. Because most mini-DV camcorders today use a FireWire connection to transfer clips, you're all set. (And even if your snazzy new DV camcorder uses a USB 2.0 connection, you're still in the zone, although you may need to modify the steps I provide in this section for your particular device.) Oh, and if your Mac has an iSight camera on board, you're a self-contained movie studio!

Here's the drill if your clips are on your FireWire-equipped mini-DV camcorder:

1. **Plug the proper cable into your Mac.**

2. **Set the DV camcorder to VTR (or VCR) mode.**

   Some camcorders call this Play mode.

3. **Click the Camera Import button (labeled in Figure 4-2).**

   iMovie opens a new window.

4. **Click the Camera pop-up menu (at the bottom of the Import window) and select your DV camcorder or iSight camera.**

   Playback controls appear under the Camera Import window, mirroring the controls on your DV camcorder. This allows you to control the unit from iMovie. *Keen!* Depending on your camcorder and the type of connection you're using, you may also get Import All and Import Checked buttons as a bonus.

   To capture video from your iSight camera, click the Video Size pop-up menu to choose the dimensions of the clip; click Capture. On the sheet that appears, choose the location where the video will be saved, and choose whether to add this video to an existing event or create a new event. Click Capture to start recording, and click Stop when your video is complete. (You can skip the rest of the steps in this section, which deal only with DV camcorders.)

   iMovie can analyze your incoming video for one of three different post-recording procedures. Click the After Import Analyze For check box to select it, and then choose *Stabilization* (which helps smooth shaky camera work), *People* (which marks a clip as including people, making it easier to locate) or Stabilization and People (which, predictably, does both). The Stabilization option is especially good if your camcorder doesn't have a built-in stabilization function, but beware: Any of these settings will add significant time to the import process!

5. **To import selected clips from your DV camcorder, set the Automatic/ Manual switch to Manual and advance the video to the point where you want to start your capture, and then click Import.**

To import all clips, set the Automatic/Manual switch to Automatic, and click Import.

6. **(Optional) Click the check boxes next to the clips that you don't want to import to deselect them and click the Import Checked button.**

7. **Click the Save To pop-up menu and choose the drive that should store your clips.**

You can choose to add the new clips to an existing Event or create a new Event. Heck, if the event spanned more than one day, you can create a new Event for each day. (How do they think up these things?)

8. **Click OK and admire your handiwork.**

iMovie begins transferring the footage to your Mac and automatically adds the imported clips to your Event Library.

If your clips are already on your hard drive, rest assured that iMovie can import them, including those in *high-definition video* (HDV) format. iMovie also recognizes a number of other video formats, as shown in Table 4-1.

Table 4-1	Video Formats Supported by iMovie
File Type	*Description*
DV	Standard 4:3 digital video
DV Widescreen	Widescreen 16:9 digital video
MOV	QuickTime movies
HDV & AVCHD	High-definition (popularly called *widescreen*) digital video, in 720p and 1080i
MPEG-2	Digital video format used for DVD movies
MPEG-4	A popular format for streaming Internet and wireless digital video

To import a movie file, follow this bouncing ball:

1. **Choose File⇨Import and choose Movies from the submenu.**

2. **If you're importing 1080i video clips, click the Optimize Video pop-up menu and choose the Full quality setting.**

   The Large setting saves you a significant amount of hard drive space, but the Full setting preserves the original resolution and detail. (If you're not importing 1080i video, use the default Large setting and click OK. The Full setting demands all the CPU and RAM resources your Mac can offer, so don't expect to do much else while importing.)

3. **Click the drive that should store your clips in the sidebar and then navigate to the desired location.**

4. **Specify whether you want to add the imported video to an existing Event or create a new Event.**

   If you choose to add the video to an existing Event, click the pop-up menu and select an Event.

5. **Specify whether you want to copy the video (leaving the original movie intact) or whether the original movie should be moved (the original deleted after a successful import).**

6. **Click Import.**

   Alternatively, you can also drag a video clip from a Finder window and drop it in the Project pane.

Making use of still images

Still images come in handy as impressive-looking titles or as ending credits to your movie. (Make sure you list a gaffer and a best boy to be truly professional.) However, you can use still images also to introduce scenes or to separate clips according to your whim. For example, I use stills when delineating the days of a vacation within a movie or different Christmas celebrations over time.

Here are two methods of adding stills to your movie:

✦ **Adding images and video clips from iPhoto:** Click the Photo Browser button in the Browser toolbar (or press ⌘+2) and you'll experience the thrill that is your iPhoto Library, right from iMovie (as shown in Figure 4-3). You can elect to display your entire iPhoto Library or more selective picks such as specific albums or Events. When you find the image you want to add, just drag it to the right spot in the Project pane. Videos from your iPhoto Library are automatically added to your iMovie Event Library — it doesn't get much easier than that.

✦ **Importing images from your hard drive:** If you're a member of the International Drag-and-Drop Society, you can drag TIFF, JPEG, GIF, PICT, PNG, and PSD images directly from a Finder window and drop them into the Project pane as well.

Figure 4-3:
Pulling still images from iPhoto is child's play.

Importing and adding audio from all sorts of places

You can pull in everything from Wagner to Weezer as both background music and sound effects for your movie. In this section, I focus on how to get those notes into iMovie and then how to add them to your movie by dragging them to the Project pane.

You can add audio from a number of sources:

✦ **Adding songs from iTunes:** Click the Show Music and Sound Effects button in the Browser toolbar (or press ⌘+1) to display the contents of your iTunes Library. Click the desired playlist in the scrolling list box, such as the dynamite ABBA playlist I selected in Figure 4-4. (If you've exported any original music you've composed in GarageBand to your iTunes Library, you can use those songs in your own movie!) You can add a track to your movie by dragging the song entry from the Music and Sound Effects list to the desired spot in the Project pane.

✦ **Adding sound effects:** Yep, if you need the sound of a horse galloping for your Rocky Mountain vacation clips, click either iMovie Sound Effects or iLife Sound Effects in the scrolling list box. iMovie includes a number of top-shelf audio effects that you can use in the second audio track on the timeline viewer. This way, you can add sound effects even when you've already added a background song. Again, to add a sound effect, drag it to the perfect spot in the Project pane.

Figure 4-4:
Calling on
my iTunes
Library to
add ABBA
to my
iMovie.

If you have several gigabytes of music in your iTunes Library, it might be more of a challenge to locate "Me and Bobby McGee" by Janis Joplin, especially if she's included in a compilation. Let your Mac do the digging for you! Click in the Search box below the track list and begin typing a song name. iMovie narrows down the song titles displayed to those that match the characters you type. To reset the search box and display all your songs in the Library or selected playlist, click the X icon that appears to the right of the box.

✦ **Ripping songs from an audio CD:** Load an audio CD and then choose Audio CD from the scrolling list box. iMovie displays the tracks from the CD, and you can add them at the current playhead position the same way as iTunes songs.

✦ **Recording directly from a microphone:** Yep, if you're thinking voiceover narration, you've hit the nail on the head. Check out the sidebar, "Narration the easy way," for the scoop.

You can fine-tune both the audio within a video clip or the audio clips that you add to your project. With the desired clip selected, click the Inspector button in the Editing toolbar (it bears a proud letter *i*) and click the Audio tab. The Audio Adjustments window that appears includes an array of audio controls that allow you to change the volume of the selected clip or to give that audio priority — or *ducking* — over other audio playing simultaneously (such as a sound effect that needs to be clearly heard over background music and the video clip). If your clips dramatically vary in volume, click the Normalize Clip Volume button and then select each clip that you want to set to the same volume; click Normalize Clip Volume again for each clip. You can also set an automatic or manual Fade-in/Fade-out for the audio. When you're done tweaking, click Done. (Oh, and don't forget that you can always return the clip to its original volume; just open this window again and click Revert to Original.)

On the Video tab within the Inspector window, you can vary the exposure, brightness, contrast, and saturation of your clip. Click the Auto button, and iMovie will perform what it considers the best job of improving your video.

Narration the easy way

Ready to create that award-winning nature documentary? You can add voiceover narration to your iMovie project that would make Jacques Cousteau proud. In fact, you can record your voice while you watch your movie playing, allowing perfect synchronization with the action! To add narration, follow these steps:

1. **Click the Voiceover button in the Editing toolbar — it sports a microphone icon — to open the Voiceover window.**

2. **Click the Record From pop-up menu and select the input device.**

   Most Macs sport a decent internal microphone, but you can always add a USB microphone to your system.

3. **Drag the input volume slider to a comfortable level.**

   You can monitor the volume level of your voice with the left and right input meters — try to keep the meters at 50 percent or so for the proper volume level.

4. **To block out ambient noise levels around you, drag the Noise Reduction slider to the right if necessary.**

If you'd like iMovie to enhance your voice electronically for a more professional sound, click the Voice Enhancement check box to select it. If you need to hear the audio from your movie project while you speak, click the Play Project Audio While Recording check box to select it — note, however, that you'll need to listen to the audio while using a set of headphones (plugged into your Mac's headphone jack) to avoid feedback problems.

5. **Click in the desired spot within a clip in the Project pane where the narration should begin.**

6. **Begin speaking when prompted by iMovie.**

7. **Watch the video while you narrate so that you can coordinate your narration track with the action.**

8. **Click anywhere in the iMovie window to stop recording (or wait until the clip ends).**

   iMovie adds an icon to the Project pane underneath the video with the voiceover.

9. **Click the Close button in the Voiceover window.**

Building the Cinematic Basics

Time to dive in and add the building blocks to create your movie. Along with video clips, audio tracks, and still images, you can add Hollywood-quality transitions, optical effects, and animated text titles. In this section, I demonstrate how to elevate your collection of video clips into a real-life furshlugginer *movie*.

Adding clips to your movie

You can add clips to your movie by using the Project pane and the Event pane. The Dynamic Duo works like this:

✦ **Project pane:** This displays the media you've added to your project so far, allowing you to rearrange the clips, titles, transitions and still images in your movie. (If the pane is titled Project Library, remember that you have to double-click on the desired project to select it. After you've selected a project, the Project Library pane turns into the Project pane.)

✦ **Event pane:** This displays your video clips arranged by Event (the date they were shot or the date they were imported), acting as the source repository for all your clips. Movies pulled into iMovie, imported into iPhoto, or added manually from the Finder appear here.

To add a clip to your movie:

1. **Move your mouse pointer across clips in the Event pane to watch a preview of the video.**

2. **When you've decided what to add to your project, you can either add the entire clip or a selection.**

   • To select an entire clip, right-click the clip's thumbnail and choose Select Entire Clip from the menu that appears.

   • To select a portion of a clip, drag your mouse cursor across the thumbnail. A yellow frame appears around your selection. To change the length of the selected video, drag the handles that appear on either side. If you make a mistake while selecting video, just click any empty space within the Event pane to remove the selection frame and try again.

3. **Drag the selection from the Event pane to the spot where it belongs in the Project pane.**

   Alternatively, you can press the E key or click the Add to Project button (the first button in the Editing toolbar).

Do this several times, and you have a movie, which you've created just as the editors of old used to by working with actual film clips. This is a good point to mention a moviemaking Mark's Maxim:

Preview your work — and do it often.

iMovie offers two Play Full Screen buttons: one under the Event Library and one under the Project Library. Select the project or Event you want to play and then click the corresponding button (or press ⌘+G). You can also choose View➪Play Full Screen to watch the selection. Press the spacebar to pause, and press Esc to return to iMovie. You can also move your mouse to display a filmstrip that you can click to skip forward or backward in the project or Event.

To play a selection from the beginning, press \ (the slash that leans to the left). (If you've ever watched directors at work on today's movie sets, you may have noticed that they're constantly watching a monitor to see what things will look like for the audience. You have the same option in iMovie!)

While you're watching video in the Event pane, you may decide that a certain clip has a favorite scene or that another clip has material you don't want, such as Uncle Ed's shadow puppets. (Shudder.) iMovie '11 features *Favorite* and *Rejected* frames, allowing you to view and use your best camera work (and ignore the worst stuff). To mark video, select a range of frames or an entire clip and then click the Mark as Favorite button in the Editing toolbar. Click the Reject button to hide the selected video or frames from view. (You can always unmark a Favorite or Rejected scene using the Unmark button in the Editing toolbar.)

Removing clips from your movie

Don't like a clip? Bah. To banish a clip from your movie, follow these steps

1. **Click the offending clip in the Project pane to select it.**

2. **Press Delete.**

   Alternatively, you can right-click the clip (or a selection you've made by dragging) and choose either Delete Entire Clip or Delete Selection from the menu that appears.

If you remove the wrong clip, don't panic. Instead, use iMovie's Undo feature (press ⌘+Z) to restore it.

Reordering clips in your movie

If Day One of your vacation appears after Day Two, you can easily reorder your clips and stills by dragging them to the proper space in the Project pane. When you release the mouse, iMovie automatically moves the rest of your movie aside with a minimum of fuss and bother.

Editing clips in iMovie

If a clip has extra seconds of footage at the beginning or end, you don't want that superfluous stuff in your masterpiece. Our favorite video editor gives you the following functions:

✦ **Crop:** Removes unwanted material from a video clip or still image, allowing you to change the aspect ratio of the media

✦ **Rotate:** Rotates a clip or image on its center axis

✦ **Trim:** Trims frames from a video clip

Before you can edit, however, you have to select a section of a clip:

1. **Click a clip or image in either the Project pane (where changes you make are specific to this project) or the Event pane (where edits you make are reflected in any project using that footage).**

   iMovie displays the clip or image in the monitor.

2. **To select the entire clip or image, simply click it.**

3. **Drag your mouse cursor across the thumbnail to select the section of the media you want to edit. (Note that some editing functions, such as Crop and Rotate, will automatically apply to the entire clip.)**

   The selected region is surrounded by a yellow frame. You're ready to edit that selected part of the clip.

Note the handles that appear at the beginning or ending of the selection. You can make fine changes to the selected section by dragging them.

✦ **To crop:** Click the Crop button in the Edit toolbar to display the frame in the Monitor pane and then click Crop at the top of the Monitor pane. Drag the edges of the frame and the handles to select the section you want to keep. To preview your selection, click the Play button at the top right corner of the monitor. When you're ready, click Done, and everything but the selected region is removed.

✦ **To rotate:** Click the Crop button in the Edit toolbar and then click one of the two rotation buttons (which carry a curved arrow icon). Each click rotates the media 90 degrees in that direction. Click Done when the clip or image is properly oriented.

✦ **To trim:** Right-click on the selection and choose Trim to Selection from the contextual menu. iMovie removes the frames from around the selected video.

Edits that you make to one clip or still image can actually be copied to multiple items! Select the edited clip and click Edit➪Copy from the iMovie menu. Now you can select one or more clips and choose Edit➪Paste Adjustments to apply Video, Audio, or Crop edits. (To apply all three type of edits, just choose All.)

Transitions for the masses

Many iMovie owners approach transitions as *visual bookends:* They merely act as placeholders that appear between video clips. Nothing could be farther from the truth, because judicious use of transitions can make or break a scene. For example, which would you prefer after a wedding ceremony — an abrupt, jarring cut to the reception or a gradual fadeout to the reception?

Today's audiences are sensitive to transitions between scenes. Try not to overuse the same transition. Also weigh the visual impact of a transition carefully.

iMovie includes a surprising array of transitions, including old favorites (such as Fade In and Dissolve) and some nifty stuff you might not be familiar with (such as Cube and Page Curl). To display your transition collection (Figure 4-5), click the Show Transitions button on the Browser toolbar (or press ⌘+4).

Figure 4-5: Add transitions for flow between clips in iMovie.

To see what a particular transition looks like, move your mouse pointer over the thumbnail to display the transition in miniature.

Adding a transition couldn't be easier: Drag the transition from the list in the Transitions Browser pane and drop it between clips or between a clip and a still image in the Project pane. In iMovie '11, transitions are applied in real time.

Even Gone with the Wind had titles

The next stop on our iMovie Hollywood Features Tour is the Titles Browser, shown in Figure 4-6. You'll find it by clicking the Title button on the Browser toolbar (which bears a big capital T), or by pressing ⌘+3. You can add a title with a still image, but iMovie also includes everything you need to add basic animated text to your movie.

Most of the controls you can adjust are the same for each animation style. You can change the font, the size of the text, and the color of the text.

Figure 4-6: Add titles for your next silent film.

To add a title manually:

1. **Select an animation thumbnail from the Title Browser pane and drag it to the desired spot in the Project pane.**

2. **Click a background thumbnail to select a background for your title.**

   Note that these are the same backgrounds you'll see in the Map, Background, and Animatic browser, which I'll discuss in the next section.

3. **Press ⌘+T (or choose Text⇨Show Fonts) to make any changes to the fonts or text attributes.**

4. **Click in a text box to type your own line of text.**

5. **Click the Play button to preview your title.**

   iMovie displays a preview of the effect in the monitor with the settings that you choose.

6. **Click Done.**

   The title appears in the Project pane.

Adding Maps and Backgrounds

iMovie '11 includes easy-to-use animated maps — think Indiana Jones traveling by airplane from place to place — and static backgrounds that can be used with your titles. To display them, click the Map, Background, and Animatic Browser button on the Browser toolbar, or press ⌘+5.

To use an animated map, drag one of the globe or map thumbnails to the Project pane. After the globe or map is created, click it to display the Inspector — now you can click the Start Location button (and optionally, the End Location button) to enter the start and stop points for the animation. Type a city or place name to see your choices. (Heck, you can even type in an airport code or decimal coordinates to specify the spot.) After you're done, click OK, and then click Done within the Inspector window. Now play the clip, and watch as iMovie animates your location (or your trip) in seconds!

To add a static background from the browser, drag it to the desired spot within the Project pane.

Creating an Honest-to-Goodness Movie Trailer

Yes, friends, you read that correctly! As I mentioned at the beginning of the chapter, iMovie '11 introduces a new Movie Trailer feature that can actually turn your film clips into a Hollywood-class preview, complete with genre transitions and background music.

To create a trailer project, follow these steps:

1. **Click the File menu and choose New Project (or press ⌘+N).**

2. **Type a name for your project.**

3. **Select the aspect ratio for your movie.**

4. **Choose the frame rate.**

5. **Click a Movie Trailer thumbnail to select it.**

iMovie displays a nifty preview of the trailer style that you've selected. You can click on different thumbnails to preview their look before you make your decision — naturally, you'll want to choose a trailer style that most closely matches the mood you want to project with your movie.

Note that each trailer has a suggested number of cast members. This number reflects the number of people that will appear in the clip "place-holders" during the editing process. (More on this in a page or two.)

6. **Click Create.**

iMovie replaces the Project Library pane with the Trailer pane, as shown in Figure 4-7. On the Outline tab, you can edit the titles used in the trailer, as well as pop-up lists for information like the gender of the star(s) and the logo style you want for your "studio" at the beginning of the trailer. To change a text field, click in it and type the new text. You'll see the changes you make in the Trailer display appear in the monitor in real time.

After you've completed your edits to the titles, click the Storyboard tab. Now you can edit the text for each transition — simply click the text to display the edit box and type. You can also drag clips from your Event Library (or from a Finder window) to fill the storyboard's placeholders for video clips. To delete a clip from the storyboard, click it to select it and press Delete.

To preserve the "look and feel" of the trailer storyboard, try to match your clips with the description and suggested activity indicated by the place-holder. (In other words, don't stick a wide-angle video clip of the family dog cavorting in the yard in a placeholder marked "Closeup" — you get the idea.)

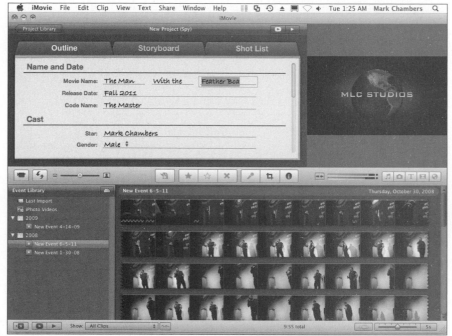

Figure 4-7:
Build your movie trailer from the Trailer pane.

The Storyboard tab might not look like an editing timeline, but you can move the cursor anywhere within the storyboard to preview your trailer! You'll see that the playhead indicator appears wherever the cursor appears, allowing you to watch the clip or transition that it's resting upon. You'll soon be sweeping your mouse to the left or right to move through each section of your trailer.

For an overall listing of each clip required for the full trailer, click the Shot List tab. On this tab, clips are organized by type — for example, all the action clips appear in one section, and all the landscape and closeup clips are grouped together as well. If necessary, you can also add, delete, or swap video clips from the Shot List.

To preview your trailer in its entirety, click the Play Full-Screen button at the top right corner of the Trailer pane. (Naturally, any storyboard placeholder that you haven't filled with a clip will display just the placeholder.)

After you're satisfied with your finished trailer — or you'd like to work on another project — click the Project Library button at the top of the Trailer pane, and you'll see that iMovie has added your trailer as a new project in the Library list.

**Book III
Chapter 4**

**Making Magic
with iMovie**

I bet all those hard-working Hollywood video editors are fuming at how easy it is to create a trailer in iMovie!

Sharing Your Finished Classic with Others

Your movie or trailer is complete, you've saved it to your hard drive, and now you're wondering where to go from here. Click Share on the application menu bar, and you'll see that iMovie can unleash your movie upon your unsuspecting family and friends (and even the entire world) in a number of ways:

✦ **iTunes:** Send your movie to your iTunes Library as a movie.

✦ **iDVD:** Create a new iDVD project automatically, using your movie.

✦ **Media Browser:** Make your iMovie project available within other iLife '11 applications, in five different sizes suited to different display devices.

✦ **Podcast Producer:** You can send your movie to Apple's Podcast Producer application for incorporation into your newest podcasting epic.

✦ **YouTube/Facebook/Vimeo/CNN iReport:** Yep, you read right, you can send your iMovie directly to any of these web sites! Can it get more convenient than that? (I think not.)

✦ **MobileMe Gallery:** Share your movie with the world at large by posting it within a Gallery on your MobileMe web site. (I provide more MobileMe details to chew on in Book V, Chapter 4.)

✦ **Export Movie:** Create a copy of your movie on your hard drive in one of five different sizes.

✦ **Export using QuickTime:** Create a QuickTime movie with your project using the QuickTime encoding engine (allowing greater control over the export process and the attributes of the finished movie file).

If you use this option, any computer with an installed copy of QuickTime can display your movies, and you can use QuickTime movies in Keynote presentations as well.

✦ **Export to Final Cut XML:** If you'd like to transfer your iMovie '11 project to Final Cut Pro, use this option to create a compatible XML file.

When you choose a sharing option, iMovie displays the video quality for the option and makes automatic changes to the movie attributes. (For example, choosing Tiny reduces the finished movie as far as possible in file size, and the audio is reduced to mono instead of stereo.)

Need to take a movie offline or stop sharing it? You can remove a project from iTunes, your iLife Media Browser, your MobileMe web site, or the YouTube web site from the Sharing menu as well. Just click the corresponding Remove From menu item. (Of course, you can share the project again at any time.)

If you're worried about permanently reducing the quality of your project by sharing it in a smaller size, fear not! When you choose a sharing option to export your movie, your original project remains on your hard drive, unchanged, so you can share a better-quality version at any time in the future!

After you adjust any settings specific to the desired sharing option, click Publish (or Save) to start the ball rolling.

Chapter 5: Burn Those DVDs! Using iDVD

In This Chapter

- ✔ Traversing the iDVD window
- ✔ Starting a new iDVD project
- ✔ Tweaking and adjusting your DVD Menu
- ✔ Previewing your (nearly) finished DVD
- ✔ Doing things automatically with OneStep DVD and Magic iDVD
- ✔ Burning a DVD for your friends and family

A number of years ago, I bore witness to yet another proud moment in Apple history: the arrival of a powerful DVD recorder in an affordable computer. The *SuperDrive* was revolutionary because suddenly folks could create and view their own professional-quality DVDs.

Today the tradition continues: Apple includes iDVD *free* with today's Macs as part of iLife '11. With iDVD, you can easily create beautiful presentations with animation and interactive menus that anyone can watch in a standard DVD player or computer DVD drive. And that, friends and neighbors, is the quintessential definition of *cool*.

In this chapter, I show you the basics of creating your first home-cooked DVD movie — and you'll even have fun doing it!

Introducing Your Mac to iDVD

Figure 5-1 shows iDVD in all its glory. You have to supply your own digital video clips, background audio, and digital photographs, of course.

Menu display

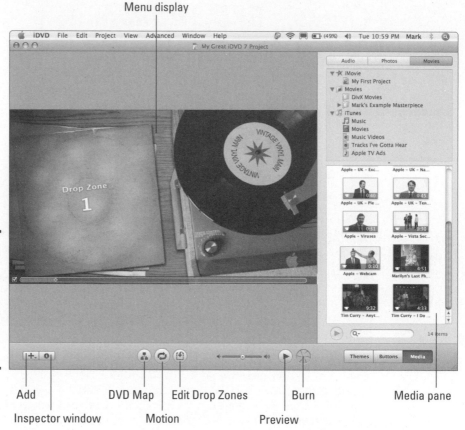

Figure 5-1:
iDVD is a jewel of an application — easy to use and powerful to boot.

Add

Inspector window

DVD Map

Motion

Edit Drop Zones

Preview

Burn

Media pane

Take a moment to appreciate iDVD — no secondary windows to fiddle with or silly palettes strung out everywhere. (Can you tell that I've had my fill of old-style DVD authoring applications?) Allow me to list the highlights of the iDVD window:

✦ **Menu display:** This section takes up the largest part of the iDVD window, with good reason. You create your project here. In this case, *Menu* refers to your DVD Menu, not the menu at the top of your Mac's display.

✦ **Media pane:** You add video, still images, and audio to your project from here, as well as tweak and fine-tune things. The Media pane actually comprises three separate panes. To choose a new pane, click one of these buttons at the bottom of the screen:

• *Themes:* You apply themes (such as Travel Cards, Wedding White, and Baby Mobile) to your DVD Menu to give it a certain look and feel.

- *Buttons:* These options apply to the item currently selected, such as drop shadows on your text titles or the appearance of your Menu buttons.

- *Media:* From here, you can add media items, such as video clips and photos, to your Menu.

✦ **Add button:** From this pop-up menu (which sports a dapper plus sign), you can choose one of three types of buttons to add to a project. The choices are

- *Add Submenu:* Choose this item to add a new submenu button to your DVD Menu. The person using your DVD Menu can click a button to display a new submenu that can include additional movies or slideshows. (If that sounds like ancient Greek, hang on. All becomes clearer later in the chapter, in the section "Adding movies.")

  A Menu can hold only a maximum of 12 buttons (depending on the theme you choose), so submenus let you pack more content on your DVD. (Older versions of the application allowed only six buttons, so don't feel too cheated.) Anyway, each submenu you create can hold another 12 buttons.

- *Add Movie:* Yep, this is the most popular button in the whole shooting match. Click this menu item to add a new movie clip to your Menu.

- *Add Slideshow:* If you want to add a slideshow to your DVD — say, using photos from your hard drive or pictures from your iPhoto library — click this menu item.

✦ **Inspector button:** Click this button to display the Inspector window for the current Menu or a highlighted object. From this window, you can change the look of an individual submenu button or an entire Menu.

✦ **DVD Map:** Click the Map button to display the organizational chart for your DVD Menu. Each button and submenu that you add to your top-level DVD Menu is displayed here, and you can jump directly to a particular item by double-clicking it. Use this road map to help design the layout of your DVD Menu system or to get to a particular item quickly. To return to the Menu display, click the Map button again.

✦ **Motion:** Click this button to start or stop the animation cycle used with the current iDVD theme. The animation repeats (just as it will on your finished DVD) until you click the Motion button again.

Need a visual indicator of the length of your Menu's animation cycle? Click View⇨Show Motion Playhead to display the animation *playhead*, which moves below the Menu display to indicate where you are in the animation cycle. As you can with other playheads in the iLife suite, you can click and drag the diamond-shaped playhead button to move anywhere in the animation cycle.

✦ **Edit Drop Zones:** This button allows you to edit the look and contents of a drop zone on your Menu. (Don't worry, I explain more about drop zones in the sidebar titled, "Taking advantage of drop zones," later in this chapter.)

✦ **Preview:** To see how your DVD Menu project looks when burned to a DVD, click Preview. You get a truly nifty on-screen remote control that you can use to navigate your DVD Menu, just as if you were watching your DVD on a standard DVD player. To exit Preview mode, click the Stop button on the remote control.

✦ **Burn:** Oh, yeah, you know what this one is for — recording your completed DVD movie to a blank disc.

That's the lot! Time to get down to the step-by-step business of making movies.

Starting a New DVD Project

When you launch iDVD for the first time (or if you close all iDVD windows), you get the sporty dialog shown in Figure 5-2. Take a moment to discover more about these four choices.

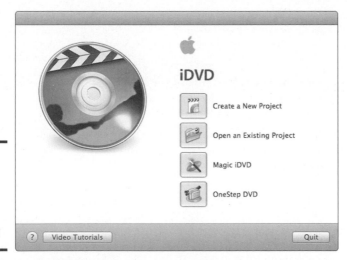

Figure 5-2:
Will that
be create
or edit,
manual or
automatic?

Creating a new project

If you choose Create a New Project, iDVD prompts you to type a name for your new DVD project and to set a location where the project files should be saved. By default, the very reasonable choice is your Documents folder. You also get to choose whether your project will display in a Standard (full-screen) aspect ratio of 4:3 or a Widescreen aspect ratio of 16:9. If you've been watching DVD movies for some time, you recognize these two terms.

You'll probably crave Widescreen format if you have a widescreen TV — go figure — but both formats will display on both types of televisions, complete with those black bars we all know and love at the top and bottom (or left and right sides) of the screen.

Click Create, and the iDVD window appears in all its glory.

Opening an existing project

If you've used iDVD and had a DVD project open the last time you quit the application, iDVD automatically loads the DVD project you were working on. However, you can open any DVD you've created by clicking Open an Existing Project. (To choose a different existing project from the iDVD window, press ⌘+O or choose File➪Open Recent.)

Automating the whole darn process

If you're a fan of click-it-and-forget-it (or are in a hurry), you can throw caution to the wind and allow iDVD to create your latest epic for you! iDVD offers two automated methods of creating a DVD movie disc.

Using OneStep DVD

With OneStep, iDVD does almost all of the work automatically, by using the media clips and photos that you specify. To allow iDVD to help you create a movie, click the OneStep DVD button on the top-level menu (refer back to Figure 5-2). If you've already opened a project, choose File➪OneStep DVD from the application's menu bar to import clips directly from your FireWire mini-DV camera (note that OneStep DVD is not compatible with USB camcorders). Alternately, click File➪OneStep DVD from Movie to select a clip to import from your hard drive. I tell you more about the OneStep DVD feature later, in the section "A Word about Automation."

Using Magic iDVD

Magic iDVD is the newcomer on the block, and it falls neatly between total automation (with OneStep DVD) and total manual control. Click the Magic iDVD button on the top-level menu (as shown in Figure 5-2). If you've already opened a project, you can choose File➪Magic iDVD from the menu bar to choose a theme, drop specific movies and specific photos into filmstrips, and choose an audio track.

In contrast to OneStep DVD, you get to preview the finished product. If it's to your liking, you can choose to either burn the disc directly or create a full-blown iDVD project with the results. *Sweet.*

You find out more about the new Magic iDVD feature later, in the section "A Word about Automation."

Creating a DVD from Scratch

Doing things the old-fashioned, creative, and manual way (following the examples in this section) involves four basic steps:

1. **Design the DVD Menu.**

Choose a theme and any necessary buttons or links.

2. **Add media.**

You can drag movie files from iMovie, still images from iPhoto, and music from iTunes.

3. **Tweak.**

Adjust and fine-tune your DVD Menu settings.

4. **Finish things up.**

Preview and burn your DVD, or save it to your hard drive.

Choosing just the right theme

The first step to take when manually designing a new DVD Menu system is to add a theme. In the iDVD world, a *theme* is a preset package that helps determine the appearance and visual appeal of your DVD Menu, including a background image, Menu animation, an audio track, and a group of settings for text fonts and button styles.

iDVD helps those of us who are graphically challenged by including a wide range of professionally designed themes for all sorts of occasions, ranging from old standbys such as weddings, birthdays, and vacations to more generic themes with the accent on action, friendship, and technology. To view the included themes, click the Themes button in the lower-right corner of the iDVD window (see Figure 5-3).

To choose a theme for your project — or to see what a theme looks like on your Menu — click any thumbnail and watch iDVD update the Menu display.

 If you decide while creating your DVD Menu that you need a different theme, you can change themes at any time. iDVD won't lose a single button or video clip that you add to your DVD Menu. You'll be amazed at how the look and sound of your DVD Menu completely change with just the click of a theme thumbnail.

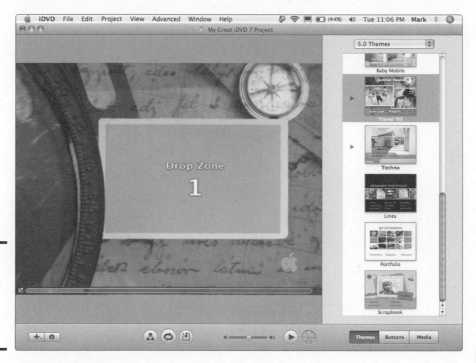

Figure 5-3:
Select a
new theme
from the
Themes
pane.

Adding movies

Drop zones and themes are cool, but most folks want to add video to their DVD. To accomplish this, iDVD uses *buttons* as links to your video clips. In fact, some iDVD Movie buttons display a preview of the video they'll display! To play the video on a DVD player, you select the Movie button with the remote control, just as you do for a commercial DVD.

To add a Movie button, drag a QuickTime movie file from the Finder and drop it onto your DVD Menu display. (Only MPEG-4 QuickTime movies and DV streams are supported — MPEG-1 and MPEG-2 movie clips may be rejected or converted.) Alternatively, click the Add button and choose Add Movie from the pop-up menu.

iDVD and iMovie are soul mates, so you can also display the iDVD Media pane and then click Movies from the pop-up menu. Now you can drag clips from your Movies folder.

**Book III
Chapter 5**

**Burn Those DVDs!
Using iDVD**

Taking advantage of drop zones

Most of Apple's animated themes include special bordered areas marked as drop zones. These locations have nothing to do with skydiving; rather, a *drop zone* is a placeholder in the Menu that can hold a single video clip or photograph. When you drag a video clip or an image to a drop zone, that clip or picture is added to the animation in Apple's theme! Think about that for a moment; I know I did. You can actually personalize a Hollywood-quality animated DVD menu with *your own photos and video!*

Most of the themes included with iDVD include at least one drop zone, and some are practically jam-packed with drop zones. For example, the amazing Forever theme has a whopping six drop zones! If you think a Menu looks just fine without anything in a drop zone, however, you don't have to put anything there. The words *Drop Zone* disappear when you preview or burn your DVD. (Empty frames do tend to look a bit silly in some themes, though.)

To add a video clip or image to a drop zone, simply drag the clip or photo from a Finder window and drop it on the desired drop zone. You can also drag clips or photos from other sources, including the Movies and Photos panes in iDVD's Media pane, the iMovie window, or the iPhoto window. (Remember, Apple is anything but strict on these matters.) Remember, drop zones don't act as links or buttons to other content; the stuff you add to a Menu's drop zones appears only as part of the theme's animation cycle. You can even drag an iPhoto event or album to a drop zone, and it will continuously cycle through the images. *Wowsers!*

To see all the drop zones at one time (without cycling through the animation), click the Edit Drop Zones button at the bottom center of the iDVD window; when you do, you see a thumbnail display of each zone. You can drag items to these thumbnails or jump right to one in the animation by clicking the thumbnail. To delete the contents of a drop zone, click the thumbnail in the editor and press the Delete key.

If you're adding something to a dynamic drop zone (which disappears and reappears during the menu animation cycle), click the Motion button to activate the animation and then click it again to stop the animation cycle. Now click and drag the scrubber bar until the desired drop zone is in view. To delete the contents of a drop zone, Control-click (or right-click) the drop zone and choose Clear.

No matter the source of the clip, when you drop it onto your DVD Menu, iDVD adds a Movie button, as you can see in Figure 5-4. Note that some buttons appear as text links rather than actual buttons. The appearance of a Movie button in your DVD Menu is determined by the theme you choose.

A Movie button doesn't have to stay where iDVD places it! By default, iDVD aligns buttons and text objects using an invisible grid, but if you don't want such order imposed on your creativity, just drag the object to where you'd like it to be to turn on Free Positioning. (You can also right-click the object and select the Free Positioning item from the menu that appears.) iDVD even provides cool new automatic guides that help you align objects when you're using Free Positioning! You'll see them as yellow lines that appear when objects are aligned along a vertical or horizontal plane.

Book III
Chapter 5

Burn Those DVDs!
Using iDVD

Figure 5-4:
A new
Movie
button
appears on
your pristine
DVD Menu.

You can have up to 12 buttons on your iDVD Menu (the theme you choose determines the maximum number of buttons you can add). To add more content than 12 buttons allow, add a submenu by clicking the Add button and choosing Add Submenu from the pop-up menu. Now you can click the submenu button to jump to that screen and drag up to another 12 movie files into it.

Keep your target audience in mind while you create your DVD. Standard TV sets have a different *aspect ratio* (height to width) and *resolution* (number of scan lines on the screen) than a digital video clip, and a standard TV isn't as precise in focusing that image on the tube. If you selected the Standard aspect ratio when you created the project, you can make sure that your DVD content looks great on a standard TV screen by following these steps:

1. **Click View on the old-fashioned iDVD menu (the one at the top of the screen).**

2. **Choose the Show TV Safe Area command.**

    You can also press the convenient ⌘+T shortcut. iDVD adds a smaller rectangle within the iDVD window to mark the screen dimensions of a standard TV.

If you take care that your Menu buttons and (most of) your background image fit within this smaller rectangle, you're assured that folks with a standard television can enjoy your work. To turn off the TV Safe Area rectangle, press ⌘+T again.

If your entire family is blessed with a fleet of HD TVs (or you chose the Widescreen aspect ratio for this project), leave the Show TV Safe Area option off. Today's widescreen displays can handle just about any orientation.

Great, now my audience demands a slideshow

Many Mac owners don't realize that iDVD can use not only video clips but also digital photos as content. In fact, you can add a group of images to your DVD Menu by using Slideshow buttons, which allow the viewer to play back a series of digital photographs. iDVD handles everything for you, so there's no tricky timing to figure out or weird scripts to write. Just click the Add button at the bottom of the iDVD window and choose Add Slideshow. iDVD places a Slideshow button on your DVD Menu.

After the Slideshow button is on tap, add the content — in this case, by choosing the images that iDVD adds to your DVD Menu. Follow these steps to select your slideshow images:

1. **Double-click the Slideshow Menu button — the one you just added to the Menu — to open the Slideshow display (see Figure 5-5).**

A word on image dimensions

For best playback results on a standard TV, make sure that your background image has the same dimensions as standard digital video — 640 x 480 pixels. If the dimensions of your image don't match the dimensions of digital video, iDVD will stretch or shrink the image to fit, which might have undesirable effects. When your image is stretched and skewed to fit the DVD Menu, Aunt Harriet might end up looking like Shrek.

You can use QuickTime player or iPhoto to change the dimensions of your background image for import into iDVD. For example, you can use the iPhoto crop feature to alter the overall shape of the image and then resize it within iPhoto. Use the Size setting when you export the image from iPhoto and then save the file in the Pictures folder located in your Home folder so that you can find it easily later. (For more on working in iPhoto, see Book III, Chapter 3.)

If you enjoy a cutting-edge widescreen (16:9) or HD (high-definition) TV display, you won't have the standard TV dimension restriction of 640 x 480 pixels. And because iDVD supports HD video and 16:9 video with a number of widescreen themes, be prepared to kiss the phrases *pan-and-scan* and *full-screen* goodbye and forget about the Show TV Safe Area feature. If your completed DVD projects are purely for your own enjoyment, that's a great idea. However, don't forget that if you distribute your discs to others with old-fashioned TVs dating back to the archaic '80s and '90s, they might not be pleased with what they see!

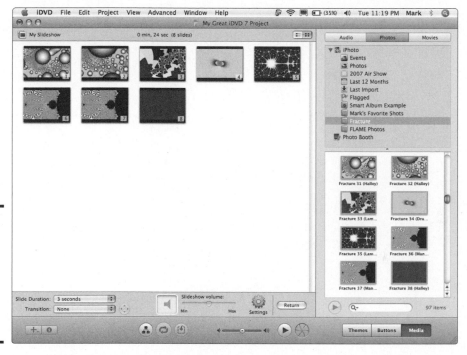

Figure 5-5:
Who needs
a projector
anymore?
iDVD can
create
a great
slideshow!

2. **Click the Media button (bottom right of the screen).**

3. **Click the Photos tab (top right of the screen) to display your iPhoto library and photo albums.**

4. **Drag your favorite image thumbnails from the Photos list and drop them into the My Slideshow window.**

   You can also drag images straight from a Finder window or the iPhoto window itself. (Those Apple folks are sooooo predictable.)

5. **Drag around the photos in the My Slideshow window to set their order of appearance in your slideshow.**

6. **To add audio to these pictures, drag your favorite audio file from the Finder and drop it in the Audio well in the My Slideshow window.**

   The *Audio well* is the box bearing the speaker icon, next to the volume control below the My Slideshow window.

   Alternatively, click the Audio button to select an audio track from your iTunes library, iTunes playlists, or GarageBand creations.

7. **Click the Return button to return to your DVD Menu.**

If you're using a Menu with animated buttons that display an image (rather than text buttons), you can choose which image you want to appear on the Slideshow button. Click the Slideshow button that you added and see the slider that appears above the Slideshow button. Drag this slider to scroll through the images you added. When you find the image that you want to use for the Slideshow button in the DVD Menu, click the Slideshow button again to save your changes.

Now for the music . . .

Most of the Apple-supplied themes already have their own background music, so you might not even need to add music to your DVD Menu. However, if you want to change the existing background music (or if your DVD Menu currently doesn't have any music), adding your own audio to the current Menu is child's play!

1. **Click the Media button.**

2. **Click the Audio tab to reveal the musical Shangri-La, as shown in Figure 5-6.**

3. **Drag an audio file from the iTunes playlist or GarageBand folder display and drop it on the Menu background.**

    iDVD accepts every sound format that you can use for importing encoding in iTunes: AIFF, MP3, AAC, Apple Lossless, and WAV audio files.

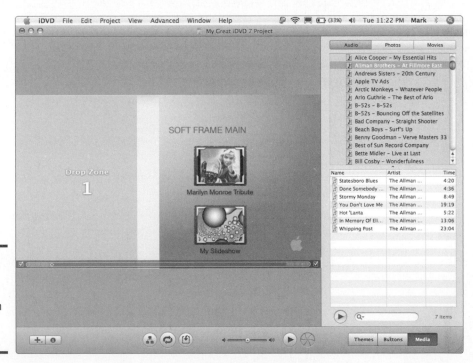

Figure 5-6:
You do a lot of fine-tuning from the Audio pane.

4. **Click the Motion button (labeled in Figure 5-1) to watch your DVD Menu animation cycle set to the new background audio.**

5. **Click the Motion button again to stop the animation and return to serious work.**

Giving Your DVD the Personal Touch

You can easily make changes to the default settings provided with the theme you chose. iDVD offers all sorts of controls that allow you to change the appearance and behavior of buttons, text, and the presentation of your content. In this section, I show you how to cast out iDVD's (perfectly good) defaults and then tweak things to perfection.

Using Uncle Morty for your DVD Menu background

Hey, Uncle Morty might not be a supermodel, but he has birthdays and anniversaries, and iDVD is more than happy to accommodate you in documenting those milestones! Follow these steps to change the background of your DVD Menu:

1. **Click the Inspector button.**

2. **Get an image using one of the following methods:**

    * *Drag an image from the Finder* and drop it into the Background well.

    * *Drag the image directly into the Menu display.*

    * *To use an image from your iPhoto library,* click the Media button and click the Photos tab, and then drag the desired image into the Menu display.

    iDVD updates the DVD Menu to reflect your new background choice.

Adding your own titles

The one tweak you'll probably have to perform in every iDVD project is changing titles. Unfortunately, the default labels provided by iDVD are pretty lame, and they appear in two important places:

✦ **Menu title:** Your large main title usually appears at the top of the DVD Menu.

✦ **Button captions:** Each Submenu, Movie, and Slideshow button that you add to your Menu has its own title.

To change the text in your Menu title or the titles below your buttons, follow these steps:

1. **Select the text by clicking it.**

2. **Click it again to edit it.**

   A rectangle with a cursor appears to indicate that you can now edit the text.

3. **Type the new text and press Return to save the change.**

Changing buttons like a highly paid professional

Customizing Movie buttons? You can do it with aplomb! Follow these steps:

1. **Click Buttons.**

2. **Click any Movie button from the DVD Menu to select it.**

   A slider appears above the button, which you can drag to set the thumbnail picture for that button in your DVD Menu. (Naturally, this is only for animated buttons, not text buttons.)

   Enable the Movie check box to animate the button.

3. **To create a Movie button with a still image, drag a picture from a Finder window or the Media pane and drop it on top of the button.**

4. **To adjust the properties for the button, click the Inspector button.**

Table 5-1 describes the button properties — note that some properties won't appear for text buttons.

Table 5-1	Button Settings You Can Customize
Movie Button Property	*What It Does*
Label Font	Changes the label font, text size, color and attributes.
Label Attributes	Specifies the position of the label and whether it has a shadow.
Custom Thumbnail	Selects the image that will be shown in the button. Drag an image to the Custom Thumbnail well. For Slideshow buttons, drag the Thumbnail slider to select the image.
Transition	Determines the transition that occurs when the button is clicked (before the action occurs).
Size	Adjusts the size of the button. Move the slider to the right to increase the button size.

Give my creation motion!

Earlier in this chapter, you find out how to use a different image for your background, but what about using an animated background? You can use any QuickTime movie from your iMovie library to animate your DVD Menu background! Didn't I tell you that this iDVD thing was *huge?*

Keep in mind that your background movie should be a short clip; 20–30 seconds is optimal. A clip with a fade-in at the beginning and a fade-out at the end is the best choice because iDVD loops your background clip continuously, and your animated background flows seamlessly behind your Menu.

I'm not talking drop zones here. (See the sidebar "Taking advantage of drop zones," earlier in this chapter, for an explanation of drop zones.) You can add a movie to a drop zone, of course, but by using a movie clip as a background, you're replacing the entire animation sequence rather than just a single area of the background. Drop zones also don't provide audio, whereas a clip background does include the clip audio.

Follow these steps to add a new animated background:

1. **Click your old friend, the Inspector button.**

Make sure that no individual objects are highlighted so that the Inspector window displays the Menu properties instead.

2. **Drag a movie from the Finder and drop it into the Background well.**

You can click the Movies tab in the Media pane to instantly display your iMovie collection.

3. **Click the Motion button in the iDVD window to try out your new background.**

4. **Click the Motion button again to stop the animation cycle.**

Previewing Your Masterpiece

Figure 5-7 captures the elusive Preview remote control — truly an awesome sight. When you click Preview, the Media pane disappears, and your DVD Menu appears exactly as it will on the finished DVD.

Ah, but appearances aren't everything: You can also use your DVD Menu! Click the buttons on the remote control to simulate the remote on your DVD player, or think outside the box and click a Menu button directly with your mouse pointer. iDVD presents the video clip, runs the slideshow, or jumps to a submenu, just as it will with the completed disc.

Book III
Chapter 5

Burn Those DVDs! Using iDVD

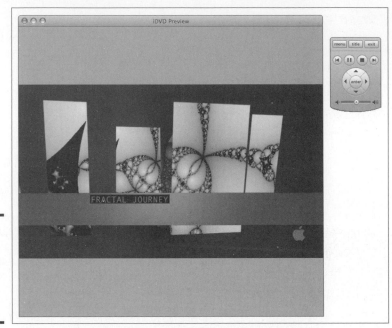

Figure 5-7:
Preview
mode — an
incredible
simulation
indeed.

This is a great time to test-drive a project before you burn it to disc. To make sure you don't waste a blank DVD, make certain that everything you expect to happen actually happens. Nothing worse than discovering that Aunt Edna's slideshow from her Hong Kong trip actually displays your family's summer trip to the zoo (whoops). If you made a mistake or something needs tweaking, click the Preview button again, and you're back to the iDVD window proper, where you can edit or fine-tune your project.

iDVD allows you to save your project as a standard Mac OS X *disc image* rather than as a simple project file (or a physical DVD) — a good idea for those Macs without a SuperDrive on board because you can use Apple's Disk Utility to open and mount the disc image as if it were a burned disc. If you move the disc image to another Mac with a SuperDrive, you can use Disk Utility to burn it on that machine. To save an iDVD project as a disc image, choose File➪Save as Disc Image (or press ⌘+Shift+R).

Interested in tweaking settings across your entire project? Perhaps you'd like to reduce the time it takes to create and edit your DVD, or you'd like to switch video modes from NTSC to PAL for a DVD that's to be sent overseas. If you'd like to view or change the overall settings for your entire DVD, click Project➪Project Info to display the Project Info dialog. Heck, you can even switch aspect ratios, or change the project name . . . . Thanks, Apple!

A Word about Automation

At the beginning of the chapter, I mention the easy way to produce an iDVD disc or project, using either OneStep DVD (for complete automation) or Magic iDVD (for partial automation). In this section, I provide you with the details.

One-click paradise with OneStep DVD

If you're in a hurry to create a DVD from clips on your tape-based DV camcorder and you don't mind losing your creative input, OneStep DVD is just the ticket. In short, iDVD allows you to plug in your FireWire-equipped mini-DV camcorder, answer a question or two, and then sit back while the application does *all* the work. iDVD imports the DV clips, creates a basic Menu design, and burns the disc automatically!

Using OneStep DVD will appeal to any laptop owner with a SuperDrive. Why not produce a DVD right after a wedding or birthday that you can give as a gift? Photographers who cover those same special events might consider selling a DVD made with OneStep DVD. If you happen to capture something incredibly unique — such as a UFO landing or an honest politician — you can use OneStep DVD to create an instant backup of the clips on your DV camcorder. You could even keep your friends and family up-to-date with the progress of your vacation by sending them a daily DVD of your exploits! (You gotta admit, even Grandma would consider that eminently *sassy!*)

Follow these steps to start the OneStep DVD process:

1. **Click the OneStep DVD button on the iDVD top-level menu (refer to Figure 5-2).**

   Alternatively, choose File➪OneStep DVD.

   iDVD displays the dialog shown in Figure 5-8.

Figure 5-8: Connect your DV camcorder, and OneStep DVD does the rest.

OneStep DVD

To use OneStep DVD, connect your digital video camera to your computer using a FireWire cable. Then turn on your camera and make sure it's in VCR mode.

Click OK and insert a blank disc. OneStep DVD rewinds the tape, imports your video, and burns it to a DVD.

OK

If you want to use OneStep DVD with an existing movie on your Mac's hard drive, choose File➪OneStep DVD from Movie instead. iDVD prompts you for the video file to use.

2. Following the prompts, connect the FireWire cable from your DV camcorder; then turn on the camcorder and set it to VCR mode.

3. Click OK.

4. Load a blank DVD.

Exercising control with Magic iDVD

Got a little extra time? For those who prefer to make just a few choices and let iDVD do the rest, the Magic iDVD feature just plain rocks! However, you can't import clips directly from your mini-DV camcorder as you can with OneStep DVD; instead, you select one of the following:

+ **An iDVD theme**

+ **Video clips** you've already created with iMovie or dragged from the Finder (perfect for use with a USB 2.0 DV camcorder)

+ **Photos** from your iPhoto library or dragged from the Finder

+ **Audio** from your iTunes playlist or dragged from the Finder

Follow these steps to start the OneStep DVD process:

1. Click the Magic iDVD button on the iDVD top-level dialog (refer to Figure 5-2).

   iDVD displays the window you see in Figure 5-9.

2. Click in the DVD Title box and type a name for your disc (or project).

3. Click to select a theme from the Theme strip.

4. Click the Movies tab and drag the desired clips into the Drop Movies Here strip.

5. To add a slideshow, click the Photos tab and drag the desired photos into the Drop Photos Here strip.

6. To add audio for your slideshow, click the Audio tab and drag the desired song into the Drop Photos Here strip (a speaker icon appears in the first cell of the strip to indicate that you've added a soundtrack).

7. Click Preview to see a preview of the finished project, complete with remote control. To exit Preview mode, click Exit.

8. To open the project in its current form in the main iDVD window, click Create Project.

9. To record your completed project directly to DVD, load a blank DVD and click Burn.

To return to the iDVD main window at any time, just click the Close button on the Magic iDVD window.

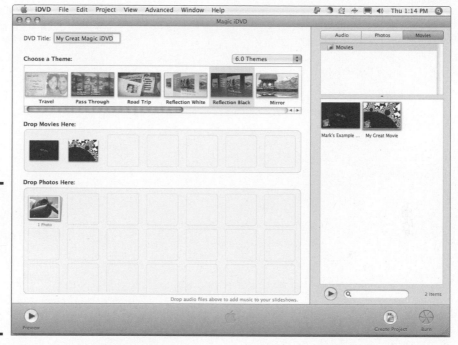

Figure 5-9:
With Magic
iDVD,
you make
some basic
choices,
and iDVD
does the
work.

**Book III
Chapter 5**

**Burn Those DVDs!
Using iDVD**

Recording a Finished Project to a Shiny Disc

When you're ready to record your next Oscar-winning documentary on family behaviors during vacation, just follow these simple words:

1. **Click the Burn button at the bottom of the iDVD window.**

   I have to admit, the Burn button that appears has to be my favorite single control in all my 20+ years of computing! It looks powerful, it looks sexy . . . it wants to *burn.* (Sorry about that.)

2. **After iDVD asks you to insert a blank DVD-R into the SuperDrive, load a single or dual-layer blank DVD-R, DVD-RW, DVD+R, or DVD+RW (depending on the media your Mac can handle).**

   Your SuperDrive might be able to burn and read a DVD+R, DVD-RW, or DVD+RW, but what about your DVD player? Keep in mind that only DVD-Rs are likely to work in older DVD players. The latest generation of DVD players is likely DVD+R compatible as well, but I've seen only a handful of DVD players that can handle rewriteable media at the time of this writing. Therefore, remember the destination for the discs you burn and choose your media accordingly.

   After a short pause, iDVD begins burning the DVD. The application keeps you updated with a progress bar.

When the disc is finished, you're ready to load it into your favorite local DVD player, or you can load it back into your Mac and enjoy your work using Apple's DVD Player.

Either way, it's all good!

Chapter 6: Becoming a Superstar with GarageBand

In This Chapter

✓ Navigating the GarageBand window

✓ Adding tracks and loops to your song

✓ Repeating loops and extending your song

✓ Building arrangements

✓ Adding effects to instruments

✓ Exporting your work to iTunes and iWeb

✓ Burning your song to an audio CD

*W*hen I was a kid, I always thought that *real* rock stars trashed their instruments after a hard night's worth of jamming — you know, like The Who, Led Zeppelin, KISS, and the Rolling Stones. Guitars got set on fire, or pounded into the stage, or thrown into the crowd like beads during a Mardi Gras parade.

I can make my own music now, but you'll never see me trash my instrument! I compose music on my Mac with *GarageBand,* Apple's music-making component in the iLife application suite. You can solo on all sorts of instruments, and even add horns, drums, and a funky bass line for backup . . . all with absolutely no musical experience (and, in my case, very little talent, to boot)!

Oh, and did I mention that GarageBand '11 also produces podcasts? That's right, you can record your voice and easily create your own show, and then share it with others from your iWeb site! Heck, add photos if you like. You'll be the talk of your family and friends and maybe even your Mac user group.

This chapter explains everything you need to know to create your first song (or your first podcast). I also show you how to import your hit record into iTunes so that you can listen to it on your iPod with a big, silly grin on your face (as I do) or add it to your next iMovie or iDVD project as a royalty-free soundtrack.

Shaking Hands with Your Band

As you can see in Figure 6-1, the GarageBand window isn't complex at all, and that's good design. In this section, I list the most important controls so that you know your Play button from your Loop Browser button.

Track list   Timeline

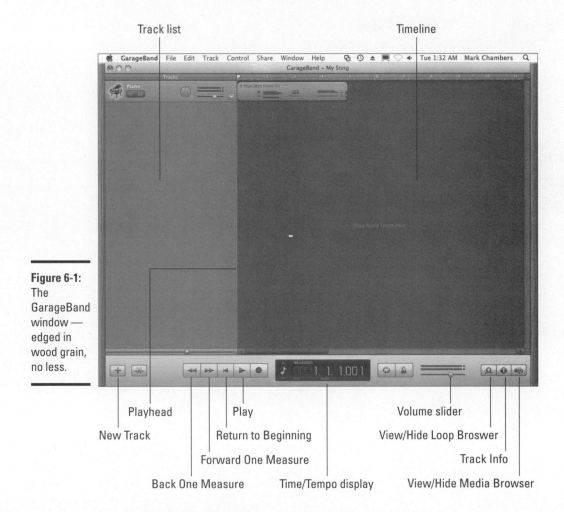

Figure 6-1:
The GarageBand window — edged in wood grain, no less.

Playhead   Play   Volume slider

New Track   Return to Beginning   View/Hide Loop Broswer

Forward One Measure   Track Info

Back One Measure   Time/Tempo display   View/Hide Media Browser

Your music-making machine includes

✦ **Track list:** In GarageBand, a *track* is a discrete instrument that you set up to play one part of your song. For example, a track in a classical piece for string quartet would have four tracks — one each for violin, viola, cello, and bass. This list contains all the tracks in your song arranged so that you can easily see and modify them, like the rows in a spreadsheet.

A track begins in the list, stretching out to the right all the way to the end of the song. As you can see in the upper left of Figure 6-1, I already have one track defined — a Grand Piano.

If you're creating a podcast, a *Podcast artwork track* can also appear.

✦ **Timeline:** This scrolling area holds the loops (see the following bullet) that you add or record, allowing you to move and edit them easily. When a song plays, the Timeline scrolls to give you a visual look at your music. (Bear with me; you'll understand that cryptic statement in a page or two.)

✦ **Loop:** This is a prerecorded clip of an instrument being played in a specific style and tempo. Loops are the building blocks of your song. You can drag loops from the Loop Browser to a track and literally build a bass line or a guitar solo. (It's a little like adding video clips in iMovie to build a film.)

✦ **Playhead:** This vertical line is a moving indicator that shows you the current position in your song while it scrolls by in the Timeline. You can drag the playhead to a new location at any time. The playhead also acts like the insertion cursor in a word processing application: If you insert a section of a song or a loop from the Clipboard, it appears at the current location of the playhead. (More on copying and inserting loops later, so don't panic.)

✦ **Create a New Track button:** Click this button to add a new track to your song.

✦ **Track Info button:** If you need to display the instrument used in a track, click the track to select it and then click this button. You can also control settings, such as Echo and Reverb, from the Edit pane of the Track Info display.

✦ **View/Hide Loop Browser button:** Click the button with the loop icon to display the Loop Browser at the right side of the window; click it again to close it. You can see more of your tracks' contents without scrolling by closing the Loop Browser.

✦ **View/Hide Media Browser button:** Click this button (which bears icons of a filmstrip, slide, and musical note) to display the media browser at the right side of the window; click it again to close it. By closing the media browser, you'll see more of your tracks. If you're already familiar with iDVD, iWeb, or iMovie, you recognize this pane in the GarageBand window; it allows you to add media (in this case, digital song files, still images, or movies) to your GarageBand project for use in a podcast.

✦ **Go to Beginning button:** Clicking this button immediately moves the playhead back to the beginning of the Timeline.

✦ **Move Back/Forward One Measure buttons:** To move quickly through your song by jumping to the previous or next measure, click the corresponding button.

✦ **Play button:** Hey, old friend! At last, a control that you've probably used countless times before — and it works just like the same control on your audio CD player. Click Play, and GarageBand begins playing your entire song. Notice that the Play button turns blue. To stop the music, click Play again; the button loses that sexy blue sheen and the playhead stops immediately. (If playback is paused, it begins again at the playhead position when you click Play.)

✦ **Time/Tempo display:** This cool-looking LCD display shows you the current playhead position in seconds.

You can click the icon at the left of the display to choose other modes, such as

- **Measures** (to display the current measure and mark the beat)

- **Chord** (to display note and chord names)

- **Project** (to show or change the key, tempo, and signature for the song)

✦ **Volume slider:** Here's another familiar face. Just drag the slider to raise or lower the volume.

Of course, more controls are scattered around the GarageBand window, but these are the main controls used to compose a song . . . which is the next stop!

Composing and Podcasting Made Easy

In this section, I cover the basics of composition in GarageBand, working from the very beginning. Follow along with this running example:

1. **Close all existing GarageBand windows.**

GarageBand displays the top-level New Project dialog shown in Figure 6-2.

2. **Click New Project on the list at the left.**

3. **Click the Piano icon and click Choose.**

By choosing the Piano, my new GarageBand project will have one track already in place — a grand piano. If you choose Electric Guitar or Voice, you'll have a project automatically created with an electric guitar track or male and female voice tracks. To create a completely empty project, choose Loops.

GarageBand displays the New Project from Template Save As dialog.

Figure 6-2:
Start
creating
your new
song here.

4. **Type a name for your new song and then drag the Tempo slider to select the beats per minute (bpm).**

   A GarageBand song can have only one *tempo* (or speed) throughout, expressed as beats per minute.

5. **If you want to adjust the settings for your song, you can select the**

   • *Time signature (the Time box, expressed as beats per minute)*

   • *Key (the Key box)*

   If you're new to music *theory* (the rules and syntax by which music is created and written), just use the defaults. Most of the toe-tappin' tunes that you and I are familiar with fit right in with these settings.

6. **Click the Create button.**

   You see the window shown in Figure 6-1. (The Blue Jazz Piano 01 section at the top of Figure 6-1 — which I show you how to add in the next section — is an example of a typical loop.)

Adding tracks

Although I'm not a musician, I am a music lover, and I know that many classical composers approached a new work in the same way you approach a new song in GarageBand: by envisioning the instruments that they wanted to hear. (I imagine Mozart and Beethoven would've been thrilled to use GarageBand, but I think they did a decent job with pen and paper, too.)

In fact, GarageBand '11 includes a *Songwriting* project (also available from the top-level New Project dialog). When you choose the Songwriting project, GarageBand presents you with a full set of four instrument tracks, plus a real instrument track for your voice. (More on software versus real instrument tracks in a page or two.) You're instantly ready to start adding loops and recording your own voice!

If you've followed along to this point, you've noticed two problems with your GarageBand window:

✦ **There's no keyboard.** You can record the contents of a software instrument track by "playing" the keyboard, clicking the keys with your mouse. (As you might imagine, this isn't the best solution, especially with a trackpad.) If you're a musician, the best method of recording your own notes is with a MIDI instrument, which I discuss later in the chapter. For now, you can display the keyboard window by pressing ⌘+K. If the keyboard window is on the screen and you don't need it, banish the window by clicking the Close button.

Even if you're not interested in the "point-and-click" keyboard, GarageBand offers a musical typing keyboard, where you press the keys on your keyboard to simulate the keys on a musical keyboard. (Hey, if you don't have a MIDI instrument, at least it's better than nothing.) To display the musical typing keyboard window, press Shift+⌘+K.

✦ **The example song has only one track.** If you want to write the next classical masterpiece for Grand Piano, that's fine. Otherwise, on the GarageBand menu bar, choose Track⇨Delete Track to start with a clean slate. (I know, I could have started with a Loops project, but this way you get to see how to delete a track.)

These are the five kinds of tracks you can use in GarageBand '11:

✦ **Software instrument tracks:** These tracks aren't audio recordings. Rather, they're mathematically precise algorithms that your Mac *renders* (or builds) to fit your needs. If you have a MIDI instrument connected to your Mac, you can create your own software instrument tracks. (More on MIDI instruments later in this chapter.)

In this chapter, I focus on software instrument tracks, which are the easiest for a nonmusician to use.

✦ **Real instrument tracks:** A real instrument track is an actual audio recording, such as your voice or a physical instrument without a MIDI connection. (Think microphone.)

✦ **Electric Guitar tracks:** GarageBand includes a real instrument track especially made for an electric guitar, which allows you to use one of five different amplifiers and a number of stompboxes (those effect pedals that guitarists are always poking with their foot to change the sound of their instruments).

+ **Podcast artwork track:** You get only one of these; they hold photos that will appear on a video-capable iPod, iPhone, or iPad (or a window on your iWeb site) when your podcast is playing.

+ **Video tracks:** The video sound track appears if you're *scoring* (adding music) to an iMovie movie. Along with the video sound track, you get a cool companion video track that shows the clips in your movie. (More on this in the "Look, I'm John Williams!" sidebar, later in this chapter.)

Time to add a software instrument track of your very own. Follow these steps:

1. **Click the New Track button (which carries a plus sign), labeled in Figure 6-1.**

GarageBand displays the New Track dialog.

2. **Click the Software Instrument icon and then click Create.**

See all those great instruments in the Track Info pane on the right?

3. **Choose the general instrument category by clicking it.**

I chose Drum Kits.

4. **From the right column, choose your specific style of weapon, such as Rock Kit for an arena sound.**

Figure 6-3 illustrates the new track that appears in your list when you follow these steps.

Figure 6-3:
The new track appears, ready to rock.

If you're creating a podcast and you want to add a series of still images that will appear on a device's screen (or on your iWeb page), follow these steps:

1. **Click the View Media Browser button (labeled in Figure 6-1).**

2. **Click the Photos button.**

   GarageBand displays all the photos in your iPhoto library and Events.

3. **Drag an image from your iPhoto library in the media browser to the Track list.**

   The Podcast track appears at the top of the Track list, and you can add and move images in the list at any time, just like the loops that you add to your instrument tracks. (More on adding and rearranging the contents of a track later in this section.)

Choosing loops

When you have a new, empty track, you can add something that you can hear. You do that by adding loops to your track from the Loop Browser — Apple provides you with thousands of loops to choose among — and photos from your media browser. Click the Loop Browser button (which bears the loop, somewhat like a roller coaster) to display your collection, as shown in Figure 6-4.

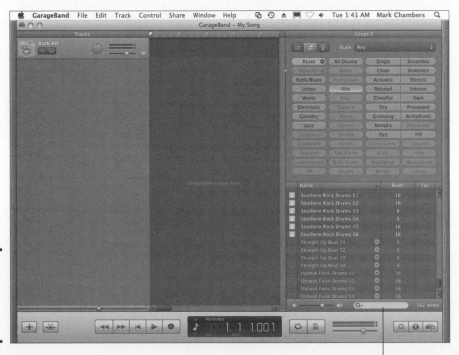

Figure 6-4: The Loop Browser, shown in button view.

Search

If your browser looks different from what you see in Figure 6-4, that's because of the view mode you're using, just like the different view modes available for a Finder window. The three-icon button in the upper-left corner of the Loop Browser toggles the browser display between column, musical button, and podcast sounds view. Click the middle of the three buttons to switch to musical button mode.

Looking for just the right loop

The track in this running example uses a Rock drum kit, but we haven't added a loop yet. (Refer to Figure 6-3.) Follow these steps to search through your loop library for just the right rhythm:

1. **Click the button that corresponds to the instrument you're using.**

In our example, this is the Kits button in the Loop Browser. Click it, and a list of different beats appears in the pane at the bottom of the Loop Browser window. (Check out Figure 6-4 for a sneak peek.)

2. **Click one of the loops with a green musical-note icon.**

Go ahead; this is where things get fun! GarageBand begins playing the loop nonstop, allowing you to get a feel for how that particular loop sounds.

Because I'm using only software instruments in this track (and throughout this chapter), you should choose only software instrument loops, which are identified by a green musical-note icon.

3. **Click another entry in the list, and the application switches immediately to that loop.**

Now you're beginning to understand why GarageBand is so cool for both musicians and the note-impaired. It's like having your own band, with members who never get tired, never miss a beat, and play whatever you want while you're composing. (Mozart would've *loved* this.)

If you want to search for a particular instrument, click in the Search box (labeled in Figure 6-4) and type the text you want to match. GarageBand returns the search results in the list.

4. **Scroll down the list and continue to sample the different loops until you find one that fits like a glove.**

For this reporter, it's Southern Rock Drums 01.

5. **Drag the entry to your Rock Kit track and drop it at the very beginning of the Timeline (as indicated by the playhead).**

Your window will look like Figure 6-5.

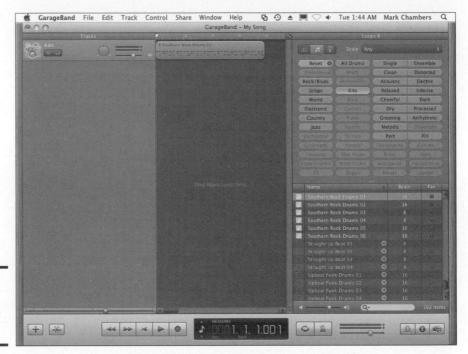

Figure 6-5:
A track
with a loop
added.

If you want that same beat throughout the song, you don't need to add any more loops to that track. (More on extending that beat in the next section.) However, if you want the drum's beat to change later in the song, you add a second loop after the first one in the *same* track. For now, leave this track as is.

Whoops! Did you do something that you regret? Don't forget that you can undo most actions in GarageBand by pressing the old standby ⌘+Z immediately afterward.

Second verse, same as the first

When you compose, you can add tracks for each instrument that you want in your song:

✦ Each track can have more than one loop.

✦ Loops *don't* have to start at the beginning; you can drop a loop anywhere in the Timeline.

For example, in Figure 6-6, you can see that my drum kit kicks in first, but my bass line doesn't begin until some time later (for a funkier opening).

Look, I'm John Williams!

You, too, can be a famous composer of soundtracks . . . well, perhaps not quite as famous as Mr. Williams, but even he had to start somewhere. To add a GarageBand score to an iMovie, click the Track menu and then click Show Movie Track to display the Movie track. Choose a movie to score from the familiar confines of the Media Browser, and drag it to the Movie Track.

At this point, you add and modify instrument tracks and loops just as you would any other GarageBand project. The existing sound for the iMovie project appears in the Movie Sound

track. A Video Preview thumbnail appears within the Movie track. When you click the Play button, the video is shown as well so that you can check your work and tweak settings (as described later in the chapter).

After you've finished composing, you can click Share on the menu bar and choose to export your work to iDVD, as a QuickTime movie directly to your hard drive, or to iTunes or iWeb as a movie. Note that you can't return to iMovie with your project, so scoring should be a final step in the production of your movie.

You put loops on separate tracks so that they can play simultaneously on different instruments. If all your loops in a song are added on the same track, you hear only one loop at any one time, and all the loops use the same software instrument. By creating multiple tracks, you give yourself the elbow room to bring in the entire band at the same time. It's über-convenient to compose your song when you can see each instrument's loops and where they fall in the song.

Click the Reset button in the Loop Browser to choose another instrument or genre category.

Resizing, repeating, and moving loops

If you haven't already tried listening to your entire song, try it now. You can click Play at any time without wreaking havoc on your carefully created tracks. Sounds pretty good, doesn't it?

But wait: I bet the song stopped after about five seconds, right? (You can watch the passing seconds using either the Time/Tempo display or the second rule that appears at the very top of the Timeline.) I'm sure that you want your song to last more than five seconds! After the playhead moves past the end of the last loop, your song is over. Click Play again to pause the playback; then click the Return to Beginning button (labeled in Figure 6-1) to move the playhead back to the beginning of the song.

**Book III
Chapter 6**

Becoming a
Superstar with
GarageBand

Figure 6-6:
My Timeline
with a
synth and
an electric
bass
onboard.
Let's rock!

The music stops so soon because your loops are only so long. Most are five seconds in length, and others are even shorter. To keep the groove going, you have to do one of three things:

✦ **Resize the loop.** Hover your mouse cursor over either the left or right edge of most loops, and an interesting thing happens: Your cursor changes to a vertical line with an arrow pointing away from the loop. That's your cue to click and drag — and as you drag, most loops expand to fill the space you're making, repeating the beats in perfect time. By resizing a loop, you can literally drag the loop's edge as long as you like.

✦ **Repeat the loop.** Depending on the loop that you chose, you might find that resizing it doesn't repeat the measure. Instead, the new part of the loop is simply dead air. In fact, the length of many loops is limited to anywhere from one to five seconds. However, if you move your cursor over the side of a loop that you want to extend, it turns into a circular arrow, which tells you that you can click and *repeat* the loop. GarageBand actually adds multiple copies of the same loop automatically, for as far as you drag the loop. In Figure 6-7, I've repeated the bass loop that you see in Figure 6-6.

✦ **Add a new loop.** You can switch to a different loop to change the flow of the music. Naturally, the instrument stays the same, but there's no reason you can't use a horn-riff loop in your violin track (as long as it sounds good played by a violin)! To GarageBand, a software instrument track is compatible with *any* software instrument loop that you add from the Loop Browser as long as that loop is marked with our old friend the green musical note.

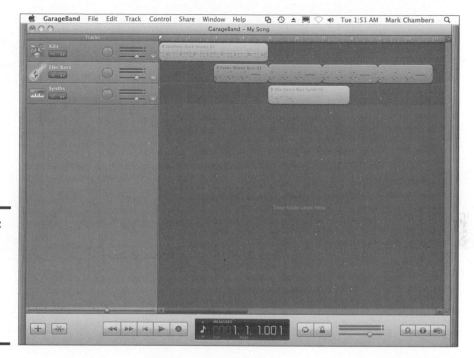

Figure 6-7:
By repeating the bass loop, you can keep the thump flowing.

You can also use the familiar cut (⌘+X), copy (⌘+C), and paste (⌘+V) editing keys to cut, copy, and paste loops from place to place — both on the Timeline and from track to track. And you can click a loop and drag it anywhere. After all, you're working under Mac OS X.

Each track can be adjusted so that you can listen to the interplay between two or more tracks or hear how your song sounds without a specific track:

✦ Click the tiny speaker button under the track name in the list, and the button turns blue to indicate that the track is muted. To turn off the mute, click the speaker icon again.

✦ You can change the volume or balance of each individual track by using the mixer that appears next to the track name. This comes in handy if you want an instrument to sound louder or confine that instrument to the left or right speaker.

A track doesn't have to be filled for every second with one loop or another. Most of my songs have a number of repeating loops with empty space between them as different instruments perform solo.

Using the Arrange track

GarageBand includes another method you can use to monkey with your music: The *Arrange track* can be used to define specific sections of a song, allowing you to reorganize things by selecting, moving, and copying entire sections. For example, you're probably familiar with the chorus (or refrain) of a song and how often it appears during the course of the tune. With the Arrange track, you can reposition the entire chorus within your song, carrying all the loops and settings within the chorus along with it! If you need another chorus, just copy that arrangement.

To use the Arrange track, display it by clicking Track⇨Show Arrange Track. The Arrange track then appears as a thin strip at the top of the track list. Click the Add Region button in the Arrange track (which carries a plus sign) and you'll see a new, untitled region appear (as shown in Figure 6-8). You can drag the right side of the Arrangement region to resize it, or drag it to move it anywhere in the song.

Who wants an arrangement full of regions named "untitled"? To rename an Arrangement region, click the word *untitled* to select it (the Arrange track turns blue) and then click the title again to display a text box. Type a new name for the region and press Return.

Now, here's where Arrangement regions get *cool:*

✦ To move an entire Arrangement region, click the region's title in the Arrange track and then drag it anywhere you like in the song.

✦ To copy an Arrangement region, hold down the Option key and drag the desired region's title to the spot where you want the copy to appear.

✦ To delete an Arrangement region, select it and press ⌘+Option+Delete.

✦ To replace the contents of an Arrangement region with those of another Arrangement region, hold down the ⌘ key and drag the desired region's title on top of the offending region's title.

✦ To switch two Arrangement regions in your song — swapping the contents completely — drag one of the Arrangement region titles on top of the other and release the mouse button.

Tweaking the settings for a track

You don't think that John Mayer or U2 just "play and walk away," do you? No, they spend hours after the recording session is over, tweaking their music in the studio and on the mixing board until every note sounds just as it should. You can adjust the settings for a track, too. The tweaks that you can perform include adding effects (pull a Hendrix and add echo and reverb to your electric guitar track) and kicking in an equalizer (for fine-tuning the sound of your background horns).

Figure 6-8:
I've just added a new region in my song's Arrange track.

To make adjustments to a track, follow these steps:

1. **Click the desired track in the track list to select it.**

2. **Click the Track Info button (labeled in Figure 6-1).**

3. **Click the Edit tab to show the settings shown in Figure 6-9.**

4. **Click the button next to each effect you want to enable. (The button glows green when enabled.)**

Each of the effects has a modifier setting. For example, you can adjust the amount of echo to add by dragging its slider.

GarageBand offers a Visual Equalizer window that you can use to create a custom equalizer setting for each track. You can display the Visual EQ window by clicking the animated button next to the Visual EQ control on the Edit pane. To change the Bass, Low Mid, High Mid, or Treble setting for a track, click and drag the equalizer waveform in the desired direction. And yep, you can do this while your song is playing, so you can use both your eyes *and* ears to define the perfect settings!

Figure 6-9:
Finesse
your tune
by tweaking
the sound
of a specific
track.

5. **To save the instrument as a new custom instrument — so that you can choose it the next time you add a track — click the Save Instrument button.**

6. **Click the Track Info button again to return to GarageBand.**

Time for a Mark's Maxim:

Save your work often **in GarageBand, just as you do in the other iLife applications. One power blackout, and you'll never forgive yourself. Press ⌘+S and enjoy the peace of mind.**

Join in and jam . . . or talk!

As I mention elsewhere in this chapter, GarageBand is even more fun if you happen to play an instrument! (And yes, I'm envious, no matter how much I enjoy the techno and jazz music that I create. After all, take away my Mac, and I'm back to playing the kazoo . . . at least until I absorb all the Learn to Play lessons for the guitar.)

Most musicians use MIDI instruments to play music on the computer. That pleasant-sounding acronym stands for *Musical Instrument Digital Interface*. A wide variety of MIDI instruments is available these days, from traditional MIDI keyboards to more exotic fun, such as MIDI saxophones. For example, Apple sells a 49-key MIDI keyboard from M-Audio for around $100; it uses a USB connection to your Mac.

Most MIDI instruments on the market today use a USB connection. If you have an older instrument with traditional MIDI ports — they're round, so you'll never confuse them with USB connectors — you need a USB-to-MIDI converter. You can find this type of converter for around $50 on web sites catering to musicians. (If you're recording your voice for a podcast, things are easier because you can use your Mac's built-in microphone.)

After your instrument is connected, you can record tracks using any software instrument. Create a new software instrument track as I demonstrate in this chapter, select it, and then play a few notes. Suddenly you're playing the instrument you chose! (If nothing happens, check the MIDI status light — which appears in the time display — to see whether it blinks with each note you play. If not, check the installation of your MIDI connection and make sure you've loaded any required drivers.)

Drag the playhead to a beat or two before the spot in the Timeline where you want your recording to start. This gives you time to match the beat. Then click the big red Record button and start jamming or speaking! When you're finished, click the Play button to stop recording.

Automatic Composition with Magic GarageBand

In a hurry? Too rushed to snag loops and tweak effects? Never fear, GarageBand '11 can even compose a song *automatically*! The Magic GarageBand feature provides a wide range of nine different genres of music to choose among — everything from blues to reggae to funk and rock.

To create a song automatically, follow these steps:

1. **Close all GarageBand windows.**

   If you're currently working on a song, GarageBand will prompt you to save it before closing the window.

2. **Click the Magic GarageBand button in the New Project dialog.**

3. **Click the desired genre button and click Choose.**

   Hover your mouse cursor over a genre button to get a preview of the song for that genre.

4. **To hear the entire song with the default instruments, click Entire Song and press the Play button.**

Alternatively, to hear a short sample of the song, click Snippet and press the Play button.

As shown in Figure 6-10, you see each instrument on stage. To choose a different musical style for an instrument (or a variation of the instrument), click it and then select the desired sound from the menu below the stage.

Click the My Instrument pop-up menu at the lower left corner of the window to add your own voice or instrumental using your Mac's keyboard, a microphone, or MIDI instrument.

5. **When the song fits like a glove, click Open in GarageBand to open the song as a project in GarageBand.**

Now you can edit and tweak the song to your heart's delight as you can any other GarageBand project, adding other software or real instrument tracks as necessary.

Figure 6-10: Creating my own arena-rock classic with Magic GarageBand.

Sharing Your Songs and Podcasts

After you finish your song, you can play it whenever you like through GarageBand. But then again, that isn't really what you want, is it? You want to share your music with others with an audio CD or download it to your iPod so that you can enjoy it yourself while walking through the mall!

iTunes to the rescue! As with the other iLife applications that I cover in this book, GarageBand can share the music you make through the digital hub that is your Mac.

Creating MP3 and AAC files and ringtones

You can create an MP3 or AAC file (or even an iPhone ringtone) from your song or podcast project in just a few simple steps:

1. **Open the song that you want to share.**

2. **Choose Share⇨Send Song to iTunes.**

   GarageBand displays the settings you see in Figure 6-11.

   To create a ringtone and send it to iTunes, choose Share⇨Send Ringtones to iTunes.

3. **Click in each of the four text boxes to type the playlist, artist name, composer name, and album name for the tracks you create.**

   You can leave the defaults as they are, if you prefer. Each track that you export is named after the song's name in GarageBand.

Hey, GarageBand, teach me how to play!

Until the arrival of GarageBand '09, you were limited to creating music — and if you were a nonmusician like yours truly, GarageBand had no practical use as a tool for teaching yourself how to actually *play* an instrument.

Ah, but Apple's introduction of Learn to Play actually turned GarageBand into your private video tutor for basic piano and guitar! From the New Project dialog, click the Learn to Play heading to display your lessons. Right out of the box, you have an Introduction to both instruments, but you can download more free lessons for each instrument from the Lesson Store — and they cover more advanced topics such as fingering and chords. Your on-screen instructor can even record what you play.

In fact, GarageBand '11 introduces the new *How Did I Play* feature, which can pinpoint the portions of a lesson that you played correctly and which spots in the song you need to work on. (I'm told musicians call such trouble spots *flubs* — having no musical talent whatsoever,

anything I attempt to play would be one giant flub.) To try How Did I Play, open your favorite lesson and move your pointer to the left side of the window, and then click the Play button that appears. Click the Record button (with the red dot in the center) and begin playing. To stop recording, click the Play button. Now you can see the portions of the song that you played correctly (where the notation area is green) and those spots where you flubbed (the notation area turns red). Oh, and make sure that your instrument is in tune because even correct notes played on an instrument that's out of tune produce errors for How Did I Play!

If you find the free Learn to Play lessons valuable, you can move up to the Artist lessons, which are taught by famous musicians (including favorites of mine such as Alex Lifeson, John Fogerty, and Sting, who actually teaches you how to play "Roxanne")! Each Artist lesson is $4.99 — well worth the price.

4. **Click the Compress Using pop-up menu and choose the encoder GarageBand should use to compress your song file.**

   The default is AAC, but you can also choose MP3 encoding for compatibility with a wider range of devices.

5. **Click the Audio Settings pop-up menu to select the proper audio quality for the finished file.**

   The higher the quality, the larger the file. GarageBand displays the approximate file size and finished file information in the description box.

6. **Click Share.**

After a second or two of hard work, your Mac opens the iTunes window and highlights the new (or existing) playlist that contains your new song.

Figure 6-11: Tweaking settings for iTunes song files.

Sending a podcast to iWeb or iTunes

If you've prepared a new podcast episode in GarageBand, you can send it automatically to iWeb or iTunes by following these steps:

1. **Open the podcast that you want to export to iWeb.**

   Make sure that the Podcast track is displayed. If necessary, click Track⟹Show Podcast Track to display it.

2. **Choose Share⟹Send Podcast to iWeb (or Share⟹Send Podcast to iTunes).**

3. **Click the Compress Using pop-up menu and choose the encoder that GarageBand should use to compress your podcast file.**

   Your choices are AAC and MP3 format.

4. **Click the Audio Settings pop-up menu to select the proper audio quality for the finished file.**

5. **Click Share.**

Burning an audio CD

Ready to create a demo CD with your latest GarageBand creation? Follow these steps to burn an audio disc from within GarageBand:

1. **Open the song that you want to record to disc.**

2. **Choose Share⟹Burn Song to CD.**

3. **Load a blank disc into your optical drive.**

Chapter 7: Crafting a Web Site with iWeb

In This Chapter

✔ Introducing the iWeb window

✔ Planning your site

✔ Adding a new site and pages

✔ Editing pages

✔ Setting site and page attributes with the Inspector

✔ Publishing sites to the Internet

I keep telling everyone who'll listen: The web is *simple.* Or at least it *should* be.

Kids in preschool these days know how to use a browser. Millions of people contribute to Facebook pages, help to create the dynamic reference wonder that is Wikipedia, and correspond effortlessly through web-based e-mail. Yet there's one untamed wilderness that many Mac owners haven't explored — or even set foot in! That's the jungle of *HTML,* the language used to create web pages. HTML is complex, and it's not particularly fun, either. Have you thrown up your hands and declared, "I guess I'll never get my own web site on the Internet?"

Forget your web site envy, fellow Mac enthusiast! With iWeb, Apple has provided a guide through that untamed wilderness . . . and suddenly it's as easy and fun to create a web site as it is to make a movie or write a song with your Mac. In this chapter, you discover how to design a site, import your own photos, and add all sorts of different pages.

Soon, you'll proudly hold your head up high and declare to the world, "I am a webmaster!"

Looking around the iWeb Window

All of iWeb's features and controls fit into a single window, naturally, just as they do in iPhoto and iMovie. (I agree with the Apple software designers: *Multiple windows* equals *confusing.*) Figure 7-1 illustrates the iWeb window, complete with a web site in progress. The stuff to keep your eye on includes

Figure 7-1:
The iWeb
window
holds
everything
you need
to put your
mark on the
web.

✦ **Toolbar:** Located at the bottom of the window, the iWeb toolbar keeps all your major controls one or two clicks away.

The iWeb toolbar contains different buttons, depending on the chore you're handling at the moment. Figure 7-1 shows the set of toolbar buttons that you see when you're editing a page.

✦ **Layout:** You need elbow room to build a web page, so the Layout section of the iWeb interface dominates the window. You create and edit your pages in the Layout display and then use it to preview and test-drive your finished site.

✦ **Site Organizer:** The strip to the left of the layout display is the Site Organizer, which allows you to organize your web sites, add new pages to a site, and select an existing page for editing.

Before we get down to business, it's overview time. You essentially follow three phases to put your new site on the web:

1. **Decide which pages you need.**

2. **Create a new site and build those pages.**

3. **Publish your site to your MobileMe account (or to a web server using FTP).**

I go over each of these phases in order. (They taught me that in college . . . along with the history of the Aztecs and the wonders of FIFO accounting.)

Planning Your Pages

Every properly designed web site has a purpose: to inform, to entertain, or to provide downloads or contact information. The pages you add to your site should all reflect that common purpose.

iWeb can produce the following types of pages for your site:

✦ **Welcome:** This is the default first page that iWeb adds to a site you create. The Welcome page familiarizes your visitor with the idea behind your site, and perhaps offers a snippet of the latest developments on the site in a "What's New" paragraph.

✦ **About Me:** This page provides a biography of you or another person, listing things like your age, favorite songs, and favorite foods. (After all, that's important stuff.) Links are provided to your photo album pages and other web sites you want to share.

✦ **Photos:** Oh, this is good stuff here — iWeb makes it easy to add one of those cool online photo galleries for your snapshots, complete with a web slideshow! You can add Events and albums from iPhoto, too.

✦ **My Albums:** You can organize all your Photos and Movie pages on a single My Albums page. Visitors click a thumbnail to jump to the corresponding page Photos or Movies page — it's a visual index done the *right* way.

✦ **Movie:** Got a QuickTime movie you've created with iMovie to share with others? This is the page that presents it to your adoring fans.

✦ **Blog:** Adding a *Blog* (or personal web journal) page is a somewhat different beast: iWeb keeps track of each addition you make in an entry list so that you can quickly add or delete entries without requiring tons of scrolling, cutting, and pasting. A Blog page also includes an archive so that deleted entries aren't lost forever.

✦ **Podcast:** Consider a podcast as an audio (or audio/visual) blog — it's designed to be downloaded to a visitor's iPod for later enjoyment. As does the Blog page, a Podcast page has an entry list and an archive list attached to it.

✦ **Blank:** Yep, an old-fashioned blank page, ready for you to fill with whatever you like.

Before you even launch iWeb, jot down on a piece of paper (or put in a Sticky) these important points:

✦ **What message do I want to communicate to visitors?**

✦ **What tone will I use — funny, serious, or businesslike?**

✦ **What stuff do I want to offer: photos, movies, or podcasts?**

Now you have the starting point for your site and you know what you want to include . . . so let's get down with the web!

Adding a New Site

When you open iWeb for the first time, the application creates a new site for you, and you can rename and modify this default site to your heart's content. In fact, for many of us, one site is all we ever create — but iWeb can easily handle multiple web sites, keeping them separate in the Site Organizer.

If there's at least one existing site in your Site Organizer, iWeb automatically displays the last site you were working on. Therefore, if you want to create an entirely new site, you have to perform a little manual labor. Here are a number of different ways to add a site:

✦ **Choose File➪New Site.**

✦ **Press ⌘+Shift+N.**

✦ **Control-click (or right-click) in the Site Organizer and click New Site.**

iWeb leaps into action and displays the template sheet you see in Figure 7-2. Scroll through the template themes in the list at the left of the sheet until you find one that matches the tone you decided on in the previous section. (Informal, formal, or silly, iWeb has templates that match every mood!) Click a template on the left, and the application automatically updates the page type thumbnails on the right.

When you choose a template, iWeb automatically provides your pages with a common background, color scheme, and fonts so that your finished web site has a common theme throughout.

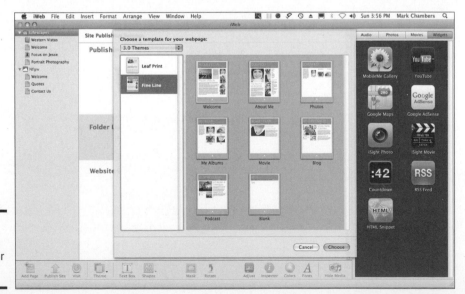

Figure 7-2:
Choosing a
template for
a new site.

After you find the right look and feel, click the desired template in the scrolling list at the left, click the Welcome page thumbnail, and then click the Choose button. iWeb creates a new site heading in the Site Organizer, complete with the default Welcome page. Figure 7-1, shown previously, illustrates the Welcome page from a new site I created with the Main Event template.

Adding a New Page

Time to add the pages you plan for your site! For example, I've decided to add Photo and About Me pages to the new site I've created. In the following section, I discuss how to edit these pages to personalize them . . . but for now, I just want you to add the pages.

If you have multiple sites in your Site Organizer list, click the top-level heading for the desired site to select it. You can add pages by

✦ **Clicking the Add Page button on the toolbar at the bottom of the iWeb window**

✦ **Choosing File⇨New Page**

✦ **Pressing ⌘+N**

✦ **Control-clicking or right-clicking the site header in the Site Organizer and clicking New Page**

TIP

Want to start with an existing page as a basis for a new page? Right-click that page entry in the Site Organizer and choose Duplicate. iWeb creates a new page with exactly the same contents and adds it to the site.

Pages are listed under the main site heading in outline format, making it easy to expand or collapse a site by clicking the familiar rotating triangle icon next to the site heading. (Apple calls these *disclosure triangles*. Wowzers!)

Deleting a page — or a whole site, for that matter — is easy in iWeb. Right-click the offending page or site heading in the Site Organizer and choose Delete Page/Delete Site. Note that iWeb doesn't prompt you for confirmation here, so these aren't commands to toy with.

Editing a Page

If you have your site framework complete, you can actually put your site on the Internet as is! Of course, the photos would all be of good-looking strangers, and most of the text would read like Pig Latin nonsense. (Come to think of it, I've been on some real sites that aren't much better. Go figure.)

I think we both agree, however, that *you* want to personalize your pages with your *own* information. To begin editing a page, click it in the Site Organizer.

Book III
Chapter 7

Crafting a Web
Site with iWeb

Modifying text

First, update the text with your own information by following these steps:

1. **Click the text you want to replace.**

   As do most desktop publishing applications, iWeb uses boxes to enclose text. When you click the text, the box appears, with handles that you can drag to resize the box.

2. **Begin typing your text.**

   iWeb replaces the existing template text with the text you type, using the text formatting taken from the template. Don't forget that you can paste text from the Clipboard by pressing ⌘+V. To match the text style of the template, though, press Option+Shift+⌘+V.

   Mistakes are passé in iWeb. To undo your last action, you can always press the familiar ⌘+Z keyboard shortcut or choose Edit⇨Undo.

3. **Highlight and format your new text as necessary.**

   To make changes easier, click the Inspector button in the iWeb toolbar. The window you see in Figure 7-3 appears, allowing you to change text color, alignment, and spacing with aplomb. (You find more about the Inspector later.) You can click the Colors or Fonts buttons on the iWeb toolbar to display a Color Picker or Font Panel for the selected text.

4. **Click outside the text box after you're satisfied with the text.**

Because you're likely modifying everything on the template pages from the title to the last box on the page, repeat Steps 1–4 for each section of text you want to change.

Don't I have to slave over a hot menu?

You would if you were building a web site by hand or if you were using an old-fashioned web creation application not designed by our favorite company! (Insert smug expression here.)

Let me explain . . . . Every web site needs a series of links called a *menu* that allows you to jump from one page of the site to another. (For instance, you're probably already familiar with the "tabbed" menu at the top of the Apple web site that you use to flit from the Mac OS X section to the Support section to the Store section and back again.) In days of old, a site menu was often a nightmare to maintain, especially if your site changed often.

iWeb creates and maintains a menu for each of your sites *automatically* and places it at the top of your pages for you! (You might have noticed that the Welcome menu item already appears in Figure 7-1.) When you add or delete pages, the application updates your menu in the background.

This is the way software is supposed to be designed. Don't you agree?

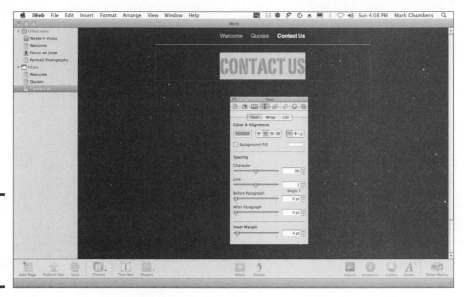

Book III
Chapter 7

Crafting a Web
Site with iWeb

Figure 7-3:
Using the
Inspector
dialog to
format text.

Replacing images

If your page includes photographs that you want to change, follow these steps:

1. **Click the image you want to replace.**

As it does a block of text, iWeb displays a box around the image, complete with resizing handles.

2. **Drag an image to the image box from a Finder window.**

Alternatively, you can click the Show Media button in the toolbar, which displays the Media Browser you see in Figure 7-4. From this window, you can click the Photos tab to choose an image from your iPhoto library.

You can hide the Media Browser to make more room for your page layout. Just click the Hide Media Browser button in the Toolbar.

3. **Adjust your new image if necessary.**

Click the Adjust button, and iWeb displays a cool, semi-opaque dialog that allows you to tweak image settings, such as tint, brightness, and sharpness (see Figure 7-5). Click Enhance to allow iWeb to choose the settings it considers best for the image or click Reset Image to restore the photo to its original appearance. When you're satisfied with the image, click the Close button on the dialog to return to the image box.

4. **Click outside the image box (usually the page background) after you're satisfied with the photo.**

Again, lather/rinse/repeat for each image you want to change on your page.

Figure 7-4:
Browsing
my iPhoto
library for
the right
image.

Figure 7-5:
Adjusting
an image in
iWeb.

Adding new elements

iWeb also makes it easy to add new items to a page. The list of extras includes

✦ **Audio:** You can add a song (complete with volume control, Play/Pause
button, and progress slider) to your page! Either drag an audio file from

a Finder window to your page, or click the Audio button in the Media Browser to select a song from your iTunes collection. You can drag any image to the player that appears. (How about a photo of your daughter instead of album art?)

✦ **Photos:** To add a new image box to your page, drag a photo from a Finder window to the iWeb layout section. Click the Photos button in the Media Browser to choose an image from your iPhoto library, or throw caution to the wind and drag an entire Event or an album to your new page! iWeb takes care of all the details.

✦ **Movies:** Yep, you guessed it: You can drag a movie clip from a Finder window to your page, or click the Movies button in the Media Browser to choose a movie from iMovie or your Movies folder.

✦ **Text:** Choose Insert⇨Text or click the Text button in the toolbar.

✦ **Shapes:** Click the Shape button in the toolbar to display the pop-up menu and then click the desired shape. (Don't forget to resize it as you desire with the box handles.)

✦ **Widgets:** Click this button in the Media Browser to insert a *widget* (a web applet) to your page. For example, HTML Snippet allows you to type HTML code directly into place on the page, or paste HTML code that you've copied from another web site. You can also insert interactive Google Adsense advertisements or a Google Map. To populate the page with a MobileMe Gallery, choose the MobileMe Gallery widget and select a Gallery you've created using the iPhoto MobileMe Gallery feature. (For the complete scoop on iPhoto, cruise over to Chapter 3 in this mini-book.) Other widgets include a countdown timer and YouTube videos.

You can move a widget anywhere on a page by dragging it, and it can be resized just as a text box can.

Doing the slideshow thing

Ready to offer a slideshow on your web site? Again, we're talking automation here! Add a Photo page to your site and notice that the Start Slideshow button is already in place at the top of the page. All you need to do is add the photos to the page, using the Media browser or dragging them from a Finder window. When your visitors click the Start Slideshow button, all the photos on the page are displayed in a pop-up window.

It's important to note, however, that some Windows (and older Mac) browsers don't support this Slideshow feature. Other Mac owners using Safari can enjoy the show, but don't count on older versions of Internet Explorer (or Firefox) to be able to handle it.

✦ **Links:** If you're editing text and you want to insert a web link, choose Insert➪Hyperlink and choose from the menu that appears. You can choose to link to another web page, go to another location on the same page, or insert a link that automatically sends an e-mail message to the mail address you provide. You can also offer a file for downloading.

iWeb can automatically detect e-mail and web addresses that you type in a text box, so you don't have to use the Links menu. To enable this feature, choose iWeb➪Preferences and click the Automatically Detect Email and Web Addresses check box to select it.

✦ **Button.** Your web page can include buttons that allow your visitors to e-mail you or display the number of hits (visits) your page has received. Choose Insert➪Button and click an option to add or remove a specific button. (If the menu option is selected, the button appears on your page.) Blog and Podcast pages can also offer *RSS feeds* (for automated retrieval of new entries within a web browser), subscriptions to your podcasts, and slideshows.

With these tools, you can use the Blank page template to create your own new pages. Personally, I prefer to use the professionally designed templates offered by Apple as starting points, removing whatever I don't need and adding new content.

Most web designers would strongly recommend that you use a common theme for all the pages within a site (to lend continuity). Of course, you can also stick your tongue out at those very same web designers and select a different theme for every page! To select a different theme for a page, open the page in iWeb and click the Theme button in the toolbar; then click the desired thumbnail from the pop-up menu. Nothing's lost but the old look of the page, so feel free to experiment to your heart's content.

Tweaking with the Inspector

Earlier, you used the Inspector to change text formatting attributes — but this star performer can do much more than just that! To modify page characteristics, click the page in the Site Organizer, display the Inspector, and click the Page Inspector button (which carries a document icon). These settings allow you to change the name of a page; you can also elect to include or exclude this page from the site menu, or to drop the site menu from this page.

If your site contains a Blog or Podcast page, you can click the RSS button to provide an automated RSS *(RDF Site Summary)* feed to your visitors. (For more information on RSS and how it works in Safari, see Chapter 5 of Book V.)

Don't forget your site properties!

To make global changes to a site, click the site name in the Site Organizer. iWeb switches to the Site Properties screen (Figure 7-6), where you can change settings such as

✔ The name of the site

✔ Your contact e-mail

✔ Where the site is published (more on this in the next section)

✔ Password protection for MobileMe sites

You can also verify how much space is available on your iDisk, which is where iWeb stores your web sites if you're a MobileMe member. Heck, iWeb can even update your Facebook profile automatically when you publish your site! What will those Apple designers think of next?

Publishing Your Web Site

After you finish with a new site — or you're satisfied with the edits you make to existing pages — it's time to get your masterpiece on the web! Even the best web site design is worth next to nil if it isn't available on the Internet, and in this last section, I demonstrate how to publish your web site to your MobileMe account or to a separate server maintained by a third party (perhaps your ISP, your company, or Dave down the street).

As I mention in the "Don't forget your site properties!" sidebar, you specify where your iWeb site will be published from the Site Properties screen. Click the site name in the Site Organizer to display the Publish To pop-up menu (Figure 7-6). iWeb offers the following publishing options:

✦ **Publish to MobileMe:** Your site is hosted by Apple as part of your MobileMe subscription. The application takes care of everything, uploading any changed pages or media.

✦ **Publish to FTP Server:** This publishing option provides you with a completely different collection of settings on the Site Properties screen. You'll need to furnish iWeb with your web server's FTP settings (which should be furnished to you by the host) and your site's address (or *URL*).

✦ **Publish to a Local Folder:** The final publishing option creates a folder on your hard drive that contains all the files to display your web site. This is the option to choose if you're not a MobileMe subscriber and you don't use a third-party hosting service. You can add these files directly to your home or business web server. Once again, you must supply the site URL as it will appear on the Internet after you copy or upload the site files to the server. (I describe how to set up Lion's built-in Apache web server in Book VIII, Chapter 4.)

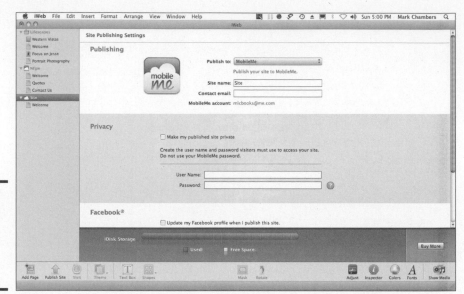

Figure 7-6:
Setting the publishing method for an iWeb site.

After you've set the type of publishing the site will use, it's time to take care of business! Click the site to select it in the Site Organizer and then click the Publish Site button on the toolbar. The application takes care of everything else, automatically uploading all pages and media (if you choose MobileMe or FTP publishing) or saving them on your hard drive (if you chose the Local Folder option).

In a hurry? You can elect to publish just the changes necessary to update your site: Instead of clicking the Publish Site button on the toolbar, click the File menu and choose Publish Site Changes.

Chapter 8: No, It's Not Called iQuickTime

In This Chapter

✓ Viewing movies

✓ Listening to audio

✓ Converting media to different formats

✓ Keeping track of your favorite media

✓ Tweaking QuickTime preferences

QuickTime is a set of exciting technologies that gives you access to the greatest multimedia experience around. Despite its power, don't be surprised if you don't even realize that you're using it sometimes. Built with the average Joe in mind, QuickTime Player takes multimedia to new heights without forcing its users to become rocket scientists in the process.

QuickTime Can Do That?

QuickTime was created by Apple to perform all sorts of multimedia functions. Although normally associated with movie playback, QuickTime Player can do much more. Whether it's playing movies, audio, animation, or music, QuickTime acts as the main engine that drives all your multimedia needs.

✦ **Media player:** QuickTime Player's main claim to fame is playing all sorts of media — and I do mean *all* sorts. Table 8-1 lists the most popular of the media types that QuickTime can play.

The real beauty of QuickTime Player is that it transparently handles playback of all these media formats and more. You don't even really have to know what each of these formats is to play them. QuickTime Player takes care of that for you.

✦ **Internet media tool:** When it comes to using media from the Internet, QuickTime is in a league all its own. In addition to playing the usual movies and audio files found on the web, QuickTime can play (or display) 3-D scenes and animations. As if that weren't enough, QuickTime even lets you interact with some media. For example, with QuickTime, you can navigate within 3-D worlds or play Flash games.

Table 8-1	QuickTime Playback Formats
Media Type	*File Types*
Movie	.mov*, .avi*, .mpg, .dv, .mp4, 3g (cell phones), h.263, h.264
Audio	.aiff, .wav, .mp3, .au, .sfil, .aac, .amr
Music	.mid, .kar
3-D	QTVR (QuickTime Virtual Reality)
Animation	.swf

Movies in MOV and AVI formats use a wide range of compression schemes, many of them pro-prietary. For this reason, QuickTime might not be able to play some MOV or AVI movies that you download.

Playing Media with QuickTime

QuickTime makes a world of movies, audio, graphics, and music instantly available to you. Whether you want to view professional movie trailers or listen to a garage band's new single, QuickTime faithfully reproduces nearly any media format that you feed it.

To launch QuickTime Player, double-click its icon in the Finder, or click the Launchpad icon in the Dock and then click on the QuickTime Player icon that appears. You can also launch QuickTime Player from the Finder by double-clicking a media file that QuickTime can play. (See Table 8-1 earlier in this chapter for a listing of these file types.)

Don't make the mistake of thinking that QuickTime and QuickTime Player are the same thing: *QuickTime* is a technology that hides in the background waiting for instructions to do something with media; *QuickTime Player* is an application that uses the QuickTime technologies. You'll do recording, media conversions, playback, and editing with QuickTime Player. What you won't see is the QuickTime technology in action behind the scenes.

You can also launch QuickTime Player from an oh-so-convenient Dock icon. For more on the Dock, read Book II, Chapter 2.

Opening QuickTime movies

To begin viewing and hearing — aw, what the heck, how about *absorbing* — multimedia files, choose File⇨Open File from the QuickTime Player application.

This isn't the only way to open a file with QuickTime Player, though. Some of the other ways to open files with QuickTime Player are

✦ **Drag a file to the QuickTime Player icon in the Dock.**

✦ **Right-click a movie and choose Open With; choose QuickTime Player from the pop-up menu.**

✦ **Double-click the media file in the Finder.**

Operating QuickTime Player

When you open a QuickTime file, QuickTime Player creates a new window to display it. All QuickTime Player windows have some common features:

✦ **Close, Minimize, and Zoom controls**: These three controls appear at the top-left corner of most windows in Mac OS X. You probably recognize them by their colors: red, yellow, and green, respectively.

✦ **Resize handle:** Drag the lower-right corner of QuickTime Player to resize its movie for playback. Hold Shift while dragging to break free from constrained resizing. If the document contains only sound media, the window grows or shrinks in a horizontal direction when you resize it.

Any resizing that you perform makes no changes to the original file. QuickTime provides it for your convenience during playback.

Although some window features are common to all QuickTime Player windows, many features depend on the type of media that you wish to play. Table 8-2 lists some of the window features that you might find and the media types associated with those features.

Table 8-2   QuickTime Player Window Features Based on Media

Window Feature	Media Type That Uses This Feature
Play button	All time-based media: movies, audio, animations, and MIDI
Rewind button	All time-based media: movies, audio, animations, and MIDI
Fast Forward	All time-based media: movies, audio, animations, and MIDI
Timeline	All time-based media: movies, audio, animations, and MIDI
Volume slider	All media with one or more audio tracks
Toggle Full Screen	All movies and animations
Zoom buttons	QTVR 3-D media
Rotate buttons	QTVR 3-D media
Mute	All media with one or more audio tracks

To make your life easier, QuickTime does a lot of work for you behind the scenes each time that it opens a media file. Although you might think that there are different combinations of controls in QuickTime Player, the reality is that the various media windows are more similar than they are different. Figure 8-1 shows the location of various QuickTime Player controls.

Figure 8-1: QuickTime Player sports different controls, depending on the media you play.

Playing media

Playback begins as you might suspect — by clicking the Play button. While a file is playing, the Play button toggles to a Pause button. Click that button to pause playback, which toggles the button back to Play.

Clicking the buttons with double arrows on them advances the playback head at high speed in the direction of the arrows. (Click once to advance at 2x speed; click again to increase the speed.) If the file has audio in it, you hear the playback at high speed, which sounds like an episode of those helium-inhaling Chipmunks. (Remember? *Meee, I waaant a hooola hooop.*) Despite its comical sound, it's helpful for quickly scanning through a file.

You can also advance through the file by dragging the playback head — an action called *scrubbing* — in either direction. Scrubbing is permissible while the file is playing or when it's stopped. When you drag the playback head, however, you miss out on the high-speed sound and video that you would get if you used the buttons.

To adjust the volume of a movie, simply move the volume slider left or right. To mute the volume, click the speaker icon to the left of the volume slider.

You can control playback by using the keyboard as well. Table 8-3 summarizes the keyboard shortcuts for playback.

Table 8-3	Common Playback Keyboard Shortcuts
Keyboard Shortcut	*What It Does*
Spacebar	Starts or stops the player
Left/right arrow	Advances the playback head (either one frame at a time or in slow motion)
Option+Up/down arrow	Sets the volume to Maximum and Minimum, respectively
Up/down arrow	Increases/decreases the volume of the current movie

Sometimes you might want to play a piece of media more than once. In these situations, you need to loop the playback. To force a movie to loop, choose View⇨Loop or press ⌘+L. Press ⌘+L again to turn off looping.

Movie info

To see more information about the files that you're playing, ask the expert: QuickTime Player. To view basic information about a movie, choose Window⇨ Show Movie Inspector or press ⌘+I. The resulting window displays the following data:

+ **Source:** Location of the file

+ **Format:** Compressor and dimensions of the file

+ **FPS:** Preferred rate of playback in frames per second (fps), shown only for video

+ **Data Size:** Size of the file

+ **Data Rate:** Preferred rate of playback (in bits per second)

+ **Current Time:** Position of the playback head (in units of time)

+ **Current Size:** Actual movie dimensions

These bits and pieces of information are *read-only* — you can't change them from the Movie Inspector window.

Recording audio, video, and screens in QuickTime Player

Most folks don't think of QuickTime Player as a recording application. That's because Apple provides applications (such as Photo Booth, iMovie, and iTunes) that have long been the recording tools of choice in the Mac universe. However, you can indeed record audio, video, and your Mac's screen display with QuickTime Player, as long as your Mac is equipped with the proper hardware (a microphone or line-in device for audio, and an iSight camera or external video camera for video).

When you're ready to record, click File and choose either New Movie Recording, New Audio Recording, or New Screen Recording. You can select your input sources, recording quality, and saved file location by clicking the button with the down arrow. When all the settings are correct, the process itself is a one-click operation: Click the Big Red Button to start and stop recording. QuickTime displays both the recording time and the approximate hard drive space used so far. 'Nuff said.

If you'd like to share a multimedia file with others from your MobileMe home page on the web, choose File⇨Share⇨MobileMe Gallery. After you've typed a name and description for your new file, you can optionally click the Allow Movies to be Downloaded check box to let others download the movie from your MobileMe page. Click Publish, and QuickTime automatically takes care of the rest. Slick as a wet toad!

Chapter 9: Turning Your Mac into a DVD Theater

In This Chapter

✓ **Understanding what you need to watch DVDs on your Macintosh**

✓ **Using the DVD Player software**

✓ **Unearthing the mysteries of the hidden controls**

A ll the creative capabilities of the Mac OS X digital hub are a lot of fun, but at some point, you'll want to take a break from work. Because of its high fidelity, convenience, and seemingly limitless storage capacity, the DVD has taken consumers by storm. The idea of an honest-to-goodness theater in your home is now within the grasp of mere mortals (with, coincidentally, merely average budgets). Mac OS X has everything that you'll need to enjoy a night at the movies without ever leaving home. In fact, I highly recommend the 27-inch iMac or the 17-inch MacBook Pro for those widescreen classics.

Getting the Right DVD Hardware

Before you watch one second of video, get your setup in order. Playing DVDs requires a bit of hardware; fortunately, virtually all recent Macintosh computers come equipped with the stuff that's necessary to watch DVDs.

To play DVD movies, you need either an internal DVD-compatible drive in your Macintosh or an external DVD drive with a FireWire or USB 2.0 connection. DVD-ROM drives can only play discs, whereas others, such as the SuperDrive, can both play and record discs. Either type of drive works fine for watching movies on your Mac.

You can watch any standard DVD that you purchase at your local video store as well as any DVD that you create with iDVD. (For more on iDVD, read Book III, Chapter 5.)

Watching Movies with DVD Player

To watch Frodo Baggins, Don Corleone, or James Bond, you need DVD player software. Mac OS X comes stocked with the perfect tool for the task: DVD Player.

Apple's DVD Player application is included with Mac OS X; you can find it within the confines of your Applications folder. But instead of rooting through the Finder, you can launch DVD Player an even easier way: Simply insert a DVD into the drive. As soon as you do, your Mac recognizes the disc and launches DVD Player by default for you. (Time for another round of well-deserved gloating about your choice of personal computer.)

This automatic behavior (the DVD playing — not necessarily the gloating) can be curbed, however. You can control what action Lion takes (if any) when you load a DVD via the CDs & DVDs pane within System Preferences. For all the details, visit Book II, Chapter 3.

However you choose to start DVD Player, you'll notice that it offers two windows:

✦ **Controller:** The small, silver-colored, remote control–looking interface that holds all the controls for the Player

✦ **Viewer:** The large window where you view your DVD movies

In Full-Screen mode, of course, you won't see the Viewer window, and the video takes up the entire screen. The controller appears as a floating opaque strip of controls along the bottom of the screen. To display the controls, move your mouse cursor to the bottom of the screen. Move the cursor to the top of the screen and you can switch chapters and jump to bookmarks. (I talk about both later in the chapter.)

If you're already using a traditional DVD player, you'll be right at home with Apple's DVD Player. Even if you've never used a traditional DVD player, you'll find that it's not much different from using a software-based audio player such as iTunes.

Using the Controller

The *Controller* is the command center of the DVD Player software. Arranged much the same as a VCR or tape deck, all the familiar controls are present. Check it out in Figure 9-1.

Figure 9-1:
Use the
Controller
for mundane
playback
chores.

Table 9-1 details the fundamental commands present in the DVD Player Controller. Apple software usually has some goodies hidden beneath the surface, and DVD Player is no exception. The controls in DVD Player have a few functions that might not be obvious to the casual user. These are listed in the third column of Table 9-1.

Table 9-1	Basic DVD Controls	
Control Name	*What It Does*	*Other Functions*
Play	Plays the DVD	Switches into a Pause button anytime a movie is playing.
Stop	Stops playback of the DVD	
Previous Chapter	Skips to the previous chapter	Click and hold the button to quickly scan through the movie in reverse.
Next Chapter	Skips to the next chapter	Click and hold the button to quickly scan forward through the movie.
Playback Volume	Adjusts the volume of the DVD audio	
Arrow Buttons	Navigates through the menu items of the DVD	
Enter	Selects the currently high-lighted menu item	
Eject	Ejects the DVD from the drive	
Title	Jumps immediately to the DVD's title menu	
Menu	Displays the menu of the current DVD	

Book III
Chapter 9

Turning Your Mac into a DVD Theater

Jumping right to the flying-monkey action

Movies on DVD usually are divided into *chapters* that enable you to jump directly to specific points. That way, you can jump right to the scene, say, where the flying monkey guards march into the Wicked Witch's castle in *The Wizard of Oz.* (Or skip that egg-hatching scene in *Alien* that always makes you nauseated.)

You can navigate to chapters, play the movie from the beginning, or check out special bonus features (such as trailers and documentaries) from the DVD's main menu. To switch to a different chapter in Full-Screen mode, move your mouse to the top of the screen.

Keeping your eyes on the Viewer

As soon as you begin playing with the DVD Player controls, you'll notice activity in the Viewer window, as shown in Figure 9-2.

Figure 9-2:
The Viewer is the real star of Lion's DVD Player.

You can think of the Viewer window as a television inside your Macintosh, if it helps, but DVD Player goes one step further. Unlike a television screen, the Viewer has some nice tricks up its sleeve: For example, you can resize the Viewer window by using one of the five sizes listed in the View menu (Half, Actual Size, Double Size, Fit to Screen, and Full-Screen sizes). This is useful for watching a movie in a small window on your Desktop while you work with other applications. You can toggle your Viewer size from the keyboard; for example, select Half Size with ⌘+0 (zero), Actual Size with ⌘+1 (one), and Double Size with ⌘+2 (two).

If you're only in it for the entertainment factor, you'll probably want to resize the Viewer to fill the screen. I like to watch movies in Full-Screen mode, which you can toggle with the ⌘+F keyboard shortcut. If you want to take full advantage of all your screen space yet leave the Viewer window on-screen for occasional resizing, choose Fit to Screen mode with ⌘+3 (three).

Watching video in the raw

That sounds a little racy, but I'm talking about viewing digital video directly from your hard drive to your HDTV! Many Mac owners prefer to leave their high-definition video content on a hard drive, instead of burning those huge clips and movies to DVD using iLife's iDVD application — if you're one of this crowd, consider a peripheral like the WD Elements Play from Western Digital (www.wdc.com), which connects directly to your TV's HDMI port.

In fact, your Mac isn't involved at all, since the device includes its own internal hard drive, and you can even plug in an external hard drive containing your video. The Elements Play supports a bewildering range of video formats at up to AVCHD 1080p, including MPEG-1, MPEG-2, AVI (divx, xvid, and avc), H.264, and mkv. The Elements Play is available online for under $100, complete with a remote control.

Taking Advantage of Additional DVD Features

As anyone with a little DVD experience knows, DVDs can do a lot more than those archaic tapes that you used to feed your VCR. Apple has included several functions that allow you to explore the extra features and content provided with a DVD movie.

Controller extras

To use the additional Controller features, double-click the small tab at the rightmost (or bottom) edge of the DVD Player Controller. After you do, a trick drawer slides out, displaying the extra controls. (See Figure 9-3.) You can also display or hide the drawer with the Controls➪Open/Close Control Drawer menu command or by pressing ⌘+] (that's the right bracket key).

Figure 9-3:
Expand the Controller to view additional controls.

Are you interested in fine-tuning the audio from your DVD movies? If so, choose Window⇨Audio Equalizer, and DVD Player displays a ten-band equalizer. (I often use this feature to add extra bass to a concert DVD.) To turn the equalizer on, click the On check box to select it. Click the pop-up menu at the upper right of the Equalizer window, and you can choose a preset (such as Bass Boost or Vocal Boost), or even create your own custom audio presets.

Table 9-2 summarizes the functions that you can perform with these additional controls.

Table 9-2	Additional Controller Features
Control	*What It Does*
Slow Motion (half speed)	Plays a DVD in slow motion at half the original speed
Step Button (frame speed)	Steps through a DVD in ultra-slow motion, one frame at a time
Return	Navigates to the previous menu
Subtitle/Closed Captioning	Displays alternate subtitles and closed captioning on the DVD
Audio	Plays alternate audio tracks on the DVD
Angle	Displays the current video footage from different camera angles

Although you won't find a Bookmark button on the Controller, DVD Player can set them nonetheless. A *bookmark* is a spot, like a favorite scene, that you specify in a movie so that you can return to it at any time. To set a bookmark at the current spot in the movie, click the Controls menu and choose New Bookmark, or press ⌘+= (the equal sign key). DVD Player even allows you to name the bookmark so that it's easier to remember. To return to a bookmark, choose Go⇨Bookmarks and click the desired bookmark. (If you're enjoying your movie in Full-Screen mode, move your cursor to the top of the screen to use the Bookmarks strip.)

DVD Player preferences

The DVD Player application has a variety of settings that you can access and adjust via its Preferences window. To open the Preferences window, choose DVD Player⇨Preferences. This brings up the Preferences dialog.

This window consists of six panes:

✦ **Player:** Settings that affect how DVD Player operates

✦ **Disc Setup:** Settings for Audio, Subtitles, Language, and the web

✦ **Full Screen:** Settings that determine your full-screen viewing configuration

✦ **Windows:** Settings for displaying on-screen information during playback

✦ **Previously Viewed:** Settings that determine what happens when you load a DVD that you watched already

✦ **High Definition:** Settings that specify how high-definition video from Apple's DVD Studio Pro application is displayed on your Mac

The advantage of these Preference settings is that you can customize your copy of DVD Player to match your needs or desires. (Thanks yet again to the Cupertino Crowd!)

Player

The Player settings take care of much of the automation within DVD Player:

✦ **When DVD Player Opens:** These two check boxes affect what happens when you launch the DVD Player application. You can force DVD Player to play in full-screen mode and automatically begin playback every time you start the application.

✦ **When DVD Player Is Inactive:** If you're multitasking while watching your movie in windowed mode, you can click another window to make it active. This check box determines whether DVD Player automatically pauses while you're working in that other application.

✦ **When a Disc Is Inserted:** Besides automatic playback on startup, you can also make DVD Player start playing a disc automatically when the application is running already. (To illustrate: If this check box is deselected, loading a new disc won't automatically start it playing if DVD Player is already running.)

✦ **When Playing Using Battery:** If you're using a MacBook, you can conserve power while using DVD Player by selecting this check box. The DVD Player will "spin down" the DVD whenever possible, which may cause a short delay when you fast forward or rewind.

✦ **When Muted:** Do you answer a lot of telephone calls while you sneak a quick DVD movie at work? If so, be sure to enable this option. If you have to press the Mute button on your keyboard while a movie is playing, DVD Player automatically adds the subtitles/closed captions so that you can keep up with the dialog. *Super sassy!*

✦ **During iChat with Audio:** Another option for those who like to run multiple applications simultaneously. If you're watching a DVD and start an audio chat in iChat AV, you can choose to either mute the DVD audio or pause the DVD playback until you click Play again.

✦ **When Viewer Is Minimized:** Watching a DVD at the office, eh? Enable this check box, and DVD Player automatically pauses the movie when you minimize the DVD Player window. (Managers label this feature *downright sneaky*.)

Disc Setup

The second tab of the Player Preferences window consists of these controls:

✦ **Language:** Sprechen Sie Deutsch? DVDs are designed to be multi-language-aware. Feel like brushing up on your German, Spanish, or Chinese? You can control the language used for the audio, subtitling, and menus in this section.

✦ **Internet:** Some DVDs with DVD@ccess support can access information on the Internet. Mark this check box to allow that function.

✦ **Audio:** Click this pop-up menu to specify the default audio output signal that you'd like to use. You can also choose to disable the Dolby dynamic range compression feature, which might enhance the sound for two-speaker systems; however, you don't want to damage the lower-output speakers on a MacBook or MacBook Pro, so I recommend that laptop owners leave dynamic range compression enabled.

Multiple languages and web access are not mandatory features of a DVD, so don't be surprised if you see variations of support when it comes to these settings.

Full Screen

These Preference settings control the default screen display settings within DVD Player:

✦ **Controller:** I generally like to hide the Controller after a defined time of inactivity; select the Hide Controller If Inactive for *xx* Seconds check box if you agree. To set the delay period, click in the seconds box and type a new value.

✦ **Displays:** These options specify how DVD Player shares your Desktop with others: politely or downright rudely. You can choose to automatically dim other monitors while a movie is playing (if you have more than one display connected to your Mac), and DVD Player can stay in full-screen mode even if another application actually has the active window. Normally, DVD Player displays video at the full resolution of your desktop in full screen mode, but you can use the current video size instead (which generally results in a small video centered within a black border). Finally, you can choose to remove the menu bar altogether (often called *kiosk mode*), which helps cut down on interruptions and accidents if small hands are nearby — and you can optionally allow Lion's screen saver to appear on the DVD menu in kiosk mode.

Windows

This pane gives you the chance to configure the behavior of the Controller and status information for the Viewer window:

✦ **Options:** Mark the Display Status Information check box, and DVD Player adds a small text box at the top-left corner of the Viewer window. In this text box, you see the name of the last task that you performed with DVD Player. For example, click the Stop button to see the word Stop displayed in the Viewer on top of the video beneath it. You can also set the Controller to fade away instead of just disappear — it's eye candy, but doggone it, it's *good* eye candy!

✦ **Closed Captioned:** If you do decide to display the closed-caption text from a DVD movie, you can click the color buttons to specify the text color. You can also choose the font for your text.

Previously Viewed

This pane controls what happens when you load a disc that you've seen already . . . or perhaps your significant other watched it and didn't tell you. (Insert growling noise here.)

✦ **Start Playing Discs From:** If you have to quit DVD Player for some reason, the application is smart enough to remember where you were, and you can choose to begin watching from the beginning, from the last position (where you were when you stopped the last time), or from a default bookmark. Alternatively, just select Always Ask, and DVD Player will prompt you each time this situation crops up.

✦ **Always Use Disc Settings For:** Select these check boxes to specify whether DVD Player should use the same settings you used the last time you watched this disc.

High Definition

The final DVD Player Preferences panel specifies how both standard DV and high-definition video from a disc you've created in DVD Studio Pro are displayed within the Viewer window. (As I mention earlier, the Viewer window size can also be changed from the View menu, but the settings in this pane control what defaults DVD Player uses.)

✦ **For Standard Definition:** You can choose to display the actual video size by default, or to use the default size provided by the DVD.

✦ **For High Definition:** These options affect how a high-definition video signal is displayed. Your choices include the actual video size, a height of 720 pixels, and a height of 1,080 pixels.

Don't forget to click OK to save any changes you make to your DVD Player preferences.

After you have your DVD Player customized to your liking, get out the popcorn, pull up your favorite recliner, and let the movies roll!

Book IV

Using iWork

The 5th Wave   By Rich Tennant

©RICHTENNANT

" Ms. Gretsky, tell the employees they can have
internet games on their computers again."

Contents at a Glance

Chapter 1: Desktop Publishing with Pages

In This Chapter

✓ Creating a Pages document

✓ Entering and editing text

✓ Formatting text

✓ Inserting tables and graphics

✓ Resizing objects

✓ Checking your spelling

✓ Printing Pages documents

✓ Sharing your work

What's the difference between word processing and desktop publishing? In a nutshell, it's in how you *design* your document. Most folks use a word processor like an old-fashioned typewriter. Think Microsoft Word and a typical business letter. (Yawn.)

On the other hand, a desktop publishing application typically allows you far more creativity in choosing where you place your text, how you align graphics, and how you edit formats. I think desktop publishing is more visual and intuitive, allowing your imagination a free hand at creating a document.

In this chapter, I show you how to set your inner designer free from the tedious constraints of word processing! Whether you need a simple letter, a stunning brochure, or a multipage newsletter, Pages '09 can handle the job with ease — and you'll be surprised at how simple it is to use.

Creating a New Pages Document

Every visual masterpiece starts somewhere, and with Pages, the first stop in creating your document is the Template Chooser window. To create a new Pages document from scratch, follow these steps:

1. **Double-click your hard drive icon and click the Applications entry in the Finder window sidebar. Double-click the iWork folder to open it.**

   The iWork installation program offers to add a Pages icon to your Dock. If you'll be using Pages often, it's a good idea to use this option!

2. **Double-click the Pages icon.**

   Pages displays the Template Chooser window that you see in Figure 1-1.

3. **Click the type of document you want to create in the list to the left. The thumbnails on the right are updated with templates that match your choice.**

4. **Click the template that most closely matches your needs.**

5. **Click Choose to open a new document by using the template you selected.**

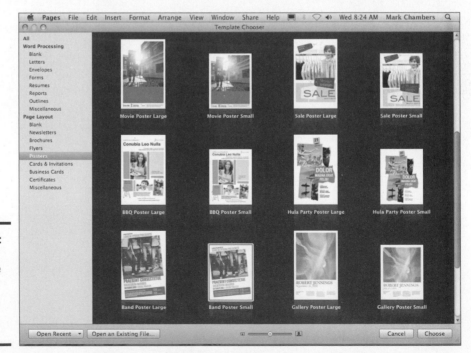

Figure 1-1:
Selecting a template from the Template Chooser window.

Open an Existing Pages Document

Of course, you can always open a Pages document from a Finder window —
just double-click the document icon. However, you can also open a Pages
document from within the program. Follow these steps:

1. **Double-click the Pages icon to run the program.**

2. **Press ⌘+O to display the Open dialog.**

   The Open dialog operates much the same as a Finder window in icon,
   list, or column view mode.

3. **Click the desired drive in the Devices list at the left of the dialog and then
   click folders and subfolders until you've located the Pages document.**

4. **Double-click the filename to load it.**

If you want to open a Pages document that you've edited in the recent past,
things get even easier! Just click File➪Open Recent, and you can open the
document with a single click from the submenu that appears.

Saving Your Work

To save a Pages document after you finish it (or to take a break while designing), follow these steps:

1. **Press ⌘+S.**

2. **Type a filename for your new document.**

3. **Click the Where pop-up menu and choose a location to save the
   document.**

4. **Click Save.**

You can create a version of a Pages document by clicking File➪Save
a Version. To revert the current document to an older version, click
File➪Revert Document. Pages gives you the option of reverting to the
last saved version, or you can click Older Version to browse multiple
versions of the document and choose one of those to revert to.

Touring the Pages Window

Before we dive into any real work, let me show you around the Pages window!
You'll find the following major components and controls, as shown in Figure 1-2:

✦ **Pages list:** This thumbnail list displays all the pages you've created within your document. (For a single-page document, of course, the Page list will contain only a single thumbnail.) You can switch instantly between different pages in your document by clicking the desired thumbnail in the list.

✦ **Layout pane:** This section takes up most of the Pages window — it's where you design and edit each page in your document.

✦ **Toolbar:** Yep, Pages has its own toolbar. The toolbar keeps all the most common application controls within easy, one-click reach.

✦ **Styles Drawer:** This window extension allows you to quickly switch the appearance of selected paragraphs, characters, and lists. You can hide and display the Styles Drawer from the View menu or from the View drop-down menu on the toolbar.

✦ **Format Bar:** This button strip runs underneath the Pages toolbar, allowing you to format selected text, paragraphs, and lists on the fly.

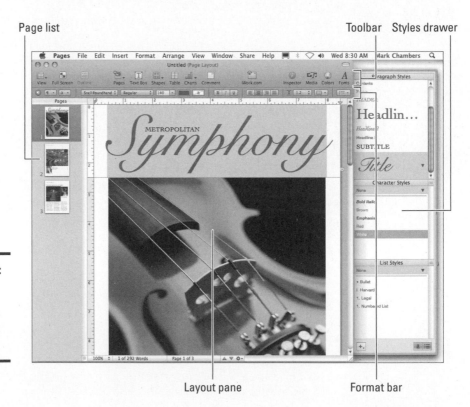

Page list   Toolbar   Styles drawer

Figure 1-2: The major points of interest in the Pages window.

Layout pane   Format bar

Entering and Editing Text

If you've used a modern word processing program on any computer — including "freebies" such as TextEdit on a Mac or WordPad on a PC — you'll feel right at home typing within Pages. Just in case, however, let's review the high points:

✦ The bar-shaped text cursor, which looks like a capital letter *I,* indicates where the text you enter will appear within a Pages document.

✦ To enter text, simply begin typing. Your characters appear at the text cursor.

✦ To edit existing text in your Pages document, click the insertion cursor at any point in the text and drag the insertion cursor across the characters to highlight them. Type the replacement text, and Pages automatically replaces the existing characters with the ones you type.

✦ To delete text, click and drag across the characters to highlight them; then press Delete.

Using Text and Graphics Boxes

Within Pages, text and graphics appear in *boxes*, which can be resized by clicking and dragging on one of the handles that appear around the edges of the box. (Hover your mouse cursor over one of the square handles and you'll see that it changes to a double-sided arrow, indicating that Pages is ready to resize the box.)

You can also move a box, including all the stuff it contains, to another location within the Layout pane. Click in the center of the box and drag the box to the desired spot. Note that Pages displays blue alignment lines to help you align the box with other elements around it (or with regular divisions of the page, such as the vertical center of a poster or flyer). Figure 1-3 illustrates a box containing text that I'm moving; note the vertical alignment line that automatically appears.

To select text or graphics within a box, you must first click the box to select it and then click again on the line of text or the graphic that you want to change.

Figure 1-3:
Moving a
text box
within the
Layout
pane.

The Three Amigos: Cut, Copy, and Paste

"Hang on, Mark, you've covered moving stuff, but what if you want to *copy* a block of text or a photo to a second location? Or how about cutting something from a document open in another application?" Good questions, dear reader! That's when you can call on the power of the cut, copy, and paste features within Pages. The next few sections explain how you do these actions.

Cutting stuff

Cutting selected text or graphics removes it from your Pages document and places that material within your Clipboard. (Think of the Clipboard as a holding area for snippets of text and graphics that you want to manipulate.) To cut text or graphics, select some material and do one of the following:

✦ Choose Edit➪Cut.

✦ Press ⌘+X.

If you simply want to remove the selected material from your Pages document (and you don't plan to paste it somewhere else), just select the text and press the Delete key.

Copying text and images

When you copy text or graphics, the original selection remains untouched, but a copy of the selection is placed in the Clipboard. Select some text or graphics and do one of the following:

✦ Choose Edit➪Copy.

✦ Press ⌘+C.

If you cut or copy a new selection into the Clipboard, it erases what was there. In other words, the Clipboard holds only the latest material you cut or copied.

You can also let your cursor do the work! Hold down the Option key while dragging selected items to copy them to a new location.

Pasting from the Clipboard

Are you wondering what you can do with all that stuff that's accumulating in your Clipboard? Pasting the contents of the Clipboard places the material at the current location of the insertion cursor. You can repeat a paste operation as often as you like because the contents of the Clipboard aren't cleared. However, remember that the Clipboard holds only the contents of your *last* copy or cut operation, so you must paste the contents before you cut or copy again to avoid losing what's in the Clipboard.

To paste the Clipboard contents, click the insertion cursor at the location you want and do one of the following:

✦ Choose Edit➪Paste.

✦ Press ⌘+V.

Formatting Text the Easy Way

If you feel that some (or all) of the text in your Pages document needs a facelift, you can format that text any way you like. Formatting lets you change the color, font family, character size, and attributes as necessary.

After the text is selected, you can apply basic formatting in two ways:

✦ **Use the Format bar.** The Format bar appears directly underneath the Pages toolbar (refer to Figure 1-2). Click to select a font control to display a pop-up menu and then click your choice. For example, click the Font Family button and you can change the font family from Arial to a more daring font. You can also select characteristics such as the font's background color (perfect for "highlighting" items) or choose italicizing or bolding. The Format Bar also provides buttons for text alignment (Align Left, Center, Align Right, and Justify).

✦ **Use the Format menu.** Most controls on the Format Bar are also available from the Format menu. Click Format and hover the mouse cursor over the Font menu item, and you can then apply bolding, italicizing, and underlining to the selected text. You can also make the text bigger or smaller. To change the alignment from the Format menu, click Format and hover the mouse cursor over the Text menu item.

Adding a Spiffy Table

In the world of word processing, a *table* is a grid that holds text or graphics for easy comparison. Many computer owners think of a spreadsheet program like Numbers when they think of a table (probably because of the rows and columns layout used in a spreadsheet), but you can create a custom table layout within Pages with a few simple mouse clicks.

Follow these steps:

1. **Click the insertion cursor at the location where you want the table to appear.**

2. **Click the Table button on the Pages toolbar.**

   Pages inserts a simple table and displays the Table Inspector. (Both are visible in Figure 1-4.)

By default, Pages creates a table with three rows and three columns, with an extra row for headings at the top. You can change this layout from the Table Inspector — just click in the Body Rows or Body Columns box and type a number.

3. **Click within a cell in the table to enter text. The table cell automatically resizes and "wraps" the text you enter to fit.**

   You can paste material from the Clipboard into a table. See the earlier section "Pasting from the Clipboard" for details on pasting.

4. **To change the borders on a cell, click the cell to select it and then click one of the Cell Border buttons to change the border.**

   Select multiple cells in a table by holding down Shift as you click.

5. **To add a background color (or even fill cells with an image for a background), click the Cell Background pop-up menu and choose a type of background.**

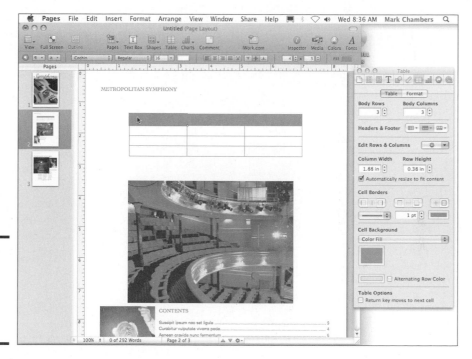

Figure 1-4:
Preparing
to tweak
a table in
my Pages
document.

Adding Alluring Photos

You can choose from two methods of adding a picture within your Pages document: as a *floating* object, meaning that you can place the image in a particular spot and it doesn't move, even if you make changes to the text; and as an *inline* object, which flows with the surrounding text as you make layout changes.

✦ **Add a floating object.** Drag an image file from a Finder window and place it at the spot you want within your document. Alternatively, you can click the Media button on the toolbar and click Photos, navigate to the location where the file is saved, and drag the image thumbnail to the spot you want in the document. Figure 1-5 illustrates the Media Browser in action.

Note that a floating object (such as a shape or image) can be sent to the *background,* where text will not wrap around it. To bring a background object back as a regular floating object, click the object to select it and click Arrange➪Bring Background Objects to Front. (More about background objects later in this chapter.)

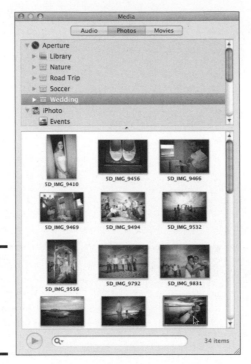

Figure 1-5:
Hey, isn't that the Pages Media Browser?

✦ **Add an inline object.** Hold down the ⌘ key as you drag an image file from a Finder window and place it where you want within your document. You can also click the Media toolbar button and click Photos to display the Media Browser. Navigate to the location where the file is saved, hold down the ⌘ key, and drag the image thumbnail to the spot where you want it in the document.

Manipulating images for fun and profit

If you add an image that appears too large or distorted within your Pages document, you can resize it at any time to correct the problem. To resize an image object, click the image to select it and then drag one of the selection handles that appear along the border of the image. (They look like tiny squares.) The side-selection handles drag only that edge of the frame, whereas the corner-selection handles resize both adjoining edges of the selection frame.

When you hold down the Shift key as you drag, Pages preserves the aspect ratio of the image so that the vertical and horizontal proportions remain fixed.

You can also flip images. Click Arrange on the Pages menu bar to flip the image horizontally or vertically.

Adding a Background Shape

To add a shape (such as a rectangle or circle) as a background for your text, follow these steps:

1. **Click the insertion cursor in the location you want.**

2. **Click the Shapes button on the Pages toolbar and choose a shape.**

   The shape appears in your document.

3. **Click the center of the shape and drag it to a new spot.**

   As can image boxes, shapes can be resized or moved.

4. **Before you can type over a shape, remember to select it and choose Arrange⇨Send Object to Background.**

Are You Sure About That Spelling?

Pages can check spelling as you type (the default setting) or check it after you complete your document. If you find automatic spell-checking distracting, you should definitely pick the latter method.

Spell-checking only confirms that a word is correctly spelled, *not* that it's the right word for the job! If you've ever "red" a document that someone else "rote," you know what he means.

To check spelling as you type, follow these steps:

1. **Click Edit and hover the mouse cursor over the Spelling menu item.**

2. **Click Check Spelling As You Type.**

   If a possible misspelling is found, Pages underlines the word with a red, dashed line.

3. **Right-click the word to choose a possible correct spelling from the list, or you can ignore the word if it's spelled correctly.**

To turn off automatic spell checking, click the Check Spelling As You Type menu item again to deselect it.

To check spelling manually, follow these steps:

1. **Click within the document to place the text insertion cursor where the spell check should begin.**

2. **Click Edit and hover the mouse cursor over the Spelling menu item; then choose Check Spelling.**

3. **Right-click any possible misspellings and choose the correct spelling, or choose Ignore if the word is spelled correctly.**

Book IV Chapter 1

Desktop Publishing with Pages

Printing Your Pages Documents

Ready to start the presses? You can print your Pages document on real paper, of course, but don't forget that you can also save a tree by creating an electronic, PDF-format document instead of a printout. (For the lowdown on PDF printing, visit Chapter 4 in Book VII.)

To print your Pages document on old-fashioned paper, follow these steps:

1. **Within Pages, click File and choose Print.**

Pages displays the Print sheet you see in Figure 1-6.

2. **Click in the Copies field and enter the number of copies you need.**

3. **Select the pages to print.**

- To print the entire document, select All.

- To print a range of selected pages, select the From radio button and enter the starting and ending pages.

4. **Click the Print button to send the document to your printer.**

Figure 1-6:
Preparing to print a work of art within Pages.

Sharing That Poster with Others

Besides printing — which is, after all, so passé — you can choose to share your Pages document electronically in a number of ways:

✦ **Sharing on iWork.com.** Apple provides a web site, iwork.com, where you can invite others to view and comment on your Pages document, complete with email notifications when a new comment is added. (If you like, you can require a password before visitors to iWork.com can see anything you've shared.) Click the iWork.com button on the Pages toolbar to get started, and the site will walk you through the rest of the process.

You'll need an Internet connection to use iWork.com (naturally), as well as an Apple ID and a working Apple Mail account. If you didn't create an Apple ID when buying your Mac or installing Lion, you can save the day by clicking the Create New Account button on the iWork.com site. If you're not using Apple Mail yet, peruse Book V, Chapter 2 for all the details.

✦ **Sharing through e-mail.** Click Share➪Send via Mail, and you can choose to add your Pages document to a Mail message in three different formats: as a native Pages document file as a Word format document; or as a PDF file. After you've selected a format, Pages obligingly launches Apple Mail for you automatically and creates a new message, ready for you to address and send!

✦ **Sharing through iWeb.** Again, click the Share menu, but this time choose Send to iWeb. Pages automatically opens the iWeb site you last edited and provides your Pages document as a native Pages document file or as a PDF file. (If your visitors may be using PCs, choose the PDF option.)

✦ **Exporting.** Don't forget that Pages can export your work in one of four different formats: a PDF document; a Word format document; an RTF (Rich Text Format) file; or even plain text. Click Share➪Export, pick your format, click Next, and then select the location where Pages should save the file. Click Export and sit back while your favorite desktop publishing application does all the work.

To keep your document as close to how it appears in Pages as possible, I recommend either PDF or Word. Your document will retain far more of your original formatting than an RTF or plain-text document would.

Chapter 2: Creating Spreadsheets with Numbers

In This Chapter

⯈ **Opening, saving, and creating spreadsheets**

⯈ **Selecting cells**

⯈ **Entering and editing cell data**

⯈ **Formatting cells**

⯈ **Adding and removing rows and columns**

⯈ **Creating simple calculations**

⯈ **Adding charts to your spreadsheets**

⯈ **Printing a Numbers spreadsheet**

Are you downright afraid of spreadsheets? Does the idea of building a budget with charts and all sorts of fancy graphics send you running for the safety of the hall closet? Well, good Mac owner, Apple has once again taken something that everyone else considers super-complex and turned it into something that normal human beings can use! (Much like video editing, songwriting, and web site creation — heck, is there *any* type of software that Apple designers can't make intuitive and easy to use?)

In this chapter, I get to demonstrate how Numbers can help you organize data, analyze important financial decisions, and yes, even maintain a household budget! You'll soon see why the Numbers spreadsheet program is specifically designed with the home Mac owner in mind.

Before We Launch Numbers . . .

Just in case you're not familiar with applications like Numbers and Microsoft Excel — and the documents they create — let me provide you with a little background information.

A *spreadsheet* organizes and calculates numbers by using a grid system of rows and columns. The intersection of each row and column is a *cell,* and cells can hold either text or numeric values (along with calculations that are usually linked to the contents of other, surrounding cells).

Spreadsheets are wonderful tools for making decisions and comparisons because they let you "plug in" different numbers — such as interest rates or your monthly insurance premium — and instantly see the results. Some of my favorite spreadsheets that I use regularly include

✦ Car and mortgage loan comparisons

✦ A college planner

✦ My household budget (not that we pay any attention to it)

Creating a New Numbers Document

As does Pages, the desktop publishing application that's included in iWork '09, Numbers ships with a selection of templates that you can modify quickly to create a new spreadsheet. (For example, after a few modifications, you can easily use the Budget, Loan Comparison, and Mortgage templates to create your own spreadsheets!)

To create a spreadsheet project file, follow these steps:

1. **Open your Applications folder and double-click the iWork '09 folder to display its contents.**

2. **Double-click the Numbers icon.**

Numbers displays the Template Chooser window you see in Figure 2-1.

If Numbers will be a favorite application on your Mac, I highly recommend that you allow the iWork '09 installation program to add a Numbers icon to your Dock.

3. **Click the type of document you want to create in the list to the left.**

The document thumbnails on the right are updated with templates that match your choice.

4. **Click the template that most closely matches your needs.**

5. **Click Choose to open a new document using the template you selected.**

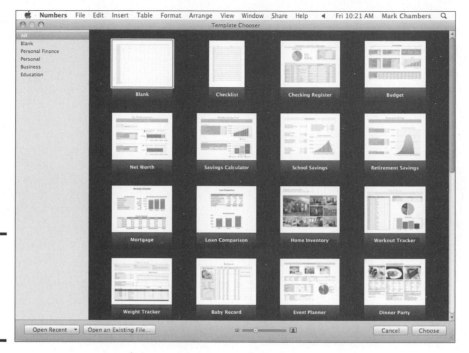

Figure 2-1:
Hey, these templates aren't frightening at all!

Opening an Existing Spreadsheet File

If a Numbers document appears in a Finder window, you can just double-click the document icon to open it; Numbers automatically loads and displays the spreadsheet.

However, it's equally easy to open a Numbers document from within the program. Follow these steps:

1. **Double-click the Numbers icon to run the program.**
2. **Press ⌘+O to display the Open dialog.**
3. **Click the desired drive in the Devices list at the left of the dialog and then click folders and subfolders until you've located the desired Numbers document.**
4. **Double-click the spreadsheet to load it.**

If you want to open a spreadsheet you've been working on over the last few days, click File ➪ Open Recent to display Numbers documents that you've worked with recently.

The Template Chooser window also sports both an Open Recent button and an Open Existing File button. Convenience is A Good Thing!

Save Those Spreadsheets!

If you're not a huge fan of retyping data a second time, I always recommend that you save your spreadsheets often (just in case of a power failure or a co-worker's mistake). Follow these steps to save your spreadsheet to your hard drive:

1. **Press ⌘+S.**

2. **Type a filename for your new spreadsheet.**

3. **Click the Where pop-up menu and choose a location to save the file.**

   This allows you to select common locations, such as your desktop, Documents folder, or Home folder.

4. **Click Save.**

After you've saved the file the first time, you can simply press ⌘+S in the future and your changes are saved.

You can also use the Save a Version and Revert Document items on the File menu to save a "snapshot" of your Numbers document, or revert the document to a past version.

Exploring the Numbers Window

Apple has done a great job of minimizing the complexity of the Numbers window. Figure 2-2 illustrates these major points of interest:

✦ **Sheets list:** Because a Numbers project can contain multiple spreadsheets, they're displayed in the Sheets list at the left of the window. To switch between spreadsheets in a project, click the top-level headings (each of which has a spreadsheet icon).

✦ **Sheet canvas:** Numbers displays the rows and columns of your spreadsheet in this section of the window; you enter and edit cell values within the sheet canvas.

✦ **Toolbar:** The Numbers toolbar keeps the most common commands you'll use within easy reach.

✦ **Formula Box:** You'll use the Formula Box to enter formulas into a cell, allowing Numbers to automatically perform calculations based on the contents of other cells.

✦ **Format Bar:** Located directly under the toolbar, the Format Bar displays editing controls for the object that's currently selected. (If you enter an equal sign into the Formula Box, the Format Bar changes into the Formula Bar. No, I'm not making this up.) My goodness, this is starting to sound like that classic movie about the chocolate tycoon and those kids!

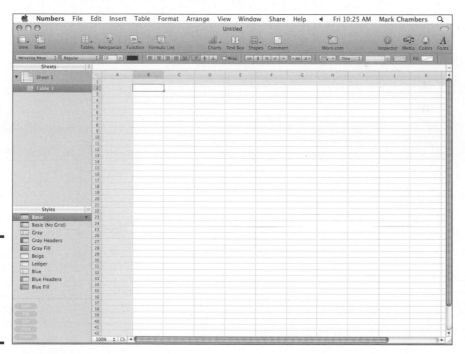

Figure 2-2: The Numbers window struts its stuff.

Book IV
Chapter 2

Creating Spreadsheets with Numbers

Navigate and Select Cells in a Spreadsheet

Before you can enter data into a cell, you need to know how to get to the cell where you want to enter that data. You can use the scroll bars to move around in your spreadsheet, but when you enter data into cells, moving your fingers from the keyboard is a hassle. For this reason, Numbers has various movement shortcut keys that you can use to navigate, and I list them in Table 2-1. After you commit these keys to memory, your productivity shoots straight to the top.

Table 2-1	Movement Shortcut Keys in Numbers
Key or Key Combination	*Where the Cursor Moves*
Left arrow (←)	One cell to the left
Right arrow (→)	One cell to the right
Up arrow (↑)	One cell up
Down arrow (↓)	One cell down
Home	To the beginning of the active worksheet
End	To the end of the active worksheet
Page Down	Down one screen
Page Up	Up one screen
Return	One cell down (also works within a selection)
Tab	One cell to the right (also works within a selection)
Shift+Enter	One cell up (also works within a selection)
Shift+Tab	One cell to the left (also works within a selection)

You can use the mouse to select cells in a spreadsheet:

✦ To select a *single* cell, click it.

✦ To select a *range* of multiple adjacent cells, click a cell at any corner of the range you want and then drag the mouse in the direction you want.

✦ To select a *column* of cells, click the alphabetic heading button at the top of the column.

✦ To select a *row* of cells, click the numeric heading button on the far left side of the row.

Entering and Editing Data in a Spreadsheet

After you navigate to the cell in which you want to enter data, you're ready to type your data. Follow these steps to enter That Important Stuff:

1. **Either click the cell or press the spacebar.**

   A cursor appears, indicating that the cell is ready to hold any data you type.

2. **Type in your data.**

   Spreadsheets can use both numbers and text within a cell — either type of information is considered data in the Spreadsheet World.

3. **To edit data, click within the cell that contains the data to select it and then click the cell again to display the insertion cursor. Drag the insertion cursor across the characters to highlight them and then type the replacement data.**

4. **To simply delete characters, highlight the characters and press Delete.**

5. **When you're ready to move on, press Return (to save the data and move one cell down) or press Tab (to save the data and move one cell to the right).**

Selecting the Right Number Format

After your data has been entered into a cell, row, or column, you still might need to format it before it appears correctly. Numbers gives you a healthy selection of formatting possibilities. *Number formatting* determines how a cell displays a number, such as a dollar amount, a percentage, or a date.

Characters and formatting rules, such as decimal places, commas, and dollar and percentage notations, are included in number formatting. So if your spreadsheet contains units of currency, such as dollars, format it as such. Then all you need to do is type the numbers, and the currency formatting is applied automatically.

To specify a number format, follow these steps:

1. **Select the cells, rows, or columns you want to format.**

2. **Click the Inspector toolbar button.**

3. **Click the Cells Inspector button in the Inspector toolbar to display the settings you see in Figure 2-3.**

4. **Click the Cell Format pop-up menu and click the type of formatting you want to apply.**

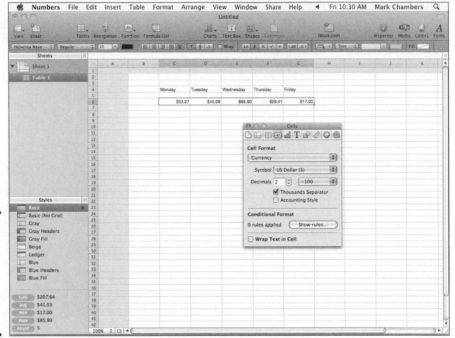

Figure 2-3:
You can format the data you've entered from the Inspector.

Aligning Cell Text Just So

You can also change the alignment of text in the selected cells. (The default alignment for text is flush left.) Follow these steps:

1. **Select the cells, rows, or columns you want to format.**

See "Navigate and Select Cells in a Spreadsheet," earlier in this chapter, for tips on selecting stuff.

2. **Click the Inspector toolbar button.**

3. **Click the Text Inspector button in the Inspector toolbar to display the settings you see in Figure 2-4.**

4. **Click the corresponding alignment button to choose the type of formatting you want to apply.**

You can choose from left, right, center, justified, and text left and numbers right. Text can also be aligned at the top, center, or bottom of a cell.

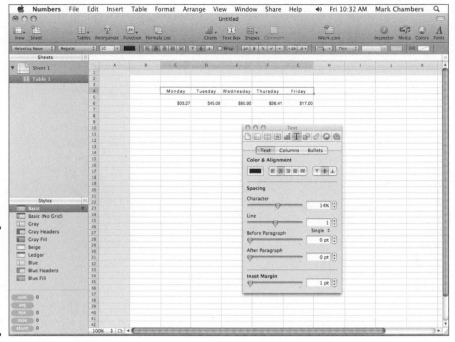

Figure 2-4:
Using the Inspector to change text alignment within a cell.

Do you need to set apart the contents of some cells? For example, you might need to create text headings for some columns and rows or to highlight the totals in a spreadsheet. To change the formatting of the data displayed within selected cells, select the cells, rows, or columns you want to format and then click the Font Family, Font Size, or Font Color buttons on the Format Bar.

Format with Shading

Shading the contents of a cell, row, or column is helpful when your spreadsheet contains subtotals or logical divisions. Follow these steps to shade cells, rows, or columns:

1. **Select the cells, rows, or columns you want to format.**

2. **Click the Inspector toolbar button.**

3. **Click the Graphic Inspector button in the Inspector toolbar.**

Numbers displays the settings you see in Figure 2-5.

**Book IV
Chapter 2**

Creating
Spreadsheets
with Numbers

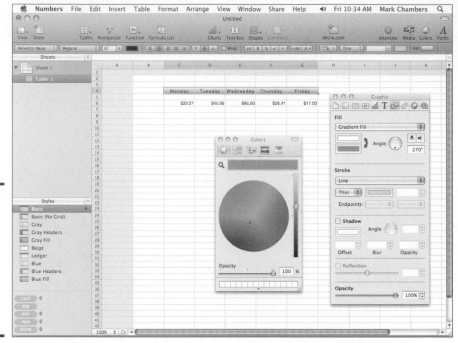

Figure 2-5:
Adding
shading
and colors
to cells,
rows, and
columns
is easy in
Numbers.

4. **Click the Fill pop-up menu to select a shading option.**

5. **Click the color box to select a color for your shading.**

   Numbers displays a color picker (also shown in Figure 2-5).

6. **Click to select a color.**

7. **After you achieve the right effect, click the Close button in the color picker.**

8. **Click the Inspector's Close button to return to your spreadsheet.**

Insert and Delete Rows and Columns

What's that? You forgot to add a row and now you're three pages into your data entry? No problem. You can easily add or delete rows and columns. Really — you can! First, select the row or column that you want to delete or that you want to insert a row or column next to, and do one of the following:

✦ **For a row:** Right-click and choose Add Row Above, Add Row Below, or Delete Row from the pop-up menu that appears.

✦ **For a column:** Right-click and choose Add Columns Before, Add Columns After, or Delete Column from the pop-up menu that appears.

Remember that you can also take care of this business from the Table menu. (Personally, I like to right-click.)

The Formula Is Your Friend

Sorry, but it's time to talk about *formulas*. These equations calculate values based on the contents of cells you specify in your spreadsheet. For example, if you designate cell A1 (the cell in column A at row 1) to hold your yearly salary and cell B1 to hold the number 12, you can divide the contents of cell A1 by cell B1 (to calculate your monthly salary) by typing this formula into any other cell:

=A1/B1

By the way, formulas in Numbers always start with an equal sign (=).

"So what's the big deal, Mark? Why not use a calculator?" Sure, but maybe you want to calculate your weekly salary. Rather than grab a pencil and paper, you can simply change the contents of cell B1 to 52, and — boom! — the spreadsheet is updated to display your weekly salary.

That's a simple example, of course, but it demonstrates the basis of using formulas (and the reason that spreadsheets are often used to predict trends and forecast budgets).

To add a simple formula within your spreadsheet, follow these steps:

1. **Select the cell that will hold the result of your calculation.**

2. **Click inside the Formula Box and type = (the equal sign).**

   The Formula Box appears to the right of the Sheets heading, directly under the Button bar. Note that the Format Bar changes to show a set of formula controls (also known as the Formula Bar).

3. **Click the Function Browser button, which bears the *fx* label.**

   It appears next to the red Cancel button on the Formula Bar.

4. **In the window that appears, as shown in Figure 2-6, click the desired formula to add it to the Formula Box.**

5. **After you finish, click the Accept button to add the formula to the cell.**

That's it! Your formula is now ready to work behind the scenes, doing math for you so that the correct numbers appear in the cell you specified.

TIP

To display all the formulas that you've added to a sheet, click the Formula List button in the toolbar.

**Book IV
Chapter 2**

Creating Spreadsheets with Numbers

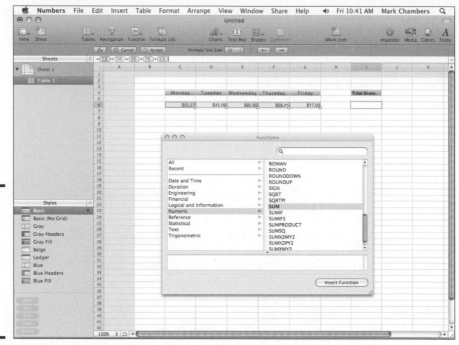

Figure 2-6:
If you have to use formulas, at least Numbers can enter them for you.

Adding Visual Punch with a Chart

Sometimes you just have to see something to believe it — hence the ability to use the data you add to a spreadsheet to generate a professional-looking chart! Follow these steps to create a chart:

1. **Select the adjacent cells you want to chart by dragging the mouse.**

To choose individual cells that aren't adjacent, you can hold down the ⌘ key as you click.

2. **Click the Charts button on the Numbers toolbar. The Charts button bears the symbol of a bar graph.**

Numbers displays the thumbnail menu you see in Figure 2-7.

3. **Click the thumbnail for the chart type you want.**

Numbers inserts the chart as an object within your spreadsheet so that you can move the chart. You can drag using the handles that appear on the outside of the object box to resize your chart. Figure 2-8 illustrates the 3-D chart I generated with just a couple of mouse clicks.

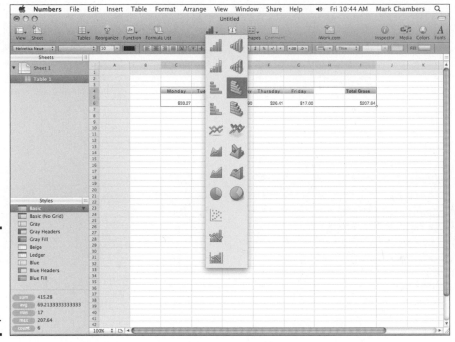

Figure 2-7:
Numbers
displays the
range of
chart styles
you can use.

Click the Inspector toolbar button and you can switch to the Chart Inspector dialog, where you can change the colors and add (or remove) the chart title and legend.

4. To change the default title, click the title box once to select it; click it again to edit the text.

After you've added your chart to the sheet, you'll note that it appears in the Sheets list, as also shown in Figure 2-8. To edit the chart at any time, just click on the corresponding entry in the Sheets list.

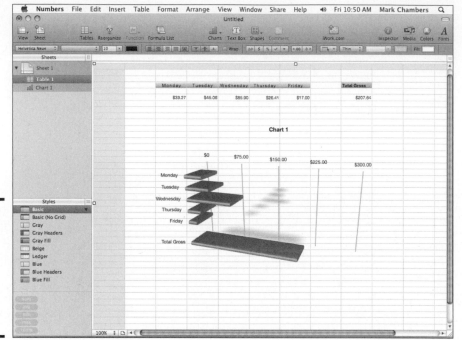

Figure 2-8:
My finished
chart
looks like
someone
with talent
drew it for
me!

Chapter 3: Building Presentations with Keynote

In This Chapter

✔ Creating a new presentation

✔ Adding slides

✔ Using selection boxes

✔ Entering and editing text

✔ Formatting text

✔ Adding presenter's notes

✔ Inserting media and shapes

✔ Running a slideshow

✔ Printing slides and notes

*I*t seems like only yesterday that I was giving business presentations with a klunky overhead projector and black-and-white acetate transparencies. Fancy color gradients and animation were unheard of, and the only sound my presentations made was the droning of the projector's fan. I might as well have been using tree bark and chalk.

Thank goodness those days are gone forever, because cutting-edge presentation software like Keynote makes slide creation easy and — believe it or not — *fun*! This is the application that Steve Jobs once used for his Macworld keynotes every year, and there's so much visual candy available that you'll never need to shout to wake your audience again.

In this chapter, I demonstrate how simple it is to build a stunning Keynote presentation, and how to start and control your slide display from your keyboard (or even your iPhone or iPod touch). Heck, we'll even print your slides and notes so that your audience can keep a copy of your brilliant work!

Creating a New Keynote Project

As do the other applications in the iWork '09 suite, Keynote begins the document creation process with a Template Chooser window. To create a new presentation project, follow these steps:

1. **Double-click your hard drive icon and click the Applications entry in the Finder window sidebar. Double-click the iWork folder to open it.**

   If presentations are your bread and butter, allow the iWork installation program to add a Keynote icon to your Dock. Your clicking finger will thank you.

2. **Double-click the Keynote icon.**

   The Theme Chooser window that you see in Figure 3-1 appears. (I have to say that these are probably the most stunning visual building blocks I've ever seen in a presentation application. You should have heard the "oohs" and "ahhs" from the Macworld faithful when Steve Jobs demonstrated Keynote for the first time on the big screen!)

3. **Click the Slide Size pop-up menu at the bottom of the screen to select the resolution for your completed slides.**

   Although you don't necessarily need to select an exact match for the screen resolution of your Mac, it's a good idea to select the closest value to the maximum resolution of your projector. (If someone else is providing the projector, the default value of 1024 x 768 is a good standard to use.)

Figure 3-1: Selecting a template from the Theme Chooser window.

4. **Click the template that most closely matches your needs.**

5. **Click Choose to open a new document by using the template you selected.**

Opening a Keynote Presentation

If an existing Keynote presentation file is visible in a Finder window, you can double-click the document icon to open the project. If Keynote is already running, however, follow these steps to load a project:

1. **Press ⌘+O to display the Open dialog.**

2. **Click the desired drive in the Devices list at the left of the dialog; then click folders and subfolders until you've located the Keynote project.**

3. **Double-click the filename to load it.**

If you want to open a Keynote document that you've edited in the recent past, things get even easier! Just click File⇨Open Recent and you can open the document with a single click from the submenu that appears. (Note that the Template Chooser window has both Open Recent and Open Existing File buttons as well.)

Saving Your Presentation

When you're done working on a Keynote presentation (or if you'd simply like to safeguard your work in a world of power failures), follow these steps:

1. **Press ⌘+S.**

2. **Type a filename for your new document.**

3. **Click the Where pop-up menu and choose a location to save the document.**

4. **Click Save.**

You can create a version of a Keynote presentation by clicking File⇨Save a Version. To revert the current presentation to an older version, click File⇨Revert Document. Keynote gives you the option of reverting to the last saved version, or you can browse multiple versions of the presentation and choose one of those to revert to.

Putting Keynote to Work

Ready for the five-cent tour of the Keynote window? Launch the application and create or load a project, and you'll see the tourist attractions shown in Figure 3-2:

✦ **Slides list:** Use this thumbnail list of all the slides in your project to help you navigate quickly. Click a thumbnail to switch instantly to that slide.

The Slide list can also display your project in outline format, allowing you to check all your discussion points. (This is a great way to ferret out any "holes" in your presentation's flow.) While in outline mode, you can still jump directly to any slide by clicking the slide's title in the outline. To display the outline, click View⇨Outline. You can switch back to the default Navigator Slide list by clicking View⇨Navigator.

✦ **Layout pane:** Your slide appears in its entirety in this pane. You can add elements and edit the content of the slide from the Layout pane.

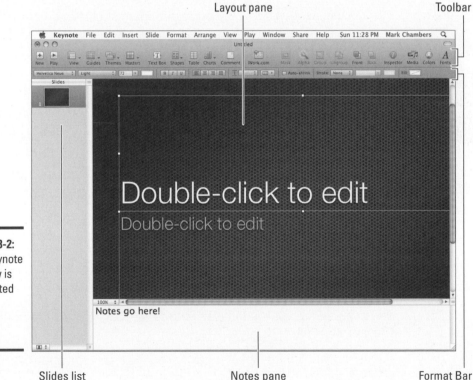

Figure 3-2:
The Keynote window is dominated by the Layout pane.

Layout pane

Toolbar

Double-click to edit

Double-click to edit

Notes go here!

Slides list

Notes pane

Format Bar

✦ **Toolbar:** As does the toolbar in Pages and Numbers, Keynote's toolbar makes it easy to find the most common controls you'll use while designing and editing your slides. Clicking an icon in the toolbar performs an action, just as selecting a menu item does.

✦ **Notes pane:** If you decide to add notes to one or more slides (either for your own use or to print as additional information for your audience), click View⇨Show Presenter Notes to open the Notes pane. This text box appears under the Layout pane.

✦ **Format Bar:** Keynote displays this button strip underneath the Keynote toolbar, allowing you to format selected text, paragraphs, and lists on the fly.

Adding Slides

Sure, Keynote creates a single Title slide when you first create a project, but not many presentations are complete with just a single slide! To add more slides to your project, use one of these methods:

✦ Click the New button on the Keynote toolbar.

✦ Choose New Slide from the Slide menu.

✦ Press ⌘+Shift+N.

✦ Right-click (or Control-click) in the Slides list and choose New Slide from the menu.

Keynote adds the new slide to your Slides list and automatically switches to the new slide in the Layout pane.

Need a slide that's very similar to an existing slide you've already designed? Right-click the existing slide and choose Duplicate to create a new slide just like it. (Consider it cloning without the science.)

To move slides to different positions in the Slides list (and therefore a different order in your Keynote slideshow), drag each slide thumbnail to the desired spot in the list.

Working with Text and Graphics Boxes

You've probably noticed that all the text within your first Title slide appears within boxes. Keynote uses boxes to manipulate text and graphics. You can resize a box (and its contents) by clicking and dragging one of the handles that appear around the edges of the box. (Your mouse cursor changes into a double-sided arrow when you're "in the zone.") The side-selection handles drag only that edge of the frame, whereas the corner-selection handles resize both adjoining edges of the selection frame.

To keep the proportions of the box constrained, hold down Shift while dragging the corner handles.

Boxes make it easy to move text and graphics together (as a single unit) to another location within the Layout pane. Click in the center of the box and drag the box to the desired spot; Keynote displays alignment lines to help you align the box with other elements around it (or with regular divisions of the slide, like horizontal center). As you can see in Figure 3-3, I'm moving a box on the slide to a new location, and Keynote has supplied alignment lines to help me place it correctly.

To select text or graphics within a box, you should double-click the box.

If you're resizing a photo in a box, don't forget to hold down the Shift key as you drag the frame. Doing so specifies that Keynote should preserve the aspect ratio of the image so that the vertical and horizontal proportions remain fixed. You can also flip images horizontally or vertically from the Arrange menu bar.

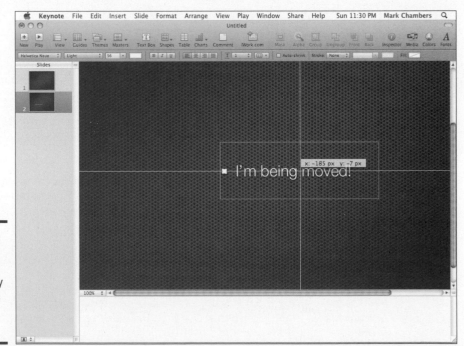

Figure 3-3: Alignment lines are provided by Keynote as you move boxes.

Adding and Editing Slide Text

As with Pages and Numbers — which also use boxes for text layout — Keynote allows you to add or edit text with ease. For example, double-click in a box with the text `Double-click to edit`, and the placeholder text disappears, leaving the field ready to accept new text. Any new text you type appears at the blinking cursor within the box.

To edit existing text in your Keynote document, click using the bar-shaped cursor to select just the right spot in the text, and drag the insertion cursor across the characters to highlight them. Type the replacement text, and Keynote obligingly replaces the text that was there with the text you type.

If you want to delete existing text, click and drag across the characters to highlight them; press Delete. You can also delete an entire box and all its contents: Right-click (or Control-click) the offending box and choose Delete from the menu that appears.

When the contents of a box are just right and you're finished entering or editing text, click anywhere outside the box to hide it from view. You can always click the text again to display the box later.

Formatting Slide Text for the Perfect Look

Keynote doesn't restrict you to the default fonts for the theme you chose. It's easy to format the text in your slides — you can choose a different font family, font color, text alignment, and text attributes such as bolding and italicizing on the fly, whenever you like.

Select the desired text by double-clicking a box and then dragging the text cursor to highlight the characters. Now apply your formatting using one of these two methods:

✦ **The Format Bar:** The font controls on the Format Bar work just like the controls on the toolbar: Either click a font control to display a pop-up menu, or click a button to immediately perform an action. Clicking the Font Size pop-up menu, for example, displays a range of sizes for the selected text; — with a single click on the B (bold) button, you'll add the bold attribute to the highlighted characters.

✦ **The Format menu:** The controls on the Format menu generally mirror those on the Format Bar. To change the alignment from the Format menu, click Format and hover the mouse cursor over the Text menu item. To change text attributes, click Format and hover your mouse over the Font menu.

Using Presenter's Notes in Your Project

As I mention earlier, you can type text notes in the Notes pane — I use them for displaying alternate topic points while presenting my slide show. However, you can also print the notes for a project along with the slides, so presenter's notes are also great for including reminders and To Do points for your audience in handouts.

To type your notes, just click within the Notes pane; if it's hidden, click View⇨Show Presenter Notes. When you're done adding notes, click in the Slide list or the Layout pane to return to editing mode.

To display your notes while practicing, use Keynote's Rehearsal feature. Click Play and choose Rehearse Slideshow, and you can scroll through the notes while the slideshow runs. (More on slideshows in a second.)

Every Good Presentation Needs Media

Adding audio, photos, and movies to a slide is drag-and-drop easy in Keynote! Simply drag an image, audio, or movie file from a Finder window and place it at the spot you want within your document.

You can also use the Media Browser — click the Media button on the toolbar and click the Audio, Photos, or Movies button to select the desired type. Keynote displays the contents of your various media collections — like your iPhoto and iTunes libraries — or you can also navigate to the file's location on your hard drive, or type in a filename in the Search box at the bottom of the browser. When you've found the file you want to add, drag it to the spot you want in the document. Figure 3-4 illustrates the Media Browser in action.

Adding a Background Shape

Text often stands out on a slide when it sits on top of a background shape. To add a shape (such as a rectangle or circle) as a background for your text, follow these steps:

1. **Click the insertion cursor in the location you want.**

2. **Click the Shapes button on the Keynote toolbar and choose a shape.**

   The shape appears in your document.

3. **Click the center of the shape and drag it to a new spot.**

   As with image boxes, shapes can be resized or moved.

4. **When the shape is properly positioned and sized, select it and choose Arrange⇨Send to Back.**

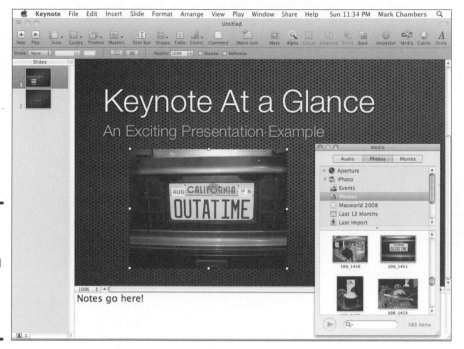

Figure 3-4:
It's not just
photos —
you can add
audio and
movie clips
to a slide,
too!

Creating Your Keynote Slideshow

The heart of a Keynote presentation is the slideshow that you build from the slides you've created. A Keynote slideshow is typically presented full screen, with slides appearing in linear order as they are sorted in the Slides list.

In its simplest form, you can always run a slideshow from a Keynote project by clicking the Play button in the toolbar, or by choosing Play➪Play Slideshow from the menu. You can advance to the next slide by clicking your mouse, or by pressing the right bracket key, which looks like this:].

Of course, other controls are available besides just the ones that advance to the next slide! Table 3-1 illustrates the key shortcuts you'll use most often during a slideshow.

Table 3-1	Keynote Slideshow Shortcut Keys
Key or Key Combination	**Action**
] (right bracket)	Next slide
P	Previous slide

(continued)

Table 3-1 *(continued)*

Key or Key Combination	Action
Home	Jump to first slide
End	Jump to last slide
C	Show or hide the pointer
(number)	Jump to the corresponding slide in the Slide list
U	Scroll notes up
D	Scroll notes down
N	Show current slide number
H	Hide slideshow and display last application used (the presentation appears as a minimized icon in the Dock)
B	Pause slideshow and display a black screen (press any key to resume the slideshow)
Esc	Quit

Keynote offers a number of settings that you can tweak to fine-tune your slideshow. To display these settings, choose Keynote➪Preferences and click the Slideshow button in the Preferences window.

If you have an iPhone or iPod touch handy and you've installed the Apple Keynote Remote application on your device, display the Preferences window and click the Remote button to link your iPhone or iPod touch to your Mac and Keynote. Now you can use your handheld device as a remote and use it during your slideshow!

Printing Your Slides and Notes

Okay, I'll be honest: I don't always print handouts for every presentation I give, just because some of the slideshows I run are short introductions to hands-on demonstrations. However, if you're presenting a lengthy slideshow with plenty of information that you'd like your audience to remember, nothing beats handouts that include scaled-down images of your slides (and, optionally, your presenter's notes).

You can also use Keynote to create an electronic PDF-format document instead of a printed handout, which your audience members can download from your web site. (For the lowdown on PDF printing, visit Chapter 4 in Book VII.)

To print a hard copy of your slides and notes, follow these steps:

1. **Within Keynote, click File and choose Print.**

Keynote displays the Print sheet you see in Figure 3-5.

2. **Click the desired format.**

   • To print each slide on a separate page at full size, click Individual Slides.

   • To print each slide on a separate page with the presenter's notes for that slide, click Slides with Notes.

   • To print the contents of your Slides list in Outline view, click Outline.

   • To print a handout with multiple slides per page (and, optionally, with presenter's notes), click Handout. Click the Slides per Page pop-up menu to specify the number of slides that Keynote should print on each page.

3. **Select the pages to print.**

   • To print the entire document, select All.

   • To print a range of selected slides, select the From radio button and enter the starting and ending pages.

4. **Select or deselect specific options from the Options column.**

   You can include elements such as the date, borders around each slide, and the slide number as part of each page of the hardcopy.

5. **Click the Print button to send the job to your printer.**

Figure 3-5: Keynote offers a wide range of printing options for your slides and notes.

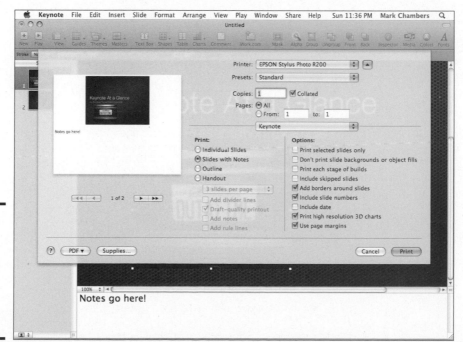

Book V

The Typical Internet Stuff

The 5th Wave   By Rich Tennant

"Are you using that 'clone' tool again?!"

Contents at a Glance

Chapter 1: Getting on the Internet

In This Chapter

✔ Selecting an Internet service provider (ISP)

✔ Understanding how your Mac gets on the Internet

✔ Setting up your Internet connection

1'll be honest — the Internet is a terribly complex monster of a network. If you tried to fathom all the data that's exchanged on the Internet and everything that takes place when you check your e-mail for Aunty Joan's fruitcake recipe, your brain would probably melt like a chocolate bar in the Sahara Desert. A shoebox *full* of archaic things is tucked under the Internet: communications protocols, routing addresses, packets, servers, and other hoo-hah that are beyond the grasp of just about everyone on the planet.

Luckily for regular folks like you and me, Mac OS X Lion closes the trapdoor on all these details, keeping them hidden (as they *should* be). You don't have to worry about them, and the obscure information that you need to establish an Internet connection is kept to a minimum. In fact, the happiest computer owners I've met think that the Internet is a little blinking light on their DSL or cable modem: If the light blinks in the proper manner, all is well. (I don't argue with them.)

In this chapter, I provide help and advice to those who are prepared to play games, download music and chat with their friends — and I lead you through the procedure of adding an Internet connection under Mac OS X. (In other words, you'll get your light blinking properly.)

If you entered your Internet configuration information while you were in the Setup Assistant during the installation of Mac OS X, *you can skip this chapter!* The information contained herein is only for those who add or change their Internet connectivity *after* installing Mac OS X.

Shopping for an ISP

Before you can connect to the Internet, you must sign up for Internet access. If you already have an ISP (acronym-speak for an *Internet service provider*) or your company or school provides Internet access, smile quietly to yourself and skip to the next section. Otherwise, hang around while I discuss what to look for in an ISP and how to locate one in your local area.

If you're unfamiliar with the term, an *ISP* is simply the company you contract with so that you can connect to the Internet. You may be contracting with a cable company, such as Comcast, Bright House, or Mediacom, or you may be using a service such as AOL, Juno, or Earthlink. All these are ISPs.

ISPs are as thick as Louisiana mosquitoes these days, and often they're judged solely by the amount that they charge for basic access. Cost definitely is a factor, but it's not the *only* thing that should determine your choice in a service provider. Consider these guidelines when choosing or switching ISPs:

✦ **Broadband service:** Virtually all ISPs now offer digital subscriber line (DSL) or cable modem access. Collectively, these connections are called *broadband* because they offer the fastest method of transferring information to and from the Internet. If you have a home business, a large family, or students — or you telecommute to your office — using broadband can make your life much simpler.

✦ **Quality technical support:** A 24-hour/7-day telephone support line is a godsend for the Internet novice — don't settle for voice support during business hours. Forget e-mail–based support, too; your e-mail application will be dead and gone if your Internet connection gives you problems. (Sound of your palm whacking your forehead.)

✦ **Static IP addresses:** A *static IP address* — the unique number that identifies your computer on the Internet — allows you to set up a professional web server or File Transfer Protocol (FTP) server. (More on these adventures later in Book VIII, Chapter 4.) Most ISPs charge an additional amount for a static IP address, so it's not really a good idea for a typical Mac owner at home. Suffice it to say, however, that a business or commercial organization running a web server or FTP server will benefit from a static IP address.

✦ **E-mail accounts:** Investigate how many individual accounts you receive with various ISPs. Also, find out whether you can maintain them yourself through a web site. If so, that's a good sign. Additionally, if the prospective ISP provides a web site where you can read and send e-mail messages, you can stay on top of your e-mail even while you're on the road or vacationing halfway across the globe.

✦ **Local calling rates:** If you live in a rural area and you're using a dial-up modem, check to make sure that all prospective ISPs offer local calling rates. Believe me, no matter how much fun and how useful the Internet is, it's not worth hours of long-distance charges. (Oh, and don't forget to make sure that your ISP has local access numbers in the cities that you visit regularly.) If your Mac doesn't have an internal modem, you can always add an external USB modem for dial-up Internet access and faxing.

✦ **Web space:** If you want your ISP to host your web site, this is a no-brainer: The more space you get, the better. A minimum of 1GB is acceptable, but most ISPs provide 3GB or more these days. Also, beware of ISPs that charge you for your web site if it receives a large amount of traffic: It can be expensive to host a popular web site if you join one of these ISPs.

✦ **Domain name service:** Finally, the better class of ISP also offers a *domain name service,* which allows you to register something like `your namehere.com`. For the most professional appearance, you can usually pay a yearly fee, and the ISP takes care of all the details in setting up your own .com or .org domain name.

Locating an ISP is easy in the modern, Internet-savvy world. In the order that you should try them, here are the tricks that I recommend for finding your local ISPs:

✦ **Check with your cable or telephone companies.** If you're already subscribing to cable service in your area, you're likely to be a candidate for cable Internet access. Also, many local phone companies offer DSL access, but that access area is often limited to certain locations. Call the customer service numbers for these companies and check out what they offer — and don't forget that a broadband cable or DSL connection is always more expensive than an old-fashioned, dial-up connection. ("Maude, did you see the Internet bill this month?")

✦ **Get recommendations from friends and neighbors.** Folks love to give free advice. Ask them how much they're paying, how reliable the connection has been, and how well they rate the ISP's technical support.

✦ **Check your phone directory.** Check the phone book for Internet service.

✦ **Investigate ISP web sites.** If you have Internet access at work, a friend's house, or your local public library, you can surf to The List (`www.the list.com`), where you can search for ISPs within your area code and location.

Investigating Various Types of Connections

Consider the types of connections that are available under Lion to link your Mac to an ISP (see the previous section for more about ISPs). You can choose among five pathways to digital freedom:

✦ **A dial-up connection:** Old-fashioned, yes. Slow as an arthritic burro, indeed. However, an *analog* (or telephone modem) connection is still a very viable method for reaching the Internet for most computer owners.

It's the cheapest method available, and all you need for this type of connection is a standard telephone jack and a modem. Apple used to include a modem with every computer, but no longer . . . these days, you'll have to buy an external USB modem to make the dial-up connection. (Apple makes one, or any Mac OS X–compatible USB modem will work fine.)

✦ **A broadband connection:** Be it through DSL (which uses a typical telephone line) or cable (which uses your cable TV wiring), broadband Internet access is many times faster than a dial-up connection. Plus, both these technologies are *always on,* meaning that your computer is automatically connected to the Internet when you turn it on and that connection stays active. With DSL or cable, no squeaky whine accompanies your modem while it makes a connection each time you want to check your movie listings web site. Both DSL and cable require a special piece of hardware (commonly called a *modem,* but it really isn't); this box is usually thrown in as part of your ISP charge. Broadband connections usually require a professional installation, too.

✦ **A cellular connection:** If you own a cell phone, you may already be using the Internet on your phone over a 3G or 4G connection. That same type of Internet connection is available for your desktop or laptop Mac from the major cellular providers. Sure, it's pricey compared to a typical broadband connection, but if you're a road warrior with a laptop — or if, for some reason, you can't get cable or DSL service in your area — then cellular Internet may be the option for you.

✦ **A satellite connection:** If you're *really* out there — miles and miles away from any cable or DSL phone service, and even out of the range of a 3G/4G cellular network — you can still get high-speed Internet access. The price for a satellite connection is usually much steeper than a standard DSL or cable connection, but it's available anywhere you can plant your antenna dish with a clear view of the sky. Plus, a satellite connection is actually faster than other types of broadband access. Older satellite technologies required you to also use a dial-up connection — and the antenna could only receive, not send — but most ISPs that can handle satellite connections now offer satellite systems that both send and receive through the dish.

✦ **A network connection:** The last type of connection concerns those Macs that are part of a local area network (LAN) either at the office or in your home. If your Mac is connected to a LAN that already has Internet access, you don't need an ISP at all, and no other hardware is required: Simply contact your network administrator, buy that important person a steak dinner, and ask to be connected to the Internet. On the other hand, if your network currently has no Internet access, you're back to Square One: You'll need one of the previous three types of connections.

After you connect one of your computers on your network to the Internet, you can use an Internet sharing device to allow all the computers to share that Internet connection. Book VI, Chapter 4 goes into all the details on sharing an Internet connection on a network.

Setting Up Your Internet Connection

Okay, so you sign up for Internet access, and your ISP sends you a sheet of paper covered with indecipherable stuff that looks like Egyptian hieroglyphics. Don't worry; those are the settings that you need to connect to your ISP. After you get them in Mac OS X, you should be surfing the web like an old pro.

Before you jump into this configuration, make sure that you've configured the Internet Accounts settings within System Preferences, as I discuss in Book II, Chapter 3. That way, you'll already have entered your default e-mail and web settings. You'll also need to be logged in using an Administrator account.

Using an external modem

Follow these steps to set up your Internet connection if you're using an external USB modem:

1. **Click the System Preferences icon in the Dock and choose Network.**

2. **Select External modem from the list at the left side of the pane.**

3. **Enter the settings for the type of connection that your ISP provides:**

   - *If your ISP tells you to use PPP (Point-to-Point Protocol):* Click the Configure IPv4 pop-up menu and choose Using PPP. If your ISP provided you with DNS Server or Search Domain addresses, type them now in the corresponding boxes.

   - *If you're using AOL:* Click the Configure IPv4 pop-up menu and choose AOL Dialup. If AOL provided you with DNS Server or Search Domain addresses, click in the corresponding box and type them now.

   - *If you're using a manual connection:* Click the Configure IPv4 pop-up menu and choose Manually. Then click in the IP Address, DNS Servers, and Search Domains fields and enter the respective settings provided by your ISP.

4. **If you need to enter PPP settings, click the Advanced button.**

5. **In their respective fields, enter the account name, password, telephone number, and (optionally) the service provider name and an alternative telephone number provided by your ISP.**

I always like Mac OS X to connect automatically when I'm using a modem. I hate excess mouse movements, which usually lead to a bad case of Rodent Elbow. To automate your dial-up connection (allowing Lion to call your ISP whenever your system needs the Internet), click the Connect Automatically When Needed check box to enable it.

6. **Press ⌘+Q to exit System Preferences and save your changes.**

Using Ethernet hardware

Follow these steps to set up your Internet connection if you're using a network, cable modem, or DSL connection:

1. **Click the System Preferences icon in the Dock and choose Network.**

2. **Select Ethernet from the list on the left of the pane to display the settings that you see in Figure 1-1.**

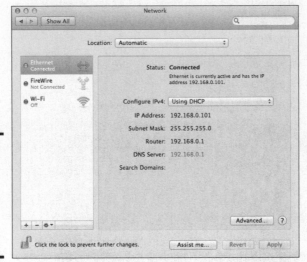

Figure 1-1: The Network settings for an Ethernet Internet connection.

3. **Enter the settings for the type of connection that your ISP provides:**

   • *If your ISP tells you to use Dynamic Host Configuration Protocol (DHCP):* Choose Using DHCP from the Configure IPv4 pop-up menu, and your ISP can automatically set up virtually all the TCP/IP settings for you! (No wonder DHCP is so popular these days.)

   • *If you won't be using DHCP:* Choose Manually from the Configure IPv4 pop-up menu. Then enter the settings provided by your ISP in the IP Address, Subnet Mask, Router, and DNS Servers fields.

4. **If your ISP uses PPPoE (Point-to-Point Protocol over Ethernet), click the Configure IPv4 pop-up menu and choose Create PPPoE Service.**

   a. Type an identifying name for the PPPoE service.

   b. Click Done.

   c. Enter the password for your PPPoE connection.

5. **Press ⌘+Q to exit System Preferences and save your changes.**

Lion can get down-and-dirty in the configuration trenches as well! To launch a wizard to help with the configuration process, click the Assist Me button and then click Assistant on the wizard's welcome screen.

Chapter 2: Using Apple Mail

In This Chapter

✔ **Adding and configuring Mail accounts**

✔ **Receiving, reading, and sending e-mail**

✔ **Filtering junk mail**

✔ **Opening attachments**

✔ **Configuring and automating Apple Mail**

Okay, how many of you can function without e-mail? Raise your hands. Anyone? Anyone at all?

I suppose that I *can* function without my Internet e-mail, but why should I? Mac OS X includes a very capable and reliable e-mail client, *Apple Mail* (affectionately called *Mail* by everyone but Bill Gates).

In this chapter, I discuss the features of Apple Mail and show you how everything hums at a perfect C pitch. However, you have to sing out, "You've got mail!" yourself. Personally, I think that's a plus, but I show you how you can add any sound you like.

Know Thy Mail Window

To begin our epic e-mail journey, click the Mail icon in the Dock. Don't worry if your display doesn't look just like Figure 2-1, which illustrates the Mail window after I've added an account — which I demonstrate in a page or two. What you'll see depends on whether you're installing a fresh copy of Lion or upgrading from an earlier version of Mac OS X, and whether or not you provided e-mail account information within the Setup Assistant.

Besides the familiar toolbar, which naturally carries buttons specific to Mail, you find the following:

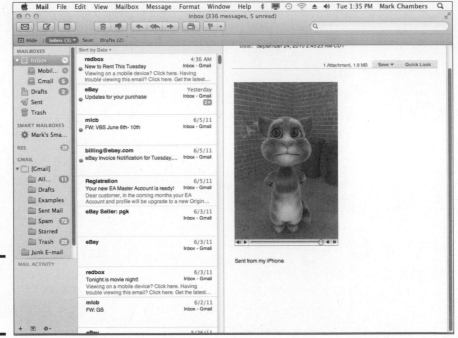

Figure 2-1:
The Apple
Mail
window.

+ **Title bar:** This heading at the top of the Mail window displays information about the current folder — typically, how many messages it contains, but other data can be included as well.

TIP

Like many other Mac OS X Lion applications, you can switch Mail to a full-screen display (which hides the title bar, window controls and menu bar). To switch to full-screen, click View➪Enter Full Screen, or click the full-screen button at the top right corner of the Mail window. If you need to use a menu command, move your mouse cursor to the top of the screen and the menu bar will temporarily reappear. To return Mail to a windowed display, display the menu bar and click View➪Exit Full Screen.

+ **Toolbar:** Yep, Mail has a high-powered, convenient-as-all-get-out toolbar of its own — and you can customize the Mail toolbar just like a Finder window toolbar! (Book II, Chapter 1 describes the process.) Click View➪Customize Toolbar, and sit back in awe of the range of menu items and features that you can activate with just one click.

If you don't use the toolbar and you'd like to reclaim the space it takes in your Mail window, click View➪Hide Toolbar, or right-click the toolbar and choose Hide Toolbar. For a "lite" version of the toolbar that takes less space, right-click the toolbar and choose Text Only.

✦ **Message list:** This resizable scrolling list box contains all the messages for the folder that you've chosen. To resize the list larger or smaller, drag the handle on the bar that runs across the window. You can also resize the columns in the list by dragging the edges of the column heading buttons.

TIP

To specify which columns appear in the message list, choose View⇨ Message Attributes. From the submenu that appears, you can toggle the display of specific columns. You can also sort the messages in the message list from the View menu; by default, messages are sorted by the Date Received. (Alternatively, use Lazy Mark's method: Just click the column that you want to sort by. To reverse the sort order, click the column again.)

✦ **Mailboxes:** The pane at the left of the main Mail window is the Mailboxes list. You can click any of the folders to switch the display in the message list. The Mailbox list can be hidden or shown from the View menu by clicking the Show Mailboxes List item, or you can press the ⌘+Shift+M keyboard shortcut to hide or show it — there's even a Hide/Show button at the top left corner of the Mailbox list! To widen or narrow the Mailboxes list, click the divider at the right side of the list. Your mouse cursor turns to a line with double arrows — and drag it in the desired direction.

✦ **Preview pane:** This resizable scrolling pane displays the contents of the selected message, including both text and any graphics or attachments that Mail recognizes.

Mail uses the following folders (some of which appear only at certain times):

✦ **Inbox:** Mail you've received already.

✦ **Outbox:** Messages that Mail is waiting to send.

✦ **Drafts:** Draft messages waiting to be completed.

✦ **Sent:** Mail you've sent already.

✦ **Trash:** Deleted mail. As with the Trash in the Dock, you can open this folder and retrieve items that you realize you still need. Alternatively, you can empty the contents of the Trash at any time by pressing the ⌘+K shortcut or by choosing Mailbox⇨Erase Deleted Messages.

✦ **Junk:** Junk mail. You can review these messages or retrieve anything you want to keep by choosing Message⇨Move To. After you're sure nothing of value is left, you can delete the remaining messages straight to the Trash. (Junk mail filtering must be enabled from the Junk Mail settings in Preferences before you see this box.)

✦ **RSS:** Messages from an RSS news feed that you've subscribed to. You find out more on RSS later in this chapter.

✦ **Notes:** This folder displays notes that you've made, like those all-important reminders about washing the car, paying taxes, and picking up dog food on the way home. I discuss how to create a new note later in this chapter.

What's a smart mailbox?

Remember the smart folders you can create in the Finder? Well, Apple Mail provides something similar for your e-mail messages: the *smart mailbox.* The contents of a smart mailbox are actually links to messages in your Mail folders; these links match the search criteria you specify, such as messages from a specific address or those that contain attachments. Other criteria include the date an item is received, the subject of a message, the mailbox a message is stored in, and so on. You can use smart mailboxes to organize your messages in different ways and identify those messages that require special (or **immediate!**) attention.

To set up a smart mailbox, choose Mailbox⇨ New Smart Mailbox, or click the Add button (which carries a plus sign) at the lower-left corner of the Mail window and choose New Smart Mailbox from the pop-up menu. Type a name to identify the mailbox and then click the Match pop-up menu to specify whether the search should match any one or all of your criteria. Now you can click the pop-up menus to specify what the search should find. To add a new criterion line, click the button with the plus sign. (To delete a criterion line that Should Not Be, click the button with the minus sign next to the offending line.) Note that you can also include messages from Mail's Trash and Sent folders. When you're ready, click OK, and the new smart mailbox appears in the Mailboxes list. It has a cool folder icon with a gear symbol, much like the gear symbol sported by smart folders in a Finder window.

If you've set up your smart folder, it automatically maintains itself when you receive, send, and delete messages, always showing whatever matches your criteria. Here's a mind-boggler: Imagine what Ben Franklin could've done if he'd been able to use smart folders!

You can add new personal folders to the Mailbox list to further organize your messages. Choose Mailbox⇨New Mailbox, or click the Add button (which bears a plus sign) at the bottom of the Mailboxes list. Choose a location where the mailbox will appear in the list (for example, within the On My Mac section) and then type the name for your new folder in the Name box. Click OK to create the new personal folder.

Messages can be dragged from the message list and dropped into the desired folder in the Mailbox list to transfer them. Alternatively, you can move 'em from the Message list by selecting the messages that you want to move, choosing Message⇨Move To, and then clicking the desired destination folder. (You can also automate the transfer of messages from folder to folder using Rules, which I'll cover later in the chapter.)

Also note that Spotlight has staked its claim with the Search box at the upper right in the Mail toolbar.

Setting Up Your Account

By default, Mail includes one (or more) of these accounts when you first run it:

✦ **The account that you entered when you first installed Mac OS X:** Go to the beginning — literally, Book I, Chapter 1 — to read about the Setup Assistant that I discuss at the beginning of this book. If you entered the information for an e-mail account, it's available.

✦ **Your MobileMe account:** If you registered for a MobileMe service account, it's included.

✦ **Upgraded accounts:** If you upgraded an existing Mac OS system, your existing Mail accounts are added to the Accounts list in Mail.

Speaking of the Accounts list, choose Mail➪Preferences and click the Accounts button to display the Accounts pane that you see in Figure 2-2. From here, you can add an account, edit an existing account, or remove an account from Mail. Although some folks still have only one e-mail account, you can use a passel of them. For example, you might use one account for your personal e-mail and one account for your business communications. To switch accounts, just click the account that you want to use from this list to make it the active account.

Figure 2-2:
The Accounts list, where all is made clear (about your e-mail accounts).

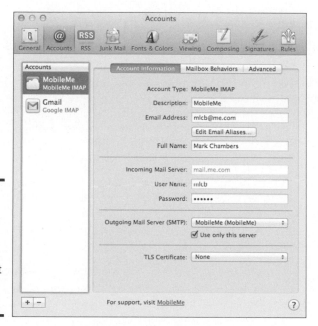

Adding an account

To add a new account within Mail, choose File⇨Add Account to open an Accounts assistant that leads you through the process. 'Nuff said.

However, I'm a manual kind of guy — at least, that's what I'm told — so I should describe the process. For our demonstration, I'll add a typical ISP POP account from the Preferences dialog, which displays the same Accounts assistant.

Open the Preferences dialog by clicking Mail and choosing Preferences; click the Accounts button on the Preferences toolbar. Follow these steps:

1. **Click the Add button at the bottom-left corner of the window, which carries a plus sign.**

2. **On the General Information pane, type your full name in the Full Name field — or, if this is to be an anonymous account, enter whatever you like as your identity — and then press Tab.**

Messages that you send appear with this name in the From field in the recipient's e-mail application.

3. **Type the e-mail address assigned to you by your ISP, and then press Tab.**

4. **In the Password field, type the password supplied by your ISP for login to your e-mail account.**

5. **Click Continue — or, if Mail can automatically set up the account, click Create.**

Yes, you read right: If Mail recognizes the type of account you're using, the assistant may offer to automatically complete all the required settings for you! (If the account is recognized, Mail displays the Account Summary pane with the configuration data it automatically entered. Smile proudly and click Create, and you're done. Sit back and watch as Mail downloads the existing messages.) If your account isn't recognized by Mail, it's no big deal — just continue with Step 6.

6. **Click the Account Type pop-up menu and choose the protocol type to use for the account.**

You can select an Apple MobileMe account, a Post Office Protocol (POP) account, a Microsoft Exchange account, an Internet Message Access Protocol (IMAP) account, or a standard Microsoft Exchange IMAP account. If you're adding an account from an Internet service provider (ISP), refer to the setup information that you received to determine which is right. Most ISP accounts are POP accounts.

When you select an Account Type, the fields may change on the Accounts assistant, but they'll still follow the same general order I give in this POP account demonstration. (In fact, there are fewer fields to fill out for IMAP accounts!) Keep the account information provided by your ISP handy because that data should include everything covered in the assistant.

7. In the Description field, name the account to identify it within Mail and then press Tab to move to the next field.

For example, *Work* and *Mom's ISP* are good choices.

8. In the Incoming Mail Server text box, type the incoming mail server address supplied by your ISP.

If your ISP requires a login for security, you need to enter your server username and password.

9. Click Continue.

10. On the Incoming Mail Security sheet, click the Authentication pop-up menu and choose the authentication scheme used by your incoming mail server.

Unless you're told differently by your ISP, the default choice — Password — is very likely correct already. Don't enable the Use Secure Sockets Layer (SSL) check box unless specifically instructed to do so by your ISP.

11. Click Continue.

12. On the Outgoing Mail Server sheet, type a description for the server and press Tab.

I typically enter the ISP name.

13. In the Outgoing Mail Server text box, type the outgoing mail server address supplied by your ISP.

14. If your ISP requires your e-mail application to authenticate the connection, select the Use Authentication check box and type the username and password supplied by your ISP into the corresponding fields.

15. Click Continue.

16. Click Continue on the Account Summary sheet.

17. Click Create on the Conclusion sheet.

You're done! The new account appears in the Accounts list.

You can specify advanced settings for an account. I cover those in the section "Fine-Tuning Your Post Office," later in this chapter.

When you add a new account within Mail — either automatically or manually — that account will also appear within the Mail, Contacts & Calendars pane within the System Preferences window.

Editing an existing account

Need to make changes to an existing account? Choose Mail⇨Preferences and click the account that you want to change. Mail displays the same settings that I explain in the preceding section.

Deleting an account

If you change ISPs or you decide to drop an e-mail account, you can remove it from your Accounts list. Otherwise, Mail can annoy you with error messages when it can no longer connect to the server for that account. Display the Mail Preferences dialog, select the account that you want to delete, and then click the Remove button (which is graced by a minus sign).

Naturally, Mail requests confirmation before deleting the folders associated with that account. Click Remove to verify the deletion or click the Cancel button to prevent accidental catastrophe.

Receiving and Reading E-Mail Wisdom

The heart and soul of Mail — well, at least the heart, anyway — is receiving and reading stuff from your friends and family. (Later in this chapter, I show you how to avoid the stuff you get promising free prizes, low mortgage rates, and improved . . . um, performance. This is a family-oriented book, so that's enough of that.)

After you set up an account (or select an account from the Accounts list), it's time to check for mail. Use any of these methods to check for new mail:

✦ **Click the Get Mail button on the toolbar, which bears an envelope icon.**

✦ **Choose Mailbox⇨Get All New Mail or press ⌘+Shift+N.**

✦ **Choose Mailbox⇨Get New Mail and then choose the specific account to check from the submenu.**

This is a great way to check for new mail in another account without going through the trouble of making it active in the Preferences window.

Mail can also check for new messages automatically; you can find more on this topic in the "Checking Mail automatically" section, later in this chapter.

If you do have new mail in the active account, it appears in the Message list. As you can see in Figure 2-3, new unread messages appear marked with a snazzy blue dot in the first column. The number of unread messages is displayed next to the Inbox folder icon in the Mailboxes list.

Mail also displays the number of new messages that you've received on its Dock icon. If you've hidden the Mail window or sent it to the Dock, you can perform a quick visual check for new mail just by glancing at the Dock.

Reading and deleting your messages

To read any message in the message list, you can either click the desired entry (which displays the contents of the message in the preview pane), or you can double-click the entry to open the message in a separate message window, complete with its own toolbar controls.

To quickly scan your mail, click the first message that you want to view in the message list and then press the down-arrow key when you're ready to move to the next message. Mail displays the content of each message in the preview pane. To display the previous message in the list, press the up-arrow key.

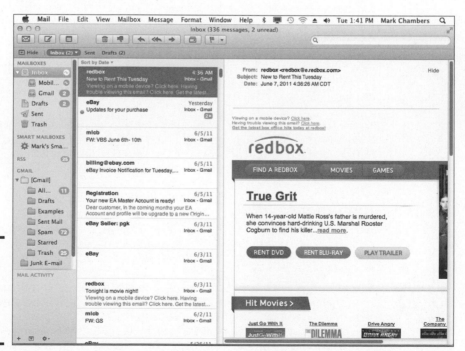

Figure 2-3:
A new
message
to read. Oh,
joy, and no
spam!

Displaying all Mail headers

Mail actually hides the majority of the heading lines that help identify and route an e-mail message to its rightful destination. By default, all you'll see is the *filtered heading,* which includes only the From, Date, To, and Subject fields. This is great unless, for some reason, you need to display the entire message header in all its arcane madness. If you do, press ⌘+Shift+H. You can toggle back to the filtered heading by pressing the same shortcut.

Mail also allows you to read your messages grouped within conversations (typically called *threads* within other e-mail applications). A *conversation* contains an original message and all related replies, which makes it easy to follow the flow of an e-mail discussion (without bouncing around within your Inbox, searching for the next message in the conversation). Conversations are indicated in the Message list by numbers at the right side of the original message, indicating how many messages are included. Choose View⇨Organize by Conversation, and the replies in the current folder are all grouped under the original messages and sorted by date. To expand a thread, click the original message to select it; then press the right-arrow key (or choose View⇨Expand All Conversations). To collapse a thread, select the original message and press the left-arrow key (or choose View⇨Collapse All Conversations).

Hey, why not let Mail *read* you your mail? (That is, if you can drive and listen to your MacBook speak at the same time!) Simply select one message or a group of messages and then choose Edit⇨Speech⇨Start Speaking. *Wowsers!*

To delete a message from the message list, click the desired entry (or entries, by holding down the ⌘ key) to select them and then click the Delete button on the toolbar (or press the Del key). To delete a message from within a message window, click the Delete button on the toolbar.

Replying to mail

What? Aunt Harriet sent you a message because she's forgotten where she parked her car last night? If you happen to know where her priceless '78 Pinto is, you can reply to her and save her the trouble of retracing her steps.

If Aunt Harriet isn't in your Address Book yet, this is a good time to add her. With the message entry selected in the list, choose Message⇨Add Sender to Address Book or just press the convenient ⌘+Shift+Y keyboard shortcut. The person's name and e-mail address are added automatically to your Address Book. To add more information in the Address Book, however, you have to open that application separately. (Read through Book I, Chapter 6 for the skinny on the Address Book.)

To reply to a message in Mail, follow these steps:

1. **To respond to a message from the message list, click the desired message entry and then click the Reply button on the toolbar (which carries a single left arrow).**

   To respond to a message that you've opened in a message window, click the Reply button on the toolbar for the message window.

   If a message was addressed not just to you but also to a number of different people, you can send your reply to all of them. Instead of clicking the Reply button, click the Reply All button on the Mail window toolbar, which bears two left arrows. (This is a great way to quickly facilitate a festive gathering, if you get my drift.)

   You can also add carbon copies of your message to other new recipients, expanding the party exponentially; more on carbon copies later, in the section "Raise the Little Flag: Sending E-Mail."

   Mail opens the Reply window that you see in Figure 2-4. Note that the address has been added automatically and that the default Subject is Re: *<the original subject>*. Mail automatically adds a separator line in the message body field that reads On *<day><date>at<time>*, *<addressee>* wrote:, followed by the text of the original message; this is done so that the addressee can remember what the heck she wrote in the first place to get you so happy/sad/angry/indifferent. The original text is indented and prefaced by a vertical line to set it apart. If you like, you can click in the Subject line and change the default subject line; otherwise, the cursor is already sitting on the first line of the text box, so you can simply start typing your reply.

   To choose the text from the original message that you want to include in a reply, select the desired text in the original message before you click the Reply button.

2. **After you complete typing your reply, you can select text in the message body and apply different fonts or formats.**

   To change your reply's formatting, click the Format button on the message window toolbar — it's the one with the capital letter A. From the buttons that appear, you can choose the font family, the type size, and formatting (such as italic or bold) for the selected text. You can also apply color to the selected text by clicking the Colors button — the black square — and then clicking anywhere in the color grid that appears to select that color.

   Click the Format button again to hide these controls. (If you like menus, you can also choose Format from the menu and make changes from there.)

   You can also apply color to the selected text. Click the Colors button — the black square — and then click anywhere in the color grid that appears to select that color.

On Jun 7, 2011, at 1:44 PM, Fuad Ramses wrote:

How about some awesome ocean-front property in Kansas? It's all the rage!

Fuad

Figure 2-4:
Replying to
an incoming
e-mail
message.

To create a bulleted list in your reply, click Format⇨Lists and choose either a bulleted or a numbered list. Mail thoughtfully prepares your first bullet item for you. Press Return to add another bullet item. Click outside the bullet formatting to complete the list.

Care to chat directly with the recipients of your message? Just click Message⇨Reply with iChat, and Mail automatically opens iChat and attempts to connect! (Note that this will work only with the recipients who have an instant messaging address in their Address Book card.) This Chat feature also appears on the New Message window toolbar, which I discuss in a page or two.

3. To add an attachment, click the Attach button (with the paper clip icon) on the toolbar.

Mail displays a familiar Open dialog. Navigate to the to-be-attached file, select it, and click the Open button to add it to the message. (More on attachments in the "Attachments on Parade" section, later in this chapter.) If the recipient is running Windows, make sure the Send Windows-Friendly Attachments check box is enabled — this results in a slightly larger e-mail message size but helps ensure that PC e-mail programs, such as Outlook and Outlook Express, can correctly open your attachments.

Hey, what does MIME mean?

First, a note of explanation about Internet e-mail. (Don't worry about notes; you won't be tested on this stuff.) Decades back, Internet e-mail messages were pure text, composed only of ASCII characters — that means no fancy fonts, colors, stationery, or text formatting. However, as more and more folks started using e-mail, the clarion call rang forth across the land for more attractive messages (as well as attachments, which I cover in the section "Attachments on Parade"). Therefore, the MIME encoding standard was developed. In case you're interested, MIME stands for *Multipurpose Internet Mail Extensions* — a rather cool (and surprisingly understandable) acronym.

Originally, virtually all e-mail programs recognized MIME, but then the Tower of Babel principle kicked in, and now there are actually multiple versions of MIME. Apple Mail uses the

most common variant of MIME, so most folks who receive your e-mail can see them in all their glory (even under Windows).

However, if one of your addressees complains that he got a message containing unrecognizable gobbledygook and a heading that mentions MIME, he's using an e-mail client application that either doesn't support MIME or supports a different version. (Of course, that person could have unknowingly turned off MIME support.) You have two possible solutions: You can ask the addressee to double-check whether MIME is enabled on his end in the e-mail application, or you can disable MIME when sending a message to that particular person. When you're composing an original message or a reply, you can use pure text by choosing Format⇨Make Plain Text. (Naturally, this prevents you from doing anything fancy, and files that you attach to a plain-text message might not be delivered correctly.)

Because most folks end up sending photos through e-mail, Apple includes a Photo Browser button on the toolbar. Click this button on the Reply or New Message window toolbars and you can choose a photo from your iPhoto library to insert directly into your message. Heck, you can even take a quick candid shot using Photo Booth! Naturally, your Mac will need an iSight camera (or other compatible video camera) to use the Photo Booth feature.

4. **Choose the message priority.**

   By default, Mail adds a normal priority flag to your e-mail message — however, you can click the Priority icon at the right side of the Reply window toolbar and choose Low or High priority as well. (Note that choosing a different priority won't actually send the message any faster or slower — it merely displays a High or Low priority notification.)

5. **When you're ready to send your reply, you have two options. You can click the Send button (which carries a cool paper airplane icon) to immediately add the message to your Outbox folder or you can click**

the Close button on the Reply window and choose to store it in your Drafts folder for later editing.

After a message is moved to the Outbox folder, it's sent either immediately or at the next connection time that you specify in Mail Preferences (more on this in the section "Checking Mail automatically," later in the chapter). However, saving the message to your Drafts folder doesn't send it. Read the following section for the skinny on how to send a message stored in your Drafts folder.

When you reply to a message, you can also *forward* your reply to another person (instead of the original sender). The new addressee receives a message containing both the text of the original message that you received and your reply. To forward a message, click the Forward button on the Mail toolbar (which bears a right arrow) instead of Reply or Reply to All.

If you don't want to include the text of the original message in a reply, choose Mail➪Preferences. Click the Composing button and disable the Quote the Text of the Original Message check box.

By default, Mail checks your spelling while you type and also underlines any words that it doesn't recognize. (Very Microsoftian.) I personally like this feature, but if you find it irritating, you can turn it off or set Mail to check the spelling just once (when you click Send). Just choose Mail➪Preferences, click Composing, and click the Check Spelling as I Type pop-up menu to choose the desired option.

Raise the Little Flag: Sending E-Mail

To compose and send a new message to someone, follow these steps:

1. **Click the New Message button on the Mail toolbar or choose File➪New Message (or avail yourself of the handy ⌘+N keyboard shortcut).**

   Mail opens the New Message window that you see in Figure 2-5.

2. **Enter the recipient's (To) address by**

   • *Typing it in directly.*

   • *Pasting it in after copying it to the Clipboard.*

   • *Dragging an e-mail address from your Address Book.*

   or

   • *(My favorite) Clicking Window➪Address Panel,* which shows you the scaled-down version of the Address Book (the Addresses panel) that you see in Figure 2-6.

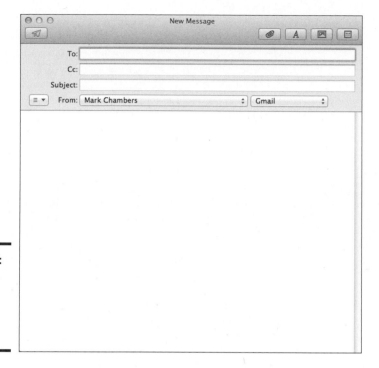

Figure 2-5:
An empty
Mail
message,
waiting to
be filled.

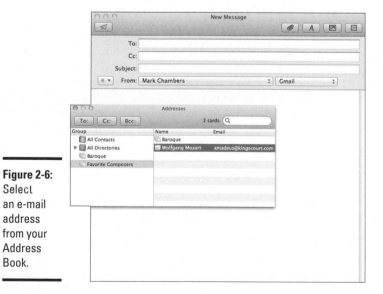

Figure 2-6:
Select
an e-mail
address
from your
Address
Book.

From the Addresses panel, click the address that you want to use and then click the To button. To pick multiple recipients, hold down the ⌘ key while you click the multiple addresses. Click the Close button on the Addresses panel to close it; then, press Tab.

If you have a huge number of entries in your Address Book, use the Search field on the Addresses panel toolbar, which operates just like the Finder window Search box.

3. **When Mail highlights the Cc field (the spot where you can send optional carbon copies of the message to additional recipients), you can type the addresses directly, use the contents of the Clipboard, or display the Addresses panel.**

   If you use the Addresses panel, select the addresses that you want to use and click the Cc button. Then click the Close button on the Addresses panel and press Tab.

Looking for the Blind Carbon Copy (Bcc) field? To display it, choose View⇨Bcc Address Field. (A *blind carbon copy* is a message sent to multiple recipients, just like a regular carbon copy, but the recipients aren't listed when the message is displayed — that way, the other recipients don't know who else got a copy of the message.) You can also click the small Field Display pop-up menu at the left side of the Subject field to toggle the display of the Bcc Address Field. Oh, and there's also a Bcc button on the Addresses panel — go figure.

4. **In the Subject field, enter the subject of the message and then press Tab.**

   Your text cursor now rests in the first line of the message text area — type, my friend, type like the wind! It's considered good form to keep this line short and relatively to the point.

5. **Click the Show Stationery button on the toolbar to display the Stationery strip above the message text box (as shown in Figure 2-7), where you can choose one of many backgrounds that Apple supplies.**

   Stationery isn't required, but it really packs a visual wallop! Double-click a thumbnail in the strip to add it to your message; to display a different category of stationery, such as a Greeting or Invitation, click the category buttons on the left side of the Stationery strip.

This one will really knock your socks off: If you choose a Photo stationery background for your new message, you can even drag an image from the Photo Browser, the iPhoto window, or a Finder window to fill the "placeholder" images on the background. (Which, when you think about it, kind of makes sense . . . after all, why send an e-mail from sunny Italy that has stock photos of a strange couple at the top? Add your own travel shots instead!) Figure 2-7 illustrates a Photo stationery background.

Figure 2-7:
Adding
visual
impact to
my e-mail
message
with a Photo
stationery
background.

Not all e-mail applications on other computers correctly display a message with a stationery background. For the whole scoop, see the "Hey, what does MIME mean?" sidebar, earlier in this chapter. Also, remember that a message with a stationery background is going to be much larger than a simple text message, especially if it contains a number of photos. (And, as you guessed, that also means that it takes longer to send and receive, which is very important for those using a dial-up analog modem connection.)

6. **After you type your message, select any of the text that you've entered and use the toolbar features I describe in the earlier section "Replying to mail" to apply different fonts or formatting.**

    Click the Format button in the message window toolbar to open a button bar of formatting choices. (Click the Format button again to hide the Format bar.) If you like menus, you can also click Format and make changes from there.

7. **To add an attachment, click the Attach button on the toolbar, navigate to the to-be-attached file in the dialog that appears, select the file, and then click Open to add it to the message.**

    Remember, if you'd like to include photos in your message, just click the Photo Browser toolbar button to select images from your iPhoto library, or take a photo with Photo Booth.

8. **When your new message is ready to post, either click the Send button to immediately add the message to your Outbox folder or click the Close button on the New Message window and click Save to store it in your Drafts folder (without actually sending it).**

To send a message held in your Drafts folder, click the Drafts folder in the Mailbox list to display all draft messages. Double-click the message that you want to send, which displays the message window (you can make edits at this point, if you like) and then click the Send button on the message window toolbar.

 If you don't have access to an Internet connection at the moment, Mail allows you to work offline. This way, you can read your unread messages and compose new ones on the road to send later. After you regain your Internet connection, you might need to choose Mailbox➪Online Status (depending on the connection type).

What? You Get Junk Mail, Too?

Spam — it's the Crawling Crud of the Internet, and I hereby send out a lifetime of bad karma to those who spew it. However, chucking the First Amendment is *not* an option, so I guess we'll always have junk mail. (Come to think of it, my paper mailbox is just as full of the stuff.)

Thankfully, Apple Mail has a net that you can cast to collect junk mail before you have to read it. The two methods of handling junk mail are

✦ **Manually:** You can mark any message in the message list as Junk Mail. Select the unwanted flotsam in the message list and then click the Junk button (which carries the very negative "thumbs down" icon) on the Mail window toolbar. Mail marks the message, as shown in Figure 2-8. (Ocean-front property in Kansas . . . yeah, right.) If a message is mistakenly marked as junk but you actually want it, display the message in the preview pane and then click the Not Junk button at the top of the preview pane.

✦ **Automatically:** Apple Mail has a sophisticated Junk Mail filter that you actually train to better recognize what's junk. (Keep reading to discover how.) After you train Mail to recognize spam with a high degree of accuracy, turn it to full Automatic mode, and it moves all those worthless messages to your Junk folder.

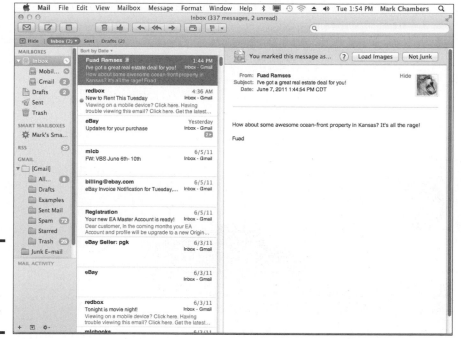

Figure 2-8:
"Be gone,
sludge
demons of
Junk Mail!"

You customize and train the Junk Mail filter from the Preferences dialog
(available from your trusty Mail menu); click Junk Mail to show the settings.
I recommend that you first try Mail in Training mode, using the Mark as Junk
Mail, But Leave It in My Inbox option. Junk Mail then takes its best shot at
determining what's junk. When you receive more mail and mark more messages as junk (or mark them as *not* junk), you're actually teaching the Junk
Mail feature how to winnow the wheat from the chaff. In Training mode, junk
messages aren't actually moved anywhere — they're just marked with a particularly fitting, grungy brown color.

After you're satisfied that the Junk Mail filter is catching just about everything
that it can (and not tagging messages it shouldn't), display the Mail preferences again and choose the Move It to the Junk Mailbox option. Mail creates
a Junk folder and prompts you for permission to move all junk messages to
this folder. After you review everything in the Junk folder, you can delete what
it contains and send it to the Trash folder. To save a message from junkdom,
click the Not Junk button in the preview window and then drag the message
from the Junk folder message list to the desired folder in the Mailbox list.

Finally, you can create a complete set of custom *rules* for your Junk Mail filtering by clicking Perform Custom Actions — the Advanced button displays your Junk Mail rule set and allows you to edit your rules. I explain rules in more depth at the end of this chapter.

If you don't receive a lot of spam — or you want to be absolutely sure that nothing gets labeled as junk until you review it — click the Enable Junk Mail Filtering check box to deselect it. (And good luck.)

By default, Mail exempts certain messages from Junk Mail status based on three criteria: if the sender is in your Address Book, if you've sent the sender a message in the past, or if the message is addressed to you with your full name. To tighten up your Junk Mail filtering to the max, you might want to disable these check boxes as well.

To reset the Junk Mail filter and erase any training that you've done, visit the Junk Mail settings in Preferences again and click Reset. Then click the Yes button to confirm your choice.

Attachments on Parade

Attachments are a fun way to transfer files through e-mail. However, it's imperative that you remember these three very important caveats:

✦ **Attachments can contain viruses.** Even a message attachment that was actually sent by your best friend can contain a virus or malevolent macro — either because your friend unwittingly passed one along or because the virus actually took control of your friend's e-mail application and replicated itself automatically. (Ugh.)

✦ **Corpulent attachments don't make it.** Most corporate and ISP mail servers have a 4–6MB limit for the total size of a message, and the attachments (and any Photo stationery background you might have added) count toward that final message size. Therefore, I recommend sending a file as an attachment only if it's less than 3MB (or perhaps 4MB) in size. If the recipient's e-mail server sends you an automated message saying that the message was refused because it was too big, this is the problem.

✦ **Not all e-mail applications and firewalls accept attachments.** Not all e-mail programs support attachments in the same way, and others are simply set for pure text messages. Some corporate firewalls even reject messages with attachments. If the message recipient gets the message text but not the attachment, these are the likely reasons.

With all that said, it's back to attachments as a beneficial feature. Follow these steps to save an attachment that you receive:

1. **Click the message with an attachment in your message list.**

   Having trouble determining which messages have attachments? Although messages with attachments appear with a tiny paper-clip icon in the Message list, it's sometimes hard to spot them. Click the Sort By pop-up menu button at the top of the Message list and choose Attachments, and Mail places all messages with attachments at the top of the list!

   If Mail recognizes the attachment format, it displays or plays the attachment in the body of the message; if not, the attachment is displayed as a file icon.

2. **To open an attachment that's displayed as a file icon, click the file icon and then choose Open Attachment from the pop-up menu that appears.**

   If you know what application should be used to open the attachment, click the Open With button and choose the correct application from the submenu that appears.

3. **To save an attachment, right-click the attachment (however it appears in the message) and then choose Save Attachment from the pop-up menu.**

   In the Save dialog that appears, navigate to the location where you want to save the file and then click Save.

Fine-Tuning Your Post Office

As is all other Apple software, Mail is easily customized to your liking. In this section, I discuss some of the preferences that you might want to change.

Adding sound

To choose a sound that plays whenever you receive new mail, choose Mail⇨Preferences and click the General button. Either click the New Messages Sound pop-up menu and choose one of the sounds that Apple provides or choose Add/Remove from the pop-up menu to choose a sound file from the Sounds folder. (You can also add a sound to your Sound folder from this sheet.) Choose None from the New Messages Sound pop-up menu to disable the new mail sound altogether.

Checking Mail automatically

By default, Mail automatically checks for new mail (and sends any mail in your Outbox folder) every five minutes. To change this delay period, display the General pane in the Preferences dialog, choose the Check for New Messages pop-up menu, and then choose one of the time periods. To disable automatic mail checking, choose Manually; you can click the Get Mail toolbar button to manually check your mail any time you like. (For example, those folks using dial-up analog modem connections may not fancy Mail taking control of the telephone line every five minutes.)

Automating junk mail and message deletion

If you like, Mail can be set to automatically delete sent mail and Junk messages (as well as permanently erase messages that you relegate to the Trash). To configure these settings, display the Accounts pane in the Preferences window, click the desired account, and then click the Mailbox Behaviors tab.

To delete Sent messages automatically, click the Delete Sent Messages When pop-up menu and choose the delay period or action. You can choose to delete mail after a day, a week, a month, or immediately upon quitting Mail. Alternatively, you can leave this field set to Never, and Mail never automatically deletes any messages from the Sent folder.

To delete Junk messages automatically, click the Delete Junk Messages When pop-up menu and choose the delay period or action. (They're the same as the options available for Sent mail.)

To delete messages from the Trash, click the Permanently Erase Deleted Messages When pop-up menu and choose the delay period or action — again, the choices are the same as those for Sent messages.

Adding signatures

To add a block of text or a graphic to the bottom of your messages as your personal signature, follow these steps:

1. **Choose Mail⇨Preferences and click the Signatures button.**

2. **From the Signatures pane that appears, click the Add Signature button (which carries a plus sign).**

3. **Type an identifying name.**

   Press Return to save the new name.

4. **Click inside the text entry box at the right to move the cursor.**

5. **Type the signature itself in the text entry box or copy the signature to the Clipboard and paste it into the text entry box.**

It's considered good "netiquette" to keep your signature to 3 lines.

Because downloading a graphic in a signature takes longer — and because some folks still use plain-text e-mail — avoid the temptation to include graphics in your signature. If you do use them, remember that a graphic used as a signature may be handled as an attachment by the recipient's e-mail application!

6. **If you have multiple signatures, click the Choose Signature pop-up menu to choose which one you want to use or to use them all randomly or in sequence.**

If you prefer the signature to appear above the quoted text in a reply, select the Place Signature above Quoted Text check box.

Changing the status of an account

Sometimes you can't reach one of your accounts. For example, maybe you're on the road with your laptop and you can't access your office network. Apple Mail allows you to enable and disable specific accounts without the hassle of deleting an account and then having to add it again.

To disable or enable an account, open the Preferences dialog, click the Accounts button, click the desired account, click the Advanced tab, and then select (or deselect) the Enable This Account check box as necessary.

If you disable an account, you should also deselect the Include When Automatically Checking for New Mail check box to make sure that Mail doesn't display an error message. You can always check any account for new mail by choosing Mailbox⇨Get New Mail and then choosing the desired account name from the submenu.

Automating Your Mail with Rules

Before I leave the beautiful shores of Mail Island, I'd be remiss if I didn't discuss one of its most powerful features: the ability to create *rules,* which are automated actions that Mail can take. With rules, you can specify criteria that can perform actions such as

✦ Transferring messages from one folder to another

✦ Forwarding messages to another address

✦ Highlighting or deleting messages

To set up a rule, follow these steps:

1. **Choose Mail⇨Preferences and then click the Rules button on the toolbar.**

   Mail displays the Rules pane.

2. **To duplicate an existing rule, highlight it in the list and then click the Duplicate button. (For this demonstration, however, create a rule from scratch by clicking the Add Rule button.)**

3. **In the Description field, type a descriptive name for the new rule and then press Tab to move to the next field.**

4. **Click the If pop-up menu to specify whether the rule is triggered if any of the conditions are met or if all conditions must be met.**

5. **Because each rule requires at least one condition, click the Target pop-up menus to set the target for the condition.**

   These include whom the message is from or to, which account received the message, whether the message is marked as junk, and whether the message contains certain content. Select the target for the condition.

6. **Click the Criteria pop-up menu to choose the rule's criteria.**

   The contents of this pop-up menu change depending on the condition's target. For example, if you choose From as the target, the criteria include Contains, Does Not Contain, Begins With, and so forth.

7. **Click in the expression box and type the text to use for the condition.**

   For example, a completed condition might read

   ```
   Subject Contains Ocean-Front
   ```

   This particular condition is true if I get an e-mail message with a subject that contains the string Ocean-Front.

8. **Add more conditions by clicking the plus sign button at the right of the first condition.**

   To remove any condition from this rule, click the minus sign button next to it. Remember, however, that every rule needs at least one condition.

9. **To specify what action is taken after the condition (or conditions) is met, click the first Perform the Following Actions pop-up menu to see the action that this rule should perform. Then click the second pop-up menu and select the action for the rule.**

   Choices include transferring a message from one folder to another, playing a sound, automatically forwarding the message, deleting it, and marking it as read.

   Each rule requires at least one action.

10. **Depending on the action that you select, specify one or more criteria for the action.**

For instance, if I select Set Color as my action, I must then choose whether to color the text or the background as well as what color to use.

As with the plus button next to the conditions, you can also click the plus button next to the first action to perform more than one action. To remove an action, click the minus button next to it.

11. **When the rule is complete, click OK to save it.**

Here's an example of a complex rule:

If the message was sent by someone in my Address Book *and* the Subject field contains the text FORWARD ME, forward the message to the e-mail address fuadramses@me.com.

This is a good example of an automated forwarding rule. With this rule in place and Mail running on Mac OS X, any of my friends, family, or co-workers can forward urgent e-mail to my MobileMe account while I'm on vacation. To trigger the rule, all the sender has to do is include the words FORWARD ME in the message subject. And if the sender isn't in my Address Book, the rule doesn't trigger, and I can read the message when I get home. Mondo *sassy*.

Each rule in the Rules dialog can be enabled or disabled by toggling the Active check box next to the rule in the Rules pane. You can also edit a rule by selecting it in the Rules pane and then clicking the Edit button. To delete a rule completely from the list, select it and then click the Remove button; Mail prompts you for confirmation before the deed is done.

If you decide to create a custom Junk mail processing rule, the process is the same, but you get to it from a different place. Click the Junk Mail button on the Preferences dialog toolbar and click the Perform Custom Actions radio button to select it. You see that the Advanced button is now enabled — click it and you can set up the custom Junk mail rules that handle stuff from any conceivable junk mail source!

Chapter 3: Staying in Touch with iChat and FaceTime

In This Chapter

✔ **Setting up iChat**

✔ **Changing modes in iChat**

✔ **Adding Buddies**

✔ **Inviting a Buddy to chat**

✔ **Sending and receiving files via iChat**

✔ **Sharing screens with another person**

✔ **Ignoring those who deserve to be shunned**

✔ **Adding visual pizzazz with video backgrounds and effects**

✔ **Chatting face-to-face with FaceTime**

*T*hroughout humankind's history, our drive has been toward communication — from the earliest cave paintings, through written language, to the telegraph, telephone, and cell phone all-in-one PDA that the guy in the SUV in front of you is using . . . and he's arguing with someone and he's not paying attention and . . . (whump).

So much for the scholarly introduction — anyway, forget that silly cellular phone and your complicated calling plan! As long as you have Mac OS X and an Internet connection, you can instantly chat with your friends and family whether they're across the aisle in another cube or halfway across the world. And, by golly, if you both have an iSight camera, Mac-compatible web camera, or digital video (DV) camcorder connected to your computers, you'll *see* each other in glorious, full-color video! These modern marvels are *iChat* and *FaceTime*, and they fulfill the decades-old promise of the video telephone quite well, thank you.

In this chapter, I show you how to gab with the following folks:

✦ Others who use iChat (either on your local network or on the Internet)

✦ Mac, iPhone 4, and iPad 2 owners with FaceTime-compatible hardware

✦ Anyone who uses AIM — that's short for *America Online (AOL) Instant Messaging* — MobileMe, Jabber, Yahoo!, or Google Talk

✦ Folks who participate in AOL chat rooms

Configuring iChat

The first time you run iChat (by clicking the iChat icon in your Applications folder or on Launchpad), you're prompted to create an iChat account.

By default, iChat uses the MobileMe (or me.com) account that you set up when you first installed Mac OS X. Type your MobileMe name and password, and you're good to go. However, if you're already using AIM, Jabber, Yahoo!, or Google Talk and you want to use your existing account, click the Account Type pop-up menu and choose the correct type; then enter your existing account name and password instead.

Alternately, select the type of account you want and click the Get an iChat Account button — iChat launches Safari and whisks you to the web page where you can sign up for that type of account.

You can also choose to set up Bonjour messaging. Think of *Bonjour* as plug-and-play for your local network. In iChat, Bonjour allows you to see (and yak with) anyone on your local network without having to know his iChat name. That's because Bonjour automatically announces all the iChat users who are available on your network. If you have others using iChat, Jabber, Yahoo!, or AIM on your local network, go for this option; if you're not connected to a local network, however, Bonjour messaging isn't necessary. Also, if you're on a public AirPort/AirPort Extreme network or if you're connecting to the Internet with an external modem through dial-up, I recommend disabling Bonjour messaging. (For all that's cool about AirPort Extreme, see Book VI, Chapter 3.) To turn on Bonjour messaging, click iChat⇨Preferences and click the Accounts tab, click the Bonjour account to select it, and then click the Enable Bonjour Instant Messaging check box.

After you finish these configuration necessities, iChat displays the Buddy List window that you see in Figure 3-1.

A few things to note here about the Buddy List window:

✦ **If you don't like your picture, don't panic.** By default, iChat uses your user account thumbnail image as your visual persona. However, you can add a picture to your iChat iDentity — sorry, I couldn't resist that — by dragging an image to the well next to your name at the top of the Buddy List window. If necessary, iChat asks you to position and size the image so that it fits in the (admittedly limited) space. This picture is then sent along with your words when you chat. In the figures for this chapter, I borrow the smiling face of Wolfgang Amadeus Mozart.

Click your image to display your recent thumbnails. This way, you can even use a different thumbnail image for each of your many moods. (Geez.) Also, you can click Edit Picture from the pop-up menu and capture a new thumbnail with your iSight camera.

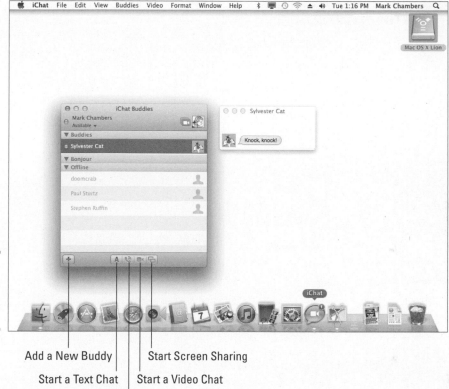

Figure 3-1:
iChat instant messaging at its finest!

Add a New Buddy

Start a Text Chat

Start an Audio Chat

Start Screen Sharing

Start a Video Chat

✦ **Check out the buttons along the bottom of the Buddy List window.** In order, these buttons are

- *Add a New Buddy* (which I cover in the following section)

- *Start a Text Chat* (plain, old-fashioned chatting via the keyboard)

- *Start an Audio Chat* (chatting with your voice, using microphones)

- *Start a Video Chat* (the ultimate chat, where the parties can both see and hear each other)

- *Start Screen Sharing* (where you can view — or even remotely control — a Buddy's computer)

Using these buttons can handle about 90 percent of the commands that you need to give while using iChat, so use 'em!

✦ **Hey, look, there's an iChat menu bar icon!** When you're running iChat, you can choose to add a balloon menu bar icon in the upper-right corner of your screen. Click it to display the options that you see in Figure 3-2.

You can change your online/offline status, immediately invite a Buddy for a chat, or display the Buddy list (which I discuss later in the section, "Will You Be My Buddy?"). The menu bar icon appears only if you select the Show Status in Menu Bar check box. Click iChat in the menu and choose Preferences; then click the General button in the Preference dialog.

Figure 3-2:
The iChat Finder menu icon leaps into action.

Changing Modes in iChat

To launch iChat, click the LaunchPad icon in the Dock and click the iChat icon (or launch it from your Applications folder). Or, you can click its menu bar icon, which is grayed out when you're offline. If you're not already familiar with the terms *online* and *offline,* here's the scoop: When you're *online,* folks can invite you to chat and communicate with you. When you're *offline,* you're disconnected: iChat isn't active, you can't be paged, and you can't chat.

Even when you're offline, you can choose Available from the friendly balloon Finder menu bar icon, which automatically switches iChat to online mode. Or you can click a Buddy name directly, which automatically switches iChat to online mode and opens the paging window for that Buddy. (Naturally, you have to have the proper network or Internet connection first.)

You can use another mode, *Away,* whenever iChat is running and you're still online but not available. For example, if I'm away from my Mac for a few minutes, I leave iChat running, but I switch myself to Away mode. My Buddies get a message saying that I'm Away, so they won't bother trying to contact me. When I return to my computer, I simply move my mouse, and iChat intelligently inquires as to whether I'd like to return to Available mode. You can also use the menu bar icon to switch from Away to Available (or my other favorite mode, *Twiddling My Thumbs*). Refer to Figure 3-2 to see these choices.

iChat can even display which iTunes song you're listening to at the moment. Pick Current iTunes Song from the menu and impress your friends with your digital audio techno-powers.

Speaking of modes, you, too, can create a custom mode — like *Bored stiff!* or *Listening to the Pointy-Haired Boss* — and use it instead of the somewhat mundane choices of *Available* and *Away.* To do this, display the Buddy List window, click the word *Available* beneath your name (refer to Figure 3-2), and a pop-up menu appears. Click Custom Available or Custom Away to create your new mode. An edit box appears, in which you can type the new mode; press Return to automatically add the newcomer to your mode list. You can also switch modes from this pop-up menu.

To choose an existing mode, click it; modes with a green bullet are online modes, and red bullet modes are offline modes. (Apple provides you with some starting choices, like *Surfing the Web* for *Available* and *In a Meeting* for *Away.*) Notice in Figure 3-2 that I created a custom mode called *Getting Another Diet Coke . . .* cAfFeInE fills my life.

If you decide your status list is getting a bit too lengthy with all those custom messages, click the Available pop-up menu in the Buddy List window and choose Edit Status Menu. Both the Available and Away list boxes have a Delete button (which bears a minus sign) — click the offending status message to select it and click the Delete button to take care of business.

Will You Be My Buddy?

I know that question sounds a little personal, but in iChat, a *Buddy* is anyone with whom you want to chat, whether the topic is work related or your personal life. iChat keeps track of your Buddies in the Buddy list. You can also add them to your Address Book or use the AIM entry in an Address Book contact to generate a new Buddy identity.

To add a new Buddy, follow these steps:

1. **Choose Buddies➪Add Buddy, or click the Add Buddy button at the bottom of the iChat window and click Add Buddy from the pop-up menu, or press ⌘+Shift+A.**

2. **To create a Buddy entry from an Address Book contact who has an Instant Messaging username, click the down-arrow button next to the Last Name box to display the Address Book list. Click the entry to select it.**

   As a shortcut, you can also click in the First Name box and then type the person's first name or click in the Account Name box and type the person's Instant Messaging account name.

3. **To add a brand-new person who's not already in your Address Book, type the person's Instant Messaging account name.**

4. **Click Add to save the Buddy information.**

Even when you add a new Buddy and that name appears in the Buddy list, don't be surprised if the name actually fades out after a few seconds — that indicates that the person is offline and unavailable. You can also tell when a person is available if her name appears with a green bullet in the Buddy list.

You can also specify a number of actions that iChat should take if a Buddy logs in or out of Instant Messaging, or if a Buddy changes his or her status to Available. To display these actions, click the desired Buddy's entry in your Buddy list and then press ⌘+Shift+I (from the menu, click Buddies➪Show Info). Click the Alerts button and then choose the event that should trigger the action from the Event pop-up menu. Select the desired check box to specify whether iChat should play the sound that you select, run an AppleScript, speak an announcement or animate the iChat icon by "bouncing" it in the Dock.

Click the Address Card button on the Info dialog to enter or edit the person's

✦ Real name

✦ Nickname

✦ E-mail

✦ Buddy icon

Click Show in Address Book, and iChat obligingly creates an entry in your Address Book for your new Buddy. (Apple, you truly rock.)

Chat! Chat, 1 Say!

Turn your attention to getting the attention of others — through inviting others to chat. Good chatting etiquette implies inviting someone to a conversation rather than barging in unannounced.

If you want to join a chat already in progress, choose File⇨Go to Chat Room (or press ⌘+Control+G). Depending on the service being used, you might have to specify both the type of chat and the specific chat room name.

At this point, it's time to draw your attention to the green phone and video icons next to each person in your Buddy list (as well as next to your own name at the top of the list). If the green phone icon appears next to both your name and your Buddy's name, you can enjoy a two-way audio (or voice) chat. If both you and your Buddy (or Buddies) are lucky enough to have iSight, UVC webcams, or DV cameras connected to your Macs, you can jump into a real-time, two-way video chat room, complete with audio. Time for a very important Mark's Maxim that's violated a surprising number of times:

> **Always wear a shirt while chatting with video, no matter your impressive physique.** *Always.*

If your Mac has a microphone or video camera hooked up but you don't see these icons, click the Video menu and make sure that the Microphone Enabled and Camera Enabled menu items are selected.

To invite someone, click the desired Buddy from the Buddy list, click Buddies, and then choose Invite to Chat. (Using the mouse, right-click the Buddy in the list and click Invite to Chat.) You can also click directly on the phone or camera icon next to the person's name in your Buddy list. iChat displays the Group Chat window that you see in Figure 3-3, which also doubles as an Invitation window.

You can invite additional Buddies to enter the chat by clicking the plus button at the bottom left of the Participants list and choosing another Buddy. If the Participants list isn't visible, click the View menu and choose Show Chat Participants.

Type your invitation text into the entry box at the bottom of the window. If you want to use bold or italic text, highlight the text and press ⌘+B for Bold (**B**) or ⌘+I for Italic (*I*). You can also add an *emoticon* (often called a *Smiley*) to your invitation text: Click in the desired spot in the text, click the Emoticon button to the right of the text entry field, and then choose the proper symbol from the list. To send the invitation text, press Return.

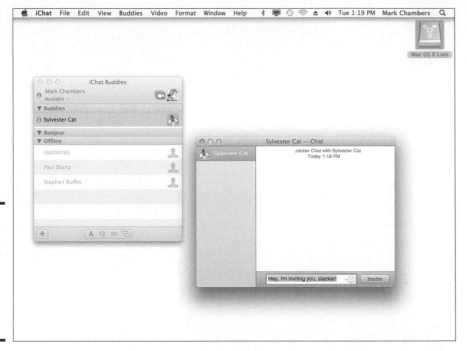

Figure 3-3:
Inviting
that special
someone.
(Actually,
this guy
owes me
money.)

The recipient of your chat invitation can decline or accept your chat invitation. You're notified (as delicately as possible) if the chat has been declined.

To invite a Buddy to an audio chat, select that person in the Buddy list, click the Buddies menu, and then choose Invite to Audio Chat (or One-Way Audio Chat, if only one of you has a microphone). A video invitation works in a similar fashion: Click Buddies and choose either Invite to Video Chat or Invite to One-Way Video Chat, depending on the hardware available. (Need I mention that you can just right-click the person in your Buddy list and choose these commands from the shortcut menu that appears?)

If the chat is accepted, iChat displays a message saying that the Buddy whom you invited has joined the chat, and you now can begin the chat. You don't have to alternate sending messages back and forth between participants — everyone in a chat can compose and send messages at the same time — but I personally like to alternate when I'm chatting one on one. By the way, you might notice that AIM users are represented by the AIM Running Dude icon (unless the AOL user changes it, or you assign an icon picture of your own, as I describe in the "Configuring iChat" section, earlier in the chapter).

Sending SMS messages and e-mail within iChat

iChat doesn't limit you to just a chat between computers! Choose File⇨New SMS and you can hold an SMS (Short Message Service) conversation with anyone using a digital mobile phone. iChat prompts you for the mobile-phone number, and the connection is made automatically. The SMS chat window looks just like the standard iChat text chat window. (Need I warn you that the charge for text messaging can bankrupt an unsuspecting teenager in an hour?)

You can also choose to ship off an e-mail message from within iChat. Click a person in the Buddy list and click the Buddies menu; click Send Email to automatically launch Apple Mail.

If you're ready to video chat with a FaceTime-compatible iPhone or iPad owner, you'll find a complete discussion of FaceTime at the end of this chapter.

If someone invites you to a chat, you get the opposite side of the coin: A prompt dialog appears, and you can choose to accept or decline the invitation. (If it's a video chat, you even get a video preview of the person inviting you.)

You can resize the Chat window by using the dragging any edge of the window (or any of the corners), just as you can most other application windows in Mac OS X Lion.

You can also change fonts and colors while composing a line of text. Simply select the text and then choose Format⇨Show Fonts or Format⇨Show Colors (or press ⌘+T or ⌘+Shift+C) to display the Font panel and Color Picker, respectively. These windows can be resized and moved wherever you like.

To save the discussion in a chat, choose File⇨Save a Copy As. In the dialog that appears, type a name for the chat file, select a location where you want to store the file, and then click Save. To automatically save transcripts of all your chats, choose iChat⇨Preferences and click Messages; then select the Save Chat Transcripts To check box. By default, the transcripts are saved in an iChats folder that's created inside your Documents folder in your Home folder. You can, however, click the pop-up menu to choose another location if you like.

When the iChat window is active, a number of display choices can be made from the View menu. Click the Messages item in the View menu to display these options, including

✦ **Show as Text:** Each line that you write and receive in a chat can be displayed in *balloons,* just like your favorite comic — the default — or as simple text. You can also choose to display text lines in the more traditional boxes or as compact text (allowing more room for more characters in the iChat window).

✦ **Show Names and Pictures:** Each line can be displayed with the individual's picture, just the name, or both the name and picture.

If you're tired of the default background for the chat window, click View and choose the Set Chat Background menu item to choose a graphic to use for the Chat window. To return to the original appearance, choose the Clear Background menu item.

Click the Buddy list, and the View menu offers a different set of controls: You can sort your Buddy list by first name, last name, or availability; you can also toggle the display of offline Buddies.

Curious about the capabilities of your Mac hardware in iChat? Choose Video⇨Connection Doctor, where you can view statistics and information about your current chat, display the features of iChat that are supported by your Mac and your connection, and view any error messages that are generated by iChat during this session.

If you're conversing within multiple iChat windows, you can switch between windows by clicking on the desired window to make it active. To close a chat, click the Close button on the Chat window.

Sharing Screens and iChat Theater

How often have you wanted to show someone a neat new application, or lead your Aunt Mildred through the paces of setting up an Apple TV connection on her system? That's the idea behind the ultimate collaboration tool, *sharing* screens, where you can watch (or even remotely control) the display on another person's Mac — across any broadband Internet or local network connection!

Screen sharing must be turned on for you to send or receive sharing invites. Choose Video⇨Screen Sharing Enabled — a check mark appears next to the menu item when the feature is enabled.

If a Buddy invites you to share a screen, you receive a prompt that lets you accept or decline. (You can also request to share a Buddy's screen by clicking Buddies⇨Ask to Share Screen.) If you accept the sharing invitation, iChat automatically initiates an audio chat (so that you can gab away to each other while things are happening on-screen). Suddenly, you're seeing the Desktop and applications that your Buddy is running, and you can both control the cursor and left- or right-click the mouse.

Throughout the screen-sharing session, iChat maintains a semi-opaque panel on your screen that has three buttons:

✦ **End the Shared Screen Session:** Click this button to exit shared screen mode.

✦ **Switch Desktops:** Click this button to swap between your Mac's screen and the remote Mac's screen. (Those Mac owners who have enabled Fast User Switching will recognize the cool screen swap animation.)

✦ **Mute Audio:** Click this button to mute the audio during the screen-sharing session.

To invite a Buddy to share your screen, choose Buddies⟹Share My Screen.

Okay, if sharing a screen with someone you don't absolutely know and trust doesn't set off alarm bells in your cranium, it **should.** Remember, anyone with shared screen access can perform most of the same actions as you can, just as if that person were sitting in front of your Mac. Granted, most of the truly devastating things would require you to type your admin password, but a malicious individual could still delete files or wreak havoc any number of ways on your system. **Be careful with whom you share your screen!**

But wait . . . What if you don't *want* to control Aunt Mildred's Mac? Perhaps you just want to share a document instead? For example, you could show off some photos or a movie you've just finished, or visit your family web page. That's the idea behind iChat Theater, where you can share a document, web page, or video and hold a conversation while viewing the content! iChat Theater falls in between Screen Sharing and a simple file download, which I cover in the next section.

To select one or more items for your Theater show, choose File⟹Share iPhoto with iChat Theater (to share images from your iPhoto library), File⟹ Share Webpage with iChat Theater (to share a web page within Safari) or File⟹Share a File with iChat Theater (to share movies and other documents). iChat displays a standard Open dialog, in which you can select one or more items — or, if you're showing a web page, you're prompted for the page's address (URL) to share. When you're ready to begin your Theater presentation, click Share. If you're using a video camera, your video appears as a thumbnail, while your content gets center stage.

iChat Theater works with anything that can be displayed in Quick Look or located with Spotlight, including slideshows from iPhoto, a Keynote presentation, or a QuickTime movie.

Sending Files with iChat

To send a file to a Buddy, click the desired entry in the Buddy list and then choose Buddies⇨Send File. Alternatively, you can use the ⌘+Option+F keyboard shortcut; right-click and choose Send a File; drag the file from a Finder window to the person's entry in the Buddy list; or even drag the file into the text typing window. (How's that for convenience?) A dialog appears to indicate that the recipient is being offered a file transfer request. If the file transfer request is accepted by your Buddy, the transfer begins and is saved where the recipient specifies on her system.

If a Buddy sends you a file, the Incoming File Request pane appears. You can then either click the Decline button (to decline the file transfer) or the Save File button (to save the incoming file to any spot on your system).

Always check any files that you receive from iChat with your antivirus scanning software before you run them!

If you're looking for another easy method of sending files between Mac computers running Lion, don't forget to check out AirDrop! I discuss this new feature in Book VI, Chapter 2. iChat does, however, have two important advantages over AirDrop: The two computers don't have to be within Wi-Fi range of each other, and iChat can transfer files with PCs running Windows or Linux.

Eliminating the Riffraff

Here I need to explain something that I hope you won't have to use — what I like to call the *Turkey Filter*. (iChat is a little more subtle — you just *ignore* people.)

To ignore someone in a chat group, click her name in the list and choose Buddies⇨Ignore *<person>*. When someone is ignored in a chat group, you don't see anything that she types or have to respond to any file transfer requests from that person.

If only it were that easy to ignore someone when he's standing close to you.

Anyway, if the person becomes a royal pain, you can also choose to *block* that person entirely. That way, the offensive cur doesn't even know that you're online, and he can't reach you at all. Click the person in the list and choose Buddies⇨Block *<person>* — the deed is done.

Adding Visual Effects

Our esteemed Apple software developers decided to bring a little Hollywood special effects "flash" to iChat with video backdrops. You can also use many of the special effects filters provided by Photo Booth to keep your video chat room laughing!

To add a video backdrop to your video feed, choose Video⇨Video Preview to display your stunning self in a live video feed; then choose Video⇨Show Video Effects. Use the scroll buttons to move to the backdrop thumbnails toward the end of the Effects library. When you click one, iChat prompts you to leave the frame for a few seconds so that the plain background behind you can be correctly "masked" (just like those blockbuster special effects used in today's films). When your background has been captured and masked, iChat prompts you to return to your spot, and you'll see that your new static or animated backdrop is in place. *Just plain cool!*

The plainer the background behind you, the better iChat can process and mask your background. A plain wall painted a single color works best.

"But, Mark, I want my *own* movies and photos for backgrounds!" No problem — you'll notice that iChat provides six user-defined backdrop slots for your own selections at the end of the Video Effects collection. (Click the right scroll arrow in the Video Effects window until you reach the last couple of pages.) To add your own visuals, you can

- ✦ Drag a video from iMovie to an empty User Backdrop well in the Video Effects window.

- ✦ Drag a photo from iPhoto to an empty User Backdrop well in the Video Effects window.

- ✦ Drag a video or photo from a Finder window to an empty User Backdrop well in the Video Effects window.

As long as an item can be displayed in Quick Look, it can be used as a video background. Think of the possibilities!

To try out a Photo Booth effect in iChat, choose Video⇨Video Preview to display your live video feed; then choose Video⇨Show Video Effects (or press ⌘+Shift+E). Figure 3-4 illustrates the Video Preview and Video Effects windows; click a video effect thumbnail to see how it looks on you in the Preview window! Effects range from simple Black & White to a Thermal Camera look, an Andy Warhol–style Pop Art display, and a number of really cool optical distortions (such as Twirl and Light Tunnel).

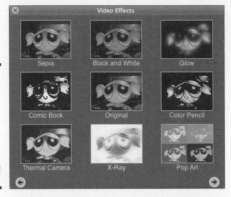

Figure 3-4:
Andy
Warhol
would be
impressed
by my iChat
video effect!

After you find just the right video effect, close the two windows and start chatting. If you decide you'd rather return your video persona to something more conventional, display the Video Effects window again and click the Normal thumbnail (which appears in the center of the first screen of thumbnails).

Conversing with FaceTime

Although iChat's standard video chat is downright nifty, it has limits: You're confined to your instant messaging buddies, and those folks may not have the necessary video hardware. With Apple's FaceTime technology, however, you can video chat with owners of iPhone 4s, iPad 2s, and Macs without the constraints of instant messaging accounts — and if they can run FaceTime, they're guaranteed to have the right video hardware!

At the time of this writing, FaceTime-compatible devices include

✦ Macs running Lion. (Mac owners running Snow Leopard 10.6.6 or later can also buy the FaceTime application from the App Store.)

✦ An iPhone 4 running iOS 4.1 or higher.

✦ An iPad 2.

✦ An iPod Touch running iOS 4.1 or higher.

You need a Wi-Fi connection to use FaceTime with a mobile device — a 3G cellular connection will not work — and a Mac requires either a wired or Wi-Fi connection to the Internet.

To launch FaceTime, click the jaunty-looking video camera icon in the Dock. The first time you use the application, you have to enter your Apple ID and your e-mail address. The folks you chat with on the other end use that same e-mail address to call you via FaceTime. (iPhone 4 owners can be called using their telephone numbers.)

TIP

To change the e-mail address that other FaceTime users use to call you, click FaceTime⇨Preferences and click the E-mail link under the heading You Can Be Reached For Calls At.

After you've signed in, FaceTime displays your Address Book Contacts list by default, as shown in Figure 3-5. To initiate a call with any contact, click the name in the list — FaceTime displays the e-mail and telephone numbers for the contact (once again, taken from your Address Book). Click the e-mail or telephone number that FaceTime should use, and the connection process begins. To return to the Contacts list and choose another person, click the All Contacts button at the top of the window.

Figure 3-5:
FaceTime offers a contact list taken from your Address Book.

Apple isn't satisfied with a mere contacts list, however! You can use a number of other methods of selecting someone to call:

✦ **Recent Calls:** Click the Recents button to choose a contact that you've called (or attempted to call) within the recent past. Click the All or Missed buttons at the top of the window to further filter the Recents list.

✦ **Groups:** If you've set up one or more groups within your Address Book, you can display them by clicking the Groups button. For example, if you've created an Address Book group containing all those fellow employees within your company, you can easily locate and call a specific person without wading through all your friends and family as well.

✦ **FaceTime Search:** Click within the familiar Search box and begin typing the contact's first or last name, and FaceTime displays the matching entries.

✦ **Favorites:** Sure, you have folks you like to chat with all the time, and it's easy to add them to the Favorites list. (Those who don't make the Favorites list don't have to know, right?) Click the desired contact, and then click the Add to Favorites button. To display your favorite contacts at any time, click the Favorites button in the FaceTime window.

When the call is accepted, you'll see a large video window with a smaller "picture-in-picture" display — the video from the other person fills the large window, and the video that you're sending to them appears in the small display, as shown in Figure 3-6.

Figure 3-6:
The
FaceTime
window in
action.

Move your mouse cursor into the FaceTime window, and you'll see the window controls appear, as well as three icons at the bottom of the window:

✦ **Mute:** Click the mute icon to turn off the sound coming from your Mac. FaceTime displays a reminder that mute is enabled. (You'll continue to hear the audio from the other person.) To restore your audio feed, click the mute icon again.

✦ **End:** Click this icon to end the FaceTime call.

✦ **Full-screen:** Click the full-screen icon (or press ⌘+Shift+F) to switch FaceTime into full-screen display mode. To return to windowed mode, press ⌘+Shift+F again, or move your mouse and click the full-screen icon again.

You can switch FaceTime into landscape mode and take advantage of your Mac's widescreen display — click Video⇨Use Landscape, or press ⌘+R. (Why let the iPhone 4 and iPad 2 owners have all the landscape fun?)

Chapter 4: Expanding Your Horizons with iCloud and iDisk

In This Chapter

✔ **Introducing iCloud**

✔ **Setting up iDisk**

✔ **Using files and folders on your iDisk**

✔ **Using public files**

*I*f you ask the average MacBook owner about what's available on the Internet, you likely hear benefits such as e-mail, web surfing, RSS feeds, Google, and instant communication via iChat. What you may *not* hear is "instant syncing among all my Apple iOS devices" and "convenient, trouble-free storage for my files and folders."

If you have an iPhone, iPad or iPod touch, you may be experiencing what I like to call the Synchronizing Blues: When you take a photo with your iPhone or create a new document with your iPad, your new additions just *sit* there (in their original location) until you have a chance to sync your device with your MacBook. Ah, but with Apple's new iCloud functionality, your stuff gets automatically synchronized across the Internet, automatically, and you can even keep your iTunes music library stored online!

Speaking of storage, you might have tried to use one of the dozens of storage sites on the Internet that allows you to upload and download files from a personal file area via your web browser. Unfortunately, these web-based storage sites are slow in transferring files and lacking in convenience, and they typically offer only a small amount of space. As a result, most computer owners decide that the idea of online storage is neat . . . but impractical.

In this chapter, I show you what's *really* exciting for your MacBook about the online world. I'm talking about Apple's new iCloud feature (which offers synchronization betwixt all many Apple devices and online storage for your media) and *iDisk* (Apple's existing online storage feature for current MobileMe members that's integrated into the Mac OS X Finder). With iCloud, you can automatically synchronize your stuff and easily make use of online storage for backups and sharing files with your friends . . . from anywhere on the planet, road warrior!

Apple's existing iDisk functionality is still available for a limited time as a part of Apple's MobileMe service for existing subscribers. As I write this, however, Apple has announced that MobileMe is being phased out in June 2012, and new subscribers are no longer being accepted. Therefore, you may not be able to use the MobileMe-specific features within this chapter for long.

Keeping Track of Your iCloud

As I mentioned earlier, today's Apple iOS devices can all display or play the same media: photos, music, books, TV shows and such. Heck, some iOS devices can even share applications that you install, such as your iPhone and iPod touch. Therefore, it makes sense to effortlessly share all your digital media across these devices, and that's what iCloud is all about. Apple calls this synchronization *pushing*.

Let's take a look at how the pushing process works. Imagine that you've just completed a Pages document on your MacBook (an invitation for your son's birthday party), but you're currently traveling on the road, and you need to get the document to your family so that they can edit and print it using your son's iPad.

Before iCloud, you'd have to attach the document to an e-mail message, or upload it to some type of online storage, and then a family member would have to download and save the document to the iPad before working with it. With iCloud, you simply save the document, and your MacBook automatically pushes the document to the iPad! Your document appears on the iPad, ready to be opened, edited, and printed. (And on any other iOS devices as well.)

iCloud isn't limited to just digital media, though. Your MacBook can also automatically synchronize your e-mail, iCal calendars, and Address Book contacts with other iOS5 devices across the Internet, making it much easier to stay in touch (no matter which device you happen to be using at the moment).

Apple also throws in 5GB of free online storage that you can use for all sorts of things: not only digital media files but also documents and anything else that you'd like to place online for safekeeping. In fact, anything you buy through the iTunes Store — music, video and applications — do not count against your 5GB limit.

Need more elbow room than 5GB? Apple is happy to provide 10, 20, or even 50GB of additional storage for an annual subscription fee of $20, $40, or $100 a year, respectively. Click the Manage button on the iCloud pane in System Preferences and then click Buy More Storage.

To join the iCloud revolution, you'll need an Apple ID, or you can upgrade your existing MobileMe account. It's important to note, however, that **upgrading your MobileMe account to an iCloud account is a one-way street!** After you've switched to iCloud, you won't be able to access MobileMe features such as your iDisk or Galleries in the future.

You control all the settings for iCloud from the new iCloud pane in System Preferences. Click the System Preferences icon in the Dock and click the iCloud icon. If you're not an iCloud member already, you'll enter your Apple ID or MobileMe account and your password, and System Preferences will guide you through basic iCloud configuration with a number of questions.

Most of the check boxes on the iCloud Preferences pane control whether a particular type of data is pushed between all your iOS devices (as I describe in Book III, Chapter III). However, you can also enable two other features from this pane:

Book V
Chapter 4

Expanding Your
Horizons with
iCloud and iDisk

✦ **Back to My Mac:** If you enable Back to My Mac, you'll be able to remotely control your MacBook from another Mac computer (or vice versa) using Lion's Screen Sharing feature. You can also transfer files between the two computers. Back to My Mac works over both a broadband Internet connection and a local network. Available Mac computers show up in the Shared section of the Finder window sidebar. Note that you must manually turn on Screen Sharing within the System Preferences Sharing pane before you can remotely control another Mac.

✦ **Find My Mac:** Talk about Buck Rogers. . . Imagine locating a lost or stolen MacBook from your iPhone or iPad. Now think about this: With Find My Mac, you can even lock or completely wipe your MacBook's hard drive *remotely*, preventing unauthorized use and erasing your private data! After you access your MacBook from another iOS device, you can play a sound, send a message to be displayed onscreen, remotely lock the machine, or remotely wipe the drive. Note that after you have locked or wiped the drive, you can't locate your MacBook again.

To monitor your iCloud storage, click the Manage button at the bottom-right corner of the iCloud Preferences pane. From the sheet that appears, you can see how much space you're using for document and data storage.

Grabbing Internet Storage for Your MacBook

So how do you actually *use* iDisk? That's the simple part! To use iDisk within Mac OS X, just do what comes naturally — it works the same as any other removable volume's Finder window. You can copy and move files and folders to and from your iDisk, create new subfolders (except in the Backup, Library, and Software root folders, which are read-only), and delete whatever you don't need.

With an existing MobileMe account, iDisk is available automatically. To see how much storage you're using and to configure access to your Public folder, open System Preferences, click the MobileMe icon, and then click the iDisk button to display the settings.

The iDisk Usage bar graph illustrates how much of your current iDisk territory you're using.

You can specify the access privilege level for other MobileMe users from this pane as well. Select the Allow Others to Write Files in your Public Folder check box to allow others to save files in your iDisk Public folder. If this check box is disabled, other MobileMe users are not allowed to copy files to your Public folder.

You can also set a password that other MobileMe users must type before they're allowed access to your Public folder. This is the very definition of *A Truly Good Idea*, so I recommend that you select the Password-Protect Your Public Folder check box to enable it. (More on the Public folder in the next section.)

If you've already set a password, you can change it by clicking the Set Password button and typing the new word in the Password box. Retype the word in the Confirm box to verify it; then click OK to save the change and return to the MobileMe System Preferences pane.

Understanding What's on Your iDisk

In contrast to the physical hard drive in your MacBook, your iDisk never needs formatting or defragmenting, and you never have to check it for errors. However, the structure of an iDisk is fixed, so you can't just go crazy creating your own folders. In fact, you can't create new folders at the *root* — the top level — of your iDisk at all, but you can create new folders inside most of the root folders.

Now that you're thoroughly rooterized, here are the folders that you find hanging out in your iDisk:

✦ **Backup:** This is a read-only folder that contains the backup files created with the Apple Backup application. You can, however, copy the files in this folder to a removable drive on your system for an additional level of safekeeping.

✦ **Documents:** This folder holds any application documents that you want to store — things like spreadsheets and letters. No one but you can access these items; you can, however, tag items in the Documents folder as *shared*, allowing individuals or groups to download them using an access code sent by MobileMe in an e-mail message. Sharing files is a great way to transfer files too big to send as e-mail attachments.

✦ **Groups:** This folder holds files that you want to share with others in any MobileMe Groups you might have joined.

✦ **Library:** Another read-only folder. This spot contains the configuration data and custom settings that you've created for other MobileMe features.

✦ **Movies:** QuickTime movies go here. Again, you can add the movies stored here to your web pages. (I cover QuickTime like a blanket in Book IV, Chapter 8.)

✦ **Music:** This is the repository for iTunes music and playlists, and the contents can be added to your web pages. (iTunes is the star of Chapter 2 in Book IV.) Mine is stuffed full of Mozart, Scarlatti, and that Bach fellow.

✦ **Pictures:** This folder is the vault for your JPEG, PNG, and GIF images, including those that you want to use with your web pages.

✦ **Public:** This is the spot to place files that you specifically want to share with others, either directly through iDisk or with your web pages. If you've allowed write access, others can copy files to your Public folder as well.

✦ **Sites:** The web pages that you store here can be created with iWeb, which I cover in Book IV, Chapter 7. In fact, you can even use your own web page design application and copy the completed site files here.

✦ **Software:** Apple provides this read-only folder as a service to MobileMe members; it contains a selection of the latest freeware, shareware, and commercial demos for you to enjoy. To try something, open the Software folder and copy whatever you like to your Mac OS X Desktop. Then you can install and run the application from the local copy of the files.

✦ **Web:** This folder holds your MobileMe Galleries created from within iPhoto and iMovie, as well as other media used by iWeb.

Opening and Using iDisk

When you're connected to the Internet, you can open your iDisk in one of the following ways:

✦ **From the Finder menu, choose Go⇨iDisk and then choose My iDisk from the submenu or use the ⌘+Shift+I keyboard shortcut.**

✦ **Click the iDisk icon in the Finder Sidebar.**

✦ **Add an iDisk button to your Finder window toolbar by choosing View⇨Customize Toolbar.**

After you add the button, you can click it to connect to your iDisk from anywhere in the Finder.

Your iDisk opens in a new Finder window. After you use one of these methods in a Mac OS X session, your iDisk icon appears on the Mac OS X Desktop and sidebar; you can control the locations where the iDisk icon shows up from the Finder menu bar (click Finder⇨Preferences and then click the General and Sidebar tabs). The iDisk volume icon remains until you shut down or restart your MacBook. (Alternatively, you can dismiss the iDisk volume icon from your Desktop using the same method by which you eject an external drive: Click the iDisk icon and press ⌘+E or click the Eject button next to the iDisk icon in the Finder window Sidebar.)

If you're using a remote PC with an Internet connection, you can log in to the MobileMe page at www.me.com/ and use your web browser to access the contents of your iDisk. (Hey, sometimes this is the only choice you have.)

However, you don't actually need to open your iDisk in a Finder window to use it, because you can also load and save files directly to your iDisk from within any application. Simply choose your iDisk as you would any of the hard drives on your system when using the application's Open, Save, or Save As commands.

You can also open an iDisk Public folder — either yours or the Public folder inside another person's iDisk — as if it were an Internet file server. As I explain earlier in the chapter, if that person has set a password, you need to enter that password to gain access to all of his or her iDisk folders. From the Finder menu, choose Go⇨iDisk⇨Other User's iDisk (or, to jump directly to their Public folder, choose Go⇨iDisk⇨Other User's Public Folder). If you choose the former, Lion prompts you for the other person's member name and password; if you pick the latter, you need only enter the other MobileMe member's account name.

After you enter a valid iDisk member name (and password, if required), you see the MobileMe member's Public folder.

You can also use the server address

http://idisk.me.com/*username*-Public?

to connect to an iDisk from computers running Windows and Linux. Check the Help for your operating system to determine how to connect to a WebDAV server (usually called a *Web folder* in the Windows world). When prompted for your access username and password, use your MobileMe account name and password. If you're using Windows XP, Vista, or Windows 7, Apple has provided an even easier way to manage your iDisk: Use MobileMe Control Panel for Windows, which you can download from www.me.com/.

Chapter 5: Going Places with Safari

In This Chapter

✔ **Introducing the Safari window and controls**

✔ **Visiting web sites with Safari**

✔ **Moving between sites**

✔ **Creating and using bookmarks**

✔ **Receiving files with Safari**

✔ **Surfing with your tabs showing**

✔ **Saving web pages to disk**

✔ **Protecting your privacy on the web**

✔ **Blocking those irritating pop-ups**

When I was designing the Table of Contents for this book, I seriously considered leaving this chapter out. After all, more people use a web browser now than any other software application. Who really needs a guide to mowing a lawn?

But then again, I suddenly thought of all the hidden features that folks don't know about Apple's Safari browser — for example, the tips and tricks that can help you organize your online visits. It's a little like finding out more about the lawn mower itself: Even though you might not need tips on mowing, many people don't know how to remove the spark plug in the winter or how to sharpen the blade so that you can handle taller grass. To paraphrase a favorite author of mine, Arthur C. Clarke, *magic is nothing more than technology that someone understands.*

In this chapter, I show you how to use those other controls and toolbar buttons in Safari — you know, the ones in addition to the Forward and Back buttons — and you'll discover how to keep track of where you've been and where you'd like to go. (Oh, and did I mention that you'll need a network connection?)

One note: Many authors have written entire books on web browsing with Safari. As you might guess, this chapter is far narrower in scope than those books — I've got more ground to cover before dinner — and it doesn't include every one of Safari's features. However, I think the coverage that you find here will explain all that you're likely to need for most surfing sessions.

Pretend You've Never Used This Thing

Figure 5-1 illustrates the Safari window. You can launch Safari directly from the Dock, or you can click the Safari icon within your Applications folder.

Major sections of the Safari window include

✦ **The toolbar:** You'll find the most often used commands on this toolbar — for tasks such as navigation, adding bookmarks, and searching Google. Plus, here you can type or paste the address for web sites that you'd like to visit. The toolbar can be hidden to provide you with more real estate in your browser window for web content. To toggle hidden mode, press ⌘+| (the vertical bar right above the backslash) or choose View➪Hide/Show Toolbar.

✦ **The Bookmarks bar:** Consider this a toolbar that allows you to jump directly to your favorite web sites with a single click or two. I show you later, in the section "Adding and Using Bookmarks," how to add and remove sites from your Bookmarks bar. For now, remember that you can toggle the display of the Bookmarks bar by choosing View➪Hide/Show Bookmarks Bar or by pressing ⌘+Shift+B.

Figure 5-1:
Safari at a
glance.

✦ **The Content pane:** Congratulations! At last, you've waded through all the pregame show and you've reached the area where web pages are actually displayed. As can any other window, the Content window can be scrolled; when you minimize Safari to the Dock, you get a *thumbnail* (minimized) image of the Content pane.

The Content pane often contains underlined text and graphical icons that transport you to other pages when you click them. These underlined words and icons are *links,* and they make it easy to move from one area of a site to another or to a completely different site. You can tell when your mouse pointer is resting on a link because the pointer changes to that reassuring gloved hand.

✦ **The status bar:** The status bar displays information about what the mouse pointer is currently resting upon, such as the address for a link or the name of an image; it also updates you on what's happening while a page is loading. To hide or display the status bar, press ⌘+/ (forward slash) or choose View➪Hide/Show Status Bar.

Visiting Web Sites

Here's the stuff that virtually everyone over the age of five knows how to do . . . but I get paid by the word, and some folks might just not be aware of all the myriad ways of visiting a site. You can load a web page from any of the following methods:

✦ **Type (or paste) a web site address into the Address box on the Toolbar and then press Return.**

If you're typing in an address and Safari recognizes the site as one that you've visited in the past, it helps by completing the address for you. Press Return if you want to accept the suggested site. If this is a new site, just keep typing.

Safari also includes a *Smart Address* field that displays a new pop-up menu of sites that match the text you've entered. Safari does this by using sites taken from your History file and your bookmarks. If the site you want to visit appears in the list, click it to jump there immediately.

✦ **Click a Bookmarks entry within Safari.**

✦ **Click the Home button, which takes you to the home page that you specify.**

More on this in the section "Setting Up Your Home Page," later in this chapter.

✦ **Click the Show Top Sites button on the Toolbar.**

Safari displays a wall of preview thumbnail pages from your most frequently visited sites, and you can jump to a site just by clicking on
the preview. Click the Edit button on the Top Sites screen to delete a
preview thumbnail — click the X — or you can "anchor" a thumbnail to
keep it on the screen permanently by clicking the pin icon next to the
desired thumbnail. You can also choose the size of the preview thumbnails in Edit mode.

Because each thumbnail is updated with the most current content, the
Top Sites wall makes a great time-saver — you can quickly make a visual
check of all your favorite haunts from one screen!

✦ **Click a page link in Apple Mail or another Internet-savvy application.**

Some Mac applications require you to hold down ⌘ while clicking to
open a web page.

✦ **Click a page link within another web page.**

✦ **Use the Search box in the Toolbar.**

By default, Safari uses Google as a search engine, but you can also use
Yahoo! or Bing if you prefer. To set the search engine, click Safari⇨
Preferences, click the General tab, and click the Default Search Engine
drop-down menu.

Click in the Google box, type the contents that you want to find, and
then press Return. Safari presents you with the search results page on
Google for the text that you entered. (In case you've been living under
the Internet equivalent of a rock for the last five years, *Google* (www.
google.com) is the preeminent search site on the web — people use
Google to find everything from used auto parts to ex-spouses.)

✦ **Click a Safari page icon in the Dock or a Finder window.**

Drag a site from your Bookmarks bar and drop it on the right side of the
Dock. Clicking the icon that you add launches Safari and automatically
loads that site.

This trick works only on the side of the Dock to the right of the
vertical line.

If you minimize Safari to the Dock, you'll see a thumbnail of the page with the
Safari logo superimposed on it. Click this thumbnail in the Dock to restore
the page to its full glory.

Navigating the Web

A typical web surfing session is a linear experience — you bop from one
page to the next, absorbing the information that you want and discarding
the rest. However, after you visit a few sites, you might find that you need

to return to where you've been or head to the familiar ground of your home page. Safari offers these navigational controls on the Toolbar:

+ **Back:** Click the Back button (the left-facing arrow) on the toolbar to return to the last page you visited. Additional clicks take you to previous pages, in reverse order. The Back button is disabled if you haven't visited at least two sites.

+ **Forward:** If you've clicked the Back button at least once, clicking the Forward button (the right-facing arrow) takes you to the next page (or through the pages) where you originally were, in forward order. The Forward button is disabled if you haven't used the Back button.

+ **Home:** Click this button (look for the little house) to return to your home page.

Not all these buttons and controls must appear on your Toolbar. To display or hide Toolbar controls, choose View⊏⊃Customize Toolbar. The sheet that appears works just like the Customize Toolbar sheet within a Finder window: Drag the control you want from the sheet to your Safari Toolbar or drag a control that you don't want from the Toolbar to the sheet.

+ **New Tab:** Click this button (it looks like a little tab with a plus sign) to open a new tab in the Content pane. I'll get knee-deep into tabbed browsing later in the chapter.

+ **AutoFill:** If you fill out a lot of forms online — when you're shopping at web sites, for example — you can click the AutoFill button (which looks like a little text box and a pen) to complete these forms for you. You can set what information is used for AutoFill by choosing Safari⊏⊃Preferences and clicking the AutoFill toolbar button.

To be honest, I'm not a big fan of releasing *any* of my personal information to *any* web site, so I don't use AutoFill often. If you do decide to use this feature, make sure that the connection is secure (look for the padlock icon in the Address box) and read the site's Privacy Agreement page first to see how your identity data will be treated.

+ **Top Sites:** Click this button to display the Top Sites screen I discussed earlier. (If you're having trouble finding it, the button bears a tiny, fashionable grid of squares.)

+ **Reading List:** Click this icon to display or hide the Reading List pane, where you can save links (and entire pages) for later perusal. (From the keyboard, press ⌘+Shift+L.) When the Reading List pane is visible, click the Add Page button to add the current page to the list — you can quickly add a link to the list by holding down the Shift key and clicking the link.

+ **Zoom:** Shrinks or expands the size of text on the page, offering smaller, space-saving characters (for the shrinking crowd) or larger, easier-to-read text (for the expanding crowd). Hence the button, which is labeled with a small and large letter *A*.

✦ **Bookmarks Bar:** Click this button (which carries the Bookmarks symbol sandwiched between two horizontal lines) to display or hide the Bookmarks bar.

✦ **Stop/Reload:** Click Reload (which has a circular arrow in the Address box) to *refresh* (reload) the contents of the current page. Although most pages remain static, some pages change their content at regular intervals or after you fill out a form or click a button. By clicking Reload (look for the curvy arrow in the Address box), you can see what's changed on these pages. (I use Reload every hour or so with CNN.com, for example.) While a page is loading, the Reload button turns into the Stop button — with a little X mark — and you can click it to stop the loading of the content from the current page. This is a real boon when a download takes *foorrevverr,* which can happen when you're trying to visit a very popular or very slow web site (especially if you're using a dial-up modem connection to the Internet). Using Stop is also handy if a page has a number of very large graphics that are likely to take a long time to load.

✦ **Bookmark:** Click this Toolbar button (which carries an open book icon) to hide or display the Bookmark Window. You'll find the complete description of the Bookmark window in an upcoming section.

✦ **History:** Click this button (which bears a clock symbol) to display or hide the History list, which I'll discuss later in the chapter.

✦ **Downloads:** Click this toolbar button to display the files you've downloaded recently. Click the Clear button to clear the contents of the Download list — note that clearing the list does not delete the files you've downloaded, it simply cleans things up. (More on downloading in a page or two.)

✦ **Open in Dashboard:** Click this button to create a Dashboard widget using the contents of the currently displayed web page. Safari prompts you to choose which clickable section of the page to be included within the widget's borders (such as the local radar map on your favorite weather web site). Click Add, and Dashboard loads automatically with your new widget. (More on widgets in Book II, Chapter 2.)

✦ **Mail:** Click this button (bearing an envelope icon) to send an e-mail message with a link to the current page, just as if you had selected File⇨Mail Link to This Page. Safari automatically opens Apple Mail and creates a new message with the link already in the body. *Shazam!*

✦ **Add Bookmark:** Click this Toolbar button (which carries a plus sign) to add a page to your Bookmarks bar or Bookmarks menu. (More on this in a tad.)

✦ **Search:** As I mention earlier, you can click in this box and type text that you want to find on the web via the Google (or Yahoo!, or Bing) search engine; press Return to display the results. To repeat a recent search, click the down arrow in the Search box and select it from the pop-up menu.

✦ **Print:** Click this convenient button to print the contents of the Safari window. (Dig that crazy printer icon!)

✦ **Report Bug:** A rather strange creature, the Report Bug button makes it easy to alert Apple when you encounter a page that doesn't display properly in Safari. (Software developers call such glitches *bugs* — hence the name.) When you click the Bug button, you'll see a sheet with the settings shown in Figure 5-2; take time to enter a short description of the problem that you're having. (I also click More Options to enable the Send Screen Shot of Current Page and the Send Source of Current Page check boxes, giving the Apple folks more to work with while they're debugging Safari.) Then click the Submit button to send the bug report to Apple.

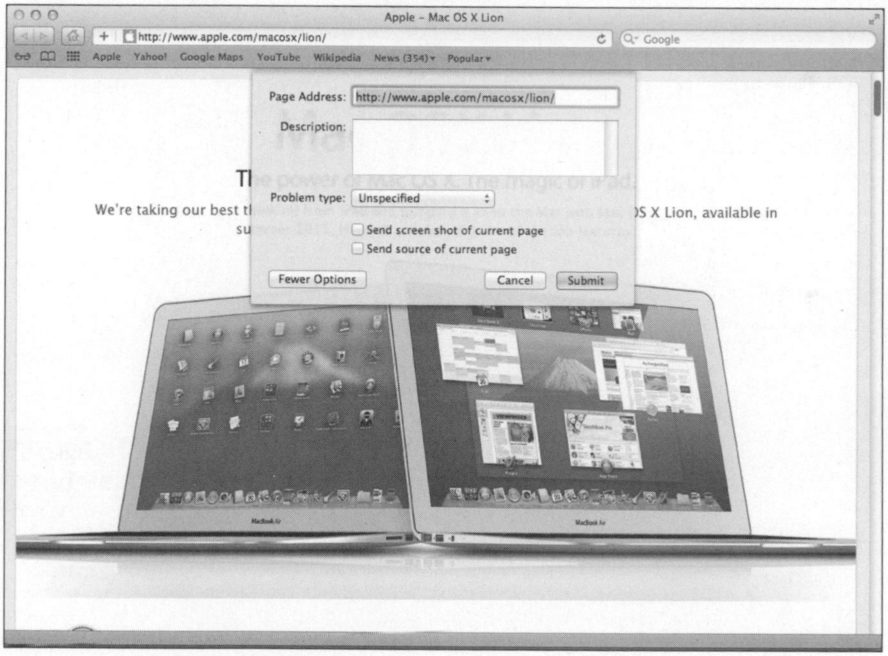

Figure 5-2: Have at thee, troublesome buggy page!

Setting Up Your Home Page

Choosing a home page is one of the easiest methods of speeding up your web surfing, especially if you're using a dial-up modem connection. However, a large percentage of the Mac owners whom I've talked with have never set their own home page; instead, they simply use the default home page provided by their browser! With Safari running, take a moment to follow these steps to declare your own freedom to choose your own home page:

1. **If you want to use a specific web page as your new home page, display it in Safari.**

   I recommend selecting a page with few graphics or a fast-loading popular site.

2. **Choose Safari⇨Preferences or press ⌘+, (comma).**

3. **Click the General button.**

   You see the settings shown in Figure 5-3.

Figure 5-3: Adding your own home page is an easy change you can make.

4. **Click the Set to Current Page button.**

5. **Alternatively, click the New Windows Open With pop-up menu and choose Empty Page if you want Safari to open a new window with a blank page.**

   This is the fastest choice of all for a home page.

6. **Click the Close button to exit the Preferences dialog.**

Visit your home page at any time by pressing the Home button on the Toolbar.

Adding and Using Bookmarks

No doubt about it: Bookmarks make the web a friendly place. As you collect bookmarks in Safari, you're able to immediately jump from one site to another with a single click of the Bookmarks menu or the buttons on the Bookmarks bar.

Lean, fast, and mean — That's RSS

Well, maybe not *mean* — after all, I don't want you to be afraid of RSS (RDF Site Summary) pages! RSS web sites display updated information using a shortened list format, rather like a newspaper headline, without unnecessary graphics or silly advertisements. You can tell when a web site has RSS pages available because Safari displays an RSS icon at the right side of the Address box on the toolbar. (When you click the RSS icon, the web address switches to a `feed://` prefix — another indication that you're not in Kansas reading HTML pages anymore.)

To display more information about a news item on an RSS page, click the item headline. Safari opens the corresponding web page — yep, once again you're back in the world of HTML —

and you can read the full story. To return to the RSS feed, click the Back button on the toolbar. Naturally, RSS feed pages can be bookmarked. In fact, Apple gives you a number of RSS sites that you can explore immediately.

To customize your RSS display, choose Safari➪Preferences and then click the RSS tab. By default, Safari checks for updated RSS headlines every 30 minutes, but you can change this to an hourly or daily check. (Of course, you can also check for updates manually by reloading the RSS page, just as you would any other web page.) New articles can be assigned a highlighted color, and you can specify the amount of time an item should remain on the RSS page after it's published.

To add a bookmark, first navigate to the desired page and then do any of the following:

✦ **Choose Bookmarks➪Add Bookmark.**

✦ **Press the ⌘+D keyboard shortcut.**

Safari displays a sheet where you can enter the name for the bookmark and also select where it appears (on the Bookmarks bar, Reading List, Top Sites display or the Bookmarks menu).

✦ **Drag the icon next to the web address from the Address field to the Bookmarks bar.**

This trick also works with other applications besides Safari, including within a Mail message or iChat conversation — drag the icon from the Safari Address field to the other application window, and the web page link is added to your document!

You can also drag a link on the current page to the Bookmarks bar, but note that doing this adds a bookmark only for the page corresponding to the link — not the current page.

To jump to a bookmark

✦ **Choose it from the Bookmarks menu.**

  If the bookmark is contained in a folder, which I discuss later in this section, move your mouse pointer over the folder name to show its contents and then click the bookmark.

✦ **Click the bookmark on the Bookmarks bar.**

  If you've added a large number of items to the Bookmarks bar, click the More icon on the edge of the Bookmarks bar to display the rest of the buttons.

✦ **Click the Show All Bookmarks button (which looks like a small, opened book) on the Bookmarks bar and then click the desired bookmark.**

  The Bookmarks window that you see in Figure 5-4 appears — complete with swank Cover Flow display — where you can review each collection of bookmarks at your leisure. As you might expect, Safari's Cover Flow works just as the Cover Flow view does in a Finder window.

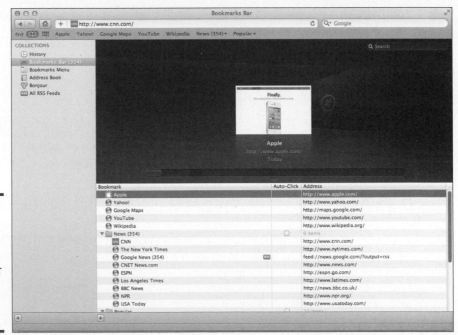

Figure 5-4: The Bookmarks window puts all your bookmarks within easy reach.

The more bookmarks you add, the more unwieldy the Bookmarks menu and the Bookmarks window become. To keep things organized, choose Bookmarks⇨Add Bookmark Folder and then type a name for the new folder. With folders, you can organize your bookmarks into *collections,* which appear in the column at the left of the Bookmarks window and as menus on the Bookmarks bar. (Collections also appear as separate submenus within the Bookmarks menu on the Safari menu bar). You can drag bookmarks into the new folder to help reduce the clutter.

To delete a bookmark or a folder from the Bookmarks window, click it and then press Delete.

Downloading Files

A huge chunk of the fun that you'll find on the web is the ability to download images and files. If you've visited a site that offers files for downloading, typically you just click the Download button or the download file link, and Safari takes care of the rest. You'll see the Downloads status window, which keeps you updated as to the progress of the transfer. While the file is downloading, feel free to continue browsing or even download additional files; the Downloads status window helps you keep track of what's going on and when everything will be finished transferring. To display the Download status window from the keyboard, press ⌘+Option+L. You can also click the Download button at the upper right corner of the window to display the Download list.

By default, Safari saves any downloaded files to the Downloads folder that appears in your Dock, which I like and use. To specify the location where downloaded files are stored — for example, if you'd like to scan them automatically with an antivirus program — follow these steps:

1. **Choose Safari⇨Preferences or press ⌘+, (comma).**

2. **Click the General tab and then click the Save Downloaded Files To pop-up menu.**

3. **Choose Other.**

4. **Navigate to the location where you want the files stored.**

5. **Click the Select button.**

6. **Click the Close button to exit Preferences.**

To download a specific image that appears on a web page, move your mouse pointer over the image and right-click. Then choose Save Image As from the pop-up menu that appears. Safari prompts you for the location where you want to store the file.

You can choose to automatically open files that Safari considers safe — things like movies, text files, and PDF files that are **very** unlikely to store a virus or a damaging macro. By default, the Open "Safe" Files after Downloading check box is selected on the General pane. However, if you're interested in preventing *anything* you download from running until you've manually checked it with your antivirus application, you can deselect the check box and breathe easy.

Luckily, Safari has matured to the point that it can seamlessly handle virtually any multimedia file type that it encounters. However, if you've downloaded a multimedia file and Safari doesn't seem to be able to play or display it, try loading the file within QuickTime Player. As you can read in Book III, Chapter 8, *QuickTime Player* is the Swiss Army knife of multimedia players, and it can recognize a huge number of audio, video, and image formats.

Using Subscriptions and History

To keep track of where you've been, you can display the History list by clicking the History menu. To return to a page in the list, just choose it from the History menu. Note that Safari also arranges older history items by the date you visited the site, so you can easily jump back a couple of days to that page you forgot to bookmark!

In fact, Safari also searches the History list automatically, when it fills in an address that you're typing — that's the feature I mention in the earlier section "Visiting Web Sites."

To view your Top Sites thumbnail screen, press ⌘+Shift+1 or choose Show Top Sites from the History menu. You can also click the Top Sites button on the toolbar.

If you're worried about security and would rather not keep track of where you've been online, I show you how to clear the contents of the History file in the "Handling ancient history" section, later in this chapter.

Tabs Are Your Browsing Friends

Safari also offers *tabbed browsing,* which many folks use to display (and organize) multiple web pages at one time. For example, if you're doing a bit of comparison shopping for a new piece of hardware between different online stores, tabs are ideal.

When you hold down the ⌘ key and click a link or bookmark using tabs, a tab representing the new page appears at the top of the Safari window. Just click the tab to switch to that page. By holding down Shift+⌘, the tab is both created and opened. (If you don't hold down ⌘, things revert to business as usual, and Safari replaces the contents of the window with the new page.) Figure 5-5 illustrates a number of pages that I've opened in Safari using tabs.

You can also open a new tab by clicking the plus sign that appears at the upper-right corner of the Safari window, or by pressing ⌘+T.

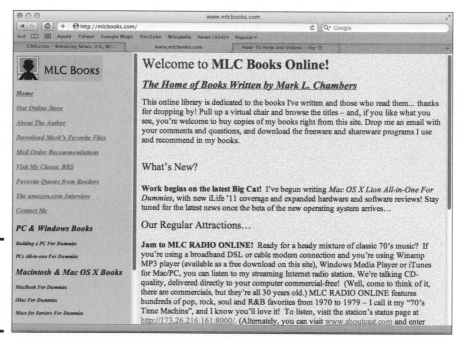

Figure 5-5:
Hang on, Martha; we've struck tabs!

To fine-tune your tabbed browsing experience, choose Safari⇨Preferences to display the Preferences dialog; then click Tabs. From here, you can specify whether a new tab or window automatically becomes the active window within Safari.

Done with a page? You can remove a tabbed page by clicking the X button next to the tab's title.

Saving Web Pages

If you've encountered a page that you'd like to load later, you can save it to disk in its entirety. (Just the text, mind you, not the images.) Follow these steps:

1. **Display the desired page.**

2. **Choose File⇨Save As or press ⌘+S.**

3. **In the Save As text field, type a name for the saved page.**

4. **From the Where pop-up menu, navigate to the location where you want to store the file on your system.**

   To expand the sheet to allow navigation to any location on your system, click the button with the downward arrow.

5. **Click the Format pop-up menu to choose the format for the saved page.**

   Usually, you'll want to choose a Web Archive, which saves the entire page and can be displayed just as you see it. However, if you want to save just the HTML source code, choose Page Source.

6. **Click Save to begin the download process.**

   After the Save file has been created, double-click it to load it in Safari.

A quick word about printing a page within Safari: Some combinations of background and text colors might conspire together to render your printed copy practically worthless. In a case like that, use your printer's grayscale setting (if it has one) or deselect the Print Backgrounds check box in the Print dialog. Alternatively, you can simply click and drag to select the text on the page, press ⌘+C to copy it, and then paste the text into TextEdit, Word, or Pages, where you can print the page on a less offensive background (while still keeping the text formatting largely untouched). You can also save the contents of a page as plain text, as I just demonstrated.

If you'd rather mail the contents of a web page to a friend — or just a link to the page, which is faster to send over a dial-up Internet connection — choose either File⇨Mail Contents of This Page or File⇨Mail Link to This Page. (From the keyboard, press ⌘+I to send the contents in an e-mail message or press ⌘+Shift+I to send a link in e-mail. Alternately, if you've added the Mail button to your toolbar, one click does the job.) Mail loads automatically, complete with a prepared e-mail message. Just address it to the recipients and then click Send!

Protecting Your Privacy

No chapter on Safari would be complete without a discussion of security, against both outside intrusion from the Internet and prying eyes around your Mac. Hence this last section, which covers protecting your privacy.

Although diminutive, the padlock icon that appears at the right side of the Address box when you're connected to a secure web site means a great deal! A *secure site* encrypts the information that you send and receive, making it much harder for those of unscrupulous ideals to obtain things such as credit card numbers and personal information. You can click the padlock icon (next to the site name) to display the security certificate in use on that particular site.

Yes, there are such things as bad cookies

First, a definition of this ridiculous term: A *cookie,* a small file that a web site automatically saves on your hard drive, contains information that the site will use on your future visits. For example, a site might save a cookie to preserve your site preferences for the next time or — in the case of a site such as Amazon.com — to identify you automatically and help customize the offerings that you see.

In and of themselves, cookies aren't bad things. Unlike a virus, a cookie file isn't going to replicate itself or wreak havoc on your system, and only the original site can read the cookie that it creates. However, many folks don't appreciate acting as a gracious host for a slew of little snippets of personal information. (Not to mention that some cookies have highly suggestive names, which could lead to all sorts of conclusions. End of story.)

You can choose to accept some or all cookies, or you can opt to disable cookies altogether. You can also set Safari to accept cookies only from the sites you choose to visit. To change your *Cookie Acceptance Plan* (or CAP, for those who absolutely crave acronyms), follow these steps:

1. **Choose Safari⇨Preferences.**

2. **Click the Privacy toolbar button.**

Safari displays the preference settings shown in Figure 5-6.

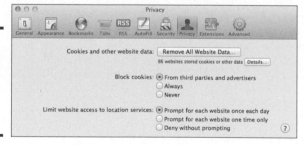

Figure 5-6:
Specifying who's welcome in my cookie jar.

3. **Choose how to block cookies via these radio button choices:**

> *Never:* Accept all cookies.

> *Always:* Block cookies entirely.

> *From Third Parties and Advertisers:* Personally, I use this option, which allows sites like Amazon.com to work correctly without allowing a barrage of superfluous cookies.

4. **To view the cookies currently on your system, click the Details button.**

If a site's cookies are blocked, you might have to take care of things manually, such as by providing a password on the site that used to be read automatically from the cookie.

5. **Click the Close button to save your changes.**

Feeling nervous about the data stored by the web sites you visit? You can always delete *all* of that stored information with a single click — from the Privacy pane in the Safari Preferences window, click the Remove All website Data button. You'll be asked to confirm your draconian decision.

Cleaning your cache

Safari speeds up the loading of web sites by storing often-used images and multimedia files in a temporary storage, or cache, folder. Naturally, the files in your cache folder can be displayed (hint), which could lead to assumptions (hint, hint) about the sites you've been visiting (hint, hint, hint). (Tactful, ain't I?)

Luckily, Safari makes it easy to dump the contents of your cache file. Just choose Safari⇨Empty Cache; then click Empty to confirm that you want to clean up your cache.

Handling ancient history

As you might imagine, your History file leaves a very clear set of footprints indicating where you've been on the web. To delete the contents of the History menu, choose History⇨Clear History (at the very bottom of the History menu).

Safari also allows you to specify an amount of time to retain entries in your History file. Open the Safari Preferences dialog, click the General tab, and then click the Remove History Items pop-up menu to specify the desired amount of time. Items can be rolled off daily, weekly, biweekly, monthly, or yearly.

Avoiding those @*!^%$ pop-up ads

I hate pop-up ads, and I'm sure you do, too. To block most of those pop-up windows with advertisements for everything from low-rate mortgages to "sure-thing" Internet casinos, click the Safari menu and verify that Block Pop-Up Windows is selected. (If it's not selected, click the menu item to toggle the menu item on.)

From time to time, you might run across a web site that actually does something *constructive* with pop-up windows, such as present a download or login prompt. If you need to temporarily deactivate pop-up blocking, press ⌘+Shift+K to toggle it off. Then press ⌘+Shift+K again to turn pop-up blocking back on after you've finished with the site.

Chapter 6: Staying Secure Online

In This Chapter

✔ **Understanding the dangers of going online**

✔ **Using a firewall**

✔ **Avoiding trouble online**

I know that you've heard horror stories about hacking: Big corporations and big government installations seem to be as open to hackers as a public library. Often, you read that even entire identities are stolen online. When you consider that your Mac can contain very sensitive and private information in your life — such as your Social Security number and financial information — it's enough to make you nervous about turning on your computer long enough to check your eBay auctions.

But how much of that is Hollywood? How truly real is the danger, especially to Mac owners? And how can you protect yourself? The good news is that you can *easily* secure your data from all but the most determined hacker — in fact, depending on the hardware that you're using to connect to the Internet, you might be well guarded right now without even knowing it.

In this chapter, I continue a quest that I've pursued for over two decades now — to make my readers feel comfortable and secure in the online world by explaining the truth about what can happen and telling you how you can protect your system from intrusions.

One quick note: This chapter is written with the home and small-business Mac owner in mind. Macs that access the Internet through a larger corporate network are very likely already protected by that knight in shining armor, the network system administrator. (Insert applause here.) Of course, if you're using Mac OS X in your office, you're still welcome to read and follow this material — especially if you have a laptop that could act as a carrier for viruses from home; however, check with your system administrator before you attempt to implement any of the recommendations that I make.

What Can Happen if I Don't Take Security Seriously?

Before I begin, I want to offer you a moment of reassurance and a little of my personal background to explain that I'm well qualified to be your guide through this online minefield. (After all, you don't want Jerry Lewis lecturing you on how to maintain your Internet security. He's a funny guy, though, *convenez-vous?*)

If it smells phishy . . .

Ever heard of the word *phishing?* Con artists and hackers create web sites that look just like major online stores — including big names such as eBay, PayPal, and Amazon. These turkeys then send out junk e-mail messages that tell you that you must log on to this web site to "refresh" or "correct" your personal information. As you've no doubt already guessed, that information is siphoned off and sold to the highest bidder. *Your* credit card, *your* password, and *your* address. Luckily, if you follow the tips that I give later in this chapter in the section "A Dose of Common Sense: Things Not to Do Online," you'll avoid these phishing expeditions!

✦ I've been running and managing all sorts of online systems since the days of the BBS *(Bulletin Board System),* the text-based dinosaurs that used to rule the online world in the early '80s to early '90s. (In fact, my first book was on this very subject — and it contained a chapter on viruses long before they were the darlings of the techno-media.)

✦ As a consultant, I run web sites and squash virus attacks for a number of companies and organizations.

✦ I run a popular Internet radio station that serves up '70s hits in CD-quality to anyone with a high-speed DSL or cable Internet connection and a copy of iTunes. (More on this broadcasting revolution in Book III, Chapter 2.)

✦ I keep my own office network of six computers safe from attack while still providing readers all over the world with web sites and the afore-mentioned radio station and BBS.

With that understood, here's what can happen to you online *without* the right safeguards, on *any* computer:

✦ **Hackers can access shared information on your network.** If you're running an unguarded network, others can gain access to your documents and applications or wreak havoc on your system.

✦ **Your system could be infected with a virus or dangerous macro.** Left to their own devices, these misbehaving programs and macro commands can delete files or turn your entire hard drive into an empty paperweight. (Although Mac viruses are very, *very* rare as I write this, I don't think we'll enjoy such luxury for long. Plus, if you dual-boot your Intel Mac into Windows XP, Vista, or Windows 7, you've suddenly entered a veritable minefield of PC viruses and spyware. More on this in a page or two.)

✦ **Unsavory individuals could attempt to contact members of your family.** This kind of attack may take place through iChat, e-mail, or web discussion boards, putting your family's safety at risk.

✦ **Hackers can use your system to attack others.** Your computer can be tricked into helping hackers when they attempt to knock out web servers and public-access File Transfer Protocol (FTP) sites on the Internet. Along the same lines, that innocent web server you put online can be misused by spam-spewing, online "entrepreneurs." (Cute name, right?)

✦ **Criminals can attempt to con you out of your credit card or personal information.** The Internet is a prime tool used by those trying to steal identities.

To be absolutely honest, some danger is indeed present every time you or any user of your Macintosh connects to the Internet. However, here's the good news. With the right safeguards, it's literally impossible for most of those worst-case scenarios to happen on your Macintosh, and what remains would be so difficult that even the most die-hard hacker would throw in the towel long before reaching your computer or network.

More of Mark's totally unnecessary computer trivia

The term *hacker* dates far back in the annals of the personal computer — in fact, it originally had nothing to do with networks, the Internet, or illegal activities at all . . . because In The Beginning, there was no public Internet!

"Explain yourself, Chambers!" All right. The original hackers were electronics buffs, ham radio operators, computer hobbyists, and engineers who built (or *hacked*) a working computer out of individual components with a soldering gun and a whole lotta guts. At the time, you didn't simply order a computer from Dell or visit your local Maze o' Wires store in the mall to select your favorite system. You built it from a kit, or even from scratch!

Remember, I'm talking about the mid-'70s, in the halcyon time before IBM even introduced the IBM PC (and when the only folks using the Internet, which wasn't called that back then,

were military folks and researchers). Even the simplest computer — really nothing more than a glorified calculator by today's standards — had to be lovingly assembled by hand. These early personal computers didn't run software as we know it. Instead, you programmed them manually through a bank of switches on the front, and they responded with codes displayed on a bank of lights. (Think about that the next time you launch Microsoft Word 2011 with a single click of a Dock icon.)

Today, of course, the need to assemble a computer from individual transistors is nonexistent, and the word *hacker* has an entirely different connotation — but don't be surprised if you meet an older member of your Macintosh user's group who's proud to be an old-fashioned hacker! (Look for the soldering gun, usually worn in a holster like a sidearm.)

Using a Macintosh gives you an advantage: Hackers and virus developers (there's a career for you) are traditionally interested only in "having fun" with PCs running Windows, so the likelihood that Lion could pick up a virus is far less than it would be if you were using Windows XP, Vista, or 7. As I mentioned earlier, if you boot into Windows using Lion's dual-boot feature on your Intel-based Macintosh, you need to pay heed to Windows security — the same warning also applies to those running Windows in a virtual machine (using programs like Parallels Desktop or VMWare).

Because this is a book that focuses on Mac OS X Lion, I won't be spending much time covering Windows. If you'd like a comprehensive guide to Windows 7 and the PC world, however, I can heartily recommend the sister volume to this book, *PCs All-in-One For Dummies,* Fifth Edition, published by Wiley. Why the strong recommendation? Well, I wrote that book as well!

Evidently, Apple just doesn't have the numbers to attract the attention of the Bad Guys *yet* . . . another reason to enjoy the exclusive nature of the Mac universe (and its UNIX foundation)! (Heck, I even know a couple of fellow Mac owners who feel they just don't need antivirus protection — but believe me, this is *not* an area where you want to be lax and lazy, and you *still need* an antivirus application! More on antivirus software later in this chapter.)

I also want to point out that virtually everyone reading this book — as well as the guy writing it — really doesn't have anything that's worth a malicious hacking campaign. Things like Quicken data files, saved games of Sims 3, and genealogical data might be priceless to us, of course, but most dedicated hackers are after bigger game. Unfortunately, the coverage that the media and Hollywood give to corporate and government attacks can turn even Aunt Harriet more than a little paranoid. Therefore, time for another of Mark's Maxims:

It's not really necessary to consider the FBI or Interpol each time you poke your Mac's power button. A few simple precautions are all that's required.

"Shields Up, Chekov!"

"Okay, Mark, now I know the real story on what can happen to my computer online. So what do I do to safeguard my Macintosh?" You need but two essential tools to protect your hardware (besides a healthy amount of common sense, which I cover in the upcoming section "A Dose of Common Sense: Things Not to Do Online"): a firewall and an antivirus program.

Firewall basics

First, a definition: a *firewall* is a piece of hardware or software that essentially builds an impermeable barrier between the computers on your side of the wall (meaning your Mac and any other computers on your network) and all external computers on the other side of the wall (meaning the rest of the Internet).

"But wait a second — if other computers can't reach me and my Mac can't reach them, how can I use the Internet at all?" Ah, that's the beauty of today's firewalls. By using a series of techniques designed to thwart attacks from the outside, a firewall allows you to communicate safely, even monitoring what you send and what you receive for later examination. Figure 6-1 illustrates the basics of a firewall.

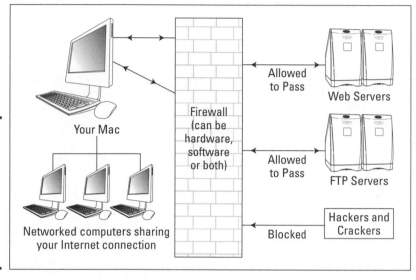

Figure 6-1:
A firewall, hard at work. (They're not actually made of brick, though.)

A firewall sounds grand and incredibly complex and highly technical — and sometimes it is — but it can also be incredibly simple. For example:

✦ You can spend anywhere from $50 to thousands of dollars installing sophisticated firewall hardware and/or software.

or

✦ You can activate your firewall by disconnecting your Mac's dialup, digital subscriber line (DSL), or cable modem from the wall socket.

Believe it or not, both of those examples technically involve a firewall. In the first case, the firewall is a physical, tangible presence on the network; in the second case, the lack of a connection to the Internet actually acts as a firewall. (Think of it as the Air Firewall.) I've spoken to a number of readers who actually do this; however, if you're running a web site or downloading a file from your company's FTP site, yanking the connection when you head to bed isn't an option. Therefore, most of us will install a physical firewall through hardware or software.

Do I already have a firewall?

In some cases, you might already be using a hardware firewall and not even know it. For example, many Internet-sharing devices include a built-in NAT firewall. NAT stands for *Network Address Translation,* and it's the most effective and popular hardware firewall standard in use by consumer devices. If you're using an Internet sharing hub or router, check its manual to determine whether it offers NAT as a firewall feature — and if so, turn it on if NAT isn't enabled by default. (See Book VI, Chapter 2 for more on Internet sharing, routers, and firewalls.)

For instance, Figure 6-2 illustrates the configuration screen for my Internet router. Note the options to disable port scanning and ping responses, which are two tricks that hackers often use to detect what's often called a *hot computer* — meaning that the computer can be identified and is accessible to attack. (Wireless networks are notoriously hot — for more information on securing your wireless connections, visit Book VI, Chapter 4.)

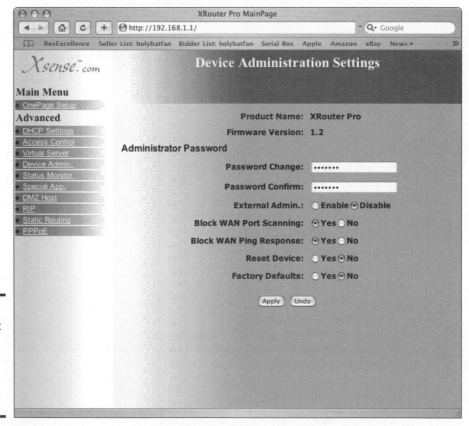

Figure 6-2: My Internet router is set to be downright rude to hackers.

Using the internal Mac OS X firewall

Mac OS X includes a powerful internal firewall, which Lion makes very simple to use! Most Mac owners will be perfectly satisfied with this built-in firewall, which is configured through System Preferences — find more information on setting up your firewall in Book VI, Chapter 2.

Using a commercial software firewall

You'll also find a number of popular alternatives to Lion's built-in firewall on the market that offer more control over individual applications and more configuration options than your Mac OS X firewall. For example, consider these commercial software firewall applications:

✦ **Symantec, Norton Internet Security for Mac, $80 (www.symantec.com):** Symantec provides both antivirus and firewall protection for the PC and the Macintosh. Frequent updates and top-of-the-line technical support ensure that your firewall stays current and that you can get help when you need it.

✦ **Intego, Internet Security Barrier X6, $80 (www.intego.com):** Along with antispam and antiphishing features, Internet Security Barrier X6 comes with a number of preset configurations that allow you to choose a basic firewall for your network environment with a single click.

Whether you set up the internal firewall, a shareware firewall, or a commercial firewall, visit a favorite site of mine on the web: www.grc.com, the home of Gibson Research Corporation. There you'll find the free online utility ShieldsUP!!, which automatically tests just how tight your firewall is and how susceptible your Mac could be to hacker attacks. Visit this site often because this service is updated periodically to reflect new hacking techniques.

Antivirus basics

Next, consider your antivirus protection (both under Lion and Windows XP/Vista/7, if you're running Boot Camp on an Intel-based Mac). *Viruses* are typically transmitted through applications — you run a program, and the virus is activated. (Although they don't meet the traditional definition of a virus, both scripts and macros can be used to take control of your system and cause trouble, as well.) Therefore, you need to closely monitor what I call The Big Three:

✦ **Web downloads:** Consider every file that you receive from the Internet as a possible viral threat.

✦ **Removable media:** Viruses can be stored on everything from CD-ROMs and DVD-ROMs to USB flash drives.

✦ **E-mail file attachments:** A "Trojan Horse" or "worm" application sent to you as an e-mail attachment is an easy doorway to your system.

Horrors! Mac OS X has no built-in antivirus support. (Then again, neither does Windows.) However, a good antivirus program will take care of any application that's carrying a virus. Some even handle destructive macros within documents. Make sure that the antivirus program you choose offers *real-time scanning,* which operates when you download or open a file. Periodic scanning of your entire system is important, too, but only a real-time scanning application such as Norton AntiVirus can immediately ensure that the StuffIt and Zip archives or the application you just received in your e-mail Inbox is actually free from viruses. (Oh, and don't forget that many of the Software Updates released by Apple for Lion will plug security holes in our favorite operating system.)

Virus technology continues to evolve over time, just as more beneficial application development does. For example, viruses have been developed that are actually contained in both JPEG image files and ebooks (electronic books)! With a good antivirus application that offers regular updates, you'll continue to keep your system safe from viral attack.

I heartily recommend both ClamXav 2 (free for personal use at www. clamxav.com) and Intego's VirusBarrier X6 for Mac antivirus protection. Both programs include automatic updates delivered while you're online to make sure that you're covered against the latest viruses.

A Dose of Common Sense: Things Not to Do Online

One more powerful weapon that you can use to make sure that your Mac stays safe from unlawful intrusion is this: Practicing common sense on the Internet is just as important as adding a firewall and an antivirus application to your Mac.

With this in mind, here's a checklist of things that you should never do while you're online:

✦ **Never download a file from a site you don't trust.** And make sure that your antivirus software is configured to check downloaded files before you open them.

✦ **Never open an e-mail attachment until it has been checked.** Don't give in to temptation, even if the person who sent the message is someone you trust. (Many macro viruses actually replicate themselves by sending copies to the addresses found through the victim's e-mail program. Of course, this problem crops up regularly in the Windows world, but it's been known to happen in the Macintosh community as well.)

+ **Never enter any personal information in an e-mail message unless you know the recipient.** Sure, I send my mailing address to friends and family, but no one else. In fact, e-mail can be intercepted by a determined hacker, so if you're sending something truly important like personal data, use an encryption application, such as PGP Personal Desktop (www.pgp.com).

+ **Never enter any personal information on a web site provided as a link in an e-mail message.** Don't fall prey to phishing expeditions. Some of these e-mail-message/web-site combinations look authentic enough to fool anyone! No reputable online company or store will demand or solicit your personal information through e-mail or through a linked web site. In fact, feel free to contact the company through its *real* web site and report the phishing attempt!

+ **Never include any personal information in an Internet newsgroup post.** (In case you're not familiar with the term, *newsgroups* are public Internet message bases, often called Usenet groups. Many ISPs offer a selection of newsgroups that you can access.) Newsgroup posts can be viewed by anyone, so there's no such thing as privacy in a newsgroup. (For a glimpse of just how long one of these posts can linger in the great Internet continuum, visit www.google.com, click the Groups button, and search for your name. I can pull up newsgroup messages that I posted back in 1995!)

+ **Never buy from an online store that doesn't offer a secure, encrypted connection when you're prompted for your personal information and credit card number.** If you're using Apple's Safari browser, the padlock icon appears next to the site name in the title bar. When the padlock icon appears in the title bar, the connection is encrypted and secure — you'll also note that the web address begins with *https:* rather than *http:*

+ **Never divulge personal information to others over an iChat connection.**

+ **Never use the same password for all your electronic business.** Use different passwords that include both letters and numbers, change them often, and never divulge them to anyone else.

+ **Never give anyone else administrative access to your web server.**

+ **Never allow any type of remote access (such as sharing screens) to your Macintosh or your network without testing that access first.** It's very important to restrict remote access to visitors whom you trust.

Find more details on securing your network from intrusion — including Internet hacker attacks — in Book VI. I cover System Preferences that can affect the security of your system in Book II.

Book VI

Networking in Mac OS X

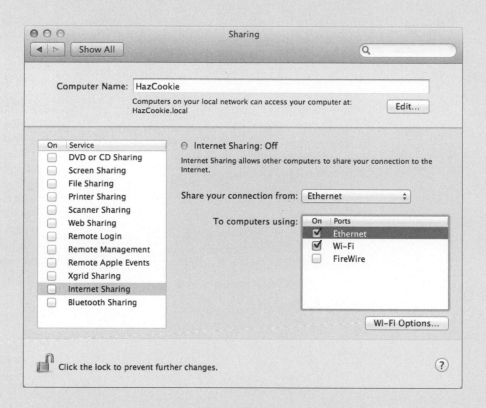

Contents at a Glance

Chapter 1: Setting Up a Small Network

In This Chapter

✔ Finding out what a network is and why you might want one

✔ Setting up the network hardware

✔ Configuring network system preferences

✔ Troubleshooting your network

*I*n the not-so-distant past — I'm talking 20–25 years ago — networks were found only in huge companies that had the money and the workforce to pay for and maintain them. But now, as technology rolls on, a home or small office network is both very affordable and relatively easy to create. In this chapter, I introduce you to this helpful beastie: You discover what networks are, what you can do with them, and how to set up a small network of your own for your home or small business.

Networks can be used for many things. Computers exchange all types of data over a network: files that you want to send between computers or to networked printers, streaming audio or video broadcasts, data for multiplayer computer games, or even a private company web site (typically called an *intranet*). Anything that you can imagine that would involve moving data between multiple computers can be done by using a network.

What Do I Need to Set Up My Network?

First, let me define network. In a nutshell, a *network* is a combination of hardware, cables, and software that allows computers and printers to talk to one another. (Heck, you don't even need cables with a wireless network, as I show you in Chapter 3 of this minibook.) To have a network, you need the right hardware and software. Some of the hardware and most of the software that you'll need probably came with your Mac, depending on which Mac you have. As you progress through this chapter, you'll discover everything that's required to set up your network so that you can pick up any additional parts you need. Any good-sized computer store (either the brick-and-mortar or online variety) has everything that you need to get up and running.

Now, back to the requirements: You need the right hardware and software to make your network sing. This section covers each component with a description about the role that each part plays on the network and other good stuff you'll want to know to get your network right the first time.

Something to network

Okay, this might be obvious, but I'm nothing if not thorough. The first thing that you need to build a network is . . . well, *stuff!* That's right, you need to have devices that you want to network. Most times these are computers (whether Macs or other PCs running Windows/Linux/UNIX), printers, personal digital assistants (PDAs), cell phones, iOS devices (like the iPad, iPhone, and iPod touch) and other stand-alone, network-capable devices (such as file servers and shared back-up drives).

Network interface card (NIC)

A *network interface card*, or NIC, is a hardware device that your computer uses to talk to the rest of the network. The NIC connects to the network cabling, and it speaks the language of electronics, sending data around the network. Nowadays, most networks use the Ethernet networking protocol, and most NICs are Ethernet-compatible. All Lion-compatible Mac models have Ethernet NIC hardware built right onto the Mac's main system board.

Switch

So you have an assortment of devices in your home or small office that you've decided to network. How do you make them all interconnect? Although you could connect just two computers by using nothing more than a single cross-over cable, you need fancier hardware to connect more than two computers: namely, a switch. The switch is used to connect everything, so it's the focal point of the network. Without a switch, you don't have a network.

A *switch* is really just a small box that has a bunch of Ethernet ports on it. A *port* is really just like an Ethernet NIC on your computer, but a switch has lots of them. Inside, all those Ethernet ports are arranged so that the talking (sending) wires from each port connect to the listening (receiving) wires on all other ports. Therefore, when one computer talks, all others listen.

Setting up a switch (and therefore giving birth to your network, which sounds more painful than it is) is usually no more difficult than connecting a power cable to the device and then plugging in your computers with their own Ethernet cables. You'll see various lights on the box — usually a power light indicating that the switch is powered on and operational. You'll also see lights that correspond to each port on the switch; these lights tell you what's going on in the box. For instance, you normally see the following types of lights:

Thirty-nine flavors of Ethernet . . . but no Rocky Road

Ethernet standards allow for operation at different speeds. Because the Ethernet standard has improved over time, some older Ethernet devices support only the older (slower) speeds. Ethernet's speed is rated by how much data it can transfer in a second — usually in millions of bits per second, or megabits per second (Mbps). Originally, Ethernet was designed to run at 10 Mbps. Now there are different speeds of Ethernet: 10 Mbps, 100 Mbps, 1000 Mbps, and even faster.

1000 Mbps Ethernet — also called *Gigabit Ethernet* or just *Gigabit* for short — is the best choice for small home or office networks. All consumer-level Gigabit Ethernet NICs also support running at 10 Mbps or 100 Mbps, so you

will hear them called *10/100/1000 Ethernet NICs*. All current Mac models (except the MacBook Air) come with a 10/100/1000 Ethernet NIC built in, including the MacBook and Mac mini. Although Gigabit switches are now priced under $50, most of the devices that can connect Gigabit NICs still cost a bit more than their 10/100 counterparts, but the performance gains are well worth a few extra dollars.

Virtually all the modern NICs and other Ethernet hardware support both 10 Mbps and 100 Mbps. Most times, you'll see this labeled as *10/100 Ethernet*. For your home networking, you probably want to invest in hardware that can deliver either Gigabit or 100 Mbps speeds.

✦ **Link light:** Each port on a switch should have a link light. *Link lights* simply tell you which ports have something alive connected to a given port — that is, a device is connected and powered on.

✦ **Speed light:** Each port on the switch should have a speed light, which tells you the speed of the device at the other end. Some switches have different lights for different speeds, and some use a single light and make it different colors for different speeds.

✦ **Activity light:** When one computer speaks, they all hear it. Typically, an entire switch has only one activity light for the entire network, indicating that someone is speaking. With heavy traffic, the light can appear solid.

Bear with me whilst I spew techno-talk for a paragraph or two. When an Ethernet switch receives a *frame* — that's the name for a standard unit, or *packet,* of network data — it reads the label on the frame to see the return address of the computer that sent the frame. In a short amount of time (after being turned on and watching the data move around), a switch figures out which computer is located on which port. Then, whenever data comes into the switch, it looks at the *header* (some information on the front of all frames, much like a mailing label on a package that you send) and sees which computer should receive the frame. The switch then sends the frame out the port for that computer only.

This is A Good Thing. Instead of forcing all computers on the network to listen while one Mac speaks (as antique network hubs did) — known as *half-duplex* — a switch sends the data directly to the only computer that needs to hear it.

Cables

Cables are the ties that bind . . . literally. *Cables* are used to connect the Ethernet port on each computer to the switch, the central hardware of the network. With a little experience, you'll be a cable-wielding superhero with hundreds of feet of cable draped across every piece of furniture in your place for your first LAN party. (A *LAN party,* by the way, is when way too many techies bring their computers into a very small space, connect them, and play games for 48 hours straight. Oh, and we eat a lot, too. Good stuff!)

Here's the scoop on what kind of cables to use. Technically, you can run 100 Mbps Ethernet over *Cat-5* cable (like a super-version of the wire that you use for your telephones).

Although you can do 10/100 Mbps Ethernet over Cat-5 cable, any new cables that you buy should be Cat-5E or Cat-6 — which I talk about in the following section — because these types of cables are specifically meant for use with 1000 Mbps (or Gigabit) Ethernet. I'm sure you noticed that the common denominator here is the Cat-5 cable. That's because fiber optic cable, although supporting speeds of 100 Mbps, 1 Gbps, and even 10 Gbps, is much more expensive and more difficult to install.

Hey, did I mention that you can eschew cables entirely? For more information on the lean, mean (but significantly slower) world of wireless networking, see Chapter 3 of this minibook.

Be sure to buy *straight-through* Cat-5E/Cat-6 cables (also called *patch* cables) and not *crossover* cables, which are used only in certain circumstances. Crossover cables are mainly used to connect two computers directly (to form a tiny, two-computer network), connect a cable/DSL modem directly to a computer, or connect multiple switches.

Cat-5 cable supports speeds of 100 Mbps. 1000 Mbps Ethernet, of course, is designed to run ten times faster than that; luckily enough, it was engineered to be compatible with 90 percent of Cat-5 installations. Having said that, I must also point out that some Cat-5 cables don't stick to the stringent specifications that 1000 Mbps Ethernet requires. The newer version of Cat-5 cable is *Category 5 Enhanced*, or Cat-5E for short. Cat-5E is recommended for any new installation because it can easily handle 10/100 Mbps Ethernet and yet can handle 1000 Mbps Ethernet as well. Even if you're using 10/100 Mbps Ethernet, you can upgrade someday to 1000 Mbps without having to worry about upgrading your cabling. You may also find Cat-6 cabling in your network travels, which can also easily handle 1000 Mbps speeds.

Setting Up Your Network

After you collect the hardware components I list earlier in this chapter, you're ready to connect things. Here's a quick list of things to do to get your network fired up:

1. Find the best location for placing your switch.

To keep costs down, try to place the switch in a location close to a power outlet that's centrally located so that you can use the least amount of cable. If cost isn't an issue, hide the unit in a closet and just run all the cables along the walls to the hub or switch. And if cost *really* isn't an issue, get your house fully wired with Cat-5E or Cat-6 cable.

2. Plug the switch into the power socket.

Some switches come on automatically when you plug them in and can never be turned off. Others have a power switch that you need to turn on the first time that you plug them in.

3. Verify that the switch is working by looking at the lights on the front. Check the manual that came with the switch to see what light configuration is normal for that particular unit.

Until you have computers or printers attached to it, you might just have a status light that shows the switch is powered on. But if the lights on your unit don't match up with what the manual says, you could have a bum unit that you need to return.

4. Verify that all your devices are near enough to the switch to be connected by your cables; then turn them all on.

5. Get one of your Cat-5E or Cat-6 cables and connect one cable from the Ethernet jack on your computer, usually on the side or back, to an open port on the switch.

You should see a link light or speed light come on that verifies that the two devices sense each other. (You might also have a link light on your NIC where you plug in the cable, but that depends on the Mac you're using.)

6. Repeat Step 5 until each device is attached to the switch.

Congratulations, you're a network technician! (Don't forget to call your friends and brag.) The first phase of the network, the physical connection, is complete; the next step is the configuration of Mac OS X.

Understanding the Basics of Network Configuration

Take a deep breath; there's no need to panic — in fact, configuring your network software basically involves entering a lot of numbers and other stuff in dialogs. (In fact, most folks can just allow Lion to take care of network settings automatically.) But just so that you'll understand what's involved, this section explains what those numbers are, what they do, and why you ought to know it. Because this is a Mac OS X book, I stick with configuring Macs running the Big X.

TCP/IP

First things first: *Protocol* is just the techno-nerd word for a set of rules or a language. A *protocol* is a language that computers use to communicate. Without protocols, the computers on your network would never be able to speak to one another even though you have NICs, cables, and a hub or a switch. The Internet Protocol (IP) part of the TCP/IP suite is what you're really interested in because it's the most important part of your network configuration chore.

IP addresses

IP addresses are like street addresses for computers on a network. Each computer on the network has an IP address, and it needs to be unique because no other computer can share it. When a computer wants to communicate with another computer, it can simply send the data on the network in a nice package that has its address as well as the address of the computer that it's trying to talk to. (Remember frames? If not, take a refresher in the earlier section "Switch.")

An IP address is just a number, but it's written in a strange way. (Go figure.) All IP addresses are written as four sets of numerals between 0 and 255 with a dot (period) between each set. For instance, a common IP address that you might run into is 192.168.0.1. As everyone knows, engineers can't sleep unless they have three or four ways to write the same thing, including IP addresses. The form shown above — which is by far the most common — is *dotted notation.* Each number, such as 192, is an *octet.*

Don't worry too much about this stuff: You don't have to remember terms like *octet* to create your own network. They could be helpful, however, if something goes wrong and you need to place a call to tech support. Plus, you can impress the computer salesperson (gleefully called a *wonk* by Mac power users) at your local Maze 'o Wires store with your mastery of techno-babble.

IP addresses at home versus on the Internet

One very important thing to keep in mind is that the Almighty IP Address Police — *Internet Assigned Numbers Authority* (www.iana.org) — has broken IP addresses into groups. The two main types of IP addresses are public and private:

✦ **Public IP addresses** can be used on the Internet and are unique throughout the whole world.

✦ **Private IP addresses** are used in homes or businesses and can't be used to talk to the public Internet. Private IP addresses are used over and over by many people and most commonly take the form 192.168.*x.x*, 172.16.x.x, or 10.0.x.x (Apple routers, such as the TimeCapsule or AirPort Extreme, set up private networks in the last range).

You'll almost always get a public IP address from your Internet service provider (ISP), whether you're using a cable modem, digital subscriber line (DSL), or a regular dial-up modem. If you use a cable/DSL router or Lion's built-in sharing software to share your Internet connection among multiple computers, you'll be using private IP addresses on your network while using a single public IP address to talk to the Internet. (More on that in Chapter 4 of this minibook.)

"Great! I get an IP address, put it into my Network settings in System Preferences, and off I go. Right?" Well, you're close, but here are a few other pieces of information that you might need before you can go surfing around the world:

✦ **Default gateway:** When you send information to other networks — whether in another building or around the world on the Internet — your computer needs to know the IP address of the gateway that will forward your data down the line. The *default gateway* is really just the IP address of a *router,* which is a device that connects multiple networks. A *gateway* gets its name because it really is your gateway to all other networks.

✦ **Subnet mask:** A *subnet mask* is a number that helps your computer know when it needs to send stuff through the router. It's a group of four octets with dots, just like an IP address, but almost always uses 0 or 255 for each of the four octets. Most often, the subnet mask is 255.255.255.0. If the wrong number is entered for the subnet mask, it could keep you from talking to the Internet or even to computers on your own network.

Software applications

After you have the hardware in place and you've chosen and configured a protocol to allow the computers to all talk to one another, you need software to make use of your new network connections. Time for more good news: A lot of the software that you need to move data on your network is included already in Mac OS X! Here are brief descriptions of some of the network software and protocols already built into Mac OS X and what they're used for:

✦ **FTP:** *File Transfer Protocol* (FTP), part of the TCP/IP protocol suite, allows computers of any type — Mac, PC, Linux, UNIX, mainframe, or whatever — to transfer files back and forth.

✦ **Telnet:** *Telnet* is also part of the TCP/IP suite — you can use it to remotely connect to a computer and execute commands on the remote machine.

✦ **Samba:** *Samba* (or *SMB*) enables Mac OS X users to share files with people using Windows computers and allows the Mac users to connect to files that the Windows computers share.

✦ **HTTP:** *HyperText Transfer Protocol* (HTTP), also part of the TCP/IP suite, is used by web browsers to provide access to all the various pages on the World Wide Web.

Configuring Network System Preferences

In this section, I show you how to configure your Mac to communicate with other computers on a local network.

Leave it to Lion to provide you with assistance — in this case, when you first open the Network pane, you might be greeted with a dialog offering you assistance on setting up the stuff I cover in this section. (Whether you get this *absolutely free* offer of aid depends on whether you upgraded your Mac from a previous version of Mac OS X or whether you entered your network and Internet settings within the Lion Setup Assistant.) If you do decide to allow the Lion Internet/Network assistant to guide you through your network setup, I'll meet back up with you at the next section. (Note that you can also start the assistant manually at any time by clicking the Assist Me button at the bottom of the Network pane.)

Using DHCP for automatic IP address assignment

Now I'd like to introduce you to a **very** dear friend of mine — an abbreviation that you will soon grow to love, as does everyone else who's set up a small Mac network. *Dynamic Host Configuration Protocol,* or DHCP for short, is a protocol that enables a computer to automatically get all the information that I've talked about to this point. (Check in your *Webster's* . . . this is the very definition of the word *godsend.*)

You're saying, "Mark, there's gotta be a catch, right?" Well, here's the bad news: Before you can use DHCP, you have to add a *DHCP server,* which provides other computers on the network with their configuration settings. Here's the good news: Most Internet connection-sharing hardware devices (and software-sharing implementations as well) provide a DHCP server as part of the price of admission. (*Internet connection sharing* allows all your networked computers to access the Internet through a single Internet connection. I cover it more in Chapter 4 of this minibook.) Most wired and wireless routers can provide DHCP services these days. Technology marches on.

If you plan to use Internet connection sharing or you know that you have a DHCP server on your network, you can set up your Mac to automatically obtain the required IP address and information. Open System Preferences from the Dock or the Apple menu and choose Network. From the Network dialog that appears, click the Ethernet entry in the list on the left. Choose Using DHCP from the Configure IPv4 pop-up menu; click the Apply button. Mac OS X contacts the DHCP server to obtain an IP address, a subnet mask, a gateway router IP address, and a Domain Name System (DNS) address. (*DNS servers* convert a human-friendly address, like www.yahoo.com, to a computer-friendly IP address, like 66.218.71.86.)

A few seconds after clicking the Apply button, you should see the information come up, as provided by the DHCP server. This lets you know that the process worked and configuration is complete. You might also notice that the DNS Servers information is empty (or grayed out). Fear not: Mac OS X is really using DNS information provided by the DHCP server. Press ⌘+Q to quit System Preferences and save your settings.

**Book VI
Chapter 1**

Setting Up a Small Network

If you ever make a network change that screws things up, such as entering the wrong subnet mask or an IP address that isn't in the same range as others on your LAN, you can always click the Revert button to get back your old settings.

One DHCP server on a network is princely, but two or more DHCP servers on a single network will fight like alley cats and grind everything to a halt. Therefore, if you're considering adding a DHCP server to an existing network, make *doggone* sure that you're not treading on another server's toes. (Ask that network administrator person.)

Manually choosing an IP address range

You say you don't have a DHCP server, and you need to manually assign IP addresses? This configuration means two things: You need to manually configure the Transmission Control Protocol/Internet Protocol (TCP/IP) Properties. Keep in mind that for now, you're not concerned with the Internet — just computers on the local network.

A result of being on a *local* network — because it's not connected to the Internet, it's also called a *private* network — is that you must use IP addresses that are reserved for private network use. You can use a few different ranges of IP addresses, but I recommend that you choose an address range from the 192.168.*x.x* networks. In the next section, I show you how.

Down to business: *I recommend that you use IP addresses in the 192.168.x.x range.* What does this mean exactly? Well, here's the scoop:

✦ **Use IP addresses where the first two octets are 192 and 168 (192.168).**

Octet numbers are conjoined by periods.

✦ **For the third octet, select any number between 1 and 254.**

It doesn't matter which one you choose as long as you use this same third number on all computers on your network.

✦ **For the fourth octet, select any number between 1 and 254.**

Make sure that every computer on your local network has a different fourth octet number. This is very important — your network doesn't work otherwise.

✦ **Use 255.255.255.0 as your subnet mask.**

For instance, suppose that you're using three computers on your network. All the IP addresses that you use will start with *192.168.* Next, suppose you choose *123* for the third octet. (Remember that you can choose any number between 1 and 254.) Finally, for the fourth octet, choose the numbers 100, 105, and 110 for the three computers, respectively. (Again, you can choose any numbers between 1 and 254.) The resulting IP addresses used on the three computers are

192.168.123.100

192.168.123.105

192.168.123.110

By the way, I should mention that there are other range possibilities for reserved private networks — AirPort and AirPort Extreme hardware typically uses a 10.*x.x.x* network range, for example — but the 192.168.*x.x* range is definitely the most popular and the most common default on Ethernet network hardware.

After you know the IP addresses and the subnet mask that you're going to use, start setting up each computer. Being a nice guy, I walk you through the process of configuring Mac OS X with the 192.168.123.105 address as an example.

Be sure that you have all the physical portion of your network powered up and connected as I outline in the earlier section, "Setting Up Your Network."

1. **Select any of your Macs to start with and open System Preferences (either from the Apple menu or from the Dock).**

2. **From the System Preferences dialog, choose Network.**

   The Network pane appears.

3. **Click Ethernet in the list.**

4. **Click the Configure IPv4 pop-up menu and choose Manually.**

5. **Enter the IP address for this machine (192.168.123.105 in this example) in the IP Address text box.**

6. **Enter the subnet mask of 255.255.255.0 in the Subnet Mask text box.**

7. **If you're using a router or hardware Internet sharing device, enter the IP address used by the router in the Router text box.**

   Figure 1-1 shows how things should look at this point.

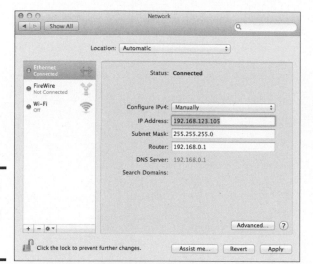

Figure 1-1:
Manually
configuring
TCP/IP
settings.

8. **Click the Apply button, and your new network settings take effect.**

9. **Press ⌘+Q to quit System Preferences.**

   Repeat this same procedure with the other IP addresses for each of the other Macs that are connected to your network.

Most ISPs also supply DNS server addresses and search domains. If your ISP included DNS server addresses or search domains, don't forget to type them into the corresponding boxes on the TCP/IP panel.

Verifying Connectivity

After you have your Macs connected and your TCP/IP configuration is done, check to make sure that everything is working. After you have at least two computers on your network, each with a TCP/IP address, you can use a simple little utility called `ping` to test the connection.

`ping` is a very simple, yet extremely helpful, utility that's the first connectivity-testing tool out of the box, even for network professionals. When you use the `ping` utility — referred to as *pinging* something — the application sends out a small packet of data to whatever destination you're trying to reach.

When the receiving computer hears the ping, it answers with a ping reply. If the original computer receives the ping reply, you know that the connection between the computers is good.

To ping a computer, you use a little application built in to Mac OS X called *Network Utility,* which allows you to work various network wonders (including checking connectivity, watching the route that your computer takes to get to another computer, and looking up information about Internet domain names). To use Network Utility to check network connectivity, follow these steps:

1. **Click the Launchpad icon in the Dock, and then click the Utilities icon.**

2. **Click the Network Utility icon to launch the application.**

3. **Click the Ping tab (see Figure 1-2).**

Figure 1-2:
Preparing to ping. (Can you say that with a straight face?)

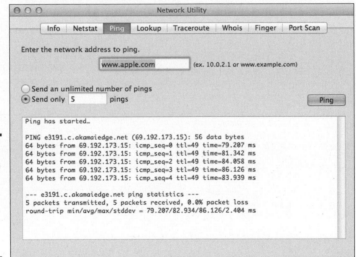

4. **In the Enter the Network Address to Ping text field, enter the IP address (or web address) of the computer that you want to ping.**

5. **To simply verify connectivity, select the Send Only *x* Pings radio button and enter a low number, such as 5, in the text field.**

Five or ten pings are plenty to see whether the connection is working.

6. **Click the Ping button.**

Your Mac sends ping packets to the IP address that you entered.

If the pings are successful, text appears in the text box at the bottom of the Ping tab: one line for each ping reply received from the other computer. The end of each line reads `time=` with a number at the end. That number is the amount of time, in 1/1000 of a second (milliseconds [ms]), that it took for the ping packet to go from your computer to the other computer and back.

If your ping is unsuccessful, you see nothing, at least for a little bit. Each ping that you send takes two seconds before it's considered missing in action. So, if you choose five pings, wait ten seconds before you see the results. After all the pings time out — a ping *times out* when it doesn't get returned in the proper amount of time — you see a line of text appear that reads `ping: sendto: No route to host` or `100% packet loss`. Both error messages mean the same thing: All the ping packets that you sent out are now in the packet graveyard, never to be seen again. As you've likely guessed already, this is *not* A Good Sign for your network connectivity. Look to the following section, "Troubleshooting Your New Network," to find out where to begin troubleshooting this problem.

If you can ping all the other computers on your network from one of the computers, you don't need to go to each computer and ping all the others. You can logically assume that all the computers can communicate. For instance, if you can ping computers B, C, and D from computer A, you don't need to bother with ping tests from computer B, C, or D.

After you have your computers configured and you've verified connectivity among them, start doing the fun stuff that a network allows you to do, such as sharing data, printing, and (most important) playing games with users on other computers.

Troubleshooting Your New Network

After a network is set up and operating, it rarely has problems — still, Murphy sometimes takes charge, and the darn thing just won't work right. When you do have problems with the network, I recommend using a standard, consistent approach to finding and fixing the problem. This section breaks down troubleshooting into two areas:

✦ **The hardware:** The best place to start troubleshooting a network problem is with the actual equipment, such as the NICs, cables, and hubs/switches. (See earlier sections on each equipment type.)

✦ **The software:** The second place to check for problems is in the configuration of the computers on the network, specifically the configuration on the computer(s) having the problem that you're troubleshooting.

Physical problems with your network

Although many things on a network can go bad or cause problems, usually network problems are caused by faulty equipment or wiring. Sometimes it's something as simple as a cable not being plugged in snugly. Looking at the physical cables, connections, and equipment is always the best place to start looking for problems. Here is a quick list of physical things to check while trying to fix network problems:

1. **Make sure that both ends of the network cable are firmly connected.**

   First check the end that plugs into the computer and then check the end that connects to the switch.

2. **Turn on the problematic computer to be sure that it's connected to a hub or switch.**

   Check the port on the switch to see whether the link/speed light is lit. (Depending on the switch that you have, you might not have a link light. Many switches use a speed light to indicate a link. Check the manufacturer's manual for your model.) If your computer is on and connected but no link/speed light is lit, try replacing the network cable.

3. **If you replace the network cable and there still isn't light, try unplugging the cable from the switch and plug it into another port.**

   Choose one of the other computers connected to the switch that works, unplug it, and plug the broken computer into that port for testing. Occasionally, a single port on a switch goes bad; if that happens, just mark it as bad and don't use it anymore. But if all computers connected to the switch stop working, it's probably the switch that's gone south. If the switch is still under warranty, I recommend getting it fixed or replaced — if the warranty has expired, it's usually cheaper to replace a switch than fix it.

4. **If you replace the cable, try a different port on the switch, and if other computers work fine on that switch, the NIC inside your computer has possibly gone bad.**

   If you reach this determination, call your local service center to have it looked at and repaired. If you have an older model on which the NIC was added instead of built in, you can simply replace the NIC yourself.

 The key when troubleshooting physical problems is the link/speed light on the switch. If the link/speed light still doesn't work, the problem likely isn't physical. Start troubleshooting the network configuration on the computer itself.

Network configuration problems

After checking the hardware, look for problems in the network settings. When using TCP/IP on your network, look for these specific things: the TCP/IP configuration mode, IP address, subnet mask, and router IP address (if you're using a router to connect to the Internet or other networks). To check these settings, open System Preferences and click the Network icon to bring up the Network pane. Click the Ethernet entry in the list and then follow these steps:

1. **Make sure that the Configure IPv4 pop-up menu is set to the appropriate option.**

   - *Using DHCP:* Select the Using DHCP option only if you're using a cable/DSL modem/router or other DHCP server. Otherwise, set this to Manually.

   - *Manually:* If the configuration is set to Manually, check the IP Address, DNS Servers, Router, and Subnet Mask fields to make sure that they're correct. If you're not sure whether your Subnet Mask field entry is correct, you can usually make it the same as other computers on the same network with you. Most times, the subnet mask is 255.255.255.0.

2. **To check your Internet connectivity to the rest of the Internet, try pinging** www.apple.com.

   This checks the router and DNS settings.

3. **If you're set up for DHCP and your TCP/IP settings remain blank, make sure that your DHCP server — which could be your cable/DSL modem/router — is turned on and working properly.**

Book VI
Chapter 1

Setting Up a Small
Network

Chapter 2: Using Your Network

In This Chapter

✔ Finding out what you can do with your network

✔ Sharing your files and printers with other Macs

✔ Sharing your files with Windows computers

✔ Accessing files on Windows computers

✔ Configuring the built-in firewall

✔ Remote-controlling your Mac from afar

Here's one of those incredibly complex concepts that you always find in these computer books: After you have your network all set up and ready to go, you can do *all kinds of really cool things with it.* (Highly technical.) You can use your network to share files, share printers, remotely control your Mac, or even play multiuser games against other friends. To keep your files safe from unwanted snoops, you can configure the Mac OS X built-in firewall. In this chapter, I cover the basics of file sharing, sharing printers, and using the firewall to protect yourself from intruders.

It's All about (File) Sharing

One of the main reasons for building a network is sharing files between computers. You might even want to set up a *server,* which is a computer with shared files that are always available to anyone on the network. Think of a server as a common file storage area for the rest of the network. Really, any computer that shares files is technically a server because it's serving, so to speak. But most people use the word *server* only to mean a computer that's dedicated solely to serving files, printers, and so on for the rest of the network.

Creating an account

Sharing files on your Mac with other Mac users is a piece of cake. Remember, however, that you need to create an account for anyone who you want to have access to your files. The accounts that you create can access only three folders, as shown in Figure 2-1:

Figure 2-1:
The location of user folders and the Shared folder on your hard drive.

✦ **The account's Home folder:** That specific account's Home folder carries a short version of the username that's in the Users folder on your hard drive. Figure 2-1 shows the Home folder, which is noted with an icon that looks like a house, for the mark account (where *mark* is the short account name for Mark Chambers). The Home folder icon always bears the short account name for the user who's currently logged in.

✦ **Each account's Public folder:** Each user account you create also has a Public folder located within its Home folder. Any files you place in the Public folder can be accessed by any user on your Mac, local or remote.

✦ **The Shared folder:** This folder is also in the Users folder on your hard drive. Anyone with an admin-level account on your Mac can access the Shared folder across the network, and any user account on your Mac can access the Shared folder locally, so it's a great place to keep common files that everyone wants to copy or use.

To create an account, you need to be logged in as an Admin user. Follow these steps:

1. **Open System Preferences from the Apple menu (⌘) or the Dock.**

2. **Click the Users & Groups icon.**

3. **Click the New User button, which carries a plus sign.**

   If the New User button is grayed out, you need to unlock the Users & Groups pane first. Click the padlock icon in the lower left corner and type your Admin user account password, and then click Unlock.

4. **Fill in the appropriate information, including the name for the account and a password.**

   Note that the name that appears as the short name determines the name of that user's Home folder.

5. **Click Create User.**

6. **Press ⌘+Q to exit System Preferences.**

I cover creating accounts in greater detail in Book II, Chapter 5, but that's the short version.

Enabling file sharing

When you enable file sharing, your files are exchanged over Transmission Control Protocol/Internet Protocol (TCP/IP).

Follow these steps to turn on sharing:

1. **Open System Preferences.**

2. **Click the Sharing icon to open the Sharing Preferences pane.**

3. **Select the File Sharing check box to turn File Sharing on.**

**Book VI
Chapter 2**

Using Your Network

This provides the default system of file sharing, where your account's Public folder is accessible to all users. You can give other users access to additional folders on your Mac by clicking the Add button (with the plus sign) under the Shared Folders list.

Connecting to a shared resource

At the top of the Sharing pane, you can see that other Macintosh users can access your computer at `afp://<ip address>`, where `ip address` is the IP address for your specific computer. When another Mac user wants to connect to your shared files, that person can do the following:

1. **Choose Go⇨Connect to Server from the Finder menu bar.**

2. **After the Connect to Server dialog opens, other Mac users can type afp://<*ip address*> (where ip address is the IP address of your Macintosh) into the Server Address box and then click the Connect button.**

You can also browse for a shared resource in the Connect to Server dialog. Choose Go⇨Connect to Server or press ⌘+K. Click Browse to locate the shared computer. Note that you might be prompted to choose whether you want to connect as a Guest or a Registered User. To connect to the server as a Registered User, you must supply the right username and password. If you connect as Guest, you don't have to supply a password, but you will have restricted access to only the Public folder for each account on the system that you connect to. If you need to connect as a Registered User, ask an Admin user who controls that Mac to supply you with the correct username and password.

Give the username and password that you created to the person using the other Mac, and he can now access files in that account's Home folder as well as any other Public folders on your computer.

The sidebar that appears in Finder windows offers a Shared heading. Click the arrow next to Shared to display other shared resources on your network, just as if you had clicked Browse from the Connect to Server dialog. (I'm starting to think *Lion* might be a synonym for *convenience*.)

Sending files the easy AirDrop way

AirDrop is the local Mac-to-Mac file transfer feature built-in to Mac OS X Lion — and it couldn't be much easier to use, since there's literally no setup and no passwords involved! However, there are three caveats (aren't there always?):

✔ AirDrop only works with Macs running Lion.

✔ AirDrop uses the Wi-Fi hardware built-in to today's Mac laptops and desktops, so don't forget to turn Wi-Fi on first. (If you're displaying the Wi-Fi status icon in your Finder menu bar, click the icon and choose Turn Wi-Fi On.)

✔ You'll have to be within Wi-Fi signal range of another Mac to use AirDrop. Note, however, that the two computers *don't* have to be using the same Wi-Fi network. (For example, my iMac uses a wired connection to my network, but since the iMac has internal Wi-Fi hardware, I can use AirDrop to send files to my MacBook Pro.)

To use AirDrop to transfer files to another Mac, both users should click the AirDrop icon in any Finder window sidebar to join the AirDrop group. After a short delay, you'll see the account pictures for all of the Macs within signal range that have AirDrop open — drag the files you want to transfer to the person's picture. Both you and the recipient are prompted for confirmation before the transfer begins. Once the transfer is completed, the files you sent are saved in the recipient's Downloads folder.

Once you're done using AirDrop, just close the Finder window displaying the account pictures, and you'll exit from the AirDrop group. (Don't forget, you have to open AirDrop again if someone wants to send you files, so I personally leave my AirDrop Finder window open and minimized to the Dock!)

Sharing a Connected Printer

Sharing your printer for others to use is one of the best reasons to have a network. Setting up your Mac to share your printer is very easy under Mac OS X. Here's a quick rundown of what you need to do:

1. **Open System Preferences.**

2. **Click the Sharing icon under the Internet & Wireless section to open the Sharing Preferences pane.**

3. **Click the Printer Sharing check box to enable it.**

By default, when you turn on Printer Sharing, Lion automatically shares all the current printers connected to your Mac. To select which printers can be used for shared printing from the Sharing pane, click the check box next to each printer — select the check box to share that printer, or deselect it to block others from using it. (Alternately, you can click the Print & Scan icon in System Preferences. From this pane, you can also enable and disable sharing of individual printers.)

**Book VI
Chapter 2**

Using Your Network

After Printer Sharing is enabled, follow these steps to connect to that printer from other computers on your network:

1. **Click System Preferences in the Dock.**

2. **Click the Print & Scan icon.**

3. **Click the Add button (which carries a plus sign).**

If the Add button is disabled, click the padlock icon in the lower left corner and type your Admin user account password, and then click Unlock.

You might be prompted to add a printer automatically when the Printer Setup Utility opens. Click the Add button to begin the addition. (For more on adding a printer with the Printer Setup Utility, see Book VII, Chapter 4.)

4. **From the Browser window that opens, click the Default button on the toolbar.**

5. **Click the shared printer you want to use and then click the Add button.**

Already have the Printer Browser open? Then follow the easier path: Clicking the Default toolbar button displays all the available local shared printers. Click the desired printer and then click Add.

Sharing Files with Windows Computers

If you've deigned to allow PCs running Windows on your network (a generous gesture to the lower classes), you'll probably want to also share files with those computers. Sharing files with a Windows PC — actually a Windows user — is very similar to sharing files with other Mac users.

File sharing must be enabled, as I demonstrated earlier in this chapter. (When you share with other Macs, you're also making those files available to PCs.)

To allow file sharing with Windows computers, follow these steps:

1. **Click the System Preferences icon in the Dock.**

2. **Click the Sharing icon to open the Sharing Preferences pane.**

3. **Click the File Sharing entry.**

4. **Click the Options button.**

5. **Click the On check box next to the user account (or accounts) that will be accessible by Windows PCs.**

Lion will growl while you try to enable SMB sharing. That's because you have to enable Windows access on the desired account before it can be used. Lion prompts you for your password, smugly informing you that the account password will be stored "in a less secure manner." (Take that, Mr. Gates!) Generally, this isn't a problem, but never enable an account for Windows access unless trusted individuals will use it.

6. **Click the Share files and folders using SMB check box to enable it.**

7. **Click Done to exit the Advanced dialog, and close the System Preferences window to save the changes.**

Accessing File Shares on Windows Computers

If you allow a Windows PC to access your files, you'll also probably want to putter around with files on a Windows PC. Easy!

Accessing files on Windows computers relies on the Samba component (a part of the UNIX foundation of Mac OS X). Follow these steps:

1. **Choose Go⇨Connect to Server from the Finder.**

The Connect to Server dialog opens.

2. **In the Address box, enter** smb://*<ip address>*, **where** ip address **is the IP address of the Windows computer that you want to connect to.**

3. **Click the Connect button.**

   Depending on the type of account you have on the Windows PC, Mac OS X might display an SMB (Server Message Block) authentication dialog in which you can enter your username and password. (Think security for the Windows crowd.)

4. **Select the desired shared folder or drive to mount from the pop-up menu.**

5. **Mount the shared folder or drive according to the Windows version:**

   ✦ *If you're accessing a file shared on a Windows 95 or Windows 98 computer:* Simply click OK to mount the share.

   ✦ *If you're accessing a file shared on a Windows NT, 2000, XP, Vista, or 7 computer:* Click the Authenticate button. Then enter your username and password, click OK, and then click OK again to mount the share.

After you mount the shared location, you'll see it appear on your Desktop, just as you see a Mac volume. You can use this drive just as you do any other drive on your system. To disconnect from the Windows share, you can

✦ Drag the icon to the Trash in the Dock (which changes to an Eject icon when you start dragging).

✦ Press ⌘+E.

   or

✦ Right-click the icon, and then choose Eject from the menu that appears.

Using FTP to Access Files

FTP is part of the TCP/IP protocol suite; the hoary acronym FTP stands for *File Transfer Protocol*. FTP is one of the oldest methods for sharing files between computers; however, because it's part of the TCP/IP protocol suite, it can be used on many different kinds of computers, including those running just about any type of strange and arcane operating system. You can still manage to exchange files regardless of whether you're using Mac OS X, Windows, Linux, or UNIX. (Heck, even dinosaurs like DOS can join the party.)

FTP is a *client/server* application. In plain English, this means that two pieces make things tick: the *server* (which hosts the connection, rather like a file server) and the *client* (which connects to the server, and which you control). Mac OS X, thanks to its UNIX foundation, has an FTP client built in. To use FTP, you need a computer running the FTP server software to give others access to files; then the other computer, or client, can connect to the FTP server. After the connection is made, the client can either send files to the server *(uploading)* or get files from the server *(downloading)*. In this section, I cover how to use FTP to access files on a server as well as talk about the FTP applications that come with Mac OS X.

Using FTP on the Internet

Because File Transfer Protocol (FTP) is a part of the TCP/IP suite, it works on virtually every type of computer (over both the Internet and your local area network). So, assuming that you have your computer connected to the Internet through a modem or a local area network (LAN) connection, everything that I discuss about FTP and how to use it applies to connecting to FTP servers on the Internet as well. When you connect to FTP servers on the Internet, you can use the Fully Qualified Domain Name (or FQDN for short), such as `ftp.apple.com`, instead of an actual IP address.

Using FTP from Terminal to transfer files

You can use FTP to transfer files with an FTP server by using the command-line interface (CLI); to use the CLI, open a Terminal, or shell, session. To use a Terminal session, double-click the Terminal icon in the Utilities folder inside the Applications folder. When you open a Terminal session, you're presented with a window that accepts text commands. You'll see a prompt that consists of your computer's name and the folder that you're currently in, followed by your user ID. It's at this prompt where you type various FTP commands.

If you'd rather use a drag-and-drop graphical client application for transferring files using ftp, I recommend the freeware FileZilla application (available at `filezilla-project.org`).

After you're in the Terminal session, you'll use a series of commands to connect to another computer, move in and out of folders, and transfer files. Following is a list of the basic commands that you need to use FTP as well as a brief description of what each command does.

✦ `ftp`: This command starts the FTP command line interface session. You can tell that you're in the FTP client application when you see `ftp>` as your command prompt. This is where you type all other FTP commands to do things.

✦ `open`: This command is used to start your connection to another computer. Type this command followed by the IP address of the FTP server that you want to connect to.

✦ `ls`: Use this command to see a listing of all files and folders in the current folder on the FTP server.

✦ `cd`: This command allows you to change the folder that you're in. Type **cd** <folder> (where *folder* is a specific folder name) to move into a sub-folder on the FTP server. Type **cd ..** (that's c, d, space, and two periods) to go back out a folder level.

✦ lcd: This command acts exactly like cd except that it changes the folder that you're currently in on your local system, not the FTP server. Use this command to put yourself in the folder on the local drive that you want to transfer files to and from.

✦ bin: Type this command to get in binary mode to transfer files that aren't plain-text files. (Always use binary mode unless you're specifically transferring plain-text files.)

✦ ascii: This command puts you in ASCII mode for transferring text files.

✦ get or mget: To retrieve a single file, use the get command followed by the filename of the file that you want to retrieve. If you want to get multiple files at one time, use the mget command followed by a filename, possibly containing * and/or ? as wildcards.

✦ put or mput: To send a single file, use the put command followed by the filename to send a file to the FTP server. To send multiple files, use the mput command followed by a filename, possibly containing * and/or ? as wildcards.

✦ quit: Use the quit command to end your FTP session.

**Book VI
Chapter 2**

Using Your Network

To end a Terminal session and exit Terminal at any time, press ⌘+Q. Terminal prompts you for confirmation if necessary.

Many FTP servers will let you send files only to certain folders. Most times this folder is named *Upload, Uploads,* or something similar.

Using these commands will enable you to exchange files with an FTP server. Here's an example of how to use these commands within the Terminal window:

1. **Type** ftp **to get into FTP mode.**

2. **Type** open *<ip address>* **(where** *ip address* **is the server's network IP address) to open your connection to the FTP server.**

3. **At this point, you're asked for a username and password.**

   For many FTP servers, using the username anonymous and your e-mail address as the password is enough to get you logged in. Some sites even allow you to log in without any username or password at all. On secure sites, however, you must use an assigned username and password provided by the administrator of that particular server.

4. **Type** lcd <folder> **(where** folder **is a specific folder name) to change into the folder on your local drive that you want files to come to or from.**

5. **Type the** ls **and** cd **commands to place yourself into the desired folder on the FTP server.**

6. **Type the** ascii **or** bin **command to set your file transfer mode to ASCII or binary, respectively.**

   This is important because choosing the wrong type will likely cause the transfer to fail. Unless it's a plain-text file, always use binary mode.

7. **Type the** get, mget, put, **and** mput **commands to send or receive the desired files.**

8. **Type the** quit **command to close the connection and exit the FTP session.**

Using the Built-in Firewall

A *firewall* watches all the network communications coming into your Mac. It automatically plays the role of security guard, blocking, or denying certain network traffic that you want to prevent from reaching your Mac. It acts as another layer of security to help keep you safe from unwanted attacks. That's all well and good, but you must be careful to set up your firewall correctly before you turn it on: A configuration mistake could make your Mac inaccessible from the network.

For instance, if you want to enable screen sharing on your Mac (which I'll discuss in the next section) but you also want to keep all other traffic from coming into your Mac, you can tell the built-in firewall to allow only screen sharing. The firewall on the Mac will follow the rules you set up on what to block or allow.

When enabled, the firewall blocks all traffic that comes into your Mac. By default, however, the firewall is turned off. So, your first job is to activate the firewall, which you can do by following these steps:

1. **Click the System Preferences icon in the Dock.**

2. **Click the Security & Privacy icon.**

3. **Click the Firewall tab.**

4. **Click the Start button to turn on your firewall.**

   Is the Start button disabled? Don't panic — just click the padlock icon in the lower left corner and type your Admin user account password, and then click Unlock.

   This enables the firewall. And, by default, virtually all incoming TCP/IP traffic is blocked.

5. **Click the Advanced button to show the settings that you see in Figure 2-2.**

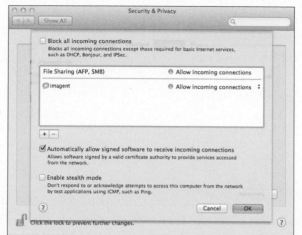

Figure 2-2:
You can help protect your Mac by using Lion's built-in firewall.

6. **Click the Automatically Allow Signed Software to Receive Incoming Connections radio button to select it.**

   As I mentioned earlier, you must enable each sharing method that you want to be able to use — however, when you enable different sharing methods from the Sharing pane in System Preferences (such as File Sharing or Screen Sharing), you'll notice that those types of traffic now appear in the Firewall list. (In other words, when you turn on a sharing method, the firewall automatically allows traffic for that sharing method, which Lion calls a *service*. Most excellent.)

   Click the up/down arrow icon to the right of any service to specify whether the firewall should allow or block connections.

   Sometimes, you might want to allow other traffic through your firewall that isn't on the firewall list of recognized services and applications. At that point, you can click the Add button (which bears a plus sign) to specify the application that your firewall should allow. Lion presents you with the familiar Add dialog, and you can choose the application that needs access.

7. **Click OK to save your changes and return to the Security & Privacy pane, and then click the Close button to close the System Preferences window.**

Remote Control of Your Mac

Forgive me whilst I wax techno-nerd here: One of the coolest advantages to a network is the ability to take control of one computer from another computer. For example, sometimes you might need to access files on your Mac while you're on a trip, but you don't have File Sharing enabled. What can you do? You can remotely connect into your Mac and then — just as if you were sitting in front of it — enable File Sharing (as I demonstrate earlier in the chapter). Perhaps you have a file on your computer with someone's phone number that you suddenly need on the road. With remote control, it's at your fingertips! (Sigh . . . ah, technology.)

Using Screen Sharing

Lion's Screen Sharing feature, which is available from iChat, can be turned on for individual users from the Sharing pane in System Preferences. You can allow access for all user accounts on your Mac, or limit remote access to selected users. Screen Sharing is Apple's implementation of VNC technology.

To set up Screen Sharing, follow these steps:

1. **Click the System Preferences icon in the Dock.**

2. **Click the Sharing icon to open the Sharing Preferences pane.**

3. **Click the Screen Sharing check box to select it.**

4. **To limit remote access for specific accounts, click the Only these users radio button, and click the Add button (which bears a plus sign) to select a user.**

5. **Close the System Preferences window to save the change.**

After you've enabled screen sharing, you can use the Buddies ➪ Share My Screen menu item in iChat to share your screen with another person. To view another person's screen, use the Buddies ➪ Ask to Share Remote Screen menu item. (For the details on iChat and Screen Sharing, see Book V, Chapter 3.)

Remotely control your Mac (for free, no less!)

Virtual Network Computing (or VNC, available for many platforms at www. realvnc.com) is a very nice application that enables you to remotely control a computer from pretty much anywhere that has an Internet connection. VNC is easy to install and configure, and it runs on many different platforms, ranging from Windows 7 and UNIX on desktop computers and servers to iPhones, iPads, and Windows CE on personal digital assistants (PDAs). Wrap your mind around this: You could be at a friend's house on her wireless network and use your iPhone to remotely control your Mac at home over the Internet. Pure, undiluted *sassy!*

Some networks have proxies and firewalls that might interfere with VNC's operation. You can remotely control a computer that's behind a firewall or cable/DSL router, but the firewall/router needs to be configured properly. Because the process varies from one manufacturer to the next, check your cable/DSL router manual for instructions on how to do this.

How VNC works

In a nutshell, VNC takes the graphical interface on your monitor, turns it into data, and sends it to the computer that you're using to remotely control it. The computer that you're using sends keyboard presses, mouse movements, and clicks to it, acting just the same way as it would if you were sitting right in front of it.

As I mentioned earlier, you can use Lion's Screen Sharing feature in iChat to make a remote connection from another Mac to your Mac. However, you're not limited to using just another Mac using Lion and Screen Sharing in iChat — you can control your Mac from a Windows PC, or from an older version of Mac OS X as well! If you've already enabled Screen Sharing (as I demonstrate earlier in this chapter), follow these steps to enable *any* VNC connection:

1. **Click the System Preferences icon in the Dock.**

2. **Click the Sharing icon to open the Sharing Preferences pane.**

3. **Click the Screen Sharing entry.**

4. **Click the Computer Settings button.**

5. **Click the VNC Viewers May Control Screen with Password check box to select it.**

6. **Click within the password text box and enter a password for VNC applications.**

7. **Click OK to exit the Computer Settings sheet, and close the System Preferences window to save the changes.**

Mr. Paranoia speaks again: **Make doggone sure that you set up the password access correctly for VNC or don't run it!** I can't stress enough how much fun a hacker would have with free remote control over your Mac OS X Desktop.

Remote control of another computer from your Mac

A few different VNC viewers exist for Mac OS X. A *VNC viewer* is just an application you use to remotely control your computer running VNC. You can download them at `www.realvnc.com/download.html`. If you find yourself on a computer without a VNC viewer — heaven forbid — VNC server actually runs over the web as well! As long as the computer that you're using has a web browser that supports Java — which Safari does — you can still remotely control your computer. (You may have to download the Java runtime package from the Apple web site at `support.apple.com`. Click in the web site Search box and type *Java runtime* to locate the latest version.)

When you connect to the computer running VNC using a web browser, the web server sends a default page that contains a Java applet. That Java applet asks you for the password to connect; upon entering the correct password, it brings up the remote control session right in the web browser.

Chapter 3: Going Wireless

In This Chapter

✔ **Finding out how wireless networking works**

✔ **Discovering wireless security**

✔ **Connecting to other Macs without a wireless access point**

✔ **Connecting to and disconnecting from AirPort networks**

Nowadays, wireless connectivity is king. For example, mobile phones have gone from being a toy of the technological elite to a permanent fixture on the hip of the common man. The shorts that I'm wearing right now have a special pocket just for a cell phone to ride in; when I'm without my phone, it usually carries a 5th Avenue candy bar. (Perhaps that was too personal . . . sorry.)

Because people have become accustomed to being able to keep in touch wherever they are, they also want to be able to have access to their network, at least within their house or workplace, without the hassle of cables. (Which, by the way, are magnets for pets that enjoy a good chew toy.) This desire for convenience and the advances in wireless technology have combined to bring you the concept of the wireless network — as well as wireless coffee shops, wireless access providers, and even wireless gaming centers. (In fact, Apple's iPad 2 is a wireless Internet marvel, with instant connectivity to any Bluetooth-enabled Mac and full-featured e-mail and browsing that'll knock your socks off.)

Now you can be connected to your home local area network (LAN) and your shared Internet connection (which I cover in Book VI, Chapter 4) from your balcony, deck, lounge chair in the yard, or even your bedroom. In this chapter, I talk about how wireless networks work, and then I give you a lot of information to help you get the right pieces to free yourself — *securely*, mind you — from the world of the wired.

Speaking the Wireless Lingo

Wireless networks aren't all that different from their wired siblings. In this chapter, I discuss some of the features and limitations of wireless networking, but you must first be familiar with a foundation of information.

Because of the technology involved in wireless networks and how things are changing rapidly in this area, you'll find yourself swimming in a sea of acronyms and other techno-babble. Although you don't need to know every little detail to be able to set up your own wireless network, you should know some of these terms so that you can avoid getting stung by hackers or stuck with equipment that's on the verge of obsolescence.

Here's a quick list of terms that you'll see on your road to becoming a wireless network guru:

✦ **WLAN:** WLAN stands for *Wireless LAN.* If you've already read previous chapters in this minibook, you know that a LAN (local area network) is just a bunch of connected computers and other devices.

✦ **IEEE:** This stands for *Institute of Electrical and Electronics Engineers,* which is an organization that approves standards that allow computers, network equipment, and just about anything else electronic to play nicely together. Sometimes IEEE helps create these standards before approving them, and sometimes it just approves standards that others have produced.

✦ **802.11:** This is the part of the IEEE standards that deals specifically with wireless networking.

Although wireless is usually generically referred to as *wireless networks* (or sometimes even *Wi-Fi*), it's all really a wireless form of Ethernet.

✦ **Wireless access point:** A *wireless access point,* or WAP, is a device that allows wireless network devices to connect to a wired Ethernet network.

✦ **Service Set Identifier:** The *Service Set Identifier,* or SSID, is used to tell your computer the name of the wireless network that you want to use.

✦ **Wired Equivalency Privacy:** *Wired Equivalency Privacy,* or WEP, is an encryption that wireless networks can use to keep your wireless network more secure from snoopers and hackers.

✦ **Wi-Fi Protected Access:** Usually referred to as WPA, this is a security protocol that's more robust and harder to crack than WEP. The latest version, WPA2, is a common security feature on today's wireless hardware.

✦ **Ad Hoc mode:** An *Ad Hoc* wireless network is one in which each wireless device talks directly with all other wireless devices.

Apple calls Ad Hoc mode a *computer-to-computer network.*

✦ **Infrastructure mode:** This is where all wireless devices talk to a WAP, and the WAP then talks to other wireless devices and the wired network.

As I cover the different parts of wireless networking and how to set it up, you'll find yourself using these terms over and over. Before you know it, you'll be spouting these wireless-related acronyms like a pro. (No, really. I'm not kidding.)

Figuring Out the Different Flavors of Wireless Ethernet

One of the first things that you might notice when you start looking into wireless networking is the existence of different wireless standards. You should at least be aware that these different standards exist: That way, you can be sure to get wireless network components that will work together because *some of the different wireless standards are not compatible.* (Feel free to photocopy this list and stick it on your fridge door.)

Basic Wi-Fi: 802.11b

IEEE 802.11b has another name that you'll likely see on product advertisements, literature, or boxes in stores: *Wi-Fi,* which stands for Wireless Fidelity. (Kinda like that cutting-edge Hi-Fi stereo from the '60s and '70s, where *Hi-Fi* stands for *High Fidelity.*) Most folks proclaim Wi-Fi as only 802.11b. Wi-Fi was the first version of wireless Ethernet. This version of wireless runs at speeds up to 11 million bits per second, or 11 Mbps. The reason I say that it runs at speeds *up to* 11 Mbps is because the actual speed at which the data is transferred depends on things like signal strength and quality. When the conditions are such that your signal strength or quality is decreased — such as an inconvenient concrete wall or a circuit breaker box between you and your AirPort Base Station — you might find that your wireless connection changes down to 5.5 Mbps, 2 Mbps, or even as slow as 1 Mbps.

802.11b has been largely supplanted in current wireless networking, and almost all the equipment you can buy today is either 802.11g or 802.11n (both of which I cover in a moment). However, if you're working with older computers and existing 802.11b hardware, any networking equipment you buy should be backward-compatible with 802.11b.

Apple's original AirPort network cards and standard-issue AirPort Base Station used 802.11b. In fact, it's time for Mac owners to swell with pride yet again: Apple was the first computer company to ship 802.11b hardware. (Back then, in 1999, it was the original AirPort Base Station.) Now, of course, Apple has raised the bar with AirPort Extreme, which I discuss later in this chapter, and the AirPort Express mobile Base Station.

In theory, Wi-Fi network cards have the ability to communicate with other Wi-Fi devices and WAPs that are up to 1,000 feet away. Having said that, realize that 1,000 feet is a generous estimate (and that's outdoors on a clear day with no wind blowing) — you see what I'm getting at. In reality, when you set up your wireless network, things such as walls — especially concrete walls, as in basements — and areas with lots of electrical wiring decrease the distance that you can cover. If you use a WAP, plan on no more than 150 feet between wireless computers and the WAP. However, your mileage might vary.

That 11 Mbps bandwidth is shared between all computers using it. Collisions can also occur if more than one computer tries to communicate at the same time. If you have a lot of people on your wireless network, the network will get noticeably slower because of increased collisions. Remember that the total bandwidth is shared among the computers on the wireless network. This applies not only to Wi-Fi but also to the 802.11a (which I cover in the nearby sidebar) and the 802.11g standards.

One last thing about 802.11b networking: Wi-Fi uses the 2.4 GHz frequency range. It actually uses 11 different channels, but they're all around the 2.4 GHz range. If you're using a 2.4 GHz cordless phone or even a microwave, using either device can definitely interfere with or even shut down your wireless network. Keep this in mind when you buy your next phone or wonder why your file transfers stop when you're communing with Orville Redenbacher in the microwave.

Let's get Extreme: 802.11g

Apple's release of the first generation of AirPort Extreme provided both the speed of 802.11a and the compatibility with Wi-Fi. That's because it used the *802.11g* standard, which operates at speeds up to 54 Mbps (as did 802.11a) but will also operate at the same frequency ranges and play nicely with existing 802.11b equipment. (Notice that we're heading in the right direction again when it comes to naming conventions. Go figure.)

Apple was once again the *first* company to offer 802.11g hardware as standard equipment. Feel free to enjoy the Superiority Dance yet again.

Naturally, there's a downside: 802.11g returned to that pesky 2.4 GHz range, so your cordless phone and microwave can also wreak the same havoc that they did with your original AirPort equipment.

Raising the bar to 802.11n

I would be remiss if I didn't mention the current wireless standard from IEEE: 802.11n. Most third-party manufacturers (including Apple) now offer only 802.11n wireless equipment. Apple's 802.11n products include the current AirPort Extreme base station, the AirPort Express, the AirPort Extreme hardware in most of the Macintosh computer line, the iPod touch, iPad and iPhone, and the spiffy Apple TV.

Why the hubbub? Oh, I forgot to mention that 802.11n can deliver throughput in excess of 100 Mbps! Don't bet your house that you'll get that kind of speed, though — as with the other members of the 802.11 family, that's likely to be a theoretical maximum speed.

You can't go wrong with the 802.11n standard: think superfast wireless connections in your household or office. Ahh, technology . . . .

802.11a networks

802.11a was a newer version of wireless Ethernet than 802.11b. 802.11b came out first, and 802.11a came out next. (I guess someone ran into a doorframe.) 802.11a doesn't have a generally recognized handy nickname like *Wi-Fi*, so just call it 802.11a.

802.11a equipment isn't compatible with Wi-Fi or older 802.11b AirPort Base Stations, so don't make the mistake of buying both 802.11b and 802.11a network equipment. Instead, I strongly recommend that you follow the AirPort Extreme course charted by Apple and use the 802.11g or 802.11n standards (which are backward compatible with Wi-Fi). Just in case, the current AirPort Extreme base station (which uses 802.11n) does support 802.11a — hats off again to the folks in Cupertino!

802.11a can run at speeds up to 54 Mbps — almost *five times* faster than Wi-Fi. This is because 802.11a uses the 5 GHz frequency range instead of the cluttered 2.4 GHz range that Wi-Fi uses. The powers that be set aside the 5 GHz range just for wireless networking, so cordless phones and microwaves (or any other wireless devices, for that matter) can't interfere with the network. The downside to using the higher 5 GHz range, though, is that the distances that can be covered are even less than that of Wi-Fi — no more than about 60 feet to maintain the highest speeds.

Because of the incompatibilities with 802.11b and the arrival of 802.11g and 802.11n, 802.11a equipment has all but disappeared, and you should steer clear of it with a wide berth. (In fact, good luck finding 802.11a hardware anywhere but eBay and craigslist.)

The guy with the turquoise teeth

I should also mention *Bluetooth* — a strange name for a wireless standard, I admit, but it works like a charm. Bluetooth devices use 2.4 GHz as well, but they're designed only for very short distances . . . up to only about 30 feet. Bluetooth is the future for linking mobile devices (such as personal digital assistants and cell phones) and external peripherals (such as wireless keyboards and mice) to your Mac. In fact, Bluetooth is built into all current Macs, which can turn your iMac or Mac Pro into a completely cordless machine — except for the power cord, of course. Lion provides built-in support for Bluetooth through the Bluetooth pane in System Preferences.

Keeping Your Wireless Network Secure

Are you worried about the security of your AirPort wireless network? You should be, bunkie. Imagine someone in the next apartment or house — or standing right in your street — intercepting and monitoring your data from your wireless network.

But before you decide to toss the idea of a wireless network, keep this in mind: Even though it is technically *possible* that someone might camp out on your doorstep in order to gain access to your wireless network, for most home networks, this possibility isn't very probable. Even if someone tries to gain access to your wireless network and perhaps even sniff your network — a techno-nerd term meaning to record all the data flying around a network — there isn't a whole lot someone can do with that information.

If a friend invites you for an evening of war driving, think "recreational mobile hacking." *War driving* is the act of driving through neighborhoods in a car equipped with a laptop computer and a wireless network card. The payoff? If the hacker is lucky enough to locate a house with an open wireless network, we're talking free wireless Internet access . . . from the comfort of his car! (Not to mention any shared files or information that's available on that network.) Again, keep security in mind when installing wireless hardware, and these bozos will get nothing from your network.

You might say, "But I use my credit card on the Internet to buy stuff." Sure, this is a valid concern; however, if you purchase things on the Internet with your credit card, you should already be using a secure connection provided by the web site for your personal information so that the data you're sending across your wireless network is already encrypted and relatively safe from thieves. (You can find more on this when I discuss Safari in detail in Book V, Chapter 5.)

"I have shared my files on my computer. Can the Bad Guys access those shared files?" Another good question, but if you read Book VI, Chapter 2, you know that you have to create an account for those whom you want to access your files. Unless the would-be hacker is very good at guessing usernames and passwords, your files are pretty safe, too.

This is not to say that you bear absolutely no risk of being hacked. If a legitimate user on your wireless network connects to your computer and starts transferring a file, a would-be hacker could potentially record all the traffic and then reconstruct the file that was sent from the data that was recorded. In other words, a hacker could grab that user's username and password. That's where the following encryption standards come in handy!

WPA and WPA2

Wi-Fi Protected Access, or WPA, is A Good Thing (even if it makes for a silly-sounding acronym). It's currently the standard encryption protocol offered for home wireless networking — WPA2 standard is the latest version — and is even better at defending your wireless network. As you might expect, all of Apple's current AirPort wireless hardware uses WPA2 security, as does most of the wireless hardware you'll find on the shelf at your local Hardware Heaven electronics store. (It's still a good idea to check the specifications on the box, though, to make sure that WPA2 is supported.)

WPA2 works well as a deterrent to keep the wrong people out of your stuff. Although WPA2 isn't going to ward off the spies at the National Security Agency, it's good enough to protect home and small-business networks.

WEP

WEP is an old friend of mine. Short for *Wired Equivalency Privacy,* it's another ridiculous acronym for another wireless security system. WEP was one of the first widely supported wireless encryption schemes, but in today's world, WEP is now outdated and pretty easy for a hacker to outwit. I strongly recommend that your network use WPA2 whenever possible.

Apple's implementation of WEP comes in two varieties: 40 bit and 128 bit. The more bits used in the encryption, the more secure (and the better) it is.

To use WEP, you need to select a WEP *key,* which is really just a code word:

**Book VI
Chapter 3**

Going Wireless

✦ The longer the key, the better.

✦ When making a key, use something like *ab8sher7234ksief87* (something that's random with letters and numbers) as opposed to something, like *mykey,* that's easily guessed.

If you're using an Ad Hoc wireless network, all the computers need to have their wireless network card configured with the same WEP key in order to communicate. If you're using a WAP to connect to the rest of the network, you need to use the same key on your computers that you've configured on your WAP.

One thing to note about WEP is that it's been *broken,* meaning that someone has figured out how to undo the encryption that WEP provides. For businesses, especially those with sensitive data, WEP isn't a good security solution.

The LEAP security standard

Lightweight Extensible Authentication Protocol (LEAP) is an encryption protocol developed by Cisco Systems for superior security in the business world. To use LEAP, you need to have a server that's set up to enable users to log in to gain permission to the wireless network. After you initially log in (*authenticate*) to your network, LEAP changes encryption keys on the fly at a time interval that you determine. You could set it so that every 15 minutes your encryption key is changed: Even if someone is in that hypothetical tent on your front lawn, he could never record enough packets to figure out your key because it changes so often.

Setting up a server so that you can use LEAP isn't something for the novice to attempt. I would encourage you to read up on LEAP only if you're very serious about airtight security on your WLAN. The Cisco web site (www.cisco.com) is a good place to read about LEAP.

Using non-Apple wireless equipment with AirPort Extreme equipment

Because of Apple's implementation of wireless standards within the AirPort Extreme product line, keep in mind some things when trying to mix Apple wireless equipment with other vendors' 802.11b, 802.11g, or 802.11n equipment. As you discover elsewhere in this chapter, using AirPort wireless networks can require a WEP password that corresponds to the 802.11b/g/n WEP key for encryption. However, the password that you enter for AirPort networks isn't exactly the same as the WEP key for that same network. If you're using an AirPort network card and are trying to connect to a non-Apple WAP, you need to follow a specific procedure. You can find this procedure by going to **http://search.info.apple.com** and searching on the words *802.11 Compatibility.* You'll also find helpful information at this same spot if you're using a non-Apple 802.11b/g/n network card and are trying to connect to an Apple AirPort Base Station. (If you're using WPA2 encryption, no special configuration is needed. Go figure.)

You want my opinion? Because of the issues of using non-AirPort 802.11b/g/n hardware with The Real Thing (AirPort/AirPort Extreme stuff), I recommend that you stick with Apple equipment if possible.

All current AirPort Extreme wireless network cards and Base Stations are compatible with the Cisco LEAP for higher security.

Setting Up Your Wireless Network

On to the good stuff. This section describes how to set up an Ad Hoc or infrastructure-based WLAN (wireless LAN).

In case you have any issues using AirPort or need more information about anything related to AirPort, check this page at the Apple web site: www.apple.com/support/airport.

Setting up an Ad Hoc wireless network

Using an Ad Hoc network — also called a *computer-to-computer* network — is a fairly easy thing to accomplish in Mac OS X. Plus, you're not limited to just Macs: With an Ad Hoc network, you can also swap niceties with PCs and PDAs that have 802.11b/g/n network interface cards (NICs) installed. This Ad Hoc network is great for setting up an impromptu network in a classroom, exchanging recipes and pictures at a family reunion in a park, or blowing your friend up while gaming across the aisle of a Greyhound bus at 70 mph.

To set up an Ad Hoc network, you first have to create the computer-to-computer network on one of your Macs. This takes advantage of the AirPort Software Base Station that's built into Lion.

To create a computer-to-computer network, follow these steps:

1. **Click the Wi-Fi status icon on the menu bar.**

   If you haven't set Lion to display your Wi-Fi status in the Finder menu bar, follow these steps:

   a. *Open the Network pane in System Preferences and choose the Wi-Fi entry in the list at the left of the pane.*

   b. *Enable the Show Wi-Fi Status in Menu Bar check box.*

   c. *Close the System Preferences window to save your changes.*

2. **Click Create Network to display the dialog that you see in Figure 3-1.**

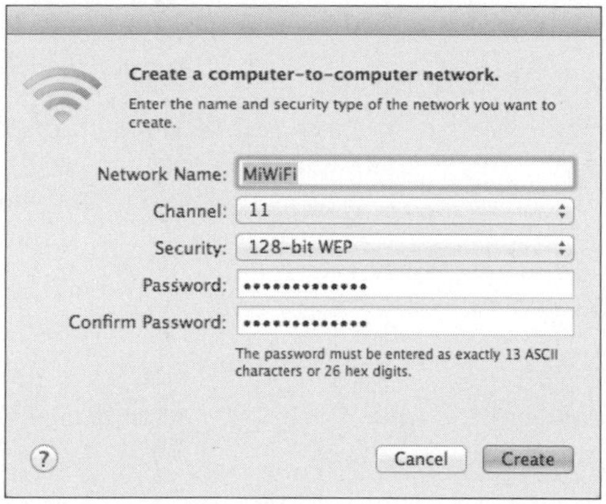

Figure 3-1:
Creating a computer-to-computer wireless network through software. *Excellent.*

> **Create a computer-to-computer network.**
> Enter the name and security type of the network you want to create.
>
> Network Name: MiWiFi
> Channel: 11
> Security: 128–bit WEP
> Password: ••••••••••••
> Confirm Password: ••••••••••••
> The password must be entered as exactly 13 ASCII characters or 26 hex digits.
>
> Cancel   Create

3. **Enter a name for your network.**

4. **Click the Security pop-up menu and choose 128-bit WEP to turn on WEP encryption.**

5. **Enter a password for your network and then enter it again to confirm it.**

Although you can leave encryption disabled, I highly recommend that you turn it on and choose a password for that extra bit of security. (Just call me Security Man.) Note that the password must be an exact length (which is determined by whether you choose a 40-bit [5-character] key or a 128-bit [13-character] key).

In general, channels 1, 6, and 11 are the only ones that don't overlap other channels — and are therefore the best choices to use. If you're close to other WAPs, AirPort Base Stations, or other Ad Hoc networks, try to find a channel that's not being used, or performance can be degraded. (If you have only one access point, it doesn't matter which channel you select — just allow Lion to automatically select a channel, which is typically channel 11.)

6. **Click Create.**

Creating a computer-to-computer network gives the illusion of having an AirPort Base Station. So for people to join your network, they would follow the same steps as those they would use to join any other AirPort Wi-Fi network, as I cover in the next section.

Setting up wireless networks with an AirPort Base Station

After one computer is running a computer-to-computer network or you've set up and configured an AirPort/AirPort Extreme Base Station/AirPort Express, you're ready to invite other computers with wireless hardware to the party.

Joining in an existing AirPort network

After you have a network set up on one of your wireless-enabled computers, you just need to have the other wireless-enabled computers join that network. You can use the same process, as I describe here, to join any wireless network:

1. **Click the Wi-Fi status icon on the menu bar.**

A list of existing network connections appears in the Wi-Fi menu.

2. **Select an existing network connection that you'd like to join.**

If you want to join a network whose name doesn't appear in the list — also called a *closed network* — follow these steps:

a. *Select Join Other Network from the Wi-Fi status menu.*

b. *Enter the name of the network that you want to join.*

c. *If the network uses security encryption, click the Security pop-up menu and choose the proper encryption format — the administrator of the network should be able to tell you the correct format — then type the password. If you plan on using the network in the future, make sure the Remember This Network check box is enabled.*

d. *Click Join.*

A closed network is another added measure of security — one that's good enough for most people because it's very unlikely that a hacker is going to try to hack a hidden network.

Disconnecting from a Wi-Fi network

To disconnect from an AirPort/AirPort Extreme network, you can turn off your Wi-Fi hardware altogether, which I cover in the next section. (Simplicity, they say, is an art.) Another way is to simply connect to another Wi-Fi network — but this option is really only useful if you actually *want* to connect to another network.

Turning your Wi-Fi hardware on or off

Being able to turn your Wi-Fi hardware on and off actually has its uses:

✦ You might want to use your Mac, usually your laptop, in a place where your wireless hardware shouldn't be used, like

- An airplane (when they tell you to turn off all cell phones)
- A hospital area that doesn't allow cell phones or other wireless devices

✦ Turning off your Wi-Fi hardware conserves your MacBook's battery life.

To turn your Wi-Fi equipment on or off via the Wi-Fi status icon on the menu bar, give it a click and choose Turn Wi-Fi On/Off from the resulting menu.

**Book VI
Chapter 3**

Going Wireless

Chapter 4: Sharing That Precious Internet Thing

In This Chapter

↙ **Finding out how Internet sharing works**

↙ **Choosing between hardware and software Internet sharing**

↙ **Connecting your Macs to a cable/DSL router**

↙ **Adding wireless support to a shared Internet connection**

Although I discuss lots of fun stuff that you can do with your network in previous chapters, this has to be my favorite: sharing a single Internet connection between *all* the computers on your network. If you have more than one computer, I'm sure that you've had to deal with the dilemma that pops up whenever more than one person wants or needs to access the Internet at the same time.

Luckily, because small home and office local area networks (LANs) use our old friend TCP/IP for network communications, connecting an entire network to the Internet isn't as troublesome a task as you might think. In this chapter, I talk about different hardware and software options for sharing your Internet connection as well as how to include your wireless devices.

Sharing the Internet

Sharing a single Internet connection among all your computers can be a boon simply because of the reduced chances of random acts of violence. (Internet deprivation can be an ugly thing, you know.) Although I won't claim that Internet sharing will save lives, it can indeed save you from headaches and arguments when more than one person wants to use the Internet at a time.

Throughout this chapter, I talk a lot about *cable* modems and *Asynchronous Digital Subscriber Line* (ADSL) modems. Both of these are high-speed Internet connections — and both are relatively inexpensive — that are offered by your local cable company and your local phone company, respectively. The phone company offers different kinds of digital subscriber line (DSL) connections, the most common of which is ADSL. However, because different kinds of DSL connections exist, in this chapter I refer to them all generically as *DSL*.

To share your Internet connection, you need a few things, so here's a brief checklist:

✦ **An Internet connection:** Typically, this is a cable or DSL modem connection, but older versions of the AirPort Base Station can use a dial-up Internet connection that's accessed via a standard v.90/v.92 analog telephone modem. (Note that recent models of the AirPort Extreme Base Station do not have the capability to use analog dial-up connections.)

✦ **A LAN:** You need a standard LAN (which is connected with cables) or a wireless LAN. (Heck, you can even have a hybrid that has both wired and wireless access.) See Book VI, Chapter 1 for more information about setting up a LAN and Book VI, Chapter 3 for more on setting up a Wireless LAN (WLAN).

✦ **An Internet-sharing device:** I use the word *device* because the method that you use to share your Internet connection could be through software that you run on one of your computers or hardware that is stand-alone, depending on how you connect to the Internet and what best fits your needs.

When you have these three things ready to go, you can share your Internet connection. However, you need to know some background information to help you choose the right components and get everything up and running.

Using Network Address Translation

You must determine one thing before you start your Internet sharing quest: the set of network Internet Protocol (IP) addresses that you'll use. If you used Book VI, Chapter 1 to set up and configure your LAN, you might recall that I suggest a specific range of IP addresses to use on your LAN. In case you missed out on Chapter 1 of this minibook, I briefly cover this important topic again so that you can share your Internet connection smoothly. (Forgive me if I wax technical, but 'tis only for the moment.)

When talking about IP addresses, the ruling body that tracks IP addresses and where they're used has broken all IP addresses up into two parts:

✦ **Public IP addresses:** *Public* IP addresses are used to communicate on the Internet, and only one device in the entire world can use a given public IP address at any given time.

✦ **Private IP addresses:** *Private* addresses, on the other hand, are supposed to be used only on networks (such as your home LAN) and do *not* connect directly to the Internet. Lots of people can use the same private address because their networks never go public; that is, they never directly access the Internet, so their IP addresses never conflict.

Typically, you'll use addresses in the form of 192.168.*x.x* on your LAN. See Book VI, Chapter 1 for an overview of IP addresses and how they work.

You might be wondering to yourself thusly: "If I use private IP addresses on my LAN at home or in the office and I have to use a public IP address to communicate on the Internet, how can my private IP addresses on my LAN communicate with public IP addresses on the Internet?" That is an excellent question, and the answer is *Network Address Translation* (or NAT, for short).

NAT acts as a gatekeeper between your private IP addresses on your LAN and the public IP addresses on the Internet. When you connect to the Internet, your Internet service provider (ISP) gives you one — and usually *only* one — public IP address that can be used on the Internet. Instead of one of your computers using that public IP address and depriving all the other computers on the LAN, the hardware or software that you use to share the Internet will take control of that public IP address. Then, when any computer on your LAN tries to communicate on the Internet, your NAT software/hardware intercepts your communications and readdresses the traffic so that it appears to be coming from your allotted public IP address. (Think of a funnel that collects water from several different sources and then directs all the water into a single stream.)

When the web site, File Transfer Protocol (FTP) server, or whatever strange Internet intelligence you're using on the Internet replies, it replies to your NAT device. The NAT device remembers which private IP address it should go to on the LAN and sends the information to that computer. See NAT at work in Figure 4-1.

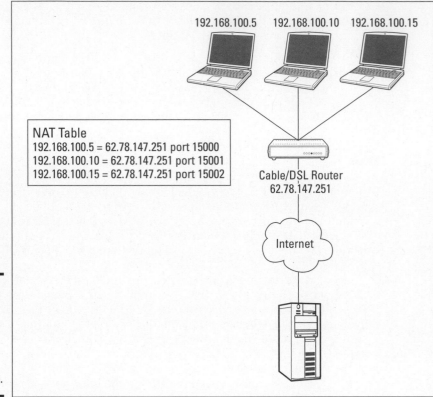

Figure 4-1:
NAT hard at work — for the betterment of Macs everywhere.

Ways to Share Your Internet Connection

After you have an Internet connection and your LAN is set up, you need something to make this NAT thing work. You have two different options to take care of NAT for your shared Internet connection: hardware or software. (Go figure.) Each has pros and cons, so take a look at each option individually.

If you read Chapter 3 of this minibook, you know that Lion has AirPort software built in. So, if you have an AirPort Extreme wireless network card in your Mac and you're using Lion, you can have your Mac act like an AirPort Extreme Base Station for all the wireless computers on your network, which in turn can use a software NAT.

Using hardware for sharing an Internet connection

Probably the most popular way to share an Internet connection is to buy a hardware device that connects to your Internet connection, which then connects to your LAN. These devices are referred to as *cable/DSL routers*. The main downside to a hardware Internet connection-sharing device is that it costs more than a software solution.

Cable/DSL routers are nice because they're easy to set up and configure. You can also leave them on, which means constant Internet access for those on your LAN. You don't have to worry about turning on another computer to connect to the Internet as you do with a software solution. Sounds like a good spot for a Mark's Maxim:

Hardware routers are the best choice for sharing your Internet connection, so if you can afford one, you should get one!

Apple's AirPort Extreme Base Station is not only a *Wireless Access Point* (WAP) for your network, as I discuss in Chapter 3 of this minibook, but also acts as an Internet connection-sharing device. (AirPort Express can't share an Internet connection . . . sorry.) Some older flavors of AirPort Base Station even have a built-in v.90 modem for sharing a single 56 Kbps connection using a dialup account! A base station typically has several Ethernet connections for sharing a high-speed Internet connection, including a dedicated port to connect to a cable/DSL router and two or four ports to connect to other computers on the LAN.

If you think that a cable/DSL router or an AirPort Extreme Base Station could be the karmic pathway for you to achieve your goal of sharing your Internet connection, here are some things to consider when deciding which device to buy for your LAN:

Book VI Chapter 4

Sharing That Precious Internet Thing

✦ **Do you need a switch?** Most cable/DSL routers have a small 3-, 4-, or 5-port switch built in. See Chapter 1 of this minibook to discover more about switches. This multiport capability is nice because the same cable/DSL router that shares your Internet connection is also the centerpiece of your LAN where all your connections meet, thus saving you from having to buy a switch on top of the cost of the cable/DSL router.

Some cable/DSL routers, however, have only a single Ethernet connection to connect to your LAN. So keep in mind that if you choose a device with a single LAN connection, you must supply your own switch that would then connect the cable/DSL router to the rest of your LAN.

✦ **Got modem?** If your only Internet connection is through a dial-up modem account, look for a built-in analog telephone modem on your cable/DSL router. You must have this feature if you want to use a hardware device to share your Internet connection. (Again, older versions of the AirPort Base Station are great for this because the modem is built in, but you'll have to do some shopping on eBay.) Even if you have cable/DSL service, some ISPs also include a dial-up account with your broadband access. With such a bountiful selection of connections, you can plug in your cable or DSL service to the cable/DSL router as well as use the dial-up account as a back-up in case your main service has problems.

✦ **Want a printer with that?** Some cable/DSL routers also have a port for connecting a printer — a great feature to have because it allows you to leave the printer connected and turned on so that anyone on the network can print to it anytime. (This is much better than connecting the printer to a computer and sharing it because then the computer doing the sharing must always be on in order to make the printer available.) Mac OS X can send a print job to a printer by using Bonjour or TCP/IP, so just make sure that your printer is compatible with TCP/IP printing, also called *LPR* (Line Printer Remote).

Using software for sharing an Internet connection

As I mention earlier, if you're using Mac OS X Lion and have an AirPort or AirPort Extreme wireless network card installed, your Mac can act like an AirPort/AirPort Extreme Base Station, providing both wireless Ethernet connectivity for other computers on the LAN *and* a shared Internet connection.

Lion also has built-in software that allows a single computer on your network to share its Internet connection with others on the LAN. To share your Internet connection, follow these quick steps:

1. **Click the System Preferences icon in the Dock.**

2. **Click the Sharing icon.**

3. **Click the Internet Sharing entry at the list on the left side of the pane.**

   This brings up the settings, as shown in Figure 4-2.

4. **Click the Share Your Connection From pop-up menu and choose Ethernet.**

5. **Select the Ethernet check box (in the To Computers Using list) to enable it.**

   When you do, you're issued a warning that enabling this could affect your ISP or violate your agreement with your ISP. In my experiences, this step has never caused any networking problems. However, if you have any doubts, contact your ISP and verify this.

6. **Click OK in the warning dialog to continue.**

   You go back to the Sharing dialog, where you'll notice that the Internet Sharing check box is conveniently ready for you to select it — feel free to click it now.

Figure 4-2:
Turning on Internet sharing with Lion.

If you're using a dial-up modem to access the Internet, you need to also make sure that the computer that has the modem also has an Ethernet or wireless LAN connection. Unfortunately, no Mac that can run Lion has a built-in modem, but if you buy an external USB modem from Apple (or a third-party vendor), you can still use this feature.

If you're using a cable or DSL modem for your Internet connection, the Mac that you want to run the sharing software on should have two Ethernet connections: one to connect to the cable/DSL modem and one to connect to the rest of the LAN.

The main disadvantage to using a software solution for Internet connection sharing is that the computer that connects to the Internet must be turned on and ready to go all the time so that others on the network can get to the Internet. And although the sharing software operates in the background on the machine it's running on, it still chews up some of that Mac's processing power and memory, so it could slow down other applications that you're running on that computer.

Connecting Everything for Wired Sharing

After you decide whether to use a software or hardware solution, it's time to get your hands dirty: All the pieces of the puzzle must be set up and connected. In this section, I tell you how to connect things for either the software or hardware method of sharing the Internet connection.

Using the software method

When you use the software method to share your Internet connection, one of the computers on your network has both the connection to the Internet and a connection to the LAN. Figure 4-3 shows a typical setup for software Internet sharing, whether you're using a dial-up modem account or a cable/DSL modem for your Internet connection.

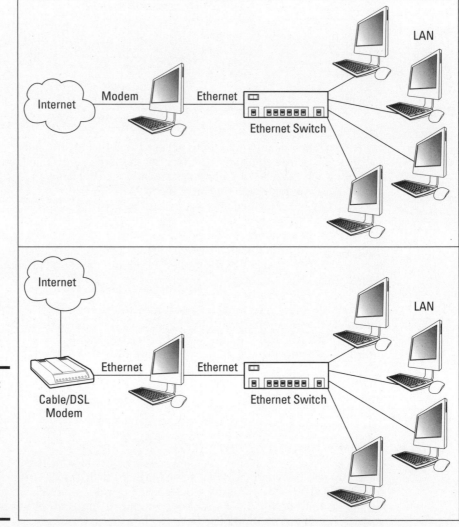

Figure 4-3: Two different configurations for Internet sharing through software.

Keep in mind, though, that when using a cable/DSL modem for your Internet connection, the computer running the sharing software *must* have two Ethernet connections.

Using the hardware method

Not only does using a dedicated piece of hardware free one of the Macs on your network from the onerous job of hosting the shared connection, but it also keeps you from having to have more than one Ethernet connection on a single computer if you're using a cable/DSL modem for your Internet access. Figure 4-4 shows how you would connect your devices for hardware Internet sharing by using either a cable/DSL router with a built-in Ethernet switch or a cable/DSL router with a stand-alone Ethernet switch, as you would need to use AirPort or AirPort Extreme.

If you choose to buy a cable/DSL router that has a built-in Ethernet switch, you can simply connect all your computers on the LAN to the built-in switch. However, if you buy a cable/DSL router that has only a single LAN connection, as with older versions of the AirPort Base Station, you must connect that single LAN connection to an external switch in order to get all the computers on the same network.

We're talking wired Ethernet here — of course, wireless connections don't require a port on your router or base station. (More on this in the next section.)

Regardless of whether you use the hardware or software method to share your Internet connection, all the computers on your LAN — except the one that's doing the sharing, if you're using software sharing — should be configured to obtain its IP address automatically through our old friend, Dynamic Host Configuration Protocol (DHCP). (See Chapter 1 of this mini-book for details on how to do this in Lion.) Although it's not a requirement that you set up your other devices with DHCP, it's recommended unless you understand the IP addressing scheme required by your cable/DSL router and you're willing to set up the addresses manually. You need to follow the instructions that come with the cable/DSL router or software that you purchase for detailed information on how to configure that.

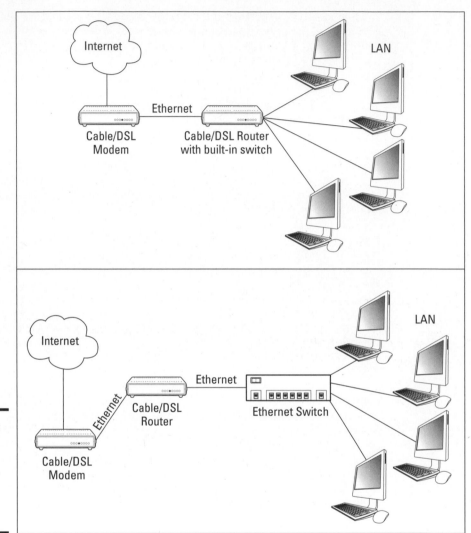

Figure 4-4:
A comely
pair of
hardware
Internet
sharing
solutions.

Adding Wireless Support

You might have noticed that I mention *wireless* here and there in this chapter. This section covers in a bit more detail how you can add wireless capabilities to your shared Internet party. To discover more about how wireless networks work and how to set up one, see Book VI, Chapter 3.

Basically, you can encounter a couple of situations when trying to add wireless capabilities into the mix. Either you already have an Internet connection-sharing mechanism in place (either hardware or software), or you don't yet have your Internet connection shared.

If you already have a cable/DSL router or are using software Internet sharing

If you already have a cable/DSL router or if you're using software Internet sharing, like that built into Lion, you can simply buy a WAP (short for *Wireless Access Point*) and connect it to your LAN. Adding a WAP enables anyone using wireless Ethernet access to your network and thus to your shared Internet connection.

There are many WAPs that you can buy to add wireless to your network. AirPort Extreme is a good example; however, because AirPort Extreme also can do Internet sharing, make sure that you *don't* enable Internet sharing through software on your Mac! (In this case, you don't want or need this feature because it can conflict with your cable/DSL router operation.)

If you do not have a cable/DSL router or an AirPort Extreme Base Station

If you don't have a cable/DSL router or an AirPort Extreme Base Station for Internet sharing, you have a few options. Each option has an upside and a downside.

One option is to get an AirPort Extreme Base Station, which provides both wireless access for AirPort-enabled wireless computers and Internet sharing for the entire network. Because today's AirPort Extreme Base Stations also feature three built-in Ethernet ports for wired connections, you won't need an additional switch to connect up to three Macs (or PCs, or printers, or even network file servers) using Ethernet cables.

The other option is to buy a combination cable/DSL router, which has a built-in WAP. Most cable/DSL routers — including the ones that have wireless built in — also have multiple Ethernet ports on them, so connecting computers by using wired Ethernet can be done without buying an external switch.

The final option is that you can use the AirPort software built into Lion to turn your Mac into an AirPort/AirPort Extreme Base Station, as I discuss earlier. This is a great, low-cost way to add wireless and Internet sharing to your network, but remember that the software will still eat up processor time and memory, and your Mac must remain turned on to supply the connection to your network. For more on wireless networking, read Chapter 3 of this minibook.

Book VII

Expanding Your System

Contents at a Glance

Chapter 1: Hardware That Will Make You Giddy

In This Chapter

✔ Using digital cameras, digital video camcorders, and scanners

✔ Adding keyboards, trackballs, joysticks, and drawing tablets

✔ Using optical recorders

✔ Adding speakers, subwoofers, and an iPod

Hardware. We love it. To a Mac power user, new hardware holds all the promise of Christmas morning, whether your new toys are used for business or for pleasure. We pore over magazines and visit our favorite Mac web sites like clockwork to check on new technology.

These hardware devices don't come cheap, however, forcing you to make the painful decision regarding which new hardware you really need in order to accomplish what you want and which hardware is a luxury. Also, if you're a new Mac owner, you might not know what's available. For example, I constantly get e-mail from readers, asking, "What can I connect to my new computer?" I guess I could reply, "Why, the kitchen sink!" To that end, I decided to add this chapter to the book to let you know how you can expand the hardware for your Mac OS X Lion powerhouse.

Each section in this chapter provides a description of what a particular device does, an idea of how much it costs, and a set of general guidelines that you can use when shopping. Although this isn't in-depth coverage — after all, the book is supposed to be about Lion — it will serve to get you started if you've just become a Mac owner. If you're especially interested in a specific piece of hardware, I recommend other books that you can read for the exhaustive details.

Ready? To quote a great line from the first *Batman* film: "Alfred, let's go shopping!"

Parading Pixels: Digital Cameras, DV Camcorders, and Scanners

The first category of hardware toys revolves around images — hardware for creating original images, capturing images in real time, and reading images from hard copy.

Digital cameras

A digital camera shares most of the characteristics of a traditional film camera. It looks the same, and you use the same techniques while shooting photographs. The difference is in the end result. With a digital camera, instead of a roll of film that has to be developed, you have an image in JPEG, RAW, or TIFF format that's stored on a memory card. The contents of the memory card can be downloaded to your Mac from within iPhoto (which I discuss with great pleasure in Book III, Chapter 3) and then the real fun begins. Here are some things that you can do with a digital photograph:

✦ Edit it with an image editor such as iPhoto or Adobe Photoshop Elements (or their more professional-level brethren, Photoshop and Aperture)

✦ Print it with an inkjet, dye-sublimation, or color laser printer

✦ Record it to a CD or DVD

✦ Add it to a web page

✦ Print several of them in a coffee-table book (using iPhoto or Photoshop Elements)

✦ Mail it to friends and family

What they cost

Consumer-level digital cameras typically sell for anywhere from under $100 (for a 10-megapixel [MP] model) to $300 (for a 14MP point-and-shoot camera). *Megapixel* is a general reference to the *resolution* (the size of the image, measured in individual dots called *pixels*) and detail delivered by the camera. Such digital cameras can produce photographs that are well suited for just about any casual shutterbug. Professional digital cameras, which capture far more detail and offer designs that more closely resemble the best SLR film camera, can set you back $600 or $1,000. Because of their cost and complexity, I wouldn't recommend them to someone who's just discovered digital photography.

What to look for

Here are some general guidelines that I recommend when selecting a digital camera:

+ **At least a 10MP camera:** As a general rule, the higher the megapixel value, the better the camera.

+ **At least a 4GB internal memory card:** The *memory card* stores the images that you capture.

+ **A Universal Serial Bus (USB) 2.0 connection to your Macintosh:** I cover USB in all its glory in Chapter 3 of this minibook.

+ **A burst mode feature:** A digital camera with burst mode can take a number of consecutive images quickly, without the shutter lag that other cameras experience.

+ **An optical zoom feature:** *Optical zoom* allows you to draw closer to subjects that are farther away.

Note that I recommended *optical* zoom there and not *digital* zoom. Essentially, digital zoom is a silly feature that simply resizes a portion of your image, providing a blocky close-up. In fact, an image editor like Photoshop Elements can produce exactly the same result as a camera with digital zoom . . . and it looks almost as bad. Only an optical zoom results in a sharper magnification of the subject.

+ **A self-timer:** With a self-timer, your camera can snap a photo automatically, allowing you to finally be seen in your own pictures!

+ **A manual flash setting:** Although automatic flash is a good thing most of the time, a manual setting allows you to disable your camera's flash for artistic shots (or just to prevent the glare on subjects with polished surfaces).

**Book VII
Chapter 1**

DV camcorders

Like digital cameras, digital video (DV) camcorders are the counterpart to the familiar video camcorder. A *DV camcorder* looks and operates like an analog VHS camcorder, but you can connect it to your Macintosh via a FireWire or USB cable and download your video clips directly into iMovie. Today's crop of DV camcorders can also record in High Definition (HD for short) for your widescreen TV or monitor. (Chapter 4 of Book III explains all about iMovie, and both FireWire and USB connections are tackled in Chapter 3 of this minibook.)

Besides the higher quality of digital video, it has a number of other real advantages over analog video:

+ Digital video can be edited with applications such as iMovie or Final Cut Express.

+ Digital video can be recorded to a CD or DVD.

+ Digital video can be copied endlessly, with no loss of quality.

+ Digital video can be posted for downloading on a web page.

Hardware That Will
Make You Giddy

What they cost

The least expensive DV camcorders start at about $100. You'll find camcorders that record in HD below $200.

What to look for

I recommend the following when shopping for a DV camcorder:

✦ **The highest optical zoom in your price range:** Again, as with a digital camera, it's important to be able to capture subjects and action when you can't get any closer — think the lion exhibit at the zoo.

✦ **Image stabilization:** This helps steady the picture when you're holding the camcorder without a tripod.

✦ **Onboard effects:** These effects generally include some snazzy things like black-and-white footage, fades, and wipes.

✦ **AV connectors:** Use these to display your video by connecting the camcorder directly to your TV.

✦ **Digital still mode:** This enables you to take still photographs if your digital camera isn't handy; however, the image quality isn't as good as a bona fide digital camera.

For a closer look at digital video, iMovie and iDVD, check out *iLife '11 For Dummies* by Tony Bove (Wiley).

Scanners

Figure 1-1 illustrates a typical flatbed scanner, which is the tool of choice for those Macintosh owners who want to digitize images and text from printed materials. Although you can also connect a sheet-fed scanner, flatbed models are much more versatile and produce better-quality scans.

Figure 1-1:
The flatbed
scanner,
King of
Digitizing.

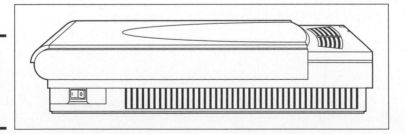

Images produced by a scanner can be edited, mailed, displayed on the web, or added to your own documents, just as the images from a digital camera can be.

What they cost

A good-quality scanner should cost anywhere from $50–$200, with the best models — featuring the fastest scanning speeds, best color depth, and highest resolutions, or those meant for scanning film negatives — going for around $400. Many multifunction printers can also perform good-quality scanning.

What to look for

Try to get the following features in a scanner:

+ **The highest color depth that you can afford:** Get a minimum of 48-bit.

+ **The highest resolution that you can afford:** Get a minimum of 2400 dots per inch (dpi) (optical).

+ **Single-pass scanning:** This feature results in a faster scan with less chance of error.

+ **Transparency adapter for scanning film negatives:** If you're a traditional film photographer, you'll find that a transparency adapter turns a standard flatbed scanner into an acceptable negative scanner.

+ **One-touch buttons for e-mailing your scanned images or uploading them to the web:** These are controls of convenience — pressing one of these buttons automatically scans the item and prepares the image to be e-mailed or uploaded to a web site.

+ **USB 2.0 or FireWire connection:** I cover the advantages of both in Chapter 3 of this minibook.

Incredible Input: Keyboards, Trackballs, Joysticks, and Drawing Tablets

Although your Mac probably came equipped with a keyboard and a mouse or trackpad, you can replace them with enhanced hardware that will add functionality and precision to your work. (Or you can buy a joystick and spend your days wreaking havoc on your enemies.)

Keyboards

If you're using the latest Intel iMac or Mac Pro tower model, you may not need to upgrade your keyboard at all (unless you prefer the response of an after-market keyboard instead). However, if you're using an older Macintosh — or you have a Mac mini (which requires an external keyboard) or a MacBook and you want to add an external keyboard — you can take advantage of the convenience of a USB keyboard like the one in Figure 1-2.

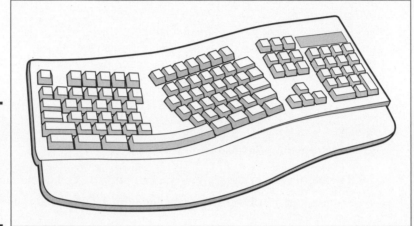

What they cost

Aftermarket (nonstandard-issue) keyboards generally cost anywhere from $30–$100.

What to look for

Look for the following keyboard features when shopping for a keyboard:

✦ **Programmable buttons:** Configure these to launch applications or run macros.

✦ **Additional USB ports:** Use these to turn your keyboard into a USB hub. The best keyboards offer *powered* USB hubs, which allow you to connect devices that draw their power from the USB port (and therefore don't require a separate power supply).

✦ **One-touch buttons to launch your browser or e-mail application:** Press one of these buttons to launch your web browser or Mail.

✦ **Ergonomic wrist pad:** Use these to help prevent wrist strain and repetitive joint injuries.

Trackballs

Some folks prefer using a trackball, like the one shown in Figure 1-3, over a mouse any day . . . even the Magic Mouse now included with Mac desktops. Graphic artists find that trackballs are more precise and offer better control, including a secondary button to display contextual menus. (One model on the market has eight buttons. Who needs a keyboard?)

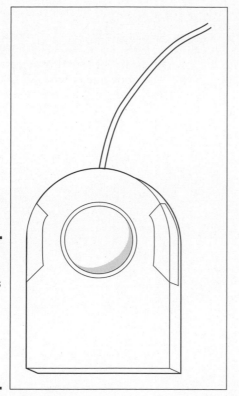

Figure 1-3:
Many Mac power users (myself included) favor a trackball over a mouse.

What they cost

Trackballs range in price from $20–$90. Most are optical (see the following section), so they need little cleaning, and they'll last for many years of precise pointing at things.

What to look for

Look for the following features when shopping for a trackball:

✦ **More programmable buttons:** Opt for at least two buttons, of course, but the more the merrier!

✦ **Optical tracking:** An *optical* trackball — one that doesn't use rollers, instead using a photo-sensitive sensor to record the movement of the ball — is more precise and easier to keep clean.

✦ **A scroll wheel:** Use this gizmo to scroll documents up and down.

✦ **Ergonomic design:** Look for a wrist pad or slanted buttons.

Joysticks and steering wheels

Game players, unite! For arcade and sports games, using a joystick results in increased maneuverability, more realistic action, higher scores, less wear and tear on your keyboard . . . and just plain more fun. Joysticks range from the traditional USB aircraft controller, as shown in Figure 1-4, to USB controllers, steering wheels and gamepads that rival anything offered on today's console game machines.

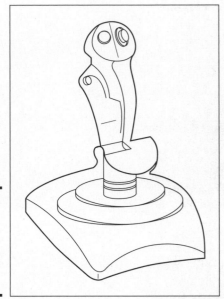

Figure 1-4: The secret weapon of Mac gaming — a joystick.

What they cost

Joysticks vary in price from $30–$120. At the low end, you'll usually find the gamepad-type controllers, whereas aircraft controllers carry the highest price tag.

What to look for

Get the following features in a joystick:

✦ **Yet even more programmable buttons.**

✦ **Pitch and yaw controls.** These are for the flight simulator crowd.

✦ **Force feedback.** A *force feedback* joystick or gamepad rumbles and moves in tandem with the action in the game, providing an extra feeling of realism.

Drawing tablets

A drawing tablet like the one you see in Figure 1-5 might be pricey, but if you're a graphic artist or a designer, using a tablet will revolutionize the way that you work with your Mac. Rather than use a mouse or trackball to sketch, you can draw on the tablet freehand, just as you would draw on paper or canvas. Tablets can recognize different levels of pressure, allowing applications, such as Photoshop and Painter, to re-create all sorts of photo-realistic brush effects. Most drawing tablets will also allow you to use Ink (Lion's built-in handwriting recognition feature, which I discuss in Book VIII, Chapter 3).

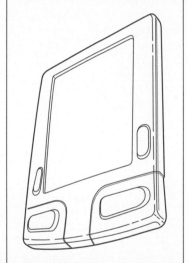

Figure 1-5:
Professional artists and designers swear by the graphics tablet.

What they cost

Depending on the size of the tablet and the pressure levels that you need, you'll pay anywhere from just under $100 to a whopping $500.

What to look for

I recommend the following tablet features:

+ **Programmable buttons:** See a trend here?

+ **Accessory mouse:** Some high-end tablets include a mouse that you can use along with the tablet.

+ **A cordless stylus:** Make sure that it doesn't require batteries.

✦ **The highest number of pressure levels possible:** The more levels that the tablet offers, the more subtle and precise your control is over painting effects.

Sublime Storage: DVD/Blu-Ray Recorders

Ready to talk storage? Consider a rewriteable DVD-RW drive which can store 4.7GB on a single disc, or dual-layer drives, which can store 8.5GB! (And don't even get me started on the latest generation of optical technology — the Blu-ray recorders — they can store 50GB on a single disc!)

If you'd like to trade data with another Mac or a PC via floppy disks, you can get an external USB floppy drive for under $50; however, I personally eschew floppy disks, which are very unreliable and carry a mere 1.44MB of data. Pick up a USB Flash drive instead.

All recent Mac models (except the MacBook Air) include a rewriteable DVD-RW SuperDrive — but if you're using a MacBook Air (or you want the latest Blu-ray storage capacity, or the ability to burn odd-sized media), you can always add an external model.

What they cost

A FireWire DVD-RW drive averages about $100.

What to look for

Get the following features in an external DVD recorder:

✦ **An internal buffer of at least 8MB:** The larger the buffer, the less chance that you'll encounter recording errors and the faster your drive will burn.

✦ **At least 16X DVD recording speed:** A no-brainer here. The faster the recording speed, the less time you'll wait for the finished disc.

✦ **AC power through the USB 2.0 or FireWire cable:** This eliminates the need for a separate AC power supply.

✦ **Burn-proof technology:** This virtually eliminates recording errors because of multitasking so that you can continue to work on other applications while you record.

Awesome Audio: Subwoofer Systems and MP3 Hardware

Although virtually all Macs ship with speakers, I'll be honest — the "stock" speakers don't measure up to the standards of a true audiophile. For those who really enjoy their music and their game audio, this last section covers the world of Macintosh aftermarket sonic enjoyment.

Subwoofer speaker systems

The ever-popular USB port again comes to your rescue. This time, it enables you to connect a more powerful speaker system with a *subwoofer*. In case you've never heard a subwoofer — think chest-rattling *thump, thump, thump* — you should know that they provide the basement-level bass that can add power and punch to both your music and your games. Being hit by an asteroid is a rather flat, tinny experience with a pair of battery-powered speakers that you salvaged from your Walkman years ago. With a new set of speakers and a subwoofer, you'll swear that Han Solo is sitting in the cockpit chair next to you!

With the growing importance of the computer as a replacement for your home entertainment center, investing in a more powerful set of speakers will help you enjoy all those audio CDs and MP3s that you've added to your iTunes Playlists. (Read all about iTunes in Book III, Chapter 2.)

What they cost

Most USB-powered speakers with a subwoofer are priced below $100, but true audiophiles looking for surround sound can spring for a better $300 system that includes five satellite speakers and a subwoofer.

What to look for

Get these features in a subwoofer:

✦ **At least 30 watts of power:** The higher the wattage rating, the more powerful the speakers (and the louder your music can be).

✦ **Additional headphone jacks and stereo mini-plug input jacks:** Use these for connecting your iPod or MP3 player directly to your speaker system. (Read all about iPods in the next section.)

✦ **Magnetic shielding:** This helps prevent your speakers from distorting your monitor display.

MP3 players (well, actually, just the iPod)

I've lusted after Apple's iPod MP3 player ever since it arrived on campus. Depending on which model you get, this incredible device can hold up to 160GB of digital audio — that's 40,000 songs — as well as digital photographs and full-length movies! Plus, the iPod also acts as your personal data butler by carrying your files; it's an honest-to-goodness, external USB 2.0 hard drive. You can download your contacts and appointments from Mac OS X and view them wherever you go. Just think: Carry your files to and from your office *and* carry DEVO and the Dead Kennedys *and* watch a movie you downloaded as well! Oh, and did I mention that you can play games and use all sorts of applications with the iPod touch model?

All this fits into a beautiful, stylish package about the size of a pack of cigarettes, with up to a 36-hour lithium rechargeable battery, high-quality earbud headphones, and automatic synchronization with your iTunes music library. (The iPod Shuffle is the smallest member of the iPod family — it's just a little over an inch square.) Life just doesn't get any better for a technoid like me. If you think that your Mac is a well-designed piece of equipment, you'll understand why this little box is so alluring. (And why I have one now.)

Sure, other MP3 players are out there, but many of them share the same following problems:

✦ They use digital memory cards, which offer far less capacity than the iPod Classic's built-in hard drive.

✦ They use standard batteries, or you have to furnish rechargeable batteries (which don't last 36 hours).

✦ They don't operate as an external hard drive, photo slideshow repository, game machine, movie theater, or contacts/appointment database.

I say forget 'em. The iPod is worth every cent that you'll pay.

The 2GB iPod Shuffle is around $50 at the time of this writing, while the 8GB iPod nano runs $149 and the 160GB iPod Classic model costs $249. Finally, you can opt for the svelte and sexy iPod touch, which runs $229 for the 8GB model.

Chapter 2: Add RAM, Hard Drive Space, and Stir

In This Chapter

✔ **Understanding the advantages of extra RAM**

✔ **Shopping for a RAM upgrade**

✔ **Choosing between internal and external hard drives**

✔ **Determining your hard drive needs**

✔ **Shopping for a new hard drive**

✔ **Installing your upgrades**

Most Macintosh owners will make two upgrades — adding more memory (RAM) and additional hard drive space — during the lifetime of their computers. These two improvements have the greatest effect on the overall performance of Mac OS X. By adding RAM and additional hard drive space, not only do you make more elbow room for your applications and documents, but everything runs faster: Think of the Six Million Dollar Man, only a heck of a lot cheaper to operate (and no strange noises accompanying your every move).

In this chapter, for those who aren't well versed in selecting memory modules or weighing the advantages of different types of hard drives, I steer you around the hidden potholes along the way. However, if you buy the wrong piece of hardware, remember that using a hammer to make it fit is *not* a workable option.

Adding Memory: Reasons for More RAM

Of all the possible upgrades that you can make to your Macintosh, adding more random access memory (RAM) is the single most cost-effective method of improving the performance of Mac OS X. (In fact, your machine will likely run faster with more memory than a reasonably faster processor!) Here is exactly what Mac OS X uses available RAM for:

✦ **Applications:** Naturally, Mac OS X needs system RAM to run the applications that you launch. The more memory in your machine, the larger the applications that you can open and the faster they'll run.

✦ **Overhead:** This includes the operating system itself, as well as various and sundry buffers and memory areas devoted for temporary work. As you would guess, the more memory here, the merrier.

✦ **Virtual memory:** Aha! Now here's something that I mentioned lightly and politely in Book I, but hasn't really amounted to a hill of beans until this moment. (Can you tell I'm a big fan of Bing Crosby?) *Virtual memory* allows Mac OS X to use empty hard drive space as temporary system memory, as shown in Figure 2-1. Data is written to your hard drive instead of being stored in RAM, and then it's erased when it's no longer needed. This is a neat trick that's also used by Windows and Linux. Virtual memory works automatically within Mac OS X.

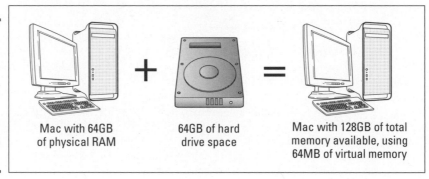

Figure 2-1: The mysterious beauty of virtual memory — but it still doesn't beat real RAM!

Mac with 64GB of physical RAM

64GB of hard drive space

Mac with 128GB of total memory available, using 64MB of virtual memory

At first, virtual memory sounds like absolute bliss, and it does indeed allow your Macintosh to do things that would otherwise be impossible, such as running an application that requires 2GB of RAM in just 1GB of actual physical RAM. However, here come the caveats:

✦ Virtual memory is as slow as molasses in December. Today's fastest magnetic hard drive is many, *many* times slower than real silicon (and even solid-state hard drives, which actually use memory chips as well, are still much slower than your Mac's system RAM), so any use of virtual memory instead of RAM slows down Mac OS X significantly.

✦ Virtual memory abuses your hard drive. If you've ever run Photoshop on a Windows PC with 128MB of RAM, you're having flashbacks right now. Whenever your Macintosh is using virtual memory, your hard drive remains almost constantly active. (Hardware types, like myself, call this phenomenon *thrashing* because we know what's happening inside that poor hard drive.) Over time, running any computer with insufficient RAM and behemoth applications will result in a significant increase in hard drive wear and tear.

✦ Virtual memory costs you processing power. With sufficient RAM, Mac OS X gleefully runs as efficiently as it can. When virtual memory kicks in, however, your Mac has to spend part of its quality time shuttling data to and from the hard drive, which robs your computer of processing power.

The moral of the story is very simple, so it's time for another of Mark's Maxims:

The less Mac OS X needs to use virtual memory, the better.

To put it another way, *physical memory* (meaning memory modules) is always a better choice than virtual memory. This is why power users and techno-types crave as much system memory as possible.

A little over five years ago, 128MB of RAM was a quite comfortable figure for most folks, but all of today's Macs can accept *at least* a whopping 4GB (that's short for *gigabyte,* or 1,024 megabytes) of system RAM. (At the extreme end of the scale, the King Kahuna — Apple's latest Mac Pro — can now accommodate an unbelievable *64 gigabytes* of RAM!)

If you'll be keeping your current Macintosh for a few years more, install as much memory as you can afford — you'll thank me every time Mac OS X Lion boots.

Shopping for a RAM Upgrade

Before you click some online computer store's Buy button, you need to determine two things that will help you determine which memory module to buy: how much RAM you already have and how much more your system can handle.

Finding out the current memory in your Mac

Memory modules are made in standard sizes, so you need to determine how much memory you already have and which of your memory slots are filled. To do this, click the Apple menu and choose About This Mac. On the dialog that appears, click the Memory toolbar button.

Here you can see exactly how many memory modules you have, what type they are, and how much memory each provides. For example, in Figure 2-2, my iMac has two memory slots, both of which use a 667 MHz DDR2 SDRAM module. Both those slots are filled to the brim with a 1GB module each, giving me a total physical memory of 2048MB, or 2GB. Jot down the name and contents of each slot on a piece of paper — or, if you're a real Mac OS X power user, add a Sticky to your Desktop with this information. (Stickies are covered in Book II, Chapter 2.)

Did you notice the link at the bottom of the dialog — the one that reads *Memory Upgrade Instructions*? Click this link, and Mac OS X Lion automatically opens a Safari browser window with online instructions on how to upgrade the RAM in your specific Mac model. If you're confident about your technical skills, you can use this documentation as a guide to installing and removing memory modules. (Because I can't cover the process for every Mac model, I highly recommend that you review these instructions closely!)

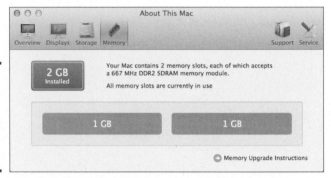

Figure 2-2:
Look under the hood with Apple's About This Mac dialog.

Unfortunately, on some machines only one memory module can be upgraded by a mere mortal, and the memory in the MacBook Air laptop can't be upgraded at all.

Potentially confusing? You bet. This arrangement differs on just about every model of Macintosh ever made — some have more memory slots, and others allow you to upgrade all the system memory instead of just one module. The only way to determine which modules are accessible on your Mac is to identify the exact model of your computer.

Determining the exact model of your computer

Most folks know the type and model of their computers, but there's a catch here, too: Sometimes the memory that you need varies by the processor in your Macintosh. For instance, many different versions of iMacs have been made since the Bondi Blue Beast debuted, and over the course of those years, Apple has made a slew of changes inside. Your eye should be on the actual processor speed and *bus speed* — the transfer speed that data reaches whilst speeding across your motherboard — because they're the identifying factors here. An older iMac with a 2.4 GHz Intel Core 2 Duo processor, for example, will use a different type of memory from the latest iMac with a 2.93 GHz Intel Core i7 processor.

Again, your salvation turns out to be the About This Mac dialog. Just click the Overview toolbar button to display both the machine speed (or *processor speed*) and the common identifier that Apple uses to refer to your specific model. (For example, my machine has a 2.4 GHz Intel Core 2 Duo CPU, and it's identified as a 20-inch, Mid 2007 model.) Grab that same piece of paper (or open that same Sticky) and add these two figures to your list.

Now you're armed with the information that you need to go online and buy the right memory — or, if you'd rather work directly with a human being, you can visit your local Apple dealer, present that most august personage with the list, and have the memory upgrade ordered for you.

Buying memory online is much cheaper. I recommend the following online stores:

✦ **MacMall:** www.macmall.com

✦ **Other World Computing:** www.macsales.com

✦ **MacConnection:** www.macconnection.com

The Tao of Adding Hard Drive Territory

Next, turn your attention to the other popular Mac upgrade — adding extra hard drive space. With today's cutting-edge, 3-D games using a couple of gigabytes of space each and Photoshop CS5.5 expanding to a minimum of 2GB, IDC (short for *Insidious Data Creep*) is a growing problem. (Bad pun most certainly intended.)

You can save space by deleting those files and folders you don't need, but what fun is that? To reduce your Mac's waistline before you consider adding more room, I recommend using Spring Cleaning from Smith Micro Software, which you can find at mysmithmicro.com. It's a great tool for locating duplicates, removing empty folders, and uninstalling old programs that you no longer use.

And yes, you guessed it, you can even determine how much free space remains on a hard drive from the About This Mac dialog! Click the Storage toolbar button to display all your glorious hard drive information, as shown in Figure 2-3. (I'm a major-league Mozart fan-boy, hence the name of my internal hard drive — my other drives are named after other composers as well.)

As a general rule, the following factors indicate that you're ready to upgrade your hard drive territory:

✦ You have less than 20GB of space on your current hard drive.

✦ You've cleaned *all* unnecessary files, and your Mac is still lagging behind in storage.

✦ You need to share a large amount of data between computers that aren't on the same network. (Read on to discover why.)

Figure 2-3:
Checking
your drive's
free space.

Internal versus External Storage

Most people who upgrade their existing hard drive do so because they need extra space; however, you might also need to add a hard drive to your system that can go mobile whenever necessary. Unlike an *internal* drive — which resides hidden inside your Mac's case — an *external* drive is a lean, mean, self-contained traveling storage machine that's perfect for road warriors.

External drives

Although most external drives carry their own power supply, some models actually don't need a separate power supply because they draw their power through your Mac's Universal Serial Bus (USB), FireWire port, or Thunderbolt port. (The next chapter in this minibook tells all about Thunderbolt, USB, and FireWire.) If you have an older MacBook Pro with an ExpressCard/34 slot and an eSATA card adapter — or if you're using a Mac Pro with an eSATA expansion card — you can also use an external SATA (eSATA) drive.

External drives also have a number of other advantages:

✦ **No installation hassle:** You can easily install a Thunderbolt, USB, or FireWire drive in seconds. Simply plug in the drive to the proper connector on the side or back of your Mac, connect the power supply (if necessary), and turn it on. (No software installation necessary. As the folks in Cupertino are fond of saying, "Look, Ma — no drivers!")

✦ **No extra space needed:** Many Macs simply don't have the internal space for another drive — laptops, iMacs, and the Mac mini are good examples. Therefore, if you want to keep your existing internal drive as-is while you're adding more storage, an external drive is your only choice.

✦ **File sharing with ease:** With an external drive, you can share your data between multiple computers or bring your files with you on your next trip.

✦ **Safe from prying eyes:** Unlike an internal drive, external drives are easy to secure. Take your sensitive information home with you or lock it in a safe.

After you plug in an external drive, Mac OS X displays it just like any other hard drive volume. Figure 2-4 illustrates my 60GB FireWire drive in action — note the drive bears the FireWire symbol as an icon, marking it as an external drive.

Figure 2-4:
A typical
FireWire
external
drive.

I'd be remiss if I didn't mention that all modern Macs (except for the MacBook Air) now have a DVD-R drive, which makes it easy to send up to 9GB of data through the mail on a single recordable disc. No one wants to box up an expensive external hard drive to transport 4GB worth of photos to Aunt Martha!

Internal drives

Your other alternative is to upgrade your internal drive, which can be a hassle. As does a memory upgrade, adding or swapping an internal drive involves opening your Mac's case. In fact, it's a somewhat more complex procedure than adding memory.

I usually recommend that folks add a second drive rather than swap out their existing drive. You'll avoid the hassle of backing up and restoring your system on a new drive or (even worse) reinstalling Mac OS X and then reinstalling all the applications that you use. (Swapping a hard drive should be the definition of the word *hassle*.) Instead, add a second drive and leave your current hard drive as-is.

However, here are a number of very important reasons why many Mac owners choose updating internal drives, even with the hassle of swapping:

✦ **They're cheaper.** You'll spend significantly less on an internal drive because it doesn't need the case and additional electronics required by an external drive.

✦ **They're faster.** A typical USB 2.0 or FireWire 400 drive isn't as fast as an internal drive.

✦ **They take up less space in your work area.** An internal drive eliminates the space taken by an external drive, which can range anywhere from the size of a paperback to the size of a hardback book.

After you establish that you are in fact ready for more space — and you've decided whether you want to add an internal drive, an external drive, or (if you enjoy punishment) upgrade your existing internal drive — you're ready to consider how big a drive you need.

Determining How Much Space You Need

Your next step is to decide just how much hard drive space is enough. I suppose that if your last name is Zuckerberg and you had something to do with that Facebook thing, you can probably pick just about any drive on the market. However, I have a family, a mortgage, a car payment, and lust in my heart for the latest computer games; therefore, I must be a little more selective.

I have two hard-and-fast rules that I follow when I'm determining the capacity of a new drive:

✦ If you're buying a *replacement* for your existing drive, shop for a drive with at least twice the capacity of the existing drive (if possible).

✦ If you're buying an *external drive,* shop for a drive with at least the same capacity as your existing internal drive (if possible). One exception: If you're adding an external drive for use with Time Machine, you'll want at least twice the capacity of your existing drive.

Those rules seem to work pretty doggone well in most circumstances, with these two exceptions: gamers and digital video gurus. These folks need to shoehorn as much space as they possibly can into their systems. If you're a hardcore gamer or if you work primarily with digital video, you need a wheelbarrow's worth of hard drive capacity. Trust me: Buy the biggest hard drive that you can afford.

Shopping for a Hard Drive

Ready to brave the local Wireless Shed superstore (or perhaps its web site)? Here's a list of guidelines to keep handy while you're shopping for a new internal or external hard drive:

✦ **Faster is indeed better.** You'll pay more for a 10,000 revolutions per minute (rpm) drive than a slower 5,400 or 7,200 rpm drive, but the extra expense is worth it. Faster drives can transfer more data to your Mac in less time, especially if you're replacing your Mac's internal Serial ATA drive.

Faster drives are especially important for storing digital video.

✦ **Serial ATA and EIDE drives are different.** If you're replacing your internal drive, you have to get the same type of drive that you already have: *EIDE* or *Serial ATA.* (EIDE, short for Enhanced Integrated Drive Electronics, is a common *parallel ATA* standard hard drive used in PCs and older Macs.) Again, System Profiler can tell you which type of drive your Mac is currently using.

✦ **Solid-State drives are hot.** An SSD drive has no moving parts — instead, it uses RAM modules to store your data, much like the USB flash drives so common today. Silicon storage allows for superfast performance (and avoids the possibility of a hard drive *crash*, where the internal moving parts in a traditional magnetic hard drive decide to take a permanent vacation). Unfortunately, at the time of this writing, you'll pay more for a solid-state drive than a standard magnetic hard drive. (Go figure.) Check the specifications on any SSD drive you're considering to make sure it's compatible with your Mac.

Book VII
Chapter 2

Add RAM, Hard
Drive Space, and
Stir

✦ **Avoid used or refurbished drives.** Hard drives are one of the few components in your computer that still have a large number of moving parts. (Again, the exception is a solid-state drive.) Therefore, buying a used drive isn't a good idea unless it's priced very low.

Because the prices on new hard drives are constantly dropping, make sure that you check on the price for a new, faster drive of the same capacity before you buy that "bargain" used drive.

✦ **Pick FireWire over USB.** Compared with a FireWire 400 connection, a USB 2.0 external hard drive is less efficient and slightly slower. Because most Macs with USB ports also have FireWire ports, make very sure that you buy a FireWire drive! (Of course, you can buy a USB 2.0 drive without being embarrassed. Or invest in a drive that has both FireWire and USB 2.0 connectors! Heck, if you're running one of the latest Mac models with a Thunderbolt port, you can invest in the fastest external performance on the planet — but you'll pay a premium price.)

Don't forget, a FireWire 800 port is roughly twice as fast as either a USB 2.0 port or the older FireWire 400 port. (For a complete discussion of USB, FireWire, and Thunderbolt, turn to the next chapter in this section. It's *thrilling* reading, let me tell you.)

✦ **Watch the size of the drive when buying internal drives.** Most SATA (Serial ATA) and EIDE drives are standard half-height 3.5-inch units, but check to make sure that you're not investing in a laptop drive — unless, of course, you're upgrading a laptop.

Installing Your New Stuff

After you get your memory modules or hard drive, pick one of two methods of installing them: easy or hard. Guess which method will cost you money?

The easy way

Your Apple dealer can perform either type of hardware installation for you. You can rest easy knowing that the job will be done right, but money will definitely change hands.

Personally, I always recommend that owners of MacBook and MacBook Pro laptops allow their dealers to install hard drives because these laptops are much more complex than a desktop, and they're much easier to damage. (The Mac mini is a bear to work on, as well.)

The hard way

If you're familiar with the inside of your Macintosh, you can install your own upgrade and save that cash. A memory upgrade is one of the simpler chores to perform, but that doesn't mean that everyone feels comfortable taking the cover off and jumping inside a computer; hard drives are a tad more complex.

If you have a knowledgeable friend or family member who can help you install your hardware, buy him the proverbial NSD (short for *Nice Steak Dinner*) and enlist him in your cause. Even if you still do the work yourself, it's always better to have a second pair of experienced eyes watching, especially if you're a little nervous.

Because the installation procedures for both memory modules and hard drives are different for *every* model of Mac — heck, even removing the cover on each model of Macintosh involves a different challenge — I can't provide you with any step-by-step procedures in this chapter. (As I mentioned earlier, Apple provides instructions from the About This Mac dialog.) Many online stores include installation instructions with their hardware. Other sources for installation instructions include the Apple web site (www. apple.com) and your Apple dealer. You can use Safari's Google search feature to scan the Internet for installation information for your particular model. However, here are guidelines to follow during the installation:

✦ **Watch out for static electricity.** When opening your Macintosh and handling hardware, make certain that you've touched a metal surface beforehand to discharge any static electricity on your body. (You can also buy a static wrist strap that you can wear while working within the bowels of your Mac.)

✦ **Check the notches on memory modules.** Most types of memory modules have notches cut into the connector. These notches make sure that you can install the module only one way, so make certain that they align properly with the slot.

✦ **Make sure you're using the right memory slot.** As I mention earlier in this chapter, most Macs have multiple memory slots, so check the label on the circuit board to make sure that you're adding the memory to the correct slot. (Naturally, this won't be a problem if you're installing a module into an unoccupied slot.)

✦ **Take good care of older hardware.** If you replace an existing memory module or hard drive with a new one, put the old hardware in the left-over anti-static bag from your new hardware and immediately start thinking of how you'll word your eBay auction . . . *Used 1GB Memory Module for Intel iMac,* for example. (Heck, some online stores will even give you a rebate if you return the original Apple memory modules.)

✦ **Check your hard drive jumper settings.** If your Mac uses EIDE hard drives, you must set the Master and Slave jumpers correctly on the back (or underside) of the new drive. A *jumper* is simply a tiny metal-and-plastic connector that is used to change the configuration on a hard drive. Setting jumpers indicates to your Mac which drive is the primary drive and which is the secondary drive. (I don't know how engineers got into the whole Master/Slave thing . . . they're normally not quite so exotic when naming things.)

Book VII
Chapter 2

Add RAM, Hard Drive Space, and Stir

If you're adding a second drive to a desktop with an EIDE drive, you'll probably have to change the jumper settings on the original drive as well. (If you're replacing the existing drive, you're in luck; simply duplicate the jumper settings from the old drive and use them on the new drive.) Because the configuration settings are different for each hard drive model, check the drive's documentation for the correct jumper position.

To determine whether a memory upgrade was successful, you can again turn to the About This Mac dialog. Display the dialog again and click the Memory toolbar button, and then compare the memory overview specifications with the original list that you made earlier. If the total amount of memory has increased and the memory module is recognized, you've done your job well. If not, switch off the Mac and check the module to make sure it's completely seated in the slot.

Chapter 3: Port-o-Rama: Using Thunderbolt, USB, and FireWire

In This Chapter

✔ **Using FireWire, USB, and Thunderbolt with Mac OS X**

✔ **Adding a USB or FireWire hub**

✔ **Troubleshooting external connections**

✔ **Adding and updating drivers**

A pple's list of successes continues to grow over the years — hardware, applications, and (of course) Mac OS X — but the FireWire standard for connecting computers to all sorts of different devices is in a class by itself. For many years, FireWire was the port of choice for all sorts of digital devices that needed a high-speed connection. Even Windows owners have grudgingly admitted that FireWire just plain rocks. Ya gotta love it.

And let us not forget that Apple was the first major computer manufacturer to include Intel's Universal Serial Bus (or USB) ports as standard equipment — and, most recently, the new Thunderbolt external port (providing the fastest connection speed *ever*) has made its debut on the MacBook Pro!

In this chapter, I discuss the importance of all three of these connections to the digital hub that I discuss in Book III, and I compare FireWire with both Thunderbolt and USB version 2.0 connection technology. I also talk troubleshooting and expansion using a hub.

Appreciating the Advantage of a FireWire Connection

So what's so special about FireWire, anyway? Why does Apple stuff at least one FireWire port in almost all of its current Macintosh models? (The exceptions are the MacBook Air and MacBook models.) Heck, even the *iPod* (Apple's MP3 player, which you can read more about in Book III, Chapter 2) originally used only a FireWire connection. (Its *official* name is IEEE 1394, but even the Cupertino crew doesn't call it that — at least not very often.)

First things first. As countless racing fans will tell you, it's all about the *speed,* my friend. The original FireWire 400 port delivered 400 Mbps (megabits per second), which proved fast enough for most peripherals of the day to communicate with a Macintosh. The following list includes a number of hardware toys that are well known for transferring prodigious file sizes:

✦ Digital video (DV) camcorders

✦ High-resolution digital cameras

✦ Scanners and some printers

✦ External hard drives and CD/DVD recorders

✦ Networking between computers

For example, consider the sheer size of a typical digital video clip captured by one of today's DV camcorders. DV buffs commonly transfer several hundred megabytes of footage to their computers at one time. Check out the relative speeds of the different types of ports in Table 3-1, and you'll see a big attraction of FireWire 800 and Thunderbolt connections.

Table 3-1	Transfer Speeds for Ports through the Ages	
Port	*Appeared on Personal Computer When*	*Transfer Speed (in Megabits)*
PC Serial	1981	Less than 1 Mbps
PC Parallel	1981	1 Mbps
USB (version 1.1)	1996	12 Mbps
FireWire 400	1996	400 Mbps (version 1)
USB (version 2.0)	2001	480 Mbps
FireWire 800	2002	800 Mbps
USB (version 3.0)	2010	5 Gbps (5,000 Mbps)
Thunderbolt	2011	10 Gbps (10,000 Mbps)

Ouch! Not too hard to figure that one out. Here are three other important benefits to FireWire:

✦ **Control over connection:** This is a ten-cent term that engineers use, meaning that you can control whatever gadget you've connected using FireWire from your computer. This is pretty neat when you think about it; for example, you can control your mini-DV camcorder from the comfort of your computer keyboard, just as though you were pressing the buttons on the camcorder.

✦ **Hot-swapped:** You don't have to reboot your Mac or restart Mac OS X every time that you plug (or unplug) a FireWire device. Instead, the FireWire peripheral is automatically recognized (as long as the operating system has the correct driver) and ready to transfer.

✦ **Power through the port:** FireWire can provide power to a device through the same wire — typically, enough power is available for an external drive or recorder — so you don't need an external AC power cord for some FireWire devices. (Apologies to owners of DV camcorders, but those things eat power like a pig eats slop.)

You'll note from Table 3-1 that the cleverly named *IEEE 1394 B* (called *FireWire 800* by anyone with any sense, including the folks at Apple) delivers a whopping 800 Mbps. Although nowhere near as fast as a Thunderbolt connection, FireWire 800 peripherals are much easier to find at the time of this writing than Thunderbolt devices — and FireWire 800 ports appear on most of the top-of-the-line Apple desktop and laptop models at the time of this writing.

Oh, and as you would expect from Apple, FireWire 800 ports are backward-compatible with older FireWire 400 hardware. However, the ports aren't exactly the same, so you'll need a plastic port converter to connect FireWire 400 devices to a FireWire 800 port. (Such important little conversion fixtures are commonly called *dongles*. No, I'm not making that up. Ask your favorite techno-wizard.)

Travelling at Warp Speed with Thunderbolt

Did you notice that Thunderbolt, Apple's latest external connection, is listed at 10 *gigabits* per second (or Gbps) instead of megabits per second (Mbps) in Table 3-1? Here's your technonerd trivia for the day: data on a 1 Gbps connection is moving as fast as data on a 1,000 Mbps connection. Therefore, Thunderbolt is literally more than *12 times faster* than FireWire 800! Heck, Thunderbolt trumps even the recently-released USB 3.0 technology, which has a maximum speed of only 5 Gbps.

Thunderbolt's sheer jump-to-warp speed performance allows something that's never been possible before: Mac owners can edit uncompressed digital video in real-time on an external Thunderbolt hard drive! (That's a chore that requires moving huge amounts of data very fast between your computer's processor and hard drive, which until now simply wasn't possible on an external drive.) Thunderbolt is also versatile — it even allows a direct high-definition connection between your Mac and your HDMI flat-screen TV, or a superfast high-resolution monitor like the Apple LED Cinema Display.

A single Thunderbolt port can handle up to six peripherals, including a mixture of a high-resolution display and devices like hard drives and Blu-Ray recorders. And, like FireWire, Thunderbolt can provide plenty of power to a connected device as well. Probably the only downside to Thunderbolt (at least at the time of this writing) is that Thunderbolt devices are not generally available yet, and are likely to be significantly more expensive than their USB or FireWire counterparts. Such is the sad lament of the early adopter of cutting-edge computer hardware!

Understanding USB and the Tale of Two Point Oh

The other resident port on today's Apple computers is the ubiquitous USB 2.0, which is short for *Universal Serial Bus.* (By the way, ubiquitous means *ever-present* or *universal,* which I quickly looked up by using my Dictionary widget — read all about this super sleuth in Book VIII, Chapter 1.) USB has taken the world by storm. It's used for everything from mice to keyboards, speakers, digital cameras, and even external drives and DVD recorders. (A friend of mine never misses the chance to point out that USB — which was originally developed by Intel, the makers of the Core 2, i5, and i7 processors — was given its first widespread implementation on the original iMac. *You're welcome,* Intel.)

USB 2.0 delivers performance comparable to the original FireWire standard: USB 2.0 can transfer 480 Mbps, although far less efficiently than FireWire, so the FireWire connection is still faster overall. These ports are backwards-compatible — meaning they work with the original USB 1.1 ports as well. (Don't call Apple a snob . . . at the time of this writing, all the Mac models in Apple's current stable have USB 2.0 ports.)

As is FireWire, USB connections are hot-swappable and *may* provide power over the connection. (Some USB ports don't supply all the power that devices need — more on this later in this chapter.) A USB port offers a more limited version of Control over Connection as well, making it a good choice for virtually all digital cameras.

The latest USB 3.0 connections offer speeds of 5 Gbps, but that's half the performance of a Thunderbolt port. At the time of this writing, Apple has not released a computer with a USB 3.0 port, so I would be wary of jumping on the USB 3.0 bandwagon — at least, until it's clear whether Apple will ever support USB 3.0. Owners of current Mac Pro models will need to add a USB 3.0 adapter card to use the faster peripherals.

Hey, You Need a Hub!

Suppose that you've embraced FireWire and USB and you now have two USB 2.0 drives hanging off the rear end of your Mac — and suddenly you buy an iPod. (Or you get another USB device that's as much fun as an iPod, if that's actually possible.) Now you're faced with too many devices for too few ports. You *could* eject a drive and unhook it each time that you want to connect your iPod, but there *must* be a more elegant way to connect. Help!

Enter the hub. Both the FireWire and USB specifications allow you to connect a device called a *hub,* which is really nothing more than a glorified splitter adapter that provides you with additional ports. With a FireWire or USB hub at work, you do lose a port; however, most hubs multiply that port into four or eight ports. Again, all this is transparent, and you don't need to hide anything up your sleeve. Adding a hub is just as plug-and-play easy as adding a regular FireWire/USB device.

When shopping for a USB hub, make sure you choose a model that provides full power to each port! As I'll discuss later in the chapter, many USB peripherals draw their AC power from the port itself — these devices won't work with a cheaper hub that doesn't supply that juice.

I should also mention that FireWire supports *daisy-chaining* — a word that stretches all the way back to the days of the Atari and Commodore computers, when devices had extra ports in the back so that additional stuff could be plugged in. However, not every FireWire drive has a daisy-chain port (also called a *passthru port*). With daisy-chaining, you can theoretically add 63 FireWire devices (or 127 USB devices) to your Mac — talk about impressing them at your next Mac user group meeting!

Uh, My External Device Is Just Sitting There: Troubleshooting

Man, I *hate* it when FireWire and USB devices act like boat anchors. FireWire and USB peripherals are so doggone simple that when something goes wrong, it really aggravates you. Fortunately, I've been down those roads many a time before, so in this section, I unleash my experience. (That sounds a little frightening, but it's a *good* thing. Really.)

Common FireWire and USB headaches

Because FireWire and USB are so alike in so many ways, I can handle possible troubleshooting solutions for both types of hardware at one time:

✦ **Problem: Every time I turn off or unplug my external peripheral, Mac OS X gets irritated and displays a nasty message saying that I haven't properly disconnected the device.**

Solution: This happens because you haven't *ejected* the peripheral. I know that sounds a little strange for a device like an external hard drive or a digital camera, but it's essentially the same reasoning as ejecting a CD or DVD from your Desktop. When you click your USB or FireWire device and hold the mouse button down, you see that the Trash icon turns into an Eject icon; drag the device icon to the Eject icon and drop it, and the external device disappears from your Desktop. (You can also click the device icon to select it and press ⌘+E. And don't forget the right-click menu . . . right-click the device and choose Eject.) At that point, you're safe to turn it off or unplug the FireWire/USB cable.

If Lion recognizes the device as an external drive, which is usually the case with a digital camera, external hard drive, or external DVD/Blu-Ray recorder, you can simply click the Eject button next to the device icon in the Finder window's sidebar.

✦ **Problem: The device doesn't show a power light.**

Solution: Check to make sure that the power cable is connected — unless, of course, you've got a device that's powered through the connection itself. This can sometimes pose its own share of problems, however, when using USB devices. Not all USB ports provide power to devices because some are designed only for connecting mice, keyboards, and joysticks.

To check whether an unpowered USB port is your problem, either connect the device to a USB port on your Mac or connect it to a powered hub or another computer. If the device works when it's connected to another port, you've found the culprit.

✦ **Problem: The device shows a power light but just doesn't work.**

Solution: This can be because of problems with your cable or your hub. To check, borrow a friend's cables and test to see whether the device works. If you're testing the hub, try connecting the device directly to your Mac using the same cable to see whether it works without the hub.

If you're attempting to connect a FireWire device through another FireWire device, try connecting that first device directly to see whether it works. If so, the middleman device either needs to be switched on to pass the data through or it doesn't support daisy-chaining at all — in which case, you may be able to place the "problem" device at the *end* of the chain. Of course, you can always connect both devices to a powered FireWire hub.

✦ **Problem: Mac OS X reports that I have a missing driver.**

Solution: Check the manufacturer's web site and download a new copy of the USB or FireWire drivers for your device because they've been corrupted, overwritten, or erased entirely. Because Mac OS X loads the driver for a USB or FireWire device when it's connected, sometimes just unplugging and reconnecting a peripheral will do the trick.

Check those drivers

Speaking of drivers . . . old and worn-out drivers are a sore spot with me. *Drivers* are simply programs that tell Mac OS X how to communicate with your external device. Each new version of Mac OS X contains updated drivers, but make certain that you check for new updates on a regular basis. That means using both the Software Update feature in Mac OS X (which I cover briefly in Book II, Chapter 3 and much more in Book I, Chapter 7) *and* going to the web sites provided by your USB and FireWire hardware manufacturers.

Chapter 4: I'm Okay, You're a Printer

In This Chapter

✔ Adding a local printer

✔ Adding a non-USB printer

✔ Managing print jobs

✔ Sending and receiving faxes

✔ Setting up a shared printer

*O*f all the features Mac owners appreciate in Lion, one of the most important is the support the operating system provides for Universal Serial Bus (USB), network and Bluetooth printers. As I discuss in Book I, Chapter 3, if your USB printer is recognized by Lion, you can print within seconds of plugging it in, with no muss or fuss. A USB printer is connected physically to your Mac, but you can also send print jobs over the network to a network printer or even to a wireless printer. (Unfortunately, if that network printer is in another room, you do have to get out of your comfortable chair to retrieve your printed document . . . not even Lion is that powerful.)

But what if you want to send documents to a printer over TCP/IP (Transmission Control Protocol/Internet Protocol)? To take care of tasks like that, you need to dig a little further — and I do so in this chapter. You also discover here how to use the features of the System Preferences Print & Scan pane and how to juggle print jobs like a circus performer.

Meet the Printer Browser

The Printer Browser runs automatically whenever it's needed by Lion, but you can always summon it at any time by clicking the plus sign (or Add) button on the Print & Scan pane within System Preferences.

If your USB printer is already *natively supported* (has a preloaded driver in Lion), you might not need to go through the trouble of clicking the Add button on the Print & Scan pane. Mac OS X can add a new USB printer automatically, so don't be surprised if your Mac swoops in and does it for you as soon as you plug in a new printer. Also, the manufacturer's installation program for your printer might add the printer for you in a behind-the-scenes way, even if Mac OS X lies dormant.

Although the Printer Browser doesn't look like much (as shown in Figure 4-1), power lurks underneath.

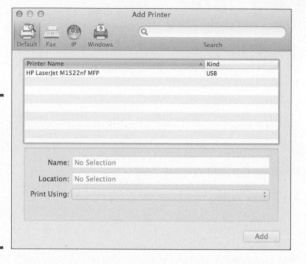

Figure 4-1: The rather plain-looking Printer Browser is actually a rugged adventurer.

Along the top of the Printer Browser, you'll find four toolbar icons that display the different types of printer connections possible in Lion. From the Browser, you can add these printers to your system. The four buttons are

+ **Default:** Click this button to add or display the entry for the default printer, which always appears in bold type.

To choose your default printer that you've already added, click the Default Printer pop-up menu in the Print & Scan list and choose that printer. You can also choose the Last Printer Used option, which automatically makes the default printer the last printer you used.

+ **Fax:** Click this button to add a fax connection as a printer selection.

+ **IP:** Click this button to add a remote printer to your Mac through an Internet connection or a local network connection. Sending a job to an Internet Protocol (IP) printer actually shoots the document across a network or Internet connection by using a target IP address or domain name. Generally, it's best to have a *static* (unchanging) IP address for a network printer; if the IP address changes often, for example, you have to reconfigure your connection to your IP printer each time it changes.

+ **Windows:** Click this button to add a shared printer that's connected to a PC on your local network. "Hey, I get to use the enemy's printers, too?" That's right, as long as a Windows user on your network has shared his printer (via the ubiquitous Windows File and Printer Sharing feature). *Sweet.*

PDF printing for your big cat

In the Windows world, Adobe Acrobat is the most popular program for creating electronic PDF documents. Although you certainly can install Adobe Acrobat under Lion, I'd be remiss if I didn't mention that you don't *have* to! That's because the operating system provides built-in support for printing documents in Adobe's PDF format (which can then be viewed and printed on any other computer with Acrobat Reader or added to your web site for downloading). Acrobat has more features, naturally, but — wait for it — don't pay for Acrobat unless you need it!

In fact, you don't even have to install a PDF print driver or display the Printer Browser! To print a document as a file in PDF format, click the PDF drop-down button in the application's Print dialog, click Save as PDF from the menu, navigate to the desired folder and enter a file-name, and then click Save.

Oh, and there's one additional important control on the toolbar that isn't actually a button: You can click in the Search field and type text to locate a particular printer in any of these dialog lists. (Personally, I don't have that many printers on my network, but in a larger company, this field can save you the trouble of scrolling through several pages of shared printers.)

Adding a Funky Printer

"And what," you might ask, "is a *funky* printer?" Well, you have a number of possibilities, but they all add up to a non-USB connection. (Remember, I said that USB connections to a printer are generally automatic, or at least handled by the printer's installation software.) Some of the non-USB connections I mention in the previous section include Windows shared printers and IP printers.

No matter which type of funky printer you add, it needs a driver installed in the Printers folder, which resides inside your Library folder. (A *driver* is a software program provided by the printer manufacturer that tells Mac OS X how to communicate with your printer.) Also, if the printer is PostScript compatible, it needs a Postscript Printer Description (PPD) file installed in your PPD folder, which also appears in the Printers folder. Luckily, Lion comes complete with a long list of drivers and PPD files already installed and available — bravo, Apple dudes and dudettes!

To add a funky printer that supports Lion, follow these steps:

1. **Launch the manufacturer's installation application, which should copy the driver and PPD files for you.**

If you have to do things the hard way, manually copy the driver file into the Library/Printers folder and then copy the PPD file (if required) into the Library/Printers/PPD folder.

2. **If you're adding a physical printer — instead of an application printer driver — verify that the printer is turned on and accessible.**

   If you're printing to a shared printer connected to another Mac or PC, that computer has to be on. Luckily, most network printers (and their computer hosts) remain on all the time.

3. **Display the Print & Scan pane within System Preferences and click the Add button.**

   You see the familiar Printer Browser. Shared printers using Bonjour network technology should show up on the default list, so you can click the printer to select it.

4. **To add an IP printer, click the IP Printer button on the browser toolbar.**

   Click the Protocol pop-up menu to choose the IP printing protocol (typically either IPP or the manufacturer-specific socket protocol). If you have a choice, it's always a good idea to use the manufacturer-specific socket.

   Click in the Address box and type the printer's IP address or Domain Name System (DNS) name, which should be provided by your network administrator or the person running the print server. You can use the default queue on the server by leaving the Queue box blank — which I recommend — or select the Queue text box and type a valid queue name for the server.

   If you don't know a valid queue name, you're up a creek — hence, my recommendation to use the default queue.

   If you like, you can type a name and location for the remote printer; this is purely for identification purposes. Finally, click the Print Using pop-up menu, choose the brand and model of the remote printer, and then click Add.

5. **To add a Windows printer, click the Windows button on the Printer Browser toolbar.**

   Click the correct Windows workgroup that includes the printer(s) that you want to use in the left column. After a scan of the specified workgroup, Printer Browser displays the list of printers that it can access. (Don't forget to thank His Billness later.)

6. **After everything is tuned correctly, click the Print Using pop-up menu and choose the brand and model of the remote printer.**

7. **Click Add to complete the process and admire your new printer on the Print & Scan panel in System Preferences.**

Heck, Lion even allows you to *order supplies* for your printer from the comfort of System Preferences! Sure, you'll pay a premium price, but think of the techno-nerd bragging rights you'll enjoy at your next Mac user group meeting! Click a printer in the Print & Scan panel and click the Options & Supplies button; then click the Supply Levels tab. When you click the Supplies button, System Preferences automatically launches Safari with the proper web page from the Apple Store.

Managing Your Printing Jobs

You can also exercise some control over the documents — or, in technoid, *print jobs* — that you send to your printer. To display the jobs that are *active* (in line and preparing to print), open the Print & Scan pane in System Preferences and click the Open Print Queue button.

The actions that you can perform from the Print Queue window (as shown in Figure 4-2) are

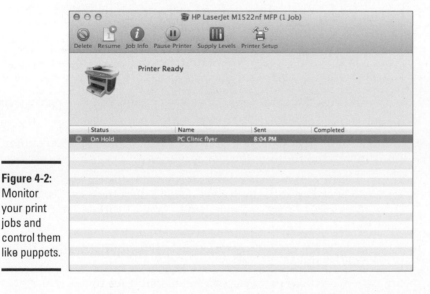

Figure 4-2: Monitor your print jobs and control them like puppets.

✦ **Delete:** When you click a print job in the list and then click the Delete icon, the print job is removed from the queue. You might need to delete a print job if you discover a mistake in the document while printing.

If the job is currently printing, several additional pages might be printed before the job is finally canceled. In other words, information already sent to the printer might have to be printed before the cancel request can be processed.

Where's the chapter on faxing?

Good question, and here's the answer: Lion handles faxing so seamlessly that you don't need a chapter's worth of instruction! As long as your Mac has an external analog (dial-up) modem connected to a phone line, you're a lean faxing machine.

To fax any open document within an active application, just choose File⇨Print or press ⌘+P. Click the PDF button at the bottom of the Print dialog and click Fax PDF. Type the destination telephone number in the To field. Next, type a dialing prefix if one is necessary to reach an outside line.

If you need a spiffy-looking cover page, select the Use Cover Page check box. Click in the Message box directly below it and type whatever you like. You can optionally type a subject as well. When all is ready, throw caution utterly to the wind and click the Fax button. The Printer Browser treats a fax just as it does any other printed document, so you can cancel it or monitor its progress, as I discuss in the section, "Managing Your Printing Jobs."

Your Mac can also receive faxes. To enable this feature, open System Preferences and click the Print & Scan icon. Click the entry for your fax in the list, click the Receive Options button, and then select the Receive Faxes on This Computer check box. Set the number of rings Lion should wait before answering the call. You can save your incoming faxes as files within a folder you specify or e-mail the contents automatically to any e-mail address you like. (Perfect for vacations!) If you like, you can even take the mundane route and print them on your system printer.

If you're going to use your Mac as a fax machine often, I definitely recommend selecting the Show Fax Status in Menu Bar check box, which appears when you click the entry for your fax modem in the list. That way, you can monitor what's happening as your Mac sends and receives throughout the day.

✦ **Hold:** Click the Hold toolbar icon to pause printing of the current print job. The status of the print job changes to Hold.

✦ **Resume:** Click a print job in Hold status in the list and then click the Resume icon to resume printing.

✦ **Job Info:** Click this button to display basic information about the selected print job, such as number of pages and page size.

✦ **Pause Printer:** Click this icon to stop all printing to this printer. Note, however, that unlike using the Delete command, Pause Printer doesn't *remove* any print jobs from the list. When jobs are stopped, the Pause Printer icon morphs into Resume Printer — click it to restart all jobs in the queue list.

This is a good feature to use when your printer is about to run out of paper.

✦ **Supply Levels:** If your printer supports remote supply monitoring, you can click this icon to display the current levels of ink and paper in your printer. (Thus saving your feet from the wear and tear of walking.)

✦ **Printer Setup:** Click this icon and Lion displays the model-specific configuration settings and features (if any) that are available for the selected printer. Of course, these settings vary for every printer produced by the hand of Man — they're actually determined by the manufacturer's printer driver — but they usually include actions (such as cleaning and alignment) and settings (such as print quality).

Sharing a Printer across That There Network

Before we leave the Island of Big X Printing, I'd like to show you how to share a printer with others on your local network, using Lion's super-easy Bonjour network sharing feature. (Earlier in this chapter, I show you how to connect to other shared printers around you. Here, you're going to share a printer that's connected directly to your Mac.)

If you decide to share your printers, don't be surprised if Mac OS X seems to slow down slightly from time to time. This is because of the processing time necessary for your Mac to store queued documents from other computers. The hard drive activity on your Mac is likely to significantly increase as well.

Once again, turn to System Preferences! Click the Sharing icon; then click the Printer Sharing check box to select it. (When it comes to printing, Lion gives you more than one way to skin a . . . well, you get the idea, even without the bad pun.) To share a printer, click the check box next to the desired printer (as shown in Figure 4-3) and click the Add button to select which users will have access to the shared printer. (By default, a shared printer can be accessed by everyone.) To prevent someone from printing, click that user's entry in the list and click the Delete button (look for the minus sign). *Voilà!* You're the guru!

"Hey, what about my firewall?" Perhaps you would worry *if* you were using that Other Operating System — which shall remain nameless here — but you're using Lion, and everything is set *automatically* for you the moment you click the Printer Sharing check box! Lion automatically opens the correct port in your firewall to allow printer sharing. (And yes, if you decide not to share your printers and you deselect the Printer Sharing check box later, Lion cleans up after you. It closes the port in your firewall for you.) Super-flippin' *sweet.*

The printers that you specify are available to other computers within the same IP subnet. In other words, someone in your local network can use your printers, but no one outside your network has access.

If you haven't already assigned a printer a descriptive name, click the desired printer from the list in the Print & Scan pane and then click the Options & Supplies button. Click the General button on the sheet that appears and enter a descriptive name in the Name text field. You can also identify that printer's location in the Location text field. For example, in an office environment, I like to add the room number to a shared printer name (as well as the Location field).

Figure 4-3:
Lion takes care of everything when you want to share a printer.

Chapter 5: Applications That You've (Probably) Gotta Have

In This Chapter

✔ **Using Microsoft Office for Mac 2011**

✔ **Using disk repair applications**

✔ **Editing images**

✔ **Editing digital video**

✔ **Using Internet applications**

✔ **Burning discs with Toast**

✔ **Running Windows with Parallels Desktop**

✔ **Adding third-party utilities**

✔ **Playing games with Mac OS X**

*I*n Chapter 1 of this minibook, I present you with an overview of the most popular hardware that you can add to your Mac — and where there's hardware, software can't be far behind. (Somebody famous said that — I think it was Mark Twain.)

Anyway, a new Mac comes with a full suite of software tools right out of the box. You get Internet connectivity, disk repair, a digital audio and video player, image editing and cataloging, digital video editing, and — depending on the price that you paid or the Mac model configuration that you bought — even a complete set of productivity applications. However, if you're willing to pay for additional features and a manual (at least what passes for a manual in the manufacturer's opinion), you can make all these tasks easier and accomplish them in even shorter time.

Read on for an overview of the most popular third-party software applications for Mac OS X: what everyone's using, how much they cost, and why they're (usually) better. However, before you drop a *wad* of cash on a fancy new application (or even an expensive upgrade to an existing application), remember yet another of Mark's Maxims:

If an application you already have does everything you really need — and you like the way it works — you *don't* have to buy a new application. Honest and truly.

The Trundling Microsoft Mammoth

Yes, I know I've been poking fun at His Gatesness for much of this book — you have to admit, he makes a pretty good target in the Apple world — but he *did* pull PC owners out of the character-based world of DOS, and I'll be the first to say that he does get things right from time to time. (Witness my bestselling book *PCs All-in-One For Dummies* [Wiley], recently revised for a fifth edition!)

For example, I've always been more impressed with Microsoft Office than I've been with Microsoft Windows. (At least Windows 7 is a step in the right direction, but it still has a long way to go to match Mac OS X.) Office has long been the productivity suite of choice in the Windows world, and it's also been a popular favorite in years past on the Macintosh side. Perhaps this is a good spot to remind everyone that Excel originated on the Mac!

A lot of hard work was put into the latest Mac version of Microsoft Office, and it shows. Office 2011 for Mac more closely mirrors the design of the PC version of Office (as you can see by Microsoft Word for Mac in Figure 5-1), but it still includes everything you'd demand from a native Mac OS X application (such as Pages from *iWork*, which is Apple's competing office productivity suite).

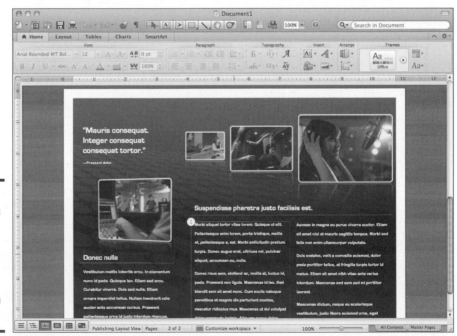

Figure 5-1:
Man, that is one good-looking Office. Thanks, Microsoft (and I mean that).

However, as with Mac OS X itself, Office 2011 for Mac isn't just an attractive exterior. Consider some of the advantages of Office 2011:

✦ **Perfect document compatibility with the Windows version of Office:** You can both read and write documents with transparent ease, no matter which platform gets the file. Documents can be shared between platforms on the same network.

✦ **Mirrored commands:** Office 2010 and Office for Mac 2011 have very similar menu items, dialogs, and settings, thus making Mac OS X instantly familiar to anyone who's used Office on a Windows PC.

✦ **Support for native Aqua features:** This includes transparent graphics within your documents, input and confirmation sheets, and palettes for formatting.

✦ **Tons of templates, samples, and support files:** Microsoft doesn't scrimp on ready-to-use documents and templates, as well as additional fonts, clip art, and web samples.

✦ **Outlook:** Office for Mac 2011 now includes a version of Outlook that's very similar to the Windows version in scope and power. It combines most of the same features that you'll find in the Apple Mail, iCal, and Address Book applications. (Read about Apple Mail in Book V, Chapter 2; read about the Address Book in Book I, Chapter 6.)

What about iWork?

If you're already using iWork '09, you might have noticed that the Office applications Excel, Word, and PowerPoint provide roughly the same features. Therefore, you might wonder whether you should scrap iWork.

Remember my maxim — if the iWork suite that you're familiar with is doing the job, I recommend that you keep it. After all, iWork is a powerful productivity suite on its own, capable of producing results that are easily as good as or better than Office 2011, and you can buy the iWork applications individually from the App Store. Also, Apple provides conversion filters that can allow you to open and save Office documents so that you're not isolated from the Office crowd.

On the other side of the coin, I *do* recommend that you buy Office if

✔ You prefer the Office 2011 menu design and features.

✔ You'd like to keep most of the same commands replicated in the same places as the Windows version of Office.

✔ You want to seamlessly share documents with co-workers who use Windows Office 2010 on your network or through e-mail.

Besides Outlook, Office for Mac 2011 includes four applications:

✦ **Word:** The word processing application that rules the planet

✦ **Excel:** The leading spreadsheet application

✦ **Messenger:** Microsoft's answer to iChat, an instant messaging program compatible with the Windows version of Messenger

✦ **PowerPoint:** A favorite presentation development application

The Office for Mac 2011 suite costs about $150 at the time of this writing. You might save a few dollars if you buy it online from a web store such as MacMall (www.macmall.com).

Your Mac OS X Toolbox: TechTool Pro

My favorite native Mac OS X disk repair application is TechTool Pro from Micromat (www.micromat.com).

More than just about any other type of application, it's important for a disk maintenance program to be built "from the ground up" for Mac OS X. **Never** attempt to repair a Mac OS X disk using an older repair utility that wasn't designed for Lion.

With TechTool Pro (as shown in Figure 5-2), you can thoroughly check a hard drive for both *physical* errors (such as faulty electronics or a bad sector on the disk surface) and *logical* errors (incorrect folder data and glitches in the file structure). The Disk Utility that's included with Mac OS X does a fine job of checking the latter, but it doesn't perform the physical testing — and TechTool Pro does both.

I should note, however, that TechTool Pro doesn't take care of viruses. Pick up a copy of VirusBarrier X6 (www.intego.com) to protect yourself against viral attack.

TechTool Pro also takes care of disk optimization, which is a feature that's been conspicuously absent from Mac OS X ever since the beginning. As I explain in Book I, Chapter 7, defragmenting your disk will result in better performance and a faster system overall.

TechTool Pro 6, which will set you back about $100, comes on a self-booting DVD-ROM, so you can easily fix your startup volume by booting your system from the TechTool Pro installation disc.

Figure 5-2:
Use
TechTool
Pro to check
for all sorts
of hardware
errors.

Image Editing for the Masses

The only one true King of the Retouching Hill in Mac OS X, Adobe Photoshop (www.adobe.com/products/photoshop) has been the digital-image editing favorite of Mac owners for many years now. As does Office for Mac 2011, the latest version of Photoshop (cs5) takes full advantage of the Aqua standard.

You can find more three-pound Photoshop books on the shelf than politicians in trouble, so it's no surprise that I can't provide you with a sweeping list of its features in this section. However, here's a summary of what you can expect from Adobe's crown jewel:

✦ **Superior editing:** The most sophisticated image editing possible for a digital photograph. If you can accomplish an image-editing task in software, it's very likely that Photoshop can do it. You can even combine and splice parts of different images to produce a new work of art or perhaps distort and liquefy an image to produce a new look.

✦ **Image retouching tools:** These help you rescue images with problems, such as overexposure and color imbalance. (You can also use tools such as the Healing brush to erase imperfections in the photograph's subject.)

✦ **Plug-ins:** Photoshop has been a standard for plug-in functionality since it first appeared. If you need features that aren't in the application out of the box, you can add them through third-party plug-ins.

✦ **Web posting:** Prepare images for use on the web.

✦ **Painting tools:** Use these gems to simulate different types of inks, paints, and brushes on different types of media.

 Although Photoshop is a hefty $699 for the full package, Adobe has also created a kid brother, Photoshop Elements, which sells for a mere $99. Designed for the novice or intermediate-level photographer, Elements has most of the functionality of the full package that you're likely to need. Elements can also automate the most common image-editing tasks, as well as one of the most comprehensive Help systems I've ever used.

The Morass of Digital Video

Two types of applications make up the DV market: *digital video editing* (in which you create a movie) and *DVD mastering* (in which you take that movie and create a DVD movie). You can find a number of great applications on the market in both these categories, all at different price points and different levels of complexity. They include

✦ **iMovie:** I cover this easy-to-use video editing iApp in Book III, Chapter 4. A good choice for any novice, it's usually bundled for free with today's new Mac models, and you get it as part of the iLife suite.

✦ **iDVD:** This is the DVD mastering counterpart to iMovie. Although it's a snap to use, it doesn't offer a lot of advanced features. (Book III, Chapter 5 explains iDVD in detail.) Again, you receive it free with your Mac.

✦ **DVD Studio Pro:** Apple's entry into the ranks of DVD mastering can produce a commercial-quality DVD movie disc, but don't expect any hand holding or assistants with this application. This is a serious tool for professionals, and as part of Apple's Final Cut Studio, it'll set you back $999. With DVD Studio Pro 4 (www.apple.com/finalcutstudio/dvd studiopro), you can add interactive, animated menus, subtitles, multiple audio tracks, and Web interactivity to your DVD projects.

✦ **Final Cut Pro 7:** As another part of that über $999 Final Cut Studio package, you'd assume Final Cut Pro (www.apple.com/finalcutstudio/finalcutpro) to be the best DV editing package on the market for Mac OS X . . . and you wouldn't get any argument from me. It offers real-time playback with RT Extreme HD — no waiting for rendering — and high-definition support over a FireWire connection. *Sassy.*

Yes, It's Really Called "Toast"

Time to turn your attention to a subject near and dear to my heart: recording data CDs, audio CDs, and DVDs on the Macintosh. Of course, Mac OS X can burn basic data CDs that you can share with your Windows and UNIX friends without any add-on software. If you have a Mac equipped with a SuperDrive, you can create standard, cross-platform data DVDs, too. But what if you need an exotic format, such as CD Extra, that allows data and digital audio tracks to co-exist peacefully on one disc? Or perhaps you need a self-booting disc, or you just got a Blu-ray external recorder?

There's one clear choice: When you're ready to seriously burn, you're ready for Roxio Toast Titanium (www.roxio.com), the CD and DVD recording choice for millions of Mac owners. (No snickering about the name, please.) Figure 5-3 illustrates this powerhouse of an application, which is an elegant design that's both simple to use and perfectly Aqua. Files, folders, and digital audio tracks that you want to record are simply dropped into the application window.

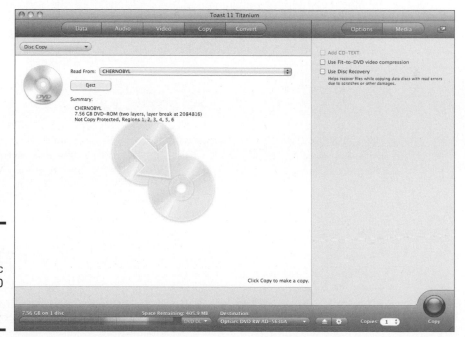

Figure 5-3: Toast is the classic Mac CD and DVD recording application.

As for exotic formats, here's a list of some types of discs you can record with Toast:

✦ Standard data CDs and DVDs

✦ Standard audio CDs

✦ Video CDs

✦ MP3 discs (which store MP3 audio tracks)

✦ Discs recorded from an image file

✦ Mac volumes

✦ Hybrid PC/Mac discs

✦ ISO 9660 discs

✦ Multisession discs

✦ CD Extra discs

Toast works with both internal and external CD, DVD, and Blu-ray recorders, taking advantage of the latest features on today's drives. You can also copy existing discs, using one or multiple drives.

Toast is quite affordable at $80. You can buy it directly from the Roxio online store at `www.roxio.com`.

If You Positively Have to Run Windows . . .

Here's where Mac power users usually start grinning from ear to ear like Santa's elves on the day after Christmas, because — get this — many of the great Unwashed Windows Horde still actually think that you *can't* run Windows on a Macintosh! Can you believe that? Obviously, they haven't heard of Boot Camp, which is built into Lion (and covered in Book I, Chapter 10) . . . but what if you don't want to reboot to switch operating systems? What if you need to share data between both Mac and PC applications running simultaneously? Well, that's where Parallels Desktop from Parallels (`www.parallels.com`) comes in. It's without a doubt one of the coolest applications ever written for the Mac.

No, my friend, your eyes aren't deceiving you — you're indeed looking at Windows 2000 running along with Mac OS X, in blissful cohabitation, on my MacBook in Figure 5-4. Parallels Desktop (which requires Mac OS X) provides a near-perfect PC environment for any version of Windows from 95 all the way up to Windows 7; literally, Windows has *no* idea that it's not running on a typical piece of PC iron.

**Book VII
Chapter 5**

**Applications That
You've (Probably)
Gotta Have**

Figure 5-4:
Take *that*,
Bill! I get
to play in
your pool,
without
rebooting!

Parallels Desktop simulates everything necessary for you to get the full functionality out of Windows. For example, this jewel automatically (and transparently) handles your Windows Internet connection, network tasks, and CD and DVD access. You can run full-screen or run Windows in a window. (Pun joyfully intended.)

As if that weren't enough, you can also run multiple operating systems. So if you need Linux, Ubuntu, or Windows 2000 along with your Windows system, no problem — all it takes is the install disc for those operating systems and the hard drive space to hold 'em. Outstanding!

Naturally, performance is an issue — and, to be honest, Parallels Desktop isn't for the PC gamer, even with the newest Macs and their super-duper GeForce and Radeon video cards. Because today's PC games push an actual PC to the limit, they just run too sluggishly on a Mac emulating a PC — they do run, just slowly. (Also, virtually all of today's blockbuster PC games are also being ported to Mac OS X, so why not just run the Mac version?) If I must run a Windows game on my Mac, I almost always use Boot Camp to boot directly into Windows 7, which allows my system to devote all of its resources to the game at hand.

However, when it comes to just about any other type of application, Parallels Desktop running on a late-model Intel-based Mac can deliver performance equal to a typical Intel PC. The more memory that your Mac has, the more you can give your virtual PC, so it also pays to have 4GB or more of RAM. I use this application with niche Windows programs that have never appeared on the Mac as well as native Mac versions of all other applications. Again, you don't need to use Mac to run the Windows version of Photoshop CS5 because Photoshop CS5 is also available for the Mac.

If you're tired of the undeserved taunts from your clueless Windows friends — you know, the ones who say that you can't run both Mac and Windows programs at the same time — head to your browser and order a copy of Parallels Desktop. The program is a very affordable $80 — but don't forget: You have to supply your own copy of Windows.

All Hail FileMaker Pro

If databases are the name of your game, you've already been using FileMaker Pro for years (on both Mac and Windows, more than likely). For the uninitiated, *FileMaker Pro* (www.filemaker.com) is the premier database creation, editing, and maintenance application for Mac OS X. It comes with dozens of ready-made database templates for business, home, and education use, or you can construct your own database in surprisingly short order. If you use AppleScript, you'll also be glad to hear that FileMaker Pro is a highly-scriptable application.

Right out of the box, FileMaker Pro can create

✦ Business databases and forms for inventory, personnel, purchase orders, and product catalogs

✦ Home databases for budgeting, recipes, music CDs, DVD movies, family medical records, and event planning

✦ Education databases for student records, expense reports, field trip planning, book and multimedia libraries, and class scheduling

FileMaker Pro 11 can add images and multimedia to your database, and you can quickly and easily publish your databases on your web site by using one of the built-in theme designs. (In fact, visitors to your web site can update your database online, if you like.) FileMaker Pro can also allow multiple users to share data across your network, no matter whether they're running the Mac or Windows version. The latest version even runs scripts automatically based on user input.

At $299, FileMaker Pro 11 is one of the least expensive — and most powerful — applications that you can buy for the Big X.

Utilities That Rock

The next stop on this Cavalcade of Software is an assortment of the absolute best you've-got-to-get-this utility applications. Sooner or later, you're likely going to buy (or register) these utilities because you'll use them every day.

StuffIt

In the Windows world, the Zip archive is the king of archiving formats. An *archive* contains one or more compressed files that you can uncompress whenever you need them. Folks store files in archives to save space on their hard drives; archiving is also a neat way to package an entire folder's worth of files in a single convenient file, which you can attach to an e-mail message or send via File Transfer Protocol (FTP). Mac OS X includes built-in support for zip files.

Manage your archives with StuffIt Deluxe 2011, from Smith Micro Software (`mysmithmicro.com`). StuffIt Deluxe 2011 can both archive and unarchive `.sit` files (the common name for StuffIt archives) as well as Zip archives from your Windows friends. You can also encrypt the contents of a StuffIt archive for those "sensitive" transfers. The application runs $50 at the Smith Micro Software online web store.

QuicKeys 4

QuicKeys 4, from Startly Technologies (`www.startly.com`), is another example of someone's thinking properly. This time, the idea is to auto-mate repetitive tasks by allowing Mac OS X to memorize what you do. Think of QuicKeys 4 as a system-wide, macro playback application. Unlike AppleScript, however, QuicKeys 4 works within any application and can play back mouse movement and clicks/double-clicks. (And unlike Automator, you can perform any action that you could normally perform within an applica-tion by typing.)

I've used QuicKeys 4 for a number of different tasks, including

✦ Typing a commonly used block of text (such as my address) into applications that don't support macros

✦ Launching applications at specific times and dates

✦ Operating menus within programs to automate complex tasks

✦ Launching Classic or choosing a specific startup disk with a single key sequence

QuicKeys 4 sells for $80 on the Startly Technologies web site.

BBEdit

Although we all know and love Mac OS X as a graphical operating system, folks still need a powerful text editor for creating and modifying text files. For example, software developers and webmasters still use text editors daily to write applications or apply a quick fix to the HyperText Markup Language (HTML) that makes up a web page. (I use a text editor to make minor changes to my web site, MLC Books Online, without firing up a horrendous web design application. Talk about overkill!)At first, you might think of TextEdit, which is the free application that ships with Mac OS X. It's not a bad editor, either, with features that far surpass Notepad in the Windows environment. However, serious text and code editing requires a more powerful tool, and the text editor of choice for Mac owners is universally considered to be BBEdit, from Bare Bones Software (`www.barebones.com`). Figure 5-5 shows a document open within BBEdit 9.

Figure 5-5: For editing text, you'll find no better tool than BBEdit.

Bare Bones Software pulls no punches in describing BBEdit — its advertising still proclaims, "It doesn't suck." Gotta give Bare Bones credit; this incredibly popular editor includes features such as

✦ **Support for DOS/Windows, Mac, and UNIX text files:** Yes, differences do exist among the platforms, even with a so-called *pure* text file.

✦ **Works with text files over 2GB in size:** Try that with TextEdit. Hmm . . . on second thought, please don't.

✦ **HTML tools for web design:** These tools include syntax checking and browser preview.

✦ `grep` **pattern-based, multifile search and replace:** In nonprogrammer/non-UNIX English, that means a very sophisticated search-and-replace function that can span more than one text file.

✦ **Syntax coloring:** Use this to help you quickly locate commands and qualifiers in programming languages.

✦ **Built-in FTP transfer commands:** No need to launch a separate FTP application: You can send your files right from within BBEdit.

You can even expand the functionality of BBEdit with plug-ins, many of which are free extensions written by programmers and developers specifically for languages such as C/C++, Java/JavaScript, Perl, and Pascal.

BBEdit 9 is available from the Bare Bones Software site for $100.

Real Studio

The final application that I want to mention really isn't a utility as such; however, you can use it to write your own software, so I guess that it should qualify. As an ex-COBOL programmer, reluctant Visual Basic shareware developer, and recalcitrant dBASE coder, I can tell you that Real Studio (from REAL Software) is definitely the easiest visual drag-and-drop programming environment that I've ever used on a personal computer. If you want to develop your own productivity applications, Mac OS X utilities, or — dare I say it? your own game! — award-winning Real Studio is the way to go.

Development in Real Studio is as simple as designing the application window by first simply adding controls, text, and multimedia wherever you like. Then just fill in the blanks, such as by setting variables and specifying what happens when the controls are triggered, which you do by using a new implementation of the tried-and-true BASIC language. Of course, some programming knowledge is required, but far less than you'd need with Visual Basic. And the results look as good as anything you can accomplish in those so-called real programming languages.

Check out these features:

✦ **Cross-platform support so that you can write your program once and compile it for Linux, Mac OS X, *and* Windows.** Code it once; then release three versions with no extra work. This is a *very* superb thing.

✦ **Support for all sorts of multimedia,** including QuickTime.

✦ **Ability to animate and rotate text and objects,** or tap the 3-D power of OpenGL graphics.

✦ **Capability to allow printing, network, and Internet communications** within your application.

✦ **Automation of Microsoft Office applications** and connection of your Real Studio application to business databases (such as FileMaker Pro).

✦ **Completely royalty-free applications,** so you can give them away or release them as shareware.

Real Studio has been such a popular development tool on the Macintosh for so many years that dozens of user-supported web sites and mailing lists have sprung up, offering all sorts of plug-ins, tutorials, and sample code for you to use in your own projects.

I recommend the Personal Edition of Real Studio for programming novices. It's $99, and you can order it from `www.realsoftware.com`.

At Least One Game

To be completely accurate, Mac OS X already comes with at least one game — a very good version of chess, which I cover in the next section — but the Macintosh has never been considered a true gaming platform by most computer owners. Until recently, many popular Windows games were never ported (or converted) for the Mac, and only the most expensive Mac models had the one important component that determines the quality of today's games: a first-rate, 3-D video card.

However, within the last three or four years, all that has changed dramatically. *All* of today's Mac models feature muscle-car-quality video cards that use the NVIDIA GeForce or ATI Radeon chipsets; they can handle the most complex 3-D graphics with ease. Match that with the renewed popularity of the Macintosh as a home computer and the performance of the current crop of Intel-based processors, and — wham! Suddenly you've got the best game developers in the business — id Software (`www.idsoftware.com`) and Blizzard (`www.blizzard.com`), to name two — releasing Macintosh versions of their newest games concurrently with the Windows version.

For the gamer in you, allow me to take you on a tour of the best of the new generation of entertainment.

Mac OS X Chess

No mercenaries, no rail guns, and no cities to raze — but chess is still the world's most popular game, and Mac OS X even includes a little 3-D as well. Figure 5-6 illustrates the Chess application at play; you'll find it in your Applications folder.

Mark Chambers — Computer (White to Move)

Figure 5-6:
Lion says,
"How about
a nice game
of chess?"

The game features speech recognition, move hints, take back (or undo) for your last move, and a 2-D or 3-D board. You can also list your games in text form and print them or save games in progress. Maybe it's not a complete set of bells and whistles as commercial chess games offer, but the price is right, and the play can be quite challenging when you set it at the higher skill levels.

World of WarCraft

I end this chapter with Blizzard's best: the online megahit that is World of WarCraft. This MMORPG (short for *massive multiplayer online role-playing game*) is yet another wrinkle in the popular WarCraft game series. World of WarCraft puts the character you create in the boots of human princes, Orc battle generals, undead champions, trolls, gnomes, and elfin lords — in fact, you can create multiple characters and play them as you choose. My recommendation: Stick with the Undead, my friend.

Combat, however, is only half the job. By finishing quests and killing various nasties, you earn experience, upgrade your armor and weapons, and build a reputation with various groups throughout the land. You can take to the air, buy goods from mercenaries, and even hone your skills with a trade like leatherworking or enchanting. Spells abound, and you can join a guild and chat with the new friends you make online. . . . I've played for over four years now, and I'm still excited by this incredible game.

Control is by both keyboard and mouse; the game is easy to understand, but you'll always find someone to kick your posterior in battlegrounds or dungeons over the Internet.

You'll pay about $50 online for World of WarCraft and then you'll be charged a set fee for each month's subscription . . . and it'll be worth every single penny you spend. (Remember, this is a program you'd buy on your own; it doesn't come with your Mac or with Lion.) For all the details and some great desktop backgrounds, check the official site at www.blizzard.com.

Book VIII

Advanced Mac OS X

Contents at a Glance

Chapter 1: . . . And UNIX Lurks Beneath

In This Chapter

✔ Why use UNIX?

✔ Doing things with the keyboard

✔ Introducing UNIX commands

✔ Creating text files

✔ Exploring deep inside Mac OS X

As I mention in the first chapter of the book — at the beginning of our Lion odyssey — UNIX lurks deep beneath the shiny Aqua exterior of Mac OS X. UNIX is a tried-and-true operating system that's been around for decades, since the days when mainframe computers were king. If you don't believe that it's a powerful (and popular) operating system, consider that over half of all web servers on the Internet use some variety of UNIX as their operating system of choice.

Besides being battle-tested and having a long history, UNIX offers some fantastic features. Unlike the graphical world of Mac OS X, the keyboard plays an integral role in using a UNIX-based operating system. Because UNIX is text-based, you'll find that it's evolved a large set of useful keyboard-driven commands that can perform powerful feats that a mouse user just can't easily equal. This chapter examines the role of the keyboard in UNIX operating systems and describes how to execute standard file system commands. You also discover how to use Apple's additional set of commands and install your own commands (and simple programs) from the Internet.

Why Use the Keyboard?

To begin benefiting from the UNIX underpinnings of Mac OS X, get used to doing things with the keyboard. Although mouse skills can be applied to UNIX, you'll generally find performing UNIX functions faster and easier with the keyboard.

UNIX keyboarding is fast

Why on Earth would any red-blooded Macintosh owner want to leave the comfort of the mouse to use a keyboard? After all, the graphical user interface is what made the Macintosh great in the first place. With the Finder, you can navigate and manage the various files on your hard drive with a few clicks. This sounds simple enough, but for some tasks, using the keyboard can be just as fast, if not faster.

Suppose, for example, that you need to copy a file from somewhere on your hard drive to somewhere else on that same drive. To do so with the Finder, you must first open a Finder window (by clicking the Finder icon in the Dock or by double-clicking a drive icon on your Desktop). Then, by using a succession of mouse clicks, you navigate to where the file that you wish to copy resides. Next, you might open another Finder window and navigate to the folder where you wish to copy the file. (Note that opening the second Finder window requires pressing ⌘+N; clicking the Finder icon in the Dock doesn't open a second Finder window.) Finally, you duplicate the original file and drag that copy to its intended destination.

Comparatively, by using the keyboard and the power of UNIX, you can accomplish the same task with a one-line command. For some tasks, the mouse is definitely the way to go, but you can perform some other tasks just as quickly, if not faster, with the keyboard. For the skinny on one-line commands, skip down to the upcoming section "Uncovering the Terminal."

The UNIX keyboard is a powerful beast

So maybe you're not an expert typist, and using the mouse still sounds inviting. For many scenarios, you'd be correct in assuming that a mouse can handle the job just as quickly and easily as a bunch of commands that you have to memorize. Using the keyboard, however, offers some other distinct advantages over the mouse. To allow you to control your computer from the keyboard, all UNIX operating systems offer the *command-line tool*. With this tool, you can enter commands one line at a time: hence, its name. Mac OS X ships with the command-line application, Terminal. You can find it here:

```
/Applications/Utilities/Terminal
```

One shining feature of the command line is its efficiency. To wit: When you use a mouse, one mouse click is equal to one command. When you use the command line, on the other hand, you aren't limited to entering one command at a time; rather, you can combine commands into a kind of *supercommand* (minus the silly cape, but with bulging muscles intact), with each command performing some action of the combined whole. By using the command line, you can string together a whole bunch of commands to do a very complex task.

For example, consider how many times you'd have to click a mouse in the Finder to do the following:

1. Find all files that begin with the letters *MyDocument.*

2. From this list of files, add a number to the beginning of the filename, indicating its size in kilobytes.

3. Save the names of all altered files to a text file.

By using the command line, you could accomplish all these tasks by typing only one *super-command:* that is, a collection of three simple commands combined to form one instruction. The built-in Terminal program that ships with Mac OS X Lion gives you everything that you need to start using the command line. I show you how in the section "Uncovering the Terminal," later in this chapter.

Delving further into super-commands isn't for the faint-hearted; things get pretty ugly pretty quickly, and this chapter can only show you the very beginning of the UNIX Yellow Brick Road. Therefore, if your thirst for UNIX dominance so compels you, I invite you to do a little independent study to bone up on the operating system. Pick up a copy of the great book of lore entitled *UNIX For Dummies, 5th Edition*, written by John R. Levine and Margaret Levine Young (Wiley).

Go where no mouse has gone before

The Finder is generally a helpful thing, but it makes many assumptions about how you work. One of these assumptions is that you don't have any need to handle some of the files on your hard drive. As I mention in Book II, Chapter 6, Mac OS X ships with its system files marked Off Limits, and I generally agree with that policy (which keeps anyone from screwing up the delicate innards of Mac OS X). To secure your system files, Apple purposely hides some files from view.

But what road do you take if you actually need to view or modify those system files? Yep, you guessed it: The command line comes to the rescue! You can use the command line to peer inside every nook and cranny of your Mac's vast directory structure on your hard drive. It also has the power to edit files that aren't normally accessible to you. With the command line, you can pretend to be other users — even users with more permissions. By temporarily acting as another more powerful user, you can perform actions with the command line that would be impossible in the Finder. (Just remember to make sure that you know *exactly* what you're doing, or you're working with an Apple technical support person — a wrong move, and it'll be time for an Ominous Chord.)

**Book VIII
Chapter 1**

. . . And UNIX Lurks
Beneath

Automate to elevate

If all these benefits are beginning to excite you, hold on to your socks! Not only can you perform complex commands with the command line, you can go even one step further: *automation.* If you find yourself using the same set of commands more than once, you're a likely candidate for using automation to save time. Instead of typing the list of commands each time, you can save them to a text file and execute the entire file with only one command. Now that's power, right up there with the dynamic duo of AppleScript and Automator! (Granted, it's not graphical like Automator, but then again UNIX has been around for decades.)

Of course, you probably don't like doing housekeeping tasks while you're busy on other things, so schedule that list of commands to run in the middle of the night while you're fast asleep. The command line lets you do that, too.

Note that automation of UNIX commands is totally separate from automation of Mac OS X applications with AppleScript and Automator, which I cover in Book VIII, Chapter 2.

Remote control

"So, Mark, the command line is the cat's meow for efficiently accessing and working with files on my Mac, and I can use it to automate many operations. Anything else?" I'm glad you asked! By using the command line, you can also send commands to another computer anywhere in the world (as long as you know the right login and password). After you log into another computer, you can use the same commands for the remote computer.

UNIX was created with multiple users in mind. Because computers used to be expensive (and honking *huge* machines to boot), UNIX was designed so that multiple users could remotely use the same machine simultaneously. In fact, if Mac OS X is your first encounter with UNIX, you might be surprised to know that many UNIX beginners of the past weren't even in the same room, building, state, or even country as the computer that they were using.

Not only can you work with a computer that's in a different physical location, but it's also very fast to do so. Instead of the bandwidth hog that is the Internet, the command line is lean and mean. This permits you to use a remote computer nearly as fast as if it were sitting on the desk in front of you. (This is a great advantage for road warriors who need to tweak a web or an e-mail server from a continent away.)

Uncovering the Terminal

The best way to find out how to use the command line is to jump right in. Mac OS X comes stocked with an application named *Terminal.* As I mentioned earlier, the Terminal application is where you enter commands in the command line, and it's located in the Utilities folder within the Applications folder on your hard drive — choose Applications⇨Utilities (from the keyboard, press Shift+⌘+U).

Double-click the icon, as shown in Figure 1-1, to launch Terminal.

Figure 1-1:
Find the
Terminal
application
in your
Utilities
folder.

By the way, feel free to make Terminal more accessible by dragging its icon to the Dock or the toolbar. That way, you won't have to dive this deep into the Applications folder in the future.

What's a prompt?

Upon launch of the Terminal application, you'll immediately notice some text in the window that appears on-screen:

```
Last login: Sun Jun 23 17:51:14 on console
WHITEDRAGON:~ markchambers$
```

As you might guess, this text details the last time that you logged into the Terminal. The last line, however, is the more important one. It's called the *prompt*.

The prompt serves some important functions. First, it lists the current directory, which is listed as ~ in the above example. A tilde character (~) denotes a user's Home directory. By default, you're always in your Home folder each time you begin a new session on the Terminal. After the current directory, the Terminal displays the name of the current user, which is markchambers in this example.

The final character of the prompt is a $. Consider this your cue because immediately after this character is where you enter any command that you wish to execute. Go ahead; don't be shy. Try out your first command by typing **uptime** in the Terminal application. (It's a good idea to type UNIX commands in lowercase.) Your text appears at the location of the cursor, denoted by a small square. If you make a mistake while entering the command, press the Delete key to back up and then type the characters again. (If the typing error is stuck deep in a longer command, press the left- or right-arrow key to move the cursor immediately after the incorrect character and press Delete to back up; then type the correct characters.) After you type the command, press Return to execute it.

```
WHITEDRAGON:~ markchambers$ uptime
6:24PM  up  2:42, 4 users, load averages: 2.44, 2.38, 1.90
WHITEDRAGON:~ markchambers$
```

If all goes well, you should see a listing of how long your Mac has been running since the last reboot or login. In the example listing, the computer has been running for 2 hours and 42 minutes (2:42 in line 2). Simple, eh? Immediately following the listing of the uptime command, the Terminal displays another prompt for you to enter more commands. I examine many more commands later in this chapter.

Prefer a different appearance for the Terminal window? Click the Terminal menu and choose Preferences; then click the Settings toolbar button to choose the color combinations for the Terminal window background and text.

A few commands to get started

Using the command line is simply a matter of entering simple instructions — or *commands* — into the Terminal application and pressing Return to execute them. It's easy to use the command line to navigate through the various folders on your hard drive. You'll become accustomed to using two vital commands: ls and cd. The ls command is shorthand for *list,* and it does just that: It lists the contents of the current directory. Enter **ls** at your prompt, and you should see a listing of your Home folder.

The complementary cd command (lowercase) — which incidentally stands for *change directory* — opens any folder that you specify. It works much the same as double-clicking a folder in the Finder: The difference is that following the cd command, you don't immediately see all the folder's content. However, the cd command requires a *parameter* (extra options or information that appear after the command) so that your Mac knows which folder to open.

For example, to open the Documents folder that resides in your Home directory, type **cd Documents** and press Return. When you do, you might be surprised to see another prompt displayed immediately. So where are all the files in the Documents folder? You must enter another command to see what items are in the folder that you just opened. Type **ls** again to see the contents of the Documents folder.

If you try to open a folder that has a space in its name, make sure to enclose the folder's name in quotation marks, like this:

```
cd "My Picture Folder"
```

Read more about using quotation marks in your commands in the upcoming section "Command-line gotchas." You can also precede a space in a name with a backslash, like this:

```
cd My\ Picture\ Folder
```

To return to your Home folder in this example, enter a modified version of the cd command:

```
cd ..
```

This causes your Mac to move back up the folder hierarchy one folder to your Home directory. By using these three simple commands — ls, cd *foldername*, and cd .. — you can traverse your entire hard drive.

After you successfully enter a command, you can recall it by pressing the up-arrow key. Press the up-arrow key again to see the command prior to that, and so forth. This is an extremely useful trick for retyping extra long file paths.

Using the skills you already have

Just because the Terminal is text based doesn't mean that it doesn't act like a good Macintosh citizen. All the usual Mac features that you know and love are there for you to use. Copy and Paste functions work as you might expect — but only at the prompt position.

Drag-and-drop is also at your disposal. After you play around with the Terminal for a while, you'll find yourself bored to tears typing the long paths that represent the files on your hard drive. To automatically enter the path of a file or folder to a command, simply drag it to the active Terminal window, as shown in Figure 1-2. The file's full path instantly appears at the location of your cursor. (Thanks, Apple!)

You can even use the mouse while entering commands in the Terminal. Click and drag your mouse over text to select it. From there, you can copy to the Clipboard as you might expect with any other application.

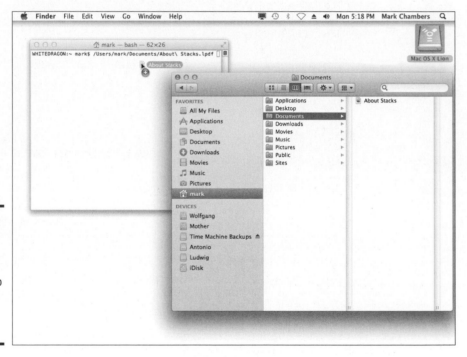

Figure 1-2:
Drag a file from a Finder window into Terminal to display its path.

UNIX Commands 101

To use the command line effectively, familiarize yourself with the commands that are available to you. After all, how can you use a tool without knowing what it can do? Despite having to memorize a few commands, UNIX usually makes it easy on you by abbreviating commands, by following a standard grammar (so to speak), and by providing you with extensive documentation for each command.

Anatomy of a UNIX command

UNIX commands can perform many amazing feats. Despite their vast abilities, all commands follow a similar structure:

```
command <optional flag(s)> <optional operand(s)>
```

The simplest form of a UNIX command is the command itself. (For a basic discussion on UNIX commands such as ls, see the earlier section, "A few commands to get started.") You can expand your use of the ls command by appending various *flags,* which are settings that enable or disable optional features for the command. Most flags are preceded by a dash (-) and always follow the command. For instance, you can display the contents of a directory as a column of names by tacking on a -1 flag to the ls command.

```
ls -1
```

Besides flags, UNIX commands sometimes also have operands. An *operand* is something that is acted upon. For example, instead of just entering the ls command, which lists the current directory, you can add an operand to list a specific directory:

```
ls ~/Documents/myProject/
```

The tilde (~) denotes the user's Home directory.

Sometimes a command can take multiple operands, as is the case when you copy a file. The two operands represent the source file and the destination of the file that you want to copy, separated by a space. The following example copies a text file from the Documents folder to the Desktop folder by using the cp command (short for *copy*).

```
cp ~/Documents/MyDocument ~/Desktop/MyDocument
```

You can also combine flags and operands in the same command. This example displays the contents of a specific folder in list format:

```
ls -1 ~/Documents/myProject/
```

Command-line gotchas

In earlier sections, I describe a few simple command-line functions. All these commands have something in common: You might not have noticed, but every example thus far involved folder names and filenames that contained only alphanumeric characters. Remember what happens if you have a folder name that has a space in it? Try the following example, but don't worry when it doesn't work.

**Book VIII
Chapter 1**

...And UNIX Lurks
Beneath

The cd command stands for *change directory*.

```
cd /Desktop Folder
```

The result is an error message:

```
-bash: cd: /Desktop: No such file or directory
```

The problem is that a space character isn't allowed in a path. To get around this problem, simply enclose the path in double quotation marks, like this:

```
cd "/Desktop Folder"
```

Mac OS X lets you use either double *or* single quotation marks to enclose a path with spaces in it. Standard UNIX operating systems, however, use double quotation marks for this purpose.

In a similar vein, you can get the space character to be accepted by a command by adding an escape character. To *escape* a character, add a backslash (\) immediately prior to the character in question. To illustrate, try the last command with an escape character instead. Note that this time, no quotation marks are necessary.

```
cd /Desktop\ Folder
```

You can use either quotation marks or escape characters because they're interchangeable.

Help is on the way!

By now, you might be wondering how a computer techno-wizard is supposed to keep all these commands straight. Fortunately, you can find generous documentation for nearly every command available to you. To access this built-in help, use the man command. Using the man command (shorthand for *manual*) will display a help file for any command that it knows about. For example, to read the available help information for the ls command, simply type **man ls** at the prompt. Figure 1-3 illustrates the result.

Autocompletion

To speed things along, the bash shell can automagically complete your input for you while you type. (A *shell* takes the commands you type and submits them to the operating system, which then performs the tasks.) Although the Terminal permits you to enter commands via the keyboard, it is the shell that interprets those commands. Many kinds of shells are available to UNIX users. The shell that Lion uses by default is bash — another common shell is tcsh. Use the autocompletion features of bash to autocomplete both commands and filenames. To demonstrate, begin by typing the following:

```
cd ~/De
```

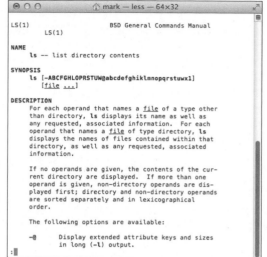

Figure 1-3:
Use the man
command to
display help
information.

Then press the Tab key. The result is that the shell predicts that you will
want to type

```
cd ~/Desktop/
```

Of course, if you have another folder that begins with the letters *De* in the
same folder, you might need to type a few additional characters. This gives
the autocompletion feature more information to help it decide which characters you want to type. In other words, if you don't type enough characters,
autocompletion ends up like a detective without enough clues to figure
things out.

Working with Files

If you've used a computer for any time at all, you're no doubt familiar with
the idea of files. Even before the first floppy drive appeared in personal computers, operating systems have stored data in files . . . they date back to the
days when a mainframe computer occupied an entire floor of an office building. Mac OS X is no exception, and it's important to understand how Mac OS
X arranges them into folders and how you go about accessing them via the
command line. This section describes the basic file and folder information
that you need to know to tame the beast that is UNIX.

Paths

Before you dive into UNIX commands, you should first know a few facts . . . nasty things, facts, but you can't earn your pair of techno-wizard suspenders without 'em. For starters, as a Mac user, you might not be familiar with how paths work in UNIX. A *path* is simply a textual representation of a folder or file. The simplest path is your Home directory, which is denoted by a tilde character (~) — the tilde character acts as the equivalent of /Users/<your short account name> (in my case, /Users/markchambers). Any folder within the Home directory is represented by the folder's name preceded by a forward slash (/). For example, a document entitled myDoc that resides in the current user's Documents folder would have a path like this:

```
~/Documents/myDoc
```

Similarly, a folder named *myFolder* that resides in the current user's Documents folder would have a path like this:

```
~/Documents/myFolder/
```

 As you've probably surmised, a *folder* and a *directory* are two different names for the same thing. *Folder* is the name with which most Mac users are familiar, and *directory* is a term that UNIX power users prefer. I use the terms interchangeably throughout the remainder of the chapter.

Because Mac OS X is a multiuser environment, you might sometimes want to work with folders or files somewhere other than in your Home folder. Starting from your Home folder, enter the following command:

```
cd ..
```

This moves you to the folder right above your Home folder, which happens to be the Users folder. Using another quick ls command will show you all users who are permitted to use the machine. (By the way, Shared isn't a user — it's a folder with privileges set so that any user can access its contents.)

Enter **cd ..** once again, and you find yourself at the root of your main hard drive. The *root directory* is what you see in the Finder when you double-click your hard drive icon on the Desktop. A user's Home directory is represented by a tilde character (~), and the root of the hard drive is denoted by a forward slash (/), as displayed by the prompt:

```
WHITEDRAGON:/ markchambers$
```

It's easy to return to your Home directory by following this sequence:

```
WHITEDRAGON:/ markchambers$ cd Users
WHITEDRAGON:/Users markchambers$ cd markchambers
WHITEDRAGON:~ markchambers$
```

Here's a faster way. Instead of moving through each successive folder until you reach your intended destination, you can specify the path by using just one cd command:

```
WHITEDRAGON:/ markchambers$ cd /Users/markchambers
WHITEDRAGON:~ markchambers$
```

Of course, the Home directory is a special folder in that you can also navigate there by simply entering **cd ~**, but the main point here is that you can navigate directly to specific folders by using that folder's path in conjunction with the cd command.

Furthermore, when you navigate your hard drive by using paths, you can jump directly to your desired destination from any place. When you enter **cd ..**, it is in relation to your current position, whereas entering

```
cd /Users/markchambers
```

always takes you to the same directory, regardless of your starting point.

Copying, moving, renaming, and deleting files

After you're comfortable with moving around the hierarchy of your hard drive, it's a cinch to copy, move, and rename files and folders.

To copy files from the command line, use the cp command. Because using the cp command will copy a file from one place to another, it requires two operands: first the source and then the destination. For instance, to copy a file from your Home folder to your Documents folder, use the cp command like this:

```
cp ~/MyDocument ~/Desktop/MyDocument
```

Keep in mind that when you copy files, **you must have proper permissions to do so!** Here's what happens when I try to copy a file from my Desktop to another user's Desktop (strangely named fuadramses):

```
WHITEDRAGON:~ markchambers$ cp ~/Desktop/MyDocument/Users/fuadramses/Desktop/
    MyDocument
```

Denied! Thwarted! Refused!

```
cp: /Users/fuadramses/Desktop/MyDocument: Permission denied
```

If you can't copy to the destination that you desire, you need to precede the cp command with sudo. Using the sudo command allows you to perform functions as another user. The idea here is that the other user whom you're "emulating" has the necessary privileges to execute the desired copy operation. When you execute the command, the command line asks you for a

Book VIII Chapter 1

...And UNIX Lurks Beneath

password. If you don't know what the password is, you probably shouldn't be using sudo. Your computer's administrator should have given you an appropriate password to use. After you enter the correct password, the command executes as desired.

In case you're curious, sudo stands for *set user and do*. It sets the user to the one that you specify and performs the command that follows the username.

```
sudo cp ~/Desktop/MyDocument /Users/fuadramses/Desktop/MyDocument
Password:
```

A close cousin to the cp (copy) command is the mv (move) command. As you can probably guess, the mv command moves a folder or file from one location to another. (I told you that all this character-based stuff would start to make sense, didn't I?) To demonstrate, this command moves MyDocument from the Desktop folder to the current user's Home folder:

```
mv ~/Desktop/MyDocument ~/MyDocument
```

Ah, but here's the hidden surprise: The mv command also functions as a rename command. For instance, to rename a file MyDocument on the Desktop to MyNewDocument, do this:

```
mv ~/Desktop/MyDocument ~/Desktop/MyNewDocument
```

Because both folders in this example reside in the same folder (~/Desktop/), it appears as though the mv command has renamed the file.

Again, like the cp command, the mv command requires that you have proper permissions for the action that you want to perform. Use the sudo command to perform any commands that your current user (as displayed in the prompt) isn't allowed to execute. On UNIX systems, not all users are necessarily equal. Some users can perform functions that others can't. This is handy for keeping your child's mitts off important files on your computer. It also creates a hurdle should you choose to work on files while using your child's restricted user account. The sudo command lets you temporarily become another user — presumably one that has permission to perform some function that the current user can't.

What would file manipulation be without the ability to delete files? Never fear; UNIX can delete anything that you throw at it. Use the rm (short for *remove*) or rmdir (short for *remove directory*) command to delete a folder or file. For example, to delete MyNewDocument from the Desktop folder, execute the rm command like this:

```
rm ~/Desktop/MyNewDocument
```

Once again, deleting files and folders requires that you have permission to do so. In other words, any time that you manipulate files with the command line, you're required to have the proper permission. If your current user lacks these permissions, using sudo helps. You should also check to make sure that your target is correctly spelled and that no pesky spaces that could wreak carnage are lurking in the command.

Opening documents and launching applications

Launching applications and opening documents is child's play for a UNIX pro like you. The open command does it all. For example, to bring the Finder to the foreground without touching the mouse, use

```
open /System/Library/CoreServices/Finder.app
```

To open a document from the command line, follow a similar scheme. For example, to view an image named myImage.tif that's stored in your Documents folder, try this:

```
open ~/Documents/myImage.tif
```

Useful Commands

Manipulating files and viewing folder content is fun, but the command line is capable of so much more! Now I focus your attention on some of the other useful tasks that you can perform with the command line.

Mac OS X comes stocked with a full set of useful commands. You can discover many of the commands that are installed by viewing the files in /usr/bin. Type **cd /usr/bin** to navigate there. Other locations to peruse include /bin and /usr/local/bin.

Calendar

One of my favorite command-line functions is the cal command, which displays a calendar in text form. Simply entering **cal** at the prompt displays a calendar for the current month, as shown in Figure 1-4.

Append a number to the cal command to display a 12-month calendar for that year. The number that follows the cal command is the year for which you'd like to see a calendar. For example, to view a calendar for 1970, type **cal 1970**. The result appears in Figure 1-5.

**Book VIII
Chapter 1**

**. . . And UNIX Lurks
Beneath**

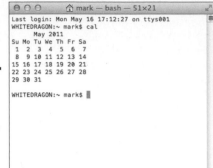

Figure 1-4:
Type **cal** to view a calendar for the current month.

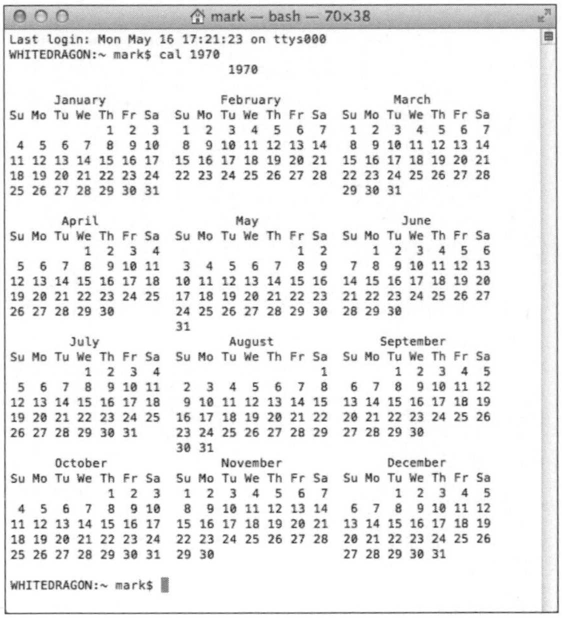

Figure 1-5:
Type **cal** followed by a year to view the 12 months of that year.

TIP

Append a month number and a year number to display the calendar for that month. For example, to view a calendar for April 2010, type **cal 04 2010**.

Use the –m flag to specify the current year, as in **cal –m 08** for August of this year.

Another useful command that's related to the cal command is date. Type **date** at the command line to display the day, date, time, and year based on your computer's settings.

```
WHITEDRAGON:~ markchambers$ date
Mon Jan 15 11:32:20 CDT 2009
```

Processes

Have you ever been curious as to why your hard drive seems to spin and grind on occasion while your system is seemingly inactive? Mac OS X sometimes has a lot of stuff going on behind the scenes. To discover just what your computer is busy doing at any time, use the `top` command to display all the actions that your computer is currently performing, as shown in Figure 1-6. These activities are called *processes;* some are created when you launch applications, and others are simply tasks that Mac OS X has to take care of to keep things running smoothly.

Figure 1-6: The `top` command displays all running processes.

```
000                    ↟ mark — top — 93×37
Processes: 59 total, 2 running, 1 stuck, 56 sleeping, 267 threads        17:45:09
Load Avg: 0.22, 0.21, 0.22  CPU usage: 0.96% user, 3.38% sys, 95.65% idle
SharedLibs: 848K resident, 0B data, 0B linkedit.
MemRegions: 7660 total, 303M resident, 33M private, 156M shared.
PhysMem: 312M wired, 678M active, 134M inactive, 1123M used, 923M free.
VM: 157G vsize, 1091M framework vsize, 59515(0) pageins, 0(0) pageouts.
Networks: packets: 2632/435K in, 2651/352K out. Disks: 70965/1227M read, 14145/210M written.

PID  COMMAND      %CPU TIME     #TH  #WQ #POR #MRE RPRVT RSHRD RSIZE VPRVT VSIZE  PGRP
527  top          3.1  00:01.31 1/1  0   29   33   1016K 680K  1092K 17M   2379M  527
524  bash         0.0  00:00.00 1    0   20   23   344K  216K  1108K 17M   2378M  524
523  login        0.0  00:00.02 2    1   34   61   644K  680K  2828K 30M   2392M  523
505  quicklookd   0.0  00:00.25 4    1   72   83   2904K 12M   9816K 43M   2922M  505
496  mdworker     0.0  00:00.11 4    1   56   71   1332K 15M   7488K 24M   2414M  496
494  mdworker     0.0  00:00.18 3    1   51   76   3548K 14M   7816K 34M   2415M  494
433  Terminal     0.6  00:05.58 5    1   144  273  9948K 22M   27M   32M   2469M  433
340  imklaunchage 0.0  00:00.11 2    1   49   64   2388K 3172K 4764K 40M   2404M  340
283  aosnotifyd   0.0  00:00.12 2    1   46   216  3496K 9460K 9776K 177M  18G    283
274  AppleSpell   0.0  00:00.15 2    1   47   50   912K  13M   4456K 30M   2413M  274
265  Grab         0.2  00:09.12 5    3   244  642  50M   38M   76M   75M   2572M  265
260  filecoordina 0.0  00:00.02 2    2   39   46   544K  9460K 2856K 22M   2406M  260
252  distnoted    0.0  00:00.01 2    1   40   53   460K  704K  1240K 22M   2391M  252
249  launchd      0.0  00:00.02 2    0   53   46   392K  416K  804K  38M   2399M  249
241  Image Captur 0.0  00:00.19 2    1   89   65   2168K 9600K 9428K 30M   2407M  241
235  applepusher  0.0  00:00.34 3    1   56   56   2712K 9960K 9532K 21M   2407M  235
228  AirPort Base 0.0  00:00.03 3    1   39   54   500K  684K  3220K 22M   2392M  228
217  warmd_agent  0.0  00:00.02 2    2   36   54   500K  684K  2684K 23M   2392M  217
215  PTPCamera    0.0  00:00.70 4    1   100  93   3256K 13M   10M   41M   2438M  215
213  imagent      0.0  00:00.63 4    1   90   94   1884K 9656K 6100K 23M   2411M  213
198  fontd        0.0  00:00.44 2    1   77   104  2116K 1080K 4844K 23M   2424M  198
194  pboard       0.0  00:00.00 1    0   28   47   352K  684K  1092K 20M   2381M  194
190  coreaudiod   0.4  01:28.24 7    5   247+ 90+  2592K+1356K 5548K+34M+ 2398M+ 190
189  Finder       0.0  00:17.09 3    1   234  875  19M   39M   53M   48M   2565M  189
188  talagent     0.0  00:00.21 2    1   88   81   1896K 12M   8572K 30M   2410M  188
187  SystemUIServ 0.0  00:05.49 5    3   278  319  7360K 28M   28M   31M   2486M  187
186  Dock         0.0  00:01.50 3    1   175  389  9300K 19M   21M   33M   2441M  186
181  distnoted    0.0  00:00.34 2    1   77   53   1752K 704K  2532K 22M   2391M  181
```

Besides listing the names of the various processes currently in use, `top` tells you how much of your CPU is being devoted to each process. This lets you know what process is currently hogging all your computing power.

Sometimes a process stalls, effectively freezing that action. By using the `top` command to find the Process ID (PID) of the offending process, you can halt the process. Simply use the `kill` command followed by the PID of the process that you want to stop. (The `man` help page for the `kill` command gives more options that may help terminate stubborn processes with prejudice.)

Do *not* go killing processes with a cavalier attitude! Although Mac OS X is extremely stable, removing the wrong process — such as `init` or `mach_init` — is rather like removing a leg from one of those deep-sea drilling platforms: the very *definition* of Not Good. You could lock up your system and lose whatever you're doing in other applications. If you simply want to shut down a misbehaving program, go graphical again (at least for a moment) and use the Force Quit menu command from the Apple menu.

Like `top`, another handy command for examining process info is `ps` (short for *process status*). Most often, you'll want to append a few flags to the `ps` command to get the information that you desire. For example, try the following command:

```
ps -aux
```

The `man` page for `ps` explains what each flag means. (Read more about using the `man` command in the earlier section "Help is on the way!")

UNIX Cadillac Commands

Besides working with files and processes, the command line has all kinds of sophisticated commands. For example, with the command line, you have instant access to a variety of tools for finding files or even stringing together commands.

Finding files

The command line gives you a number of ways to search for files on your hard drive. The two most commonly used commands are `find` and `locate`.

To use `find`, specify a starting point for the search followed by the name of the file or folder that you want to find. For example, to find the Fonts folder that belongs to your user, enter the command like this:

```
find ~/ -name "Fonts"
```

You should see at least one result of the `find` command.

```
/Users/markchambers/Library/Fonts
```

One great feature of the `find` command is that you can look for a file or folder in more than one location. Suppose you want to find a file named `MyDocument` that you know resides either in your Documents folder or on your Desktop. For this kind of search, use the `find` command like this:

```
find ~/Documents ~/Desktop -name "MyDocument"
```

In this example, you are telling the `find` command which folders it should search when looking for the file named `MyDocument`.

Using pipes

Nearly all UNIX commands can take on greater abilities by using a construct called the *pipe*. A pipe (|) is represented by that funny little vertical line that shows up when you press Shift+\. The pipe routes data from one command to another one that follows — for example, many UNIX commands produce large amounts of information that can't all fit on one page. (You might have noticed this behavior when you used the `locate` command.) Joining two commands or functions together with the pipe command is *piping*. To tame the screens full of text, pipe the `find` function to the `less` command. The `less` command provides data one page at a time.

```
find ~/ -name "Fonts" | less
```

When the results fill up one page, the data stops and waits for you to press any key (except the Q key) to continue. When you reach the end of the results, press Q to quit and return to a command-line prompt.

UNIX Programs That Come in Handy

As a Macintosh user, you might be surprised to know that many applications on your hard drive don't reside in one of the typical Applications folders of Mac OS X. These applications, in fact, don't have any graphical user interface like what you're accustomed to. They're accessible only from the command line. The remainder of this chapter covers some of these applications.

Text editors

UNIX has many text-editing applications for use at the command line. Some of the more popular ones include `nano`, `vi`, and `emacs`. Each of these text editors has its pros and cons — and say thanks to the thorough folks at Apple, because all three are included with Lion! For my examples here, however, I use `nano` because it's simple to use and sufficient for our needs.

Creating a new document

To create a text file by using `nano`, simply type **nano** at the command line. The result looks like Figure 1-7.

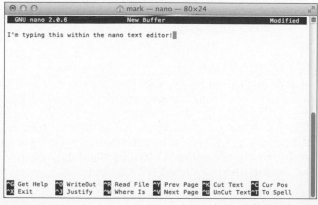

Figure 1-7: The `nano` program is a full-strength text editor, right from the command line.

This is the rough-and-tumble world of UNIX, which preceded the Macintosh by many years. Perhaps this will also help you to appreciate why the Macintosh was so revolutionary when it was introduced. (You can just hear the designers crowing, "We'll call this a *menu!* Yeah, that's the ticket!" The only graphics that you'd see on your monitor were the comics and sticky notes that you stuck to the bottom.)

At the bottom of the screen is a menu of common commands. Above the menu is a large, empty space where you can enter text, much the same as in the word processors that you already know and love. (For those of us that remember the halcyon character-based days of DOS, think older versions of Word and WordPerfect . . . or, if you're a *real* computing dinosaur like I am, consider the original WordStar.) Type some text in that area. Anything will do . . . a letter to a friend, a grocery list, or your school homework.

When you're finished entering your desired text, save the document with the `WriteOut` command in the `nano` menu. Directly next to each command in the `nano` menu is a keyboard sequence used to perform that command. (Refer to the bottom of Figure 1-7.) The ⌃ character is shorthand for the Control key on your keyboard. Thus, to save a file, press ⌃+O. This flies in the face of standard Mac keyboard conventions, where the letter *O* is traditionally used to mean *Open*.

After pressing the Control+O sequence, `pico` prompts you for a filename. As with most UNIX files, you're permitted to enter a simple filename here or a full path to a file. For this example, save the file to your Documents folder, naming it `MyNanoDocument`.

After you've completed and saved the document, pressing Control+X will transport you away from Planet Nano and back to the command line.

Networking with the Terminal

Because UNIX isn't a new phenomenon, it has many useful networking abilities built into it. In fact, UNIX was instrumental in creating much of what we now take for granted: e-mail, the Internet, and the World Wide Web. Thus, you'll be happy to know that you can communicate over networks with the Terminal in practically any manner that you can dream of . . . and then some!

WWW and FTP

If you've used the Internet for any time, you're probably familiar with the various means to transport data over a network. From FTP (short for *File Transfer Protocol*) and Telnet to e-mail and the web, UNIX can handle it all. In fact, UNIX has a command for each of these functions (and many more that have passed into historical obscurity). Rather than use each individual command to send and retrieve data with the Terminal, Apple has conveniently provided a command that can handle them all: `curl`. The `curl` command is competent at all the standard network protocols. To see it in action, pass a web address (or URL, to The Enlightened) to the curl command:

```
curl http://www.mlcbooks.com
```

The result is that you see the HyperText Markup Language (HTML) page that's located at www.mlcbooks.com. Because this isn't particularly useful for most people (it's not very easy to read), you need to add the letter o as a flag. This specifies where you would like to save this file upon download. To save the HTML page to your Home directory, add the -o flag and a path to the destination file.

Don't forget to precede all flags with a hyphen. For this example, it would be -o.

```
curl -o ~/mlcbooks.html http://www.mlcbooks.com
```

If you now perform an ls command, you see that curl has, in fact, down-loaded the HTML found at www.mlcbooks.com and saved it to a file named mlcbooks.html in your Home directory.

The beauty of curl is that it does much more than just retrieve web pages: It's equally comfortable with FTP transfers. FTP is used to *download* (or receive) files from a server as well as *upload* (or send) them. Like the previous HyperText Transfer Protocol (HTTP) examples, you only have to provide an FTP address in Uniform Resource Locator (URL) format, and curl will take care of the rest. Of course, most people want to save any files that they download via FTP — not view them in the Terminal as I did the HTML file. Therefore, as in the previous example, you should add the -o flag and a path to the destination of your download. This time, I download a README file about curl directly from the makers of curl.

```
curl -o ~/Desktop/README.curl ftp://ftp.sunet.se/pub/www/utilities/curl/README.
    curl
```

If you're familiar with FTP, you might be wondering whether curl can upload, too. Yes, indeed! Instead of using the -o flag, you need to use two flags: -T and -u. The -T flag denotes which file you want to upload. The -u flag denotes the username and password. Then, specify the FTP destination address of where you want to upload it. Because this example deals with an upload, the remainder of this example is for an imaginary FTP server. In real life, you'd use the appropriate FTP address, username, and password for an FTP server where you are allowed to upload.

```
curl -T /Desktop/README.curl -u username:passwd ftp://ftp.yoursitehere.com
/myfiles/README.curl
```

This example uploads the README.curl file from the Desktop folder that I downloaded earlier to an imaginary FTP server.

How do you spell success? C-u-r-l!

Sure, HTTP and FTP are handy, but did you know that there are many other protocols for network communications? One of the niftier ones is the *Dictionary protocol*. With it, you can look up words from any server that understands the protocol. Suppose, for example, that you want to know the meaning of the term *DVD*. Enter the following command to find out:

```
curl dict://dict.org/d:DVD
```

With `curl`, Dictionary, and your Dictionary Dashboard widget on the same Macintosh, you might never use a "real" paper dictionary again!

Chapter 2: AppleScript Just Plain Rocks

In This Chapter

↙ Simplifying your life with AppleScript

↙ Letting AppleScript create scripts for you

↙ Writing scripts on your own

↙ Using Automator to create your own applications

↙ Searching for AppleScript help elsewhere

*U*sing a Macintosh is supposed to make your life easier — and in many ways, it does. But there's a limit to how much your Mac can do by itself, right? After all, you still have to move the mouse, press keys on the keyboard, and read information on the screen to get things done . . . or do you? Why not let your computer do the dull chores — such as renaming a thousand digital photographs from your family vacation and organizing them into folders based on the subject of each photo — for you? Although most people are familiar with controlling their Macs with the mouse and keyboard, few realize that they can operate their machines without touching a key or a mouse button, or even glancing at the screen.

What's So Great about AppleScript?

If one word could describe what AppleScript is all about, it'd be *automation*. *AppleScript* is a technology for automating practically any action that you perform with your Macintosh, including both common tasks in the Finder and those that you perform in other applications.

Automate common tasks in the Finder

If you've ever found yourself repeating some task more than once, you're an ideal candidate for becoming an AppleScript techno-wizard. AppleScript is particularly good at taking the boredom and tedium out of using your Macintosh by performing all sorts of tasks automatically. To illustrate, consider a few jobs that would take a fair amount of time to do by hand but are a snap with AppleScript:

✦ While writing your next best-selling Great American Novel — or *For Dummies* book on Mac OS X — you make a mistake and misnumber the chapters. All the chapters have a filename bearing the chapter number, but they're all off by one. Sure, you could rename each file by hand, but your book is a large tome and renumbering 42 chapters manually doesn't sound like much fun. (Take my word for it. *Please*.) It'll require several minutes and lots of tedious attention on your part, not to mention introduce the likelihood of human error. But wait, there's another way! When using a simple AppleScript of only a few lines of code, you can rename the chapters in seconds whilst you go grab another Diet Coke.

✦ You're a neat individual and think that your Mac should reflect your penchant for order — in fact, you like your Desktop icons to be placed just so. Being left-handed, you prefer the icons over on the left side of the Desktop, like some of those *inferior* operating systems. In this situation, an AppleScript can help you do things that aren't humanly possible; not only can you rapidly rearrange the icons on your Desktop, but you can do so with pixel-point accuracy. Without AppleScript, it'd be nearly impossible to precisely align dozens of icons. And if you could, it would take a long time and probably cause you to go blind.

✦ After a font-download binge, you find yourself with hundreds of fonts. You really want to organize them into separate folders based on the date that you downloaded them. AppleScript comes to the rescue again! With a brief script, you could knock out this challenge without ever looking at a single date. Add a couple more lines of code to the script, and AppleScript will take care of creating the folders, too. Right, you know the word: *sassy*.

Automate tasks in other applications

By using AppleScript, you can also often automate your work from beginning to end, despite the fact that you need multiple applications to do so. Look at a few scenarios, and you'll begin to appreciate why AppleScript is such a powerful technology:

✦ You've just completed creating the ultimate library of bagpipe songs in iTunes — no, really! — and you want to share the list with your friends at the next Bagpipers Anonymous meeting. You could easily send everyone in the group an iTunes Playlist, but not everyone in the club has iTunes installed, let alone a computer. This is going to require creating a hard copy for those members without a computer. Because your bagpipe song list contains thousands of songs, you don't want to retype the name of each song. AppleScript can save the day by extracting the song titles for you and compiling them into a list just in time for your meeting.

✦ AppleScript can take care of your computer-owning bagpipe friends, too. With a few extra steps, you can e-mail all of them the list as well.

✦ Being so doggone fond of bagpipes, you want to send your bagpiping friends a special note during the holidays. To help manage your holiday greeting cards, you can create a record in FileMaker Pro or some other database listing the name and address of each person who should receive a card. If you've entered their street addresses in the Contacts section of your e-mail application, AppleScript can aid in transferring the addresses from your e-mail application to the database. Never again will your bagpiping friends miss a holiday greeting . . . and the world is a much better place.

As you can imagine, there are literally thousands of ways that you can use AppleScript to automate your workflow. (Whoops, I just used a BST, or *Business Software Term*. A *workflow* is a single document or project that one or more people work on using multiple applications. In other words, your document can be automatically manipulated in multiple applications using the same script.)

Running a Script

The easiest way to get started with AppleScript is to use some scripts that others have written already. *Scripts* are small files that contain a list of commands; this list of commands tells your Mac what functions to perform and when to perform them. Fortunately, Apple is kind enough to provide you with several completed scripts with your installation of Lion. You can find a large cache of scripts in the scripts folder, found in the Library folder, under Scripts.

Many scripts (but not all) end with the extension .scpt. Before you get started running scripts, however, you should know a few things.

Identifying scripts in the field

Each script that you encounter will be in one of these three formats:

✦ **Script application:** Some AppleScripts act much like an application. To use one, simply double-click it in the Finder, and off it goes to perform whatever tasks it was meant to do. Depending on an internal setting of the script, it might quit when it's finished doing its thing. Most often, the script completes its mission and quits. Scripts are typically identified by the icon that you see in Figure 2-1.

✦ **Compiled script:** You might also encounter AppleScripts that won't run without the aid of another application. Apple calls these *compiled scripts*. Although they can't execute on their own, they do have the abilities of a script built-in. They just require a host application to use them.

✦ **Text file:** In addition to compiled scripts and those that act like applications, a third category of AppleScript that you might encounter is a script stored in a text file. Scripts that are stored in a text file also need a host application before they'll do anything. The main difference between a text file script and a compiled script is that you can read a text file script with any application that can open a text file.

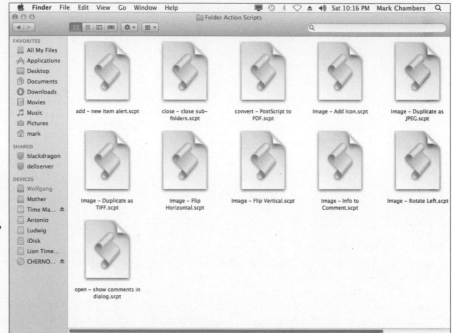

Figure 2-1:
A gaggle of typical script icons caught by the camera.

The AppleScript Editor application

Two of the three possible script types (compiled scripts and text files) require some sort of host application before they'll perform any action. Luckily, Lion provides you with just such a host: the AppleScript Editor application, which comes with Mac OS X and can execute any AppleScript with ease. With the AppleScript Editor, you can also do much more, including

✦ View or modify an AppleScript

✦ Create a new AppleScript

✦ Check an AppleScript for errors

✦ Save scripts in one of the three possible formats

To launch the AppleScript Editor application, navigate to the Utilities folder (open your Applications folder and then open the Utilities folder) and double-click the AppleScript Editor icon. The AppleScript Editor application displays an empty, script-editing window, as shown in Figure 2-2.

Figure 2-2:
The
AppleScript
Editor slices
and dices . . .
and even
checks
syntax.
Order now!

Executing a script

After you have the AppleScript Editor application running, you can run any AppleScript that you can find. To get you started, Apple has conveniently provided a handful of useful scripts. Navigate to the Scripts folder, which is located in the Library folder.

The scripts are divided into folders based on functionality, such as fonts, mail, and navigation. For example, open the Font Book folder, where you'll find a script named `Delete Empty Collections.scpt`.

Double-click the script to open it. Because it's a compiled script and not an application script, the AppleScript Editor automatically loads the script and comes to the foreground (see Figure 2-3). This particular script opens the Font Book application and checks for empty font collections. If it finds any, the script displays a prompt asking for confirmation and then deletes the empty collection if you click the OK button. To see the script in action, click the Run button or press ⌘+R.

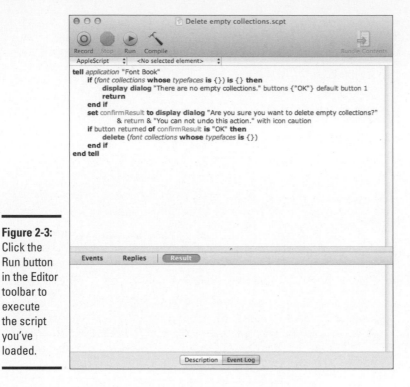

Figure 2-3:
Click the
Run button
in the Editor
toolbar to
execute
the script
you've
loaded.

Writing Your Own Simple Scripts

Using someone else's scripts is fun and all, but the real joy of AppleScript comes when you create your own. Not only can you customize a script to your own needs and desires, but saving all those keystrokes can really produce a feeling of euphoria. (Okay, perhaps just Lion power users will actually experience a heightened sense of existence . . . you'll be there soon.)

Create a script without touching a key

You needn't wear a pocket protector or tape the bridge of your glasses to become proficient with AppleScript. In fact, the AppleScript Editor can get you up and running with AppleScript in no time at all. The secret weapon of the AppleScript author is the Record function of the AppleScript Editor. You click the Record button, perform one or more actions in a recordable application, and then return to the AppleScript Editor, where you click the Stop button. The AppleScript Editor stores each of your actions and compiles the whole list into an AppleScript.

In *theory,* this is how it should all work, but in reality, finding recordable Macintosh applications isn't always so easy. The Finder is, perhaps, the most recordable application on the Mac. Although some other applications support recording, so few do that the Finder could be the only recordable application most Mac users ever see.

To try it yourself, take the following steps to automate actions in the Finder:

1. **Bring AppleScript Editor to the foreground.**

   If AppleScript Editor isn't currently running, double-click its icon in a Finder window. If it is running, click its icon in the Dock.

2. **Create a new script by pressing ⌘+N.**

3. **Click the Record button.**

   The Record button is one of four buttons positioned near the top left of a new script window. Refer to Figure 2-3.

4. **Switch to the Finder and perform the actions that you want to automate.**

   When the Finder is active, you can select some icons on the Desktop and move them around, resize any open Finder windows, or navigate to your home directory. Any action that you perform in the Finder should be acceptable fodder for the AppleScript Editor. When you perform tasks in the Finder, the AppleScript Editor automatically generates a script that replicates your actions.

5. **Return to the AppleScript Editor and click the Stop button.**

   To reactivate the AppleScript Editor, click its icon in the Dock. Click the Stop button to cease the recording of your script.

When you're finished, you should be looking at a complete AppleScript. To test your work, return to the Finder and return any icons or windows that you might have moved or repositioned to their original locations. (You don't want to run a script that doesn't appear to have any effect.) Then return to the AppleScript Editor and click the Run button to watch your automated Finder tasks being performed.

Building your own scripts

An AppleScript novice can perform all kinds of amazing feats with the recording features of the AppleScript Editor. Because AppleScript uses a kind of pseudo-English language, it's usually pretty easy to figure out what's going on behind the scenes. Consider the following script for an example:

```
tell app "Finder"
   activate
   set windowList to every window -- save list of open
   windows
```

```
repeat with theWindow in windowList
    tell theWindow
        if collapsed is true then
        -- do nothing, because the window is collapsed
        else
            set collapsed to true
        end if
    end tell
end repeat
end tell
```

By the way, in the preceding code, I bolded and italicized the commands you'll be working with, but they don't have to be bolded for the script to work. Anyway, the first thing that you might notice about this script is the first line: the tell command, which indicates that this script relates to the Finder. This script activates the Finder, creates a list of open windows, and then examines the state of each window: Is it collapsed or not collapsed? (By default, a *collapsed,* or minimized, window appears in the Dock.)

One of two possible results occurs:

✦ **If the window is already minimized,** nothing happens and the script continues through the list of windows.

✦ **If the window isn't minimized,** the script collapses it.

This continues until the script has examined all open windows. The end result? All open windows end up minimized in the Dock.

Another thing to note about this script is that it has two comments in it (save list and do nothing). Comments can help you remember what you were thinking months later when you open the script again. Although comments help us humans know what's happening, they don't really have any other function. An AppleScript comment begins with two dashes (–).

Here's a big-time Mark's Maxim that every script author should remember:

Comments are your friend in any script!

One Step Beyond: AppleScript Programming

Creating AppleScripts can soon become very involved, bordering on *programming.* Don't let that term *programming* scare you away, though. You needn't be a software developer to take advantage of AppleScripts. Apple provides a lot of help to get you started along the AppleScript trail.

Grab the Dictionary

Perhaps the greatest resource for AppleScript novices and experts alike is the AppleScript Dictionary. Although many applications are scriptable, not all are. To be scriptable, an application must contain an AppleScript Dictionary. An AppleScript Dictionary details the various commands and objects of an application that you can access via AppleScript.

The AppleScript Editor application allows you to peer inside an application and view its AppleScript Dictionary. To open an application's Dictionary, choose File➪Open Dictionary. Mac OS X searches through your installed applications and presents you with the Open Dictionary dialog, as shown in Figure 2-4, which lists all applications that have a dictionary and are therefore scriptable.

Figure 2-4:
Viewing the AppleScript Dictionary within the AppleScript Editor.

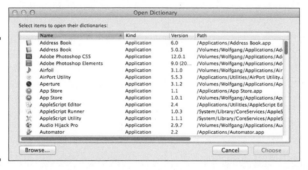

If you don't see your favorite application in the list, alas, it's probably not scriptable. To make certain, click the Browse button and navigate to the application location — if the application is disabled, you're out of luck.

After you select an application and click Choose, the AppleScript Editor displays that application's AppleScript Dictionary. An application's dictionary lists all the features of that application that are scriptable.

Scriptable features are divided into categories, called *Suites,* which you can see on the left side of the AppleScript Dictionary. Every Mac application is supposed to support the Standard Suite, which lists common terms that most applications should support.

Click an item in the Suite on the left side of the Dictionary to view detailed information about its capabilities, as shown in Figure 2-5.

**Book VIII
Chapter 2**

**AppleScript Just
Plain Rocks**

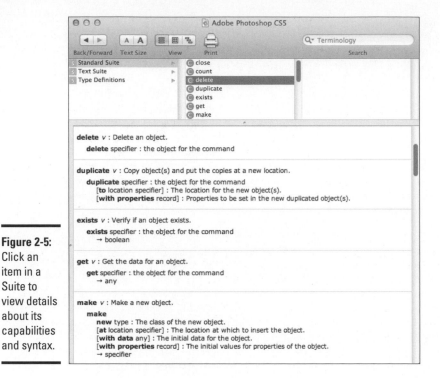

Figure 2-5:
Click an
item in a
Suite to
view details
about its
capabilities
and syntax.

By surveying the various Suites of an application, you begin to see what tasks you can automate. The Finder, with its huge AppleScript Dictionary, is perhaps the most scriptable of all applications.

Anatomy of a simple script

Although a full discussion of AppleScript programming is beyond the scope of this book — after all, we have other things to talk about, too — that doesn't mean that you can't produce some quick and useful scripts. Most AppleScripts begin with a command that addresses the application that you want to automate. Enter this command into a new AppleScript document, which you create by pressing ⌘+N.

```
tell application "Finder"
```

This is like saying, "Hey, Finder, listen up! I'm going to send commands your way!" The double quotation marks surround the application name that you're addressing in the command.

Similarly, after you finish instructing the Finder what tasks you want performed, you must also tell it to stop listening. As such, typical scripts end with

```
end tell
```

With the shell of a script in place, all you have to do is add commands between the `tell` and `end tell` commands of the script. If you want your script to force an application to the foreground, an `activate` command is usually the first line within the shell of your script.

```
tell application "Finder"
  activate
end tell
```

Believe it or not, this is technically a complete and valid script! It doesn't do much, though, so add some more functionality to make it accomplish something worthwhile. For example, suppose you want to perform some housekeeping chores each time you log in to your Macintosh. Some desirable tasks might include

- ✦ Emptying the Trash
- ✦ Having your Mac say "Hello!" to you

(Okay, I'll grant that hearing your Mac say "Hello!" isn't a housekeeping chore, but it makes the whole script that much more fun — and really impresses your visitors, too. No one ever said programming had to be boring!)

To add these functions, you can do so by using a language you already know: English. As I mention earlier, Apple tries (and sometimes succeeds) to make AppleScript as English-like as possible. That way, you don't have to know some silly computer language; just use your native tongue. For example, to empty the Trash, tell the Finder to do so.

```
empty trash
```

The trickiest line of code might be the speech, and that's only because you need to remember to add quotation marks. AppleScript thinks that anything without quotation marks is an AppleScript command.

```
say "Hello!"
```

The result is a super-simple script that anyone can read but that performs two powerful functions. The completed script looks like this:

```
tell app "Finder"
  activate
  empty trash
  say "Hello!"
end tell
```

After you complete the script, choose File⇨Save to save your script. Because you want the script to execute and then quit, use the File Format field to save it as an Application. Also, make sure that the Stay Open check box and the Startup Screen check box are deselected. And don't forget to name your script in the Save As text field.

To have the script automatically run each time you log in to your Mac, save the script anywhere you wish. (Assign its location in the Where field of the Save window.) Open System Preferences by clicking its icon in the Dock; click the Users & Groups icon. Make sure that your account is selected (if the pane is locked, click the padlock icon and type your admin password to continue) and then click Login Items. Click the Add button (which proudly bears a plus sign) and navigate to your script in the Open dialog that appears. After you click the Add button of the Open dialog, you see the script in the Login Items window.

1 Summon Automator — the Silicon Programmer!

Okay, perhaps I've watched too much *Iron Chef* over the years. Anyway, Lion features *Automator* (as shown in Figure 2-6) — he's your own personal robotic automation assistant. In fact, Automator can help you create custom applications that can handle your repetitive tasks. Again, you're creating *workflows* here, which are sequential (and repeatable) operations that are performed on the same files or data, and your Automator application can automatically launch whatever applications are necessary to get the job done.

Figure 2-6: Automator is a dream come true for those who hate repetitive tasks.

Here's a great example: You work with a service bureau that sends you a CD every week with new product shots for your company's Marketing department. Unfortunately, these images are flat-out *huge* — taken with a 12-megapixel camera — and they're always in the wrong orientation. Before you move them to the Marketing folder on your server, you have to laboriously resize each image and rotate it, and then save the smaller version.

With Automator's help, you can build a custom application that automatically reads each image in the folder, resizes it, rotates it, and even generates a thumbnail image or prints the image, and then moves the massaged images to the proper folder. You'd normally have to manually launch Preview to perform the image operations and then use a Finder window to move the new files to the right location. But now, with Automator, double-clicking your custom application icon does the trick.

You'll find Automator in your Applications folder. Currently, Automator can handle specific tasks within more than 80 applications (including the Finder), but both Apple and third-party developers are busy adding new Automator task support to all sorts of new and existing applications.

To create a simple application using Automator, follow these steps:

1. **Select Application and click Choose.**

2. **Click the desired application in the Library list.**

   Automator displays the actions available within that application.

3. **Drag the desired action from the Library pane to the workflow pane.**

4. **Modify any specific settings provided for the action you chose.**

5. **Repeat Steps 1–3 to complete the workflow.**

6. **Click Run (upper right) to test your script.**

   Use sample files (copies) while you're fine-tuning your application lest you accidentally do something deleterious to an original (and irreplaceable) file!

   Figure 2-7 illustrates a workflow that will take care of the earlier example — resizing and rotating a folder full of images, and then moving them to the Pictures folder.

7. **When the application is working as you like, press ⌘+Shift+S to save it.**

8. **In the Save dialog that appears, type a name for your new workflow.**

9. **Click the Where pop-up menu and specify a location where the file should be saved.**

10. **Click Save.**

Figure 2-7:
Now I'm ready to handle 10 or 1,000 images in a folder — my application does the work!

To find all the actions of a certain type within the Library list, click in the Search box at the bottom of the Library window and type in a keyword, such as **save** or **burn**. You don't even need to press Return!

Help 1s at Your Fingertips

If you want to explore AppleScript further, you have many resources on hand. Sometimes the easiest way to use AppleScript is to copy existing scripts and modify them as necessary; other times, it's a good idea to read the documentation included in Apple's Help system. Whichever approach you use, with a little practice and guidance, you'll soon be doing stupendous tasks with your Mac.

Built-in AppleScript Help

The most readily available AppleScript reference is built into Mac OS X. From within Automator, choose Help⇨Automator Help to launch the Automator Help Guide, or choose Help⇨AppleScript Help from the AppleScript Editor. The latter is a great place to begin your AppleScript exploration. It includes detailed documentation about the AppleScript language and loads of demonstration scripts for you to try (or alter) yourself.

AppleScript on the Web

In addition to the built-in AppleScript help in the Finder, the Internet has much to offer in the way of AppleScript training and examples. Like so many other excellent web resources, AppleScripts are free!

Not all AppleScripts are created equal: When downloading scripts from the Internet, make sure that they're compatible with Lion (Mac OS X v. 10.7).

Mac OS X Automation

Although the built-in OS X help offers a lot, this web site offers even more scripts, tutorials, and general AppleScript and Automator goodness. Furthermore, the site maintains an extensive list of links to other useful AppleScript/Automator sites.

```
www.macosxautomation.com/applescript
```

Automator World

Automator World devotes its site to all Macintosh scripting. Because AppleScript is such a huge part of scripting the Mac OS, you can be certain that there's something here for you. Besides offering up-to-date news on Automator scripting for the Mac OS, Automator World also gives you access to many scripts, information about scripting books, and details on AppleScripts with interfaces. The sheer volume of information at this site makes it one you shouldn't skip.

```
automatorworld.com
```

Chapter 3: Talking and Writing to Your Macintosh

In This Chapter

✔ **Using handwriting recognition to control Mac OS X**

✔ **Speaking to your Mac**

✔ **Having your Mac speak back**

✔ **Using VoiceOver to provide feedback in Lion**

*I*f you're a hunt-and-peck typist — leaving you certain that there *must* be some better way to get information into your computer — you'll be happy to know that Apple has you in mind. Since the very first Mac rolled off the assembly line, Apple has had a keen interest in alternative modes of interaction between human and machine. Mac OS X continues in this tradition of alternative computer controls, offering two options for controlling Mac OS X without the keyboard: handwriting and speech.

✦ **Handwriting:** By using a pen and computer tablet, you can enter text into your Mac by simply writing as you would on a sheet of paper.

✦ **Speech:** Talk to your Mac to make it listen and obey your commands. It even talks back!

This chapter guides you through the various options that you have for controlling your Macintosh without using the keyboard. First, I cover the Mac OS X *Ink* feature (also called *Inkwell*), which you use to write on a tablet to enter data into your computer. (Although it sounds a bit ironic, think of Ink as your "digital paper" for the new millennium.) Whatever you write on the tablet appears on the screen as text.

I also take a look at the more space-age speech capabilities available to you in Mac OS X. With your voice, you can command a Macintosh to perform all sorts of interesting feats. And just so you don't get lonely, the Mac even talks back to you. (Now you can control your computer just as Spock from *Star Trek* could!) And Lion's VoiceOver feature makes it easy for your Mac to read aloud all sorts of text, including web pages, Mail messages, and word processing documents.

So scoot away from your computer, lean that chair back, and let your Mac take care of the rest.

Using Ink with a Tablet

Typing on a keyboard can be a tedious and error-prone experience for even the best typists. To help out, Apple included some useful handwriting features in Mac OS X. Based in part on some of Apple's handheld software for the *Newton* (one of the first personal digital assistants [PDAs] and a product released before its time), the handwriting recognition in Mac OS X gives you the ability to write text on a compatible tablet for use in your favorite applications.

The basic process of working with handwriting on Mac OS X goes like this:

1. **Attach a tablet to your Mac.**

   Most tablets use a Universal Serial Bus (USB) connection, so connecting one to your computer is as simple as plugging in the cable from your tablet to the USB port on your Mac.

2. **Write on the tablet with the stylus that accompanies it.**

   A *stylus* is the name given the fake "pen" that accompanies most tablets. A stylus doesn't have any ink in it: It's just a pen-shaped tool with a plastic tip meant for writing on a tablet.

3. **Your Mac interprets your handwriting.**

   After your Mac recognizes the handwriting, it sends that text to the foremost application at the cursor location where you would normally type with the keyboard. You're spared the whole training bit, too.

You aren't restricted to writing just text on the tablet, naturally. You can use it to control the interface of your Mac as you would a mouse. A tablet also works great for graphics applications, such as Corel Painter, Adobe Illustrator, and Adobe Photoshop. Many artists are frustrated when drawing with a mouse; when you use a tablet, though, you can feel right at home with the natural pen or brush movements that you've always used.

Although Lion takes care of handwriting recognition, it does offer you a few settings in the Ink pane within System Preferences. To view the System Preferences, click the System Preferences icon in the Dock. From there, click the Ink icon to adjust settings for your tablet.

If you don't have a tablet connected to your Macintosh, you can't view the System Preferences pane for Ink. Mac OS X is smart enough to show you only the settings for your current hardware setup.

Hey, there's a keyboard on my screen!

Although Lion's Ink feature is nifty, it is sometimes less than precise — unfortunately, handwriting recognition is nowhere near 100% accurate. However, many Mac OS X power users overlook one alternative method of input: the virtual keyboard, which you can click with your mouse to type text into a document, System Preferences field, or anything else that needs completing.

To display the keyboard, open System Preferences and click Language & Text, and then click the Input Sources tab and select the Keyboard & Character Viewer check box. (To make things easier, make sure that the Show Input Menu in Menu Bar check box is also enabled.)

Close System Preferences and click the Input Menu icon that appears in your menu bar — depending on your settings, it looks like a square containing an asterisk, or a country's flag — and choose Show Keyboard Viewer. You can type by clicking the buttons on this floating keyboard, including all the navigation and cursor control keys. To hide the keyboard, just click the Input Menu icon in the menu bar again and choose Hide Keyboard Viewer, or click the Close button on the keyboard viewer.

Computer, Can You Hear Me?

Remember that classic scene from the movie *Star Trek IV: The Voyage Home* in which Scotty picks up the mouse on a Macintosh and tries to talk directly to the computer? Since the very early days of the Mac OS, Apple has included some form of speech recognition in its computers. Lion continues to improve on speech recognition by offering a host of tools that let you get more work done in a shorter amount of time. (We're not to that point yet, Scotty, but we're working on it.)

The Speech Recognition features of Mac OS X let you speak a word, phrase, or sentence. After you've spoken, your Mac goes to work translating what you said — and if it understands the phrase, it then performs an action associated with that phrase. The great part about this system is that you can say any phrase in continuous speech and have your Mac perform any sort of action that you can imagine. In fact, you aren't limited to just one action: You can perform dozens of actions upon speaking a particular phrase.

Before you get started using Speech Recognition, you need a microphone to get sound into your Mac. Virtually all current Macintosh models have a built-in microphone; for example, if you use an Intel iMac, your microphone is built into the monitor. MacBooks have a similar microphone built into the screen. If your Mac doesn't have a microphone, connect one to the rear of your Macintosh by plugging it into the microphone jack.

**Book VIII
Chapter 3**

**Talking and Writing
to Your Macintosh**

If you're looking for the best quality audio input from your microphone for use with iChat, check out a microphone with a USB connection. You'll get far better sound quality than a microphone that connects to your analog jack.

The Speech Recognition tab

To get started with Speech Recognition in Mac OS X, open the System Preferences window by clicking its icon in the Dock and then clicking the Speech icon. This brings up the Speech pane, as shown in Figure 3-1.

Figure 3-1:
Hail and well met, good Speech pane (and Feedback window)!

You'll find that two tabs comprise the speech settings of Mac OS X:

✦ Speech Recognition

✦ Text to Speech

In this section, I'm concerned only with the Speech Recognition tab. Later, in the "Your Mac Talks Back!" section, I explore the Text to Speech tab.

The Speech Recognition tab consists of two subtabs:

✦ **Settings:** The Settings tab provides a number of settings that control how your Mac listens to Its Master's Voice. (Meaning you, friend reader.) From here, you can set the sound input, adjust the key on the keyboard that toggles speech recognition on and off, change microphone settings, and name your computer with a keyword. (You *do* want to call your computer by name as any techno-wizard does, don't you?)

✦ **Commands:** When Speech Recognition is active, your Mac can understand any number of commands. From the Commands tab, you tell the Mac what type of command it should expect you to give. You can also specify whether you'll be giving the commands word for word or your Mac should be prepared to interpret paraphrasing. A number of specific applications and menus can be configured with speakable items, such as contact names within Lion's Address Book.

Crowning the Speech Recognition pane are the Speakable Items On and Off radio buttons. You've probably already guessed how to use 'em to switch Speech Recognition features on and off.

When you select the On radio button, the small circular Speech Recognition Feedback window appears on your screen, floating above all other windows. Know this face well because the Feedback window (also shown in Figure 3-1) is your friend and partner. If you use Speech Recognition often, it'll become a constant companion on your Desktop. (More on it in the next section.)

The Settings pane

At the bottom of the Settings pane is the Upon Recognition section. When your Mac comprehends one of your stentorian commands, you can set it to respond by playing a sound, speaking a confirmation, or both. This is helpful when you're not sure whether your Mac understands you. Like handwriting recognition, one hundred percent speech recognition isn't a reality on any computer at this point, so sometimes it helps to have any feedback you can get. Otherwise, you might feel silly shouting at your machine while it sits there doing nothing. (Or perhaps not, if you're into really inexpensive anger management.)

You can choose between two styles of listening with the Listening Method options:

✦ **Listen Only While Key Is Pressed:** Speech Recognition works only while the designated key is held down.

✦ **Listen Continuously with Keyword:** When you speak the keyword, listening turns on and remains on.

To change what key must be toggled or held down, click the Change Key button.

Why change the keyword? Instead of saying, "Computer, empty the Trash!" you might prefer, "Elrond, empty the Trash!" This adds a little bit of personality to the interaction and also gives your computer a slightly longer time to react to your command. (As a general rule, the longer the spoken phrase, the more likely your Mac will understand it.) If you select the Listen Continuously with Keyword feature, you can change your computer's name via the Keyword text box.

Finally, you can select the microphone that you want to use from the Microphone pop-up menu on the Settings pane — a great feature if you have more than one microphone connected to your Mac. Click the Calibrate key to adjust the sound volume for better recognition.

The Commands pane

When Speech Recognition is active, your Mac listens for whatever phrases appear in your Speakable Items folder (a directory on your hard drive that holds a number of scripts). The Commands tab (shown in Figure 3-2) allows you to view the contents of this folder. When you speak a phrase that matches one of these filenames, your Mac automatically executes that script. The script can perform any number of actions, which is what makes Speech Recognition so powerful. Apple includes a large number of scripts with Mac OS X, but you're free to create your own, too.

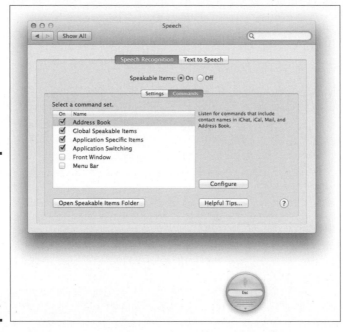

Figure 3-2:
The Commands tab allows you to specify which commands your Mac should hear.

To make something speakable, select the item and then speak the command "Make this speakable." The new speakable command is based upon the item's name.

To view the contents of the Speakable Items folder, click the Open Speakable Items Folder button on the Commands pane. The Finder comes to the foreground and navigates to the folder that holds the scripts. This is handy because each item in the Speakable Items folder is speakable.

To the right of the Open Speakable Items Folder button is another button: Helpful Tips. Click it to get some pointers on how to get the best performance from your microphone.

As I mention in the preceding section, the Speech Recognition features of Mac OS X aren't restricted to items in the Speakable Items folder. Any application that supports Speech Recognition is also fair game for your verbal manipulation. To control commands within other applications, use the Commands tab (refer to Figure 3-2). Here you can select the following check boxes:

✦ Address Book

✦ Global Speakable Items

✦ Application Specific Items

✦ Application Switching

✦ Front Window (requires that you activate assistive devices in the Universal Access panel within System Preferences)

✦ Menu Bar (requires that you activate assistive devices in the Universal Access panel within System Preferences)

Mark any one of these options to allow your Mac to listen to those kinds of commands.

The Feedback window

After you activate Speech Recognition, you instantly see the Feedback window. You can click and drag the edge of the window to position it anywhere on your Desktop.

The Feedback window includes controls and displays of its own:

✦ **Microphone Level Meter:** The Feedback window displays indicators to let you know how loud the input to your microphone is.

✦ **Visual Indicator:** The Feedback window displays visual feedback to let you know what mode it is in: idle, listening, or hearing a command. When the microphone isn't grayed out but there are no arrows on either side of the microphone, you're in listening mode. When the microphone is flanked by animated arrows, your computer is hearing a command spoken. When Speech Recognition is idle, no arrows are present and the microphone is grayed out.

✦ **Quick-Access Menu:** You can quickly access the Speech preferences for the System or view the Speech Commands window. Just click the downward-pointing arrow at the bottom of the Feedback window, and a menu appears, giving you one-click access to both.

As soon as you disable speech recognition in the System Preferences, the Feedback window disappears.

The Speech Command window

Because Speech Recognition might be listening for different sets of commands from the Finder or many other applications, Mac OS X provides you with a single listing of all commands that you might speak at any given time: the Speech Commands window. To open the Speech Commands window, click the triangle at the bottom of the Feedback window and choose Open Speech Commands Window from the menu that appears.

The Speech Commands window is a simple one, but it serves an important purpose: to let you know what commands Mac OS X understands. The Speech Commands pane, as shown in Figure 3-3, organizes commands into categories that match the settings in the Speech pane of the System Preferences.

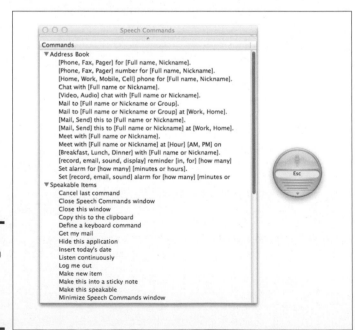

Figure 3-3:
The Speech Commands window, hard at work.

If you launch another application that supports Speech Recognition, Mac OS X adds that application's commands to the Speech Commands window. Speak any of these commands to make your Mac execute that function. For example, Mac OS X ships with speech commands for Address Book, such as Mail To and Video Chat With.

Apple might be a big, serious, computer company — yeah, right — but it isn't without a humorous side! With Speech Recognition enabled, say the phrase, "Tell me a joke." Your Mac replies with a random joke. Say it again, and your Mac tells you another joke. (Brace yourself, these jokes were likely written by preschoolers . . . they're really, really bad.) Oh, and if you get a "Knock, Knock" joke, remember that you have to actually say, "Who's there?"

Your Mac Talks Back!

Mac OS X is great at listening to your speech, but the fun doesn't stop there . . . your Mac can talk to you, too! By using one of the many available voices — including the default Lion voice, *Alex* — you can make your computer talk or even sing. (Not as well as Sinatra, but better than Bob Dylan.) And although Speech Recognition lets you speak to your Macintosh, the VoiceOver feature gives your Mac the ability to speak text. This is an especially useful feature because it lets you listen to your e-mails, web pages, or even your homework — sometimes the eyes need a break. The text-to-speech capability gives you the opportunity to lean back in your chair or even get up and walk around while still using your Macintosh.

Text-to-speech settings appear in three places within System Preferences: our old friend, the Speech pane; the Date & Time pane; and the VoiceOver settings within the Universal Access pane.

The Text to Speech panel

The text-to-speech engine that comes with Lion has a collection of many different voices to choose among; some voices are male, some are female, and some aren't human at all. To select your Mac's voice in Mac OS X, follow these steps:

1. **Click the System Preferences icon in the Dock.**

2. **Click the Speech icon.**

3. **Click the Text to Speech tab, as shown in Figure 3-4.**

Figure 3-4:
You can select your Mac's voice from the Text to Speech pane.

4. **Click the System Voice pop-up menu to choose a voice for your Mac.**

   To hear the voice, click Play; Lion speaks a sentence as a demonstration. To the left of the Play button is a slider for adjusting the speed of the speech. Move the slider to the right to increase the speed at which your Mac speaks and to the left to slow it down.

Naturally, Alex receives the most attention these days, because he's the default voice for Lion . . . and Alex definitely provides the most natural-sounding tone and best pacing of the bunch. However, I also think that the old-school voices, like Bruce and Vicki, are still quite intelligible. (I'm a Vicki kinda guy myself.)

Talking alerts

After you select a voice, you have a variety of ways to make your Macintosh speak automatically to you, based on some simple rules. For example, every Mac owner has run into an Alert dialog. (*Alert dialogs* are typically accompanied by a select group of words — better left unspoken — from the human behind the keyboard.) An Alert dialog usually displays some kind of icon from the following list:

✦ **Stop sign:** Indicates that something particularly important requires your attention — usually an error or a dire warning.

✦ **Yield sign:** Signals that you should proceed cautiously; not as severe as the Stop sign, but important nonetheless.

✦ **Notification:** Looks like the profile of a person speaking; displays an informative message, but not a warning. You could use this feature, for example, to have a calendar application alert you when you have a meeting or a deadline.

From the Text to Speech panel, you can choose to have your Mac speak a specific phrase or the contents of the Alert dialog by selecting one of the check boxes at the middle of the panel. If you enable the Announce When Alerts Are Displayed check box, click the Set Alert Options button to set alert-specific options:

✦ **Voice:** Choose the voice that should speak alerts. (By default, it's the voice you chose earlier.)

✦ **Phrase:** Click this pop-up menu to choose a "prefix" phrase that's spoken before the actual alert text. By default, Lion speaks the name of the application that displayed the alert, but you can also choose a phrase from the list or choose to mix up the phrases for a little variety. To add or remove phrases, click the Edit Phrases item.

✦ **Delay:** Drag this slider to control the increment of time that Lion allows to pass before it speaks.

To hear what your spoken alert settings sound like in use, click the Play button.

If you click the Play button on the Set Alert Options sheet and don't hear anything right away, remember that it doesn't begin speaking until the time has elapsed that you set with the Delay slider. To hear the spoken alerts speak as soon as you click the Play button, move the slider to 0 (zero).

Other spoken items

In addition to spoken alerts, you can allow your Mac to speak when other actions occur. Again, these settings are found on the Text to Speech pane. Your Mac can speak in the following circumstances:

✦ **Announce when an application requires your attention:** In case you have your Dock hidden from view, it's not always clear when an application needs your attention. In these instances, Mac OS X grabs your attention via speech.

✦ **Read a selection of text when you press a particular key:** If you have a child who's learning to read, the Mac can help him or her by reading a selection of text. Kids can figure out how to drag and select text often more quickly than they can read that text.

✦ **Announce the time:** Are you like me, constantly getting lost in time while immersed in your work? (Not to mention your favorite game.) I've set my MacBook Pro to announce the hour, which always keeps my time sense firmly planted.

**Book VIII
Chapter 3**

Talking and Writing
to Your Macintosh

The Date & Time pane

There you are, deep in concentration as you finish up the final chapter of your Great American Novel, when you glance at the clock in the Finder menu bar and realize that you were *supposed* to pick up your kids at soccer practice a full hour ago!

You can avoid this shameful lapse of parental responsibility by turning on Lion's automatic spoken time feature, which is controlled from the Date & Time pane within System Preferences (and is much more effective than a mechanical cuckoo clock). But why go to all the trouble of clicking Show All when you can just click the Open Date & Time Preferences button on the Text to Speech pane? Lion immediately switches to display the Date & Time pane. You can even click the Clock on the Finder menu bar and click Open Date & Time. (Again, it's all about the convenience when it comes to the geniuses at Apple.)

From the Date & Time pane, click the Clock tab and select the Announce the Time check box to enable your Mac to speak the time; use the Period pop-up menu to choose spoken time at the quarter, half, or full hour. You can also customize the voice for spoken time as well.

After you're done, zip back to the Speech pane by clicking the Back button at the top-left corner of the System Preferences window.

Configuring VoiceOver within the Universal Access pane

With Lion's VoiceOver utility, your Mac can provide you with all sorts of verbal feedback, creating a spoken English interface with Lion — a valuable addition to the operating system for the physically impaired. The feedback includes

+ **Announcing when certain keys are pressed:** Lion can tell you when a modifier key (such as Control, Option, or ⌘) is pressed or when the Caps Lock key is pressed.

+ **Announcing cursor movements:** You hear an audible alert when your mouse cursor switches between windows or when you've clicked a menu.

+ **Announcing the position of the VoiceOver cursor:** VoiceOver can audibly identify all operating system controls (such as buttons, sliders, and list boxes) by using a special on-screen cursor.

+ **Reading documents, web pages, and Mail messages:** VoiceOver can read aloud the contents of all sorts of documents and application windows.

+ **Speaking the characters you type:** You can set VoiceOver to speak every character or each word you type.

Here is how to enable VoiceOver (or to launch the VoiceOver utility, as shown in Figure 3-5):

Figure 3-5:
You can customize the VoiceOver audible feedback with the VoiceOver Utility.

1. **Click the Open Universal Access Preferences button on the Text to Speech pane.**

2. **Select the On radio button (or press ⌘+F5) to enable VoiceOver. (If you're using one of the latest Apple keyboards, press ⌘+Fn+F5 instead.)**

   To customize how VoiceOver operates, click the Open VoiceOver Utility button.

Speaking text through applications

Although VoiceOver provides a comprehensive text-to-speech interface for Mac OS X, it might be more than you need. If you simply want to hear text spoken within your applications, a number of alternative methods are included in Lion that don't require VoiceOver.

One of the simplest ways to hear spoken text in Mac OS X is by using the TextEdit application. *TextEdit* is a simple text processor that accompanies every copy of Mac OS X. Besides its handy word processing features, TextEdit can also speak text. This is good for reviewing a document after you've written it by listening to it. To hear spoken text with TextEdit, follow these steps:

1. **Launch TextEdit from the Applications folder.**

   To open the Applications folder, choose Go➪Applications from the Finder. In the window that appears, double-click the TextEdit application.

Book VIII Chapter 3

Talking and Writing to Your Macintosh

This launches the TextEdit application and opens a new document.

2. **Enter some text.**

   Either type some text on the keyboard or paste some into the document from the Clipboard. Here's an example:

   ```
   Billy Gates has lots of cash
   Lots of cash
   Lots of cash
   Billy Gates has lots of cash
   I'd like $10 please!
   ```

3. **Choose Edit⇨Speech⇨Start Speaking.**

   Your Mac begins speaking the text from the document. The speech engine has some intelligence, so you can enter dollar amounts (such as $25,423.12) or Roman numerals (such as Chapter XIV), and the speech engine reads them back in plain English. The result of these two strings would be "twenty-five thousand, four-hundred twenty-three dollars, and twelve cents" and "chapter fourteen."

4. **Choose Edit⇨Speech⇨Stop Speaking.**

   Your Mac stops speaking. It also stops speaking when it reaches the end of the text.

Speaking text through services

You can also speak text within most applications by using the Services menu, located under the application's named menu. To speak text from an application, first select that text. Then, choose *Application*⇨Services⇨Speech⇨Start Speaking to speak text from many applications (where *Application* is the name of the currently running application). If you don't want to use VoiceOver, this works great for doing things like

✦ **Reading a web page aloud**

✦ **Reading your e-mail**

✦ **Listening to a speech you've written in Pages**

As you might expect, choosing Application⇨Services⇨Speech⇨Stop Speaking ceases the banter emanating from your Mac's speaker.

Alas, not all applications are created equal. Some applications can't access the Services offered in the Services menu. If you don't see Speech in the list of services, you're out of luck.

Chapter 4: Hosting a Web Site with Mac OS X

In This Chapter

✔ Creating your own web site

✔ Adding web pages manually using MobileMe

✔ Hosting your own web server

✔ Sharing files with FTP

In a little more than a decade, surfing the Internet has gone from a nerd's hobby to a fun activity enjoyed by the whole family. For children and grandparents alike, web surfing has become one of the world's most popular spectator sports — and at some point, you'll probably get the itch to become more involved. Everyone else has a web site, so why not you?

Creating and hosting your own web site can be a rewarding experience, and with some help from Apple and Mac OS X, it's a cinch to do. I devote Book III, Chapter 7 to *iWeb*, the web page–creation application that's part of iLife, but that's not the only way to get your message on the web! Whether you want to share your favorite eggplant recipes, display pictures of your aubergine Auburn, or just post a purple résumé, Mac OS X has you covered in more ways than one.

So put on your seat belts — you're now entering a strange world of servers, mysterious codes, and things that go bump in the Net. No need for alarm, though . . . Apple has made the topic so simple that even a politician can do it.

Building a Site with MobileMe

To get you up and running on the web quickly, Apple offers a suite of online web-publishing tools. The toolbox, collectively known as *MobileMe,* gives you easy and fast access to a variety of Internet functions, including e-mail and your iDisk online storage — and you also get a dedicated web page, which you can create with iWeb. A MobileMe membership costs $99.95 per year direct from Apple, although you can save a significant amount of money by buying your membership from online retailers such as Amazon.com.

I should introduce everyone around the table here: *iDisk* is a space on the Apple servers designated just for you, where iWeb stores the elements of your site when you add or change web pages.

Registering as a MobileMe user

You can visit Apple's home on the Internet to register as a MobileMe user:

`www.me.com`

To register for your free 60-day trial, you must create a username and password. The username that you select is an important part of the MobileMe experience, so choose it carefully. Your username plays a part in your e-mail address, your web address, your login name, and even the bar code on your forehead. (Okay, the bar code is a joke — for now, anyway — but the rest aren't.) Take a few minutes to carefully plan your MobileMe username. Your username saves you some typing, is easier for your friends to remember, and (like a customized license plate for your car) can convey a certain personality to others on the web.

Creating a web page manually on MobileMe

For those folks who like driving a car without knowing what goes on under the hood, the combination of iWeb and MobileMe is perfect: You just use it to create and post web pages without knowing what makes it all work. On the other hand, some folks are born mechanics and like to get under the hood. If you're itching to see what goes on behind the scenes, Apple gives you a chance to get your hands dirty. Of course, you don't *have* to use iWeb to work on your web site. If you're well versed in HTML, you can edit your web page files on your iDisk just as you would any file on your hard drive.

You aren't limited to iDisk access via iWeb: Simply choose the iDisk menu from the Finder's Go menu to mount your iDisk. (No need for a saddle — I explain more about mounting volumes in Book I.) When you mount an iDisk, it shows up as an icon on your Desktop, just as you might see when you insert a CD into your Mac. The icon for your iDisk, however, looks like a purple hard drive.

Within your iDisk, open the Sites folder to see the various files that compose your web page. If you're an old pro at HTML, you can add your own pages to your iDisk with your favorite text editor. In other words, the iDisk acts much the same as any other disk that you're accustomed to using. (For all the inside information on iDisk, see Chapter 4 of Book V.)

Moving stuff is easy: With your iDisk mounted, double-click its icon to view its contents. If you need an image for your web page, stick it in the Pictures folder. If you need a movie for your web page, copy it to the Movies folder. Your HTML pages themselves go into the Sites folder.

Using Mac OS X Web Sharing

With MobileMe, Apple takes care of the web server for you, but you aren't limited to just iWeb and MobileMe: You have other options when it comes to posting web pages. Mac OS X comes stocked with its own high-powered web server, so you can run things without MobileMe. Consider the advantages, won't you?

✦ **Privacy:** Everyone in the house wants access to the family phone book. You want all computers on your home network — but not the whole world — to see the telephone list. Posting the list on the home network keeps it secure from prying eyes outside your home.

✦ **Your own domain:** Want a name like `www.size14feetphotos.com`? (Don't even think about it; I've already taken it.) Anyway, if you run your own web server, you can arrange for your own domain name.

✦ **Speed:** Your friend needs a copy of your iMovie masterpiece for a class project. Rather than wait for you to post the file to your iDisk, he decides to download it directly from your computer. If he's outside the range of an AirDrop connection (or he's not using a Mac running Mac OS X Lion), a web site is a great choice for transferring your stuff — it's my preferred method of distributing files, no matter what type of computer or operating system my visitors are using.

✦ **Coolness factor:** It's fun, it's easy, and your mother will *truly* be proud. Seriously, it's fun and easy to run your own web server. (And although your mother might not actually give a hoot, companies appreciate employees who know useful skills; therefore, web server stuff is good to know.)

I love Apache: Confessions of a UNIX webmaster

Deep in the guts of Mac OS X lies one of the most popular web servers around: *Apache*, which turns your Macintosh into a full-featured web server. The Apache web server is well known around the world and comprises about half of all personal and commercial web servers in use today. Yes, that's right! You have one of the world's most-used web servers installed already on your Mac!

Apache's first appealing feature is its price — absolutely free. *Free* is *sassy!* Free isn't any good without quality, though. Fortunately, Apache is extremely reliable — and combined with the crash-proof Mac OS X, you can be almost certain that your web server is always available. Besides being rock-solid and free, Apache sports all the features you'd expect from a top-notch web server, such as techno-wizard integration with databases and scripting languages. Believe me, it can serve anything you throw at it.

Configuring and running Apache

In addition to all its great qualities, Apache is dead simple to operate in Mac OS X. Open System Preferences and click the Sharing icon; then select the check box next to Web Sharing to launch Apache. That's it! It doesn't get any easier . . . at least, when it comes to turning on Apache. (See Figure 4-1.)

Figure 4-1: Turning on Apache is a cinch.

To begin using your web server, open a Finder window and navigate to the Sites folder that resides in your Home folder; this is the root of your personal space on the web server. Any files that you add to this folder are accessible via your web server.

Don't feel like digging through a Finder window for the Sites folder? You can also reach the Sites folder from the Sharing pane in System Preferences — click Sharing and then click the Web Sharing entry in the list. Now click the handsome Open Personal Website Folder button.

You might find a file named `index.html` installed already in the Sites folder. This is the default file for your web site. To view it, open your favorite web browser and load this URL, replacing *~username* with the username that you're currently using:

```
http://127.0.0.1/~username/
```

The 127.0.0.1 address is a generic Internet Protocol (IP) address, which means *self*. (In other words, your Mac is connecting to itself. Faintly unsettling, but absolutely legal.) You can also use your real IP address, which appears at the bottom of the Sharing pane in System Preferences when you turn on web Sharing.

To see the web page from another computer, you must use the real IP address. The 127.0.0.1 address is merely a convenience for when you're using the actual machine that runs the web server.

Because Mac OS X is a multiuser environment, each user can host a web site. The key is the username found at the end of the URL; replace it with the appropriate username and you're ready to go. If everything goes smoothly, you should be viewing the default Mac OS X web page, as shown in Figure 4-2. The default page displays a welcome message and some important information for web-sharing beginners. Make sure that you read the information carefully.

In addition to a main page for any individual who logs in, the web server also has a global default page. To find the global default page, follow these steps:

1. **Open a new Finder window.**
2. **Double-click the drive that contains your Mac OS X installation.**
3. **Choose Library⇨WebServer⇨Documents.**

Again, Lion makes it easy to open the WebServer Documents folder from the Sharing pane in System Preferences. Click the Web Sharing entry in the list, and then click the Open Computer Website Folder button.

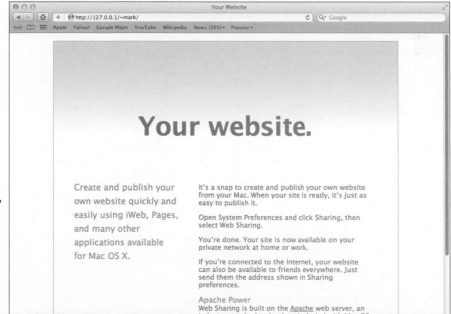

Figure 4-2: Replace this default web page with something more interesting.

Your website.

Create and publish your own website quickly and easily using iWeb, Pages, and many other applications available for Mac OS X.

It's a snap to create and publish your own website from your Mac. When your site is ready, it's just as easy to publish it.

Open System Preferences and click Sharing, then select Web Sharing.

You're done. Your site is now available on your private network at home or work.

If you're connected to the Internet, your website can also be available to friends everywhere. Just send them the address shown in Sharing preferences.

Apache Power
Web Sharing is built on the Apache web server, an

Here you find dozens of HTML files. These files are the default global home pages for many different languages. For English versions of the Mac OS, this means that the file named `index.html.en` serves as the default home page for the server. To view this file in your browser, try this URL:

```
http://127.0.0.1/
```

Serving static information

To change the default web page, simply open it in iWeb . . . or use your favorite HTML editor and start editing. An *HTML editor* is an application that lets you lay out your web page with ease. If you're familiar with a word processor, you're well on your way to using an HTML editor. Of the many HTML editors available, VersionTracker (`www.versiontracker.com`) gives you a good head start on finding some of the most popular ones.

You aren't limited only to HTML editors, of course. Many word processors support HTML export — I particularly like Microsoft Word — so it's *trés* easy to create web pages with them by simply choosing File➪Save As.

If you already know HTML (webmasters might say, "If you can bang out raw HTML code"), you can edit your web pages by hand. Open the existing index. html file with a text editor, such as TextEdit or BBEdit (`www.barebones. com`), by choosing File➪Open, and change the code to suit your needs. For example, a simple web page might read like this:

```
<html>
<head><title>My First web Page</title></head>
<body>
Welcome to my web site!
</body>
</html>
```

If you're using TextEdit, don't forget to save your files as plain text — click TextEdit➪Preferences and click the New Document tab, then click the Plain Text radio button to select it. Click the Close button on the Preferences dialog. Now each time you create a new document using TextEdit, it'll be in plain text format.

Plain-old HTML pages are handy for displaying the same information repeatedly. Computer web-wizards call this type of information *static.* (That is, it doesn't change. It's like a fully grown Chia Pet: You can set it once and forget about it.)

Serving information dynamically

Although static displays are good for things like your copy of the Magna Carta or sports stats from the past 20 years, they're not so great for data that changes a lot (usually referred to as *dynamic,* in case you hadn't guessed already). Some good examples of dynamic information are the date, the time, your age, and the weather. If you were to display your age on a web page by using only HTML, you'd have to change it only once every year. This isn't so bad, but consider what happens if you want to post the date on a web page: Now you have to update the web page once per day. Add the time, and now you're down to HTML changes every hour, minute, or second, depending on how reliable you want to make the clock. Clearly, you need something besides static HTML for *dynamic* information.

The Apache web server allows you to use a variety of tools to produce dynamic web pages. The most basic tool for serving dynamic data is the *Server Side Include.* The web server executes a small piece of code in your HTML; then the web server replaces that code with some text and sends the page to whomever requested it. The result is dynamic text in your web page.

Adding Server Side Includes requires that you perform a few preparatory steps beforehand. To alter Apache settings, you must change text in its settings file. The file is named `httpd.conf` and is located here:

```
/etc/apache2/httpd.conf
```

You probably can't find this file if you go searching for it in the Finder because it's a hidden file. Some text editors, such as BBEdit, can open hidden files, but you might not have that editor on hand. You do have the Terminal application, though. Launch the Terminal by double-clicking its icon. (You can find it in the Utility folder that resides in your Applications folder.) Book VIII, Chapter 1 has more information about the Terminal in case you need a refresher. At the prompt that appears, enter this command:

```
sudo pico /etc/apache2/httpd.conf
```

You are then nudged to provide a password at the following prompt:

```
Password:
```

When prompted for a password, use an administrator account password on your machine. If you're the only user, this might be the password of the user you're currently signed in as. Press Return and you're looking at the innards of the Apache setup file. There's a lot of what I call *Programmer Pig Latin* in this file, but don't be discouraged. Scroll down through the file (use the arcane UNIX Control+V key sequence) and look for this chunk of text:

```
# Note that "MultiViews" must be named *explicitly* --- "Options All"
# doesn't give it to you.
#
    Options Indexes FollowSymLinks MultiViews
```

If you don't feel like scrolling through a bunch of text, you can jump to the text by pressing Control+W (shorthand for *where*), entering the text that you want to find (for example: **Options Indexes FollowSymLinks**), and then pressing Return.

Whenever you find the desired text in the file, add the word **Includes** to the end of the last line of this text.

```
# Note that "MultiViews" must be named *explicitly* --- "Options All"
# doesn't give it to you.
#
    Options Indexes FollowSymLinks MultiViews Includes
```

Notice the many pound (#) characters. A *pound character* denotes a comment: Think of comments as notes to yourself that help you remember what the heck you were doing at this point in the file. Techno-wizard coders would say it this way: When a comment character (#) precedes a line, that line of text performs no function. You can use this to your advantage to turn settings on and off for the server. Add a pound character to the beginning of a line, and that function stops working. Remove the character, and the function works again. Continue scrolling through the httpd.conf file by using the arrow keys or the Control+W search trick, looking for the following:

```
# To use server-parsed HTML files
#
AddType text/html .shtml
AddHandler server-parsed .shtml
```

Make sure that no # characters precede the AddType and AddHandler lines. After you finish, press Control+O, press Return to save the file, and then press Control+X to exit the pico text editor. After you finish editing Apache's settings, you have to restart it for the changes to take effect. Open System Preferences and click the Sharing tab. Deactivate Web Sharing and then reactivate it.

Open your favorite text editor and add some text to a new file:

```
<html>
<head><title>My First web Page</title></head>
<body>
Welcome to my web site!<br>
Today's date: <!--#echo var="DATE_LOCAL" -->
</body>
</html>
```

The <!--#echo var="DATE_LOCAL" --> part is a Server Side Include. The server understands the "DATE_LOCAL" message, and in its place, adds text that displays today's date. Save the text file and give it the name index.shtml.

Make sure that you include the .shtml extension. It's important for making the Server Side Includes work properly.

Save the file in your global web folder, located here:

```
/Library/WebServer/documents/index.shtml
```

Finally, it's time to check out your handiwork and rest your fingers from all this typing. Open a web browser and navigate to the URL of your global web folder:

```
http://127.0.0.1/index.shtml
```

The result should be a web page that displays today's date. (I know, it's not exactly material for the Louvre at this point, but I think you can appreciate the possibilities.)

If you're not content with appending `.shtml` to your files to take advantage of Server Side Includes, you need to perform another step. When you view your web site with a web browser, it's customary to use default pages for a particular directory. For example, when loading the following URL

```
http://127.0.0.1/
```

the server looks for a default page to load on the server because you didn't specify one. This is normally a file named `index.html`, which causes problems for Server Side Includes because they require a filename ending with `.shtml`. The easiest way to fix this is to tell the server that `index.shtml` can also be a default page. To fix this discrepancy, reload the Apache configuration file by using this command line:

```
sudo pico /etc/apache2/httpd.conf
```

If you perform this step within 15 minutes of your last `sudo` command, you don't have to reenter a password. If it's been longer, you might have to enter the password. (As I tell you in Chapter 1 of this minibook, UNIX has sophisticated security.) Then scroll down through the `httpd.conf` file and find this bit of text:

```
# DirectoryIndex: Name of the file or files to use as a pre-written HTML
# directory index.  Separate multiple entries with spaces.
#
<IfModule mod_dir.c>
    DirectoryIndex index.html
</IfModule>
```

Change it by adding `index.shtml` to it:

```
# DirectoryIndex: Name of the file or files to use as a pre-written HTML
# directory index.  Separate multiple entries with spaces.
#
<IfModule mod_dir.c>
    DirectoryIndex index.shtml index.html
</IfModule>
```

Notice that `index.shtml` precedes `index.html`. This line indicates which filenames you can use for the default filename of any folder on the web server. In this case, I'm forcing `index.shtml` as the default filename before `index.html`. This means that when you load a web page from your server without specifying a specific file, Apache looks for a file named `index.shtml` in that folder first. If it can't find one, it looks for a file named `index.html`. With that change in place, press Control+O to write the file to disk and then press Control+X to quit the pico text editor. To see your work in action, stop and restart Web Sharing on the Sharing pane in System Preferences; load this URL with your web browser:

`http://127.0.0.1/`

The result should be that your `index.shtml` page loads with Server Side Includes intact.

Server Side Includes can perform a few other simple functions besides the date, including

✦ `DATE_GMT`: Today's date in Greenwich Mean Time.

✦ `DATE_LOCAL`: Today's date in your local time zone. (You're already an expert with this one.)

✦ `DOCUMENT_NAME`: The name of the document.

✦ `LAST_MODIFIED`: The date when this document was last modified.

To see them all in action, alter your `index.shtml` file to read like this:

```
<html>
<head><title>My First web Page</title></head>
<body>
Welcome to my web site! <br><br>
GMT date: <!--#echo var="DATE_GMT" --> <br>
Today's date: <!--#echo var="DATE_LOCAL" --><br>
Name of this document: <!--#echo var="DOCUMENT_NAME" --><br>
Last Modified: <!--#echo var="LAST_MODIFIED" --><br>
</body>
</html>
```

Reload your web server's main page to see the results.

Fancier dynamic stuff

Another common use of Server Side Includes gives you a chance to remove whole chunks of your HTML files and put them into another file. (Sounds messy, doesn't it?) You might want to do this for HTML that appears on each page of your web site: For example, you might like for today's date and the page's last modified date to appear at the bottom of any page of your whole web site. Webmasters, being the sedentary, nerd-beast crowd that they are, don't want to type this information repeatedly for each HTML page that they create. Furthermore, they don't want to have to retype all that information for every file if it should change. What's a lazy techno-wizard to do? Server Side Includes come to the rescue!

The first step is to modify your main page: in this case, `index.shtml`:

```
<html>
<head><title>My First Web Page</title></head>
<body>
Welcome to my web site!<br>
<!--#include virtual="footer.shtml"-->
</body>
</html>
```

You might notice that I removed all the Server Side Includes from before and added a new one. The new line

```
<!--#include virtual="footer.shtml"-->
```

tells the web server to load the file named `footer.shtml` and dump its contents into `index.shtml` in place of this Server Side Include. Save this file.

Create a new text file. To the new file, add this code:

```
<center>
<hr width="50%">
Today's date: <!--#echo var="DATE_LOCAL" --><br>
Last Modified: <!--#echo var="LAST_MODIFIED" --><br><br>
</center>
```

If you're familiar with HTML, the first thing that might strike you is that this file doesn't follow proper HTML formatting. Because this file is just a chunk of HTML that's going to be part of a fully formed HTML file, it doesn't need the full treatment. Otherwise, this code is standard HTML with a few Server Side Includes tossed in for good measure. Just to spruce things up a bit, the text is centered with a small horizontal line above it. Save this file, giving it the name footer.shtml.

Now, whenever you want this footer to be at the bottom of any web page on the server, add the `<!--#include virtual="footer.shtml"-->` line from before. Besides saving you time from reconstructing the footer each time in an HTML file, you have to add only one line of code, and Server Side Includes take care of the rest. Even better, you can alter the footer file whenever you want, and the changes appear in the HTML of every page that contains the footer.

When bad things happen to good webmasters

If you've browsed the web for any time at all, you've no doubt stumbled across a *dead link*. This phenomenon occurs when you attempt to load a web page that no longer exists on a particular server. If you were lucky and the server still existed, you probably saw a boring error message telling you that the page no longer exists. Apache provides default error messages like this for you, but that doesn't mean you can't improve the messages that your visitors see. A true power user eschews defaults when creativity kicks in!

Open your `httpd.conf` file for editing with pico as before.

```
sudo pico /etc/apache2/httpd.conf
```

Scroll through the file until you find the `ErrorDocument` directives.

```
#    2) local redirects
#ErrorDocument 404 /missing.html
#  to redirect to local URL /missing.html
```

Whenever a server can't find a page, it produces a `404` error — also well known as "That Blankety-Blank Screen" to web surfers around the world. (Please excuse my clarity there.) In fact, the number *404* has entered popular slang, meaning *dead* or *broken*. Normally, Apache directs itself to a default error message, but by removing one comment (note the now-absent pound character at the beginning of the second line), you can specify which file you want to display (in the form of a page for the viewer) in the case of a `404` error.

```
#    2) local redirects
ErrorDocument 404 /missing.html
#  to redirect to local URL /missing.html
```

Press Control+O to save the `httpd.conf` file and then press Control+X to exit pico. Now whenever someone comes across a missing web page on your site, your server redirects him to a file named `missing.html`. Of course, you also need to create this `missing.html` file. Use your favorite text editor to create a new HTML file. To your file, add this code:

```
<html>
<head><title>Uh-oh!</title></head>
<body>
Holy Toledo! <br><br>
We can't find the page you requested. <br>
Would you like to <a href="index.shtml">return to the main page</a>?
<!--#include virtual="footer.shtml"-->
</body>
</html>
```

Save this file, giving it the name `missing.html`. Save it in your web server's root directory.

```
/Library/WebServer/Documents/missing.html
```

Return to the System Preferences Sharing pane and toggle Web Sharing off and on again. This forces your web server to read in the changes to the `httpd.conf` file.

To test it, load a URL that you know doesn't exist. Anything will do.

```
http://1270.0.0.1/some_missing_page_I_forgot_to_add.html
```

If you've configured things properly, you see a personalized web error page. This way, perhaps your visitor will chuckle instead of curse when a dead link is encountered.

Index

1

M

O

P

X

Y

Z

Apple & Macs

iPad For Dummies
978-0-470-58027-1

iPhone For Dummies,
4th Edition
978-0-470-87870-5

MacBook For Dummies, 3rd
Edition
978-0-470-76918-8

Mac OS X Snow Leopard For
Dummies
978-0-470-43543-4

Business

Bookkeeping For Dummies
978-0-7645-9848-7

Job Interviews
For Dummies,
3rd Edition
978-0-470-17748-8

Resumes For Dummies,
5th Edition
978-0-470-08037-5

Starting an
Online Business
For Dummies,
6th Edition
978-0-470-60210-2

Stock Investing
For Dummies,
3rd Edition
978-0-470-40114-9

Successful
Time Management
For Dummies
978-0-470-29034-7

Computer Hardware

BlackBerry
For Dummies,
4th Edition
978-0-470-60700-8

Computers For Seniors
For Dummies,
2nd Edition
978-0-470-53483-0

PCs For Dummies,
Windows
7 Edition
978-0-470-46542-4

Laptops For Dummies,
4th Edition
978-0-470-57829-2

Cooking & Entertaining

Cooking Basics
For Dummies,
3rd Edition
978-0-7645-7206-7

Wine For Dummies,
4th Edition
978-0-470-04579-4

Diet & Nutrition

Dieting For Dummies,
2nd Edition
978-0-7645-4149-0

Nutrition For Dummies,
4th Edition
978-0-471-79868-2

Weight Training
For Dummies,
3rd Edition
978-0-471-76845-6

Digital Photography

Digital SLR Cameras &
Photography For Dummies,
3rd Edition
978-0-470-46606-3

Photoshop Elements 8
For Dummies
978-0-470-52967-6

Gardening

Gardening Basics
For Dummies
978-0-470-03749-2

Organic Gardening
For Dummies,
2nd Edition
978-0-470-43067-5

Green/Sustainable

Raising Chickens
For Dummies
978-0-470-46544-8

Green Cleaning
For Dummies
978-0-470-39106-8

Health

Diabetes For Dummies,
3rd Edition
978-0-470-27086-8

Food Allergies
For Dummies
978-0-470-09584-3

Living Gluten-Free
For Dummies,
2nd Edition
978-0-470-58589-4

Hobbies/General

Chess For Dummies,
2nd Edition
978-0-7645-8404-6

Drawing
Cartoons & Comics
For Dummies
978-0-470-42683-8

Knitting For Dummies,
2nd Edition
978-0-470-28747-7

Organizing
For Dummies
978-0-7645-5300-4

Su Doku For Dummies
978-0-470-01892-7

Home Improvement

Home Maintenance
For Dummies,
2nd Edition
978-0-470-43063-7

Home Theater
For Dummies,
3rd Edition
978-0-470-41189-6

Living the
Country Lifestyle
All-in-One
For Dummies
978-0-470-43061-3

Solar Power Your Home
For Dummies,
2nd Edition
978-0-470-59678-4

Internet

Blogging For Dummies,
3rd Edition
978-0-470-61996-4

eBay For Dummies,
6th Edition
978-0-470-49741-8

Facebook For Dummies,
3rd Edition
978-0-470-87804-0

Web Marketing
For Dummies,
2nd Edition
978-0-470-37181-7

WordPress
For Dummies,
3rd Edition
978-0-470-59274-8

Language & Foreign Language

French For Dummies
978-0-7645-5193-2

Italian Phrases
For Dummies
978-0-7645-7203-6

Spanish For Dummies,
2nd Edition
978-0-470-87855-2

Spanish
For Dummies,
Audio Set
978-0-470-09585-0

Math & Science

Algebra I
For Dummies,
2nd Edition
978-0-470-55964-2

Biology For Dummies,
2nd Edition
978-0-470-59875-7

Calculus For Dummies
978-0-7645-2498-1

Chemistry For Dummies
978-0-7645-5430-8

Microsoft Office

Excel 2010 For Dummies
978-0-470-48953-6

Office 2010 All-in-One
For Dummies
978-0-470-49748-7

Office 2010 For Dummies,
Book + DVD Bundle
978-0-470-62698-6

Word 2010 For Dummies
978-0-470-48772-3

Music

Guitar For Dummies,
2nd Edition
978-0-7645-9904-0

iPod & iTunes For
Dummies, 8th Edition
978-0-470-87871-2

Piano Exercises
For Dummies
978-0-470-38765-8

Parenting & Education

Parenting For Dummies,
2nd Edition
978-0-7645-5418-6

Type 1 Diabetes
For Dummies
978-0-470-17811-9

Pets

Cats For Dummies,
2nd Edition
978-0-7645-5275-5

Dog Training For Dummies,
3rd Edition
978-0-470-60029-0

Puppies For Dummies,
2nd Edition
978-0-470-03717-1

Religion & Inspiration

The Bible For Dummies
978-0-7645-5296-0

Catholicism For Dummies
978-0-7645-5391-2

Women in the Bible
For Dummies
978-0-7645-8475-6

Self-Help & Relationship

Anger Management
For Dummies
978-0-470-03715-7

Overcoming Anxiety
For Dummies,
2nd Edition
978-0-470-57441-6

Sports

Baseball
For Dummies,
3rd Edition
978-0-7645-7537-2

Basketball
For Dummies,
2nd Edition
978-0-7645-5248-9

Golf For Dummies,
3rd Edition
978-0-471-76871-5

Web Development

Web Design
All-in-One
For Dummies
978-0-470-41796-6

Web Sites
Do-It-Yourself
For Dummies,
2nd Edition
978-0-470-56520-9

Windows 7

Windows 7
For Dummies
978-0-470-49743-2

Windows 7
For Dummies,
Book + DVD Bundle
978-0-470-52398-8

Windows 7 All-in-One
For Dummies
978-0-470-48763-1

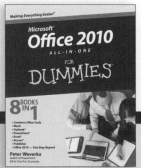

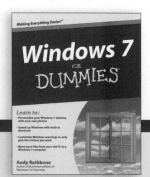

Available wherever books are sold. For more information or to order direct: U.S. customers visit www.dummies.com or call 1-877-762-2974.
U.K. customers visit www.wileyeurope.com or call (0) 1243 843291. Canadian customers visit www.wiley.ca or call 1-800-567-4797.

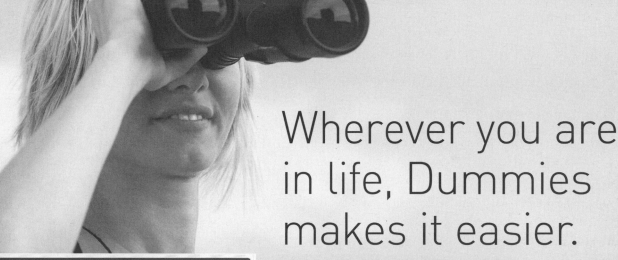

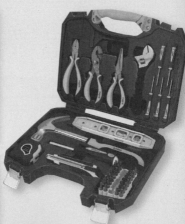